GREAT INTERDISCIPLINARY IDEAS

ABOUT THE AUTHOR

PENGUIN ACADEMICS

GREAT INTERDISCIPLINARY IDEAS

A READER FOR WRITERS

William Vesterman

Rutgers University

PEARSON
Longman

New York   Boston   San Francisco
London   Toronto   Sydney   Tokyo   Singapore   Madrid
Mexico City   Munich   Paris   Cape Town   Hong Kong   Montreal

Senior Vice President and Publisher: Joseph Opiela
Senior Acquisitions Editor: Katherine Meisenheimer
Senior Marketing Manager: Sandra McGuire
Production Manager: Savoula Amanatidis
Project Coordination and Electronic Page Makeup: Electronic Publishing
    Services Inc., NYC
Cover Design Manager: Nancy Danahy
Cover Image: © Dod Miller, Reportage/Getty Images, Inc.
Senior Manufacturing Buyer: Dennis J. Para
Printer and Binder: Courier Corporation—Westford
Cover Printer: Phoenix Color Corporation

Library of Congress Cataloging-in-Publication Data

Great interdisciplinary ideas: a reader for writers/[compiled by]
    William Vesterman.
        p. cm.
    Includes bibliographical references and index.
    ISBN-13: 978-0-321-45001-2 (pbk.)
    ISBN-10:   0-321-45001-9 (pbk.)
    1. College readers. 2. English language—Rhetoric. 3. Report writing.
I. Vesterman, William, 1942–

PE1417.G664 2007
808'.0427—dc22   2007022678

Please visit us at www.ablongman.com

ISBN-13: 978-0-321-45001-2
ISBN-10:   0-321-45001-9

    2 3 4 5 6 7 8 9 10—CRW—10 09 08

brief contents

CHAPTER 1
Evolution: Inceptions and Implications 1

CHAPTER 2
Economics: The Production and Consumption of Wealth 76

CHAPTER 3
Human Rights: Liberty and Law   164

CHAPTER 4
Literature: Life's Mirror and Life's Lamp   245

CHAPTER 5
Utopias and Dystopias: Secular Heavens and Secular Hells   345

CHAPTER 6
Gender: Human Conditioning and the Human Condition   421

detailed con

CHAPTER 1   Evolution: Inceptions and Implications   1

CHAPTER 3   Human Rights: Liberty and Law   164

But this natural equality of power led (in his famous phrases) to "a war of all against all" and a life that was "solitary, poor, nasty, brutish, and short." To improve such a life, civil society was established and people surrendered their natural rights and powers to the sovereign for the sake of individual security.

"The Origins of Civil Society" from *Social Contract*

"Man is born free but everywhere is in chains"—so begins a revolutionary book by one of the most important thinkers of the eighteenth century. Rousseau's central concept is "liberty" and here he analyzes the reasons men might surrender their liberty to a government which derives its rights and powers only from the people. He concludes that the people have a right to rescind their part of the bargain, if their government fails to live up to its part.

"The Declaration of Independence"

In some ways Jefferson's argument for independence follows the implications of Rousseau's ideas, accounting for the preponderance of legalistic reasoning in one of the world's most famous documents. This milestone in American democracy might be partly seen as outlining a breach of contract suit between the American people and the British sovereign.

"Pernicious Effects Which Arise from the Unnatural Distinctions Established in Society"

One of the first great modern feminists (and the mother of Mary Shelley, whose work appears in Chapter 5), this author analyzes some assumptions of laws, property rights, and class division. Though often taken as a reflection of nature, these distinctions, she says, are in fact man-made mechanisms of social control with unusually harsh results for women.

"Awakening and Revolt" from *My Fight for Birth Control*

Sanger led the battle for birth control in America in the early decades of the twentieth century. In the first of these excerpts, she describes her own awakening to the need for strong action and her revolt against the appalling ignorance and apathy shared by most of the rest of the medical community. In the second excerpt, she examines the issue of responsibility for contraception.

"The Nonviolent Society"

By the early twentieth century, the British empire included much of the earth's surface and hundreds of millions of its people. Both the dissolution of that empire and the national independence of its subject peoples were in very large part the result of the power of one man who successfully encouraged the use of spiritual force rather than armed rebellion. In his advocacy of nonviolence he was a follower of Thoreau (Chapter 5) and an influence on Martin Luther King, Jr., who appears later in this chapter.

| CHAPTER 5 | Utopias and Dystopias: Secular Heavens and Secular Hells   345 |

independence from conventional wisdom was further expressed in another essay, "On Civil Disobedience," a major influence on Mahatma Gandhi and Martin Luther King, Jr., both of whom appear in Chapter 3.

The Time Traveler learns in a shocking way that human evolution does not necessarily equate with human progress, when he discovers that the people of the future have evolved into two different races—one of which literally feeds on the other.

Gilman was one of the most important women in the feminist movement of the late nineteenth and early twentieth centuries. Her essay from *Women and Economics* appears in Chapter 2. Here she describes the discovery by an exploring party of an isolated race of women who have evolved to reproduce by parthenogenesis and who therefore no longer need the male intruders in any way.

Is literature the mirror and lamp of life? In this twenty-fourth century world, firemen are paid to burn books—the novel's title refers to the kindling point of paper. Rightly suspecting that Fireman Montag loves to read, Chief Beatty visits and gives him a fatherly talk and historical explanation of why books must go. The spread of mass literacy quickly dumbed them down and TV and film make ideas much more easily available and digestible. Moreover, there are so many minorities and special interest groups that any book will inevitably have material objectionable to one of them and so lead to social instability. His argument continues in this excerpt.

Trying to turn China into a workers' paradise would cost tens of millions of Chinese lives whose loss did not disturb this dictator. His initial repression silenced opposition without ending it. Yet Chairman Mao soon found a way to bring opponents out of hiding by proposing a model of freely evolving Darwinian diversity. When the flowers of diverse opinion he seemed to call for did blossom, they could be (and were) all the more easily nipped in the bud.

| CHAPTER 6 | Gender: Human Conditioning and the Human Condition   421 |

preface—to the instructor

The purpose of this book is to introduce students of composition to some major ideas by major thinkers in different fields of study by showing through representative examples how that thinking and those fields have interacted to create and define some central issues of civilization. The goal is to make students not only more aware of the historical interplay of intellect, but to help make students better readers and writers in their engagement with many academic areas throughout their college careers.

For better or for worse, the core curriculum of yesteryear has vanished, and introductory composition remains the last universally required common course. As one result of that solitary status, writing courses have often been required to assume duties well beyond the certification of literacy or literary skills by taking on greater responsibility for a student's general education. *Great Interdisciplinary Ideas* is designed to help students begin to understand the modern world through some of the great issues that have claimed widespread attention in the past and still claim our attention today. The thinkers and writers in the book are introduced not only through their individual contributions, but also through illustrations of the ways they themselves have been illuminated by earlier thinkers from other fields, just as they have stimulated those who followed them in many different disciplines. That is, just as Darwin's insights in biology were precipitated by his reading in geology and economics, so the idea of evolution went on to influence thought in many areas of study beyond biology including economics, sociology, and fiction, among others.

The book's 58 selections of varying lengths have been chosen both for the high quality and importance of their thought and for their capacities to stimulate critical reading and critical thinking along with analytic and argumentative writing. The authors here do not appear as part of a collection of famous fragments or solely as objects of cultural contemplation and admiration, admirable as they are. The book attempts to show ideas at work as they interact through time within and among different disciplines. Students are thereby invited not only into a conversation with a given author, but into an extended conversation with many writers past and present, so that the students may more fully understand how interdisciplinary thinking has operated and continues to operate.

In *Great Interdisciplinary Ideas*, questions about major issues are asked and answered both within and among chapters thematically focused on **Evolution, Economics, Human Rights, Literature, Utopias and Dystopias**, and **Gender**. The book's critical apparatus is designed to support the goals of the book without overwhelming its readers or remaining tangential to any individual course design. A brief **Introduction** to each chapter defines the theme and previews the variety of approaches taken by the different authors. Each selection opens with biographical facts and introduces the author's particular focus. Each essay is followed by **Suggestions for Writing** designed to address the particulars of the piece. Each chapter ends with a pair of essays that promote writing arguments by disagreeing or differing with one another regarding some important aspect of the chapter's theme. At the conclusion of each chapter, **Interdisciplinary Connections** provide more general writing assignments that invite the readers to explore interactions within and among chapters.

Composition remains the last required common course because writing is itself an interdisciplinary matter and the major means of academic inquiry into the structures, values, and purposes of civilization. Whatever major fields of study students may go on to pursue, they need to confront the great issues of the world they live in from the points of view of many different disciplines. In any field of inquiry, they will need to know how to read critically and write effectively. It is hoped that the contents and organization of this book will contribute in some small way to the realization of these great educational goals.

William Vesterman
Rutgers University

introduction—to the student

This book is designed to introduce you to some great ideas in the history of civilization, where they came from, and what grew out of them. You will read these ideas not only in the forms of their original expression, but also in the context of their creation and their results. By this method, you will be able to see by means of representative examples how some great thinkers have thought—where their thoughts came from and how their ideas have influenced subsequent thinking in many fields of study or *disciplines*.

You may already be familiar with some of the documents included here—the Declaration of Independence, for example. But in this book you will also read some of the authors, thinkers like Thomas Hobbes and Jean-Jacques Rousseau, that Thomas Jefferson read on the issue of human rights and government. You will also see how other authors have reacted to some of the rights and issues of government that Jefferson did not address—the rights of women and black Americans, for example. Similarly, you may already know something about Darwin's theory of evolution. But here again you will read not only Darwin's original formulation of his concept, but also how his thinking was influenced by writing in fields other than biology and how that thinking went on to influence authors who followed him and worked in different areas—the field of economics, for example. You will learn that economics was one of the fields of study that stimulated Darwin. He therefore in effect repaid his debt to economics by giving economists new ways to look at the creation and consumption of wealth. You will further learn how evolution led to new thinking about the future of human societies imagined as ideal utopias or their opposites—frighteningly flawed dystopias. In these and other ways, your reading of these selections will lead you through a process of cross-fertilization to new ways of thinking about all the fields of study you will encounter throughout your college career.

This book addresses you not only as a reader but as a writer. Because writing is generally required throughout the college curriculum, composition is itself an interdisciplinary matter. For this reason, the questions and suggestions for writing that follow each selection and each chapter will help you to form the writing skills involved in creating written analyses and arguments through the critical thinking needed to succeed in any field. Because you will be encouraged to write about the great ideas presented here both on their own and in relation to one another, you will be better able to make conclusions about what the great ideas really mean. That is, like the authors included here, you yourself will be engaged in a process of intellectual cross-fertilization by seeing the same issue in different contexts and from different points of view.

CHAPTER 1

Evolution
Inceptions and Implications

Charles Darwin

Thomas Malthus

William Vesterman

Theodore Baird

Jorge Luis Borges

H. L. Mencken

Joseph Schumpeter

Stephen Jay Gould

Rachel Carson

Phyllis Schlafly

Introduction

Charles Darwin published his revolutionary book *On the Origin of Species by Means of Natural Selection* in 1859, but the concept he announced is still very much in the news today, early in the twenty-first century some 150 years later. A key interdisciplinary idea in the future history of ideas, evolution had its own origins when new discoveries in geology and economics intersected with biology in Darwin's thinking. For their own part, his new proposals quickly went on to repay their debt by influencing new thought, not only in the same fields of study that had nurtured them, but also in many other diverse areas of inquiry. Essays in this chapter and in other chapters throughout this book will provide a wide variety of evidence for this process of inter-disciplinary cross-fertilization.

The intellectual interaction of evolutionary biology with other fields shows no signs of halting or even slowing down. A partial list of the public attention paid by the press to Darwin in just one month—November 2005—offers a fair and representative sample of the impact that the concept of evolution continues to exert.

■ The American Museum of Natural History opens an exhibition on Darwin's life and works.

■ An article in the NY Times Magazine appears: "The Literary Darwinists: Can Evolutionary Principles Shed New Light on the Literary Canon? And Why, As A Species Do We Read Anyway?" The essay claims that literary Darwinism may go on to broaden still other fields—such as psychology—and may have already done so.

■ The New York Times reports a forum on intelligent design. This currently controversial idea provides a challenge to Darwinism that preserves God as creator. The feature reports that: "The proponents of intelligent design do not claim to have a coherent scientific theory about how life actually changed over time on earth. They offer arguments about what evolution could *not* do, and then conclude that a designer is the best hypothesis."

■ A new business book is published: *Dealing With Darwin: How Great Companies Innovate at Every Stage of the Evolution*. The book deals with finding strategies for businesses to survive in the competitive world of globalization.

The selections in this chapter explore some aspects of evolution in its conceptual nature, in its origins, and in some of its impact on intellectual history as an interdisciplinary idea. We begin with Darwin himself and the key chapter of his great book in which he explains the concept of natural selection. Just as human breeders of animals select qualities such as color or shape that they wish to foster in ongoing generations, nature "selects" those fittest to survive in the struggle for existence. Darwin goes on to sketch out how sexual selection in nature makes an aspect of this general process before giving some examples from his own research that confirm how evolution has acted through time to evolve new species from an ancestral population.

We next get an insight into the very instant of inspiration for the idea of evolution through natural selection, as recorded in Darwin's own *Autobiography*. There he describes how, on reading the economist Thomas Malthus while relaxing from his own work, he was able to see how Malthus's ideas on the limits of human population could be applied to any living population with natural selection as the inevitable result. This "Eureka moment" makes one of the most famous examples of the stimulus to thought provided by interdisciplinarity.

The original passages that Darwin read in Malthus' *Essay on the Principle of Population* come next. Malthus uses mathematical insights into the different rates of growth population and the cultivatable land that feeds it to make alarming predictions about the future of humanity. His book became a great factor in giving the name of "The Dismal Science" to the field of economics, though Darwin was able to see the creative aspect of the same destructive process.

"A Note on the Explosion of Geological Time" by your editor follows Malthus. Here we see the new ideas proposed by nineteenth-century geology about the quantity of time in the earth's history. Time makes the other factor Darwin needed in his evolutionary equation. Without the newly discovered vastness of time, small modifications would not be able to make the changes in species he describes.

The next essay gives an appreciation of Darwin as an artist as well as a scientist. The literary critic Theodore Baird in "Darwin and the Tangled Bank" demonstrates through the analysis of Darwin's writing style how science and literature were combined in Darwin's great book. By doing justice to the complexities of nature as imaged in a "tangled bank," Baird shows how Darwin was able the better to understand life by continuing to respect its essential mystery.

"Intelligent Design" names what is currently the most publicized disagreement with Darwin's explanation of the past and present facts of life on earth, and the concept attempts to provide an alternative explanation for those facts. But aren't such attempts *illogical*? How can they reconcile the geological evidence of the earth's vast age with the creation described in the bible whose own evidence makes the world only some 6,000 years old? The great Argentine writer Jorge Luis Borges shows in "The Creation and P. H. Gosse" that whatever problems there might be with the bible story, the strictly logical difficulties are more apparent than real.

Gosse was a contemporary of Darwin, but Darwin's ideas continued to create opposition in the early part of the twentieth century and those ideas even went to court in Tennessee in the famous Scopes Trial, or as the famous political reporter and cultural critic H. L. Mencken calls it in his essay "The Monkey Trial: A Reporter's Account." That account includes a description of the clash between two famous figures of the early twentieth century, the liberal lawyer Clarence Darrow and the spokesman for rural America, William Jennings Bryan.

Darwin's ideas were stimulated in part by his reading of economics, but economists in their turn have been stimulated by reading Darwin. Joseph Schumpeter was a radically original Harvard economist who sought to explain by evolutionary analogy how the standard of living could appear continually to improve over the long run while over the short run—particularly in the midst of the Great Depression— businesses were failing, millions of workers were laid off, and capitalism seemed doomed. The selection from his book, *Capitalism, Socialism, and Democracy,* attempts to explain the paradox by means of the phrase "creative destruction."

Another paradox created by Darwin's thinking involved the apparent opposition between his concept of the struggle for existence and the longstanding belief that the natural world manifested the goodness of God. Nature could no longer be viewed as providing pleasant examples of universal ideals—the cooperation and harmony exemplified in a colony of bees for example. In "Nonmoral Nature," Stephen Jay Gould takes us on a tour of insect parasites that have troubled even Darwin himself in his hope that nature manifested a higher purpose.

The chapter ends with a pair of essays by famous women who disagree on what might be seen as a moral topic related to evolution and the dangers and opportunities provided by the human power to intervene in the struggle for existence. Rachel Carson was the first scientist to warn the world about the dangers of overuse for a new miracle weapon (DDT) in the fight against insect pests. Phyllis Schlafly thinks that there has been an overreaction to that warning with the result that preventable deaths from malaria continue to take a toll on poor nations.

Natural Selection   1859

From *On the Origin of Species by Means of Natural Selection*

CHARLES DARWIN

Charles Darwin (1809–1882) was the son of a highly suceesful physician famous for his acute and at times almost occult powers of observation and diagnosis. One grandfather, Erasmus Darwin was a great horticulturist and author of a long poem in couplets about biological concepts that it was his grandson's destiny to clarify and transform. His mother's father was Josiah Wedgewood, the great industrial potter and creator of the line of china still sold today.

Given such a family background, Charles was not thought very promising as a young man. He began training as a doctor, but was so sickened by witnessing operations in that pre-anesthetic time that he could not continue. He then half-heartedly pursued a clerical career at Cambridge, but was more interested in hunting and collecting insects. Always a keen lover of natural history, he seized the chance to delay a decision about his professional future by joining as a civilian naturalist a Royal Navy ship, HMS Beagle which was engaged in a mapping voyage around the world 1832–1836.

Darwin's observations published in The Voyage of the Beagle (1839) made him professionally respected and decided him on a career as a gentleman scientist unaffiliated with any university or institution. The most famous of his observations had to do with the slight variations among isolated but nearby species of birds that seemed to give them advantages in feeding—beaks particularly suited to opening difficult seed pods, for example. The new and rapidly growing science of geology seemed to show an earth hundreds of millions of years older than the 6,000 years bible scholars had ascribed to the age of the planet. Darwin saw that even slight variations over such a vast extent of time might add up to changes in a type of organism that eventually distinguished it as a separate species from its near relatives. He knew that breeders of animals could make striking changes in a line of creatures by carefully selecting the parents of the next generation, and so he called his own suggested mechanism of change natural selection.

Working for nearly twenty years on his ideas (as he describes in the second selection of his writing to follow), Darwin published his Origin of Species by Means of Natural Selection in 1859 and only then because a fellow scientist had hit upon the same general idea. Though he began a controversy with some religious believers that continues to this day, Darwin saw the wide acceptance of his ideas in his own lifetime and he died an internationally famous and respected scientist.

Can the principle of selection, which we have seen is so potent in the hands of man, apply under nature? I think we shall see that it can act most efficiently. Let the endless number of slight variations and individual differences occurring in our domestic productions, and, in a lesser degree, in those under nature, be borne in mind; as well as the strength of the hereditary tendency. Under domestication, it may be truly said that the whole organisation becomes in some degree plastic.

But the variability, which we almost universally meet with in our domestic productions, is not directly produced, as Hooker and Asa Gray have well remarked, by man; he can neither originate varieties, nor prevent their occurrence; he can preserve and accumulate such as do occur. Unintentionally he exposes organic beings to new and changing conditions of life, and variability ensues; but similar changes of conditions might and do occur under nature. Let it also be borne in mind how infinitely complex and close-fitting are the mutual relations of all organic beings to each other and to their physical conditions of life; and consequently what infinitely varied diversities of structure might be of use to each being under changing conditions of life. Can it, then, be thought improbable, seeing that variations useful to man have undoubtedly occurred, that other variations useful in some way to each being in the great and complex battle of life, should occur in the course of many successive generations. If such do occur, can we doubt (remembering that many more individuals are born than can possibly survive) that individuals having any advantage, however slight, over others, would have the best chance of surviving and of procreating their kind? On the other hand, we may feel sure that any variation in the least degree injurious would be rigidly destroyed. This preservation of favourable individual differences and variations, and the destruction of those which are injurious, I have called Natural Selection, or the Survival of the Fittest. Variations neither useful nor injurious would not be affected by natural selection, and would be left either a fluctuating element, as perhaps we see in certain polymorphic species, or would ultimately become fixed, owing to the nature of the organism and the nature of the conditions.

Several writers have misapprehended or objected to the term Natural Selection. Some have even imagined that natural selection induces variability, whereas it implies only the preservation of such variations as arise and are beneficial to the being under its conditions of life. No one objects to agriculturists speaking of the potent effects of man's selection; and in this case the individual differences given by nature, which man for some object selects, must of necessity first occur. Others have objected that the term selection implies conscious choice in the animals which become modified; and it had even been urged that, as plants have no volition, natural selection is not applicable to them! In the literal sense of the word, no doubt, natural selection is a false term; but who ever objected to chemists speaking of the elective affinities of the various elements?—and yet an acid cannot strictly be said to elect the base which which it in preference combines. It has been said that I speak of natural selection as an active power or Deity; but who objects to an author speaking of the attraction of gravity as ruling the movements of the planets? Every one knows what is meant and is implied by such metaphorical expressions; and they are almost necessary for brevity. So again it is difficult to avoid personifying the word Nature; but I mean by Nature, only the aggregate action and product of many natural laws, and by laws the sequence of events as ascertained by us. With a little familiarity such superficial objections will be forgotten.

We shall best understand the probable course of natural selection by taking the case of a country undergoing some slight physical change, for instance, of climate. The proportional numbers of its inhabitants will almost immediately undergo a change, and some species will probably become extinct. We may conclude, from what we have seen of the intimate and complex manner in which the inhabitants of each country are bound together, that any change in the numerical proportions of the inhabitants, independently of the change of climate itself, would seriously affect the others. If the country were open on its borders, new forms would certainly immigrate, and this would likewise seriously disturb the relations of some of the former inhabitants. Let it be remembered how powerful the influence of a single introduced tree or mammal has been shown to be. But in the case of an island, or of a country partly surrounded by barriers, into which new and better adapted forms could not freely enter, we should then have places in the economy of nature which would assuredly be better filled up, if some of the original inhabitants were in some manner modified; for, had the area been open to immigration, these same places would have been seized on by intruders. In such cases, slight modifications, which in any way favoured the individuals of any species, by better adapting them to their altered conditions, would tend to be preserved; and natural selection would have free scope for the work of improvement.

We have good reason to believe, as shown in the first chapter, that changes in the conditions of life give a tendency to increased variability; and in the foregoing cases the conditions have changed, and this would manifestly be favourable to natural selection, by affording a better chance of the occurrence of profitable variations. Unless such occur, natural selection can do nothing. Under the term of "variations," it must never be forgotten that mere individual differences are included. As man can produce a great result with his domestic animals and plants by adding up in any given direction individual differences, so could natural selection, but far more easily from having incomparably longer time for action. Nor do I believe that any great physical change, as of climate, or any unusual degree of isolation to check immigration, is necessary in order that new and unoccupied places should be left, for natural selection to fill up by improving some of the varying inhabitants. For as all the inhabitants of each country are struggling together with nicely balanced forces, extremely slight modifications in the structure or habits of one species would often give it an advantage over others; and still further modifications of the same kind would often still further increase the advantage, as long as the species continued under the same conditions of life and profited by similar means of subsistence and defence. No country can be named in which all the native inhabitants are now so perfectly adapted to each other and to the physical conditions under which they live, that none of them could be still better adapted or improved; for in all countries, the natives have been so far conquered by naturalised productions, that they have allowed some foreigners to take firm possession of the land. And as foreigners have thus in every country beaten some of the natives, we may safely conclude that the natives might have been modified with advantage, so as to have better resisted the intruders.

5   As man can produce, and certainly has produced, a great result by his methodical and unconscious means of selection, what may not natural selection effect? Man can act only on external and visible characters: Nature, if I may be allowed to personify the natural preservation or survival of the fittest, cares nothing for appearances, except in so far as they are useful to any being. She can act on every internal organ, on every shade of constitutional difference, on the whole machinery of life. Man selects only for his own good: Nature only for that of the being which she tends. Every selected character is fully exercised by her, as is implied by the fact of their selection. Man keeps the natives of many climates in the same country; he seldom exercises each selected character in some peculiar and fitting manner; he feeds a long and a short beaked pigeon on the same food; he does not exercise a long-backed or long-legged quadruped in any peculiar manner; he exposes sheep with long and short wool to the same climate. He does not allow the most vigorous males to struggle for the females.

He does not rigidly destroy all inferior animals, but protects during each varying season, as far as lies in his power, all his productions. He often begins his selection by some half-monstrous form; or at least by some modification prominent enough to catch the eye or to be plainly useful to him. Under Nature, the slightest differences of structure or constitution may well turn the nicely balanced scale in the struggle for life, and so be preserved. How fleeting are the wishes and efforts of man! how short his time! and consequently how poor will be his results, compared with those accumulated by Nature during whole geological periods! Can we wonder, then, that Nature's productions should be far "truer" in character than man's productions that they should be infinitely better adapted to the most complex conditions of life and should plainly bear the stamp of far higher workmanship?

It may metaphorically be said that natural selection is daily and hourly scrutinising, throughout the world, the slightest variations; rejecting those that are bad, preserving and adding up all that are good; silently and insensibly working, *whenever and wherever opportunity offers*, at the improvement of each organic being in relation to its organic and inorganic conditions of life. We see nothing of these slow changes in progress, until the hand of time has marked the lapse of ages, and then so imperfect is our view into long-past geological ages, that we see only that the forms of life are now different from what they formerly were.

In order that any great amount of modification should be effected in a species, a variety when once formed must again, perhaps after a long interval of time, vary or present individual differences of the same favourable nature as before; and these must be again preserved, and so onwards step by step. Seeing that individual differences of the same kind perpetually recur, this can hardly be considered as an unwarrantable assumption. But whether it is true, we can judge only by seeing how far the hypothesis accords with and explains the general phenomena of nature. On the other hand, the ordinary belief that the amount of possible variation is a strictly limited quantity is likewise a simple assumption.

Although natural selection can act only through and for the good of each being, yet characters and structures, which we are apt to consider as of very trifling importance, may thus be acted on. When we see leaf-eating insects green, and bark-feeders mottled-grey; the alpine ptarmigan white in winter, the red-grouse the colour of heather, we must believe that these tints are of service to these birds and insects in preserving them from danger. Grouse, if not destroyed at some period of their lives would increase in countless numbers; they are known to suffer largely from birds of prey; and hawks are guided by eyesight to their prey—so much so, that on parts of the Continent persons are warned not to keep white pigeons, as being the most liable to destruction. Hence natural selection might be effective in giving the proper colour to each kind of grouse, and in keeping that colour, when once acquired, true and constant. Nor ought we to think that the occasional destruction of an animal of any particular colour would produce little effect: we should remember how essential it is in a flock of white sheep to destroy a lamb with the faintest trace of black. We have seen how the colour of the hogs, which feed on the "paint-root" in Virginia, determines whether they shall live or die. In plants, the down on the fruit and the colour of the flesh are considered by botanists as characters of the most trifling importance: yet we hear from an excellent horticulturist, Downing, that in the United States, smooth-skinned fruits suffer far more from a beetle, a Curculio, than those with down; that purple plums suffer far more from a certain disease than yellow plums; whereas another disease attacks yellow-fleshed peaches far more than those with other coloured flesh. If, with all the aids of art, these slight differences make a great difference in cultivating the several varieties, assuredly, in a state of nature, where the trees would have to struggle with other trees, and with a host of enemies, such differences would effectually settle which variety, whether a smooth or downy, a yellow or purple fleshed fruit, should succeed.

In looking at many small points of difference between species, which, as far as our ignorance permits us to judge, seem quite unimportant, we must not forget that climate, food, &c., have no doubt produced some effect. It is also necessary to bear in mind that, owing to the law of correlation, when one part varies, and the variations are accumulated through natural selection, other modifications, often of the most unexpected nature, will ensue.

10   As we see that those variations which, under domestication, appear at any particular period of life, tend to reappear in the offspring at the same period;—for instance, in the shape, size, and flavour of the seeds of the many varieties of our culinary and agricultural plants; in the caterpillar and cocoon stages of the varieties of the silk-worm; in the eggs of poultry, and in the colour of the down of their chickens; in the horns of our sheep and cattle when nearly

adult;—so in a state of nature natural selection will be enabled to act on and modify organic beings at any age, by the accumulation of variations profitable at that age, and by their inheritance at a corresponding age. If it profit a plant to have its seeds more and more widely disseminated by the wind, I can see no greater difficulty in this being effected through natural selection, than in the cotton-planter increasing and improving by selection the down in the pods on his cotton-trees. Natural selection may modify and adapt the larva of an insect to a score of contingencies, wholly different from those which concern the mature insect; and these modifications may effect, through correlation, the structure of the adult. So, conversely, modifications in the adult may affect the structure of the larva; but in all cases natural selection will ensure that they shall not be injurious: for if they were so, the species would become extinct.

Natural selection will modify the structure of the young in relation to the parent, and of the parent in relation to the young. In social animals it will adapt the structure of each individual for the benefit of the whole community; if the community profits by the selected change. What natural selection cannot do, is to modify the structure of one species, without giving it any advantage, for the good of another species; and though statements to this effect may be found in works of natural history, I cannot find one case which will bear investigation. A structure used only once in an animal's life, if of high importance to it, might be modified to any extent by natural selection; for instance, the great jaws possessed by certain insects, used exclusively for opening the cocoon—or the hard tip to the beak of unhatched birds, used for breaking the egg. It has been asserted, that of the best short-beaked tumbler-pigeons a greater number perish in the egg than are able to get out of it; so that fanciers assist in the act of hatching. Now if nature had to make the beak of a full-grown pigeon very short for the bird's own advantage, the process of modification would be very slow, and there would be simultaneously the most rigorous selection of all the young birds within the egg, which had the most powerful and hardest beaks, for all with weak beaks would inevitably perish; or, more delicate and more easily broken shells might be selected, the thickness of the shell being known to vary like every other structure.

It may be well here to remark that with all beings there must be much fortuitous destruction, which can have little or no influence on the course of natural selection. For instance a vast number of eggs or seeds are annually devoured, and these could be modified through natural selection only if they varied in some manner which protected them from their enemies. Yet many of these eggs or seeds would perhaps, if not destroyed, have yielded individuals better adapted to their conditions of life than any of those which happened to survive. So again a vast number of mature animals and plants, whether or not they be the best adapted to their conditions, must be annually destroyed by accidental causes, which would not be in the least degree mitigated by certain changes of structure or constitution which would in other ways be beneficial to the species. But let the destruction of the adults be ever so heavy, if the number which can exist in any district be not wholly kept down by such causes,—or again let the destruction of eggs or seeds be so great that only a hundredth or a thousandth part are developed,—yet of those which do survive, the best adapted individuals, supposing that there is any variability in a favourable direction, will tend to propagate their kind in larger numbers than the less well adapted. If the numbers be wholly kept down by the causes just indicated, as will often have been the case, natural selection will be powerless in certain beneficial directions; but this is no valid objection to its efficiency at other times and in other ways; for we are far from having any reason to suppose that many species ever undergo modification and improvement at the same time in the same area.

Sexual Selection

Inasmuch as peculiarities often appear under domestication in one sex and become hereditarily attached to that sex, so no doubt it will be under nature. Thus it is rendered possible for the two sexes to be modified through natural selection in relation to different habits of life, as is sometimes the case; or for one sex to be modified in relation to the other sex, as commonly occurs. This leads me to say a few words on what I have called Sexual Selection. This form of selection depends, not on a struggle for existence in relation to other organic beings or to external conditions, but on a struggle between the individuals of one sex, generally the males, for the possession of the other sex. The result is not death to the unsuccessful competitor, but few or no offspring. Sexual selection is, therefore, less rigorous than natural selection. Generally, the most vigorous males, those which are best fitted for their places in nature, will leave most progeny. But in many cases, victory depends not so much on general vigor, as on having special weapons, confined to the male sex. A hornless stag or spurless cock would have poor chance of leaving numerous offspring. Sexual selection, by always allowing the victor to breed, might surely give indomitable courage, length to the spur, and strength to the wing to strike in the spurred leg, in nearly the same manner as does the brutal cock-fighter by the careful selection of his best cocks. How low in the scale of nature the law of battle descends, I know not; male alligators have been described as fighting, bellowing, and whirling round, like Indians in a wardance, for the possession of the females; male salmons have been observed fighting all day long; male stag-beetles sometimes bear wounds from the huge mandibles of other males; the males of certain hymenopterous insects have been frequently seen by that inimitable observer M. Fabre, fighting for a particular female who sits by, an apparently unconcerned beholder of the struggle, and then retires with the conqueror. The war is, perhaps, severest between the males of polygamous animals, and these seem oftenest provided with special weapons. The males of carnivorous animals are already well armed; though to them and to others, special means of defence may be given through means of sexual selection, as the mane of the lion, and the hooked jaw to the male salmon; for the shield may be as important for victory, as the sword or spear.

Amongst birds, the contest is often of a more peaceful character. All those who have attended to the subject, believe that there is the severest rivalry between the males of many species to attract, by singing, the females. The rock-thrush of Guiana, birds of paradise, and some others, congregate; and successive males display with the most elaborate care, and show off in the best manner, their gorgeous plumage; they likewise perform strange antics before the females, which, standing by as spectators, at last choose the most attractive partner. Those who have closely attended to birds in confinement well know that they often take individual preferences and dislikes: thus Sir R. Heron has described how a pied peacock was eminently attractive to all his hen birds. I cannot here enter on the necessary details; but if man can in a short time give beauty and an elegant carriage to his bantams, according to the standard of beauty, I can see no good reason to doubt that female birds, by selecting, during thousands of generations, the most melodious or beautiful males according to their standard of beauty, might produce a marked effect. Some well-known laws, with respect to the plumage of male and female birds, in comparison with the plumage of the young, can partly be explained through the action of sexual selection on variations occurring at different ages, and transmitted to the males alone or to both sexes at corresponding ages; but I have not space here to enter on this subject.

15   Thus it is, as I believe, that when the males and females of any animal have the same general habits of life, but differ in structure, colour, or ornament, such differences have been mainly caused by sexual selection: that is, by individual males having had, in successive generations, some slight advantage over other males, in their weapons, means of defence, or charms, which they have transmitted to their male offspring alone. Yet, I would not wish to attribute all sexual differences to this agency: for we see in our domestic animals peculiarities arising and becoming attached to the male sex, which apparently have not been augmented through selection by man. The tuft of hair on the breast of the wild turkey-cock cannot be of any use, and it is doubtful whether it can be ornamental in the eyes of the female bird;—indeed, had the tuft appeared under domestication, it would have been called a monstrosity.

Illustrations of the Action of Natural Selection, or the Survival of the Fittest

In order to make it clear how, as I believe, natural selection acts, I must beg permission to give one or two imaginary illustrations. Let us take the case of a wolf, which preys on various animals, securing some by craft, some by strength and some by fleetness; and let us suppose that the fleetest prey, a deer for instance, had from any change in the country increased in numbers or that other prey had decreased in numbers, during that season of the year when the wolf was hardest pressed for food. Under such circumstances the swiftest and slimmest wolves would have the best chance of surviving and so be preserved or selected,—provided always that they retained strength to master their prey at this or some other period of the year, when they were compelled to prey on other animals. I can see no more reason to doubt that this would be the result, than that man should be able to improve the fleetness of his greyhounds by careful and methodical selection, or by that kind of unconscious selection which follows from each man trying to keep the best dogs without any thought of modifying the breed. I may add, that, according to Mr. Pierce, there are two varieties of the wolf inhabiting the Catskill Mountains, in the United States, one with a light greyhound-like form, which pursues deer, and the other more bulky, with shorter legs, which more frequently attacks the shepherd's flocks.

It should be observed that, in the above illustration, I speak of the slimmest individual wolves, and not of any single strongly-marked variation having been preserved. In former editions of this work I sometimes spoke as if this latter alternative had frequently occurred. I saw the great importance of individual differences, and this led me fully to discuss the results of unconscious selection by man, which depends on the preservation of all the more or less valuable individuals, and on the destruction of the worst. I saw, also, that the preservation in a state of nature of any occasional deviation of structure, such as a monstrosity, would be a rare event; and that, if at first preserved, it would generally be lost by subsequent intercrossing with ordinary individuals. Nevertheless, until reading an able and valuable article in the 'North British Review' (1867), I did not appreciate how rarely single variations, whether slight or strongly marked, could be perpetuated. The author takes the case of a pair of animals, producing during their lifetime two hundred offspring, of which, from various causes of destruction, only two on an average survive to procreate their kind. This is rather an extreme estimate for most of the higher animals, but by no means so for many of the lower organisms. He then shows that if a single individual were born, which varied in some manner, giving it twice as good a chance of life as that of the other individuals, yet the chances would be strongly against its survival. Supposing it to survive and to breed, and that half its young inherited the favourable variation; still, as the Reviewer goes on to show, the young would have only a slightly better chance of surviving and breeding; and this chance would go on decreasing in the succeeding generations. The justice of these remarks cannot, I think, be disputed. If, for instance, a bird of some kind could procure its food more easily by having its beak curved, and if one were born with its beak strongly curved, and which consequently flourished, nevertheless there would be a very poor chance of this one individual perpetuating its kind to the exclusion of the common form; but there can hardly be a doubt, judging by what we see taking place under domestication, that this result would follow from the preservation during many generations of a large number of individuals with more or less strongly curved beaks, and from the destruction of a still larger number with the straightest beaks.

It should not, however, be overlooked that certain rather strongly marked variations, which no one would rank as mere individual differences, frequently recur owing to a similar organisation being similarly acted on—of which fact numerous instances could be given with our domestic productions. In such cases, if the varying individual did not actually transmit to its offspring its newly-acquired character, it would undoubtedly transmit to them, as long as the existing conditions remained the same, a still stronger tendency to vary in the same manner. There can also be little doubt that the tendency to vary in the same manner has often been so strong that all the individuals of the same species have been similarly modified without the aid of any form of selection. Or only a third, fifth, or tenth part of the individuals may have been thus affected, of which fact several instances could be given. Thus Graba estimates that about one-fifth of the guillemots in the Faroe Islands consist of a variety so well marked, that it was formerly ranked as a distinct species under the name of Uria lacrymans. In cases of this kind, if the variation were of a beneficial nature, the original form would soon be supplanted by the modified form, through the survival of the fittest.

To the effects of intercrossing in eliminating variations of all kinds, I shall have to recur; but it may be here remarked that most animals and plants keep to their proper homes, and do not needlessly wander about; we see this even with migratory birds, which almost always return to the same spot. Consequently each newly-formed variety would generally be at first local, as seems to be the common rule with varieties in a state of nature; so that similarly modified individuals would soon exist in a small body together, and would often breed together. If the new variety were successful in its battle for life, it would slowly spread from a central district, competing with and conquering the unchanged individuals on the margins of an ever-increasing circle.

20 It may be worth while to give another and more complex illustration of the action of natural selection. Certain plants excrete sweet juice, apparently for the sake of eliminating something injurious from the sap: this is effected, for instance, by glands at the base of the stipules in some Leguminosæ, and at the backs of the leaves of the common laurel. This juice, though small in quantity, is greedily sought by insects; but their visits do not in any way benefit the plant. Now, let us suppose that the juice or nectar was excreted from the inside of the flowers of a certain number of plants of any species. Insects in seeking

the nectar would get dusted with pollen, and would often transport it from one flower to another. The flowers of two distinct individuals of the same species would thus get crossed; and the act of crossing, as can be fully proved, gives rise to vigorous seedlings which consequently would have the best chance of flourishing and surviving. The plants which produced flowers with the largest glands or nectaries, excreting most nectar, would oftenest be visited by insects, and would oftenest be crossed; and so in the long-run would gain the upper hand and form a local variety. The flowers, also, which had their stamens and pistils placed, in relation to the size and habits of the particular insects which visited them, so as to favour in any degree the transportal of the pollen, would likewise be favoured. We might have taken the case of insects visiting flowers for the sake of collecting pollen instead of nectar; and as pollen is formed for the sole purpose of fertilisation, its destruction appears to be a simple loss to the plant; yet if a little pollen were carried, at first occasionally and then habitually, by the pollen-devouring insects from flower to flower, and a cross thus effected, although nine-tenths of the pollen were destroyed it might still be a great gain to the plant to be thus robbed; and the individuals which produced more and more pollen, and had larger anthers, would be selected.

When our plant, by the above process long continued, had been rendered highly attractive to insects, they would, unintentionally on their part, regularly carry pollen from flower to flower; and that they do this effectually, I could easily show by many striking facts. I will give only one, as likewise illustrating one step in the separation of the sexes of plants. Some holly-trees bear only male flowers, which have four stamens producing a rather small quantity of pollen, and a rudimentary pistil: other holly-trees bear only female flowers; these have a full-sized pistil, and four stamens with shrivelled anthers, in which not a grain of pollen can be detected. Having found a female tree exactly sixty yards from a male tree, I put the stigmas of twenty flowers, taken from different branches, under the microscope, and on all, without exception, there were a few pollen-grains, and on some a profusion. As the wind had set for several days from the female to the male tree, the pollen could not thus have been carried. The weather had been cold and boisterous, and therefore not favourable to bees, nevertheless every female flower which I examined had been effectually fertilised by the bees, which had flown from tree to tree in search of nectar. But to return to our imaginary case: as soon as the plant had been rendered so highly attractive to insects that pollen was regularly carried from flower to flower, another process might commence. No naturalist doubts the advantage of what has been called the "physiological division of labour"; hence we may believe that it would be advantageous to a plant to produce stamens alone in one flower or on one whole plant, and pistils alone in another flower or on another plant. In plants under culture and placed under new conditions of life, sometimes the male organs and sometimes the female organs become more or less impotent; now if we suppose this to occur in ever so slight a degree under nature, then, as pollen is already carried regularly from flower to flower, and as a more complete separation of the sexes of our plant would be advantageous on the principle of the division of labour, individuals with this tendency more and more increased would be continually favoured or selected, until at last a complete separation of the sexes might be effected. It would take up too much space to show the various steps, through dimorphism and other means, by which the separation of the sexes in plants of various kinds is apparently now in progress; but I may add that some of the species of holly in North America, are, according to Asa Gray, in an exactly intermediate condition, or, as he expresses it, are more or less diœciously polygamous.

Let us now turn to the nectar-feeding insects; we may suppose the plant, of which we have been slowly increasing the nectar by continued selection, to be a common plant; and that certain insects depended in main part on its nectar for food. I could give many facts showing how anxious bees are to save time: for instance, their habit of cutting holes and sucking the nectar at the bases of certain flowers, which, with a very little more trouble, they can enter by the mouth. Bearing such facts in mind, it may be believed that under certain circumstances individual differences in the curvature or length of the proboscis, &c., too slight to be appreciated by us, might profit a bee or other insect, so that certain individuals would be able to obtain their food more quickly than others; and thus the communities to which they belonged would flourish and throw off many swarms inheriting the same peculiarities. The tubes of the corolla of the common red and incarnate clovers (Trifolium pratense and incarnatum) do not on a hasty glance appear to differ in length; yet the hive-bee can easily suck the nectar out of the incarnate clover, but not out of the common red clover, which is visited by humble-bees alone; so that whole fields of red clover offer in vain an abundant supply of precious nectar to the hive-bee. That this nectar is much liked by the hive-bee is certain; for I have repeatedly seen, but only in the autumn, many hive-bees sucking the flowers through holes bitten in the base of the tube by bumble-bees. The difference in the length of the corolla in the two kinds of clover, which determines the visits of the hive-bee, must be very trifling; for I have been assured that when red clover has been mown, the flowers of the second crop are somewhat smaller, and that these are visited by many hive-bees. I do not know whether this statement is accurate; nor whether another published statement can be trusted, namely, that the Ligurian bee which is generally considered a mere variety of the common hive-bee, and which freely crosses with it, is able to reach and suck the nectar of the red clover. Thus, in a country where this kind of clover abounded, it might be a great advantage to the hive-bee to have a slightly longer or differently constructed proboscis. On the other hand, as the fertility of this clover absolutely depends on bees visiting the flowers, if humble-bees were to become rare in any country, it might be a great advantage to the plant to have a shorter or more deeply divided corolla, so that the hive-bees should be enabled to suck its flowers. Thus I can understand how a flower and a bee might slowly become, either simultaneously or one after the other, modified and adapted to each other in the most perfect manner, by the continued preservation of all the individuals which presented slight deviations of structure mutually favourable to each other.

I am well aware that this doctrine of natural selection, exemplified in the above imaginary instances, is open to the same objections which were first urged against Sir Charles Lyell's noble views on "the modern changes of the earth, as illustrative of geology"; but we now seldom hear the agencies which we see still at work, spoken of as trifling or insignificant, when used in explaining the excavation of the deepest valleys of the formation of long lines of inland cliffs. Natural selection acts only by the preservation and accumulation of small inherited modifications, each profitable to the preserved being; and as modern geology has almost banished such views as the excavation of a great valley by a single diluvial wave, so will natural selection banish the belief of the continued creation of new organic beings, or of any great and sudden modification in their structure.

SUGGESTIONS FOR WRITING

1. The phrase "Survival of the Fittest" did not appear in the first edition of Darwin's book in 1859. Does this addition provide for you a better understanding of evolution? Write an essay that discusses the ways in which the phrase contributes explanatory power to the idea of biological evolution.

2. The section on "Sexual Selection" makes a particular instance of the general principle of natural selection. Write an essay explaining how Darwin's particular points about sexual selection support his general contentions about natural selection.

3. Dogs have been associated with mankind for at least 12,000 years, but one well-known type—the German shepherd or Alsatian—was created by a dedicated breeder over just a few decades in the early twentieth century. One of his techniques was to award prizes for individual characteristics—coloration, for example—at special dog shows he arranged, and then to breed prize-winning dogs together. Write an essay in which you describe and justify the prize categories you would employ to create a new breed of a domesticated animal or pet.

How Reading Malthus on Economics Sparked the Idea of Natural Selection   1887

From *The Autobiography of Charles Darwin*

CHARLES DARWIN

In the following selection from Darwin's delightfully informal autobiography, he records the crucial moment in his thinking when the idea occurred to him for the mechanism of natural selection in a struggle for existence among all the creatures of the earth. As he says, the idea occurred to him even before the publication of The Voyage of the Beagle *when he read the economist Thomas Malthus, who appears in a selection that follows this one. As you will see, Malthus posited a severe limit to the possibilities for the growth of the human population because of the finite resources available to feed it. Population naturally tended to grow in a geometric proportion: 2: 4: 8:, etc. but land put under cultivation for the production of food could only increase arithmetically: 1: 2: 3: 4, etc. Darwin reasoned similarly that a limit on food supplies would naturally force a struggle for existence and just as naturally lead to the survival of the fittest for such a struggle, beings which would pass on their fitness or what we now call "adaptive advantages" to their offspring.*

In October 1838, that is, fifteen months after I had begun my systematic enquiry, I happened to read for amusement Malthus on *Population*, and being well prepared to appreciate the struggle for existence which everywhere goes on from long-continued observation of the habits of animals and plants, it at once struck me that under these circumstances favourable variations would tend to be preserved, and unfavourable ones to be destroyed. The result of this would be the formation of new species. Here, then, I had at last got a theory by which to work; but I was so anxious to avoid prejudice, that I determined not for some time to write even the briefest sketch of it. In June 1842 I first allowed myself the satisfaction of writing a very brief abstract of my theory in pencil in 35 pages; and this was enlarged during the summer of 1844 into one of 230 pages, which I had fairly copied out and still possess.

But at that time I overlooked one problem of great importance; and it is astonishing to me, except on the principle of Columbus and his egg, how I could have overlooked it and its solution. This problem is the tendency in organic beings descended from the same stock to diverge in character as they become modified. That they have diverged greatly is obvious from the manner in which species of all kinds can be classed under genera, genera under families, families under suborders, and so forth; and I can remember the very spot in the road, whilst in my carriage, when to my joy the solution occurred to me; and this was long after I had come to Down. The solution, as I believe, is that the modified offspring of all dominant and increasing forms tend to become adapted to many and highly diversified places in the economy of nature.

Early in 1856 Lyell advised me to write out my views pretty fully, and I began at once to do so on a scale three or four times as extensive as that which was afterwards followed in my *Origin of Species*; yet it was only an abstract of the materials which I had collected, and I got through about half the work on this scale. But my plans were overthrown, for early in the summer of 1858 Mr Wallace, who was then in the Malay archipelago, sent me an essay *On the Tendency of Varieties to depart indefinitely from the Original Type*; and this essay contained exactly the same theory as mine. Mr Wallace expressed the wish that if I thought well of his essay, I should send it to Lyell for perusal.

The circumstances under which I consented at the request of Lyell and Hooker to allow of an extract from my MS., together with a letter to Asa Gray, dated September 5, 1857, to be published at the same time with Wallace's Essay, are given in the *Journal of the Proceedings of the Linnean*

Society, 1858, p. 45. I was at first very unwilling to consent, as I thought Mr Wallace might consider my doing so unjustifiable, for I did not then know how generous and noble was his disposition. The extract from my MS. and the letter to Asa Gray had neither been intended for publication, and were badly written. Mr Wallace's essay, on the other hand, was admirably expressed and quite clear. Nevertheless, our joint productions excited very little attention, and the only published notice of them which I can remember was by Professor Haughton of Dublin, whose verdict was that all that was new in them was false, and what was true was old. This shows how necessary it is that any new view should be explained at considerable length in order to arouse public attention.

5   In September 1858 I set to work by the strong advice of Lyell and Hooker to prepare a volume on the transmutation of species, but was often interrupted by ill-health, and short visits to Dr. Lane's delightful hydropathic establishment at Moor Park. I abstracted the MS. begun on a much larger scale in 1856, and completed the volume on the same reduced scale. It cost me thirteen months and ten days' hard labour. It was published under the title of the *Origin of Species*, in November 1859. Though considerably added to and corrected in the later editions, it has remained substantially the same book.

It is no doubt the chief work of my life. It was from the first highly successful. The first small edition of 1250 copies was sold on the day of publication, and a second edition of 3000 copies soon afterwards. Sixteen thousand copies have now (1876) been sold in England and considering how stiff a book it is, this is a large sale. It has been translated into almost every European tongue, even into such languages as Spanish, Bohemian, Polish, and Russian. It has also, according to Miss Bird, been translated into Japanese, and is there much studied. Even an essay in Hebrew has appeared on it, showing that the theory is contained in the Old Testament! The reviews were very numerous; for a time I collected all that appeared on the *Origin* and on my related books, and these amount (excluding newspaper reviews) to 265; but after a time I gave up the attempt in despair. Many separate essays and books on the subject have appeared; and in Germany a catalogue or bibliography on "Darwinismus" has appeared every year or two.

The success of the *Origin* may, I think, be attributed in large part to my having long before written two condensed sketches, and to my having finally abstracted a much larger manuscript, which was itself an abstract. By this means I was enabled to select the more striking facts and conclusions. I had, also, during many years, followed a golden rule, namely, that whenever a published fact, a new observation or thought came across me, which was opposed to my general results, to make a memorandum of it without fail and at once; for I had found by experience that such facts and thoughts were far more apt to escape from the memory than favourable ones. Owing to this habit, very few objections were raised against my views which I had not at least noticed and attempted to answer.

It has sometimes been said that the success of the *Origin* proved "that the subject was in the air," or "that men's minds were prepared for it." I do not think that this is strictly true, for I occasionally sounded not a few naturalists, and never happened to come across a single one who seemed to doubt about the permanence of species. Even Lyell and Hooker, though they would listen with interest to me, never seemed to agree. I tried once or twice to explain to able men what I meant by natural selection, but signally failed. What I believe was strictly true is that innumerable well-observed facts were stored in the minds of naturalists, ready to take their proper places as soon as any theory which would receive them was sufficiently explained. Another element in the success of the book was its moderate size; and this I owe to the appearance of Mr Wallace's essay; had I published on the scale in which I began to write in 1856, the book would have been four or five times as large as the *Origin*, and very few would have had the patience to read it.

I gained much by my delay in publishing from about 1839, when the theory was clearly conceived, to 1859; and I lost nothing by it, for I cared very little whether men attributed most originality to me or Wallace; and his essay no doubt aided in the reception of the theory. I was forestalled in only one important point, which my vanity has always made me regret, namely, the explanation by means of the Glacial period of the presence of the same species of plants and of some few animals on distant mountain summits and in the arctic regions.

This view pleased me so much that I wrote it out *in extenso*, and it was read by Hooker some years before E. Forbes published his celebrated memoir on the subject. In the very few points in which we differed, I still think that I was in the right. I have never, of course, alluded in print to my having independently worked out this view.

Hardly any point gave me so much satisfaction when I was at work on the *Origin*, as the explanation of the wide difference in many classes between the embryo and the adult animal, and of the close resemblance of the embry same class. No notice of this point was taken, as far as

10

I remember, in the early reviews of the *Origin*, and I recollect expressing my surprise on this head in a letter to Asa Gray. Within late years several reviewers have given the whole credit of the idea to Fritz Müller and Häckel, who undoubtedly have worked it out much more fully, and in some respects more correctly than I did. I had materials for a whole chapter on the subject, and I ought to have made the discussion longer; for it is clear that I failed to impress my readers; and he who succeeds in doing so deserves, in my opinion, all the credit.

This leads me to remark that I have almost always been treated honestly by my reviewers, passing over those without scientific knowledge as not worthy of notice. My views have often been grossly misrepresented, bitterly opposed and ridiculed, but this has been generally done as I believe in good faith. I must, however, except Mr Mivart, who as an American expressed it in a letter has acted towards me "like a pettifogger", or as Huxley has said "like an Old Bailey lawyer." On the whole I do not doubt that my works have been over and over again greatly overpraised. I rejoice that I have avoided controversies, and this I owe to Lyell, who many years ago, in reference to my geological works, strongly advised me never to get entangled in a controversy, as it rarely did any good and caused a miserable loss of time and temper.

Whenever I have found out that I have blundered, or that my work has been imperfect, and when I have been contemptuously criticised, and even when I have been overpraised, so that I have felt mortified, it has been my greatest comfort to say hundreds of times to myself that "I have worked as hard and as well as I could, and no man can do more than this." I remember when in Good Success Bay, in Tierra del Fuego, thinking, (and I believe that I wrote home to the effect) that I could not employ my life better than in adding a little to natural science. This I have done to the best of my abilities, and critics may say what they like, but they cannot destroy this conviction.

SUGGESTIONS FOR WRITING

1. In paragraph 1 Darwin mentions the economist Thomas Malthus (who appears as the next selection of this chapter) and in paragraph 2 he speaks of "the economy of nature." Does the analogy between nature and economics seem illuminating to you? Write an essay in which you explain how the language of economics does or does not help to explain the idea of the origin of species through natural selection.

2. In paragraph 2 Darwin refers to "Columbus and his egg." The legend is that Columbus challenged some skeptics to stand an egg on end. After failing, they declared it impossible. Columbus gently tapped one end of the egg to create tiny cracks that made its point flat without breaking the shell entirely. Then he easily stood the egg up. "The simplest thing in the world," he said. "Anyone can do it *after one has been shown how*." Write an essay in which you describe how this anecdote illuminates Darwin's discovery of evolution by natural selection.

3. At the end of the selection Darwin expresses his satisfaction in the fulfillment of his early ambition of "adding a little to natural science." In this and other ways within the passage he makes implicit analogies between human learning and evolution. Earlier, for example, he describes the potential "struggle" for scientific priority of publication between Wallace and himself. Write an essay in which you describe some of the ways in which Darwin views evolution in an evolutionary way.

Food Production Increases in an Arithmetic Ratio, Population in a Geometric One 1803, 1826

From *An Essay on The Principle of Population*

THOMAS MALTHUS

The Church of England clergyman Thomas Malthus (1766–1834) along with his friend and sometime adversary David Ricardo were among the founding fathers of economics following Adam Smith. Yet unlike the optimistic Smith (who appears in the next chapter), these men were instrumental in the pessimistic outlook for the economic future that resulted in the discipline's being called "The Dismal Science" by the novelist and historian Thomas Carlyle. Malthus's studies led him to conclude that a very unequal race was being run between human fertility and the possibilities for the earth to produce food supplies. In the famous passage that makes up the selection, he looks to the future from his position in the early 1800s and sees disaster ahead for the human race.

From the accounts we have of China and Japan, it may be fairly doubted, whether the best directed efforts of human industry could double the produce of these countries even once in any number of years. There are many parts of the globe, indeed, hitherto uncultivated, and almost unoccupied; but the right of exterminating, or driving into a corner where they must starve, even the inhabitants of these thinly peopled regions, will be questioned in a moral view. The process of improving their minds and directing their industry would necessarily be slow; and during this time, as population would regularly keep pace with the increasing produce, it would rarely happen that a great degree of knowledge and industry would/ have to operate at once upon rich unappropriated soil. Even where this might take place, as it does sometimes in new colonies, a geometrical ratio increases with such extraordinary rapidity, that the advantage could not last long. If [the United States of] America continue increasing, which [they] certainly will do, though not with the same rapidity as formerly, the Indians will be driven further and further back into the country, till the whole race is ultimately [exterminated, and the territory is incapable of further extension.]

These observations are, in a degree, applicable to all the parts of the earth, where the soil is imperfectly cultivated. To exterminate the inhabitants of the greatest part of Asia and Africa, is a thought that could not be admitted for a moment. To civilize and direct the industry of the various tribes of Tartars and negroes, would certainly be a work of considerable time, and of variable and uncertain success.

Europe is by no means so fully peopled as it might be. In Europe there is the fairest chance that human industry may receive its best direction. The science of agriculture has been much studied in England and Scotland; and there is still a great portion of uncultivated land in these countries. Let us consider at what rate the produce of this island might be supposed to increase under circumstances the most favourable to improvement.

If it be allowed that by the best possible policy, and great encouragements to agriculture, the/ average produce of the island could be doubled in the first twenty five years, it will be allowing, probably, a greater increase than could with reason be expected.

5   In the next twenty five years, it is impossible to suppose that the produce could be quadrupled. It would be contrary to all our knowledge of the properties of land. The improvement of the barren parts would be a work of time and labours and it must be evident to those who have the slightest acquaintance with agricultural subjects, that in proportion as cultivation extended, the additions that could yearly be made to the former average produce must be gradually and regularly diminishing. That we may be the better able to compare the increase of population and food, let us make a supposition, which, without pretending to

accuracy, is clearly more favourable to the power of production in the earth, than any experience we have had of its qualities will warrant.

Let us suppose that the yearly additions which might be made to the former average produce, instead of decreasing, which they certainly would do, were to remain the same; and that the produce of this island might be increased every twenty five years, by a quantity equal to what it at present [produces. The] most enthusiastic speculator cannot suppose a greater increase than this. In a few centuries it would make every acre of land in the island like a garden.

If this supposition be applied to the whole earth, and if it be allowed that the subsistence for/ man which the earth affords might be increased every twenty five years by a quantity equal to what it at present produces, this will be supposing a rate of increase much greater than we can imagine that any possible exertions of mankind could make it.

It may be fairly pronounced, therefore, that, considering the present average state of the earth, the means of subsistence, under circumstances the most favourable to human industry, could not possibly be made to increase faster than in an arithmetical ratio.

The necessary effects of these two different rates of increase, when brought together, will be very striking. Let us call the population of this island 11 millions; and suppose the present produce equal to the easy support of such a number. In the first twenty five years the population would be 22 millions, and the food being also doubled, the means of subsistence would be equal to this increase. In the next twenty five years, the population would be 44 millions, and the means of subsistence only equal to the support of 33 millions. In the next period the population would be 88 millions, and the means of subsistence just equal to the support of half that number. And, at the conclusion of the first century, the population would be 176 millions, and the means of subsistence only equal to the support of 55 millions, leaving a population of 121 millions totally unprovided for.

10 Taking the whole earth, instead of this island, emigration would of course be excluded; and, supposing the present population equal to a thousand millions, the human species would increase as the numbers, 1, 2, 4, 8, 16, 32, 64, 128, 256, and subsistence as 1, 2, 3, 4, 5, 6, 7, 8, 9. In two centuries the population would be to the means of subsistence as 256 to 9; in three centuries as 4096 to 13, and in two thousand years the difference would be almost incalculable.

In this supposition no limits whatever are placed to the produce of the earth. It may increase for ever and be greater than any assignable quantity; yet still the power of population being in every period so much superior, the increase of the human species can only be kept down to the level of the means of subsistence by the constant operation of the strong law of necessity, acting as a check upon the greater power.

	Malthus's Principle in Tabular Form									
Year	1	25	50	75	100	125	150	175	200	225
Population	1	2	4	8	16	32	64	128	256	512
Food supply	1	2	3	4	5	6	7	8	9	10

SUGGESTIONS FOR WRITING

1. Writing in the early nineteenth century, Malthus uses conditions in the United States of that time as an example. Write an essay in which you evaluate the accuracy of his analyses and predictions concerning the future of the United States.

2. Surely—on the principle of Columbus and his egg—the famous formula by which Malthus contrasts the arithmetic and geometric ratios involved in food production and population growth—might be expressed more clearly than Malthus does here. Using some of the materials Malthus provides, rewrite his essay to make his formula and the reasoning behind it more clear.

3. Malthus discusses only human survival in the face of population growth, while Darwin says that the populations of *all* species of life tend to reach a limit point. Pick a nonhuman example of a species that potentially can produce hundreds or hundreds of thousands of descendents in a very short time—mosquitoes, say. Now write an essay in which you explain using Malthusian principles how the population of your species will quickly tend to reach a limit point.

A Note on the Explosion of Geological Time

WILLIAM VESTERMAN

William Vesterman (b. 1942) is the editor of this book. He received a B.A. from Amherst College and a Ph.D. from Rutgers University. Author of The Stylistic Life of Samuel Johnson *and articles on English and American literature, he teaches English at Rutgers.*

When the grandfather of the American novelist Henry James came from Ireland to the United States shortly after the Revolution intent on visiting its battlefields, the world was still very young. In the long established common sense of cosmic time, a large but fully conceivable number of human generations led back to the creation of the universe some 6,000 years earlier at a date often calculated as 4004 B.C., most conclusively by Bishop Ussher (1581–1656) in the middle of the previous century. A few of those who followed closely on Ussher like the great classifier of natural history, John Ray (1627–1705)—but unlike a rival calculator of creation, Sir Isaac Newton (1642–1727)—had noted geological evidence that appeared very much at odds with the biblical account of the earth's history. However, it was not until 1788 that a Scot, James Hutton, first raised a revolt in geology, one that struggled at first and was almost put down, until its leadership passed to the Cambridge Professor of Geology, Charles Lyell in the early nineteenth century. After Lyell adopted Hutton's cause, the revolution quickly spread throughout the republic of letters, transforming the values and assumptions that had informed its understanding of time as radically as the American Revolution transformed values and assumptions underlying ideas about government.

Rock-solid evidence proved that the world was enormously old, and the more evidence was uncovered, the older it grew. Throughout the nineteenth century the age of the earth grew by leaps and bounds of millions and tens of millions and hundreds of millions of years. By 1907 when Henry James, then in his 60s, was at work on the New York edition of his collected works, techniques involving newly discovered radioactivity set a range for the age of the planet at 400 million to 2,200 million years, an enormous increase since his grandfather's time, to say the least. Today with better radiological techniqes scientist believe the age of the earth to be 4.6 billion years. Yet even contemporary readers of Henry James would have every reason to feel as lost in time as their ancestors had been lost in space after the Copernican revolution, when the long familiar and fully comprehensible Ptolemaic universe had exploded, shattering the beauty of its transparent and musical spheres to reveal for Blaise Pascal one fearful sphere whose center was everywhere and whose circumference was nowhere.

James Hutton's discoveries, like those of Copernicus, were stimulating as well as depressing. Spreading out from the explosion of geological time, shock waves of creative destruction demolished many intellectual structures in other areas of inquiry, but also promoted the building of new ones. When Henry James was still in his teens, one of Charles Lyell's disciples, Charles Darwin, demonstrated that the new vast stretches of geological time could be applied to the problem of species. Minute changes in an individual organism that gave it even the slightest advantage in the struggle for existence could be inherited; and if such changes, however minute, added up eon after eon in subsequent generations, new species unable to interbreed with fertile offspring would eventually appear. People suddenly found themselves no longer uniquely formed by God to rule over the earth's other creatures, but placed on a continuum of life that stretched back through a length of history expressible by the brute force of the number system but scarcely conceivable in any other language of the human imagination.

SUGGESTIONS FOR WRITING

1. The first paragraph claims that "the values and assumptions" underlying the human understanding of time were radically transformed by James Hutton. Pick one of those assumptions—the history of the human race, for example—and write an essay in which you agree or disagree with the essay's claim that the assumption was radically transformed.

2. In the passage from his *Autobiography* that describes his moment of insight Darwin does not mention his mentor in geology Charles Lyell or the issue of geological time. Based on your reading of the selection from *The Origin of Species,* write an imaginary addition to Darwin's *Autobiography* that sketches out Darwin's debt to Lyell.

3. Surely it is extremely difficult to conceive of the age of the earth, though scientists can give us a figure for the number of years that make up that age. Write an essay on the psychological difficulties involved for you in imagining time in terms of a few human generations and then imagining geological time as a scientific fact.

Darwin and the Tangled Bank 1946

THEODORE BAIRD

Theodore Baird was born in Ohio in 1902 and graduated from Hamilton College. He undertook the graduate study of literature at Harvard where he earned a Ph. D. After teaching at Western Reserve University and Union College, he came to Amherst where he spent the rest of his career and became the Samuel Williston Professor of English.

In "Darwin and the Tangled Bank," Baird examines Darwin's science from the point of view of his use of language and respect for the limitation of knowledge. Starting with the description of a meeting between Darwin and a much more obvious representative of literary talent—the novelist and historian Thomas Carlyle—Baird traces Darwin's relation to the great drama of natural history and the story he made out of it that largely replaced the biblical story and continues to dominate modern views of nature. Darwin's story, as Baird shows, is made up of metaphors as much as facts. Baird looks at Darwin's writing with the same intense critical attention that made Baird himself a strikingly original writer of literary criticism.

Details of the scene can be filled in. They were both very great men. Carlyle was eighty. On his latest birthday he had been much honored. From Prussia came a decoration—"The Star . . . is really very pretty . . . hung with a black ribbon, with silver edges. . . . Had they sent me a 1/4 lb. of good Tobacco the addition to my happiness had probably been . . . greater!" From America and Harvard came an honorary LL.D., and Disraeli, beginning his letter, "A Government should recognize intellect," offered him the Grand Cross of the Bath.

Darwin was sixty-six, and the *Origin* had been published for sixteen years. At home and abroad learned societies had delighted in recognizing him, and he too was entitled to wear the star with the black silver-edged ribbon, the Prussian *Pour le Mérite*. In the public mind he played a unique part, for his name had been appropriated to stand for what vast numbers of people professed to be against, Darwinism. He had been abused, denounced and reviled. Carlyle, in ordinary conversation, but not to the man's face, had had his say often enough: our descent from the apes is a humiliating discovery, which scientists had much better have kept to themselves, and, in short, he would like to lay his stick over Darwin's back. "I find no one," he told Allingham, "who has the deep abhorrence of [Darwinism]. . . . that I have in my heart of hearts!" Here then was a combination of persons more crucial than in the famous meeting of the libertine Wilkes and the moralist Johnson; here was personified the clash between science and literature, empiricism and intuition.

We own our knowledge of what they talked about to Carlyle's brief report. "I asked him," he said, "if he thought there was a possibility of men turning into apes again. . . . [Darwin] laughed much at this, and came back to it over and over again." Completely won over by Darwin personally, Carlyle was pleased with the meeting, and he told Allingham, who thought the phrase curious, that Darwin was a "pleasant, *jolly-minded* man." What Darwin thought of this exchange may well be contained in the sentence where he says of Carlyle, "As far as I could judge, I never met a man with a mind so ill adapted for scientific research."

Plainly Carlyle belongs to literature. Darwin's position is obscure. A popular textbook places him at the opposite pole, remarking that his work "cannot be said to belong to literature, if in the definition of literary work is presupposed an effort towards artistic expression." Yet Darwin, who certainly never thought of himself as a writer like Carlyle, was deeply concerned with literary composition, as the extensive remarks to Bates of the *Amazon* reveal. There were people who were born writers, he admitted, but he found the work hard. He had found it a good plan whenever he was in difficulties to fancy that someone had entered the room and asked him what he is doing; then he would try to explain "what it is all about." He added, "I think too much pains cannot be taken in making the style transparently clear and throwing eloquence to the dogs." The effort toward expression was there, and it would be a harsh critic who did not find artistic the result in *The Voyage of the Beagle.*

5 Darwin's subject—the face of the earth, the processes of nature— had long been within the scope of literature, and in his attitude there was nothing consciously novel. In the presence of the mystery or the beauty or the violence of nature, with the accompanying possible responses of worship or pleasure or shock, a writer could say, "Here it is, look at it," while simultaneously he communicated to the reader the effect, "How divine"; "How lovely" or "How horrible." This, indeed, is the literary experience—seeing the object, feeling an emotion. And it is this which Darwin communicates on page after page of the *Journal and Remarks* made on the voyage around the world of H.M.S. Beagle. His emotions he records in the plain and modest language of the eighteenth century. They are none the less strong.

Naturally many were pleasurable. In reflecting on the five years' experience, he says he enjoyed himself deeply. His biggest word, *sublime,* he applies to large effects, like the forests of Brazil, "where

Death powers of life are predominant," or to Tierra del Fuego, "where Death and Decay prevail." Milder adjectives are *glorious, beautiful, delicious, striking, pretty*, and he is moved to speak of the "inexpressible charm" of life in the open air: the deathlike stillness of the plains, the Gauchos making their beds round the fire, the dogs keeping watch. More than once he deliberately took thought how to convey to the reader the pleasure he felt: "I wished to find language to express my ideas. Epithet after epithet was found too weak to convey to those who have not visited the intertropical regions the sensations of delight which the mind experiences."

Yet violence, destruction and death were everywhere part of the charming landscape, like the slowly wheeling condor in the sky. The observer's experience is complicated, and the emotions mixed. In the foreground there is ever present the human being—the Fuegian savage, described in pages comparable to Swift on the Yahoo, slavery in Brazil, the conflict of races in New Zealand. "Wherever the European has trod, death seems to pursue the aboriginal." The same kind of fact met him everywhere. There was the cormorant playing with the fish it caught: "Eight times successively the bird let its prey go, then dived after it." There were the seals lying in astonishing numbers on the rocks, watched in the sky all the while "by the patient but inauspicious eyes of the turkey-buzzard. This disgusting bird . . ."

Inanimate nature provoked even more violent response. The concepts of time and space, which might be enlarged by the attentive perusal of the paragraphs in Lyell's *Principles of Geology* on prepossessions in regard to the duration of past time, were shattered by the presence before his eyes of bones and shells and mountain ranges and in his ears the sound of running water. By immediate observation Darwin was forced to review his prepossessions, to consider how time in sufficient quantities could be conceived of; and the language he uses indicates how great was his perplexity. "It is impossible to reflect on the changed state of the American continent," he says, "without the deepest astonishment. . . . Certainly, no fact in the long history of the world is so startling as the wide and repeated exterminations of its inhabitants."

He returns to this problem, and once with especial solemnity. Climbing a pass in the Andes he saw and heard the muddy, steeply inclined mountain streams, whose roar was like that of the sea. "Amidst the din of rushing waters, the noise of the stones, as they rattled one over another, was most distinctly audible even from a distance. . . . The sound spoke eloquently to the geologist; the thousands and thousands of stones, which, striking against each other, made the one dull uniform sound, were all hurrying in one direction. It was like thinking on time, where the minute that now glides past is irrecoverable. So it was with these stones; the ocean is their eternity, and each note of that wild music told of one more step toward their destiny."

10 Often he had seen beds of mud and sand and shingle thousands of feet thick, and he had been inclined to exclaim that such enormous masses could never have been formed by natural causes, grain on grain. "But . . . when listening to the rattling noise of these torrents, and calling to mind that whole races of animals have passed away from the face of the earth, and that during this whole period, night and day, these stones have gone rattling onwards in their course, I have thought to myself, can any mountains, any continent, withstand such waste?" Any continent—as if nothing could be more stable. Yet even this prepossession was destroyed by the "perfect horror" of the earthquake at Valdivia. "I falter where I firmly trod," says Tennyson, and every reader knows his words are metaphorical, alluding to instabilities of faith, but for Darwin the quaking of the earth was a literal experience with consequences on his systematic thinking. "The earth, the very emblem of solidity, has moved beneath our feet," he says, "like a thin crust over a fluid."

In this mixed response to nature—so beautiful, so horrible—Darwin was, of course, like many another man. Among his contemporaries the serious writers were making it their business to convey this very tension, to frame statements about it, even to resolve it, and in so doing they used traditional forms of speech, metaphors. They spoke as if an analogy between their manner of speaking and the universe really existed; and their readers, making the proper allowances, knew what they meant. It is unlikely that anyone ever asked Tennyson whether "God's finger touch'd him, and he slept," is an accurate verbal equivalent for the bursting of a blood vessel, nor was Carlyle besought to define in operational language his splendid, ringing phrases. Communication between author and reader was sustained by words which always meant more than their literal paraphrase, and the meaning was an insight, an intuition.

When in the *Origin* Darwin came to express how Nature as a whole seemed to him, he, too, used a metaphor. Nature, he said, is like something else, a struggle for existence, in which the fittest survive. The public instantly knew what he meant, recognizing the similarity as true (the Social Darwinians) or as false (the anti-Darwinians). And as a metaphor it must stand for some general experience, some common feeling about life, like that contained in the comparison with a flame ("Out, out, brief candle") or with a growing thing ("All flesh is as grass"). It implies what was by the middle of the nineteenth century a familiar literary attitude, the act of witnessing and feeling about, as at a play. It involves recognition of hero and villain, conflict, victory and defeat, and the conversion of painful emotions into pleasure. The dramatist asserts that everything turns out right, and the audience is satisfied, the tension relaxed. "Now cracks a noble heart. Good night, sweet prince, and flights of angels sing thee to thy rest!"

Educated readers were accustomed to the most exquisite verbal consolations about the death of Hamlet or the fall of man or the decline of the Roman Empire, and the ultimate, the inexpressible meanings resided in metaphor, as in the similarity of "good night," "rest," and "death." The transfer of this trained literary attitude to nature and its processes was apparently not difficult. A handful of seeds thrown on the ground becomes a drama. No matter how painful some moments, the spectator is finally satisfied. True, a number of seeds did not germinate, others were starved out, parasites and disease were shockingly destructive, but the play has a good ending— the survivors are the better plants. The complicated literary expression known as tragedy had recognized a paradox, that death is sometimes better than life, so that we applaud defeat. The metaphor of struggle for existence revises this proposition to read, life *is* better than death, the living *are* better than the dead. If nature is horrible, it is finally beautiful.

This kind of interpretation was to be expected from readers brought up on the prophetic writing of the nineteenth century. Carlyle could proclaim that the Universe is made by Law, that the great Soul of the World is just. "Look thou, if thou have eyes or soul left, into this great shoreless Incomprehensible: in the heart of its tumultuous Appearances, Embroilments, and mad Time-Vortexes, is there not, silent, eternal, an All-Just, an All-Beautiful . . ." and so on, ending, "This is not a figure of speech; this is a fact."

15   But Darwin was using language in quite another manner. He took pains to say that the struggle for existence is not a fact but only a figure of speech. He stops dead in his tracks, when first using the term, to

explain, "I use this term in a large and metaphorical sense," and he defines exactly what in nature he is pointing at. Two dogs in a time of dearth may be truly said to struggle for life as they fight for a bone. Second, the phrase is extended to include the relation of dependence: a plant on the edge of a desert is dependent on sufficient moisture, a mistletoe is dependent on the apple tree. Third, the phrase includes success in leaving progeny. These three different kinds of behavior are represented by the shorthand notation, struggle for existence. And in detail Darwin was careful not to confuse his manner of speaking with the thing spoken of. Thus he writes, every single organic being *"may be said* to be striving . . . ."

Some readers knew well enough what Darwin was talking about. Asa Gray straightened out a correspondent who could not see how plants. "struggled" since they had neither consciousness nor will, by replying that something really did happen in nature, "call the action what you please—competition (that is open to the same objection), collision or what not—it is just what I should think Darwin was driving at," and he refers him to the relevant passages of definition in the *Origin.* Here is a language difficulty. What phrase can stand for "the action" of nature, since it contains in it so many separate items, capable of expression in so many possible relationships? Any one metaphor— struggle, competition, collision—is little better than another, since none can express nature in its entirety. To understand the meaning of the phrase the reader must comprehend the grandly complex context, established by the author, in which nature appears as a multiplicity, so varied in its movements, that only the most wide-ranging mind can take it in.

Yet the parallel phrase, survival of the fittest, seems to imply that nature turns out right and that the best man wins. Each creature tends to become more and more improved, and this improvement leads to gradual advance in organization. This, says Darwin, is an intricate subject. Only a careless reader could suppose that Darwin saw clear direction in any given moment or event, that he was ever in a position to applaud the hero or hiss the villain, like the spectator in the the-ater—for at great length he expresses objections and qualifications to his own theory. A sequence of events can be labeled "improvement," but this word is not a fact, it is only a figure of speech. What exactly does it refer to in nature? Naturalists are not agreed among them-selves, as they shift their points of view and adopt different scales of measurement. It can be defind—in words—as high differentiation and specialization of the several organs, but how do they apply to a particular organism, how as a means of comparison of two organisms? What, for example, is to be said of the many low forms which have not advanced since the dawn of life, where no sequence of improvement is perceptible, which, nevertheless, when dissected, reveal to the naturalist "their really wondrous and beautiful organization"? Then there are cases of "what we must call retrogression of organization," and how does that fit into movement going in one direction? As for the comparison of different types, to make an ascending scale seems hopeless, for "who will decide whether a cuttlefish be higher than a bee?"

The objection that a theory which must be so qualified is of little use is obviously wrong. Asa Gray and other readers knew what Darwin was talking about. Darwin's position as a writer was identical with that of the historian. Gibbon had been able to speak of events as true—in a certain way. He defined his scale, civilization under the Antonines, and, at the other extreme, the illiterate barbarian, so that the basic metaphor of decline and fall refers to something more expressed than the reader's personal scale of civilization. In detail, of course, he could not be sure of very much. The precise behavior of a particular Scythian during every moment of his life was unknown to him or to any man, but the general westward movement, in "waves," of the pastoral tribes of Asia, is an historical fact.

The figure of speech, then, points to a complicated event. A blow by blow account, with victory and defeat determined by the universal umpire, the score carefully kept, is impossible in the struggle of any organism's existence. How little he knew in detail Darwin is constantly reminding the reader: "We know hardly anything about. . . . If we make due allowance for our profound ignorance. . . . This ought to convince us of our ignorance. . . ." Granting, however, the enormous limitations of knowledge under which the historian and the scientist labor, we do know what they are driving at: that life has flourished in many forms, that whole races have disappeared, yet the historical record can be made out by the trained observer, and this record can be made out by the trained observer, and this record can be expressed in a large, metaphorical sense.

20   The basic figure for this process is the tree of life—the trunk, the branches and twigs, some living, some dead, all representing complex relationships. "I believe," said Darwin, "this simile largely speaks the

truth," and for a page, and item by item, he works out the similitude of that great tree "which fills with its dead and broken branches the crust of the earth, and covers the surface with its ever-branching and beautiful ramifications." The related movement which takes place while the tree grows, one part living, another part dying, one part branching out and continuing the succession—this is the struggle for existence. The way in which this movement takes place is natural selection. And as for the survival of the fittest, "The inhabitants of the world at successive periods in its history have beaten their predecessors in the race for life, and are, in so far *higher* in the scale." This is, indeed, largely the truth. On the diagram known as a family tree the living are higher on the scale than the dead. A temporal relation is represented spatially.

Darwin's use of language is consistent. If in addition to the analysis of metaphor a glossary is compiled of key words, such as *law, facts, nature, species, variety, variation,* and if the crucial word in each definition is followed up, it will appear that Darwin's verbal universe is expressed and his language system complete. From the pages of the *Origin* can be constructed a recognizable, going world. It would contain an enormous number of separate things, accurately observed: animals and insects and plants, continents and oceans. Life and death take place, the surface of the earth moves like a thin crust over a fluid, and whole races pass away. The causes are all natural. There would also be a consciously placed, self-disciplined observer, a man aware of his own ignorance. For him exists a language problem, to use words not as revelations of his own inner self but as pointers to actions outside the observer, and he solves it by limiting exactly the degree of similitude implied by his metaphor.

This observer is also much moved by what he sees. Privately, we know, Darwin took intense delight in the act of observing. His son writes: "I used to like to hear him admire the beauty of a flower; it was a kind of gratitude to the flower itself. . . ." The emotions expressed so modestly in *The Voyage of the Beagle* recur in more generalized form in the *Origin.* Wonder and amazement predominate. "No one," he says, "can have marveled more than I have done at the extinction of species." In the last stately pages of the *Origin* he, too, resolves the tension of nature, so horrible, so beautiful. "When I view all beings . . ." he says, "as the lineal descendants of some few beings which lived long before the first bed of the Cambrian system was deposited, they seem to me to become ennobled." And as he contemplated the tangled bank, clothed with plants, the birds singing, insects flitting about, and in the damp earth the worms crawling—the struggle for existence going on before his eyes while he paused in his morning stroll on the Sand Walk; as he reflected that these elaborate forms have all been produced by laws acting around us, and that from the war of nature, from famine and death, has come the production of the higher animals—then he says, "There is grandeur in this view of life. . . ."

Galton's praise of Darwin, that he had "studied veracity as the highest of arts," belongs to him both as an observer and as a writer. Actually it is hard to see how these two processes can be separated and distinguished. It is easier to conclude that in 1859, at one of the great moments in modern thought, literature and science were united.

SUGGESTIONS FOR WRITING

1. In paragraph 5 Baird says, "This, indeed, is the literary experience—seeing the object, feeling an emotion." Write an essay in which you show some of the ways in which Charles Darwin may be said to convey "the literary experience" as defined by Theodore Baird.

2. Baird's essay pays particular attention to Darwin's language. Beginning in paragraph 15, he examines particularly Darwin's use of the phrases "struggle for existence" and "survival of the fittest" as metaphors in language for what goes on in the natural world. Write an essay in which you discuss the strengths and limitations of these metaphors as expressions of the facts of nature.

3. The end of Baird's essay implicitly recalls its beginning—the meeting of Carlyle and Darwin in 1877 as honored representatives of literature and science respectively. Yet at the end of the essay he refers to the publication date of the *Origin* and claims that "in 1859, at one of the great moments in modern thought, literature and science were united." What does Baird mean by referring to this 1859 figurative "meeting" in contrast to the literal meeting in 1877? Write an essay in which you show some of the ways in which Charles Darwin may be seen as an interdisciplinary writer.

The Creation and P. H. Gosse 1941

JORGE LUIS BORGES

The great Argentine writer Jorge Luis Borges was born in 1899 on the eve of the twentieth century in Buenos Aires where his ancestors had played great roles in the foundation and early days of the republic. His father's mother was English and Jorge grew up speaking and reading English from his earliest childhood. His father's eye trouble (which Borges unfortunately inherited) led the family to seek medical help in Europe just before the outbreak of World War I in 1914. They spent the rest of the war mainly in Switzerland, where his school was conducted in French and where he also learned German, leading to that mastery of Western literature for which he was to become world famous.

On his return to Argentina, the young Borges joined an experimental literary movement called Ultraism. Very shy about his creative powers, he began writing as a critic of literature and ideas and often chose obscure or forgotten subjects like that of the selection to follow. His later fictions often seem to read like essays and his essays like short stories. Beginning in the 1950s, he achieved wide fame for himself and a new respect for Latin American literature, which soon underwent a vast renaissance in producing movements like Magical Realism.

In his essay on P. H. Gosse, Borges explores the remarkable way a scientist was able to reconcile the new facts of geology with the biblical account of creation. The result gives an example of the powers and limits of logic that still plays a part in the current controversy between evolution and what is now called intelligent design.

"The man without a Navel yet lives in me," Sir Thomas Browne curiously writes (*Religio Medici*, 1642), meaning that, as a descendant of Adam, he was conceived in sin. In the first chapter of *Ulysses*, Joyce similarly evokes the immaculate and smooth belly of the woman without a mother: "Heva, naked Eve. She had no navel." The subject (I know) runs the risk of seeming grotesque and trivial, but the zoologist Philip Henry Gosse connected it to the central problem of metaphysics: the problem of time. That was in 1857, eighty years of oblivion equal, perhaps, something new.

In two places in the Scriptures (Romans 5; I Corinthians 15), the first Adam, in whom all die, is compared to the last Adam, who is Jesus.[1]

---

[1] This conjunction is common in religious poetry. Perhaps the most intense example is in the penultimate stanza of the "Hymn to God, my God, in my sickness," March 23, 1630, composed by John Donne:

We think that Paradise and Calvary,
Christ's Cross, and Adam's tree, stood in one place,
Look Lord, and find both Adams met in me;
As the first Adam's sweat surrounds my face,
May the last Adam's blood my soul embrace.

This comparison, in order not to become mere blasphemy, must presuppose a certain enigmatic parity, which is translated into myths and symmetry. The *Legenda Aurea* states that the wood of the Cross comes from the forbidden Tree that is in Paradise; the theologians, that Adam was created by the Father and the Son at the exact age at which the Son died: thirty-three. This senseless precision must have influenced Gosse's cosmogony.

He revealed it in the book *Omphalos* (London, 1857), which is subtitled *An Attempt to Untie the Geological Knot*. I have searched the libraries for this book in vain; to write this note, I will use the summaries made by Edmund Gosse (*Father and Son*, 1907) and H. G. Wells (*All Aboard for Ararat*, 1940). I will introduce some illustrations that do not appear on those brief pages, but I believe they are compatible with Gosse's thought.

In the chapter of *Logic* that deals with the law of causality, John Stuart Mill argues that the state of the universe at any given moment is a consequence of its state at the previous moment, and that, for an infinite intelligence, the perfect knowledge of a *single moment* would be enough to know the history of the universe, past and future. (He also argues—oh Louis Auguste Blanqui, oh Nietzsche, oh Pythagoras!—that the repetition of any one state of the universe would entail the repetition of all the others and would turn universal history into a cyclical series.) In that moderate version of one of Laplace's fantasies—he had imagined that the present state of the universe is, in theory, reducible to a formula, from which Someone could deduce the entire future and the entire past—Mill does not exclude the possibility that a future exterior intervention may break the series. He asserts that state q will inevitably produce state r; state r, s; state s, t, but he concedes that before t a divine catastrophe—the *consummatio mundi*, let us say—may have annihilated the planet. The future is inevitable and exact, but it may not happen. God lies in wait in the intervals.

5   In 1857, people were disturbed by a contradiction. Genesis assigned six days—six unequivocal Hebrew days, from sunset to sunset—to the divine creation of the world, but the paleontologists impiously insisted on enormous accumulations of time. (De Quincey unavailingly repeated that the Scriptures have an obligation *not* to instruct mankind in any science, for the sciences constitute a vast mechanism to develop and train the human intellect.) How could one reconcile God with the fossils, Sir Charles Lyell with Moses? Gosse, fortified by prayer, proposed an astonishing answer.

Mill imagines a causal, infinite time that may be interrupted by a future act of God; Gosse, a rigorously causal, infinite time that has been interrupted by a past act: the Creation. State *n* will inevitably produce state *v*, but before *v* the Universal Judgment may occur; state *n* presupposes state *c*, but state *c* has not occurred, because the world was created in *f* or in *b*. The first moment of time coincides with the moment of the Creation, as St. Augustine says, but that first instant involves not only an infinite future, but an infinite past. A past that is hypothetical, to be sure, but also detailed and inevitable. Adam appears, and his teeth and his skeleton are thirty-three years old; Adam appears (Edmund Gosse writes) and he has a navel, although no umbilical cord attached him to a mother. The principle of reason requires that no effect be without a cause; those causes require other causes, which are multiplied regressively;[2] there are concrete vestiges of them all, but only those that are posterior to the Creation have really existed. There are skeletons of glyptodonts in the gorge of Luján, but there have never been glyptodonts. Such is the ingenious (and, above all, unbelievable) thesis that Philip Henry Gosse proposed to religion and to science.

Both rejected it. The newspapers reduced it to the doctrine that God had hidden fossils under the earth to test the faith of the geologists; Charles Kingsley denied that the Lord had carved a "superfluous and vast lie" into the rocks. In vain, Gosse explained the metaphysical foundation of his thesis: that one moment of time was inconceivable without the moment before it and the one after it, and so on to infinity. I wonder if he knew the ancient sentence that is quoted at the beginning of Rafael Cansinos Asséns' Talmudic anthology: "It was only the first night, but a number of centuries had already preceded it."

There are two virtues I would claim for Gosse's forgotten thesis. First: its somewhat monstrous elegance. Second: its involuntary reduction to absurdity of a *creatio ex nihilo*, its indirect demonstration that the universe is eternal, as the Vedanta and Heraclitus, Spinoza and the atomists all thought. Bertrand Russell has brought this up to date. In the ninth chapter of his book, *The Analysis of Mind* (London, 1921), he imagines that the planet was created only a few minutes ago, with a humanity that "remembers" an illusory past.

[2] Cf. Spencer, *Facts and Comments* [1902], 148–151.

Postscript: In 1802, Chateaubriand (*Génie du christianisme* I, 4, 5), for aesthetic reasons, formulated a thesis identical to that of Gosse. He denounced as banal and ridiculous a first day of the Creation, populated by baby pigeons, larvae, puppies, and seeds. "Without this original antiquity, there would have been neither beauty nor magnificence in the work of the Almighty; and, what could not possibly be the case, nature, in a state of innocence, would have been less charming than she is in her present degenerate condition," he wrote.

SUGGESTIONS FOR WRITING

1. The title of Gosse's book is *Omphalos*, which means in Greek *navel* or *belly button*. Borges shows how geological evidence in the nineteenth century seemed to disallow an earth that was only a few thousand years old. In what ways does the question of whether or not Adam had a navel address the apparent geological evidence for hundreds of millions of years in the evolution of other species? Write an essay in which you explain how the navel is for Gosse a symbol for how he proposed "to untie the geological knot."
2. Gosse has been cited by modern writers who support the account of creation found in the Judeo-Christian bible. Write an essay showing how Gosse's logic reconciles creationism or intelligent design with geological facts.
3. Borges says that he admires the "elegance" of Gosse's argument and shows that he understands its logic, but Borges seems completely unconvinced. Why? Write an essay in which you describe the different ways in which Jorges Luis Borges expresses or implies his own disagreement with P. H. Gosse.

The Monkey Trial   1925

H. L. MENCKEN

H. L. Mencken (1880–1956) was called in his own lifetime the Sage of Baltimore and from the base of his beloved hometown the reporter, editor, social critic, and political observer was happy to act the part of sage in his own high-spirited and playful way. For millions of Americans he stood for the modern in many areas of life from science to literature, and in 1925 he represented the modern point of view in reporting on the famous Scopes trial in Dayton, Tennessee.

Darwin's Origin of Species had been in print some 65 years when the State Legislature of Tennessee passed a law forbidding the teaching of evolution. Scopes, a high school teacher, was persuaded to challenge the law and the trial was the result. Though in legal terms his guilt was never in doubt, the trial became the occasion for a national debate within a population divided between the ideas and beliefs of the bible and those of Darwin. In the selection from Mencken's coverage of the trial, he makes no attempt at objectivity but dramatizes the conflict between two protagonists—the nationally known liberal lawyer Clarence Darrow and William Jennings Bryan, "The Great Commoner," many times presidential candidate of the Democrat party whose stronghold was the South.

The net effect of Clarence Darrow's great speech yesterday seems to be precisely the same as if he had bawled it up a rainspout in the interior of Afghanistan. That is, locally, upon the process against the infidel Scopes, upon the so-called minds of these fundamentalists of upland Tennessee. You have but a dim notion of it who have only read it. It was not designed for reading, but for hearing. The clanging of it was as important as the logic. It rose like a wind and ended like a flourish of bugles. The very judge on the bench, toward the end of it, began to look uneasy. But the morons in the audience, when it was over, simply hissed it.

During the whole time of its delivery the old mountebank, Bryan, sat tight-lipped and unmoved. There is, of course, no reason why it should have shaken him. He has those hill billies locked up in his pen and he knows it. His brand is on them. He is at home among them. Since his earliest days, indeed, his chief strength has been among the folk of remote hills and forlorn and lonely farms. Now with his political aspirations all gone to pot, he turns to them for religious consolations. They understand his peculiar imbecilities. His nonsense is their ideal of sense. When he deluges them with his theological bilge they rejoice like pilgrims disporting in the river Jordan.

The town whisper is that the local attorney-general, Stewart, is not a fundamentalist, and hence has no stomach for his job. It seems not improbable. He is a man of evident education, and his argument yesterday was confined very strictly to the constitutional points—the argument of a competent and conscientious lawyer, and to me, at least very persuasive.

But Stewart, after all, is a foreigner here, almost as much so as Darrow or Hays or Malone. He is doing his job and that is all. The real animus of the prosecution centers in Bryan. He is the plaintiff and prosecutor. The local lawyers are simply bottle-holders for him. He will win the case, not by academic appeals to law and precedent, but by direct and powerful appeals to the immemorial fears and superstitions of man. It is no wonder that he is hot against Scopes. Five years of Scopes and even these mountaineers would begin to laugh at Bryan. Ten years and they would ride him out of town on a rail, with one Baptist parson in front of him and another behind.

5 But there will be no ten years of Scopes, nor five years, nor even one year.

Such brash young fellows, debauched by the enlightenment, must be disposed of before they become dangerous, and Bryan is here, with his tight lips and hard eyes, to see that this one is disposed of. The talk of the lawyers, even the magnificent talk of Darrow, is so much idle wind music. The case will not be decided by logic, nor even by eloquence. It will be decided by counting noses—and for every nose in these hills that has ever thrust itself into any book save the Bible there are a hundred adorned with the brass ring of Bryan. These are his people. They understand him when he speaks in tongues. The same dark face that is in his own eyes is in theirs, too. They feel with him, and they relish him.

I sincerely hope that the nobility and gentry of the lowlands will not make the colossal mistake of viewing this trial of Scopes as a trivial farce. Full of rustic japes and in bad taste, it is, to be sure, somewhat comic on the surface. One laughs to see lawyers sweat. The jury, marched down Broadway, would set New York by the ears. But all of that is only skin deep.

Deeper down there are the beginnings of a struggle that may go on to melodrama of the first caliber, and when the curtain falls at least all the laughter may be coming from the yokels. You probably laughed at the prohibitionists, say, back in 1914. Well, don't make the same error twice.

As I have said, Bryan understands these peasants, and they understand him. He is a bit mangey and fleabitten, but no means ready for his harp. He may last five years, ten years or even longer. What he may accomplish in that time, seen here at close range, looms up immensely larger than it appears to a city man five hundred miles away. The fellow is full of such bitter, implacable hatreds that they radiate from him like heat from a stove. He hates the learning that he cannot grasp. He hates those who sneer at him. He hates, in general, all who stand apart from his own pathetic commonness. And the yokels hate with him, some of them almost as bitterly as he does himself. They are willing and eager to follow him—and he has already given them a taste of blood.

10   Darrow's peroration yesterday was interrupted by Judge Raulston, but the force of it got into the air nevertheless. This year it is a misdemeanor for a country school teacher to flout the archaic nonsense of Genesis. Next year it will be a felony. The year after the net will be spread wider. Pedagogues, after all, are small game; there are larger birds to snare—larger and juicier. Bryan has his fishy eye on them. He will fetch them if his mind lasts, and the lamp holds out to burn. No man with a mouth like that ever lets go. Nor ever lacks followers.

Tennessee is bearing the brunt of the first attack simply because the civilized minority, down here, is extraordinarily pusillanimous.

I have met no educated man who is not ashamed of the ridicule that has fallen upon the State, and I have met none, save only judge Neal, who had the courage to speak out while it was yet time. No Tennessee counsel of any importance came into the case until yesterday and then they came in stepping very softly as if taking a brief for sense were a dangerous matter. When Bryan did his first rampaging here all these men were silent.

They had known for years what was going on in the hills. They knew what the country preachers were preaching—what degraded nonsense was being rammed and hammered into yokel skulls. But they were afraid to go out against the imposture while it was in the making, and when any outsider denounced it they fell upon him violently as an enemy of Tennessee.

Now Tennessee is paying for that poltroonery. The State is smiling and beautiful, and of late it has begun to be rich. I know of no American city that is set in more lovely scenery than Chattanooga, or that has more charming homes. The civilized minority is as large here, I believe, as anywhere else.

15   It has made a city of splendid material comforts and kept it in order. But it has neglected in the past the unpleasant business of following what was going on in the cross roads Little Bethels.

The Baptist preachers ranted unchallenged.

Their buffooneries were mistaken for humor. Now the clowns turn out to be armed, and have begun to shoot.

In his argument yesterday judge Neal had to admit pathetically that it was hopeless to fight for a repeal of the anti-evolution law. The Legislature of Tennessee, like the Legislature of every other American state, is made up of cheap job-seekers and ignoramuses.

The Governor of the State is a politician ten times cheaper and trashier. It is vain to look for relief from such men. If the State is to be saved at all, it must be saved by the courts. For one, I have little hope of relief in that direction, despite Hays' logic and Darrow's eloquence. Constitutions, in America, no longer mean what they say. To mention the Bill of Rights is to be damned as a Red.

20   The rabble is in the saddle, and down here it makes its first campaign under a general beside whom Wat Tylor seems like a wart beside the Matterhorn.

SUGGESTIONS FOR WRITING

1. In his essay Jorge Luis Borges explains how the story in Genesis of the earth's creation some 5,000 years ago might be logically compatible with the geologic evidence that seems to imply a vastly older history of life. Yet H. L. Mencken appeals not to logic but to emotion in his support of a Darwinian explanation and in his ridicule of those who oppose it. Write an essay that analyzes and exemplifies the various ways in which H. L. Mencken appeals to the emotions of his audience.

2. In paragraph 7 Mencken says, "I sincerely hope that the nobility and gentry of the lowlands will not make the colossal mistake of viewing this trial of Scopes as a trivial farce." Yet doesn't Mencken himself see the whole affair as a farce? Or does he? Write an essay in which you show how Mencken's essay does or does not express the seriousness of the issues involved in the Scopes trial.

3. Though the occasion for his writing is called "The Scopes Trial," Mencken organizes his report not around Scopes but as a contest between Clarence Darrow and William Jennings Bryan. Write an essay in which you compare and contrast the ways Mencken uses language to create images of these two major figures. Mencken obviously favors Darrow, for example. Show how his descriptions express his point of view.

The Process of Creative Destruction

1942

From *Capitalism, Socialism, and Democracy*

JOSEPH SCHUMPETER

The Austrian intellectual Joseph Schumpeter (1883–1950) emigrated to the United States and became a professor of economics at Harvard. In the 1930s with the Great Depression shaking the economic beliefs of wide sectors of the world's population,

capitalism seemed doomed to many. The Marxist style socialism purportedly suc-
ceeding in the Soviet Union seemed an obvious alternative. In Capitalism,
Socialism, and Democracy, from which the following selection comes, Schumpeter
undertakes a counterattack basing his analysis on the enormous increase in the
standard of living that human beings enjoyed since the advent of the capitalist
system in spite of the gloomy predictions of Malthus and others.

In his most famous phrase, "creative destruction," Schumpeter appeals to
the model of Darwinian evolution to explain how economic disasters and industrial
failures could be reconciled with human progress. An example not included in the
passage illustrates the idea. Candles had replaced firewood and primitive lamps for
domestic illumination by the eighteenth century, but chandlers (makers of candles)
soon went the way of many woodchoppers as first coal gas and later coal oil replaced
them. When electricity came into general use in the later 1800s, makers of kerosene
lamps were put out of work. In the same way the makers of buggy whips were put
out of work by the development of the automobile. But the automobile created many
jobs including those that produced batteries, tires, and headlights. Though influen-
tial, Schumpeter's ideas were not widely recognized until the new interest in the
1990s in economic growth in general and the causes of the economic gaps between
countries and regions in particular, as discussed in chapter 2 by Jared Diamond.

The theories of monopolistic and oligopolistic competition and their
popular variants may in two ways be made to serve the view that capitalist reality is unfavorable to maximum performance in production. One
may hold that it always has been so and that all along output has been
expanding in spite of the secular sabotage perpetrated by the managing
bourgeoisie. Advocates of this proposition would have to produce evidence to the effect that the observed rate of increase can be accounted
for by a sequence of favorable circumstances unconnected with the
mechanism of private enterprise and strong enough to overcome the
latter's resistance. This is precisely the question which we shall discuss
in Chapter IX. However, those who espouse this variant at least avoid
the trouble about historical fact that the advocates of the alternative
proposition have to face. This avers that capitalist reality once tended to
favor maximum productive performance, or at all events productive
performance so considerable as to constitute a major element in any
serious appraisal of the system; but that the later spread of monopolist
structures, killing competition, has by now reversed that tendency.

First, this involves the creation of an entirely imaginary golden age
of perfect competition that at some time somehow metamorphosed
itself into the monopolistic age, whereas it is quite clear that perfect

competition has at no time been more of a reality than it is at present. Secondly, it is necessary to point out that the rate of increase in output did not decrease from the nineties from which, I suppose, the prevalence of the largest-size concerns, at least in manufacturing industry, would have to be dated; that there is nothing in the behavior of the time series of total output to suggest a "break in trend"; and, most important of all, that the modern standard of life of the masses evolved during the period of relatively unfettered "big business." If we list the items that enter the modern workman's budget and from 1899 on observe the course of their prices not in terms of money but in terms of the hours of labor that will buy them—i.e., each year's money prices divided by each year's hourly wage rates—we cannot fail to be struck by the rate of the advance which, considering the spectacular improvement in qualities, seems to have been greater and not smaller than it ever was before. If we economists were given less to wishful thinking and more to the observation of facts, doubts would immediately arise as to the realistic virtues of a theory that would have led us to expect a very different result. Nor is this all. As soon as we go into details and inquire into the individual items in which progress was most conspicuous, the trail leads not to the doors of those firms that work under conditions of comparatively free competition but precisely to the doors of the large concerns—which, as in the case of agricultural machinery, also account for much of the progress in the competitive sector—and a shocking suspicion dawns upon us that big business may have had more to do with creating that standard of life than with keeping it down.

The conclusions alluded to at the end of the preceding chapter are in fact almost completely false. Yet they follow from observations and theorems that are almost completely[1] true. Both economists and popular writers have once more run away with some fragments of reality they happened to grasp. These fragments themselves were mostly seen

---

[1] As a matter of fact, those observations and theorems are not completely satisfactory. The usual expositions of the doctrine of imperfect competition fail in particular to give due attention to the many and important cases in which, even as a matter of static theory, imperfect competition approximates the results of perfect competition. There are other cases in which it does not do this, but offers compensations which, while not entering any output index, yet contribute to what the output index is in the last resort intended to measure—the cases in which a firm defends its market by establishing a name for quality and service for instance. However, in order to simplify matters, we will not take issue with that doctrine on its own ground.

correctly. Their formal properties were mostly developed correctly. But no conclusions about capitalist reality as a whole follow from such fragmentary analyses. If we draw them nevertheless, we can be right only by accident. That has been done. And the lucky accident did not happen.

The essential point to grasp is that in dealing with capitalism we are dealing with an evolutionary process. It may seem strange that anyone can fail to see so obvious a fact which moreover was long ago emphasized by Karl Marx. Yet that fragmentary analysis which yields the bulk of our propositions about the functioning of modern capitalism persistently neglects it. Let us restate the point and see how it bears upon our problem.

5   Capitalism, then, is by nature a form or method of economic change and not only never is but never can be stationary. And this evolutionary character of the capitalist process is not merely due to the fact that economic life goes on in a social and natural environment which changes and by its change alters the data of economic action; this fact is important and these changes (wars, revolutions and so on) often condition industrial change, but they are not its prime movers. Nor is this evolutionary character due to a quasi-automatic increase in population and capital or to the vagaries of monetary systems of which exactly the same thing holds true. The fundamental impulse that sets and keeps the capitalist engine in motion comes from the new consumers' goods, the new methods of production or transportation, the new markets, the new forms of industrial organization that capitalist enterprise creates.

As we have seen in the preceding chapter, the contents of the laborer's budget, say from 1760 to 1940, did not simply grow on unchanging lines but they underwent a process of qualitative change. Similarly, the history of the productive apparatus of a typical farm, from the beginnings of the rationalization of crop rotation, plowing and fattening to the mechanized thing of today—linking up with elevators and railroads—is a history of revolutions. So is the history of the productive apparatus of the iron and steel industry from the charcoal furnace to our own type of furnace, or the history of the apparatus of power production from the overshot water wheel to the modern power plant, or the history of transportation from the mailcoach to the airplane. The opening up of new markets, foreign or domestic, and the organizational development from the craft shop and factory to such concerns as U. S. Steel illustrate the same process of industrial mutation—if I may use that biological term—that incessantly revolutionizes[2] the economic structure *from within*, incessantly destroying the old one, incessantly creating a new one. This process of Creative Destruction is the essential fact about capitalism. It is what capitalism consists in and what every capitalist concern has got to live in. This fact bears upon our problem in two ways.

First, since we are dealing with a process whose every element takes considerable time in revealing its true features and ultimate effects, there is no point in appraising the performance of that process *ex visu* of a given point of time; we must judge its performance over time, as it unfolds through decades or centuries. A system—any system, economic or other—that at *every* given point of time fully utilizes its possibilities to the best advantage may yet in the long run be inferior to a system that does so at *no* given point of time, because the latter's failure to do so may be a condition for the level or speed of long-run performance.

Second, since we are dealing with an organic process, analysis of what happens in any particular part of it—say, in an individual concern or industry—may indeed clarify details of mechanism but is inconclusive beyond that. Every piece of business strategy acquires its true significance only against the background of that process and within the situation created by it. It must be seen in its role in the perennial gale of creative destruction; it cannot be understood irrespective of it or, in fact, on the hypothesis that there is a perennial lull.

But economists who, *ex visu* of a point of time, look for example at the behavior of an oligopolist industry—an industry which consists of a few big firms—and observe the well-known moves and countermoves within it that seem to aim at nothing but high prices and restrictions of output are making precisely that hypothesis. They accept the data of the momentary situation as if there were no past or future to it and think that they have understood what there is to understand if they interpret the behavior of those firms by means of the principle of maximizing profits with reference to those data. The usual theorist's paper and the usual government commission's report practically never try to see that behavior, on the one hand, as a result of a piece of past history and, on

[2]Those revolutions are not strictly incessant; they occur in discrete rushes which are separated from each other by spans of comparative quiet. The process as a whole works incessantly however, in the sense that there always is either revolution or absorption of the results of revolution, both together forming what are known as business cycles.

the other hand, as an attempt to deal with a situation that is sure to change presently—as an attempt by those firms to keep on their feet, on ground that is slipping away from under them. In other words, the problem that is usually being visualized is how capitalism administers existing structures, whereas the relevant problem is how it creates and destroys them. As long as this is not recognized, the investigator does a meaningless job. As soon as it is recognized, his outlook on capitalist practice and its social results changes considerably.[3]

10 The first thing to go is the traditional conception of the *modus operandi* of competition. Economists are at long last emerging from the stage in which price competition was all they saw. As soon as quality competition and sales effort are admitted into the sacred precincts of theory, the price variable is ousted from its dominant position. However, it is still competition within a rigid pattern of invariant conditions, methods of production and forms of industrial organization in particular, that practically monopolizes attention. But in capitalist reality as distinguished from its textbook picture, it is not that kind of competition which counts but the competition from the new commodity, the new technology, the new source of supply, the new type of organization (the largest-scale unit of control for instance)—competition which commands a decisive cost or quality advantage and which strikes not at the margins of the profits and the outputs of the existing firms but at their foundations and their very lives. This kind of competition is as much more effective than the other as a bombardment is in comparison with forcing a door, and so much more important that it becomes a matter of comparative indifference whether competition in the ordinary sense functions more or less promptly; the powerful lever that in the long run expands output and brings down prices is in any case made of other stuff.

It is hardly necessary to point out that competition of the kind we now have in mind acts not only when in being but also when it is merely an ever-present threat. It disciplines before it attacks. The businessman feels himself to be in a competitive situation even if he is alone in his field or if, though not alone, he holds a position such that investigating government experts fail to see any effective competition

[3]It should be understood that it is only our appraisal of economic performance and not our moral judgment that can be so changed. Owing to its autonomy, moral approval or disapproval is entirely independent of our appraisal of social (or any other) results, unless we happen to adopt a moral system such as utilitarianism which makes moral approval and disapproval turn on them *ex definitione*.

between him and any other firms in the same or a neighboring field and in consequence conclude that his talk, under examination, about his competitive sorrows is all make-believe. In many cases, though not in all, this will in the long run enforce behavior very similar to the perfectly competitive pattern.

Many theorists take the opposite view which is best conveyed by an example. Let us assume that there is a certain number of retailers in a neighborhood who try to improve their relative position by service and "atmosphere" but avoid price competition and stick as to methods to the local tradition—a picture of stagnating routine. As others drift into the trade that quasi-equilibrium is indeed upset, but in a manner that does not benefit their customers. The economic space around each of the shops having been narrowed, their owners will no longer be able to make a living and they will try to mend the case by raising prices in tacit agreement. This will further reduce their sales and so, by successive pyramiding, a situation will evolve in which increasing potential supply will be attended by increasing instead of decreasing prices and by decreasing instead of increasing sales.

Such cases do occur, and it is right and proper to work them out. But as the practical instances usually given show, they are fringe-end cases to be found mainly in the sectors furthest removed from all that is most characteristic of capitalist activity.[4] Moreover, they are transient by nature. In the case of retail trade the competition that matters arises not from additional shops of the same type, but from the department store, the chain store, the mail-order house and the supermarket which are bound to destroy those pyramids sooner or later.

SUGGESTIONS FOR WRITING

1. Schumpeter calls his economic theory of capitalism "creative destruction" and links it to the biological theory of evolution that Charles Darwin describes in the phrases "natural selection" and "survival of the fittest." Write an essay in which you analyze and describe some similarities and differences in the implications of the key phrases used by the

[4] This is also shown by a theorem we frequently meet with in expositions of the theory of imperfect competition, viz., the theorem that, under conditions of imperfect competition, producing or trading businesses tend to be irrationally small. Since imperfect competition is at the same time held to be an outstanding characteristic of modern industry we are set to wondering what world these theorists live in, unless, as stated above, fringe-end cases are all they have in mind.

two writers. For example, do you think Darwin would accept "creative destruction" as a phrase equivalent to his own as descriptions of his subject? Why or why not?

2. Think of a vanished or historically much diminished industry—buggy whips, for example. Write an essay explaining how you think Joseph Schumpeter would analyze and explain the history of your example.

3. Think of a currently threatened industry or occupation—American autoworkers, for example. Write an essay explaining how you think Joseph Schumpeter would analyze and explain the past and predict the future of your example.

Nonmoral Nature   1982

STEPHEN JAY GOULD

Stephen Jay Gould (1941–2002) was a professor of zoology and geology at Harvard University. He became famous outside the academic world for his lively and clear explanations of science in the magazine Natural History. *Gould collected his essays in many books that are still read throughout the world.*

In "Nonmoral Nature" Gould takes on a longstanding issue at the intersection of science and religion: how can a view that sees nature as a manifestation of God's goodness be reconciled with some natural facts that can horrify human observers? Gould explores the difficulties of reconciling religion with modern science while proposing a way in which the two ways of understanding the universe may not be necessarily at odds.

When the Right Honorable and Reverend Francis Henry, earl of Bridgewater, died in February, 1829, he left £8,000 to support a series of books "on the power, wisdom and goodness of God, as manifested in the creation." William Buckland, England's first official academic geologist and later dean of Westminster, was invited to compose one of the nine Bridgewater Treatises. In it he discussed the most pressing problem of natural theology: If God is benevolent and the Creation displays his "power, wisdom and goodness," then why are we surrounded with pain, suffering, and apparently senseless cruelty in the animal world?

Buckland considered the depredation of "carnivorous races" as the primary challenge to an idealized world in which the lion might dwell with the lamb. He resolved the issue to his satisfaction by arguing that carnivores actually increase "the aggregate of animal enjoyment" and "diminish that of pain." The death of victims, after all, is swift and relatively painless, victims are spared the ravages of decrepitude and senility, and populations do not outrun their food supply to the greater sorrow of all. God knew what he was doing when he made lions. Buckland concluded in hardly concealed rapture:

> The appointment of death by the agency of carnivora, as the ordinary termination of animal existence, appears therefore in its main results to be a dispensation of benevolence; it deducts much from the aggregate amount of the pain of universal death; it abridges, and almost annihilates, throughout the brute creation, the misery of disease, and accidental injuries, and lingering decay; and imposes such salutary restraint upon excessive increase of numbers, that the supply of food maintains perpetually a due ratio to the demand. The result is, that the surface of the land and depths of the waters are ever crowded with myriads of animated beings, the pleasures of whose life are co-extensive with its duration; and which throughout the little day of existence that is allotted to them, fulfill with joy the functions for which they were created.

We may find a certain amusing charm in Buckland's vision today, but such arguments did begin to address "the problem of evil" for many of Buckland's contemporaries—how could a benevolent God create such a world of carnage and bloodshed? Yet these claims could not abolish the problem of evil entirely, for nature includes many phenomena far more horrible in our eyes than simple predation. I suspect that nothing evokes greater disgust in most of us than slow destruction of a host by an internal parasite—slow ingestion, bit by bit, from the inside. In no other way can I explain why *Alien*, an uninspired, grade-C, formula horror film, should have won such a following. That single scene of Mr. Alien, popping forth as a baby parasite from the body of a human host, was both sickening and stunning. Our nineteenth-century forebears maintained similar feelings. Their greatest challenge to the concept of a benevolent deity was not simple predation—for one can admire quick and efficient butcheries, especially since we strive to construct them ourselves—but slow death by parasitic ingestion. The classic case, treated at length by all the great naturalists, involved the so-called ichneumon fly. Buckland had sidestepped the major issue.

The ichneumon fly, which provoked such concern among natural theologians, was a composite creature representing the habits of an enormous tribe. The Ichneumonoidea are a group of wasps, not flies, that include more species than all the vertebrates combined (wasps, with ants and bees, constitute the order Hymenoptera; flies, with their two wings—wasps have four—form the order Diptera). In addition, many related wasps of similar habits were often cited for the same grisly details. Thus, the famous story did not merely implicate a single aberrant species (perhaps a perverse leakage from Satan's realm), but perhaps hundreds of thousands of them—a large chunk of what could only be God's creation.

5   The ichneumons, like most wasps, generally live freely as adults but pass their larval life as parasites feeding on the bodies of other animals, almost invariably members of their own phylum, Arthropoda. The most common victims are caterpillars (butterfly and moth larvae), but some ichneumons prefer aphids and others attack spiders. Most hosts are parasitized as larvae, but some adults are attacked, and many tiny ichneumons inject their brood directly into the egg of their host.

The free-flying females locate an appropriate host and then convert it to a food factory for their own young. Parasitologists speak of ectoparasitism when the uninvited guest lives on the surface of its host, and endoparasitism when the parasite dwells within. Among endoparasitic ichneumons, adult females pierce the host with their ovipositor and deposit eggs within it. (The ovipositor, a thin tube extending backward from the wasp's rear end, may be many times as long as the body itself.) Usually, the host is not otherwise inconvenienced for the moment, at least until the eggs hatch and the ichneumon larvae begin their grim work of interior excavation. Among ectoparasites, however, many females lay their eggs directly upon the host's body. Since an active host would easily dislodge the egg, the ichneumon mother often simultaneously injects a toxin that paralyzes the caterpillar or other victim. The paralysis may be permanent, and the caterpillar lies, alive but immobile, with the agent of its future destruction secure on its belly. The egg hatches, the helpless caterpillar twitches, the wasp larva pierces and begins its grisly feast.

Since a dead and decaying caterpillar will do the wasp larva no good, it eats in a pattern that cannot help but recall, in our inappropriate, anthropocentric interpretation, the ancient English penalty for treason—drawing and quartering, with its explicit object of extracting as much torment as possible by keeping the victim alive and sentient. As the king's executioner drew out and burned his client's entrails, so does the ichneumon larva eat fat bodies and digestive organs first, keeping the caterpillar alive by preserving intact the essential heart and central nervous system. Finally, the larva completes its work and kills its victim, leaving behind the caterpillar's empty shell. Is it any wonder that ichneumons, not snakes or lions, stood as the paramount challenge to God's benevolence during the heyday of natural theology?

As I read through the nineteenth- and twentieth-century literature on ichneumons, nothing amused me more than the tension between an intellectual knowledge that wasps should not be described in human terms and a literary or emotional inability to avoid the familiar categories of epic and narrative, pain and destruction, victim and vanquisher. We seem to be caught in the mythic structures of our own cultural sagas, quite unable, even in our basic descriptions, to use any other language than the metaphors of battle and conquest. We cannot render this corner of natural history as anything but story, combining the themes of grim horror and fascination and usually ending not so much with pity for the caterpillar as with admiration for the efficiency of the ichneumon.

I detect two basic themes in most epic descriptions: the struggles of prey and the ruthless efficiency of parasites. Although we acknowledge that we witness little more than automatic instinct or physiological reaction, still we describe the defenses of hosts as though they represented conscious struggles. Thus, aphids kick and caterpillars may wriggle violently as wasps attempt to insert their ovipositors. The pupa of the tortoise-shell butterfly (usually considered an inert creature silently awaiting its conversion from duckling to swan) may contort its abdominal region so sharply that attacking wasps are thrown into the air. The caterpillars of *Hapalia,* when attacked by the wasp *Apanteles machaeralis,* drop suddenly from their leaves and suspend themselves in air by a silken thread. But the wasp may run down the thread and insert its eggs nonetheless. Some hosts can encapsulate the injected egg with blood cells that aggregate and harden, thus suffocating the parasite.

10 J.-H. Fabre, the great nineteenth-century French entomologist, who remains to this day the preeminently literate natural historian of

insects, made a special study of parasitic wasps and wrote with an unabashed anthropocentrism about the struggles of paralyzed victims (see his books *Insect Life* and *The Wonders of Instinct*). He describes some imperfectly paralyzed caterpillars that struggle so violently every time a parasite approaches that the wasp larvae must feed with unusual caution. They attach themselves to a silken strand from the roof of their burrow and descend upon a safe and exposed part of the caterpillar:

> *The grub is at dinner: head downwards, it is digging into the limp belly of one of the caterpillars. . . . At the least sign of danger in the heap of caterpillars, the larva retreats . . . and climbs back to the ceiling, where the swarming rabble cannot reach it. When peace is restored, it slides down [its silken cord] and returns to table, with its head over the viands and its rear upturned and ready to withdraw in case of need.*

In another chapter, he describes the fate of a paralyzed cricket:

> *One may see the cricket, bitten to the quick, vainly move its antennae and abdominal styles, open and close its empty jaws, and even move a foot, but the larva is safe and searches its vitals with impunity. What an awful nightmare for the paralyzed cricket!*

Fabre even learned to feed some paralyzed victims by placing a syrup of sugar and water on their mouthparts—thus showing that they remained alive, sentient, and (by implication) grateful for any palliation of their inevitable fate. If Jesus, immobile and thirsting on the cross, received only vinegar from his tormentors, Fabre at least could make an ending bittersweet.

The second theme, ruthless efficiency of the parasites, leads to the opposite conclusion—grudging admiration for the victors. We learn of their skill in capturing dangerous hosts often many times larger than themselves. Caterpillars may be easy game, but the psammocharid wasps prefer spiders. They must insert their ovipositors in a safe and precise spot. Some leave a paralyzed spider in its own burrow. *Planiceps hirsutus*, for example, parasitizes a California trapdoor spider. It searches for spider tubes on sand dunes, then digs into nearby sand to disturb the spider's home and drive it out. When the spider emerges, the wasp attacks, paralyzes its victim, drags it back into its own tube, shuts and fastens the trapdoor, and deposits a single egg upon the spider's abdomen. Other psammocharids will drag a heavy spider back to a previously prepared cluster of clay or mud cells. Some amputate a spider's legs to make the passage easier. Others fly back over water, skimming a buoyant spider along the surface.

Some wasps must battle with other parasites over a host's body. *Rhyssella curvipes* can detect the larvae of wood wasps deep within alder wood and drill down to its potential victims with its sharply ridged ovipositor. *Pseudorhyssa alpestris*, a related parasite, cannot drill directly into wood since its slender ovipositor bears only rudimentary cutting ridges. It locates the holes made by *Rhyssella*, inserts its ovipositor, and lays an egg on the host (already conveniently paralyzed by *Rhyssella*), right next to the egg deposited by its relative. The two eggs hatch at about the same time, but the larva of *Pseudorhyssa* has a bigger head bearing much larger mandibles. *Pseudorhyssa* seizes the smaller *Rhyssella* larva, destroys it, and proceeds to feast upon a banquet already well prepared.

15   Other praises for the efficiency of mothers invoke the themes of early, quick, and often. Many ichneumons don't even wait for their hosts to develop into larvae, but parasitize the egg directly (larval wasps may then either drain the egg itself or enter the developing host larva). Others simply move fast. *Apanteles militaris* can deposit up to seventy-two eggs in a single second. Still others are doggedly persistent. *Aphidius gomezi* females produce up to 1,500 eggs and can parasitize as many as 600 aphids in a single working day. In a bizarre twist upon "often," some wasps indulge in polyembryony, a kind of iterated supertwinning. A single egg divides into cells that aggregate into as many as 500 individuals. Since some polyembryonic wasps parasitize caterpillars much larger than themselves and may lay up to six eggs in each, as many as 3,000 larvae may develop within, and feed upon, a single host. These wasps are endoparasites and do not paralyze their victims. The caterpillars writhe back and forth, not (one suspects) from pain, but merely in response to the commotion induced by thousands of wasp larvae feeding within.

The efficiency of mothers is matched by their larval offspring. I have already mentioned the pattern of eating less essential parts first, thus keeping the host alive and fresh to its final and merciful dispatch. After the larva digests every edible morsel of its victim (if only to prevent later fouling of its abode by decaying tissue), it may still use the outer shell of its host. One aphid parasite cuts a hole in the belly of its victim's shell, glues the skeleton to a leaf by sticky secretions from its salivary gland, and then spins a cocoon to pupate within the aphid's shell.

In using inappropriate anthropocentric language in this romp through the natural history of ichneumons, I have tried to emphasize just why these wasps became a preeminent challenge to natural theology—the antiquated doctrine that attempted to infer God's essence from the products of his creation. I have used twentieth-century examples for the most part, but all themes were known and stressed by the great nineteenth-century natural theologians. How then did they square the habits of these wasps with the goodness of God? How did they extract themselves from this dilemma of their own making?

The strategies were as varied as the practitioners; they shared only the theme of special pleading for an a priori doctrine—they knew that God's benevolence was lurking somewhere behind all these tales of apparent horror. Charles Lyell for example, in the first edition of his epochal *Principles of Geology* (1830–1833), decided that caterpillars posed such a threat to vegetation that any natural checks upon them could only reflect well upon a creating deity, for caterpillars would destroy human agriculture "did not Providence put causes in operation to keep them in due bounds."

The Reverend William Kirby, rector of Barham and Britain's foremost entomologist, chose to ignore the plight of caterpillars and focused instead upon the virtue of mother love displayed by wasps in provisioning their young with such care.

> The great object of the female is to discover a proper nidus for her eggs. In search of this she is in constant motion. Is the caterpillar of a butterfly or moth the appropriate food for her young? You see her alight upon the plants where they are most usually to be met with, run quickly over them, carefully examining every leaf, and, having found the unfortunate object of her search, insert her sting into its flesh, and there deposit an egg.... The active Ichneumon braves every danger, and does not desist until her courage and address have insured subsistence for one of her future progeny.

20 Kirby found this solicitude all the more remarkable because the female wasp will never see her child and enjoy the pleasures of parenthood. Yet her love compels her to danger nonetheless:

> A very large proportion of them are doomed to die before their young come into existence. But in these the passion is not extinguished. . . . When you witness the solicitude with which they provide for the

*security and sustenance of their future young, you can scarcely deny to
them love for a progeny they are never destined to behold.*

Kirby also put in a good word for the marauding larvae, praising
them for their forbearance in eating selectively to keep their caterpillar
prey alive. Would we all husband our resources with such care!

*In this strange and apparently cruel operation one circumstance is truly
remarkable. The larva of the Ichneumon, though every day, perhaps for
months, it gnaws the inside of the caterpillar, and though at last it has
devoured almost every part of it except the skin and intestines, carefully
all this time it avoids injuring the vital organs, as if aware that its
own existence depends on that of the insect upon which it preys! . . .
What would be the impression which a similar instance amongst the
race of quadrupeds would make upon us? If, for example, an animal. . .
should be found to feed upon the inside of a dog, devouring only those
parts not essential to life, while it cautiously left uninjured the heart,
arteries, lungs, and intestines—should we not regard such an instance
as a perfect prodigy, as an example of instinctive forebearance almost
miraculous? [The last three quotes come from the 1856, and last pre-
Darwinian, edition of Kirby and Spence's Introduction to Entomology.]*

This tradition of attempting to read moral meaning from nature
did not cease with the triumph of evolutionary theory after Darwin
published *On the Origin of Species* in 1859—for evolution could be read
as God's chosen method of peopling our planet, and ethical messages
might still populate nature. Thus, St. George Mivart, one of Darwin's
most effective evolutionary critics and a devout Catholic, argued that
"many amiable and excellent people" had been misled by the apparent
suffering of animals for two reasons. First, however much it might
hurt, "physical suffering and moral evil are simply incommensurable."
Since beasts are not moral agents, their feelings cannot bear any ethical message. But secondly, lest our visceral sensitivities still be aroused,
Mivart assures us that animals must feel little, if any, pain. Using a
favorite racist argument of the time—that "primitive" people suffer far
less than advanced and cultured people—Mivart extrapolated further
down the ladder of life into a realm of very limited pain indeed:
Physical suffering, he argued,

*depends greatly upon the mental condition of the sufferer. Only during
consciousness does it exist, and only in the most highly organized men*

does it reach its acme. The author has been assured that lower races of
men appear less keenly sensitive to physical suffering than do more
cultivated and refined human beings. Thus only in man can there really
be any intense degree of suffering, because only in him is there that
intellectual recollection of past moments and that anticipation of
future ones, which constitute in great part the bitterness of suffering.
The momentary pang, the present pain, which beasts endure, though
real enough, is yet, doubtless, not to be compared as to its intensity
with the suffering which is produced in man through his high
prerogative of self-consciousness [from Genesis of Species, *1871].*

It took Darwin himself to derail this ancient tradition—in that
gentle way so characteristic of his radical intellectual approach to
nearly everything. The ichneumons also troubled Darwin greatly and
he wrote of them to Asa Gray in 1860:

I own that I cannot see as plainly as others do, and as I should wish to
do, evidence of design and beneficence on all sides of us. There seems to
me too much misery in the world. I cannot persuade myself that a
beneficent and omnipotent God would have designedly created the
Ichneumonidae with the express intention of their feeding within the
living bodies of Caterpillars, or that a cat should play with mice.

Indeed, he had written with more passion to Joseph Hooker in
1856: "What a book a devil's chaplain might write on the clumsy, waste-
ful, blundering, low, and horribly cruel works of nature!"

25   This honest admission—that nature is often (by our standards)
cruel and that all previous attempts to find a lurking goodness behind
everything represent just so much absurd special pleading—can lead
in two directions. One might retain the principle that nature holds
moral messages for humans, but reverse the usual perspective and
claim that morality consists in understanding the ways of nature and
doing the opposite. Thomas Henry Huxley advanced this argument in
his famous essay on *Evolution and Ethics* (1893):

The practice of that which is ethically best—what we call goodness or
virtue—involves a course of conduct which, in all respects, is opposed
to that which leads to success in the cosmic struggle for existence. In
place of ruthless self-assertion it demands self-restraint; in place of
thrusting aside, or treading down, all competitors, it requires that the

individual shall not merely respect, but shall help his fellows. . . . It
repudiates the gladiatorial theory of existence. . . . Laws and moral
precepts are directed to the end of curbing the cosmic process.

The other argument, more radical in Darwin's day but common now, holds that nature simply is as we find it. Our failure to discern the universal good we once expected does not record our lack of insight or ingenuity but merely demonstrates that nature contains no moral messages framed in human terms. Morality is a subject for philosophers, theologians, students of the humanities, indeed for all thinking people. The answers will not be read passively from nature; they do not, and cannot, arise from the data of science. The factual state of the world does not teach us how we, with our powers for good and evil, should alter or preserve it in the most ethical manner.

Darwin himself tended toward this view, although he could not, as a man of his time, thoroughly abandon the idea that laws of nature might reflect some higher purpose. He clearly recognized that the specific manifestations of those laws—cats playing with mice, and ichneumon larvae eating caterpillars—could not embody ethical messages, but he somehow hoped that unknown higher laws might exist "with the details, whether good or bad, left to the working out of what we may call chance."

Since ichneumons are a detail, and since natural selection is a law regulating details, the answer to the ancient dilemma of why such cruelty (in our terms) exists in nature can only be that there isn't any answer—and that the framing of the question "in our terms" is thoroughly inappropriate in a natural world neither made for us nor ruled by us. It just plain happens. It is a strategy that works for ichneumons and that natural selection has programmed into their behavioral repertoire. Caterpillars are not suffering to teach us something; they have simply been outmaneuvered, for now, in the evolutionary game. Perhaps they will evolve a set of adequate defenses sometime in the future, thus sealing the fate of ichneumons. And perhaps, indeed probably, they will not.

Another Huxley, Thomas's grandson Julian, spoke for this position, using as an example—yes, you guessed it—the ubiquitous ichneumons:

Natural selection, in fact, though like the mills of God in grinding
slowly and grinding small, has few other attributes that a civilized

religion would call divine. . . . Its products are just as likely to be aesthetically, morally, or intellectually repulsive to us as they are to be attractive. We need only think of the ugliness of Sacculina or a bladderworm, the stupidity of a rhinoceros or a stegosaur, the horror of a female mantis devouring its mate or a brood of ichneumon flies slowly eating out a caterpillar.

It is amusing in this context, or rather ironic since it is too serious to be amusing, that modern creationists accuse evolutionists of preaching a specific ethical doctrine called secular humanism and thereby demand equal time for their unscientific and discredited views. If nature is nonmoral, then evolution cannot teach any ethical theory at all. The assumption that it can has abetted a panoply of social evils that ideologues falsely read into nature from their beliefs—eugenics and (misnamed) social Darwinism prominently among them. Not only did Darwin eschew any attempt to discover an antireligious ethic in nature, he also expressly stated his personal bewilderment about such deep issues as the problem of evil. Just a few sentences after invoking the ichneumons, and in words that express both the modesty of this splendid man and the compatibility, through lack of contact, between science and true religion, Darwin wrote to Asa Gray,

I feel most deeply that the whole subject is too profound for the human intellect. A dog might as well speculate on the mind of Newton. Let each man hope and believe what he can.

SUGGESTIONS FOR WRITING

1. Gould warns of the dangers of an anthropomorphic view of nature—one that perceives the nonhuman in human terms. Write an essay in which you explain and exemplify the different methods Gould uses to explore the problems with anthropomorphic thinking.

2. In paragraph 27, Gould admits that even Darwin could not "thoroughly abandon the idea that the laws of nature might reflect some higher purpose." In your opinion, does Gould himself lead his reader to thoroughly abandon the idea? Write an essay explaining why or why not.

3. Gould has been much praised as a writer for his ability to make scientific issues clear to the nonscientist. Find a moment in the essay that in your view justifies such praise and write an essay to explain the basis of your choice.

Elixirs of Death

1962

From *Silent Spring*

RACHEL CARSON

Rachel Carson (1907–1964) was trained as a marine biologist. After teaching at the University of Maryland she joined the United States Fish and Wildlife Service as an editor of its publications. In 1951 she published a best-selling book—The Sea Around Us—and became famous as an advocate for the environment who could explain scientific developments to the average reader.

As Carson explains in the following excerpt from a later book, Silent Spring, chemical pesticides rapidly came into widespread use after World War II with the result that gradually many long familiar species of birds and insects began to disappear from the American landscape. It turned out the poisons used to kill harmful pests were consumed by the creatures who fed on those pests and by the creatures who fed on those creatures, all the way up the food chain. Her attack on the wholesale use of powerful pesticides was enormously successful and resulted in her almost single-handedly changing public policy on a national and international scale.

For the first time in the history of the world, every human being is now subjected to contact with dangerous chemicals, from the moment of conception until death. In the less than two decades of their use, the synthetic pesticides have been so thoroughly distributed throughout the animate and inanimate world that they occur virtually everywhere. They have been recovered from most of the major river systems and even from streams of groundwater flowing unseen through the earth. Residues of these chemicals linger in soil to which they may have been applied a dozen years before. They have entered and lodged in the bodies of fish, birds, reptiles, and domestic and wild animals so universally that scientists carrying on animal experiments find it almost impossible to locate subjects free from such contamination. They have been found in fish in remote mountain lakes, in earthworms burrowing in soil, in the eggs of birds—and in man himself. For these chemicals are now stored in the bodies of the vast majority of human beings, regardless of age. They occur in the mother's milk, and probably in the tissues of the unborn child.

All this has come about because of the sudden rise and prodigious growth of an industry for the production of man-made or synthetic chemicals with insecticidal properties. This industry is a child of the

Second World War. In the course of developing agents of chemical warfare, some of the chemicals created in the laboratory were found to be lethal to insects. The discovery did not come by chance: insects were widely used to test chemicals as agents of death for man.

The result has been a seemingly endless stream of synthetic insecticides. In being man-made—by ingenious laboratory manipulation of the molecules, substituting atoms, altering their arrangement—they differ sharply from the simpler inorganic insecticides of prewar days. These were derived from naturally occurring minerals and plant products—compounds of arsenic, copper, lead, manganese, zinc, and other minerals, pyrethrum from the dried flowers of chrysanthemums, nicotine sulphate from some of the relatives of tobacco, and rotenone from leguminous plants of the East Indies.

What sets the new synthetic insecticides apart is their enormous biological potency. They have immense power not merely to poison but to enter into the most vital processes of the body and change them in sinister and often deadly ways. Thus, as we shall see, they destroy the very enzymes whose function is to protect the body from harm, they block the oxidation processes from which the body receives its energy, they prevent the normal functioning of various organs, and they may initiate in certain cells the slow and irreversible change that leads to malignancy.

5   Yet new and more deadly chemicals are added to the list each year and new uses are devised so that contact with these materials has become practically worldwide. The production of synthetic pesticides in the United States soared from 124,259,000 pounds in 1947 to 637,666,000 pounds in 1960—more than a fivefold increase. The wholesale value of these products was well over a quarter of a billion dollars. But in the plans and hopes of the industry this enormous production is only a beginning.

A Who's Who of pesticides is therefore of concern to us all. If we are going to live so intimately with these chemicals—eating and drinking them, taking them into the very marrow of our bones—we had better know something about their nature and their power.

Although the Second World War marked a turning away from inorganic chemicals as pesticides into the wonder world of the carbon molecule, a few of the old materials persist. Chief among these is arsenic, which is still the basic ingredient in a variety of weed and insect killers. Arsenic is a highly toxic mineral occurring widely in association with the ores of various metals, and in very small amounts in volcanoes, in the sea, and in spring water. Its relations to man are varied and historic. Since many of its compounds are tasteless, it has been a favorite agent of homicide from long before the time of the Borgias to the present. Arsenic was the first recognized elementary carcinogen (or cancer-causing substance), identified in chimney soot and linked to cancer nearly two centuries ago by an English physician. Epidemics of chronic arsenical poisoning involving whole populations over long periods are on record. Arsenic-contaminated environments have also caused sickness and death among horses, cows, goats, pigs, deer, fishes, and bees; despite this record arsenical sprays and dusts are widely used. In the arsenic-sprayed cotton country of southern United States beekeeping as an industry has nearly died out. Farmers using arsenic dusts over long periods have been afflicted with chronic arsenic poisoning; livestock have been poisoned by crop sprays or weed killers containing arsenic. Drifting arsenic dusts from blueberry lands have spread over neighboring farms, contaminating streams, fatally poisoning bees and cows, and causing human illness. "It is scarcely possible . . . to handle arsenicals with more utter disregard of the general health than that which has been practiced in our country in recent years," said Dr. W. C. Hueper of the National Cancer Institute, an authority on environmental cancer. "Anyone who has watched the dusters and sprayers of arsenical insecticides at work must have been impressed by the almost supreme carelessness with which the poisonous substances are dispensed."

Modern insecticides are still more deadly. The vast majority fall into one of two large groups of chemicals. One, represented by DDT, is known as the "chlorinated hydrocarbons." The other group consists of the organic phosphorus insecticides, and is represented by the reasonably familiar malathion and parathion. All have one thing in common. As mentioned above, they are built on a basis of carbon atoms, which are also the indispensable building blocks of the living world, and thus classed as "organic." To understand them, we must see of what they are made, and how, although linked with the basic chemistry of all life, they lend themselves to the modifications which make them agents of death.

The basic element, carbon, is one whose atoms have an almost infinite capacity for uniting with each other in chains and rings and various other configurations, and for becoming linked with atoms of other substances. Indeed, the incredible diversity of living creatures from bacteria to the great blue whale is largely due to this capacity of carbon. The complex protein molecule has the carbon atom as its basis, as have molecules of fat, carbohydrates, enzymes, and vitamins. So, too, have enormous numbers of nonliving things, for carbon is not necessarily a symbol of life.

10   Some organic compounds are simply combinations of carbon and hydrogen. The simplest of these is methane, or marsh gas, formed in nature by the bacterial decomposition of organic matter under water. Mixed with air in proper proportions, methane becomes the dreaded "fire damp" of coal mines. Its structure is beautifully simple, consisting of one carbon atom to which four hydrogen atoms have become attached:

$$\begin{array}{ccc} H & & H \\ & C & \\ H & & H \end{array}$$

Chemists have discovered that it is possible to detach one or all of the hydrogen atoms and substitute other elements. For example, by substituting one atom of chlorine for one of hydrogen we produce methyl chloride:

$$\begin{array}{ccc} H & & Cl \\ & C & \\ H & & H \end{array}$$

Take away three hydrogen atoms and substitute chlorine and we have the anesthetic chloroform:

$$\begin{array}{ccc} H & & Cl \\ & C & \\ Cl & & Cl \end{array}$$

Substitute chlorine atoms for all of the hydrogen atoms and the result is carbon tetrachloride, the familiar cleaning fluid:

$$\begin{array}{ccc} Cl & & Cl \\ & C & \\ Cl & & Cl \end{array}$$

In the simplest possible terms, these changes rung upon the basic molecule of methane illustrate what a chlorinated hydrocarbon is. But this illustration gives little hint of the true complexity of the chemical world of the hydrocarbons, or of the manipulations by which the organic chemist creates his infinitely varied materials. For instead of the simple methane molecule with its single carbon atom, he may work with hydrocarbon molecules consisting of many carbon atoms, arranged in rings or chains, with side chains or branches, holding to themselves with chemical bonds not merely simple atoms of hydrogen or chlorine but also a wide variety of chemical groups. By seemingly slight changes the whole character of the substance is changed; for example, not only what is attached but the place of attachment to the carbon atom is highly important. Such ingenious manipulations have produced a battery of poisons of truly extraordinary power.

DDT (short for dichloro-diphenyl-trichloro-ethane) was first synthesized by a German chemist in 1874, but its properties as an insecticide were not discovered until 1939. Almost immediately DDT was hailed as a means of stamping out insect-borne disease and winning the farmers' war against crop destroyers overnight. The discoverer, Paul Müller of Switzerland, won the Nobel Prize.

DDT is now so universally used that in most minds the product takes on the harmless aspect of the familiar. Perhaps the myth of the harmlessness of DDT rests on the fact that one of its first uses was the wartime dusting of many thousands of soldiers, refugees, and prisoners, to combat lice. It is widely believed that since so many people came into extremely intimate contact with DDT and suffered no immediate ill effects the chemical must certainly be innocent of harm. This understandable misconception arises from the fact that—unlike other chlorinated hydrocarbons—DDT *in powder form* is not readily absorbed through the skin. Dissolved in oil, as it usually is, DDT is definitely toxic. If swallowed, it is absorbed slowly through the digestive tract; it may also be absorbed through the lungs. Once it has entered the body it is stored largely in organs rich in fatty substances (because DDT itself is fat-soluble) such as the adrenals, testes, or thyroid. Relatively large amounts are deposited in the liver, kidneys, and the fat of the large, protective mesenteries that enfold the intestines.

This storage of DDT begins with the smallest conceivable intake of the chemical (which is present as residues on most foodstuffs) and continues until quite high levels are reached. The fatty storage depots act as biological magnifiers, so that an intake of as little as $1/10$ of 1 part per million in the diet results in storage of about 10 to 15 parts per million, an increase of one hundredfold or more. These terms of reference, so commonplace to the chemist or the pharmacologist, are unfamiliar to most of us. One part in a million sounds like a very small amount—and so it is. But such substances are so potent that a minute quantity can bring about vast changes in the body. In animal experiments, 3 parts per million has been found to inhibit an essential enzyme in heart muscle; only 5 parts per million has brought about necrosis or disintegration of liver cells; only 2.5 parts per million of the closely related chemicals dieldrin and chlordane did the same.

15   This is really not surprising. In the normal chemistry of the human body there is just such a disparity between cause and effect. For example, a quantity of iodine as small as two ten-thousandths of a gram spells the difference between health and disease. Because these small amounts of pesticides are cumulatively stored and only slowly excreted, the threat of chronic poisoning and degenerative changes of the liver and other organs is very real.

Scientists do not agree upon how much DDT can be stored in the human body. Dr. Arnold Lehman, who is the chief pharmacologist of the Food and Drug Administration, says there is neither a floor below which DDT is not absorbed nor a ceiling beyond which absorption and storage ceases. On the other hand, Dr. Wayland Hayes of the United States Public Health Service contends that in every individual a point of equilibrium is reached, and that DDT in excess of this amount is excreted. For practical purposes it is not particularly important which of these men is right. Storage in human beings has been well investigated, and we know that the average person is storing potentially harmful amounts. According to various studies, individuals with no known exposure (except the inevitable dietary one) store an average of 5.3 parts per million to 7.4 parts per million; agricultural workers 17.1 parts per million; and workers in insecticide plants as high as 648 parts per million! So the range of proven storage is quite wide and, what is even more to the point, the minimum figures are above the level at which damage to the liver and other organs or tissues may begin.

One of the most sinister features of DDT and related chemicals is the way they are passed on from one organism to another through all the links of the food chains. For example, fields of alfalfa are dusted with DDT; meal is later prepared from the alfalfa and fed to hens; the hens lay eggs which contain DDT. Or the hay, containing residues of 7 to 8 parts per million, may be fed to cows. The DDT will turn up in the milk in the amount of about 3 parts per million, but in butter made from this milk the concentration may run to 65 parts per million. Through such a process of transfer, what started out as a very small amount of DDT may end as a heavy concentration. Farmers nowadays find it difficult to obtain uncontaminated fodder for their milk cows, though the Food and Drug Administration forbids the presence of insecticide residues in milk shipped in interstate commerce.

The poison may also be passed on from mother to offspring. Insecticide residues have been recovered from human milk in samples tested by Food and Drug Administration scientists. This means that the breast-fed human infant is receiving small but regular additions to the load of toxic chemicals building up in his body. It is by no means his first exposure, however: there is good reason to believe this begins while he is still in the womb. In experimental animals the chlorinated hydrocarbon insecticides freely cross the barrier of the placenta, the traditional protective shield between the embryo and harmful substances in the mother's body. While the quantities so received by human infants would normally be small, they are not unimportant because children are more susceptible to poisoning than adults. This situation also means that today the average individual almost certainly starts life with the first deposit of the growing load of chemicals his body will be required to carry thenceforth.

All these facts—storage at even low levels, subsequent accumulation, and occurrence of liver damage at levels that may easily occur in normal diets, caused Food and Drug Administration scientists to declare as early as 1950 that it is "extremely likely the potential hazard of DDT has been underestimated." There has been no such parallel situation in medical history. No one yet knows what the ultimate consequences may be.

SUGGESTIONS FOR WRITING

1. The positive and negative implications of the key words in Carson's title seem to form a paradox. Write an essay explaining how the paradoxical title manifests itself in the points she makes about the history of DDT.

2. Carson argues for a distinction between the immediate and long-term effects of DDT. Write an essay that summarizes and exemplifies her views on the importance of this distinction.

3. This selection concludes with the sentence: "No one yet knows what the ultimate consequences may be." Still, Carson's argument has had extraordinary results in the area of public policy concerned with long-term consequences. Write an essay explaining and exemplifying the ways Carson's essay *implies* particular long-term consequences for the use of DDT.

The Myth of DDT vs. the Reality of Malaria 2005

PHYLLIS SCHLAFLY

Phyllis Schlafly was born in 1924 in St. Louis. She graduated from Washington University in her hometown at the age of nineteen and went on to earn an M. A. in government from Radcliff at Harvard and a law degree from Washington University. To date she is the author of some 21 books on topics ranging from childcare to the use of phonics in education. She writes a weekly newspaper column on political topics that is reprinted in over a hundred papers.

As her selection shows, Schlafly loves a fight and an uphill, apparently unpopular fight is all the better in her view. Her perhaps most famous fight involved undertaking a grassroots campaign against the equal rights amendment to the Constitution after it had already passed in 30 of the 38 states needed for its adoption. Only 35 states ultimately ratified. Her formidable argumentative powers are placed below in the service of the hundreds of millions of people around the world still threatened by malaria.

The United States has just assumed the largest burden of forgiving $40 billion in debt owed by 18 mostly African countries. It's no wonder these countries can't repay their debts when they suffer the enormous human and economic costs of malaria.

According to Harvard development expert Jeffrey Sachs, malaria cuts in half the potential growth of African countries. Yet, new evidence has just surfaced that the U.S. Agency for International Development, to which our taxpayers give $90 million a year to fight malaria, spends 95 percent of this money on consultants, advertising, and "social marketing," and less than 5 percent on fighting the disease.

Malaria has killed more people, especially children, than any other infectious disease in history. Annual deaths from malaria, mostly in Africa, Asia and Central America, have long been estimated at between 1 million and 2.7 million.

British scientists at Oxford University recently reported that in 2002 there were 515 million people infected with the most dangerous strain of malaria. Malaria deaths could easily exceed the 3 million people killed annually by AIDS.

5   In 1998, the World Bank pledged to reduce malaria disease and fatalities by 50 percent by 2010, but instead malaria rates have increased by 15 percent. This is the same World Bank now demanding that its bad loans to African countries be reimbursed by the United States.

Malaria is a disease carried by mosquitoes, and the world knows how to kill the hated mosquitoes—it's to spray them with the insecticide called DDT. Between the end of World War II and 1970, DDT practically eliminated malaria in the United States and Europe, and successfully battled it elsewhere.

According to the National Academy of Sciences, in those years DDT saved more than 500 million lives. In India, for example, there were 1 million deaths from malaria in 1945, and DDT reduced that figure to only a few thousand in 1960.

DDT not only saved lives and prevented debilitating illnesses, it laid a more stable foundation for development and wealth creation in malaria areas of Africa and Asia. DDT's effectiveness against malaria was dramatically demonstrated and is really beyond dispute.

Then, in 1962, Rachel Carson's book *Silent Spring* created a worldwide scare about DDT, which she claimed was a danger to wildlife. Much of her so-called scientific basis for a DDT ban was soon proven either wrong or exaggerated, and the 1972 edition of her book admitted as much.

10   No study has been able to link the use of DDT with any negative human health impact, even though sprayers have worked with the chemical many hours a day.

Nevertheless, contrary to expert testimony that DDT was not harmful to humans, animals or the environment, in a raw exercise of arbitrary power in 1972 the Environmental Protection Agency banned DDT, and it has continued to be banned in most of the world. Since then, more than 50 million people have died from malaria.

The death toll from mosquitoes breeding in the contaminated water left by the tsunami that struck Indonesia, India, Sri Lanka and many more countries on the Indian Ocean could be more deadly than the tsunami itself.

DDT is cheap, easy to use, long lasting, does the job, and could save literally millions of African, Asian and Central American lives every year. Wealthy countries like the United States can afford alternate anti-mosquito repellents that you and I can buy at any supermarket, but the epidemic of malaria in poor countries makes anything other than DDT impractical.

DDT alternatives are less effective and five to 10 times more expensive. Africans and Asians threatened by hundreds of thousands of cases of the killer disease are far more worried about malaria than about any tiny theoretical threat from DDT.

15 Despite the obvious value of DDT in saving lives, environmentalist campaigns continue to prevent its use.

Due to the large influx of illegal immigrants who, of course, are not tested for disease, as are legal immigrants, mosquito-caused diseases are re-emerging as a U.S. health problem. Malaria has popped up in Texas, and dengue fever, another mosquito-borne disease, had a virulent outbreak in a Texas county on our southern border.

Another mosquito-borne disease, West Nile virus, which was unheard of in the United States prior to 1998, has come to our country from Africa. It now infects tens of thousands of people in 21 states, and many have died.

Researchers at the University of Texas Medical Branch have just discovered that mosquitoes can pass West Nile virus to each other much faster than previously thought. This is what caused the disease to spread rapidly across North America despite earlier predictions that it would spread more slowly or even die out.

The U.S. Agency for International Development and World Bank anti-DDT policy that saves mosquitoes instead of humans has stymied African countries' economic growth and is now forcing U.S. taxpayers to bail out a mountain of bad debt. When will Americans wake up to the high costs of junk environmentalism?

SUGGESTIONS FOR WRITING

1. Schlafly's title expresses an opposition. Write an essay that shows how she uses that opposition to organize her own essay.
2. Both Carson and Schlafly address issues of human interference with the 'natural' process of natural selection by choosing certain life forms for

destruction while preserving others. Write an essay in which you compare and contrast the implied positions taken by each author on the proper relation of humanity to nature and the natural process of evolution.

3. Given the context of your reading in the chapter as a whole, what do you think about the use of DDT? Write an essay that supports either Carson or Schlafly while being sure to do justice to the arguments of both writers.

INTERDISCIPLINARY CONNECTIONS

1. Chapter 2 of this book explores the topic of economics, though Chapter 1, which focuses on evolution, also includes contributions by economists. Did you find that the views of Malthus and Schumpeter are illuminated by the evolutionary context of the first chapter, or do you think that those authors would be more effectively presented in a strictly economic setting? Write an essay that explains and defends your views.

2. The main subject of Chapter 3 is human rights, but surely the issue of human rights is an important one in the controversy between Rachel Carson and Phyllis Schlafly over the consequences of whether or not human intervention in natural conditions is justified at the expense of other life forms. What are your views on human rights when they appear in opposition to nature? Write an essay explaining and defending your views.

3. Chapter 4 of this book focuses on literature, yet Theodore Baird claims that a scientist like Charles Darwin has the right to be considered a great literary figure too. In your view, which of the *other* authors in Chapter 1 deserve praise for their writing? Pick one and write an essay that discusses and exemplifies the literary qualities of the writer of your choice.

4. Chapter 5 is concerned with utopias and dystopias, ideal communities and communities that exemplify an opposite of the ideal. In Chapter 1, the views of economists Thomas Malthus and Joseph Schumpeter on future developments might be seen in the light of their utopian or dystopian implications. Write an essay in which you explain the ways in which each writer sees economic history working toward a future that approaches either the ideal or its opposite.

5. Chapter 6 explores the topic of human gender. In your view, does Darwin's discussion of sexual selection have implications for the concept of human gender as you currently understand it? Write an essay that explains the reasoning behind your answer.

Economics
The Production and Consumption of Wealth

Jared Diamond	Thorstein Veblen
Adam Smith	Hannah Arendt
Karl Marx	John Maynard Keynes
Charlotte Perkins Gilman	Milton Friedman

Introduction

After the invention of money, wealth was too often thought of only as something measured by a quantity of coins, however much philosophers such as Aristotle tried to disabuse the world of the confusion between a measuring rod and the thing measured. But why do some nations have more wealth than others and why do some within those nations command more resources than their fellow citizens? How wealth is produced and how it is consumed have always been crucial social questions.

The word *economics* originally referred to those issues pertaining to the maintaining and running of a household, but after the industrial revolution began to transform the way wealth was created, the term was employed for new ideas involved in the study of production and consumption both individual and national. The selections in this chapter represent a range of interest in economics and the writers involved are not all professional economists.

Jared Diamond began his career in medicine and moved to ecology before his studies in poorer nations of the world led him to ask the basic question: given the general intelligence and industriousness of the native populations, why are they poor? His speculations led him to an examination of root causes of differences in wealth that begin with the geography of the earth as he tells us in an excerpt from his famous book, *Guns, Germs, and Steel.* Just as biological evolution shows adaptive advantages benefit individual organisms in the struggle for existence, geographical advantages and disadvantages promote and restrain the evolutions of economic benefits.

Adam Smith began his career as a professor of moral science and rhetoric in the late eighteenth century, but is known today as the father of modern economics. In a chapter of his classic work *The Wealth of Nations,* Smith uses the example of the manufacture of common pins to show how differences in industrial organization can be made to pay huge dividends in every sense of the term. Dividing complex tasks into simple ones seems like common sense. However, the application of this principle was far from common in the ways goods were manufactured, until the industrial revolution that was gaining speed in Smith's own lifetime showed the way toward modern mass production techniques.

The factory system was well advanced in the middle of the nineteenth century when Karl Marx composed his famous document, "The Communist Manifesto." The vast increases in the quantity of goods produced had been paradoxically matched with extreme poverty among the classes of society that produced them. The proper distribution of wealth was the crucial issue for Marx who saw material progress itself as inevitable. He depicts what was to him an equally inevitable evolution in the structure of society, one that promised to give its proper share to labor—the true basis of all wealth in his view. As future selections in this book will show, Marx's ideas have influenced areas of life—literary criticism and political action— far beyond the category of economic thought.

Charlotte Perkins Gilman looks at another aspect of the problem of wealth's distribution. Gilman has been called one of the most important feminist writers of the early twentieth century and in "Personal Profit," an excerpt from her pioneering book published on the eve of that century, *Women and Economics,* she examines production and consumption from the perspective of women. Women produce and receive goods and services, but how well do the usual explanations and justifications for the dynamics of that interaction stand up under scrutiny? Gilman's answers make a foundation for the examination of issues still under scrutiny today.

Thorstein Veblen was a professional economist who published his most famous book *The Theory of the Leisure Class* in the United States around the same time that Charlotte Perkins Gilman's own book appeared there. In "Pecuniary Emulation" Veblen examines the psychological bases for the motivations that lead to the production and consumption of wealth at a rate far beyond that needed for mere material survival. Why do people strive to accumulate more than they actually use or could ever use? For many people, wealth is defined by such accumulation, but what is the rationale for this apparently irrational fact?

Hannah Arendt is known primarily as a political philosopher but in the excerpt reprinted here, "The Labour of Our Bodies and the Work of Our Hands," she addresses a basic pre-political question: What is the difference between *work* and *labor*? Surely the words are often used interchangeably in a general sense—just as the words *house* and *home* are—but in what ways do their particular and distinct linguistic implications explain different ways of thinking about productive human effort? Her philosophical and psychological analysis focuses like Veblen's on the most basic motivations behind production, though she gets at them from an entirely different angle—that of how labor promotes the mere subsistence of what already exists and how work creates something entirely new that is added to the world.

The chapter ends with two differing attitudes toward the basic economic concept of laissez faire—the doctrine claiming that the best governmental economic policy is that which interferes least in the production and consumption of wealth. Two of the most famous and influential economists of modern times address the issue. In "The End of Laissez Faire," John Maynard Keynes holds that governmental "interference" is in fact absolutely necessary and inevitable under modern economic conditions. The Noble Prize winner Milton Friedman takes a different and often comically satirical view in "Occupational Licensure," an excerpt from his book *Capitalism and Freedom*. Friedman looks at ways that regulation can take on a life of its own to impede rather than to enhance the very delivery of goods and services that it claims to regulate. He proposes that the noble ideas of public protection through licensure are often only respectable cover stories for the facts of profit seeking by means of monopoly power.

Geographical Selection and Economic Evolution   1997

From *Guns, Germs, and Steel*

JARED DIAMOND

Jared Diamond has had a truly interdisciplinary career. He was born in Boston in 1937 and graduated from Harvard in 1958. He studied at the graduate level in Cambridge University, earning a Ph. D. in physiology and membrane biophysics in 1961, subsequently becoming a professor of physiology at UCLA.

While still in his twenties Diamond began the study of the ecology and evolution of birds in New Guinea. His experiences with and admiration of the people there led him to a third career in environmental history and economic development, seeking to understand a crucial question for modern times. Since science has shown human intelligence and physical ability to be equally distributed all over the world, why is it that wealth and poverty have been so unequally distributed? His book Guns, Germs, and Steel, from which the following selection is taken, won the Pulitzer Prize in 1997 for its attempts to answer this question.

Why were the trajectories of all key developments shifted to later dates in the Americas than in Eurasia? Four groups of reasons suggest themselves: the later start, more limited suite of wild animals and plants available for domestication, greater barriers to diffusion, and possibly smaller or more isolated areas of dense human populations in the Americas than in Eurasia. . . .

. . . In addition to Eurasia's head start and wild animal and plant species, developments in Eurasia were also accelerated by the easier diffusion of animals, plants, ideas, technology, and people in Eurasia than in the Americas, as a result of several sets of geographic and ecological factors. Eurasia's east-west major axis, unlike the Americas' north-south major axis, permitted diffusion without change in latitude and associated environmental variables. In contrast to Eurasia's consistent east-west breadth, the New World was constricted over the whole length of Central America and especially at Panama. Not least, the Americas were more fragmented by areas unsuitable for food production or for dense human populations. These ecological barriers included the rain forests of the Panamanian isthmus separating. Mesoamerican societies from Andean and Amazonian societies; the deserts of northern Mexico separating Mesoamerica from U.S. southwestern and southeastern societies;

dry areas of Texas separating the U.S. Southwest from the Southeast; and the deserts and high mountains fencing off U.S. Pacific coast areas that would otherwise have been suitable for food production. As a result, there was no diffusion of domestic animals, writing, or political entities, and limited or slow diffusion of crops and technology, between the New World centers of Mesoamerica, the eastern United States, and the Andes and Amazonia.

Some specific consequences of these barriers within the Americas deserve mention. Food production never diffused from the U.S. Southwest and Mississippi Valley to the modern American breadbaskets of California and Oregon, where Native American societies remained hunter-gatherers merely because they lacked appropriate domesticates. The llama, guinea pig, and potato of the Andean highlands never reached the Mexican highlands, so Mesoamerica and North America remained without domestic mammals except for dogs. Conversely, the domestic sunflower of the eastern United States never reached Mesoamerica, and the domestic turkey of Mesoamerica never made it to South America or the eastern United States. Mesoamerican corn and beans took 3,000 and 4,000 years, respectively, to cover the 700 miles from Mexico's farmlands to the eastern U.S. farmlands. After corn's arrival in the eastern United States, seven centuries more passed before the development of a corn variety productive in North American climates triggered the Mississippian emergence. Corn, beans, and squash may have taken several thousand years to spread from Mesoamerica to the U.S. Southwest. While Fertile Crescent crops spread west and east sufficiently fast to preempt independent domestication of the same species or else domestication of closely related species elsewhere, the barriers within the Americas gave rise to many such parallel domestications of crops.

As striking as these effects of barriers on crop and livestock diffusion are the effects on other features of human societies. Alphabets of ultimately eastern Mediterranean origin spread throughout all complex societies of Eurasia, from England to Indonesia, except for areas of East Asia where derivatives of the Chinese writing system took hold. In contrast, the New World's sole writing systems, those of Mesoamerica, never spread to the complex Andean and eastern U.S. societies that might have adopted them. The wheels invented in Mesoamerica as parts of toys never met the llamas domesticated in the Andes, to generate wheeled transport for the New World. From east to west in the Old World, the Macedonian Empire and the Roman Empire both spanned 3,000 miles, the Mongol

Empire 6,000 miles. But the empires and states of Mesoamerica had no political relations with, and apparently never even heard of, the chiefdoms of the eastern United States 700 miles to the north or the empires and states of the Andes 1,200 miles to the south.

5   The greater geographic fragmentation of the Americas compared with Eurasia is also reflected in distributions of languages. Linguists agree in grouping all but a few Eurasian languages into about a dozen language families; each consisting of up to several hundred related languages. For example, the Indo-European language family, which includes English as well as French, Russian, Greek, and Hindi, comprises about 144 languages. Quite a few of those families occupy large contiguous areas—in the case of Indo-European, the area encompassing most of Europe east through much of western Asia to India. Linguistic, historical, and archaeological evidence combines to make clear that each of these large, contiguous distributions stems from a historical expansion of an ancestral language, followed by subsequent local linguistic differentiation to form a family of related languages. Most such expansions appear to be attributable to the advantages that speakers of the ancestral language, belonging to food-producing societies, held over hunter-gatherers. We already discussed such historical expansions in Chapters 16 and 17 for the Sino-Tibetan, Austronesian, and other East Asian language families. Among major expansions of the last millennium are those that carried Indo-European languages from Europe to the Americas and Australia, the Russian language from eastern Europe across Siberia, and Turkish (a language of the Altaic family) from Central Asia westward to Turkey.

With the exception of the Eskimo-Aleut language family of the American Arctic and the Na-Dene language family of Alaska, northwestern Canada, and the U.S. Southwest, the Americas lack examples of large-scale language expansions widely accepted by linguists. Most linguists specializing in Native American languages do not discern large, clear-cut groupings other than Eskimo-Aleut and Na-Dene. At most, they consider the evidence sufficient only to group other Native American languages (variously estimated to number from 600 to 2,000) into a hundred or more language groups or isolated languages. A controversial minority view is that of the linguist Joseph Greenberg, who groups all Native American languages other than Eskimo-Aleut and Na-Dene languages into a single large family, termed Amerind, with about a dozen subfamilies.

Some of Greenberg's subfamilies, and some groupings recognized by more-traditional linguists, may turn out to be legacies of New World population expansions driven in part by food production. These legacies may include the Uto-Aztecan languages of Mesoamerica and the western United States, the Oto-Manguean languages of Mesoamerica, the Natchez-Muskogean languages of the U.S. Southeast, and the Arawak languages of the West Indies. But the difficulties that linguists have in agreeing on groupings of Native American languages reflect the difficulties that complex Native American societies themselves faced in expanding within the New World. Had any food-producing Native American peoples succeeded in spreading far with their crops and livestock and rapidly replacing hunter-gatherers over a large area, they would have left legacies of easily recognized language families, as in Eurasia, and the relationships of Native American languages would not be so controversial.

Thus, we have identified three sets of ultimate factors that tipped the advantage to European invaders of the Americas: Eurasia's long head start on human settlement; its more effective food production, resulting from greater availability of domesticable wild plants and especially of animals; and its less formidable geographic and ecological barriers to intracontinental diffusion. A fourth, more speculative ultimate factor is suggested by some puzzling non-inventions in the Americas: the non-inventions of writing and wheels in complex Andean societies, despite a time depth of those societies approximately equal to that of complex Mesoamerican societies that did make those inventions; and wheels' confinement to toys and their eventual disappearance in Mesoamerica, where they could presumably have been useful in human-powered wheelbarrows, as in China. These puzzles remind one of equally puzzling non-inventions, or else disappearances of inventions, in small isolated societies, including Aboriginal Tasmania, Aboriginal Australia, Japan, Polynesian islands, and the American Arctic. Of course, the Americas in aggregate are anything but small: their combined area is fully 76 percent that of Eurasia, and their human population as of A.D. 1492 was probably also a large fraction of Eurasia's. But the Americas, as we have seen, are broken up into "islands" of societies with tenuous connections to each other. Perhaps the histories of Native American wheels and writing exemplify the principles illustrated in a more extreme form by true island societies.

SUGGESTIONS FOR WRITING

1. Diamond traces many economic developments in the Americas and brings their geographic axes into play in his explanation. Write an essay that describes how, according to Diamond, some of the ways the evolution of human society in the Americas was influenced by "geographical selection."

2. "Location, location, location!" is the traditional slogan used to explain the success of one retail operation rather than another. Write an essay in which you trace the reasoning Diamond employs to explain why Europeans conquered Americans, rather than the other way a round.

3. Diamond mentions language and its written representation as elements in cultural diffusion. Write an essay showing how language makes a representative example of one factor in the economic evolution of the Americas.

Division of Labor   1776
From *The Wealth of Nations*

Book 1
Of the Causes of Improvement in the Productive Powers of Labour, and of the Order According to Which its Produce is Naturally Distributed Among the Different Ranks of the People

ADAM SMITH

Adam Smith (1723–1790), the Scottish philosopher who began the modern study of economics, attended Glasgow University and received a degree from Oxford, though he denounced the complacency and backwardness of the latter institution where Aristotle rather than Newton still dominated the study of physics. Smith himself was abreast of all the developments in many different areas of the Enlightenment, as he demonstrated after accepting the position of professor of logic at Glasgow in 1751. There he taught and wrote on logic and rhetoric, publishing a highly successful book Theory of Moral Sentiments *in 1759.*

Smith is most remembered for An Inquiry into the Nature and Causes of the Wealth of Nations *which was published in 1776, the year of American independence, a cause Smith favored. In this classic book Smith traced the evolution of the economic function in societies from hunter-gatherer groups to modern commercial nations like his own, which was witnessing the dawn of the Industrial Revolution. To this development he brought his views on the stable nature of human moral sentiments, especially in his views on economic causation, asserting that optimal* economic results came from allowing everyone to work in the service of his own enlightened self-interest.

The selections here give first Smith's famous explication of the benefits to industrial production derived from the division of labor. Even though Smith himself had apparently never seen a pin factory, he uses that enterprise as a striking and unforgettable representative example of the powers available to human beings through the proper organization of their economic efforts. In subsequent short chapters, Smith discusses the origins and implications of the division of labor and then examines the nature of money and its relation to labor. In that discussion, he uses the word "corn" in its British sense to mean not only what Americans call sweet corn or Indian corn, but any grain, such as barley, oats, wheat, and rye.

Chapter I

Of the Division of Labour

The greatest improvement in the productive powers of labour, and the greater part of the skill, dexterity, and judgment with which it is anywhere directed, or applied, seem to have been the effects of the division of labour.

The effects of the division of labour, in the general business of society, will be more easily understood, by considering in what manner it operates in some particular manufactures. It is commonly supposed to be carried furthest in some very trifling ones; not perhaps that it really is carried further in them than in others of more importance: but in those trifling manufactures which are destined to supply the small wants of but a small number of people, the whole number of workmen must necessarily be small; and those employed in every different branch of the work can often be collected into the same workhouse, and placed at once under the view of the spectator. In those great manufactures, on the contrary, which are destined to supply the great wants of the great body of the people, every different branch of the work employs so great a number of workmen, that it is impossible to collect them all into the same workhouse. We can seldom see more, at one time, than those employed in one single branch. Though in such manufactures, therefore, the work may really be divided into a much greater number of parts, than in those of a more trifling nature, the division is not near so obvious, and has accordingly been much less observed.

To take an example, therefore, from a very trifling manufacture; but one in which the division of labour has been very often taken notice of, the trade of the pin maker; a workman not educated to this business (which the division of labour has rendered a distinct trade), nor acquainted with the use of the machinery employed in it (to the invention of which the same division of labour has probably given occasion), could scarce, perhaps, with his utmost industry, make one pin in a day, and certainly could not make twenty. But in the way in which this business is now carried on, not only the whole work is a peculiar trade, but it is divided into a number of branches, of which the greater part are likewise peculiar trades. One man draws out the wire, another straightens it, a third cuts it, a fourth points it, a fifth grinds it at the top for receiving the head; to make the head requires two or three distinct operations; to put it on, is a peculiar business, to whiten the pins is another; it is even a trade by itself to put them into the paper; and the important business of making a pin is, in this manner, divided into about eighteen distinct operations, which, in some manufactories, are all performed by distinct hands, though in others the same man will sometimes perform two or three of them. I have seen a small manufactory of this kind where ten men only were employed, and where some of them consequently performed two or three distinct operations. But though they were very poor, and therefore but indifferently accommodated with the necessary machinery, they could, when they exerted themselves, make among them about twelve pounds of pins in a day. There are in a pound upwards of four thousand pins of a middling size. Those ten persons, therefore, could make among them upwards of forty-eight thousand pins in a day. Each person, therefore, making a tenth part of forty-eight thousand pins, might be considered as making four thousand eight hundred pins in a day. But if they had all wrought separately and independently, and without any of them having been educated to this peculiar business, they certainly could not each of them have made twenty, perhaps not one pin in a day; that is, certainly not the two hundred and fortieth, perhaps not the four thousand eight hundredth part of what they are at present capable of performing, in consequence of a proper division and combination of their different operations.

In every other art and manufacture, the effects of the division of labour are similar to what they are in this very trifling one; though, in many of them, the labour can neither be so much subdivided, nor reduced to so great a simplicity of operation. The division of labour, however, so far as it can be introduced, occasions, in every art, a proportionable increase of the productive powers of labour. The separation of different trades and employments from one another, seems to have taken place, in consequence of this advantage. This separation too is generally carried furthest in those countries which enjoy the highest degree of industry and improvement; what is the work of one man, in a rude state of society, being generally that of several in an improved one. In every improved society, the farmer is generally nothing but a farmer; the manufacturer, nothing but a manufacturer. The labour too which is necessary to produce any one complete manufacture, is almost always divided among a great number of hands. How many different trades are employed in each branch of the linen and woollen manufactures, from the growers of the flax and the wool, to the bleachers and smoothers of the linen, or to the dyers and dressers of the cloth! The nature of agriculture, indeed, does not admit of so many subdivisions of labour, nor of so complete a separation of one business from another, as manufactures. It is impossible to separate so entirely, the business of the grazier from that of the corn farmer, as the trade of the carpenter is commonly separated from that of the smith. The spinner is almost always a distinct person from the weaver; but the ploughman, the harrower, the sower of the seed, and the reaper of the corn, are often the same. The occasions for those different sorts of labour returning with the different seasons of the year, it is impossible that one man should be constantly employed in any one of them.

5   This impossibility of making so complete and entire a separation of all the different branches of labour employed in agriculture, is perhaps the reason why the improvement of the productive powers of labour in this art, does not always keep pace with their improvement in manufactures. The most opulent nations, indeed, generally excel all their neighbours in agriculture as well as in manufactures; but they are commonly more distinguished by their superiority in the latter than in the former. Their lands are in general better cultivated, and having more labour and expence bestowed upon them, produce more, in proportion to the extent and natural fertility of the ground. But this superiority of produce is seldom much more than in proportion to the superiority of labour and expence. In agriculture, the labour of the rich country is not always much more productive than that of the poor; or, at least, it is never so much more productive, as it commonly is in manufactures. The corn of the rich country, therefore, will not always, in the same degree of goodness, come cheaper to market than that of the poor. The corn of Poland, in the same degree of goodness, is as cheap as that of France, notwithstanding the superior opulence and

improvement of the latter country. The corn of France is, in the corn provinces, fully as good, and in most years nearly about the same price with the corn of England, though, in opulence and improvement, France is perhaps inferior to England. The corn lands of England, however, are better cultivated than those of France, and the corn lands of France are said to be much better cultivated than those of Poland. But though the poor country, notwithstanding the inferiority of its cultivation, can, in some measure, rival the rich in the cheapness and goodness of its corn, it can pretend to no such competition in its manufactures; at least if those manufactures suit the soil, climate, and situation of the rich country. The silks of France are better and cheaper than those of England, because the silk manufacture, at least under the present high duties upon the importation of raw silk, does not so well suit the climate of England as that of France. But the hardware and the coarse woollens of England are beyond all comparison superior to those of France, and much cheaper too in the same degree of goodness. In Poland there are said to be scarce any manufactures of any kind, a few of those coarser household manufactures excepted, without which no country can well subsist.

This great increase of the quantity of work, which, in consequence of the division of labour, the same number of people are capable of performing, is owing to three different circumstances; first, to the increase of dexterity in every particular workman; secondly, to the saving of the time which is commonly lost in passing from one species of work to another; and lastly, to the invention of a great number of machines which facilitate and abridge labour, and enable one man to do the work of many.

First, the improvement of the dexterity of the workman necessarily increases the quantity of the work he can perform, and the division of labour, by reducing every man's business to some one simple operation, and by making this operation the sole employment of his life, necessarily increases very much the dexterity of the workman. A common smith, who, though accustomed to handle the hammer, has never been used to make nails, if upon some particular occasion he is obliged to attempt it, will scarce, I am assured, be able to make above two or three hundred nails in a day, and those too very bad ones. A smith who has been accustomed to make nails, but whose sole or principal business has not been that of a nailer, can seldom with his utmost diligence make more than eight hundred or a thousand nails in a day. I have seen several boys under twenty years of age who had never exercised any other trade but that of making nails, and who, when they exerted themselves, could make, each of them, upwards of two thousand three hundred nails in a day. The making of a nail, however, is by no means one of the simplest operations. The same person blows the bellows, stirs or mends the fire as there is occasion, heats the iron, and forges every part of the nail: In forging the head too he is obliged to change his tools. The different operations into which the making of a pin, or of a metal button, is subdivided, are all of them much more simple, and the dexterity of the person, of whose life it has been the sole business to perform them, is usually much greater. The rapidity with which some of the operations of those manufactures are performed, exceeds what the human hand could, by those who had never seen them, be supposed capable of acquiring.

Secondly, the advantage which is gained by saving the time commonly lost in passing from one sort of work to another, is much greater than we should at first view be apt to imagine it. It is impossible to pass very quickly from one kind of work to another, that is carried on in a different place, and with quite different tools. A country weaver, who cultivates a small farm, must lose a good deal of time in passing from his loom to the field, and from the field to his loom. When the two trades can be carried on in the same workhouse, the loss of time is no doubt much less. It is even in this case, however, very considerable. A man commonly saunters a little in turning his hand from one sort of employment to another. When he first begins the new work he is seldom very keen and hearty; his mind, as they say, does not go to it, and for some time he rather trifles than applies to good purpose. The habit of sauntering and of indolent careless application, which is naturally, or rather necessarily acquired by every country workman who is obliged to change his work and his tools every half hour, and to apply his hand in twenty different ways almost every day of his life; renders him almost always slothful and lazy, and incapable of any vigorous application even on the most pressing occasions. Independent, therefore, of his deficiency in point of dexterity, this cause alone must always reduce considerably the quantity of work which he is capable of performing.

Thirdly, and lastly, every body must be sensible how much labour is facilitated and abridged by the application of proper machinery. It is unnecessary to give any example. I shall only observe, therefore, that the invention of all those machines by which labour is so much facilitated and abridged, seems to have been originally owing to the division of labour. Men are much more likely to discover easier and readier methods of attaining any object, when the whole attention of their minds is directed towards that single object, than when it is dissipated among a great variety of things. But in consequence of the division of labour, the whole of every man's attention comes naturally to be directed towards some one very simple object. It is naturally to be expected, therefore, that some one or other of those who are employed in each particular branch of labour should soon find out easier and readier methods of performing their own particular work, wherever the nature of it admits of such improvement.

A great part of the machines made use of in those manufactures in which labour is most subdivided, were originally the inventions of common workmen, who, being each of them employed in some very simple operation, naturally turned their thoughts towards finding out easier and readier methods of performing it. Whoever has been much accustomed to visit such manufactures, must frequently have been shown very pretty machines, which were the inventions of such workmen, in order to facilitate and quicken their own particular part of the work. In the first fire engines, a boy was constantly employed to open and shut alternately the communication between the boiler and the cylinder, according as the piston either ascended or descended. One of those boys, who loved to play with his companions, observed that, by tying a string from the handle of the value, which opened this communication, to another part of the machine, the valve would open and shut without his assistance, and leave him at liberty to divert himself with his play-fellows. One of the greatest improvements that has been made upon this machine, since it was first invented, was in this manner the discovery of a boy who wanted to save his own labour.

10 All the improvements in machinery, however, have by no means been the inventions of those who had occasion to use the machines. Many improvements have been made by the ingenuity of the makers of the machines, when to make them became the business of a peculiar trade; and some by that of those who are called philosophers or men of speculation, whose trade it is, not to do any thing, but to observe every thing; and who, upon that account, are often capable of combining together the powers of the most distant and dissimilar objects. In the progress of society, philosophy or speculation becomes, like every other employment, the principal or sole trade

and occupation of a particular class of citizens. Like every other employment too, it is subdivided into a great number of different branches, each of which affords occupation to a peculiar tribe or class of philosophers; and this subdivision of employment in philosophy, as well as in every other business, improves dexterity, and saves time. Each individual becomes more expert in his own peculiar branch, more work is done upon the whole, and the quantity of science is considerably increased by it.

It is the great multiplication of the productions of all the different arts, in consequence of the division of labour, which occasions, in a well-governed society, that universal opulence which extends itself to the lowest ranks of the people. Every workman has a great quantity of his own work to dispose of beyond what he himself has occasion for; and every other workman being exactly in the same situation, he is enabled to exchange a great quantity of his own goods for a great quantity, or, what comes to the same thing, for the price of a great quantity of theirs. He supplies them abundantly with what they have occasion for, and they accommodate him as amply with what he has occasion for, and a general plenty diffuses itself through all the different ranks of the society.

Observe the accommodation of the most common artificer or day-labourer in a civilised and thriving country, and you will perceive that the number of people of whose industry a part, though but a small part, has been employed in procuring him this accommodation, exceeds all computation. The woollen coat, for example, which covers the day-labourer, as coarse and rough as it may appear, is the produce of the joint labour of a great multitude of workmen. The shepherd, the sorter of the wool, the wool-comber or carder, the dyer, the scribbler, the spinner, the weaver, the fuller, the dresser, with many others, must all join their different arts in order to complete even this homely production. How many merchants and carriers, besides, must have been employed in transporting the materials from some of those workmen to others who often live in a very distant part of the country! How much commerce and navigation in particular, how many shipbuilders, sailors, sailmakers, ropemakers, must have been employed in order to bring together the different drugs made use of by the dyer, which often come from the remotest corners of the world! What a variety of labour too is necessary in order to produce the tools of the meanest of those workmen! To say nothing of such complicated machines as the ship of the sailor, the mill of the fuller, or even the loom of the weaver, let us consider only what a variety of labour is requisite in order to form that very simple machine, the shears with which the shepherd clips the wool. The miner, the builder of the furnace for smelting the ore, the feller of the timber, the burner of the charcoal to be made use of in the smelting house, the brickmaker, the bricklayer, the workmen who attend the furnace, the millwright, the forger, the smith, must all of them join their different arts in order to produce them.

Were we to examine, in the same manner, all the different parts of his dress and household furniture, the coarse linen shirt which he wears next his skin, the shoes which cover his feet, the bed which he lies on, and all the different parts which compose it, the kitchen grate at which he prepares his victuals, the coals which he makes use of for that purpose, dug from the bowels of the earth, and brought to him perhaps by a long sea and a long land carriage, all the other utensils of his kitchen, all the furniture of his table, the knives and forks, the earthen or pewter plates upon which he serves up and divides his victuals, the different hands employed in preparing his bread and his beer, the glass window which lets in the heat and the light, and keeps out the wind and the rain, with all the knowledge and art requisite for preparing that beautiful and happy invention, without which these northern parts of the world could scarce have afforded a very comfortable habitation, together with the tools of all the different workmen employed in producing those different conveniences; if we examine, I say, all these things, and consider what a variety of labour is employed about each of them, we shall be sensible that without the assistance and cooperation of many thousands, the very meanest person in a civilised country could not be provided, even according to, what we very falsely imagine, the easy and simple manner in which he is commonly accommodated. Compared, indeed, with the more extravagant luxury of the great, his accommodation must no doubt appear extremely simple and easy; and yet it may be true, perhaps, that the accommodation of an European prince does not always so much exceed that of an industrious and frugal peasant, as the accommodation of the latter exceeds that of many an African king, the absolute master of the lives and liberties of ten thousand naked savages.

Chapter II

Of the Principle which gives occasion to the Division of Labour

This division of labour, from which so many advantages are derived, is not originally the effect of any human wisdom, which foresees and intends that general opulence to which it gives occasion. It is the necessary, though very slow and gradual consequence of a certain propensity in human nature which has in view no such extensive utility; the propensity to truck, barter, and exchange one thing for another.

Whether this propensity be one of those original principles in human nature, of which no further account can be given; or whether, as seems more probable, it be the necessary consequence of the faculties of reason and speech, it belongs not to our present subject to enquire. It is common to all men, and to be found in no other race of animals, which seem to know neither this nor any other species of contracts. Two greyhounds, in running down the same hare, have sometimes the appearance of acting in some sort of concert. Each turns her towards his companion, or endeavours to intercept her when his companion turns her towards himself.

This, however, is not the effect of any contract, but of the accidental concurrence of their passions in the same object at that particular time. Nobody ever saw a dog make a fair and deliberate exchange of one bone for another with another dog. Nobody ever saw one animal by its gestures and natural cries signify to another, this is mine, that yours; I am willing to give this for that. When an animal wants to obtain something either of a man or of another animal, it has no other means of persuasion but to gain the favour of those whose service it requires. A puppy fawns upon its dam, and a spaniel endeavours by a thousand attractions to engage the attention of its master who is at dinner, when it wants to be fed by him. Man sometimes uses the same arts with his brethren, and when he has no other means of engaging them to act according to his inclinations, endeavours by every servile and fawning attention to obtain their good will. He has not time, however, to do this upon every occasion. In civilised society he stands at all times in need of the cooperation and assistance of great multitudes, while his whole life is scarce sufficient to gain the friendship of a few persons.

In almost every other race of animals each individual, when it is grown up to maturity, is entirely independent, and in its natural state has occasion for the assistance of no other living creature. But man has almost constant occasion for the help of his brethren, and it is in vain for him to expect it from their benevolence only. He will be more likely to prevail if he can interest their self-love in his favour, and show them that it is for their own advantage to do for him what he requires of them. Whoever offers to another a bargain of any kind, proposes to do this. Give me that which I want, and you shall have this which you want, is the meaning of every such offer; and it is in this manner that we obtain from one another the far greater part of those good offices which we stand in need of. It is not from the benevolence of the butcher, the brewer, or the baker, that we expect our dinner, but from their regard to their own interest. We address ourselves, not to their humanity but to their selflove, and never talk to them of our own necessities but of their advantages. Nobody but a beggar chooses to depend chiefly upon the benevolence of his fellow-citizens. Even a beggar does not depend upon it entirely. The charity of well-disposed people, indeed, supplies him with the whole fund of his subsistence. But though this principle ultimately provides him with all the necessaries of life which he has occasion for, it neither does nor can provide him with them as he has occasion for them. The greater part of his occasional wants are supplied in the same manner as those of other people, by treaty, by barter, and by purchase. With the money which one man gives him he purchases food. The old clothes which another bestows upon him he exchanges for other old clothes which suit him better, or for lodging, or for food, or for money, with which he can buy either food, clothes, or lodging, as he has occasion.

As it is by treaty, by barter, and by purchase, that we obtain from one another the greater part of those mutual good offices which we stand in need of, so it is this same trucking disposition which originally gives occasion to the division of labour. In a tribe of hunters or shepherds a particular person makes bows and arrows, for example, with more readiness and dexterity than any other. He frequently exchanges them for cattle or for venison with his companions; and he finds at last that he can in this manner get more cattle and venison, than if he himself went to the field to catch them. From a regard to his own interest, therefore, the making of bows and arrows grows to be his chief business, and he becomes a sort of armourer. Another excels in making the frames and covers of their little huts or moveable houses. He is accustomed to be of use in this way to his neighbours, who reward him in the same manner with cattle and with venison, till at last he finds it his interest to dedicate himself entirely to this employment, and to become a sort of house-carpenter. In the same manner a third becomes a smith or a brazier, a fourth a tanner or dresser of hides or skins, the principal part of the clothing of savages. And thus the certainty of being able to exchange all that surplus part of the produce of his own labour, which is over and above his own consumption, for such parts of the produce of other men's labour as he may have occasion for, encourages every man to apply himself to a particular occupation, and to cultivate and bring to perfection whatever talent or genius he may possess for that particular species of business.

The difference of natural talents in different men is, in reality, much less than we are aware of; and the very different genius which appears to distinguish men of different professions, when grown up to maturity, is not upon many occasions so much the cause, as the effect of the division of labour. The difference between the most dissimilar characters, between a philosopher and a common street porter, for example, seems to arise not so much from nature, as from habit, custom, and education. When they came into the world, and for the first six or eight years of their existence, they were, perhaps, very much alike, and neither their parents nor play-fellows could perceive any remarkable difference. About that age, or soon after, they come to be employed in very different occupations. The difference of talents comes then to be taken notice of, and widens by degrees, till at last the vanity of the philosopher is willing to acknowledge scarce any resemblance. But without the disposition to truck, barter, and exchange, every man must have procured to himself every necessary and convenience of life which he wanted. All must have had the same duties to perform, and the same work to do, and there could have been no such difference of employment as could alone give occasion to any great difference of talents.

20   As it is this disposition which forms that difference of talents, so remarkable among men of different professions, so it is this same disposition which renders that difference useful. Many tribes of animals acknowledged to be all of the same species, derive from nature a much more remarkable distinction of genius, than what, antecedent to custom and education, appears to take place among men. By nature a philosopher is not in genius and disposition half so different from a street porter, as a mastiff is from a greyhound, or a greyhound from a spaniel, or this last from a shepherd's dog. Those different tribes of animals, however, though all of the same species, are of scarce any use to one another. The strength

of the mastiff is not, in the least, supported either by the swiftness of the greyhound, or by the sagacity of the spaniel, or by the docility of the shepherd's dog. The effects of those different geniuses and talents, for want of the power or disposition to barter and exchange, cannot be brought into a common stock, and do not in the least contribute to the better accommodation and convenience of the species. Each animal is still obliged to support and defend itself, separately and independently, and derives no sort of advantage from that variety of talents with which nature has distinguished its fellows. Among men, on the contrary, the most dissimilar geniuses are of use to one another; the different produces of their respective talents, by the general disposition to truck, barter, and exchange, being brought, as it were, into a common stock, where every man may purchase whatever part of the produce of other men's talents he has occasion for.

Chapter III

That the Division of Labour is limited by the Extent of the Market

As it is the power of exchanging that gives occasion to the division of labour, so the extent of this division must always be limited by the extent of that power, or, in other words, by the extent of the market. When the market is very small, no person can have any encouragement to dedicate himself entirely to one employment, for want of the power to exchange all that surplus part of the produce of his own labour, which is over and above his own consumption, for such parts of the produce of other men's labour as he has occasion for.

There are some sorts of industry, even of the lowest kind, which can be carried on nowhere but in a great town. A porter, for example, can find employment and subsistence in no other place. A village is by much too narrow a sphere for him; even an ordinary market town is scarce large enough to afford him constant occupation. In the lone houses and very small villages which are scattered about in so desert a country as the Highlands of Scotland, every farmer must be butcher, baker and brewer for his own family. In such situations we can scarce expect to find even a smith, a carpenter, or a mason, within less than twenty miles of another of the same trade. The scattered families that live at eight or ten miles distance from the nearest of them, must learn to perform themselves a great number of little pieces of work, for which, in more populous countries, they would call in the assistance of those workmen. Country workmen are almost everywhere obliged to apply themselves to all the different branches of industry that have so much affinity to one another as to be employed about the same sort of materials. A country carpenter deals in every sort of work that is made of wood: a country smith in every sort of work that is made of iron. The former is not only a carpenter, but a joiner, a cabinetmaker, and even a carver in wood, as well as a wheelwright, a ploughwright, a cart and wagon maker. The employments of the latter are still more various. It is impossible there should be such a trade as even that of a nailer in the remote and inland parts of the Highlands of Scotland. Such a workman at the rate of a thousand nails a day, and three hundred working days in the year, will make three hundred thousand nails in the year. But in such a situation it would be impossible to dispose of one thousand, that is, of one day's work in the year. . . .

Chapter IV

Of the Origin and Use of Money

When the division of labour has been once thoroughly established, it is but a very small part of a man's wants which the produce of his own labour can supply. He supplies the far greater part of them by exchanging that surplus part of the produce of his own labour, which is over and above his own consumption, for such parts of the produce of other men's labour as he has occasion for. Every man thus lives by exchanging, or becomes in some measure a merchant, and the society itself grows to be what is properly a commercial society.

But when the division of labour first began to take place, this power of exchanging must frequently have been very much clogged and embarrassed in its operations. One man, we shall suppose, has more of a certain commodity than he himself has occasion for, while another has less. The former consequently would be glad to dispose of, and the latter to purchase, a part of this superfluity. But if this latter should chance to have nothing that the former stands in need of, no exchange can be made between them.

25   The butcher has more meat in his shop than he himself can consume, and the brewer and the baker would each of them be willing to purchase a part of it. But they have nothing to offer in exchange, except the different productions of their respective trades, and the butcher is already provided with all the bread and beer which he has immediate occasion for. No exchange can, in this case, be made between them.

He cannot be their merchant, nor they his customers; and they are all of them thus mutually less serviceable to one another. In order to avoid the inconvenience of such situations, every prudent man in every period of society, after the first establishment of the division of labour, must naturally have endeavoured to manage his affairs in such a manner, as to have at all times by him, besides the peculiar produce of his own industry, a certain quantity of some one commodity or other, such as he imagined few people would be likely to refuse in exchange for the produce of their industry.

Many different commodities, it is probable, were successively both thought of and employed for this purpose. In the rude ages of society, cattle are said to have been the common instrument of commerce; and, though they must have been a most inconvenient one, yet in old times we find things were frequently valued according to the number of cattle which had been given in exchange for them. The armour of Diomede, says Homer, cost only nine oxen; but that of Glaucus cost an hundred oxen. Salt is said to be the common instrument of commerce and exchanges in Abyssinia; a species of shells in some parts of the coast of India; dried cod at Newfoundland; tobacco in Virginia; sugar in some of our West India colonies; hides or dressed leather in some other countries; and there is at this day a village in Scotland where it is not uncommon, I am told, for a workman to carry nails instead of money to the baker's shop or the alehouse.

In all countries, however, men seem at last to have been determined by irresistible reasons to give the preference, for this employment, to metals above every other commodity. Metals cannot only be kept with as little loss as any other commodity, scarce any thing being less perishable that they are, but they can likewise, without any loss, be divided into any number of parts, as by fusion those parts can easily be reunited again; a quality which no other equally durable commodities possess, and which more than any other quality renders them fit to be the instruments of commerce and circulation. The man who wanted to buy salt, for example, and had nothing but cattle to give in exchange for it, must have been obliged to buy salt to the value of a whole ox, or a whole sheep at a time. He could seldom buy less than this, because what he was to give for it could seldom be divided without loss; and if he had a mind to buy more, he must, for the same reasons, have been obliged to buy double or triple the quantity, the value, to wit, of two or three oxen, or of two or three sheep. If, on the contrary, instead of sheep or oxen, he had metals to give in exchange for it, he could easily proportion the quantity of the metal to the precise quantity of the commodity which he had immediate occasion for.

Different metals have been made use of by different nations for this purpose. Iron was the common instrument of commerce among the ancient Spartans; copper among the ancient Romans; and gold and silver among all rich and commercial nations.

Those metals seem originally to have been made use of for this purpose in rude bars, without any stamp or coinage. Thus we are told by Pliny, upon the authority of Timaeus, an ancient historian, that, till the time of Servius Tullius, the Romans had no coined money, but made use of unstamped bars of copper to purchase whatever they had occasion for. These rude bars, therefore, performed at this time the function of money. . . .

30   The inconvenience and difficulty of weighing those metals with exactness gave occasion to the institution of coins, of which the stamp, covering entirely both sides of the piece and sometimes the edges too, was supposed to ascertain not only the fineness, but the weight of the metal. Such coins, therefore, were received by tale as at present, without the trouble of weighing. . . .

It is in this manner that money has become in all civilised nations the universal instrument of commerce, by the intervention of which goods of all kinds are bought and sold, or exchanged for one another.

What are the rules which men naturally observe in exchanging them either for money or for one another, I shall now proceed to examine. These rules determine what may be called the relative or exchangeable value of goods.

The word VALUE, it is to be observed, has two different meanings, and sometimes expresses the utility of some particular object, and sometimes the power of purchasing other goods which the possession of that object conveys. The one may be called value in use; the other, value in exchange. The things which have the greatest value in use have frequently little or no value in exchange; and, on the contrary, those which have the greatest value in exchange have frequently little or no value in use. Nothing is more useful than water: but it will purchase scarce any thing; scarce any thing can be had in exchange for it. A diamond, on the contrary, has scarce any value in use; but a very great quantity of other goods may frequently be had in exchange for it.

In order to investigate the principles which regulate the exchangeable value of commodities, I shall endeavour to show,

First, what is the real measure of this exchangeable value; or, wherein consists the real price of all commodities,

Secondly, what are the different parts of which this real price is composed or made up.

And, lastly, what are the different circumstances which sometimes raise some or all of these different parts of price above, and sometimes sink them below their natural or ordinary rate; or, what are the causes which sometimes hinder the market price, that is, the actual price of commodities, from coinciding exactly with what may be called their natural price.

I shall endeavor to explain, as fully and distinctly as I can, those three subjects in the three following chapters, for which I must very earnestly entreat both the patience and attention of the reader: his patience in order to examine a detail which may perhaps in some places appear unnecessarily tedious; and his attention in order to understand what may, perhaps, after the fullest explication which I am capable of giving of it, appear still in some degree obscure. I am always willing to run some hazard of being tedious in order to be sure that I am perspicuous; and after taking the utmost pains that I can to be perspicuous, some obscurity may still appear to remain upon a subject in its own nature extremely abstracted.

Chapter V

Of the real and nominal Price of Commodities, or of their Price in Labour, and their Price in Money

Every man is rich or poor according to the degree in which he can afford to enjoy the necessaries, conveniences, and amusements of human life. But after the division of labour has once thoroughly taken place, it is but a very small part of these with which a man's own labour can supply him. The far greater part of them he must derive from the labour of other people, and he must be rich or poor according to the quantity of that labour which he can command, or which he can afford to purchase. The value of any commodity, therefore, to the person who possesses it, and who means not to use or consume it himself, but to exchange it for other commodities, is equal to the quantity of labour which it enables him to purchase or command. Labour, therefore, is the real measure of the exchangeable value of all commodities.

The real price of every thing, what every thing really costs to the man who wants to acquire it, is the toil and trouble of acquiring it. What every thing is really worth to the man who has acquired it, and who wants to dispose of it or exchange it for something else, is the toil and trouble which it can save to himself, and which it can impose upon other people. What is bought with money or with goods is purchased by labour as much as what we acquire by the toil of our own body. That money or those goods indeed save us this toil. They contain the value of a certain quantity of labour which we exchange for what is supposed at the time to contain the value of an equal quantity. Labour was the first price, the original purchase money that was paid for all things. It was not by gold or by silver, but by labour, that all the wealth of the world was originally purchased; and its value, to those who possess it and who want to exchange it for some new productions, is precisely equal to the quantity of labour which it can enable them to purchase or command.

Wealth, as Mr. Hobbes says, is power. But the person who either acquires, or succeeds to a great fortune, does not necessarily acquire or succeed to any political power, either civil or military. His fortune may, perhaps, afford him the means of acquiring both, but the mere possession of that fortune does not necessarily convey to him either. The power which that possession immediately and directly conveys to him, is the power of purchasing; a certain command over all the labour, or over all the produce of labour which is then in the market. His fortune is greater or less, precisely in proportion to the extent of this power; or to the quantity either of other men's labour, or, what is the same thing, of the produce of other men's labour, which it enables him to purchase or command. The exchangeable value of every thing must always be precisely equal to the extent of this power which it conveys to its owner.

But though labour be the real measure of the exchangeable value of all commodities, it is not that by which their value is commonly estimated. It is often difficult to ascertain the proportion between two different quantities of labour. The time spent in two different sorts of work will not always alone determine this proportion. The different degrees of hardship endured, and of ingenuity exercised, must likewise be taken into account. There may be more labour in an hour's hard work than in two hours easy business; or in an hour's application to a trade which it cost ten years labour to learn, than in a month's industry at an ordinary and obvious employment. But it is not easy to find any accurate measure either of hardship or ingenuity. In exchanging indeed the different productions of different sorts of labour for one another, some allowance is commonly made for both. It is adjusted, however, not by any accurate measure, but by the higgling and bargaining of the market, according to that sort of rough equality which, though not exact, is sufficient for carrying on the business of common life.

Every commodity besides, is more frequently exchanged for, and thereby compared with, other commodities than with labour. It is more natural, therefore, to estimate its exchangeable value by the quantity of some other commodity than by that of the labour which it can purchase. The greater part of people too understand better what is meant by a quantity of a particular commodity, than by a quantity of labour. The one is a plain palpable object; the other an abstract notion, which, though it can be made sufficiently intelligible, is not altogether so natural and obvious.

But when barter ceases, and money has become the common instrument of commerce, every particular commodity is more frequently exchanged for money than for any other commodity. The butcher seldom carries his beef or his mutton to the baker, or the brewer, in order to exchange them for bread or for beer, but he carries them to the market, where he exchanges them for money, and afterwards exchanges that money for bread and for beer. The quantity of money which he gets for them regulates too the quantity of bread and beer which he can afterwards purchase. It is more natural and obvious to him, therefore, to estimate their value by the quantity of money, the commodity for which he immediately exchanges them, than by that of bread and beer, the commodities for which he can exchange them only by the intervention of another commodity; and rather to say that his butcher's meat is worth threepence or fourpence a pound, than that it is worth three or four pounds of bread, or three or four quarts of small beer. Hence it comes to pass, that the exchangeable value of every commodity is more frequently estimated by the quantity of money, than by the quantity either of labour or of any other commodity which can be had in exchange for it.

45 Gold and silver, however, like every other commodity, vary in their value, are sometimes cheaper and sometimes dearer, sometimes of easier and sometimes of more difficult purchase. The quantity of labour which any particular quantity of them can purchase or command, or the quantity of other goods which it will exchange for, depends always upon the fertility or barrenness of the mines which happen to be known about

the time when such exchanges are made. The discovery of the abundant mines of America reduced, in the sixteenth century, the value of gold and silver in Europe to about a third of what it had been before. As it cost less labour to bring those metals from the mine to the market, so when they were brought thither they could purchase or command less labour; and this revolution in their value, though perhaps the greatest, is by no means the only one of which history gives some account. But as a measure of quantity, such as the natural foot, fathom, or handful, which is continually varying in its own quantity, can never be an accurate measure of the quantity of other things; so a commodity which is itself continually varying in its own value, can never be an accurate measure of the value of other commodities.

Equal quantities of labour, at all times and places, may be said to be of equal value to the labourer. In his ordinary state of health, strength and spirits; in the ordinary degree of his skill and dexterity, he must always lay down the same portion of his ease, his liberty, and his happiness. The price which he pays must always be the same, whatever may be the quantity of goods which he receives in return for it. Of these, indeed, it may sometimes purchase a greater and sometimes a smaller quantity; but it is their value which varies, not that of the labour which purchases them. At all times and places that is dear which it is difficult to come at, or which it costs much labour to acquire; and that cheap which is to be had easily, or with very little labour. Labour alone, therefore, never varying in its own value, is alone the ultimate and real standard by which the value of all commodities can at all times and places be estimated and compared. It is their real price; money is their nominal price only.

But though equal quantities of labour are always of equal value to the labourer, yet to the person who employs him they appear sometimes to be of greater and sometimes of smaller value. He purchases them sometimes with a greater and sometimes with a smaller quantity of goods, and to him the price of labour seems to vary like that of all other things. It appears to him dear in the one case, and cheap in the other. In reality, however, it is the goods which are cheap in the one case, and dear in the other.

In this popular sense, therefore, labour, like commodities, may be said to have a real and a nominal price. Its real price may be said to consist in the quantity of the necessaries and conveniences of life which are given for it; its nominal price, in the quantity of money. The labourer is rich or poor, is well or ill rewarded, in proportion to the real, not to the nominal price of his labour.

The distinction between the real and the nominal price of commodities and labour, is not a matter of mere speculation, but may sometimes be of considerable use in practice. The same real price is always of the same value; but on account of the variations in the value of gold and silver, the same nominal price is sometimes of very different values. When a landed estate, therefore, is sold with a reservation of a perpetual rent, if it is intended that this rent should always be of the same value, it is of importance to the family in whose favour it is reserved, that it should not consist in a particular sum of money. Its value would in this case be liable to variations of two different kinds; first, to those which arise from the different quantities of gold and silver which are contained at different times in coin of the same denomination; and, secondly, to those which arise from the different values of equal quantities of gold and silver at different times. . . .

50   Equal quantities of labour will at distant times be purchased more nearly with equal quantities of corn, the subsistence of the labourer, than with equal quantities of gold and silver, or perhaps of any other commodity. Equal quantities of corn, therefore, will, at distant times, be more nearly of the same real value, or enable the possessor to purchase or command more nearly the same quantity of the labour of other people. They will do this, I say, more nearly than equal quantities of almost any other commodity; for even equal quantities of corn will not do it exactly. The subsistence of the labourer, or the real price of labour, as I shall endeavour to show hereafter, is very different upon different occasions; more liberal in a society advancing to opulence than in one that is standing still; and in one that is standing still than in one that is going backwards. Every other commodity, however, will at any particular time purchase a greater or smaller quantity of labour in proportion to the quantity of subsistence which it can purchase at that time. A rent therefore reserved in corn is liable only to the variations in the quantity of labour which a certain quantity of corn can purchase. But a rent reserved in any other commodity is liable, not only to the variations in the quantity of labour which any particular quantity of corn can purchase, but to the variations in the quantity of corn which can be purchased by any particular quantity of that commodity.

Though the real value of a corn rent, it is to be observed however, varies much less from century to century than that of a money rent, it varies much more from year to year. The money price of labour, as I shall endeavour to show hereafter, does not fluctuate from year to year with the money price of corn, but seems to be everywhere accommodated, not to the temporary or occasional, but to the average or ordinary price of that necessary of life. The average or ordinary price of corn again is regulated, as I shall likewise endeavour to show hereafter, by the value of silver, by the richness or barrenness of the mines which supply the market with that metal, or by the quantity of labour which must be employed, and consequently of corn which must be consumed, in order to bring any particular quantity of silver from the mine to the market. But the value of silver, though it sometimes varies greatly from century to century, seldom varies much from year to year, but frequently continues the same, or very nearly the same, for half a century or a century together. The ordinary or average money price of corn, therefore, may, during so long a period, continue the same or very nearly the same too, and along with it the money price of labour, provided, at least, the society continues, in other respects, in the same or nearly in the same condition. In the meantime the temporary and occasional price of corn may frequently be double, one year, of what it had been the year before, or fluctuate, for example, from five and twenty to fifty shillings the quarter. But when corn is at the latter price, not only the nominal, but the real value of a corn rent will be double of what it is when at the former, or will command double the quantity either of labour or of the greater part of other commodities; the money price of labour, and along with it that of most other things, continuing the same during all these fluctuations.

Labour, therefore, it appears evidently, is the only universal, as well as the only accurate measure of value, or the only standard by which we can compare the values of different commodities at all times and at all places. We cannot estimate, it is allowed, the real value of different commodities from century to century by the quantities of silver which were given for them. We cannot estimate it from year to year by the quantities of corn. By the quantities of labour we can, with the greatest accuracy, estimate it both from century to century and from year to year. From century to century, corn is a better measure than silver, because, from century to century, equal quantities of corn will command the same quantity of labour more nearly than equal quantities of silver. From year to year, on the contrary, silver is a better measure than corn, because equal quantities of it will more nearly command the same quantity of labour. . . .

As it is the nominal or money price of goods, therefore, which finally determines the prudence or imprudence of all purchases and sales, and thereby regulates almost the whole business of common life in which price is concerned, we cannot wonder that it should have been so much more attended to than the real price.

SUGGESTIONS FOR WRITING

1. Why, according to Smith, does the division of labor allow in general for a greater quantity of goods to be produced? Write an essay explaining his reasoning in your own words.
2. According to Smith in his most particular example, an individual could hardly produce a finished pin in a day's labor, while a small group of workers can produce an extraordinary number of pins through the division of labor. Write an essay explaining how the manufacture of pins might be seen to involve a process of evolution akin to that of natural selection or survival of the fittest.
3. In British English "corn" means not only sweet corn or Indian corn, but any grain such as rye, wheat, oats, or barley. Write an essay explaining the reasoning behind Smith's claim that poor countries can rival rich ones in their production of "corn" but not in their production of manufactured goods.

The Communist Manifesto   1848

KARL MARX

Karl Marx (1818–1883)—the man in whose name enormous revolutions erupted in the century following his death—was a German born to Jewish parents who had been converted to Christianity. He earned a doctorate in philosophy but was unable to secure a university position. He entered journalism and soon became notorious for his radical views. Forced into exile from several countries, he eventually settled in London where he became associated with Friedrich Engels, the son of a wealthy industrialist. With Engels's financial and literary help, Marx worked out the economic and social theories expressed in The Communist Manifesto *appearing below.*

A specter is haunting Europe—the specter of Communism. All the Powers of old Europe have entered into a holy alliance to exorcise this specter; Pope and Czar, Metternich and Guizot, French Radicals and German police-spies.

Where is the party in opposition that has not been decried as communistic by its opponents in power? Where the Opposition that has not hurled back the branding reproach of Communism against the more advanced opposition parties, as well as against its reactionary adversaries?

Two things result from this fact.

I. Communism is already acknowledged by all European Powers to be itself a Power.

5   II. It is high time that Communists should openly, in the face of the whole world, publish their views, their aims, their tendencies, and meet this nursery tale of the specter of Communism with a Manifesto of the party itself.

To this end, Communists of various nationalities have assembled in London and sketched the following Manifesto, to be published in the English, French, German, Italian, Flemish and Danish languages.

Bourgeois and Proletarians

The history of all hitherto existing society is the history of class struggles.

Freeman and slave, patrician and plebeian, lord and serf, guildmaster and journeyman, in a word, oppressor and oppressed, stood in constant opposition to one another, carried on uninterrupted, now hidden, now open fight, a fight that each time ended, either in a revolutionary reconstitution of society at large, or in the common ruin of the contending classes.

In the earlier epochs of history we find almost everywhere a complicated arrangement of society into various orders, a manifold gradation of social rank. In ancient Rome we have patricians, knights, plebeians, slaves; in the Middle Ages, feudal lords, vassals, guild-masters, journeymen, apprentices, serfs; in almost all of these classes, again, subordinate gradations.

10   The modern bourgeois society that has sprouted from the ruins of feudal society, has not done away with class antagonisms. It has but established new classes, new conditions of oppression, new forms of struggle in place of the old ones.

Our epoch, the epoch of the bourgeoisie, possesses, however, this distinctive feature; it has simplified the class antagonisms. Society as a whole is more and more splitting up into two great hostile camps, into two great classes directly facing each other: Bourgeoisie and Proletariat.

From the serfs of the Middle Ages sprang the chartered burghers of the earliest towns. From these burgesses the first elements of the bourgeoisie were developed.

The discovery of America, the rounding of the Cape, opened up fresh ground for the rising bourgeoisie. The East Indian and Chinese markets, the colonization of America, trade with the colonies, the increase in the means of exchange and in commodities generally, gave to commerce, to navigation, to industry, an impulse never before known, and thereby, to the revolutionary element in the tottering feudal society, a rapid development.

The feudal system of industry, under which industrial production was monopolized by closed guilds, now no longer sufficed for the growing wants of the new market. The manufacturing system took its place. The guild-masters were pushed on one side by the manufacturing middle-class: division of labor between the different corporate guilds vanished in the face of division of labor in each single workshop.

15 Meantime the markets kept ever growing, the demand ever rising. Even manufacture no longer sufficed. Thereupon, steam and machinery revolutionized industrial production. The place of manufacture was taken by the giant, Modern Industry, the place of the industrial middle-class, by industrial millionaires, the leaders of whole industrial armies, the modern bourgeois.

Modern industry has established the world market, for which the discovery of America paved the way. This market has given an immense development to commerce, to navigation, to communication by land. This development has, in its turn, reacted on the extension of industry; and in proportion as industry, commerce, navigation, railways extended, in the same proportion the bourgeoisie developed, increased its capital, and pushed into the background every class handed down from the Middle Ages.

We see, therefore, how the modern bourgeoisie is itself the product of a long course of development, of a series of revolutions in the modes of production and of exchange.

Each step in the development of the bourgeoisie was accompanied by a corresponding political advance of that class. An oppressed class under the sway of the feudal nobility, an armed and self-governing association in the medieval commune, here independent urban republic (as in Italy and Germany), there taxable "third estate" of the monarchy (as in France), afterwards, in the period of manufacture proper, serving either the semi-feudal or the absolute monarchy as a counterpoise against nobility, and, in fact, corner stone of the great monarchies in general, the bourgeoisie has at last, since the establishment of Modern Industry and of the worldmarket, conquered for itself, in the modern representative State, exclusive political sway. The executive of the modern State is but a committee for managing the common affairs of the whole bourgeoisie.

The bourgeoisie, historically, has played a most revolutionary part.

The bourgeoisie, wherever it has got the upper hand, has put an end to all feudal, patriarchal, idyllic relations. It has pitilessly torn asunder the motley feudal ties that bound man to his "natural superiors," and has left no other nexus between man and man than naked self-interest, than callous "cash payment." It has drowned the most heavenly ecstasies of religious fervor, of chivalrous enthusiasm, of Philistine sentimentalism, in the icy water of egotistical calculation. It has resolved personal worth into exchange value, and in place of the numberless indefeasible chartered freedoms, has set up that single, unconscionable freedom—Free Trade. In one word, for exploitation, veiled by religious and political illusions, it has substituted naked, shameless, direct, brutal exploitation.

The bourgeoisie has stripped of its halo every occupation hitherto honored and looked up to with reverent awe. It has converted the physician, the lawyer, the priest, the poet, the man of science, into its paid wage laborers.

The bourgeoisie has torn away from the family its sentimental veil, and has reduced the family relation to a mere money relation.

The bourgeoisie has disclosed how it came to pass that the brutal display of vigor in the Middle Ages, which reactionists so much admire, found its fitting complement in the most slothful indolence. It has been the first to show what man's activity can bring about. It has accomplished wonders far surpassing Egyptian pyramids, Roman aqueducts and Gothic cathedrals; it has conducted expeditions that put in the shade all former Exoduses of nations and crusades.

The bourgeoisie cannot exist without constantly revolutionizing the instruments of production, and thereby the relations of production, and with them the whole relations of society. Conservation of the old modes of production in unaltered form was, on the contrary, the first condition of existence for all earlier industrial classes. Constant revolutionizing of production, uninterrupted disturbance of all social conditions, everlasting uncertainty and agitation distinguish the bourgeois epoch from all earlier ones. All fixed, fast frozen relations, with their train of ancient and venerable prejudices and opinions, are swept away, all new formed ones become antiquated before they can ossify. All that is solid melts into the air, all that is holy is profaned, and man is at last compelled to face with sober senses, his real conditions of life, and his relations with his kind.

25   The need of a constantly expanding market for its products chases the bourgeoisie over the whole surface of the globe. It must nestle everywhere, settle everywhere, establish connections everywhere.

The bourgeoisie has through its exploitation of the worldmarket given a cosmopolitan character to production and consumption in every country. To the great chagrin of reactionists, it has drawn from under the feet of industry the national ground on which it stood. All old-established national industries have been destroyed or are daily being destroyed. They are dislodged by new industries, whose introduction becomes a life and death question for all civilized nations, by industries that no longer work up indigenous raw material, but raw material drawn from the remotest zones; industries whose products are consumed, not only at home, but in every quarter of the globe. In place of the old wants, satisfied by the productions of the country, we find new wants, requiring for their satisfaction the products of distant lands and climes. In place of the old local and national seclusion and self-sufficiency, we have intercourse in every direction, universal interdependence of nations. And as in material, so also in intellectual production. The intellectual creations of individual nations become common property. National onesidedness and narrow-mindedness become more and more impossible, and from the numerous national and local literatures there arises a world-literature.

The bourgeoisie, by the rapid improvement of all instruments of production, by the immensely facilitated means of communication, draws all, even the most barbarian nations into civilization. The cheap prices of its commodities are the heavy artillery with which it batters down all Chinese walls, with which it forces the barbarians' intensely obstinate hatred of foreigners to capitulate. It compels all nations, on pain of extinction, to adopt the bourgeois mode of production; it compels them to introduce what it calls civilization into their midst, i.e., to become bourgeois themselves. In a word, it creates a world after its own image.

The bourgeoisie has subjected the country to the rule of the towns. It has created enormous cities, has greatly increased the urban population as compared with the rural and has thus rescued a considerable part of the population from the idiocy of rural life. Just as it has made the country dependent on the towns, so it has made barbarian and semi-barbarian countries dependent on civilized ones, nations of peasants on nations of bourgeois, the East on the West.

The bourgeoisie keeps more and more doing away with the scattered state of the population, of the means of production, and of property. It has agglomerated population, centralized means of production, and has concentrated property in a few hands. The necessary consequence of this was political centralization. Independent, or but loosely connected provinces, with separate interests, laws, governments, and systems of taxation, became lumped together in one nation, with one government, one code of laws, one national class interest, one frontier and one customs tariff.

30 The bourgeoisie, during its rule of scarce one hundred years, has created more massive and more colossal productive forces than have all preceding generations together. Subjection of Nature's forces to man, machinery, application of chemistry to industry and agriculture, steam-navigation, railways, electric telegraphs, clearing of whole continents for cultivation, canalization of rivers, whole populations conjured out of the ground—what earlier century had even a presentiment that such productive forces slumbered in the lap of social labor?

We see then: the means of production and of exchange on whose foundation the bourgeoisie built itself up, were generated in feudal society. At a certain stage in the development of these means of production and of exchange, the conditions under which feudal society produced and exchanged, the feudal organization of agriculture and manufacturing industry, in one word, the feudal relations of property became no longer compatible with the already developed productive forces; they became so many fetters. They had to burst asunder; they were burst asunder.

Into their place stepped free competition, accompanied by a social and political constitution adapted to it, and by the economical and political sway of the bourgeois class.

A similar movement is going on before our own eyes. Modern bourgeois society with its relations of production, of exchange and of property, a society that has conjured up such gigantic means of production and of exchange, is like the sorcerer, who is no longer able to control the powers of the nether world whom he has called up by his spells. For many a decade past, the history of industry and commerce is but the history of the revolt of modern productive forces against modern conditions of production, against the property relations that are the conditions for the existence of the bourgeoisie and of its rule. It is enough to mention the commercial crises that by their periodical return put on its trial, each time more threateningly, the existence of the entire bourgeois society. In these crises a great part not only of the existing products, but also of the previously created productive forces, are periodically destroyed. In these crises there breaks out an epidemic that, in all earlier epochs, would have seemed an absurdity—the epidemic of overproduction. Society suddenly finds itself put back into a state of momentary barbarism; it appears as if a famine, a universal war of devastation, had cut off the supply of every means of subsistence; industry and commerce seem to be destroyed; and why? Because there is too much civilization, too much means of subsistence, too much industry, too much commerce. The productive forces at the disposal of society no longer tend to further the development of the conditions of the bourgeois property; on the contrary, they have become too powerful for these conditions by which they are fettered, and as soon as they overcome these fetters they bring disorder into the whole of bourgeois society, endanger the existence of bourgeois property. The conditions of bourgeois society are too narrow to comprise the wealth created by them. And how does the bourgeoisie get over these crises? On the one hand by enforced destruction of a mass of productive forces; on the other, by the conquest of new markets, and by the more thorough exploitation of the old ones. That is to say, by paving the way for more extensive and more destructive crises, and by diminishing the means whereby crises are prevented.

The weapons with which the bourgeoisie felled feudalism to the ground are now turned against the bourgeoisie itself.

35   But not only has the bourgeoisie forged the weapons that bring death to itself; it has also called into existence the men who are to wield those weapons—the modern working class—the proletarians.

In proportion as the bourgeoisie, i.e., capital, is developed, in the same proportion is the proletariat, the modern working class, developed, a class of laborers who live only so long as they find work, and who find work only so long as their labor increases capital. These laborers, who must sell themselves piecemeal, are a commodity, like every other article of commerce, and are consequently exposed to all the vicissitudes of competition, to all the fluctuations of the market.

Owing to the extensive use of machinery and to division of labor, the work of the proletarians has lost all individual character, and, consequently, all charm for the workman. He becomes an appendage of the machine, and it is only the most simple, most monotonous and most easily acquired knack that is required of him. Hence, the cost of production of a workman is restricted almost entirely to the means of subsistence that he requires for his maintenance, and for the propagation of his race. But the price of a commodity, and also of labor, is equal to its cost of production. In proportion, therefore, as the repulsiveness of the work increases the wage decreases. Nay more, in proportion as the use of machinery and division of labor increases, in the same proportion the burden of toil increases, whether by prolongation of the working hours, by increase of the work enacted in a given time, or by increased speed of the machinery, etc.

Modern industry has converted the little workshop of the patriarchal master into the great factory of the industrial capitalist. Masses of laborers, crowded into factories, are organized like soldiers. As privates of the industrial army they are placed under the command of a perfect hierarchy of officers and sergeants. Not only are they the slaves of the bourgeois class and of the bourgeois state, they are daily and hourly enslaved by the machine, by the overlooker, and, above all, by the individual bourgeois manufacturer himself. The more openly this despotism proclaims gain to be its end and aim, the more petty, the more hateful and the more embittering it is.

The less the skill and exertion or strength implied in manual labor, in other words, the more modern industry becomes developed, the more is the labor of men superseded by that of women. Differences of age and sex have no longer any distinctive social validity for the working class. All are instruments of labor, more or less expensive to use, according to their age and sex.

No sooner is the exploitation of the laborer by the manufacturer, so far at an end, that he receives his wages in cash, than he is set upon by the other portions of the bourgeoisie, the landlord, the shopkeeper, the pawnbroker, etc.

The lower strata of the middle class—the small trades-people, shopkeepers and retired tradesmen generally, the handicraftsmen and peasants—all these sink gradually into the proletariat, partly because their diminutive capital does not suffice for the scale on which Modern Industry is carried on, and is swamped in the competition with the large capitalists, partly because their specialized skill is rendered worthless by new methods of production. Thus the proletariat is recruited from all classes of the population.

The proletariat goes through various stages of development. With its birth begins its struggle with the bourgeoisie. At first the contest is carried on by individual laborers, then by the workpeople of a factory, then by the operatives of one trade, in one locality, against the individual bourgeois who directly exploits them. They direct their attacks not against the bourgeois conditions of production, but against the instruments of production themselves; they destroy imported wares that compete with their labor, they smash to pieces machinery, they set factories ablaze, they seek to restore by force the vanished status of the workman of the Middle Ages.

At this stage the laborers still form an incoherent mass scattered over the whole country, and broken up by their mutual competition. If anywhere they unite to form more compact bodies, this is not yet the consequence of their own active union, but of the union of the bourgeoisie, which class, in order to attain its own political ends, is compelled to set the whole proletariat in motion, and is moreover yet, for a time, able to do so. At this stage, therefore, the proletarians do not fight their enemies, but the enemies of their enemies, the remnants of absolute monarchy, the landowners, the non-industrial bourgeois, the petty bourgeoisie. Thus the whole historical movement is concentrated in the hands of the bourgeoisie, every victory so obtained is a victory for the bourgeoisie.

But with the development of industry the proletariat not only increases in number; it becomes concentrated in greater masses, its strength grows and it feels that strength more. The various interests and conditions of life within the ranks of the proletariat are more and more equalized, in proportion as machinery obliterates all distinctions of labor, and nearly everywhere reduces wages to the same low level. The growing competition among the bourgeois, and the resulting commercial crisis, make the wages of the workers even more fluctuating. The unceasing improvement of machinery, ever more rapidly developing, makes their livelihood more and more precarious; the collisions between individual workmen and individual bourgeois take more and more the character of collisions between two classes. Thereupon the workers begin to form combinations (Trades' Unions) against the bourgeois; they club together in order to keep up the rate of wages; they found permanent associations in order to make provision beforehand for these occasional revolts. Here and there the contest breaks out into riots.

45   Now and then the workers are victorious, but only for a time. The real fruit of their battle lies not in the immediate result but in the ever-expanding union of workers. This union is helped on by the improved means of communication that are created by modern industry, and that places the workers of different localities in contact with one another. It was just this contact that was needed to centralize the numerous local struggles, all of the same character, into one national struggle between classes. But every class struggle is a political struggle. And that union, to

attain which the burghers of the Middle Ages with their miserable highways, required centuries, the modern proletarians, thanks to railways, achieve in a few years.

This organization of the proletarians into a class, and consequently into a political party, is continually being upset again by the competition between the workers themselves. But it ever rises up again, stronger, firmer, mightier. It compels legislative recognition of particular interests of the workers by taking advantage of the divisions among the bourgeoisie itself. Thus the ten hours' bill in England was carried.

Altogether collisions between the classes of the old society further, in many ways, the course of development of the proletariat. The bourgeoisie finds itself involved in a constant battle. At first with the aristocracy; later on, with those portions of the bourgeoisie itself whose interests have become antagonistic to the progress of industry; at all times, with the bourgeoisie of foreign countries. In all these battles it sees itself compelled to appeal to the proletariat, to ask for its help, and thus, to drag it into the political arena. The bourgeoisie itself, therefore, supplies the proletariat with its own elements of political and general education; in other words, it furnishes the proletariat with weapons for fighting the bourgeoisie.

Further, as we have already seen, entire sections of the ruling classes are, by the advance of industry, precipitated into the proletariat, or are at least threatened in their conditions of existence. These also supply the proletariat with fresh elements of enlightenment and progress.

Finally, in times when the class-struggle nears the decisive hour, the process of dissolution going on within the ruling class—in fact, within the whole range of an old society—assumes such a violent, glaring character that a small section of the ruling class cuts itself adrift and joins the revolutionary class, the class that holds the future in its hands. Just as, therefore, at an earlier period, a section of the nobility went over to the bourgeoisie, so now a portion of the bourgeoisie goes over to the proletariat, and in particular, a portion of the bourgeois ideologists, who have raised themselves to the level of comprehending theoretically the historical movements as a whole.

50   Of all the classes that stand face to face with the bourgeoisie today the proletariat alone is a really revolutionary class. The other classes decay and finally disappear in the face of modern industry; the proletariat is its special and essential product.

The lower middle class, the small manufacturer, the shopkeeper, the artisan, the peasant, all these fight against the bourgeoisie, to save from extinction their existence as fractions of the middle class. They are therefore not revolutionary, but conservative. Nay, more; they are reactionary, for they try to roll back the wheel of history. If by chance they are revolutionary, they are so only in view of their impending transfer into the proletariat; they thus defend not their present, but their future interests; they desert their own standpoint to place themselves at that of the proletariat.

The "dangerous class," the social scum, that passively rotting mass thrown off by the lowest layers of old society, may, here and there, be swept into the movement by a proletarian revolution; its conditions of life, however, prepare it far more for the part of a bribed tool of reactionary intrigue.

In the conditions of the proletariat, those of the old society at large are already virtually swamped. The proletarian is without property; his relation to his wife and children has no longer anything in common with the bourgeois family relations; modern industrial labor, modern subjection to capital, the same in England as in France, in America as in Germany, has stripped him of every trace of national character. Law, morality, religion, are to him so many bourgeois prejudices, behind which lurk in ambush just as many bourgeois interests.

All the preceding classes that got the upper hand sought to fortify their already acquired status by subjecting society at large to their conditions of appropriation. The proletarians cannot become masters of the productive forces of society, except by abolishing their own previous mode of appropriation, and thereby also every other previous mode of appropriation. They have nothing of their own to secure and to fortify; their mission is to destroy all previous securities for and insurances of individual property.

55 All previous historical movements were movements of minorities, or in the interest of minorities. The proletarian movement is the self-conscious, independent movement of the immense majority. The proletariat, the lowest stratum of our present society, cannot stir, cannot raise itself up without the whole superincumbent strata of official society being sprung into the air.

Though not in substance, yet in form, the struggle of the proletariat with the bourgeoisie is at first a national struggle. The proletariat of each country must, of course, first of all settle matters with its own bourgeoisie.

In depicting the most general phases of the development of the proletariat, we traced the more or less veiled civil war, raging within existing society, up to the point where that war breaks out into open revolution, and where the violent overthrow of the bourgeoisie, lays the foundations for the sway of the proletariat.

Hitherto every form of society has been based, as we have already seen, on the antagonism of oppressing and oppressed classes. But in order to oppress a class, certain conditions must be assured to it under which it can, at least, continue its slavish existence. The serf, in the period of serfdom, raised himself to membership in the commune, just as the petty bourgeois, under the yoke of feudal absolutism, managed to develop into a bourgeois. The modern laborer, on the contrary, instead of rising with the progress of industry, sinks deeper and deeper below the conditions of existence of his own class. He becomes a pauper, and pauperism develops more rapidly than population and wealth. And here it becomes evident that the bourgeoisie is unfit any longer to be the ruling class in society, and to impose its conditions of existence upon society as an over-riding law. It is unfit to rule, because it is incompetent to assure an existence to its slave within his slavery, because it cannot help letting him sink into such a state that it has to feed him, instead of being fed by him. Society can no longer live under this bourgeoisie; in other words, its existence is no longer compatible with society.

The essential condition for the existence, and for the sway of the bourgeois class, is the formation and augmentation of capital; the condition for capital is wage labor. Wage labor rests exclusively on competition between the laborers. The advance of industry, whose involuntary promoter is the bourgeoisie, replaces the isolation of the laborers, due to competition, by their involuntary combination, due to association. The development of Modern Industry, therefore, cuts from under its feet the very foundation on which the bourgeoisie produces and appropriates products. What the bourgeoisie therefore produces, above all, are its own grave diggers. Its fall and the victory of the proletariat are equally inevitable.

Proletarians and Communists

60   In what relation do the Communists stand to the proletarians as a whole?

The Communists do not form a separate party opposed to other working class parties.

They have no interests separate and apart from those of the proletariat as a whole.

They do not set up any sectarian principles of their own, by which to shape and mold the proletarian movement.

The Communists are distinguished from the other working class parties by this only: 1. In the national struggles of the proletarians of the different countries, they point out and bring to the front the common interests of the entire proletariat, independently of all nationality. 2. In the various stages of development which the struggle of the working class against the bourgeoisie has to pass through, they always and everywhere represent the interests of the movement as a whole.

65 The Communists, therefore, are on the one hand practically the most advanced and resolute section of the working class parties of every country, that section which pushes forward all others; on the other hand, theoretically, they have over the great mass of the proletariat the advantage of clearly understanding the line of march, the conditions, and the ultimate general results of the proletarian movement.

The immediate aim of the Communists is the same as that of all the other proletarian parties: formation of the proletariat into a class, overthrow of the bourgeois of supremacy, conquest of political power by the proletariat.

The theoretical conclusions of the Communists are in no way based on ideas or principles that have been invented or discovered by this or that would-be universal reformer.

They merely express, in general terms, actual relations springing from an existing class struggle, from a historical movement going on under our very eyes. The abolition of existing property relations is not at all a distinctive feature of Communism.

All property relations in the past have continually been subject to historical change consequent upon the change in historical conditions.

70 The French Revolution, for example, abolished feudal property in favor of bourgeois property.

The distinguishing feature of Communism is not the abolition of property generally, but the abolition of bourgeois property. But modern bourgeois private property is the final and most complete expression of the system of producing and appropriating products, that is based on class antagonism, on the exploitation of the many by the few.

In this sense, the theory of the Communists may be summed up in the single sentence: Abolition of private property.

We Communists have been reproached with the desire of abolishing the right of personally acquiring property as the fruit of a man's own labor, which property is alleged to be the groundwork of all personal freedom, activity and independence.

Hard won, self-acquired, self-earned property! Do you mean the property of the petty artisan and of the small peasant, a form of property that preceded the bourgeois form? There is no need to abolish that; the development of industry has to a great extent already destroyed it, and is still destroying it daily.

75 Or do you mean modern bourgeois private property?

But does wage labor create any property for the laborer? Not a bit. It creates capital, i.e., that kind of property which exploits wage labor, and which cannot increase except upon condition of getting a new supply of wage labor for fresh exploitation. Property, in its present form, is based on the antagonism of capital and wage labor. Let us examine both sides of this antagonism.

To be a capitalist is to have not only a purely personal, but a social status in production. Capital is a collective product, and only by the united action of many members, nay, in the last resort, only by the united action of all members of society, can it be set in motion.

Capital is therefore not a personal, it is a social power.

When, therefore, capital is converted into common property, into the property of all members of society, personal property is not thereby transformed into social property. It is only the social character of the property that is changed. It loses its class character.

80 Let us now take wage labor.

The average price of wage labor is the minimum wage, i.e., that quantum of the means of subsistence which is absolutely requisite to keep the laborer in bare existence as a laborer. What, therefore, the wage laborer appropriates by means of his labor, merely suffices to prolong and reproduce a bare existence. We by no means intend to abolish this personal appropriation of the products of labor, an appropriation that is made for the maintenance and reproduction of human life, and that leaves no surplus wherewith to command the labor of others. All that we want to do away with is the miserable character of this appropriation, under which the laborer lives merely to increase capital and is allowed to live only in so far as the interests of the ruling class require it.

In bourgeois society, living labor is but a means to increase accumulated labor. In Communist society accumulated labor is but a means to widen, to enrich, to promote the existence of the laborer.

In bourgeois society, therefore, the past dominates the present; in Communist society the present dominates the past. In bourgeois society, capital is independent and has individuality, while the living person is dependent and has no individuality.

And the abolition of this state of things is called by the bourgeois abolition of individuality and freedom! And rightly so. The abolition of bourgeois individuality, bourgeois independence and bourgeois freedom is undoubtedly aimed at.

85 By freedom is meant, under the present bourgeois conditions of production, free trade, free selling and buying.

But if selling and buying disappears, free selling and buying disappears also. This talk about free selling and buying, and all the other "brave words" of our bourgeoisie about freedom in general have a meaning, if any, only in contrast with restricted selling and buying, with the fettered traders of the Middle Ages, but have no meaning when opposed to the Communistic abolition of buying and selling, of the bourgeois conditions of production, and of the bourgeoisie itself.

You are horrified at our intending to do away with private property. But in your existing society private property is already done away with for nine-tenths of the population; its existence for the few is solely due to its non-existence in the hands of those nine-tenths. You reproach us, therefore, with intending to do away with a form of property, the necessary condition for whose existence is the non-existence of any property for the immense majority of society.

In one word, you reproach us with intending to do away with your property. Precisely so: that is just what we intend.

From the moment when labor can no longer be converted into capital, money, or rent, into a social power capable of being monopolized, i.e., from the moment when individual property can no longer be transformed into bourgeois property, into capital, from that moment, you say, individuality vanishes.

90 You must, therefore, confess that by "individual" you mean no other person than the bourgeois, than the middle-class owner of property. This person must, indeed, be swept out of the way and made impossible.

Communism deprives no man of the power to appropriate the products of society: all that it does is to deprive him of the power to subjugate the labor of others by means of such appropriation.

It has been objected that upon the abolition of private property all work will cease and universal laziness will overtake us.

According to this, bourgeois society ought long ago to have gone to the dogs through sheer idleness; for those of its members who work acquire nothing, and those who acquire anything do not work. The whole of this objection is but another expression of the tautology: that there can no longer be any wage labor when there is no longer any capital.

All objections urged against the Communistic mode of producing and appropriating material products have, in the same way, been urged against the Communistic modes of producing and appropriating intellectual products. Just as, to the bourgeois, the disappearance of class property is the disappearance of production itself, so the disappearance of class culture is to him identical with the disappearance of all culture.

95   That culture, the loss of which he laments, is, for the enormous majority, a mere training to act as a machine.

But don't wrangle with us so long as you apply, to our intended abolition of bourgeois property, the standard of your bourgeois notions of freedom, culture, law, etc. Your very ideas are but the outgrowth of the conditions of your bourgeois production and bourgeois property, just as your jurisprudence is but the will of your class made into a law for all, a will whose essential character and direction are determined by the economical conditions of existence of your class.

The selfish misconception that induces you to transform into eternal laws of nature and of reason the social forms springing from your present mode of production and form of property—historical relations that rise and disappear in the progress of production—this misconception you share with every ruling class that has preceded you. What you see clearly in the case of ancient property, what you admit in the case of feudal property, you are of course forbidden to admit in the case of your own bourgeois form of property.

Abolition of the family! Even the most radical flare up at this infamous proposal of the Communists.

On what foundation is the present family, the bourgeois family, based? On capital, on private gain. In its completely developed form this family exists only among the bourgeoisie. But this state of things finds its complement in the practical absence of the family among the proletarians, and in public prostitution.

100   The bourgeois family will vanish as a matter of course when its complement vanishes, and both will vanish with the vanishing of capital.

Do you charge us with wanting to stop the exploitation of children by their parents? To this crime we plead guilty.

But, you will say, we destroy the most hallowed of relations when we replace home education by social.

And your education! Is not that also social, and determined by the social conditions under which you educate; by the intervention, direct or indirect, of society by means of schools, etc.? The Communists have not invented the intervention of society in education; they do but seek to alter the character of that intervention, and to rescue education from the influence of the ruling class.

The bourgeois clap-trap about the family and education, about the hallowed correlation of parent and child, become all the more disgusting, the more, by the action of Modern Industry, all family ties among the proletarians are torn asunder and their children transformed into simple articles of commerce and instruments of labor.

105   But you Communists would introduce community of women, screams the whole bourgeoisie chorus.

The bourgeois sees in his wife a mere instrument of production. He hears that the instruments of production are to be exploited in common, and, naturally, can come to no other conclusion, than that the lot of being common to all will likewise fall to the women.

He has not even a suspicion that the real point aimed at is to do away with the status of women as mere instruments of production.

For the rest, nothing is more ridiculous than the virtuous indignation of our bourgeois at the community of women which, they pretend, is to be openly and officially established by the Communists. The Communists have no need to introduce community of women, it has existed almost from time immemorial.

Our bourgeois, not content with having the wives and daughters of their proletarians at their disposal, not to speak of common prostitutes, take the greatest pleasure in seducing each others' wives.

110   Bourgeois marriage is in reality a system of wives in common, and thus, at the most, what the Communists might possibly be reproached with, is that they desire to introduce, in substitution for a hypocritically concealed, an openly legalized community of women. For the rest, it is

self-evident that the abolition of the present system of production must bring with it the abolition of the community of women springing from that system, i.e., of prostitution both public and private.

The Communists are further reproached with desiring to abolish countries and nationalities.

The working men have no country. We cannot take from them what they don't possess. Since the proletariat must first of all acquire political supremacy, must rise to be the leading class of the nation, must constitute itself the nation, it is, so far, itself national, though not in the bourgeois sense of the word.

National differences and antagonisms between peoples are daily more and more vanishing, owing to the development of the bourgeoisie, to freedom of commerce, to the world-market, to uniformity in the mode of production and in the conditions of life corresponding thereto.

The supremacy of the proletariat will cause them to vanish still faster. United action, of the leading civilized countries at least, is one of the first conditions for the emancipation of the proletariat.

115   In proportion as the exploitation of one individual by another is put an end to, the exploitation of one nation by another will also be put an end to. In proportion as the antagonism between classes within the nation vanishes, the hostility of one nation to another will come to an end.

The charges against Communism made from a religious, a philosophical, and generally, from an ideological standpoint, are not deserving of serious examination.

Does it require deep intuition to comprehend that man's ideas, views and conceptions, in one word, man's consciousness, changes with every change in the conditions of his material existence, in his social relations and in his social life?

What else does the history of ideas prove than that intellectual production changes in character in proportion as material production is changed? The ruling ideas of each age have ever been the ideas of its ruling class.

When people speak of ideas that revolutionize society they do but express the fact that within the old society the elements of a new one have been created, and that the dissolution of the old ideas keeps even pace with the dissolution of the old conditions of existence.

120   When the ancient world was in its last throes the ancient religions were overcome by Christianity. When Christian ideas succumbed in the 18th century to rationalist ideas, feudal society fought its deathbattle

with the then revolutionary bourgeoisie. The ideas of religious liberty and freedom of conscience merely gave expression to the sway of free competition within the domain of knowledge.

"Undoubtedly," it will be said, "religious, moral, philosophical and judicial ideas have been modified in the course of historical development. But religion, morality, philosophy, political science, and law, constantly survived this change.

"There are, besides, eternal truths such as Freedom, Justice, etc., that are common to all states of society. But Communism abolishes eternal truths, it abolishes all religion and all morality, instead of constituting them on a new basis; it therefore acts in contradiction to all past historical experience."

What does this accusation reduce itself to? The history of all past society has consisted in the development of class antagonisms, antagonisms that assumed different forms at different epochs.

But whatever form they may have taken, one fact is common to all past ages, viz., the exploitation of one part of society by the other. No wonder, then, that the social consciousness of past ages, despite all the multiplicity and variety it displays, moves within certain common forms, or general ideas, which cannot completely vanish except with the total disappearance of class antagonisms.

125 The Communist revolution is the most radical rupture with traditional property relations; no wonder that its development involves the most radical rupture with traditional ideas.

But let us have done with the bourgeois objections to Communism.

We have seen above that the first step in the revolution by the working class is to raise the proletariat to the position of ruling class, to win the battle of democracy.

The proletariat will use its political supremacy to wrest, by degrees, all capital from the bourgeoisie, to centralize all instruments of production in the hands of the State, i.e., of the proletariat organized as a ruling class; and to increase the total productive forces as rapidly as possible.

Of course, in the beginning, this cannot be effected except by means of despotic inroads on the rights of property, and on the conditions of bourgeois production; by means of measures, therefore, which appear economically insufficient and untenable, but which in the course of the movement outstrip themselves, necessitate further inroads upon the old social order, and are unavoidable as a means of entirely revolutionizing the mode of production.

These measures will of course be different in different countries.

Nevertheless in the most advanced countries the following will be pretty generally applicable:

1. Abolition of property in land and application of all rents of land to public purposes.
2. A heavy progressive or graduated income tax.
3. Abolition of all right of inheritance.
4. Confiscation of the property of all emigrants and rebels.
5. Centralization of credit in the hands of the State, by means of a national bank with State capital and an exclusive monopoly.
6. Centralization of the means of communication and transport in the hands of the State.
7. Extension of factories and instruments of production owned by the State; the bringing into cultivation of waste lands, and the improvement of the soil generally in accordance with a common plan.
8. Equal liability of all to labor. Establishment of industrial armies, especially for agriculture.
9. Combination of agriculture with manufacturing industries; gradual abolition of the distinction between town and country by a more equable distribution of the population over the country.
10. Free education for all children in public schools. Abolition of children's factory labor in its present form. Combination of education with industrial production, etc., etc.

When, in the course of development, class distinctions have disappeared, and all production has been concentrated in the hands of a vast association of the whole nation, the public power will lose its political character. Political power, properly so called, is merely the organized power of one class for oppressing another. If the proletariat during its contest with the bourgeoisie is compelled, by the force of circumstances, to organize itself as a class, if, by means of a revolution, it makes itself the ruling class, and, as such, sweeps away by force the old conditions of production, then it will, along with these conditions, have swept away the conditions for the existence of class antagonism, and of classes generally, and will thereby have abolished its own supremacy as a class.

In place of the old bourgeois society, with its classes and class antagonisms, we shall have an association in which the free development of each is the condition for the free development all. . . .

Position of the Communists in Relation to the Various Existing Opposition Parties

[The preceding section] has made clear the relations of the Communists to the existing working class parties, such as the Chartists in England and the Agrarian Reforms in America.

135   The Communists fight for the attainment of the immediate aims, for the enforcement of the momentary interests of the working class; but in the movement of the present they also represent and take care of the future of that movement. In France the Communists ally themselves with the Social-Democrats against the conservative and radical bourgeoisie, reserving, however, the right to take up a critical position in regard to phrases and illusions traditionally handed down from the great Revolution.

In Switzerland they support the Radicals, without losing sight of the fact that this party consists of antagonistic elements, partly of Democratic Socialists, in the French sense, partly of radical bourgeois.

In Poland they support the party that insists on an agrarian revolution, as the prime condition for national emancipation, that party which fomented the insurrection of Cracow in 1846.

In Germany they fight with the bourgeoisie whenever it acts in a revolutionary way, against the absolute monarchy, the feudal squirearchy, and the petty bourgeoisie.

But they never cease for a single instant to instill into the working class the clearest possible recognition of the hostile antagonism between bourgeoisie and proletariat, in order that the German workers may straightway use, as so many weapons against the bourgeoisie, the social and political conditions that the bourgeoisie must necessarily introduce along with its supremacy, and in order that, after the fall of the reactionary classes in Germany, the fight against the bourgeoisie itself may immediately begin.

140   The Communists turn their attention chiefly to Germany, because that country is on the eve of a bourgeois revolution, that is bound to be carried out under more advanced conditions of European civilization, and with a more developed proletariat, than that of England was in the seventeenth and of France in the eighteenth century, and because the bourgeois revolution in Germany will be but the prelude to an immediately following proletarian revolution.

In short, the Communists everywhere support every revolutionary movement against the existing social and political order of things.

In all these movements they bring to the front, as the leading question in each, the property question, no matter what its degree of development at the time.

Finally, they labor everywhere for the union and agreement of the democratic parties of all countries.

The Communists disdain to conceal their views and aims. They openly declare that their ends can be attained only by the forcible overthrow of all existing social conditions. Let the ruling classes tremble at a Communistic revolution. The proletarians have nothing to lose but their chains. They have a world to win.

Working men of all countries, unite!

SUGGESTIONS FOR WRITING

1. Marx claims that the modern state acts in the service of the bourgeoisie. Write an essay that analyzes and discusses his reasoning and his examples.
2. According to Marx, what is the economic position of women? Write an essay that breaks down and explains the reasoning behind his contention.
3. In paragraph 54 Marx says, "All the preceding classes that got the upper hand sought to fortify their already acquired status." He says further that the proletariat will "destroy all previous securities for and insurances of individual property." Write an essay in which you describe Marx's views on the history of economic relations as a kind of evolutionary struggle for existence and survival of the fittest.

Personal Profit   1898

From *Womens and Economics*

CHARLOTTE PERKINS GILMAN

Charlotte Perkins Gilman (1860–1935), perhaps most famous for her short story "The Yellow Wallpaper," is generally considered to be the most important author in the women's movement of the early twentieth century. She energetically maintained a rigorous program of self-education and social criticism throughout a long and troubled life that began with the desertion of her father and included marriage difficulties. She is represented by two selections in this book, one below from her Women and Economics *(1898) and one in Chapter 5 from her utopian fantasy* Herland *(1915).*

Toward economics Gilman adopts a straightforward, no-nonsense style in addressing the relation of women to the classic categories and accepted nomenclature of the discipline of her day. "Women consume economic goods," she says. "What economic product do they give in exchange for what they consume?" She examines the conventional answers and dismisses them with an alternative analysis of her own. Her larger goal is to show how mothers might be transformed from "home servants" to "social servants."

The economic status of the human race in any nation, at any time, is governed mainly by the activities of the male: the female obtains her share in the racial advance only through him.

Studied individually, the facts are even more plainly visible, more open and familiar. From the day laborer to the millionaire, the wife's worn dress or flashing jewels, her low roof or her lordly one, her weary feet or her rich equipage,—these speak of the economic ability of the husband. The comfort, the luxury, the necessities of life itself, which the woman receives, are obtained by the husband, and given her by him. And, when the woman, left alone with no man to "support" her, tries to meet her own economic necessities, the difficulties which confront her prove conclusively what the general economic status of the woman is. . . . But we are instantly confronted by the commonly received opinion that, although it must be admitted that men make and distribute the wealth of the world, yet women earn their share of it as wives. This assumes either that the husband is in the position of employer and the wife as employee, or that marriage is a "partnership," and the wife an equal factor with the husband in producing wealth. . . .

Women consume economic goods. What economic product do they give in exchange for what they consume? The claim that marriage is a partnership, in which the two persons married produce wealth which neither of them, separately, could produce, will not bear examination. A man happy and comfortable can produce more than one unhappy and uncomfortable, but this is as true of a father or son as of a husband. To take from a man any of the conditions which make him happy and strong is to cripple his industry, generally speaking. But those relatives who make him happy are not therefore his business partners, and entitled to share his income.

Grateful return for happiness conferred is not the method of exchange in a partnership. The comfort a man takes with his wife is not in the nature of a business partnership, nor are her frugality and industry.

A housekeeper, in her place, might be as frugal, as industrious, but would not therefore be a partner. Man and wife are partners truly in their mutual obligation to their children,—their common love, duty, and service. But a manufacturer who marries, or a doctor, or a lawyer, does not take a partner in his business, when he takes a partner in parenthood, unless his wife is also a manufacturer, a doctor, or a lawyer. . . .

If the wife is not, then, truly a business partner, in what way does she earn from her husband the food, clothing, and shelter she receives at his hands? By house service, it will be instantly replied. This is the general misty idea upon the subject,—that women earn all they get, and more, by house service. Here we come to a very practical and definite economic ground. Although not producers of wealth, women serve in the final processes of preparation and distribution. Their labor in the household has a genuine economic value.

For a certain percentage of persons to serve other persons, in order that the ones so served may produce more, is a contribution not to be overlooked. The labor of women in the house, certainly, enables men to produce more wealth than they otherwise could; and in this way women are economic factors in society. But so are horses. The labor of horses enables men to produce more wealth than they otherwise could. The horse is an economic factor in society. But the horse is not economically independent, nor is the woman. . . .

The labor which the wife performs in the household is given as part of her functional duty, not as employment. The wife of the poor man, who works hard in a small house, doing all the work for the family, or the wife of the rich man, who wisely and gracefully manages a large house and administers its functions, each is entitled to fair pay for services rendered.

To take this ground and hold it honestly, wives, as earners through domestic service, are entitled to the wages of cooks, housemaids, nursemaids, seamstresses, or housekeepers, and to no more. This would of course reduce the spending money of the wives of the rich, and put it out of the power of the poor man to "support" a wife at all, unless, indeed, the poor man faced the situation fully, paid his wife her wages as house servant, and then she and he combined their funds in the support of their children. He would be keeping a servant: she would be helping keep the family. But nowhere on earth would there be "a rich woman" by these means. Even the highest class of private housekeeper, useful as her services are, does not accumulate a fortune. . . .

But the salient fact in this discussion is that, whatever the economic value of the domestic industry of women is, they do not get it.

The women who do the most work get the least money, and the women who have the most money do the least work. Their labor is neither given nor taken as a factor in economic exchange. It is held to be their duty as women to do this work; and their economic status bears no relation to their domestic labors, unless an inverse one. Moreover, if they were thus fairly paid,—given what they earned, and no more,—all women working in this way would be reduced to the economic status of the house servant. Few women—or men either—care to face this condition. The ground that women earn their living by domestic labor is instantly forsaken, and we are told that they obtain their livelihood as mothers. This is a peculiar position. We speak of it commonly enough, and often with deep feeling, but without due analysis. . . .

10   If this is so, if motherhood is an exchangeable commodity given by women in payment for clothes and food, then we must of course find some relation between the quantity or quality of the motherhood and the quantity and quality of the pay. This being true, then the women who are not mothers have no economic status at all; and the economic status of those who are must be shown to be relative to their motherhood. This is obviously absurd. The childless wife has as much money as the mother of many,—more; for the children of the latter consume what would otherwise be hers; and the inefficient mother is no less provided for than the efficient one. Visibly, and upon the face of it, women are not maintained in economic prosperity proportioned to their motherhood. Motherhood bears no relation to their economic status. . . . The claim of motherhood as a factor in economic exchange is false today. But suppose it were true. Are we willing to hold this ground, even in theory? Are we willing to consider motherhood as a business, a form of commercial exchange? Are the cares and duties of the mother, her travail and her love, commodities to be exchanged for bread?

It is revolting so to consider them; and, if we dare face our own thoughts, and force them to their logical conclusion, we shall see that nothing could be more repugnant to human feeling, or more socially and individually injurious, than to make motherhood a trade. Driven off these alleged grounds of women's economic independence; shown that women, as a class, neither produce nor distribute wealth; that women, as individuals, labor mainly as house servants, are not paid as such, and would not be satisfied with such an economic status if they were so paid; that wives are not business partners or co-producers of wealth with their husbands, unless they actually practise the same profession; that they are not salaried as mothers, and that it would be unspeakably degrading if they were,—what remains to those who deny that women are supported by men? This. . .—that the function of maternity unfits a woman for economic production, and, therefore, it is right that she should be supported by her husband. . . .

. . . Because of her maternal duties, the human female is said to be unable to get her own living. As the maternal duties of other females do not unfit them for getting their own living and also the livings of their young, it would seem that the human maternal duties require the segregation of the entire energies of the mother to the service of the child during her entire adult life, or so large a proportion of them that not enough remains to devote to the individual interests of the mother. . . .

Is this the condition of human motherhood? Does the human mother, by her motherhood, thereby lose control of brain and body, lose power and skill and desire for any other work? Do we see before us the human race, with all its females segregated entirely to the uses of motherhood, consecrated, set apart, specially developed, spending every power of their nature on the service of their children?

We do not. We see the human mother worked far harder than a mare, laboring her life long in the service, not of her children only, but of men; husbands, brothers, fathers, whatever male relatives she has; for mother and sister also; for the church a little, if she is allowed; for society, if she is able; for charity and education and reform—working in many ways that are not the ways of motherhood.

15 It is not motherhood that keeps the housewife on her feet from dawn till dark; it is house service, not child service. Women work longer and harder than most men, and not solely in maternal duties. . . . Many mothers, even now, are wage-earners for the family, as well as bearers and rearers of it. And the women who are not so occupied, the women who belong to rich men,—here perhaps is the exhaustive devotion to maternity which is supposed to justify an admitted economic dependence. But we do not find it even among these. Women of ease and wealth provide for their children better care than the poor woman can; but they do not spend more time upon it themselves, nor more care and effort. They have other occupation.

In spite of her supposed segregation to maternal duties, the human female, the world over, works at extra-maternal duties for hours enough to provide her with an independent living, and then is denied independence on the ground that motherhood prevents her working! . . .

With the growth of civilization, we have gradually crystallized into law the visible necessity for feeding the helpless female; and even old women are maintained by their male relatives with a comfortable assurance. But to this day—save, indeed, for the increasing army of women wage-earners, who are changing the face of the world by their steady advance toward economic independence—the personal profit of women bears but too close a relation to their power to win and hold the other sex. From the odalisque with the most bracelets to the débutante with the most bouquets, the relation still holds good,—woman's economic profit comes through the power of sex-attraction.

When we confront this fact boldly and plainly in the open market of vice, we are sick with horror. When we see the same economic relation made permanent, established by law, sanctioned and sanctified by religion, covered with flowers and incense and all accumulated sentiment, we think it innocent, lovely, and right. The transient trade we think evil. The bargain for life we think good. But the biological effect remains the same. In both cases the female gets her food from the male by virtue of her sex-relationship to him. In both cases, perhaps even more in marriage because of its perfect acceptance of the situation, the female of genus homo, still living under natural law, is inexorably modified to sex in an increasing degree. . . .

SUGGESTIONS FOR WRITING

1. According to Gilman, why does "partnership" seem the wrong kind of model to explain a married woman's economic position? Write an essay that analyzes her views with examples.

2. Gilman says, "The salient fact in this discussion is that, whatever the economic value of the domestic industry of women is, they do not get it." Write an essay that analyzes her arguments in support of this claim.

3. According to Gilman's views of her society's economic arrangements, a woman's personal profit was almost entirely due to the sex relation. In your opinion, would Darwin's views on biological sexual selection support or challenge her claim? Write an essay discussing the interaction between biological and economic aspects of life as seen by Charlotte Perkins Gilman.

Pecuniary Emulation   1899

From *The Theory of the Leisure Class*

THORSTEIN VEBLEN

Thorstein Veblen (1857–1929) was a maverick economist born in the early Scandinavian settlements of what was then the frontier and is now the Midwest. A brilliant student, his undergraduate degree was from Carleton College in Minnesota and he was among the first of those to attend a program of the new American graduate programs, earning a Ph. D. in philosophy from Yale.

For a long time, Veblen was unable to find academic employment and when he did find such work he did not last very long in any one position. His views on all topics were, to say the least, controversial, but even so he unexpectedly found a wide audience for his Theory of the Leisure Class *(1899), for which he himself had to pay the expenses of publication. The following selection from that book shows that Veblen did not disagree with contemporary economists that prices are determined as a function of supply and demand. What he did instead is to look more deeply into the psychology of consumption to find out how demand is formed. His views on "pecuniary emulation" have recently found their place in economic growth models of the early twenty-first century with their emphasis on "partly excludable goods," those that may be only partly possessed by the individual because they may be copied by others.*

In the sequence of cultural evolution the emergence of a leisure class coincides with the beginning of ownership. This is necessarily the case, for these two institutions result from the same set of economic forces. In the inchoate phase of their development they are but different aspects of the same general facts of social structure.

It is as elements of social structure—conventional facts—that leisure and ownership are matters of interest for the purpose in hand. An habitual neglect of work does not constitute a leisure class; neither does the mechanical fact of use and consumption constitute ownership. The present inquiry, therefore, is not concerned with the beginning of indolence, nor with the beginning of the appropriation of useful articles to individual consumption. The point in question is the origin and nature of a conventional leisure class on the one hand and the beginnings of individual ownership as a conventional right or equitable claim on the other hand.

The early differentiation out of which the distinction between a leisure and a working class arises is a division maintained between men's and women's work in the lower stages of barbarism. Likewise the earliest form of ownership is an ownership of the women by the able-bodied men of the community. The facts may be expressed in more general terms, and truer to the import of the barbarian theory of life, by saying that it is an ownership of the woman by the man.

There was undoubtedly some appropriation of useful articles before the custom of appropriating women arose. The usages of existing archaic communities in which there is no ownership of women is warrant for such a view. In all communities the members, both male and female, habitually appropriate to their individual use a variety of useful things; but these useful things are not thought of as owned by the person who appropriates and consumes them. The habitual appropriation and consumption of certain slight personal effects goes on without raising the question of ownership; that is to say, the question of a conventional, equitable claim to extraneous things.

5   The ownership of women begins in the lower barbarian stages of culture, apparently with the seizure of female captives. The original reason for the seizure and appropriation of women seems to have been their usefulness as trophies. The practice of seizing women from the enemy as trophies gave rise to a form of ownership-marriage, resulting in a household with a male head. This was followed by an extension of slavery to other captives and inferiors, besides women, and by an extension of ownership-marriage to other women than those seized from the enemy. The outcome of emulation under the circumstances of a predatory life, therefore, has been on the one hand a form of marriage resting on coercion, and on the other hand the custom of ownership. The two institutions are not distinguishable in the initial phase of their development; both arise from the desire of the successful men to put their prowess in evidence by exhibiting some durable result of their exploits. Both also minister to that propensity for mastery which pervades all predatory communities. From the ownership of women the concept of ownership extends itself to include the products of their industry, and so there arises the ownership of things as well as of persons.

In this way a consistent system of property in goods is gradually installed. And although in the latest stages of the development, the serviceability of goods for consumption has come to be the most obtrusive element of their value, still, wealth has by no means yet lost its utility as an honorific evidence of the owner's prepotence.

Wherever the institution of private property is found, even in a slightly developed form, the economic process bears the character of a struggle between men for the possession of goods. It has been customary in economic theory, and especially among those economists who adhere with least faltering to the body of modernized classical doctrines, to construe this struggle for wealth as being substantially a struggle for subsistence. Such is, no doubt, its character in large part during the earlier and less efficient phases of industry. Such is also its character in all cases where the "niggardliness of nature" is so strict as to afford but a scanty livelihood to the community in return for strenuous and unremitting application to the business of getting the means of subsistence. But in all progressing communities an advance is presently made beyond this early stage of technological development. Industrial efficiency is presently carried to such a pitch as to afford something appreciably more than a bare livelihood to those engaged in the industrial process. It has not been unusual for economic theory to speak of the further struggle for wealth on this new industrial basis as a competition for an increase of the comforts of life—primarily for an increase of the physical comforts which the consumption of goods affords.

The end of acquisition and accumulation is conventionally held to be the consumption of the goods accumulated—whether it is consumption directly by the owner of the goods or by the household attached to him and for this purpose identified with him in theory. This is at least felt to be the economically legitimate end of acquisition, which alone it is incumbent on the theory to take account of. Such consumption may of course be conceived to serve the consumer's physical wants—his physical comfort—or his so-called higher wants—spiritual, aesthetic, intellectual, or what not; the latter class of wants being served indirectly by an expenditure of goods, after the fashion familiar to all economic readers.

But it is only when taken in a sense far removed from its naïve meaning that consumption of goods can be said to afford the incentive from which accumulation invariably proceeds. The motive that lies at the root of ownership is emulation; and the same motive of emulation continues active in the further development of the institution to which it has given rise and in the development of all those features of the social structure which this institution of ownership touches. The possession of wealth confers honor; it is an invidious distinction. Nothing equally cogent can be said for the consumption of goods, not for any other conceivable incentive to acquisition, and especially not for any incentive to the accumulation of wealth.

It is of course not to be overlooked that in a community where nearly all goods are private property the necessity of earning a livelihood is a powerful and ever-present incentive for the poorer members of the community. The need of subsistence and of an increase of physical comfort may for a time be the dominant motive of acquisition for those classes who are habitually employed at manual labor, whose subsistence is on a precarious footing, who possess little and ordinarily accumulate little; but it will appear in the course of the discussion that even in the case of these impecunious classes the predominance of the motive of physical want is not so decided as has sometimes been assumed. On the other hand, so far as regards those members and classes of the community who are chiefly concerned in the accumulation of wealth, the incentive of subsistence or of physical comfort never plays a considerable part. Ownership began and grew into a human institution on grounds unrelated to the subsistence minimum. The dominant incentive was from the outset the invidious distinction attaching to wealth, and, save temporarily and by exception, no other motive has usurped the primacy at any later stage of the development.

Property set out with being booty held as trophies of the successful raid. So long as the group had departed but little from the primitive communal organization, and so long as it still stood in close contact with other hostile groups, the utility of things or persons owned lay chiefly in an invidious comparison between their possessor and the enemy from whom they were taken. The habit of distinguishing between the interests of the individual and those of the group to which he belongs is apparently a later growth. Invidious comparison between the possessor of the honorific booty and his less successful neighbors within the group was no doubt present early as an element of the utility of the things possessed, though this was not at the outset the chief element of their value. The man's prowess was still primarily the group's prowess, and the possessor of the booty felt himself to be primarily the keeper of the honor of his group. This appreciation of exploit from the communal point of view is met with also at later stages of social growth, especially as regards the laurels of war.

But so soon as the custom of individual ownership begins to gain consistency, the point of view taken in making the invidious comparison on which private property rests will begin to change. Indeed, the one change is but the reflex of the other. The initial phase of ownership, the phase of acquisition by naïve seizure and conversion, begins to pass into the subsequent stage of an incipient organization of industry on the basis of private property (in slaves); the horde develops into a more or less self-sufficing industrial community; possessions then come to be valued not so much as evidence of successful foray, but rather as evidence of the prepotence of the possessor of these goods over other individuals within the community. The invidious comparison now becomes primarily a comparison of the owner with the other members of the group. Property is still of the nature of trophy, but, with the cultural advance, it becomes more and more a trophy of successes scored in the game of ownership carried on between the members of the group under the quasi-peaceable methods of nomadic life.

Gradually, as industrial activity further displaces predatory activity in the community's everyday life and in men's habits of thought, accumulated property more and more replaces trophies of predatory exploit as the conventional exponent of prepotence and success. With the growth of settled industry, therefore, the possession of wealth gains in relative importance and effectiveness as a customary basis of repute and esteem. Not that esteem ceases to be awarded on the basis of other, more direct evidence of prowess; not that successful predatory aggression or warlike exploit ceases to call out the approval and admiration of the crowd, or to stir the envy of the less successful competitors; but the opportunities for gaining distinction by means of this direct manifestation of superior force grow less available both in scope and frequency. At the same time opportunities for industrial aggression, and for the accumulation of property by the quasi-peaceable methods of nomadic industry, increase in scope and availability. And it is even more to the point that property now becomes the most easily recognized evidence of a reputable degree of success as distinguished from heroic or signal achievement. It therefore becomes the conventional basis of esteem. Its possession in some amount becomes necessary in order to attain any reputable standing in the community. It becomes indispensable to accumulate, to acquire property, in order to retain one's good name. When accumulated goods have in this way once become the accepted badge of efficiency, the possession of wealth presently assumes the character of an independent and definitive basis of esteem. The possession of goods, whether acquired aggressively by one's own exertion or passively by transmission through inheritance from others, becomes a conventional basis of reputability. The possession of wealth, which was at the outset valued simply as evidence of efficiency, becomes, in popular apprehension, itself a meritorious act. Wealth is now itself intrinsically honorable and confers honor on its possessor. By a further refinement, wealth acquired passively by transmission from ancestors or other antecedents presently becomes even more honorific than wealth acquired by the possessor's own effort; but this distinction belongs at a later stage in the evolution of the pecuniary culture and will be spoken of in its place.

Prowess and exploit may still remain the basis of award of the highest popular esteem, although the possession of wealth has become the basis of commonplace reputability and of a blameless social standing. The predatory instinct and the consequent approbation of predatory efficiency are deeply ingrained in the habits of thought of those peoples who have passed under the discipline of a protracted predatory culture. According to popular award, the highest honors within human reach may, even yet, be those gained by an unfolding of extraordinary predatory efficiency in war, or by a quasi-predatory efficiency in statecraft; but for the purposes of a commonplace decent standing in the community these means of repute have been replaced by the acquisition and accumulation of goods. In order to stand well in the eyes of the community, it is necessary to come up to a certain, somewhat indefinite, conventional standard of wealth; just as in the earlier predatory stage it is necessary for the barbarian man to come up to the tribe's standard of physical endurance, cunning, and skill at arms. A certain standard of wealth in the one case, and of prowess in the other, is a necessary condition of reputability, and anything in excess of this normal amount is meritorious.

15 Those members of the community who fall short of this, somewhat indefinite, normal degree of prowess or of property suffer in the esteem of their fellow-men; and consequently they suffer also in their own esteem, since the usual basis of self-respect is the respect accorded by one's neighbors. Only individuals with an aberrant temperment can in the long run retain their self-esteem in the face of the disesteem of their fellows. Apparent exceptions to the rule are met with, especially among people with strong religious convictions. But these apparent exceptions are scarcely real exceptions, since such persons commonly fall back on the putative approbation of some supernatural witness of their deeds.

So soon as the possession of property becomes the basis of popular esteem, therefore, it becomes also a requisite to that complacency which we call self-respect. In any community where goods are held in severalty it is necessary, in order to his own peace of mind, that an individual should possess as large a portion of goods as others with whom he is accustomed to class himself; and it is extremely gratifying to possess something more than others. But as fast as a person makes new acquisitions, and becomes accustomed to the resulting new standard of wealth, the new standard forthwith ceases to afford appreciably greater satisfaction than the earlier standard did. The tendency in any case is constantly to make the present pecuniary standard the point of departure for a fresh increase of wealth; and this in turn gives rise to a new standard of sufficiency and a new pecuniary classification of one's self as compared with one's neighbors. So far as concerns the present question, the end sought by accumulation is to rank high in comparison with the rest of the community in point of pecuniary strength. So long as the comparison is distinctly unfavorable to himself, the normal, average individual will live in chronic dissatisfaction with his present lot; and when he has reached what may be called the normal pecuniary standard of the community, or of his class in the community, this chronic dissatisfaction will give place to a restless straining to place a wider and ever-widening pecuniary interval between himself and this average standard. The invidious comparison can never become so favorable to the individual making it that he would not gladly rate himself still higher relatively to his competitors in the struggle for pecuniary reputability.

In the nature of the case, the desire for wealth can scarcely be satiated in any individual instance, and evidently a satiation of the average or general desire for wealth is out of the question. However widely, or equally, or "fairly," it may be distributed, no general increase of the community's wealth can make any approach to satiating this need, the ground of which is the desire of everyone to excel everyone else in the accumulation of goods. If, as is sometimes assumed, the incentive to accumulation were the want of subsistence or of physical comfort, then the aggregate economic wants of a community might conceivably be satisfied at some point in the advance of industrial efficiency; but since the struggle is substantially a race for reputability on the basis of an invidious comparison, no approach to a definitive attainment is possible.

What has just been said must not be taken to mean that there are no other incentives to acquisition and accumulation than this desire to excel in pecuniary standing and so gain the esteem and envy of one's fellow-men. The desire for added comfort and security from want is present as a motive at every stage of the process of accumulation in a modern industrial community; although the standard of sufficiency in these respects is in turn greatly affected by the habit of pecuniary emulation. To a great extent this emulation shapes the methods and selects the objects of expenditure for personal comfort and decent livelihood.

Besides this, the power conferred by wealth also affords a motive to accumulation. That propensity for purposeful activity and that repugnance to all futility of effort which belong to man by virtue of his character as an agent do not desert him when he emerges from the naïve communal culture where the dominant note of life is the unanalyzed and undifferentiated solidarity of the individual with the group with which his life is bound up. When he enters upon the predatory stage, where self-seeking in the narrower sense becomes the dominant note, this propensity goes with him still, as the pervasive trait that shapes his scheme of life. The propensity for achievement and the repugnance to futility remain the underlying economic motive. The propensity changes only in the form of its expression and in the proximate objects to which it directs the man's activity. Under the régime of individual ownership the most available means of visibly achieving a purpose is that afforded by the acquisition and accumulation of goods; and as the self-regarding antithesis between man and man reaches fuller consciousness, the propensity for achievement—the instinct of workmanship—tends more and more to shape itself into a straining to excel others in pecuniary achievement. Relative success, tested by an invidious pecuniary comparison with other men, becomes the conventional end of action. The currently accepted legitimate end of effort becomes the achievement of a favorable comparison with other men; and therefore the repugnance to futility to a good extent coalesces with the incentive of emulation. It acts to accentuate the struggle for pecuniary reputability by visiting with a sharper disapproval all shortcoming and all evidence of shortcoming in point of pecuniary success. Purposeful effort comes to mean, primarily, effort directed to or resulting in a more creditable showing of accumulated wealth. Among the motives which lead men to accumulate wealth, the primacy, both in scope and intensity, therefore, continues to belong to this motive of pecuniary emulation.

20   In making use of the term "invidious," it may perhaps be unnecessary to remark, there is no intention to extol or depreciate, or to commend or deplore any of the phenomena which the word is used to characterize. The term is used in a technical sense as describing a comparison of persons with a view to rating and grading them in respect of relative worth or value—in an aesthetic or moral sense—and so awarding and defining the relative degrees of complacency with which they may legitimately be contemplated by themselves and by others. An invidious comparison is a process of valuation of persons in respect of worth.

SUGGESTIONS FOR WRITING

1. Veblen sees the primitive distinction between "women's work" and "men's work" as the basis of pecuniary emulation to demonstrate "prepotence." Write an essay in which you explain his reasoning in your own words while creating your own examples.

2. Does Veblen's account of a struggle for prestige parallel Darwin's account of the struggle for existence? Write an essay in which you explore your view of any similarities and differences in the processes addressed by the two writers.

3. Veblen argues that no "fair" distribution of wealth will satiate the need for pecuniary emulation. Write an essay in which you compare and contrast the views of Veblen and Marx on the human meaning of wealth.

The Labour of Our Body and the work of Our Hands   1958
From *The Human Condition*

HANNAH ARENDT

Hannah Arendt (1906–1975) was born in Germany and educated at the University of Heidelberg, earning a doctorate in philosophy when she was only 22 years old. She was among the vast number of Jewish intellectuals who fled Europe with the rise of Fascism in the 1930s. Coming to New York City on the eve of World War II she worked with Jewish relief groups and for book publishers, while learning English and continuing the work on political theory that was to make her world famous with the publication of The Origins of Totalitarianism *in 1951. In that book she analyzes the common bases of Communism and Fascism, ideologies which had been widely seen as polar opposites.*

While continuing her work on political and historical issues she returned to general philosophical topics, one of which is represented by the following selection. There she makes a crucial distinction about key concepts in the philosophy of economics—the often overlooked differences between what is expressed by the word labor *and the word* work.

11. *"The Labour of-our Body and the Work of our Hands"*

The distinction between labor and work which I propose is unusual. The phenomenal evidence in its favor is too striking to be ignored, and yet historically it is a fact that apart from a few scattered remarks, which moreover were never developed even in the theories of their authors, there is hardly anything in either the premodern tradition of political thought or in the large body of modern labor theories to support it. Against this scarcity of historical evidence, however, stands one very articulate and obstinate testimony, namely, the simple fact that every European language, ancient and modern, contains two etymologically unrelated words for what we have to come to think of as the same activity, and retains them in the face of their persistent synonymous usage.

Thus, Locke's distinction between working hands and a laboring body is somewhat reminiscent of the ancient Greek distinction between the *cheirotechnēs*, the craftsman, to whom the German *Handwerker* corresponds, and those who, like "slaves and tame animals with their bodies minister to the necessities of life," or in the Greek idiom, *tō sōmati ergazesthai*, work with their bodies (yet even here, labor and work are already treated as identical, since the word used is not *ponein* [labor] but *ergazesthai* [work]). Only in one respect, which, however, is linguistically the most important one, did ancient and modern usage of the two words as synonyms fail altogether, namely in the formation of a corresponding noun. Here again we find complete unanimity; the word "labor," understood as a noun, never designates the finished product, the result of laboring, but remains a verbal noun to be classed with the gerund, whereas the product itself is invariably derived from the word for work, even when current usage has followed the actual modern development so closely that the verb form of the word "work" has become rather obsolete.

The reason why this distinction should have been overlooked in ancient times and its significance remained unexplored seems obvious enough. Contempt for laboring, originally arising out of a passionate striving for freedom from necessity and a no less passionate impatience with every effort that left no trace, no monument, no great work worthy of remembrance, spread with the increasing demands of *polis* life upon the time of the citizens and its insistence on their abstention (*skholē*) from all but political activities, until it covered everything that demanded an effort. Earlier political custom, prior to the full development of the city-state, merely distinguished between slaves, vanquished enemies (*dmōes* or *douloi*), who were carried off to the victor's household with other loot where as household inmates (*oiketai* or *familiares*) they slaved for their own and their master's life, and the *dēmiourgoi*, the workmen of the people at large, who moved freely outside the private realm and within the public. A later time even changed the name for these artisans, whom Solon had still described as sons of Athena and Hephaestus, and called them *banausoi*, that is, men whose chief interest is their craft and not the market place. It is only from the late fifth century onward that the *polis* began to classify occupations according to the amount of effort required, so that Aristotle called those occupations the meanest "in which the body is most deteriorated." Although he refused to admit *banausoi* to citizenship, he would have accepted shepherds and painters (but neither peasants nor sculptors).

We shall see later that, quite apart from their contempt for labor, the Greeks had reasons of their own to mistrust the craftsman, or rather, the *homo faber* mentality. This mistrust, however, is true only of certain periods, whereas all ancient estimates of human activities, including those which, like Hesiod, supposedly praise labor, rest on the conviction that the labor of our body which is necessitated by its needs is slavish. Hence, occupations which did not consist in laboring, yet were undertaken not for their own sake but in order to provide the necessities of life, were assimilated to the status of labor, and this explains changes and variations in their estimation and classification at different periods and in different places. The opinion that labor and work were despised in antiquity because only slaves were engaged in them is a prejudice of modern historians. The ancients reasoned the other way around and felt it necessary to possess slaves because of the slavish nature of all occupations that served the needs for the maintenance of life. It was precisely on these grounds that the institution of slavery was defended and justified. To labor meant to be enslaved by necessity, and this enslavement was inherent in the conditions of human life. Because men were dominated by the necessities of life, they could win their freedom only through the domination of those whom they subjected to necessity by force. The slave's degradation was a blow of fate and a fate worse than death, because it carried with it a metamorphosis of man into something akin to a tame animal. A change in a slave's status, therefore, such as manumission by his master or a change in general political circumstance that elevated certain occupations to public relevance, automatically entailed a change in the slave's "nature."

5   The institution of slavery in antiquity, though not in later times, was not a device for cheap labor or an instrument of exploitation for profit but rather the attempt to exclude labor from the conditions of man's life. What men share with all other forms of animal life was not considered to be human. (This, incidentally, was also the reason for the much

misunderstood Greek theory of the non-human nature of the slave. Aristotle, who argued this theory so explicitly, and then, on his deathbed, freed his slaves, may not have been so inconsistent as moderns are inclined to think. He denied not the slave's capacity to be human, but only the use of the word "men" for members of the species man-kind as long as they are totally subject to necessity.) And it is true that the use of the word "animal" in the concept of *animal laborans*, as distinguished from the very questionable use of the same word in the term *animal rationale,* is fully justified. The *animal laborans* is indeed only one, at best the highest, of the animal species which populate the earth.

It is not surprising that the distinction between labor and work was ignored in classical antiquity. The differentiation between the private household and the public political realm, between the household inmate who was a slave and the household head who was a citizen, between activities which should be hidden in privacy and those which were worth being seen, heard, and remembered, overshadowed and predetermined all other distinctions until only one criterion was left: is the greater amount of time and effort spent in private or in public? is the occupation motivated by *cura privati negotii* or *cura rei publicae,* care for private or for public business? With the rise of political theory, the philosophers overruled even these distinctions, which had at least distinguished between activities, by opposing contemplation to all kinds of activity alike. With them, even political activity was leveled to the rank of necessity, which henceforth became the common denominator of all articulations within the *vita activa.* Nor can we reasonably expect any help from Christian political thought, which accepted the philosophers' distinction, refined it, and, religion being for the many and philosophy only for the few, gave it general validity, binding for all men.

It is surprising at first glance, however, that the modern age—with its reversal of all traditions, the traditional rank of action and contemplation no less than the traditional hierarchy within the *vita activa* itself, with its glorification of labor as the source of all values and its elevation of the *animal laborans* to the position traditionally held by the *animal rationale*—should not have brought forth a single theory in which *animal laborans* and *homo faber,* "the labour of our body and the work of our hands," are clearly distinguished. Instead, we find first the distinction between productive and unproductive labor, then somewhat later the differentiation between skilled and unskilled work, and, finally, outranking both because seemingly of more elementary significance, the division of all activities into manual and intellectual labor. Of the three, however, only the distinction between productive and unproductive labor goes to the heart of the matter, and it is no accident that the two greatest theorists in the field, Adam Smith and Karl Marx, based the whole structure of their argument upon it. The very reason for the elevation of labor in the modern age was its "productivity," and the seemingly blasphemous notion of Marx that labor (and not God) created man or that labor (and not reason) distinguished man from the other animals was only the most radical and consistent formulation of something upon which the whole modern age was agreed.

Moreover, both Smith and Marx were in agreement with modern public opinion when they despised unproductive labor as parasitical, actually a kind of perversion of labor, as though nothing were worthy of this name which did not enrich the world. Marx certainly shared Smith's contempt for the "menial servants" who like "idle guests . . . leave nothing behind them in return for their consumption." Yet it was precisely these menial servants, these household inmates, *oiketai* or *familiares*, laboring for sheer subsistence and needed for effortless consumption rather than for production, whom all ages prior to the modern had in mind when they identified the laboring condition with slavery. What they left behind them in return for their consumption was nothing more or less than their masters' freedom or, in modern language, their masters' potential productivity.

In other words, the distinction between productive and unproductive labor contains, albeit in a prejudicial manner, the more fundamental distinction between work and labor. It is indeed the mark of all laboring that it leaves nothing behind, that the result of its effort is almost as quickly consumed as the effort is spent. And yet this effort, despite its futility, is born of a great urgency and motivated by a more powerful drive than anything else, because life itself depends upon it. The modern age in general and Karl Marx in particular, overwhelmed, as it were, by the unprecedented actual productivity of Western mankind, had an almost irresistible tendency to look upon all labor as work and to speak of the *animal laborans* in terms much more fitting for *homo faber,* hoping all the time that only one more step was needed to eliminate labor and necessity altogether.

SUGGESTIONS FOR WRITING

1. As part of her effort to distinguish "work" from "labor," Hannah Arendt points out early in the selection that only the word "work" is used to designate a finished product, what human effort leaves behind in the world. So it is we speak of the "works" of Shakespeare or Marx but not of a cooked meal as a "work." Later (p. 144) she says of menial servants that their labor is only apparently "unproductive." "What they left behind them in return for their consumption was nothing more or less than their masters' freedom or, in modern language, their masters' potential productivity." That is, because he did not have to labor to sustain life, the master was free to occupy himself with higher tasks and produce "work" that has a lasting existence in the world. Given your reading of Smith and Marx in this section, do you think they would agree with Arendt's analysis of "unproductive" labor? Write an essay that explains and defends your views.

2. In your view, would Gilman agree with Arendt's analysis of domestic tasks? Write an essay that explains and defends your view.

3. In your view, would Veblen agree with Arendt's analysis of the differing levels of prestige associated with labor and work? Write an essay that explains and defends your view.

The End of Laissez-Faire   1926

JOHN MAYNARD KEYNES

John Maynard Keynes (1883–1946) was one of the most influential economists of the twentieth century and his thinking is still behind many economic policies worldwide. Keynes became famous as an economist with the publication of a book on the peace treaties that ended World War I, a topic he knew firsthand as a member of the British delegation. The Economic Consequences of the Peace *pointed out the disastrous results likely to come from the harsh financial treatment of the losing side. Though one consequence for Germany was not the Communist revolution Keynes feared, the Nazi rise to power was founded on economic issues and secured by economic success due to re-armament with the well-known result of World War II.*

Keynes's views on the place of governmental power in regulating a national economy are at odds with the tradition of laissez faire, the hands-off approach that let the economy take care of itself while the government focused on areas like national defense. Keynes explains why this separation of powers needs reexamination.

Let us clear from the ground the metaphysical or general principles upon which, from time to time, *laissez-faire* has been founded. It is *not* true that individuals possess a prescriptive "natural liberty" in their economic activities. There is *no* "compact" conferring perpetual rights on those who Have or on those who Acquire. The world is *not* so governed from above that private and social interest always coincide. It is *not* so managed here below that in practice they coincide. It is *not* a correct deduction from the Principles of Economics that enlightened self-interest always operates in the public interest. Nor is it true that self-interest generally *is* enlightened; more often individuals acting separately to promote their own ends are too ignorant or too weak to attain even these. Experience does *not* show that individuals, when they make up a social unit, are always less clear-sighted than when they act separately.

We cannot, therefore, settle on abstract grounds, but must handle on its merits in detail, what Burke termed "one of the finest problems in legislation, namely, to determine what the State ought to take upon itself to direct by the public wisdom, and what it ought to leave, with as little interference as possible, to individual exertion." We have to discriminate between what Bentham, in his forgotten but useful nomenclature, used to term *Agenda* and *Non-Agenda,* and to do this without Bentham's prior presumption that interference is at the same time, "generally needless" and "generally pernicious." Perhaps the chief task of Economists at this hour is to distinguish afresh the *Agenda* of Government from the *Non-Agenda;* and the companion task of Politics is to devise forms of Government within a Democracy which shall be capable of accomplishing the *Agenda.* I will illustrate what I have in mind by two examples.

(1) I believe that in many cases the ideal size for the unit of control and organization lies somewhere between the individual and the modern State. I suggest, therefore, that progress lies in the growth and the recognition of semiautonomous bodies within the State—bodies whose criterion of action within their own field is solely the public good as they understand it, and from whose deliberations motives of private advantage are excluded, though some place it may still be necessary to leave, until the ambit of men's altruism, grows wider, to the separate advantage of particular groups, classes, or faculties— bodies which in the ordinary course of affairs are mainly autonomous within their prescribed limitations, but are subject in the last resort to the sovereignty of the democracy expressed through Parliament.

I propose a return, it may be said, towards mediaeval conceptions of separate autonomies. But, in England at any rate, corporations are a mode of government which has never ceased to be important and is sympathetic to our institutions. It is easy to give examples, from what already exists, of separate autonomies which have attained or are approaching the mode I designate—the Universities, the Bank of England, the Port of London Authority, even perhaps the Railway Companies.

5 But more interesting than these is the trend of Joint Stock Institutions, when they have reached a certain age and size, to approximate to the status of public corporations rather than that of individualistic private enterprise. One of the most interesting and unnoticed developments of recent decades has been the tendency of big enterprise to socialize itself. A point arrives in the growth of a big institution—particularly a big railway or big public utility enterprise, but also a big bank or a big insurance company—at which the owners of the capital, i.e., the shareholders, are almost entirely dissociated from the management, with the result that the direct personal interest of the latter in the making of great profit becomes quite secondary. When this stage is reached, the general stability and reputation of the institution are more considered by the management than the maximum of profit for the shareholders. The shareholders must be satisfied by conventionally adequate dividends; but once this is secured, the direct interest of the management often consists in avoiding criticism from the public and from the customers of the concern. This is particularly the case if their great size or semimonopolistic position renders them conspicuous in the public eye and vulnerable to public attack. The extreme instance, perhaps, of this tendency in the case of an institution, theoretically the unrestricted property of private persons, is the Bank of England. It is almost true to say that there is no class of persons in the Kingdom of whom the Governor of the Bank of England thinks less when he decides on his policy than of his shareholders. Their rights, in excess of their conventional dividend, have already sunk to the neighborhood of zero. But the same thing is partly true of many other big institutions. They are, as time goes on, socializing themselves.

Not that this is unmixed gain. The same causes promote conservatism and a waning of enterprise. In fact, we already have in these cases many of the faults as well as the advantages of State Socialism. Nevertheless we see here, I think, a natural line of evolution. The battle of Socialism against unlimited private profit is being won in detail hour by hour. In these particular fields—it remains acute elsewhere—this is no longer the pressing problem. There is, for instance, no so-called important political question so really unimportant, so irrelevant to the reorganization of the economic life of Great Britain, as the Nationalization of the Railways.

It is true that many big undertakings, particularly Public Utility enterprises and other business requiring a large fixed capital, still need to be semisocialized. But we must keep our minds flexible regarding the forms of this semisocialism. We must take full advantage of the natural tendencies of the day, and we must probably prefer semiautonomous corporations to organs of the Central Government for which Ministers of State are directly responsible.

I criticize doctrinaire State Socialism, not because it seeks to engage men's altruistic impulses in the service of Society, or because it departs from *laissez-faire*, or because it takes away from man's natural liberty to make a million, or because it has courage for bold experiments. All these things I applaud. I criticize it because it misses the significance of what is actually happening; because it is, in fact, little better than a dusty survival of a plan to meet the problems of fifty years ago, based on a misunderstanding of what some one said a hundred years ago. Nineteenth-century State Socialism sprang from Bentham, free competition, etc., and is in some respects a clearer, in some respects a more muddled, version of just the same philosophy as underlies nineteenth-century individualism. Both equally laid all their stress on freedom, the one negatively to avoid limitations on existing freedom, the other positively to destroy natural or acquired monopolies. They are different reactions to the same intellectual atmosphere.

(2) I come next to a criterion of *Agenda* which is particularly relevant to what it is urgent and desirable to do in the near future. We must aim at separating those services which are *technically social* from those which are *technically individual*. The most important *Agenda* of the State relate not to those activities which private individuals are already fulfilling, but to those functions which fall outside the sphere of the individual, to those decisions which are made by *no one* if the State does not make them. The important thing for Government is not to do things which individuals are doing already, and to do them a little better or a little worse; but to do those things which at present are not done at all.

10   It is not within the scope of my purpose on this occasion to develop practical policies. I limit myself, therefore, to naming some instances of what I mean from among those problems about which I happen to have thought most.

Many of the greatest economic evils of our time are fruits of risk, uncertainly, and ignorance. It is because particular individuals, fortunate in situation or in abilities, are able to take advantage of uncertainty and ignorance, and also because for the same reason big business is often a lottery, that great inequalities of wealth come about; and these same factors are also the cause of the Unemployment of Labor, or the disappointment of reasonable business expectations, and of the impairment of efficiency and production. Yet the cure lies outside the operations of individuals; it may even be to the interest of individuals to aggravate the disease. I believe that the cure for these things is partly to be sought in the deliberate control of the currency and of credit by a central institution, and partly in the collection and dissemination on a great scale of data relating to the business situation, including the full publicity, by law if necessary, of all business facts which it is useful to know. These measures would involve Society in exercizing directive intelligence through some appropriate organ of action over many of the inner intricacies of private business, yet it would leave private initiative and enterprise unhindered. Even if these measures prove insufficient, nevertheless they will furnish us with better knowledge than we have now for taking the next step.

My second example relates to Savings and Investment. I believe that some co-ordinated act of intelligent judgment is required as to the scale on which it is desirable that the community as a whole should save, the scale on which these savings should go abroad in the form of foreign investments, and whether the present organization of the investment market distributes savings along the most nationally productive channels. I do not think that these matters should be left entirely to the chances of private judgment and private profits, as they are at present.

My third example concerns Population. The time has already come when each country needs a considered national policy about what size of Population, whether larger or smaller than at present or the same, is most expedient. And having settled this policy, we must take steps to carry it into operation. The time may arrive a little later when the community as a whole must pay attention to the innate quality as well as to the mere numbers of its future members.

These reflections have been directed towards possible improvements in the technique of modern Capitalism by the agency of collective action. There is nothing in them which is seriously incompatible with what seems to me to be the essential characteristic of Capitalism, namely the dependence upon an intense appeal to the money-making and money-loving instincts of individuals as the main motive force of the economic machine. Nor must I, so near to my end, stray towards other fields. Nevertheless, I may do well to remind you, in conclusion, that the fiercest contests and the most deeply felt divisions of opinion are likely to be waged in the coming years not round technical questions, where the arguments on either side are mainly economic, but round those which, for want of better words, may be called psychological or, perhaps, moral.

15   In Europe, or at least in some parts of Europe—but not, I think, in the United States of America—there is a latent reaction; somewhat widespread, against basing Society to the extent that we do upon fostering, encouraging, and protecting the money-motives of individuals. A preference for arranging our affairs in such a way as to appeal to the money-motive as little as possible, rather than as much as possible, need not be entirely *a priori*, but may be based on the comparison of experiences. Different persons, according to their choice of profession, find the money-motive playing a large or a small part in their daily lives, and historians can tell us about other phases of social organization in which this motive has played a much smaller part than it does now. Most religions and most philosophies deprecate, to say the least of it, a way of life mainly influenced by considerations of personal money profit. On the other hand, most men today reject ascetic notions and do not doubt the real advantages of wealth. Moreover it seems obvious to them that one cannot do without the money-motive, and that, apart from certain admitted abuses, it does its job well. In the result the average man averts his attention from the problem, and has no clear idea what he really thinks and feels about the whole confounded matter.

Confusion of thought and feeling leads to confusion of speech. Many people, who are really objecting to Capitalism as a way of life, argue as though they were objecting to it on the ground of its inefficiency in attaining its own objects. Contrariwise, devotees of Capitalism are often unduly conservative, and reject reforms in its technique, which might really strengthen and preserve it, for fear that they may prove to be first steps away from Capitalism itself. Nevertheless a time may be coming when we shall get clearer than at present as to when we are talking about Capitalism as an efficient or inefficient technique, and when we are talking about it as desirable or objectionable in itself. For my part, I think that Capitalism, wisely managed, can probably be made more efficient for attaining economic ends than any alternative system yet in sight, but that in itself it is in many ways extremely objectionable. Our problem is to work out a social organization which shall be as efficient as possible without offending our notions of a satisfactory way of life.

The next step forward must come, not from political agitation or premature experiments, but from thought. We need by an effort of the mind to elucidate our own feelings. At present our sympathy and our judgment are liable to be on different sides, which is a painful and paralysing state of mind. In the field of action reformers will not be successful until they can steadily pursue a clear and definite object with their intellects and their feelings in tune. There is no party in the world at present which appears to me to be pursuing right aims by right methods. Material Poverty provides the incentive to change precisely in situations where there is very little margin for experiments. Material Prosperity removes the incentive just when it might be safe to take a chance. Europe lacks the means, America the will, to make a move. We need a new set of convictions which spring naturally from a candid examination of our own inner feelings in relation to the outside facts.

SUGGESTIONS FOR WRITING

1. Marx is perhaps the most famous opponent of laissez-faire capitalism, the economic system in which capital is allowed to operate as free as possible from any restraint. Given your reading of Marx in his chapter and your understanding of Keynes's essay, would you consider Keynes to be a Marxist? Write an essay that explains and defends your view.

2. In your opinion, what would Veblen think of Keynes's analyses and recommendations? Write an essay that compares and contrasts the views of these two economists.

3. Keynes is concerned with the proper relation of government and individuals in an economy. Do you think he has understood and explained the proper balance between them? Write an essay that defines and defends your views.

Occupational Licensure   1962

From *Capitalism and Freedom*

MILTON FRIEDMAN

Milton Friedman, a Nobel Prize-winning economist (1976) was born to immigrant parents in 1912. Growing up in New Jersey, he graduated from Rutgers University (salve magna parens) in 1932. After World War II he largely abandoned the Keynesian views of his earlier career and went on to the University of Chicago where he helped to form a world-famous department of economics that included many future winners of the Nobel Prize.

Friedman is most widely known for his work on monetary economics, and the present economy of Chile was organized largely in accordance with his views, which are expressed by the title of his highly popular book Capitalism and Freedom *(1962). In his selection here, Friedman brings those views to bear in a common-sense analysis of an economic issue that usually seems to the general public entirely noncontroversial.*

Before discussing the advantages and disadvantages of licensing, it is worth noting why we have it and what general political problem is revealed by the tendency for such special legislation to be enacted. The declaration by a large number of different state legislatures that barbers must be approved by a committee of other barbers is hardly persuasive evidence that there is in fact a public interest in having such legislation. Surely the explanation is different; it is that a producer group tends to be more concentrated politically than a consumer group. This is an obvious point often made and yet one whose importance cannot be overstressed.[1] Each of us is a producer and also a consumer. However, we are much more specialized and devote a much larger fraction of our attention to our activity as a producer than as a consumer. We consume literally thousands if not millions of items. The result is that people in the same trade, like barbers or physicians, all have an intense interest in the specific problems of this trade and are willing to devote considerable energy to doing something about them. On the other hand, those of us who use barbers at all, get barbered infrequently and spend only a minor fraction of our income in barber shops. Our interest is casual. Hardly any of us are willing to devote much time going to the legislature in order to testify against the iniquity of restricting the practice of barbering. The same point holds for tariffs. The groups that think they have a special interest in particular tariffs are concentrated groups to whom the issue makes a great deal of difference. The public interest is widely dispersed. In consequence, in the absence of any general arrangements to offset the pressure of special interests, producer groups will invariably have a much stronger influence on legislative action and the powers that be

---

[1] See, for example, Wesley Mitchell's famous article on the "Backward Art of Spending Money," reprinted in his book of essays carrying that title (New York: McGraw-Hill, 1937), pp. 3–19.

than will the diverse, widely spread consumer interest. Indeed from this point of view, the puzzle is not why we have so many silly licensure laws, but why we don't have far more. The puzzle is how we ever succeeded in getting the relative freedom from government controls over the productive activities of individuals that we have had and still have in this country, and that other countries have had as well.

The only way that I can see to offset special producer groups is to establish a general presumption against the state undertaking certain kinds of activities. Only if there is a general recognition that governmental activities should be severely limited with respect to a class of cases, can the burden of proof be put strongly enough on those who would depart from this general presumption to give a reasonable hope of limiting the spread of special measures to further special interests. This point is one we have adverted to time and again. It is of a piece with the argument for the Bill of Rights and for a rule to govern monetary policy and fiscal policy.

Policy Issues Raised by Licensure

It is important to distinguish three different levels of control: first, registration; second, certification; third, licensing.

By registration, I mean an arrangement under which individuals are required to list their names in some official register if they engage in certain kinds of activities. There is no provision for denying the right to engage in the activity to anyone who is willing to list his name. He may be charged a fee, either as a registration fee or as a scheme of taxation.

5   The second level is certification. The governmental agency may certify that an individual has certain skills but may not prevent, in any way, the practice of any occupation using these skills by people who do not have such a certificate. One example is accountancy. In most states, anybody can be an accountant, whether he is a certified public accountant or not, but only those people who have passed a particular test can put the title CPA after their names or can put a sign in their offices saying they are certified public accountants. Certification is frequently only an intermediate stage. In many states, there has been a tendency to restrict an increasing range of activities to certified public accountants. With respect to such activities there is licensure, not certification. In some states, "architect" is a title which can be used only by those who have passed a specified examination. This is certification. It does not prevent anyone else from going into the business of advising people for a fee how to build houses.

The third stage is licensing proper. This is an arrangement under which one must obtain a license from a recognized authority in order to engage in the occupation. The license is more than a formality. It requires some demonstration of competence or the meeting of some tests ostensibly designed to insure competence, and anyone who does not have a license is not authorized to practice and is subject to a fine or a jail sentence if he does engage in practice.

The question I want to consider is this: under what circumstances, if any, can we justify the one or the other of these steps? There are three different grounds on which it seems to me registration can be justified consistently with liberal principles.

First, it may assist in the pursuit of other aims. Let me illustrate. The police are often concerned with acts of violence. After the event, it is desirable to find out who had access to firearms. Before the event, it is desirable to prevent firearms from getting into the hands of people who are likely to use them for criminal purposes. It may assist in the pursuit of this aim to register stores selling firearms. Of course, if I may revert to a point made several times in earlier chapters, it is never enough to say that there *might* be a justification along these lines, in order to conclude that there *is* justification. It is necessary to set up a balance sheet of the advantages and disadvantages in the light of liberal principles. All I am now saying is that this consideration might in some cases justify overriding the general presumption against requiring the registration of people.

Second, registration is sometimes a device to facilitate taxation and nothing more. The questions at issue then become whether the particular tax is an appropriate method to raise revenue for financing government services regarded as necessary, and whether registration facilitates the collection of taxes. It may do so either because a tax is imposed on the person who registers, or because the person who registers is used as a tax collector. For example, in collecting a sales tax imposed on various items of consumption, it is necessary to have a register or list of all the places selling goods subject to the tax.

10   Third, and this is the one possible justification for registration which is close to our main interest, registration may be a means to protect consumers against fraud. In general, liberal principles assign to the state the power to enforce contracts, and fraud involves the violation of a contract. It is, of course, dubious that one should go very far to protect in advance against fraud because of the interference with voluntary

contracts involved in doing so. But I do not think that one can rule out on grounds of principle the possibility that there may be certain activities that are so likely to give rise to fraud as to render it desirable to have in advance a list of people known to be pursuing this activity. Perhaps one example along these lines is the registration of taxicab drivers. A taxicab driver picking up a person at night may be in a particularly good position to steal from him. To inhibit such practices, it may be desirable to have a list of names of people who are engaged in the taxicab business, to give each a number, and to require that this number be put in the cab so that anyone molested need only remember the number of the cab. This involves simply the use of the police power to protect individuals against violence on the part of other individuals and may be the most convenient method of doing so.

Certification is much more difficult to justify. The reason is that this is something the private market generally can do for itself. This problem is the same for products as for people's services. There are private certification agencies in many areas that certify the competence of a person or the quality of a particular product. The *Good Housekeeping* seal is a private certification arrangement. For industrial products there are private testing laboratories that will certify to the quality of a particular product. For consumer products, there are consumer testing agencies of which Consumer's Union and Consumer's Research are the best known in the United States. Better Business Bureaus are voluntary organizations that certify the quality of particular dealers. Technical schools, colleges, and universities certify the quality of their graduates. One function of retailers and department stores is to certify the quality of the many items they sell. The consumer develops confidence in the store, and the store in turn has an incentive to earn this confidence by investigating the quality of the items it sells.

One can however argue that in some cases, or perhaps even in many, voluntary certification will not be carried as far as individuals would be willing to pay for carrying it because of the difficulty of keeping the certification confidential. The issue is essentially the one involved in patents and copyrights, namely, whether individuals are in a position to capture the value of the services that they render to others. If I go into the business of certifying people, there may be no efficient way in which I can require you to pay for my certification. If I sell my certification information to one person, how can I keep him from passing it on to others? Consequently, it may not be possible to get effective voluntary exchange with respect to certification, even though this is a service that people would be willing to pay for if they had to. One way to get around this problem, as we get around other kinds of neighborhood effects, is to have governmental certification.

Another possible justification for certification is on monopoly grounds. There are some technical monopoly aspects to certification, since the cost of making a certification is largely independent of the number of people to whom the information is transmitted. However, it is by no means clear that monopoly is inevitable.

Licensure seems to me still more difficult to justify. It goes still farther in the direction of trenching upon the rights of individuals to enter into voluntary contracts. Nonetheless, there are some justifications given for licensure that the liberal will have to recognize as within his own conception of appropriate government action, though, as always, the advantages have to be weighed against the disadvantages. The main argument that is relevant to a liberal is the existence of neighborhood effects. The simplest and most obvious example is the "incompetent" physician who produces an epidemic. Insofar as he harms only his patient, that is simply a question of voluntary contract and exchange between the patient and his physician. On this score, there is no ground for intervention. However, it can be argued that if the physician treats his patient badly, he may unleash an epidemic that will cause harm to third parties who are not involved in the immediate transaction. In such a case, it is conceivable that everybody, including even the potential patient and physician, would be willing to submit to the restriction of the practice of medicine to "competent" people in order to prevent such epidemics from occurring.

15   In practice, the major argument given for licensure by its proponents is not this one, which has some appeal to a liberal, but rather a strictly paternalistic argument that has little or no appeal. Individuals, it is said, are incapable of choosing their own servants adequately, their own physician or plumber or barber. In order for a man to choose a physician intelligently, he would have to be a physician himself. Most of us, it is said, are therefore incompetent and we must be protected against our own ignorance. This amounts to saying that we in our capacity as voters must protect ourselves in our capacity as consumers against our own ignorance, by seeing to it that people are not served by incompetent physicians or plumbers or barbers.

So far, I have been listing the arguments for registration, certification, and licensing. In all three cases, it is clear that there are also strong social costs to be set against any of these advantages. Some of these social costs have already been suggested and I shall illustrate them in more detail for medicine, but it may be worth recording them here in general form.

The most obvious social cost is that any one of these measures, whether it be registration, certification, or licensure, almost inevitably becomes a tool in the hands of a special producer group to obtain a monopoly position at the expense of the rest of the public. There is no way to avoid this result. One can devise one or another set of procedural controls designed to avert this outcome, but none is likely to overcome the problem that arises out of the greater concentration of producer than of consumer interest. The people who are most concerned with any such arrangement, who will press most for its enforcement and be most concerned with its administration, will be the people in the particular occupation or trade involved. They will inevitably press for the extension of registration to certification and of certification to licensure. Once licensure is attained, the people who might develop an interest in undermining the regulations are kept from exerting their influence. They don't get a license, must therefore go into other occupations, and will lose interest. The result is invariably control over entry by members of the occupation itself and hence the establishment of a monopoly position.

Certification is much less harmful in this respect. If the certified "abuse" their special certificates; if, in certifying newcomers, members of the trade impose unnecessarily stringent requirements and reduce the number of practitioners too much, the price differential between certified and non-certified will become sufficiently large to induce the public to use non-certified practitioners. In technical terms, the elasticity of demand for the services of certified practitioners will be fairly large, and the limits within which they can exploit the rest of the public by taking advantage of their special position will be rather narrow.

In consequence, certification without licensure is a half-way house that maintains a good deal of protection against monopolization. It also has its disadvantages, but it is worth noting that the usual arguments for licensure, and in particular the paternalistic arguments, are satisfied almost entirely by certification alone. If the argument is that we are too ignorant to judge good practitioners, all that is needed is to make the relevant information available. If, in full knowledge, we still want to go to someone who is not certified, that is our business; we cannot complain that we did not have the information. Since arguments for licensure made by people who are not members of the occupation can be satisfied so fully by certification, I personally find it difficult to see any case for which licensure rather than certification can be justified.

20 Even registration has significant social costs. It is an important first step in the direction of a system in which every individual has to carry an identity card, every individual has to inform authorities what he plans to do before he does it. Moreover, as already noted, registration tends to be the first step toward certification and licensure.

Medical Licensure

The medical profession is one in which practice of the profession has for a long time been restricted to people with licenses. Offhand, the question, "Ought we to let incompetent physicians practice?" seems to admit of only a negative answer. But I want to urge that second thought may give pause.

In the first place, licensure is the key to the control that the medical profession can exercise over the number of physicians. To understand why this is so requires some discussion of the structure of the medical profession. The American Medical Association is perhaps the strongest trade union in the United States. The essence of the power of a trade union is its power to restrict the number who may engage in a particular occupation. This restriction may be exercised indirectly by being able to enforce a wage rate higher than would otherwise prevail. If such a wage rate can be enforced, it will reduce the number of people who can get jobs and thus indirectly the number of people pursuing the occupation. This technique of restriction has disadvantages. There is always a dissatisfied fringe of people who are trying to get into the occupation. A trade union is much better off if it can limit directly the number of people who enter the occupation—who ever try to get jobs in it. The disgruntled and dissatisfied are excluded at the outset, and the union does not have to worry about them.

The American Medical Association is in this position. It is a trade union that can limit the number of people who can enter. How can it do this? The essential control is at the stage of admission to medical school. The Council on Medical Education and Hospitals of the American Medical Association approves medical schools. In order for a medical school to get and stay on its list of approved schools it has to meet the standards of the Council. The power of the Council has been demonstrated at various times when there has been pressure to reduce numbers. For example, in the 1930's during the depression, the Council on Medical Education and Hospitals wrote a letter to the various medical schools saying the medical schools were admitting more students than could be given the proper kind of training. In the next year or two, every school reduced the number it was admitting, giving very strong presumptive evidence that the recommendation had some effect.

Why does the Council's approval matter so much? If it abuses its power, why don't unapproved medical schools arise? The answer is that in almost every state in the United States, a person must be licensed to practice medicine, and to get the license, he must be a graduate of an approved school. In almost every state, the list of approved schools is identical with the list of schools approved by the Council on Medical Education and Hospitals of the American Medical Association. That is why the licensure provision is the key to the effective control of admission. It has a dual effect. On the one hand, the members of the licensure commission are always physicians and hence have some control at the step at which men apply for a license. This control is more limited in effectiveness than control at the medical school level. In almost all professions requiring licensure, people may try to get admitted more than once. If a person tries long enough and in enough jurisdictions he is likely to get through sooner or later. Since he has already spent the money and time to get his training, he has a strong incentive to keep trying. Licensure provisions that come into operation only after a man is trained therefore affect entry largely by raising the costs of getting into the occupation, since it may take a longer time to get in and since there is always some uncertainty whether he will succeed. But this rise in cost is nothing like so effective in limiting entry as is preventing a man from getting started on his career. If he is eliminated at the stage of entering medical school, he never comes up as a candidate for examination; he can never be troublesome at that stage. The efficient way to get control over the number in a profession is therefore to get control of entry into professional schools.

25   Control over admission to medical school and later licensure enables the profession to limit entry in two ways. The obvious one is simply by turning down many applicants. The less obvious, but probably far more important one, is by establishing standards for admission and licensure that make entry so difficult as to discourage young people from ever trying to get admission. Though most state laws require only two years of college prior to medical school, nearly 100 per cent of the entrants have had four

years of college. Similarly, medical training proper has been lengthened, particularly through more stringent internship arrangements.

As an aside, the lawyers have never been as successful as the physicians in getting control at the point of admission to professional school, though they are moving in that direction. The reason is amusing. Almost every school on the American Bar Association's list of approved schools is a full time day school; almost no night schools are approved. Many state legislators, on the other hand, are graduates of night law schools. If they voted to restrict admission to the profession to graduates of approved schools, in effect they would be voting that they themselves were not qualified. Their reluctance to condemn their own competence has been the main factor that has tended to limit the extent to which law has been able to succeed in imitating medicine. I have not myself done any extensive work on requirements for admission to law for many years but I understand that this limitation is breaking down. The greater affluence of students means that a much larger fraction are going to full time law schools and this is changing the composition of the legislatures.

To return to medicine, it is the provision about graduation from approved schools that is the most important source of professional control over entry. The profession has used this control to limit numbers. To avoid misunderstanding let me emphasize that I am not saying that individual members of the medical profession, the leaders of the medical profession, or the people who are in charge of the Council on Medical Education and Hospitals deliberately go out of their way to limit entry in order to raise their own incomes. That is not the way it works. Even when such people explicitly comment on the desirability of limiting numbers to raise incomes they will always justify the policy on the grounds that if "too" many people are let in, this will lower their incomes so that they will be driven to resort to unethical practices in order to earn a "proper" income. The only way, they argue, in which ethical practices can be maintained is by keeping people at a standard of income which is adequate to the merits and needs of the medical profession. I must confess that this has always seemed to me objectionable on both ethical and factual grounds. It is extraordinary that leaders of medicine should proclaim publicly that they and their colleagues must be paid to be ethical. And if it were so, I doubt that the price would have any limit. There seems little correlation between poverty and honesty. One would rather expect the opposite; dishonesty may not always pay but surely it sometimes does.

Control of entry is explicitly rationalized along these lines only at times like the Great Depression when there is much unemployment and relatively low incomes. In ordinary times, the rationalization for restriction is different. It is that the members of the medical profession want to raise what they regard as the standards of "quality" of the profession. The defect in this rationalization is a common one, and one that is destructive of a proper understanding of the operation of an economic system, namely, the failure to distinguish between technical efficiency and economic efficiency.

A story about lawyers will perhaps illustrate the point. At a meeting of lawyers at which problems of admission were being discussed, a colleague of mine, arguing against restrictive admission standards, used an analogy from the automobile industry. Would it not, he said, be absurd if the automobile industry were to argue that no one should drive a low quality car and therefore that no automobile manufacturer should be permitted to produce a car that did not come up to the Cadillac standard. One member of the audience rose and approved the analogy, saying that, of course, the country cannot afford anything but Cadillac lawyers! This tends to be the professional attitude. The members look solely at technical standards of performance, and argue in effect that we must have only firstrate physicians even if this means that some people get no medical service—though of course they never put it that way. Nonetheless, the view that people should get only the "optimum" medical service always lead to a restrictive policy, a policy that keeps down the number of physicians. I would not, of course, want to argue that this is the only force at work, but only that this kind of consideration leads many well-meaning physicians to go along with policies that they would reject out-of-hand if they did not have this kind of comforting rationalization.

30   It is easy to demonstrate that quality is only a rationalization and not the underlying reason for restriction. The power of the Council on Medical Education and Hospitals of the American Medical Association has been used to limit numbers in ways that cannot possibly have any connection whatsoever with quality. The simplest example is their recommendation to various states that citizenship be made a requirement for the practice of medicine. I find it inconceivable to see how this is relevant to medical performance. A similar requirement that they have tried to impose on occasion is that examination for licensure must be taken in English. A dramatic piece of evidence on the power and

potency of the Association as well as on the lack of relation to quality is proved by one figure that I have always found striking. After 1933, when Hitler came to power in Germany, there was a tremendous outflow of professional people from Germany, Austria and so on, including of course, physicians who wanted to practice in the United States. The number of physicians trained abroad who were admitted to practice in the United States in the five years after 1933 was the same as in the five years before. This was clearly not the result of the natural course of events. The threat of these additional physicians led to a stringent tightening of requirements for foreign physicians that imposed extreme costs upon them.

SUGGESTIONS FOR WRITING

1. Friedman says that the *announced* motive of licensure is always a concern for "quality," but that the *real* motive is always a desire to attain monopolistic economic power. Write an essay that analyzes his argument and his examples.

2. At the end of his essay, Friedman uses the example of immigrating physicians during the Great Depression of the 1930s. Write an essay describing how the facts he mentions in this regard do or do not support his arguments against licensure.

3. Friedman often uses wit and ridicule as argumentative techniques. Write an essay in which you explain and illustrate the rational arguments that underlie Friedman's humorous examples.

INTERDISCIPLINARY CONNECTIONS

1. Marx wrote "The Communist Manifesto" in 1848, well before the publication of Darwin's *On the Origin of Species* in 1859, yet Marx read Darwin's book. Based on your understanding of the two writers' views, how do you think Marx would have responded to Darwin? Write an essay that defines and explains your position.

2. Human rights and their relations with governmental power often make implicit subtexts of economic discussions. Adam Smith and Milton Friedman seem in many ways opposed to any interference with market forces, while Karl Marx and John Maynard Keynes seem to assume the need for powerful means to control market forces. Write an essay in

which you compare and contrast these writers in terms of the relations of economic power to human rights.

3. All the authors in this chapter display great powers as writers. Who do you see as the best writer? Write an essay explaining and defending your choice.

4. If we understand the word *utopian* to imply a striving for ideal human relations, which author in this section seems to you the most utopian? Which the least? Write an essay explaining and defending your choices.

5. In her discussion of the distinction between labor and work, Hannah Arendt does not explicitly discuss the issue of "women's work," as Thorstein Veblen and Charlotte Perkins Gilman do in their essays. How do you think Hannah Arendt would respond to the views of those authors? Write an essay explaining and defending your answer.

Human Rights
Liberty and Law

Queen Elizabeth I

Thomas Hobbes

Jean-Jacques Rousseau

Thomas Jefferson

Mary Wollstonecraft

Margaret Sanger

Mahatma Gandhi

George Orwell

Martin Luther King, Jr.

Malcolm X

Introduction

The political philosopher Hannah Arendt who addressed economic issues in Chapter 2 has remarked that human rights have been widely proclaimed to be natural rights, but that without proper governments artificially created with powers to secure those rights, no human liberty can survive, as the long history of high-sounding but short-lived paper constitutions witnesses. But what is the proper relation of a government to its people and their individual rights and liberties? The issues involved in answering this question have been addressed by disciplines ranging from anthropology to zoology and because those issues involve so many aspects of human life, the inquiry is interdisciplinary almost by definition as the political implications of many selections in other chapters of this book will show.

Naturally, only a small selection from the enormous range of response to the problem of government can be presented in the space available here. The selections in this chapter have been chosen for their variety and for their interrelations, and also for the fact that they represent some widely held views advanced by people who played important parts in history. The writing here is arranged historically, beginning with an example from the oldest and most widespread form of government— that of royal rule.

The first selection is a speech by Queen Elizabeth I to her troops on the occasion of their preparations to repel the expected invasion of England by the Spanish Armada in 1588. The Queen views her subjects as part of a family, and family values like mutual love, trust, and loyalty may be seen to lie at the heart of the relationship between ruler and ruled that she expresses. We know that Elizabeth was an enormously popular and respected queen, and the style and content of her speech go some way toward allowing us to understand that popularity and that respect.

Thomas Hobbes was born during the year of the Armada threat and became a great philosopher of government in the next century. In this excerpt from his famous book on government, *The Leviathan*, Hobbes seeks to explain how and why people come to be governed in the first place, whether under a queen with inherited powers or under a freely elected president. Hobbes' explanation is based on the idea of contract, and his idea of a social contract as the foundation of all relations between a government and its people became a key concept in thinking about the issue from his time onward.

One famous thinker who took up the idea of social contract in the century that followed Hobbes was Jean-Jacques Rousseau. His ideas modified those of Hobbes with what many claim were practical results that soon followed in the form of the American and French revolutions. The modifications included the idea that the people as a whole, rather than individual persons, made the true source of sovereignty. One implication of this distinction was that those natural human rights that have in part been surrendered to rulers may be reclaimed if the rulers fail to maintain their side of the social contract.

Rousseau's thinking may be seen in part to stand behind the reasoning of Thomas Jefferson in the next selection, the Declaration of Independence. Jefferson begins with the claim that governments are formed to secure natural human rights. He then alleges a long series of abuses of the American people by King George III as a justification for the formation by that people of a new government. It has been widely remarked that while Jefferson proclaimed liberty to be one of the natural human rights that his argument depended upon, he was himself an owner of slaves, even though he freed them subsequently in his will. The question remains for the reader: does this paradox invalidate his views or inevitably invite their expansion?

Slaves were not the only people excluded from political rights in the eighteenth century. A pioneering feminist of that era, Mary Woolstonecraft addresses the exclusion of women in "Pernicious Effects Which Arise from the Unnatural Distinctions Established in Society." Though Jefferson appealed to nature and nature's God for the justification of human rights, Wollstonecraft argues that there is no natural basis for the ways women's political identities are imagined and enforced. On the contrary, all such policies are unnatural and irrational.

Like many empires throughout history, the British Empire in the twentieth century excluded the people of its colonies from political rights enjoyed by British subjects of the crown. By far Britain's largest colony in area and population was British India which, until its independence, also included what is now Pakistan and Bangladesh. Mahatma Gandhi was a leader in the fight to make British India independent, but he made his eventually successful struggle in an entirely nonviolent way, a policy whose nature and virtues he explains in a selection from his voluminous writings.

Women gained political rights in twentieth century America, but are political rights necessarily coextensive with human rights? Margaret Sanger was a nurse who led the early fight for the right to birth control. She explains the horrifying and touching personal origin of her public struggle in "My Fight for Birth Control," a selection from her autobiography.

George Orwell was a leading British author and social critic whose famous novel 1984 imagined a future dystopia, a Britain in which all human rights and liberties had been eliminated by a homegrown totalitarian government. Orwell saw tendencies in his own time that, if left uncorrected, would inevitably lead to a realization of his imaginary world. One of the most fundamental of those tendencies was the abuse of language in political discussion, and he exemplifies and analyzes the problem in his much-reprinted essay, "Politics and the English Language."

The chapter closes with two writers from the civil rights era of the mid-twentieth century, both of whom were assassinated by opponents. In the struggle for civil rights Martin Luther King, Jr. supported a nonviolent approach like that of Mahatma Gandhi, and he defends the tactic in his historic essay, "Letter from Birmingham Jail." Malcolm X was a Black Muslim leader who held out the possibility of violent action if working within the political process should prove ineffective. He makes his case in his grimly titled essay, "The Ballot or the Bullet."

Address to the Troops at Tilbury 1588

QUEEN ELIZABETH I

With its control of the mines of America, Spain was the most powerful nation in Europe when it threatened the invasion and conquest of England in 1588 with the Invincible Armada. The actor/poet William Shakespeare was some 24 years of age and his queen was Elizabeth I, a daughter of Henry VIII. As her speech to the troops awaiting the invasion shows, she was a warrior queen, and the defeat of the Armada made England into a major European force and led to the beginnings of its colonial empire.

My loving people, we have been persuaded by some, that are careful of our safety, to take heed how we commit ourselves to armed multitudes, for fear of treachery; but I assure you, I do not desire to live to distrust my faithful and loving people. Let tyrants fear; I have always so behaved myself that, under God, I have placed my chiefest strength and safeguard in the loyal hearts and good will of my subjects. And therefore I am come amongst you at this time, not as for my recreation or sport, but being resolved, in the midst and heat of the battle, to live or die amongst you all; to lay down, for my God, and for my kingdom, and for my people, my honor and my blood, even the dust. I know I have but the body of a weak and feeble woman; but I have the heart of a king, and of a king of England, too; and think foul scorn that Parma or Spain, or any prince of Europe, should dare to invade the borders of my realms: to which, rather than any dishonor should grow by me, I myself will take up arms; I myself will be your general, judge, and rewarder of every one of your virtues in the field. I know already, by your forwardness, that you have deserved rewards and crowns; and we do assure you, on the word of a prince, they shall be duly paid you. In the mean my lieutenant general shall be in my stead, than whom never prince commanded a more noble and worthy subject; not doubting by your obedience to my general, by your concord in the camp, and by your valor in the field, we shall shortly have a famous victory over the enemies of my God, of my kingdom, and of my people.

SUGGESTIONS FOR WRITING

1. "Faithful," "loving," "loyal"—these are words that express highly personal relations, and all of them might well appear in a love poem. Write an essay that explains with examples some ways government is imagined by Queen Elizabeth I as a personal rather than an institutional matter.

2. *Heart* is a word used as a symbolic site of the tender emotions, but also for the symbolic site of courage. Write an essay that explains with examples how the queen's address to her troops expresses both senses of the word *heart*.

3. Like her subjects, Elizabeth's enemies are personalized in her address. Write an essay that explains with examples the particular kind of enemy and the particular kind of war that the queen seems to imagine.

The Cause of Government   1660

From *Leviathan*

THOMAS HOBBES

Thomas Hobbes was born in the year of the Armada and lived until 1679. As a young man he was astounded by his first encounter with Euclidean geometry whereby, starting with simple and apparently obvious axioms, conclusions far from simple and not at all obvious could be reached with irrefutable proofs by a long train of inexorable logic. As the following selection shows, Hobbes attempted to apply logic to the problems of politics. Here he attempts to explain and to justify the nature of government by means of the idea of a social contract.

So that in the nature of man, we find three principall causes of quarrell. First, Competition; Secondly, Diffidence; Thirdly, Glory.

The first, maketh men invade for Gain; the second, for Safety; and the third, for Reputation. The first use Violence, to make themselves Masters of other mens persons, wives, children, and cattell; the second, to defend them; the third, for trifles, as a word, a smile, a different opinion, and any other signe of undervalue, either direct in their Persons, or by reflexion in their Kindred, their Friends, their Nation, their Profession, or their Name.

Hereby it is manifest, that during the time men live without a common Power to keep them all in awe, they are in that condition which is called WARRE; and such a warre, as is of every man, against every man. For WARRE, consisteth not in Battell onely, or the act of fighting; but in a tract of time, wherein the Will to contend by Battell is sufficiently known: and therefore the notion of *Time*, is to be considered in the nature of WARRE; as it is in the nature of Weather. For as the nature of Foule weather, lyeth not in a showre or two of rain; but in an inclination thereto of many dayes together: So the nature of War, consisteth not in actuall fighting; but in the known disposition thereto, during all the time there is no assurance to the contrary. All other time is PEACE.

Whatsoever therefore is consequent to a time of Warre, where every man is Enemy to every man; the same is consequent to the time, wherein men live without other security, than what their own strength, and their own invention shall furnish them withall. In such condition, there is no place for Industry; because the fruit thereof is uncertain: and consequently no Culture of the Earth; no Navigation, nor use of the commodities that may be imported by Sea; no commodious Building; no Instruments of moving, and removing such things as require much force; no Knowledge of the face of the Earth; no account of Time; no Arts; no Letters; no Society; and which is worst of all, continuall feare, and danger of violent death; And the life of man, solitary, poore, nasty, brutish, and short.

5   It may seem strange to some man, that has not well weighed these things; that Nature should thus dissociate, and render men apt to invade, and destroy one another: and he may therefore, not trusting to this Inference, made from the Passions, desire perhaps to have the same confirmed by Experience. Let him therefore consider with himselfe, when taking a journey, he armes himselfe, and seeks to go well accompanied; when going to sleep, he locks his dores; when even in his house he locks his chests; and this when he knowes there bee Lawes, and publike Officers, armed, to revenge all injuries shall bee done him; what opinion he has of his fellow subjects, when he rides armed; of his fellow Citizens, when he locks his dores; and of his children, and servants, when he locks his chests. Does he not there as much accuse mankind by his actions, as

I do by my words? But neither of us accuse mans nature in it. The Desires, and other Passions of man, are in themselves no Sin. No more are the Actions, that proceed from those Passions, till they know a Law that forbids them: which till Lawes be made they cannot know: nor can any Law be made, till they have agreed upon the Person that shall make it.

It may peradventure be thought, there was never such a time, nor condition of warre as this; and I believe it was never generally so, over all the world: but there are many places, where they live so now. For the savage people in many places of *America*, except the government of small Families, the concord whereof dependeth on naturall lust, have no government at all; and live at this day in that brutish manner, as I said before. Howsoever, it may be perceived what manner of life there would be, where there were no common Power to feare; by the manner of life, which men that have formerly lived under a peacefull government, use to degenerate into, in a civill Warre.

But though there had never been any time, wherein particular men were in a condition of warre one against another; yet in all times, Kings, and Persons of Soveraigne authority, because of their Independency, are in continuall jealousies, and in the state and posture of Gladiators; having their weapons pointing, and their eyes fixed on one another; that is, their Forts, Garrisons, and Guns upon the Frontiers of their Kingdomes; and continuall Spyes upon their neighbours; which is a posture of War. But because they uphold thereby, the Industry of their Subjects; there does not follow from it, that misery, which accompanies the Liberty of particular men.

To this warre of every man against every man, this also is consequent; that nothing can be Unjust. The notions of Right and Wrong, Justice and Injustice have there no place. Where there is no common Power, there is no Law: where no Law, no Injustice. Force, and Fraud, are in warre the two Cardinall vertues. Justice, and Injustice are none of the Faculties neither of the Body, nor Mind. If they were, they might be in a man that were alone in the world, as well as his Senses, and Passions. They are Qualities, that relate to men in Society, not in Solitude. It is consequent also to the same condition, that there be no Propriety, no Dominion, no *Mine* and *Thine* distinct; but onely that to be every mans, that he can get; and for so long, as he can keep it. And thus much for the ill condition, which man by meer Nature is actually placed in; though with a possibility to come out of it, consisting partly in the Passions, partly in his Reason.

The Passions that encline men to Peace, are Feare of Death; Desire of such things as are necessary to commodious living; and a Hope by their

Industry to obtain them. And Reason suggesteth convenient Articles of Peace, upon which men may be drawn to agreement. These Articles, are they, which otherwise are called the Lawes of Nature: whereof I shall speak more particularly, in the two following Chapters.

Chapter XIV

Of the first and second NATURALL LAWES, and of CONTRACTS

10 THE RIGHT OF NATURE, which Writers commonly call *Jus Naturale*, is the Liberty each man hath, to use his own power, as he will himselfe, for the preservation of his own Nature; that is to say, of his own Life; and consequently, of doing any thing, which in his own Judgement, and Reason, hee shall conceive to be the aptest means thereunto.

By LIBERTY, is understood, according to the proper signification of the word, the absence of externall Impediments: which Impediments, may off take away part of a mans power to do what hee would; but cannot hinder him from using the power left him, according as his judgement, and reason shall dictate to him.

A LAW OF NATURE, (*Lex Naturalis*,) is a Precept, or generall Rule, found out by Reason, by which a man is forbidden to do, that, which is destructive of his life, or taketh away the means of preserving the same; and to omit, that, by which he thinketh it may be best preserved. For though they that speak of this subject, use to confound *Jus*, and *Lex*, *Right* and *Law*; yet they ought to be distinguished; because RIGHT, consisteth in liberty to do, or to forbeare; Whereas LAW, determineth, and bindeth to one of them: so that Law, and Right, differ as much, as Obligation, and Liberty; which in one and the same matter are inconsistent.

And because the condition of Man, (as hath been declared in the precedent Chapter) is a condition of Warre of every one against every one; in which case every one is governed by his own Reason; and there is nothing he can make use of, that may not be a help unto him, in preserving his life against his enemyes; It followeth, that in such a condition, every man has a Right to every thing; even to one anothers body. And therefore, as long as this naturall Right of every man to everything endureth, there can be no security to any man, (how strong or wise soever he be,) of living out the time, which Nature ordinarily alloweth men to live. And consequently it is a precept, or generall rule of Reason, *That every man, ought to endeavour Peace, as farre as he has hope of obtaining it; and when he cannot obtain it, that he may seek, and use, all helps, and advantages of Warre.* The first branch of which Rule, containeth the first, and Fundamentall Law of Nature; which is, *to seek Peace, and follow it.* The Second, the summe of the Right of Nature; which is, *By all means we can, to defend our selves.*

From this Fundamentall Law of Nature, by which men are commanded to endeavour Peace, is derived this second Law; *That a man be willing, when others are so too, as farre-forth, as for Peace, and defence of himself he shall think it necessary, to lay down this right to all things; and be contented with so much liberty against other men, as he would allow other men against himselfe.* For as long as every man holdeth this Right, of doing any thing he liketh; so long are all men in the condition of Warre. But if other men will not lay down their Right, as well as he; then there is no Reason for any one, to devest himselfe of his: For that were to expose himselfe to Prey, (which no man is bound to) rather than to dispose himselfe to Peace. This is that Law of the Gospell; *Whatsoever you require that others should do to you, that do ye to them.* And that Law of all men, *Quod tibi fieri non vis, alteri ne feceris.*

15   To *lay downe* a mans *Right* to any thing, is to *devest* himselfe of the *Liberty,* of hindring another of the benefit of his own Right to the same. For he that renounceth, or passeth away his Right, giveth not to any other man a Right which he had not before; because there is nothing to which every man had not Right by Nature: but onely standeth out of his way, that he may enjoy his own originall Right, without hindrance from him; not without hindrance from another. So that the effect which redoundeth to one man, by another mans defect of Right, is but so much diminution of impediments to the use of his own Right originall.

Right is layd aside, either by simply Renouncing it; or by Transferring it to another. By *Simply* RENOUNCING; when he cares not to whom the benefit thereof redoundeth. By TRANSFERRING; when he intendeth the benefit thereof to some certain person, or persons. And when a man hath in either manner abandoned, or granted away his Right; then is he said to be OBLIGED, or BOUND, not to hinder those, to whom such Right is granted, or abandoned, from the benefit of it: and that he *Ought,* and it is his DUTY, not to make voyd that voluntary act of his own: and that such hindrance is INJUSTICE, and INJURY, as being *Sine Jure*; the Right being before renounced, or transferred. So that *Injury*, or *Injustice*, in the controversies of the world, is somewhat like to that, which in the disputations of Scholers is called *Absurdity*. For as it is there called an Absurdity, to contradict what one maintained in the Beginning: so in the world, it is called Injustice, and Injury, voluntarily to undo that, which from the beginning he had voluntarily done. The way by which a man either simply Renounceth, or Transferreth his Right, is a Declaration, or Signification, by some voluntary and sufficient signe, or signes, that he doth so Renounce, or Transferre; or hath so Renounced, or Transferred the same, to him that accepteth it. And these Signes are either Words onely, or Actions onely; or (as it happeneth most often) both Words, and Actions. And the same are the BONDS, by which men are bound, and obliged: Bonds, that have their strength, not from their own Nature, (for nothing is more easily broken then a mans word,) but from Feare of some evill consequence upon the rupture.

Whensoever a man Transferreth his Right, or Renounceth it; it is either in consideration of some Right reciprocally transferred to himselfe; or for some other good he hopeth for thereby. For it is a voluntary act: and of the voluntary acts of every man, the object is some *Good to himselfe*. And therefore there be some Rights, which no man can be understood by any words, or other signes, to have abandoned, or transferred. As first a man cannot lay down the right of resisting them, that assault him by force, to take away his life; because he cannot be understood to ayme thereby, at any Good to himselfe. The same may be sayd of Wounds, and Chayns, and Imprisonment; both because there is no benefit consequent to such patience; as there is to the patience of suffering another to be wounded, or imprisoned: as also because a man cannot tell, when he seeth men proceed against him by violence, whether they intend his death or not. And lastly the motive, and end for which this renouncing, and transferring of Right is introduced, is nothing else but the security of a mans person, in his life, and in the means of so preserving life, as not to be weary of it. And therefore if a man by words, or other signes, seem to despoyle himselfe of the End, for which those signes were intended; he is not to be understood as if he meant it, or that it was his will; but that he was ignorant of how such words and actions were to be interpreted.

The mutuall transferring of Right, is that which men call CONTRACT.

SUGGESTIONS FOR WRITING

1. In contrast to the personalized nature of government implied by the language of Queen Elizabeth's address to her troops, Hobbes employs a language of impersonal logic that moves from admitted general truths to a deduction of their particular implications. In this way, he deduces an overwhelming need for government that led people to yield their natural rights in return for protection from the dangers that all people faced without government in a state of nature that he claims is really a war of all against all. Write an essay that explains in your own words the reasoning that leads Hobbes to his famous definition of life in a state of nature as "solitary, poor, nasty, brutish, and short."

2. Write an essay that explains in your own words the reasoning Hobbes uses to understand why people have been willing to surrender some of their natural rights to government.

3. Write an essay that explains in your own words the reasoning Hobbes employs to define government in terms of a legal contract.

The Origins of Civil Society   1762

From *Social Contract*

Translated from the French by Ronah Sadan

JEAN-JACQUES ROUSSEAU

Jean-Jacques Rousseau (1712–1778) was born in Switzerland and endured a troubled youth. Winning an important essay contest in Paris as a young man led to a celebrated literary career that set Europe on fire with controversy. In his political thinking represented in the following selection, he uses Hobbes's idea of a social contract, but argues against his ideas about sovereignty. Hobbes claimed that the individuals surrendered their powers to a king, but Rousseau claimed that both the king and the people were sovereign, so that any violation of the social contract on the part of the magistrate meant that the powers of government automatically reverted to the people as a whole.

Chapter I

Subject of this First Book

Man is born free, and is everywhere in chains. A man who believes himself the master of others is no less enslaved than they, if not more so. How does this change come about? I do not know. What can render it legitimate? I believe to be able to find an answer to this question.

Were I to consider nothing but force, and the effect derived from it, I should say: as long as a people is constrained to obey does obey, he does well; as soon as it can shake the yoke and succeeds in shaking it, it does even better. The fact that it recovered its liberty by the same right by which it was ravished, means either it is entitled to reclaim its liberty, or that one was not entitled to take it away in the first place. But the social order is a sacred right that serves as foundation for all the others. Nevertheless, this right does not come from nature but is founded upon conventions. The matter of our inquiry consists of discovering what these conventions are. Before proceeding, I must establish the truth of what I have so far put forth.

Chapter II

Of the First Societies

The oldest of all societies—and the only natural one—is that of the family. Children stay tied to their father only as long as they need him for their self-preservation. As soon as this need ceases the natural tie dissolves. Then, the children, exempt of the obedience they have owed to their father, and the father exempt of the debt of care he owed his children, all come into equal independence. If they remain tied to one another, they do so no longer by nature but by volition; and the family remains family only by reason of convention.

This shared liberty is a consequence of man's nature. Its first law is self-preservation, its first cares are those that it owes itself. As soon as a man reaches the age of reason, he, alone able to judge of what means will best assure his self-preservation, becomes his own master.

5   We may, if we will, consider the family as the first model of political associations: the ruler is, symbolically, the father, the people, symbolically his children, and all, both ruler and people, having been born equal and free, alienate their liberty only so far as it is to their advantage. The difference lies in that, whereas in the family the father's love for his children rewards him for the care he takes of them, in the State, the pleasure of commanding stands in for the love that the ruler lacks for his people.

Grotius denies that political power is ever used in the interests of the governed, and cites the institution of slavery as support for his stance. His constant method of reasoning is always to derive Right from Fact. One could employ a more logical method, but not one that would be more favorable to tyrants.

It is doubtful, then, according to Grotius, whether the concept "human race" belongs only to a few hundred men, or whether those few hundred men belong to the human race. He seems throughout his book to lean towards the first alternative, and Hobbes seems to agree with him. In that case, here we have humanity divided into herds of cattle, of which each has its keeper, who guards his herd so that he may finally devour it.

Just as the shepherd is of a nature superior to that of his sheep, so, too, the shepherds of men, or their rulers, are of a nature superior to that of their peoples. Thus reasoned, according to Philo, the emperor Caligula, and drew from this analogy the fine conclusion that either Kings are Gods, or that their subjects are beasts.

Caligula's reasoning harks back to that of Hobbes' and Grotius'. Even before them, Aristotle had maintained as well that men are not equal by nature, but that ones are born for slavery and others for domination.

10 Aristotle was right, but he mistakenly took the effect for the cause. Nothing is more certain than that all men born into a situation of enslavement are slaves by nature. Slaves in chains lose all they have—even the desire to be freed from them. They love their servitude, just as Ulysses' companions loved their own transformation into brutes. If there exist slaves by nature, the reason for it is that they had been made slaves *against* nature. Force has made the first slaves: cowardice has perpetuated their kind.

I have mentioned nothing of King Adam, or of Emperor Noah, the father of three great Monarchs who divided up the universe between them, as did the children of Saturn had done, whom some have been tempted to identify in them. I hope that I may be given credit for my moderation; for, being descended in a direct line from one of those princes, and possibly belonging of the elder branch, I may, for all I know, be the legitimate King of the Human Race. Be that as it may, none would disagree that Adam had been the sovereign of the world, as Robinson had been of his island, only as long as he was its only inhabitant, and that the great convenience of this kind of empire was its Monarch, seated firmly on his throne, had to fear neither rebellions, nor wars, nor conspirators.

Chapter III

Of the Right of the Strongest

Even the strongest man will never be strong enough to remain the master always, unless he transforms his Might into Right and Obedience into Duty. Hence we derive the Right of the Strongest, a right assumed ironically in appearance, and which has, in fact, become established in principle. But will anyone ever adequately explain this phrase? Strength is a physical power; I see not how any moral validity can result from its effects. To yield to another's use of force is an act of necessity, not of will; it is at best an act of prudence. In what sense could it be considered a duty?

Let us suppose for a moment this alleged Right of the Strongest exists. The conclusion that results from this is but inexplicable gabble. For to suppose that Might makes Right is to substitute an effect for its cause. The Mighty man who overpowers a formerly mightier one succeeds to his Right. So soon as we can disobey with impunity, we can disobey legitimately. And, since the Mightiest is always right, all that is left for us to do is become the mightiest. But how valid is a right that expires when the Might that supports it ceases to be mighty? If a man is constrained by Might to obey, he does not need to obey by Duty; and if he is no longer *forced* to obey, he is no longer obligated to do so. It follows, then, that the word "right" adds nothing to the concept of "might." It this context, it has no meaning.

Obey the Powers that be. If this means, Yield to Might, the precept is fine but redundant—I maintain that it will never be violated. All power comes from God, I avow it; but so do all ailments. Does this mean that we are never allowed to call for the doctor? If a bandit creeps up on me in the neck of the woods, I must perforce hand him my purse. But, if I manage to keep it from him, am I still obliged by duty to hand it over? The pistol he holds is also a form of Power.

15   Let us agree that Might does not make Right, and that no man is obliged to obey any but legitimate Powers. Hence I go back again to the question I first raised.

Chapter IV

Of Slavery

Since no man has natural authority over his peers, and since Might cannot produce any Right, Agreement remains the foundation for legitimate authority among men.

If a private citizen, says Grotius, can alienate his liberty and render himself another's slave, why should not a whole people do likewise and subject itself to the will of a king? The argument contains several ambiguous words that require explanation. Let us focus our attention solely on *alienate*. To alienate means to give or to sell. Now a man who becomes the slave of another does not give himself. He sells himself in return for at least mere subsistence. But a people—why should a whole people sell itself? Far be it from a king to furnish subjects with their subsistence, he reaps his own from them, and from a king to furnish subjects with their subsistence, he reaps his own from them, and from them alone. According to Rabelais, a King does not live on little. Does a subject, then, surrender his person on the condition that his livelihood would be taken away as well? It is hard to see what he has left to keep.

One could say in response that the despot secures his subjects' civil peace. So be it. But what do they gain if the wars that his ambition brings upon them, his insatiable greed, and the vexatious acts of his ministers afflict them than would the onset of dissentions among them? What do they gain, if Peace itself is a cause of wretchedness for them? One may live peacefully in a dungeon, but can one be happy in such peace? The Greeks penned in Cyclop's den lived peacefully while awaiting their turn to be devoured.

To say that a man gives himself for nothing is to advance an absurd and inconceivable statement. Such an act of self-abandonment is illegitimate, null, and void by the mere fact that he who commits it is not in his right mind. To say the same thing about a people is to maintain that this whole People is made up of fools. Folly does not produce Right.

20 Even if a man can alienate himself, he cannot alienate his children. They are born free, and their freedom belongs to them; no one but themselves has the right to dispose of. Before they attain the age of reason, their father can set down, on their behalf, certain conditions to facilitate their preservation and well-being. But he cannot curtail their liberty irrevocably and unconditionally, for such an action is contrary to the natural order and oversteps a father's rights. It follows that an arbitrary government can become legitimate only if each successive generation of its people has the power to either accept or reject it; but then such a government would no longer be arbitrary.

In renouncing his liberty, a man renounces the essence of his manhood, and the rights and duties of humanity. There is no possible compensation for such a total renunciation. It is incompatible with man's nature; and to deprive him of his free will is to deprive him of any moral agency. In a word, an agreement that sets up on the one hand absolute authority, and on the other hand total obedience is vain and self-contradictory. Is it not obvious that a man owes nothing to another of whom he has the right to demand everything; and that where there is no mutuality, nor any exchange of obligations, the actions demanded by one man of another have no moral value? What right could my slave have against me, when all that he has belongs to me? His right being my right, it makes no sense to suggest that I could have a right against myself.

Grotius, and the others who concur with him, considers war another genuine source of the so-called "right" of slavery. Since the victor has, according to them, the right to kill the vanquished, the former may redeem his life at the expense of his liberty, and that this agreement is the more legitimate in that it benefits both parties.

But it is clear that the right to kill the vanquished does not in any manner originate in the state of war, if only because men, living in their primitive independence, do not have contact stable enough between them to constitute either a state of peace or of war. They are not naturally enemies. It is the contact between things, not between men, that constitutes war, and since war cannot originate in simple personal relations, but only in relations between things, private man-to-man conflict cannot occur either in the state of nature, where there is no established system of private property, or in the state of society, where law holds authority over all.

Single combats, duels, and personal encounters are occurrences that do not constitute a state of anything. As for the private wars authorized by the Ordinances of King Louis IX, and suspended by the Peace of God, they were merely abuses of Feudalism, an absurd system of government if there ever was one, so contrary was it to the principles of Natural Right and to all good polity.

War then, does not occur between man and man, but between State and State. The individuals caught up in it are enemies merely accidentally. They fight neither as men nor even as citizens, but as soldiers: not at all as members of a nation, but as its defenders. A State can have as enemies only other States and not men, considering that it is impossible for things of diverse natures to have a real relation.

This principle is in keeping with maxims established in all periods of history, and with the constant practice of all civilized societies. Declarations of war are warnings not so much to the Powers that be as to their subjects. The foreigner—be it a king, a private person, or a whole people—who steals, kills or detains subjects of a country without declaring war on its Prince, is not an enemy but a brigand. Even in the midst of war, the just Prince takes possession of the public property on enemy territory, yet respects the persons and property of individuals, and in so doing upholds the rights upon which his own laws are based. The object of war being the destruction of the enemy State, a commander the right to kill its defenders

25

so long as they have weapons in their hands: but as soon as they have laid them down and give themselves up—and in so doing cease to be enemies or instruments of the enemy—they become simply men again, and no one has rightful claim over their lives any longer. On some occasions, one may kill the State without killing a single one of its members. Now war does not give any right necessary to its ends. These principles are not those of Grotius; they are not founded on the authority of poets, but they spring from the nature of things, and are founded on reason.

As to the Right of Conquest, it has no foundation other than the Law of the Mightiest. If war does not give to the victor the right to massacre his vanquished enemies, he cannot base the claim to subjugating them upon a nonexistent one. We have the right to kill our enemy only when we cannot enslave them; the right to enslave is not rooted, then, in the right to kill. To make an enemy buy his life, over which no one has any right, at the price of his liberty, is to impose upon him an iniquitous exchange. Is it not obvious that in establishing the right of life and death upon the right of slavery, and the right of slavery on the right of life and death, we get caught in a vicious circle?

Even in assuming the existence of the terrible right to kill *everything*, I still contend that a man enslaved, or a whole people conquered, in war is not under any obligation to his master, and should obey him only so much as he is forced to. By sparing his life in return for an equivalent, the victor does not show the vanquished man any mercy: instead of destroying him fruitlessly, he destroys him usefully. Far be it that in subjugating him by force, he acquires over him any genuine authority. The state of war continues between the two of them as before, and its effect is their very relationship. The enjoyment of the Right of War does not presuppose any Peace Treaty. The victor and the vanquished have established an accord of sorts: so be it, but far from ending the state of war, this accord implies its very continuance.

In whatever sense one considers the matter, the Right of Slavery is null and void not only because it is illegitimate, but also because the very term is absurd and meaningless. The words *Slavery* and *Right* are contradictory and mutually exclusive. Be it regarding the relationship of one man to another, or that of one man to a whole people, it will always be senseless to say, "You and I have made a compact all to your loss and all to my benefit, a compact which you and I shall both observe so long as it will please me."

Chapter V

That We Must Always Go Back to a First Compact

30 Even if I were to concede all that I have refuted until now, the stalwarts of despotism would not have been any further advanced in their position. There will always be a vast difference between subduing a multitude of men and governing a society. Whatever number of isolated individuals may submit themselves in succession to a single man, I can only regard their relationship as that of a master and his slaves, never that of a people and its ruler. The group of men so gathered may be called an agglomeration; it is not an association. It involves neither public welfare nor a body politic. Its master—even were he to subjugate half the world—is still merely an individual; his interests, separated from the interests of the others he controls, remain private to himself. When this man perishes, his empire is left scattered and disintegrated, like an oak that crumbles and falls in a heap of ashes after a fire has consumed it.

"A people," claims Grotius, "may give itself to a King." According to him, then, a People is already a People before it submits itself. The very act of a gift is that of a civil society and presupposed public deliberation. It is therefore appropriate, before examining the act by which a people elects a King, to examine that by which it becomes a People. For it necessarily precedes the act of gift, and is the real foundation of society.

Indeed, if this preceding compact has not been made, why, unless the election were unanimous, should the minority be bound to submit itself to the choice of the majority? What would give the hundred who want a master the right to vote for ten who do not? The rule instituting franchise constitutes, in itself, a compact, and implies that unanimity amongst the members of a society was reached at least one original time.

Chapter VI

Of the Social Contract

I assume, for argument's sake, that human kind had arrived at a certain point in its history when the obstacles to the preservation of the State of Nature prevailed over the forces that each individual could wield in order to maintain himself in it. Its original State of Nature could no longer last, and the human race would have perished had it not changed his manner of existence.

Now, as men cannot engender new powers, but only unite and direct those which they already possess, they have no means for preserving themselves except that of pooling together the sum of all their individual powers, such that together they will be able to prevail against any outside resistance they come upon. They must create some sort of central mobilizing body and learn to act in concert.

35   This concentration of powers could only be born from an accord between individual men; but, since the strength and liberty of each man are his primary instruments of self-preservation, how could he engage them in an accord with others without causing himself harm and without neglecting the cares which he owes himself? This difficulty, as it harks back to my subject, can be pronounced in these terms:

"Some form of association must be found that can mobilize the combined strength of its community to protect the person and property of each associated member, so that each, when united to his peers, nonetheless obeys only his own will and stays as free as he had been previously." Such is the fundamental problem to which the Social Contract provides the solution.

The clauses of this Contract are determined by the nature of the Act of Association in such a way that the least modification must render them vain and null and void. Even though they have, perhaps, never been formally enunciated, they must be everywhere the same and everywhere tacitly admitted and recognized. This condition must hold so totally, that should the social compact be violated, each individual would revert to his original rights and regain his natural liberty, by the fact of having lost the agreed upon liberty for which he had renounced it.

These clauses, when well understood, may all be reduced to a single one, namely, that each associate totally alienate all his original rights to the community. For, in the first place, since each individual gives himself over entirely, conditions are equal for all: and, because they are equal for all, it is in nobody's interest to render them onerous to his peers.

Moreover, this alienation having been made without reservation, the union of individuals is as perfect as it could be, no associated member having anything further to claim. For should there be any rights left to individuals, and no common authority were established to pronounce in cases between them and the public, each, being in some matters his own judge, would soon presume to be so in all. Then, the State of Nature would persist, and the association would necessarily become either tyrannical or vain.

40   In short, in giving himself to all, each individual gives himself to none. And since there exists not one member of the association over

whom we do not acquire the same rights as those what we ceded over ourselves to him, we gain the equivalent of all that we lose, as well as some more power to conserve what we already have.

If, then, we separate from the Social Contract everything that is not essential to it, we shall find it reduced to the following terms: *each one of us gives to the community his person and all his power under the supreme direction of the general will; and we receive into the body of the community each member as an indivisible part of the the whole.*

The act of association immediately replaces the person of each of its contracting parties with a collective moral body composed of as many members as the constituting assembly has votes, which body receives from this very act of association its unity, its common "me," its life and its will. The person of the public that thus forms itself by the union of all individual persons was known in former times as a *City*, and today as a *republic* or a *body politic*; that which is known by its members as *The State* when taking a passive role, as *The Sovereign People* when taking an active role, and a *Power* when it stands in comparison to similar bodies. As to its associate members, they take the collective name of *The People* and refer to themselves on an individual basis as *Citizens*, insofar as they participate in wielding sovereign authority, and *Subjects* insofar as they owe obedience to the laws of the state. But these terms often get considered as having one and the same meaning and taken one for the other. Suffice it for us to know how to distinguish between them when they are employed in a precise sense.

Chapter VII

Of the Sovereign

We may see by the above formula that the act of association involves a reciprocal commitment between the body politic and its associate members. Each individual contracts, so to speak, with himself and is bound in a relationship of a dual nature. As a member of the sovereign people, he owes his duty to each individual member of it, and as a Citizen, he owes his duty to the Sovereign People as a whole. But we cannot here apply the maxim of Civil Law that says that no man can be beholden to himself, for there is very well a difference between being under obligation to oneself and to a whole of which he is a part.

It is necessary to remark here that a public resolution that places all subjects under obligation to the sovereign, cannot, by reason of two different relations according to which each of them functions, on the contrary, make the sovereign beholden to himself. Consequently, it is against the nature of a body politic that the sovereign should impose upon himself a law that he cannot infringe. For, since he can only consider himself under a single relation, he is then in the position of an individual contracting with himself. Whence its is evident that there is not, nor can there be, any kind of fundamental law which is obligatory for the whole body of the People, not even the Social Contract itself. This does not mean that the body politic cannot very well enter into an engagement with another body politic, provided that this engagement does not derogate from the nature of the Contract; for, when considered in relation to a foreign power, the body politic becomes a simple individual.

45 But the body politic or the Sovereign deriving its existence only from the sanctity of the Contract can never commit itself, even in its relations with a foreign power, to anything that derogates from the original act. It may not, for instance, alienate some portion of itself or submit itself to the rule of another sovereign. To violate the act by virtue of which it exists would be to annihilate itself, and that which is nothing can produce nothing.

As soon as a multitude of men becomes united into one body politic, it is impossible to commit an offense against one of its members without attacking the whole body. It is even less possible to commit an offense against the body without each of its members' feeling its effects. Thus both duty and interest oblige the two contracting parties to mutually assist each other on an equal basis. The same men should seek to unite under the dual relation all the advantages that accrue from it.

Now, since the Sovereign has no existence outside that of the individuals who compose it, it has not, nor can it have, any interest contrary to theirs. Consequently, the sovereign power has no need to give guarantee to its subjects, because it is impossible that the body should wish to harm all its members; nor, as we shall see hereinafter, can it harm any one in particular. The sovereign, by merely *being*, is always all it *ought to be*.

But the case is not the same for the relation of subjects to sovereign. In spite of their sharing a common interest, there can be no guarantee the subjects will fulfill their engagements to the sovereign, unless the latter finds a way to ensure their fidelity.

Indeed, every individual may, as a man, have a particular will contrary or dissimilar to the general will in which he partakes as a citizen. His individual interest may set him upon an end completely other than that dictated by the interest of all. His absolute and naturally independent existence may lead him to consider what he owes to the common cause as a contribution made freely; and he may decide that by withholding it, he would do less harm to others than he would to himself by paying it. Regarding the moral being constituting the State as a rational abstraction because it is not a man, he might enjoy the rights of a citizen without having to fulfill his duties as a subject, thus committing an injustice the spread of which could bring ruin upon the body politic.

50   In order, then, that the social compact be not a merely vain formula, it must include, though tacitly, the only undertaking that can give force to the whole, namely, that whoever shall refuse to obey the general will must be constrained to do so by the whole body politic. This means nothing other than that it may be necessary to force an individual to be free—freedom being that condition which, in giving every citizen to his country, guarantees him from all personal dependence; that creates the artifice and game of the political machine; and that alone renders legitimate civil engagements, which without it would be absurd, tyrannical, and subject to enormous abuses.

Chapter VIII

Of Civil State

The passage from the state of nature to the state of civil society produces in man a very remarkable change. In his conduct, it substitutes justice for instinct, and thus gives his actions the moral value that they previously lacked. It is only when that the voice of duty takes the place of physical impulse and when Right takes the place of Appetite that man, who until then took only himself into consideration, can realize that he must act upon other principles, and consult his reason before responding to his base cravings. Although in this state he finds himself deprived of several advantages that he held in the state of nature, he will realize that he has gained some other great ones. His faculties will exert and develop themselves, his ideas will reach a greater scope, his sentiments will become ennobled, and his entire soul will elevate itself to such a point that, even should occasional abuses of this new condition degrade him below that from which he has emerged, he would ceaselessly bless the fortunate moment in which he was plucked out from it for good, and that turned him from a stupid and limited animal to an intelligent being and a man.

Let us reduce all this to terms easy to compare. What a man loses by the Social Contract is natural liberty and the unlimited right to all that tempts him, provided that he can procure it. What he gains is civil liberty and the ownership of all that he possesses. To prevent ourselves from erring in considering these compensations, we must clearly distinguish between natural liberty, which is limited only by the individual's strength, and between civil liberty, which is limited by the general will; between possessions that are derived from of physical strength and or the right of the first occupier, and ownership that can be founded only upon a positive title.

To the advantages attached to the civil state, one might add that of Moral Freedom, which alone renders man truly his own master. For to let one's actions be determined by one's appetite alone is to be a slave, whereas to obey the laws that one prescribes oneself is liberty. But I have already said much on this point, and the philosophical meaning of the word *liberty* is not my subject here.

Chapter IX

Of Real Property

Each member of the Community gives himself to it the moment that it forms. He gives himself as the whole man as he is then, together with all his strengths, and everything he possesses. Not that, by this act of giving, the possessions, in changing hands and becoming property of the Sovereign, change their nature. But as the strength of the City are incomparably greater than that of the individual, public ownership is also, in fact, stronger and more irrevocable. It is not, so far as it concerns foreigners, more legitimate. For within it, the State is master of all its individual members' possessions by reason of the Social Contract, which serves as basis to all rights; but in relation to other powers, it is master of its possessions only by virtue of the rights of first occupier, which it derives from the individuals who compose it.

55   The "right of first occupier," although more real that the "right of the mightiest," becomes a genuine right only after the establishment of the right of property. Every man has a natural right to all that is necessary for his existence. But the positive act that renders him proprietor of a certain item excludes him from ownership of all others. His portion having been decided, he must limit himself to it, and has no longer any right to communal proprietorship. For this reason, the right of the first occupier, as weak as it is in the state of nature, is assured to every man as citizen. In enjoying this right, he withholds his claim, less over what belongs to others than over what does not belong specifically to him.

In general terms, to authorize the right of first occupier over any territory, the following conditions are necessary. First, the terrain must not be already inhabited by anyone. Second, a man must only occupy the amount of it that he needs for subsistence. Third, a man must take possession not by mere empty ceremony, but by work and cultivation, the sole signs of property that, in the absence of a legal title, will be respected by others.

Indeed, by granting the right of first occupier by virtue of necessity and labor, do we not extend it as far as it could go? Should no limits be set to this right? Is it enough that a man place his foot on terrain belonging to a community to pretend to be its master? Does it suffice to have the momentary force to push other men away from it to forever undo any right they had to return there? How can a single man or a people take over an immense territory and deprive all the rest of human kind of it, in a way other than punishable usurpation, since this act involves taking from all other men the shelter and livelihood that nature provides for their common use? When Núñez Balboa stepped on a shoreline and claimed possession of the Southern Sea and all of South America in the name of the crown of Castille, was he thereby justified in dispossessing all its former inhabitants and in excluding from it all the Princes of the world? By that standard, vain ceremonies will abound, until His Catholic Majesty would simply claim ownership of the entire universe from his cabinet, excepting from his empire only those portions of it which have already come to the possession of other Princes.

It is conceivable how the contiguous but separate lands of individuals may be gathered together to become public territory, and how the right of sovereignty, extending itself from the subjects to the terrain that they occupy, may become at once real and personal; which puts the possessors in a state of greater dependence, and turns their very forces into a guarantee of their fidelity. This is an advantage that does not appear to have been felt by monarchs of old, who, claiming to be merely kings of the Persians, the Scythians, the Macedonians, seemed to regard themselves as the rulers of men more so than the masters of countries. Today's monarchs refer to themselves more often as kings of France, of Spain, of England etc. In thus controlling territories, they are well assured of controlling their inhabitants.

The strange thing about this act of alienation, is that, far from despoiling individuals of their goods, in accepting their surrender, the community guarantees their legitimate possession of them, thus transforming usurpation into a veritable right and the enjoyment of goods into proprietorship over them. Then the proprietors are considered as depositories of the public good, and their rights are respected by all members of the State, which wields all its forces for their protection from the usurpation of foreign powers. By ceding their property to the State—a cession advantageous to the public and even more to themselves—they have, so to speak, acquired all that they have given. This paradox is easily explained by distinguishing between rights that the Sovereign and the Proprietor have over the same piece of property, as we shall see later.

60   It may also happen that men unite into a group before possessing anything, and that after taking over a territory sufficient for them all, they benefit from it as a community or divide it between themselves either equally or according to a scale established by the sovereign. In whatever manner that this territorial acquisition is made, the claim that each individual has over his own piece of property is always subordinate to the claim that the community as a whole has over the territory in its entirety. Without this condition, there would be no strength in the social fabric, nor any real power in the exercise of sovereignty.

I will conclude this chapter and this book with a remark that should serve as the basis to every social system: that, instead of destroying natural equality, the original compact substitutes it with a moral and legitimate equality that compensates for the physical inequalities that nature may have established in mankind. Even if they are unequal in strength or in genius, they all become equal by law as a result of the agreement into which they entered.

SUGGESTIONS FOR WRITING

1. Rousseau writes "the ruler is not in a relation of love to his people" and seems to assume a very different basis for rule from that assumed by Queen Elizabeth. On the basis of your reading of this selection from Rousseau, what seems to be the relation he does imagine between ruler and people? Write an essay that explains and supports your view through the analysis of evidence from the text.

2. Rousseau claims to trace the origins of government back to the collective relations within a family and thereby differs from Hobbes, who focuses on the interactions of individuals. How else do Rousseau's views on the bases of government differ from those of Hobbes? In what way are their views alike? Write an essay that compares and contrasts the views of Hobbes and Rousseau on the bases of government.

3. Rousseau bases many of his ideas about "rights" on his views of "the people." Write an essay in which you describe the implicit and explicit qualities and characteristics that define "the people" for Jean-Jacques Rousseau.

The Declaration of Independence

In Congress, July 4, 1776

THOMAS JEFFERSON

Thomas Jefferson (1743–1826) was given the task of composing the Declaration of Independence in 1776 under the close supervision of other founding fathers, including Benjamin Franklin and John Adams. As you will see, the reasoning in the document clearly shows the influence of earlier ideas concerning social contract, particularly those of Rousseau. After the revolution, Jefferson served as the first American secretary of state and later as vice president under John Adams, becoming president himself for two terms during which he added the immense territory of the Louisiana Purchase to the growing nation.

The Unanimous Declaration of the Thirteen United States of America

When in the Course of human events, it becomes necessary for one people to dissolve the political bands which have connected them with another, and to assume among the Powers of the earth, the separate and equal station to which the Laws of Nature and of Nature's God entitle them, a decent respect to the opinions of mankind requires that they should declare the causes which impel them to the separation.

We hold these truths to be self-evident, that all men are created equal, that they are endowed by their Creator with certain inalienable Rights, that among these are Life, Liberty and the pursuit of Happiness. That to secure these rights, Governments are instituted among Men, deriving their just powers from the consent of the governed. That whenever any Form of Government becomes destructive of these ends, it is the Right of the People to alter or to abolish it, and to institute new Government, laying its foundation on such principles and organizing its powers in such form, as to them shall seem most likely to effect their Safety and Happiness. Prudence, indeed, will dictate that Governments long established should not be changed for light and transient causes; and accordingly all experience hath shown, that mankind are more disposed to suffer, while evils are sufferable, than to right themselves by abolishing the forms to which they are accustomed. But when a long train of abuses and usurpations, pursuing invariably the same Object evinces a design to reduce them under absolute Despotism, it is their right, it is their duty, to throw off such Government, and to provide new Guards for their future security.— Such has been the patient sufferance of these Colonies; and such is now the necessity which constrains them to alter their former Systems of Government. The history of the present King of Great Britain is a history of repeated injuries and usurpations, all having in direct object the establishment of an absolute Tyranny over these States. To prove this, let Facts be submitted to a candid world.

He has refused his Assent to Laws, the most wholesome and necessary for the public good.

He has forbidden his Governors to pass Laws of immediate and pressing importance, unless suspended in their operation till his Assent should be obtained; and when so suspended, he has utterly neglected to attend to them.

5   He has refused to pass other laws for the accommodation of large districts of people, unless those people would relinquish the right of Representation in the Legislature, a right inestimable to them and formidable to tyrants only.

He has called together legislative bodies at places unusual, uncomfortable, and distant from the depository of their Public Records, for the sole purpose of fatiguing them into compliance with his measures.

He has dissolved Representative Houses repeatedly, for opposing with manly firmness his invasions on the rights of the people.

He has refused for a long time, after such dissolutions, to cause others to be elected; whereby the Legislative Powers, incapable of Annihilation, have returned to the People at large for their exercise; the State remaining in the mean time exposed to all the dangers of invasion from without, and convulsions within.

He has endeavoured to prevent the population of these States; for that purpose obstructing the Laws for Naturalization of Foreigners; refusing to pass others to encourage their migration hither, and raising the conditions of new Appropriations of Lands.

10   He has obstructed the Administration of Justice, by refusing his Assent to Laws for establishing Judiciary Powers.

He has made Judges dependent on his Will alone, for the tenure of their offices, and the amount and payment of their salaries.

He has erected a multitude of New Offices, and sent hither swarms of Officers to harass our People, and eat out their substance.

He has kept among us, in times of peace, Standing Armies without the Consent of our legislature.

He has affected to render the Military independent of and superior to the Civil Power.

15 He has combined with others to subject us to a jurisdiction foreign to our constitution, and unacknowledged by our laws; giving his Assent to their acts of pretended Legislation:

For quartering large bodies of armed troops among us:

For protecting them, by a mock Trial, from Punishment for any Murders which they should commit on the Inhabitants of these States:

For cutting off our Trade with all parts of the world:

For imposing taxes on us without our Consent:

20 For depriving us in many cases, of the benefits of Trial by Jury:

For transporting us beyond Seas to be tried for pretended offences:

For abolishing the free System of English Laws in a neighbouring Province, establishing therein an Arbitrary government, and enlarging its Boundaries so as to render it at once an example and fit instrument for introducing the same absolute rule into these Colonies:

For taking away our Charters, abolishing our most valuable Laws, and altering fundamentally the Forms of our Governments:

For suspending our own Legislatures, and declaring themselves invested with Power to legislate for us in all cases whatsoever.

25 He has abdicated Government here, by declaring us out of his Protection and waging War against us.

He has plundered our seas, ravaged our Coasts, burnt our towns, and destroyed the lives of our people.

He is at this time transporting large armies of foreign mercenaries to compleat the works of death, desolation and tyranny, already begun with circumstances of Cruelty & perfidy scarcely paralleled in the most barbarous ages, and totally unworthy the Head of a civilized nation.

He has constrained our fellow Citizens taken Captive on the high Seas to bear Arms against their Country, to become the executioners of their friends and Brethren, or to fall themselves by their Hands.

He has excited domestic insurrections amongst us, and has endeavoured to bring on the inhabitants of our frontiers, the merciless Indian

Savages, whose known rule of warfare, is an undistinguished destruction of all ages, sexes and conditions.

30   In every stage of these Oppressions We have Petitioned for Redress in the most humble terms: Our repeated Petitions have been answered only by repeated injury. A Prince, whose character is thus marked by every act which may define a Tyrant, is unfit to be the ruler of a free People.

Nor have We been wanting in attention to our British brethren. We have warned them from time to time of attempts by their legislature to extend an unwarrantable jurisdiction over us. We have reminded them of the circumstances of our emigration and settlement here. We have appealed to their native justice and magnanimity, and we have conjured them by the ties of our common kindred to disavow these usurpations, which, would inevitably interrupt our connections and correspondence. They too have been deaf to the voice of justice and of consanguinity. We must, therefore, acquiesce in the necessity, which denounces our Separation, and hold them, as we hold the rest of mankind, Enemies in War, in Peace Friends.

We, therefore, the Representatives of the United States of America, in General Congress, Assembled, appealing to the Supreme Judge of the world for the rectitude of our intentions, do, in the Name, and by Authority of the good People of these Colonies, solemnly publish and declare, That these United Colonies are, and of Right ought to be Free and Independent States, that they are Absolved from all Allegiance to the British Crown, and that all political connection between them and the State of Great Britain, is and ought to be totally dissolved; and that as Free and Independent States, they have full Power to levy War, conclude Peace, contract Alliances, establish Commerce, and to do all other Acts and Things which Independent States may of right do. And for the support of this Declaration, with a firm reliance on the Protection of Divine Providence, we mutually pledge to each other our Lives, our Fortunes and our sacred Honor.

SUGGESTIONS FOR WRITING

1. For the most part, the Declaration personalizes the complaints of the colonies and blames King George III himself before going on to complain about "our British brethren." Write an essay that compares and contrasts the assumptions about personal sovereignty in Queen Elizabeth's address with those of Thomas Jefferson about two hundred years later in the Declaration of Independence.

2. In paragraph 2 Jefferson says of a people under the conditions he names that "it is their right, it is their duty to throw off such Government, and to provide new Guards for their future security." In this focus on security, he seems to resemble Hobbes to some degree. Write an essay in which you examine the entire Declaration of Independence in the light of Hobbes's ideas about the nature of social contract.

3. In his paragraph 37, Rousseau says that "the clauses in this Contract are determined by the nature of the Act of Association in such a way that the least modification must render them null and void." Write an essay in which you examine the Declaration of Independence in light of Rousseau's ideas about the nature of social contract.

Pernicious Effects Which Arise from the Unnatural Distinctions Established in Society 1792

MARY WOLLSTONECRAFT

From an early age Mary Wollstonecraft (1759–1797) was forced to support herself as a governess and a teacher, and later as a writer. She and her advanced views on political and social issues and became known to many leading intellectuals of the later eighteenth century, including Samuel Johnson (Chapter 4) and William Godwin, whom she later married. Mary Wollstonecraft died after giving birth to their daughter who later became Mary Shelley, author of Frankenstein *(Chapter 5).*

As the following selection shows, Wollstonecraft sees women's rights in political terms and it was her goal to bring to the British social order the goals of the French Revolution—liberty, equality, and fraternity.

From the respect paid to property flow, as from a poisoned fountain, most of the evils and vices which render this world such a dreary scene to the contemplative mind. For it is in the most polished society that noisome reptiles and venomous serpents lurk under the rank herbage; and there is voluptuousness pampered by the still sultry air, which relaxes every good disposition before it ripens into virtue.

One class presses on another; for all are aiming to procure respect on account of their property: and property, once gained, will procure the respect due only to talents and virtue. Men neglect the duties incumbent on man, yet are treated like demi-gods; religion is also separated from morality by a ceremonial veil, yet men wonder that the world is almost, literally speaking, a den of sharpers or oppressors.

There is a homely proverb, which speaks a shrewd truth, that whoever the devil finds idle he will employ. And what but habitual idleness can hereditary wealth and titles produce? For man is so constituted that he can only attain a proper use of his faculties by exercising them, and will not exercise them unless necessity of some kind first set the wheels in motion. Virtue likewise can only be acquired by the discharge of relative duties; but the importance of these sacred duties will scarcely be felt by the being who is cajoled out of his humanity by the flattery of sycophants. There must be more equality established in society, or morality will never gain ground, and this virtuous equality will not rest firmly even when founded on a rock, if one half of mankind be chained to its bottom by fate, for they will be continually undermining it through ignorance or pride.

It is vain to expect virtue from women till they are in some degree independent of men; nay, it is vain to expect that strength of natural affection which would make them good wives and mothers. Whilst they are absolutely dependent on their husbands they will be cunning, mean, and selfish, and the men who can be gratified by the fawning fondness of spaniel-like affection have not much delicacy, for love is not to be bought, in any sense of the words; its silken wings are instantly shrivelled up when anything beside a return in kind is sought. Yet whilst wealth enervates men, and women live, as it were, by their personal charms, how can we expect them to discharge those ennobling duties which equally require exertion and self-denial? Hereditary property sophisticates the mind, and the unfortunate victims to it, if I may so express myself, swathed from their birth, seldom exert the locomotive faculty of body or mind; and, thus viewing everything through one medium, and that a false one, they are unable to discern in what true merit and happiness consist. False, indeed, must be the light when the drapery of situation hides the man, and makes him stalk in masquerade, dragging from one scene of dissipation to another the nerveless limbs that hang with stupid listlessness, and rolling round the vacant eye which plainly tells us that there is no mind at home.

5   I mean, therefore, to infer that the society is not properly organized which does not compel men and women to discharge their respective duties, by making it the only way to acquire that countenance from their fellow-creatures which every human being wishes some way to

attain. The respect, consequently, which is paid to wealth and mere personal charms, is a true north-east blast that blights the tender blossoms of affection and virtue. Nature has wisely attached affections to duties to sweeten toil, and to give that vigour to the exertions of reason which only the heart can give. But the affection which is put on merely because it is the appropriated insignia of a certain character, when its duties are not fulfilled, is one of the empty compliments which vice and folly are obliged to pay to virtue and the real nature of things.

To illustrate my opinion, I need only observe that when a woman is admired for her beauty, and suffers herself to be so far intoxicated by the admiration she receives as to neglect to discharge the indispensable duty of a mother, she sins against herself by neglecting to cultivate an affection that would equally tend to make her useful and happy. True happiness, I mean all the contentment and virtuous satisfaction that can be snatched in this imperfect state, must arise from well regulated affections; and an affection includes a duty. Men are not aware of the misery they cause and the vicious weakness they cherish by only inciting women to render themselves pleasing; they do not consider that they thus make natural and artificial duties clash by sacrificing the comfort and respectability of a woman's life to voluptuous notions of beauty when in nature they all harmonize.

Cold would be the heart of a husband, were he not rendered unnatural by early debauchery, who did not feel more delight at seeing his child suckled by its mother, than the most artful wanton tricks could ever raise; yet this natural way of cementing the matrimonial tie and twisting esteem with fonder recollections, wealth leads women to spurn. To preserve their beauty and wear the flowery crown of the day, which gives them a kind of right to reign for a short time over the sex, they neglect to stamp impressions on their husbands' hearts that would be remembered with more tenderness when the snow on the head began to chill the bosom than even their virgin charms. The maternal solicitude of a reasonable affectionate woman is very interesting, and the chastened dignity with which a mother returns the caresses that she and her child receive from a father who has been fulfilling the serious duties of his station, is not only a respectable but a beautiful sight. So singular indeed are my feelings, and I have endeavored not to catch factitious ones, that after having been fatigued with the sight of insipid grandeur and the slavish ceremonies that with cumbrous pomp supplied the place of domestic affections, I have turned to some other scene to relieve my eye by resting it on the refreshing green everywhere scattered by nature. I have then viewed with pleasure a woman nursing her children, and discharging the duties of her station with, perhaps, merely a servant maid to take off her hands the servile part of the household business. I have seen her prepare herself and children, with only the luxury of cleanliness, to receive her husband, who returning weary home in the evening found smiling babes and a clean hearth. My heart has loitered in the midst of the group, and has even throbbed with sympathetic emotion, when the scraping of the well known foot has raised a pleasing tumult.

Whilst my benevolence has been gratified by contemplating this artless picture, I have thought that a couple of this description, equally necessary and independent of each other, because each fulfilled the respective duties of their station, possessed all that life could give. Raised sufficiently above abject poverty not to be obliged to weigh the consequence of every farthing they spend, and having sufficient to prevent their attending to a frigid system of economy, which narrows both heart and mind, I declare, so vulgar are my conceptions, that I know not what is wanted to render this the happiest as well as the most respectable situation in the world, but a taste for literature, to throw a little variety and interest into social converse, and some superfluous money to give to the needy and to buy books. For it is not pleasant when the heart is opened by compassion and the head active in arranging plans of usefulness, to have a prim urchin continually twitching back the elbow to prevent the hand from drawing out an almost empty purse, whispering at the same time some prudential maxim about the priority of justice.

Destructive, however, as riches and inherited honours are to the human character, women are more debased and cramped, if possible, by them than men, because men may still, in some degree, unfold their faculties by becoming soldiers and statesmen.

10   As soldiers, I grant, they can now only gather, for the most part, vainglorious laurels, whilst they adjust to a hair the European balance, taking especial care that no bleak northern nook or sound incline the beam. But the days of true heroism are over, when a citizen fought for his country like a Fabricius or a Washington, and then returned to his farm to let his virtuous fervour run in a more placid, but not a less salutary, stream. No, our British heroes are oftener sent from the gaming table than from the plough and their passions have been rather inflamed by hanging with dumb suspense on the turn of a die, than

sublimated by panting after the adventurous march of virtue in the historic page.

The statesman, it is true, might with more propriety quit the faro bank, or card table, to guide the helm, for he has still but to shuffle and trick. The whole system of British politics, if system it may courteously be called, consisting in multiplying dependents and contriving taxes which grind the poor to pamper the rich; thus a war, or any wild goose chase, is, as the vulgar use the phrase, a lucky turn-up of patronage for the minister, whose chief merit is the art of keeping himself in place. It is not necessary then that he should have bowels for the poor, so he can secure for his family the odd trick. Or should some show of respect, for what is termed with ignorant ostentation an Englishman's birthright, be expedient to bubble the gruff mastiff that he has to lead by the nose, he can make an empty show very safely by giving his single voice and suffering his light squadron to file off to the other side. And when a question of humanity is agitated he may dip a sop in the milk of human kindness to silence Cerberus, and talk of the interest which his heart takes in an attempt to make the earth no longer cry for vengeance as it sucks in its children's blood, though his cold hand may at the very moment river their chains by sanctioning the abominable traffic. A minister is no longer a minister than while he can carry a point which he is determined to carry. Yet it is not necessary that minister should feel like a man, when a bold push might shake his seat.

But, to have done with these episodical observations, let me return to the more specious slavery which chains the very soul of woman, keeping her for ever under the bondage of ignorance.

The preposterous distinctions of rank, which render civilization a curse by dividing the world between voluptuous tyrants and cunning envious dependents, corrupt, almost equally, every class of people, because respectability is not attached to the discharge of the relative duties of life, but to the station, and when the duties are not fulfilled the affections cannot gain sufficient strength to fortify the virtue of which they are the natural reward. Still there are some loopholes out of which a man may creep, and dare to think and act for himself; but for a woman it is a herculean task, because she has difficulties peculiar to her sex to overcome which require almost superhuman powers.

A truly benevolent legislator always endeavors to make it the interest of each individual to be virtuous; and thus private virtue becoming the cement of public happiness, an orderly whole is consolidated by the tendency of all the parts towards a common centre. But, the private or public virtue of woman is very problematical; for Rousseau, and a numerous list of male writers, insist that she should all her life be subjected to a severe restraint, that of propriety. Why subject her to propriety—blind propriety, if she be capable of acting from a nobler spring, if she be an heir of immortality? Is sugar always to be produced by vital blood? Is one half of the human species, like the poor African slaves, to be subject to prejudices that brutalize them, when principles would be a surer guard, only to sweeten the cup of man? Is not this indirectly to deny woman reason? for a gift is a mockery, if it be unfit for use.

15   Women are, in common with men, rendered weak and luxurious by the relaxing pleasures which wealth procures; but added to this they are made slaves to their persons, and must render them alluring that man may lend them his reason to guide their tottering steps aright. Or should they be ambitious, they must govern their tyrants by sinister tricks, for without rights there cannot be any incumbent duties. The laws respecting woman, which I mean to discuss in a future part, make an absurd unit of a man and his wife; and then, by the easy transition of only considering him as responsible, she is reduced to a mere cypher.

The being who discharges the duties of its station is independent; and, speaking of women at large, their first duty is to themselves as rational creatures, and the next in point of importance, as citizens, is that which includes so many, of a mother. The rank in life which dispenses with their fulfilling this duty necessarily degrades them by making them mere dolls. Or, should they turn to something more important than merely fitting drapery upon a smooth block, their minds are only occupied by some soft platonic attachment; or, the actual management of an intrigue may keep their thoughts in motion; for when they neglect domestic duties, they have it not in their own power to take the field and march and counter-march like soldiers, or wrangle in the senate to keep their faculties from rusting.

I know that, as a proof of the inferiority of the sex, Rousseau has exultingly exclaimed, How can they leave the nursery for the camp! And the camp has by some moralists been termed the school of the most heroic virtues; though, I think, it would puzzle a keen casuist to prove the reasonableness of the greater number of wars that have dubbed heroes. I do not mean to consider this question critically; because, having frequently viewed these freaks of ambition as the first natural mode of civilization, when the ground must be torn up, and the woods cleared by fire and sword, I do not choose to call them pests; but surely the present system of war has little connection with virtue of any denomination, being rather the school of *finesse* and effeminacy than of fortitude.

Yet if defensive war, the only justifiable war, in the present advanced state of society, where virtue can show its face and ripen amidst the rigours which purify the air on the mountain's top, were alone to be adopted as just and glorious, the true heroism of antiquity might again animate female bosoms. But fair and softly, gentle reader, male or female, do not alarm thyself, for though I have compared the character of a modern soldier with that of a civilized woman, I am not going to advise them to turn their distaff into a musket, though I sincerely wish to see the bayonet converted into a pruning-hook. I only recreated an imagination, fatigue by contemplating the vices and follies which all proceed from a feculent stream of wealth that has muddied the pure rills of natural affection, by supposing that society will some time or other be so constituted, that man must necessarily fulfill the duties of a citizen or be despised, and that while he was employed in any of the departments of civil life, his wife; also an active citizen, should be equally intent to manage her family, educate her children, and assist her neighbors.

But, to render her really virtuous and useful, she must not, if she discharge her civil duties, want, individually, the protection of civil laws; she must not be dependent on her husband's bounty for her subsistence during his life or support after his death—for how can a being be generous who has nothing of its own? or virtuous, who is not free?

20 The wife, in the present state of things, who is faithful to her husband, and neither suckles nor educates her children, scarcely deserves the name of a wife, and has no right to that of a citizen. But take away natural rights, and duties become null.

Women then must be considered as only the wanton solace of men when they become so weak in mind and body that they cannot exert themselves, unless to pursue some frothy pleasure or to invent some frivolous fashion. What can be a more melancholy sight to a thinking mind than to look into the numerous carriages that drive helter-skelter about this metropolis in a morning full of pale-faced creatures who are flying from themselves. I have often wished, with Dr. Johnson, to place some of them in a little shop with half a dozen children looking up to their languid countenances for support. I am much mistaken if some latent vigour would not soon give health and spirit to their eyes, and some lines drawn by the exercise of reason the blank cheeks, which before were only undulated by dimples, might restore lost dignity to the character, or rather enable it to attain the true dignity of its nature. Virtue is not to be acquired even by speculation, much less by the negative supineness that wealth naturally generates.

Besides, when poverty is more disgraceful than even vice, is not morality cut to the quick? Still to avoid misconstruction, though I consider that women in the common walks of life are called to fulfill the duties of wives and mothers, by religion and reason, I cannot help lamenting that women of a superior cast have not a road open by which they can pursue more extensive plans of usefulness and independence. I may excite laughter by dropping a hint which I mean to pursue some future time, for I really think that women ought to have representatives, instead of being arbitrarily governed without having any direct share allowed them in the deliberations of government.

But, as the whole system of representation is now in this country only a convenient handle for despotism, they need not complain, for they are as well represented as a numerous class of hard-working mechanics, who pay for the support of royalty when they can scarcely stop their children's mouths with bread. How are they represented whose very sweat supports the splendid stud of an heir apparent, or varnishes the chariot of some female favourite who looks down on shame? Taxes on the very necessaries of life enable an endless tribe of idle princes and princesses to pass with stupid pomp before a gaping crowd, who almost worship the very parade which costs them so dear. This is mere gothic grandeur, something like the barbarous useless parade of having sentinels on horseback at Whitehall, which I could never view without a mixture of contempt and indignation.

How strangely must the mind be sophisticated when this sort of state impresses it! But, till these monuments of folly are levelled by virtue, similar follies will leaven the whole mass. For the same character, in some degree, will prevail in the aggregate of society; and the refinements of luxury, or the vicious repinings of envious poverty, will equally banish virtue from society, considered as the characteristic of that society, or only allow it to appear as one of the stripes of the harlequin coat worn by the civilized man.

25   In the superior ranks of life every duty is done by deputies, as if duties could ever be waived, and the vain pleasures which consequent idleness forces the rich to pursue appear so enticing to the next rank

that the numerous scramblers for wealth sacrifice everything to tread on their heels. The most sacred trusts are then considered as sinecures, because they were procured by interest, and only sought to enable a man to keep *good company*. Women in particular, all want to be ladies. Which is simply to have nothing to do, but listlessly to go they scarcely care where, for they cannot tell what.

But what have women to do in society? I may be asked, but to loiter with easy grace; surely you would not condemn them all to suckle fools and chronicle small beer! No. Women might certainly study the art of healing, and be physicians as well as nurses. And midwifery, decency seems to allot to them, though I am afraid the word midwife in our dictionaries will soon give place to *accoucheur*, and one proof of the former delicacy of the sex be effaced from the language.

They might also study politics, and settle their benevolence on the broadest basis; for the reading of history will scarcely be more useful than the perusal of romances, if read as mere biography; if the character of the times, the political improvements, arts, &c., be not observed. In short, if it be not considered as the history of man; and not of particular men, who filled a niche in the temple of fame, and dropped into the black rolling stream of time, that silently sweeps all before it, into the shapeless void called—eternity. For shape, can it be called, "that shape hath none"?

Business of various kinds they might likewise pursue, if they were educated in a more orderly manner, which might save many from common and legal prostitution. Women would not then marry for a support, as men accept of places under government, and neglect the implied duties; nor would an attempt to earn their own subsistence—a most laudable one!—sink them almost to the level of those poor abandoned creatures who live by prostitution. For are not milliners and mantua-makers reckoned the next class? The few employments open to women, so far from being liberal, are menial; and when a superior education enables them to take charge of the education of children as governesses, they are not treated like the tutors of sons, though even clerical tutors are not always treated in a manner calculated to render them respectable in the eyes of their pupils, to say nothing of the private comfort of the individual. But as women educated like gentlewomen are never designed for the humiliating situation which necessity sometimes forces them to fill, these situations are considered in the light of a degradation; and they know little of the human heart, who need to be told that nothing so painfully sharpens sensibility as such a fall in life.

Some of these women might be restrained from marrying by a proper spirit or delicacy, and others may not have had it in their power to escape in this pitiful way from servitude; is not that government then very defective, and very unmindful of the happiness of one half of its members, that does not provide for honest, independent women, by encouraging them to fill respectable stations? But in order to render their private virtue a public benefit, they must have a civil existence in the state, married or single; else we shall continually see some worthy woman, whose sensibility has been rendered painfully acute by undeserved contempt, droop like "the lily broken down by a plowshare."

SUGGESTIONS FOR WRITING

1. Throughout the essay Wollstonecraft criticizes what she considers "unnatural" distinctions between men and women and claims that they lead to bad social and political relations. Write an essay that analyzes what Wollstonecraft understands as the causal relations between unnatural distinctions and social ills.
2. What does Wollstonecraft assume to define natural relations between the sexes? Write an essay that examines the kind of social order that Wollstonecraft holds up as ideal.
3. Throughout the essay Wollstonecraft emphasizes property and economic issues. Write an essay that explains the relations Wollstonecraft sees between economics and the rights of women.

Awakening and Revolt   1931
From *My Fight for Birth Control*

MARGARET SANGER

Margaret Sanger was a leader in the American birth control movement early in twentieth century, and she describes her personal impetus toward that movement here. She was extremely active in raising awareness about contraception and bringing the issue to public notice by organizing international conferences and establishing clinics in urban areas such as she describes below. "Awakening and Revolt" is an excerpt from My Fight for Birth Control *(1931). She tells very movingly how she was led to take up this aspect of the women's cause through her personal experience of the suffering and death that an ignorance of contraception continually produced, an ignorance to which the medical establishment persisted in turning a blind eye.*

Early in the year 1912 I came to a sudden realization that my work as a nurse and my activities in social service were entirely palliative and consequently futile and useless to relieve the misery I saw all about me. . . .

Were it possible for me to depict the revolting conditions existing in the homes of some of the women I attended in that one year, one would find it hard to believe. There was at that time, and doubtless is still today, a sub-stratum of men and women whose lives are absolutely untouched by social agencies.

The way they live is almost beyond belief. They hate and fear any prying into their homes or into their lives. They resent being talked to. The women slink in and out of their homes on their way to market like rats from their holes. The men beat their wives sometimes black and blue, but no one interferes. The children are cuffed, kicked and chased about, but woe to the child who dares to tell tales out of the home! Crime or drink is often the source of this secret aloofness, usually there is something to hide, a skeleton in the closet somewhere. The men are sullen, unskilled workers, picking up odd jobs now and then, unemployed usually, sauntering in and out of the house at all hours of the day and night.

The women keep apart from other women in the neighborhood. Often they are suspected of picking a pocket or "lifting" an article when occasion arises. Pregnancy is an almost chronic condition amongst them. I knew one woman who had given birth to eight children with no professional care whatever. The last one was born in the kitchen, witnessed by a son of ten years who, under his mother's direction, cleaned the bed, wrapped the placenta and soiled articles in paper, and threw them out of the window into the court below. . . .

5   In this atmosphere abortions and birth become the main theme of conversation. On Saturday night I have seen groups of fifty to one hundred women going into questionable offices well known in the community for cheap abortions. I asked several women what took place there, and they all gave the same reply: a quick examination, a probe inserted into the uterus and turned a few times to disturb the fertilized ovum, and then the woman was sent home. Usually the flow began the next day and often continued four or five weeks. Sometimes an ambulance carried the victim to the hospital for a curetage, and if she returned home at all she was looked upon as a lucky woman.

This state of things became a nightmare with me. There seemed no sense to it all, no reason for such waste of mother life, no right to exhaust women's vitality and to throw them on the scrap-heap before the age of thirty-five.

Everywhere I looked, misery and fear stalked—men fearful of losing their jobs, women fearful that even worse conditions might come upon them. The menace of another pregnancy hung like a sword over the head of every poor woman I came in contact with that year. The question which met me was always the same: What can I do to keep from it? or, What can I do to get out of this? Sometimes they talked among themselves bitterly.

"It's the rich that know the tricks," they'd say, "while we have all the kids." Then, if the women were Roman Catholics, they talked about "Yankee tricks," and asked me if I knew what the Protestants did to keep their families down. When I said that I didn't believe that the rich knew much more than they did I was laughed at and suspected of holding back information for money. They would nudge each other and say something about paying me before I left the case if I would reveal the "secret." . . .

Finally the thing began to shape itself, to become accumulative during the three weeks I spent in the home of a desperately sick woman living on Grand Street, a lower section of New York's East Side.

Mrs. Sacks was only twenty-eight years old; her husband, an unskilled worker, thirty-two. Three children, aged five, three and one, were none too strong nor study, and it took all the earnings of the father and the ingenuity of the mother to keep them clean, provide them with air and proper food, and give them a chance to grow into decent manhood and womanhood.

Both parents were devoted to these children and to each other. The woman had become pregnant and had taken various drugs and purgatives, as advised by her neighbors. Then, in desperation, she had used some instrument lent to her by a friend. She was found prostrate on the floor amidst the crying children when her husband returned from work. Neighbors advised against the ambulance, and a friendly doctor was called. The husband would not hear of her going to a hospital, and as a little money had been saved in the bank a nurse was called and the battle for that precious life began.

It was in the middle of July. The three-room apartment was turned into a hospital for the dying patient. Never had I worked so fast, never so concentratedly as I did to keep alive that little mother. Neighbor women came and went during the day doing the odds and ends necessary for our comfort. The children were sent to friends and relatives and the doctor and I settled ourselves to outdo the force and power of an outraged nature.

Never had I known such conditions could exist. July's sultry days and nights were melted into a torpid inferno. Day after day, night after night, I slept only in brief snatches, ever too anxious about the condition of that feeble heart bravely carrying on, to stay long from the bedside of the patient. . . .

At the end of two weeks recovery was in sight, and at the end of three weeks I was preparing to leave the fragile patient to take up the ordinary duties of her life, including those of wifehood and motherhood. Everyone was congratulating her on her recovery. All the kindness of sympathetic and understanding neighbors poured in upon her in the shape of convalescent dishes, soups, custards, and drinks. Still she appeared to be despondent and worried. She seemed to sit apart in her thoughts as if she had no part in these congratulatory messages and endearing welcomes. I thought at first that she still retained some of her unconscious memories and dwelt upon them in her silences.

15   But as the hour for my departure came nearer, her anxiety increased, and finally with trembling voice she said: "Another baby will finish me, I suppose."

"It's too early to talk about that," I said, and resolved that I would turn the question over to the doctor for his advice. When he came I said: "Mrs. Sacks is worried about having another baby."

"She well might be," replied the doctor, and then he stood before her and said: "Any more such capers, young woman, and there will be no need to call me."

"Yes, yes—I know, Doctor," said the patient with trembling voice, "but," and she hesitated as if it took all of her courage to say it, "*what can I do to prevent getting that way again?*"

"Oh ho!" laughed the doctor good naturedly, "You want your cake while you eat it too, do you? Well, it can't be done." Then, familiarly slapping her on the back and picking up his hat and bag to depart, he said: "I'll tell you the only sure thing to do. Tell Jake to sleep on the roof!"

With those words he closed the door and went down the stairs, leaving us both petrified and stunned.

20   Tears sprang to my eyes, and a lump came in my throat as I looked at that face before me. It was stamped with sheer horror. I thought for a moment she might have gone insane, but she conquered her feelings, whatever they may have been, and turning to me in desperation said: "He can't understand, can he?—he's a man after all—but you do, don't you? You're a woman and you'll tell me the secret and I'll never tell it to a soul."

She clasped her hands as if in prayer, she leaned over and looked straight into my eyes and beseechingly implored me to tell her something—something *I really did not know*. It was like being on a rack and tortured for a crime one had not committed. To plead guilty would stop the agony; otherwise the rack kept turning.

I had to turn away from that imploring face. I could not answer her then. I quieted her as best I could. She saw that I was moved by the tears in my eyes. I promised that I would come back in a few days and tell her what she wanted to know. The few simple means of limiting the family like *coitus interruptus* or the condom were laughed at by the neighboring women when told these were the means used by men in the well-to-do families. That was not believed, and I knew such an answer would be swept aside as useless were I to tell her this at such a time.

A little later when she slept I left the house, and made up my mind that I'd keep away from those cases in the future. I felt helpless to do anything at all. I seemed chained hand and foot, and longed for an earthquake or a volcano to shake the world out of its lethargy into facing these monstrous atrocities.

The intelligent reasoning of the young mother—how to *prevent* getting that way again—how sensible, how just she had been—yes, I promised myself I'd go back and have a long talk with her and tell her more, and perhaps she would not laugh but would believe that those methods were all that were really known.

25 But time flew past, and weeks rolled into months. That wistful, appealing face haunted me day and night. I could not banish from my mind memories of that trembling voice begging so humbly for knowledge she had a right to have. I was about to retire one night three months later when the telephone rang and an agitated man's voice begged me to come at once to help his wife who was sick again. It was the husband of Mrs. Sacks, and I intuitively knew before I left the telephone that it was almost useless to go.

I dreaded to face that woman. I was tempted to send someone else in my place. I longed for an accident on the subway, or on the street—anything to prevent my going into that home. But on I went, just the same. I arrived a few minutes after the doctor, the same one who had given her such noble advice. The woman was dying. She was unconscious. She died within ten minutes after my arrival. It was the same result, the same story told a thousand times before—death from abortion. She had become pregnant, had used drugs, had then consulted a five-dollar professional abortionist, and death followed.

The doctor shook his head as he rose from listening for the heart beat. I knew she had already passed on; without a groan, a sigh or recognition of our belated presence she had gone into the Great Beyond as thousands of mothers go every year. I looked at that drawn face now stilled in death. I placed her thin hands across her breast and recalled how hard they had pleaded with me on that last memorable occasion of parting. The gentle woman, the devoted mother, the loving wife had passed on leaving behind her a frantic husband, helpless in his loneliness, bewildered in his helplessness as he paced up and down the room, hands clenching his head, moaning "My God! My God! My God!"

The Revolution came—but not as it has been pictured nor as history relates that revolutions have come. It came in my own life. It began in my very being as I walked home that night after I had closed the eyes and covered with a sheet the body of that little helpless mother whose life had been sacrificed to ignorance.

After I left that desolate house I walked and walked and walked; for hours and hours I kept on, bag in hand, thinking, regretting, dreading to stop; fearful of my conscience, dreading to face my own accusing soul. At three in the morning I arrived home still clutching a heavy load the weight of which I was quite unconscious.

30   I entered the house quietly, as was my custom, and looked out of the window down upon the dimly lighted, sleeping city. As I stood at the window and looked out, the miseries and problems of that sleeping city arose before me in a clear vision like a panorama: crowded homes, too many children; babies dying in infancy; mothers overworked; baby nurseries; children neglected and hungry—mothers so nervously wrought they could not give the little things the comfort nor care they needed; mothers half sick most of their lives—"always ailing, never failing"; women made into drudges; children working in cellars; children aged six and seven pushed into the labor market to help earn a living; another baby on the way; still another; yet another; a baby born dead—great relief; an older child dies—sorrow, but nevertheless relief—insurance helps; a mother's death—children scattered into institutions; the father, desperate, drunken; he slinks away to become an outcast in a society which has trapped him. . . .

. . . For hours I stood, motionless and tense, expecting something to happen. I watched the lights go out, I saw the darkness gradually give way to the first shimmer of dawn, and then a colorful sky heralded the rise of the sun. I knew a new day had come for me and a new world as well.

It was like an illumination. I could now see clearly the various social strata of our life; all its mass problems seemed to be centered around uncontrolled breeding. There was only one thing to be done: call out, start the alarm, set the heather on fire! Awaken the womanhood of America to free the motherhood of the world! I released from my almost paralyzed hand the nursing bag which unconsciously I had clutched, threw it across the room, tore the uniform from my body, flung it into a corner, and renounced all palliative work forever.

I would never go back again to nurse women's ailing bodies while their miseries were as vast as the stars. I was now finished with superficial cures, with doctors and nurses and social workers who were brought face to face with this overwhelming truth of women's needs and yet turned to pass on the other side. They must be made to see these facts. I resolved that women should have knowledge of contraception. They have every right to know about their own bodies. I would strike out—I would scream from the housetops. I would tell the world what was going on in the lives of these poor women. I *would* be heard. No matter what it should cost. *I would be heard.*

SUGGESTIONS FOR WRITING

1. Sanger creates a sense of horror for her reader by describing her own horror at the conditions she sees. Write an essay that analyzes examples of Sanger's writing to show how she tells her story in such a moving way.

2. In paragraph 28, Sanger distinguishes her personal "revolution" from those of history, yet she was a pioneer in the history of birth control. Write an essay that explores the full meaning of the word *revolution* in Sanger's essay.

3. Sanger does not speak directly of human rights in her essay, but surely they make a major theme by implication. Write an essay in which you explore the issue of implied human rights in "Awakening and Revolt."

The Nonviolent Society   1924

MAHATMA GANDHI

The Indian people gave Gandhi (1869–1948) the honorable name of "Mahatma," which means "Great Soul." He was born Mohandas Karamchaund Gandhi and became a world famous spiritual and political leader of the Nationalist movement in its fight for independence from the British Empire. In that fight, he always maintained a policy of nonviolence, forming part of a human continuum that includes Martin Luther King, Jr. in this chapter and Henry David Thoreau (Chapter 5).

British India gained independence in 1947 after being partitioned into Pakistan and India, generally along religious lines that divided the population largely into Moslem and Hindu sections. Gandhi campaigned for a united India based on principles of religious toleration, but was assassinated by a Hindu fanatic at the beginning of 1948.

I HOLD that nonviolence is not merely a personal virtue. It is also a social virtue to be cultivated like the other virtues. Surely society is largely regulated by the expression of nonviolence in its mutual dealings. What I ask for is an extension of it on a larger, national and international scale.

All society is held together by nonviolence, even as the earth is held in her position by gravitation. But when the law of gravitation was discovered, the discovery yielded results of which our ancestors had no knowledge. Even so, when society is deliberately constructed in accordance with the law of nonviolence, its structure will be different in material particulars from what it is today. But I cannot say in advance what the government based on nonviolence will be like.

What is happening today is disregard of the law of nonviolence and enthronement of violence as if it were an eternal law.

Society based on nonviolence can only consist of groups settled in villages in which voluntary co-operation is the condition of dignified and peaceful existence.

The Government

5 The Government cannot succeed in becoming entirely nonviolent, because it represents all the people. I do not today conceive of such a golden age. But I do believe in the possibility of a predominantly nonviolent society. And I am working for it.

There remains the question as to whether in an ideal society, there should be any or no government. I do not think we need worry ourselves about this at the moment. If we continue to work for such a society, it will slowly come into being to an extent, such that the people can benefit by it. Euclid's line is one without breadth, but no one has so far been able to draw it and never will. All the same, it is only by keeping the ideal line in mind that we have made progress in geometry. What is true here is true of every ideal.

Anarchy

It must be remembered that nowhere in the world does a State without government exist. If at all it could ever come into being, it would be in India; for, ours is the only country where the attempt has, at any rate, been made. We have not yet been able to show that bravery to the degree which is necessary and for the attainment of which there is only one way. Those who have faith in the latter have to demonstrate it. In order to do so, the fear of death has to be completely shed, just as we have shed the fear of prisons.

Democracy and Nonviolence

Science of war leads one to dictatorship pure and simple. Science of nonviolence can alone lead one to pure democracy.

Democracy and violence can ill go together. The States that are today nominally democratic have either to become frankly totalitarian, or if they are to become truly democratic, they must become courageously nonviolent.

Holding the view that, without the recognition of nonviolence on a national scale, there is no such thing as a constitutional or democratic government, I devote my energy to the propagation of nonviolence as the law of our life, individual, social, political, national and international.

I fancy that I have seen the light, though dimly. I write cautiously for I do not profess to know the whole of the Law. If I know the success of my experiments, I know also my failures. But the successes are enough to fill me with undying hope.

I have often said that if one takes care of the means, the end will take care of itself. Nonviolence is the means, the end for everyone is complete independence. There will be an international League only when all the nations, big or small, composing it are fully independent. The nature of that independence will correspond to the extent of nonviolence assimilated by the nations concerned. One thing is certain. In a society based on nonviolence, the smallest nation will feel as tall as the tallest. The idea of superiority and inferiority will be wholly obliterated.

. . . The conclusion is irresistible that for one like me, wedded to nonviolence, constitutional or democratic government is a distant dream so long as nonviolence is not recognized as a living force, an inviolable creed, not a mere policy. While I prate about universal nonviolence, my experiment is confined to India. If it succeeds, the world will accept it without effort. There is however a bit of a BUT. The pause does not worry me. My faith is brightest in the midst of impenetrable darkness.

Use of Power

By its very nature, nonviolence cannot 'seize' power, nor can that be its goal. But nonviolence can do more; it can effectively control and guide power without capturing the machinery of government. That is its beauty.

15   There is an exception, of course. If the nonviolent non-co-operation of the people is so complete that the administration ceases to function or if the administration crumbles under the impact of a foreign invasion and a vaccum results, the people's representatives will then step in and fill it. Theoretically that is possible.

But the use of power need not necessarily be violent. A father wields power over his children; he may even punish but not by infliction violence. The most effective exercise of power is that which irks least. Power rightly exercised must sit light as a flower; no one should feel the weight of it.

The people accepted the authority of the Congress willingly. I was on more than one occasion invested with the absolute power of dictatorship. But everybody knew that my power rested on their willing acceptance. They could set me aside at any time and I would have stepped aside without a murmur.

Prophets and supermen are born only once in an age. But if even a single individual realizes the ideal of ahimsa in its fullness, he covers and redeems the whole society. Once Jesus had blazed the trail, his twelve disciples could carry on his mission without his presence.

It needed the perseverance and genius of so many generations of scientists to discover the laws of electricity, but today everybody, even children use electric power in their daily life. Similarly, it will not always need a perfect being to administer an ideal State once it has come into being. What is needed is a thorough social awakening to begin with. The rest will follow.

20   To take an instance nearer home, I have presented to the working class the truth that true capital is not silver or gold, but the labour of their hands and feet and their intelligence. Once labour develops that awareness, it would not need my presence to enable it to make use of the power that it will release.

SUGGESTIONS FOR WRITING

1. In paragraph 6 Gandhi speaks about the possibilities for government in an ideal society. Write an essay that explores Gandhi's use of the concept of the "ideal" throughout his essay.

2. In paragraph 11 Gandhi says "I write cautiously." Based on your reading of the essay as a whole, do you agree with his self-assessment? Write an essay that explains and defends your answer.

3. Like Rousseau earlier in this chapter, Gandhi points to the family as a model for natural government. Write an essay in which you compare and contrast the uses made of "the family" in the thoughts on government of Jean-Jacques Rousseau and Mahatma Gandhi.

Politics and the English Language

1946

GEORGE ORWELL

George Orwell was the penname of Eric Arthur Blair (1903–1950), an Englishman born in Bengal, India in a family of civil servants to the British Empire. Best known for his antitotalitarian novels Animal Farm *(1945) and* 1984 *(1949), Orwell was also a highly accomplished essayist. In the following piece, reprinted innumerable times during the Cold War of the late twentieth century, he analyzes in detail what he takes to be crippling abuses of language and posits a vital connection between clear thinking, clear writing, and "political regeneration."*

Most people who bother with the matter at all would admit that the English language is in a bad way, but it is generally assumed that we cannot by conscious action do anything about it. Our civilization is decadent and our language—so the argument runs—must inevitably share in the general collapse. It follows that any struggle against the abuse of language is a sentimental archaism, like preferring candles to electric light or hansom cabs to aeroplanes. Underneath this lies the half-conscious belief that language is a natural growth and not an instrument which we shape for our own purposes.

Now, it is clear that the decline of a language must ultimately have political and economic causes: it is not due simply to the bad influence of this or that individual writer. But an effect can become a cause, reinforcing the original cause and producing the same effect in an intensified form, and so on indefinitely. A man may take to drink because he feels himself to be a failure, and then fail all the more completely because he drinks. It is rather the same thing that is happening to the English language. It becomes ugly and inaccurate because our thoughts are foolish, but the slovenliness of our language makes it easier for us to have foolish thoughts. The point is that the process is reversible. Modern English, especially written English, is full of bad habits which spread by imitation and which can be avoided if one is willing to take the necessary trouble. If one gets rid of these habits one can think more clearly, and to think clearly is a necessary first step towards political regeneration: so that the fight against bad English is not frivolous and is not the exclusive concern of professional writers. I will come back to this presently, and I hope that by that time the meaning of what I have said here will have become clearer. Meanwhile, here are five specimens of the English language as it is now habitually written.

These five passages have not been picked out because they are especially bad—I could have quoted far worse if I had chosen—but because they illustrate various of the mental vices from which we now suffer. They are a little below the average, but are fairly representative samples. I number them so that I can refer back to them when necessary:

1. I am not, indeed, sure whether it is not true to say that the Milton who once seemed not unlike a seventeenth-century Shelley had not become, out of an experience ever more bitter in each year, more alien [sic] to the founder of that Jesuit sect which nothing could induce him to tolerate.

—Professor Harold Laski (Essay in *Freedom of Expression*)

2. Above all, we cannot play ducks and drakes with a native battery of idioms which prescribes such egregious collocations of vocables as the Basic *put up with for tolerate or put at a loss for bewilder.*

—Professor Lancelot Hogben (*Interglossa*)

3. On the one side we have the free personality: by definition it is not neurotic, for it has neither conflict nor dream. Its desires, such as they are, are transparent, for they are just what institutional approval keeps in the forefront of consciousness; another institutional pattern would alter their number and intensity; there is little in them that is natural, irreducible, or culturally dangerous. But *on the other side,* the social bond itself is nothing but the mutual

reflection of these self-secure integrities. Recall the definition of love. Is not this the very picture of a small academic? Where is there a place in this hall of mirrors for either personality or fraternity?

—Essay on Psychology in *Politics* (New York)

4. All the "best people" from the gentlemen's clubs, and all the frantic fascist captains, united in common hatred of Socialism and bestial horror of the rising tide of the mass revolutionary movement, have turned to acts of provocation, to foul incendiarism, to medieval legends of poisoned wells, to legalize their own destruction of proletarian organizations, and rouse the agitated petty-bourgeoisie to chauvinistic fervor on behalf of the fight against the revolutionary way out of the crisis.

—Communist Pamphlet

5. If a new spirit *is* to be infused into this old country, there is one thorny and contentious reform which must be tackled, and that is the humanization and galvanization of the B.B.C. Timidity here will bespeak canker and atrophy of the soul. The heart of Britain may be sound and of strong beat, for instance, but the British lion's roar at present is like that of Bottom in Shakespeare's *Midsummer Night's Dream*—as gentle as any sucking dove. A virile new Britain cannot continue indefinitely to be traduced in the eyes or rather ears, of the world by the effete languors of Langham Place, brazenly masquerading as "standard English." When the voice of Britain is heard at nine o'clock, better far and infinitely less ludicrous to hear aitches honestly dropped than the present priggish, inflated, inhibited, school-ma'amish arch braying of blameless bashful mewing maidens!

—Letter in *Tribune*

Each of these passages has faults of its own, but, quite apart from avoidable ugliness, two qualities are common to all of them. The first is staleness of imagery; the other is lack of precision. The writer either has a meaning and cannot express it, or he inadvertently says something else, or he is almost indifferent as to whether his words mean anything or not. This mixture of vagueness and sheer incompetence is the most marked characteristic of modern English prose, and especially of any kind of political writing. As soon as certain topics are raised, the concrete melts into the abstract and no one seems able to think of turns of speech that are not hackneyed: prose consists less and less of *words* chosen for the sake of their meaning, and more and more of *phrases* tacked together like the sections of a prefabricated hen-house. I list below, with notes and examples, various of the tricks by means of which the work of prose-construction is habitually dodged:

Dying Metaphors

5 A newly invented metaphor assists thought by evoking a visual image, while on the other hand a metaphor which is technically "dead" (e.g., *iron resolution*) has in effect reverted to being an ordinary word and can generally be used without loss of vividness. But in between these two classes there is a huge dump of worn-out metaphors which have lost all evocative power and are merely used because they save people the trouble of inventing phrases for themselves. Examples are: *Ring the changes on, take up the cudgels for, toe the line, ride roughshod over, stand shoulder to shoulder with, play into the hands of, no axe to grind, grist to the mill, fishing in troubled waters, on the orden of the day, Achilles' heel, swan song, hotbed.* Many of these are used without knowledge of their meaning (what is a "rift," for instance?), and incompatible metaphors are frequently mixed, a sure sign that the writer is not interested in what he is saying. Some metaphors now current have been twisted out of their original meaning without those who use them even being aware of the fact. For example, *toe the line* is sometimes written *tow the line.* Another example is *the hammer and the anvil*, now always used with the implication that the anvil gets the worst of it. In real life it is always the anvil that breaks the hammer, never the other way about: a writer who stopped to think what he was saying would be aware of this, and would avoid perverting the original phrase.

Operators or Verbal False Limbs

These save the trouble of picking out appropriate verbs and nouns, and at the same time pad each sentence with extra syllables which give it an appearance of symmetry. Characteristic phrases are *render inoperative, militate against, make contact with, be subjected to, give rise to, give grounds for, have the effect of, play a leading part (role) in, make itself felt, take effect, exhibit a tendency to, serve the purpose of,* etc., etc. The keynote is the elimination of simple verbs. Instead of being a single word, such as *break, stop, spoil, mend, kill,* a verb becomes a *phrase*, made up of a noun or adjective tacked on to some general-purpose verb such as *prove, serve, form, play, render.* In addition, the passive voice is wherever possible used in preference to the active, and noun constructions are used instead of gerunds (*by examination of* instead of *by examining*). The range of verbs is further cut down by means of the *-ize* and *de-* formations, and the banal statements are given an appearance of profundity by means of the *not un-* formation. Simple conjunctions and prepositions are replaced by such phrases as *with respect to, having regard to, the fact that, by dint of, in view of, in the interests of, on the hypothesis that;* and the ends of sentences are saved from anticlimax by such resounding common-places as *greatly to be desired, cannot be left out of account, a development to be expected in the near future, deserving of serious consideration, brought to a satisfactory conclusion,* and so on and so forth.

Pretentious Diction

Words like *phenomenon, element, individual* (as noun), *objective, categorical, effective, virtual, basic, primary, promote, constitute, exhibit, exploit, utilize, eliminate, liquidate,* are used to dress up simple statements and give an air of scientific impartiality to biased judgments. Adjectives like *epoch-making, epic, historic, unforgettable, triumphant, age-old, inevitable, inexorable, veritable,* are used to dignify the sordid processes of international politics, while writing that aims at glorifying war usually takes on an archaic color, its characteristic words being: *realm, throne, chariot, mailed fist, trident, sword, shield, buckler, banner, jackboot, clarion.* Foreign words and expressions such as *cul de sac, ancien régime, deus ex machina, mutatis multandis, status quo, gleichschaltung, weltanschauung,* are used to give an air of culture and elegance. Except for the useful abbreviations *i.e., e.g.,* and *etc.,* there is no real need for any of the hundreds of foreign phrases now current in English. Bad writers, and especially scientific, political and sociological writers, are nearly always haunted by the notion that Latin or Greek words are grander than Saxon ones, and unnecessary words like *expedite, ameliorate, predict, extraneous, deracinated, clandestine, subaqueous* and hundreds of others constantly gain ground from their Anglo-Saxon opposite numbers.[1] The jargon peculiar to Marxist writing (*hyena, hangman, cannibal, petty bourgeois, these gentry, lacquey, flunkey, mad dog, White Guard,* etc.) consists largely of words and phrases translated from Russian, German or French; but the normal way of coining a

---

[1] An interesting illustration of this is the way in which the English flower names which were in use till very recently are being ousted by Greek ones, *snapdragon* becoming *antirrhinum, forget-me-not* becoming *myosotis,* etc. It is hard to see any practical reason for this change of fashion: it is probably due to an instinctive turning-away from the more homely word and a vague feeling that the Greek word is scientific.

new word is to use a Latin or Greek root with the appropriate affix and, where necessary, the *ize* formation. It is often easier to make up words of this kind (*deregionalize, imapermissible, extramarital, nonfragmentary* and so forth) than to think up the English words that will cover one's meaning. The result, in general, is an increase in slovenliness and vagueness.

Meaningless Words

In certain kinds of writing, particularly in art criticism and literary criticism, it is normal to come across long passages which are almost completely lacking in meaning.[2] Words like *romantic, plastic, values, human, dead, sentimental, natural, vitality,* as used in art criticism, are strictly meaningless, in the sense that they not only do not point to any discoverable object, but are hardly ever expected to do so by the reader. When one critic writes, "The outstanding feature of Mr. X's work is its living quality," while another writes, "The immediately striking thing about Mr. X's work is its peculiar deadness," the reader accepts this as a simple difference of opinion. If words like *black* and *white* were involved, instead of the jargon words *dead* and *living*, he would see at once that language was being used in an improper way. Many political words are similarly abused. The word *Fascism* has now no meaning except in so far as it signifies "something not desirable." The words *democracy, socialism, freedom, patriotic, realistic, justice,* have each of them several different meanings which cannot be reconciled with one another. In the case of a word like *democracy,* not only is there no agreed definition, but the attempt to make one is resisted from all sides. It is almost universally felt that when we call a country democratic we are praising it: consequently the defenders of every kind of régime claim that it is a democracy, and fear that they might have to stop using the word if it were tied down to any one meaning. Words of this kind are often used in a consciously dishonest way. That is, the person who uses them has his own private definition, but allows his hearer to think he means something quite different. Statements like *Marshal Pétain was a true patriot, The Soviet Press is the freest in the world, The Catholic Church is*

---

[2] Example: "Comfort's catholicity of perception and image, strangely Whitmanesque in range, almost the exact opposite in aesthetic compulsion, continues to evoke that trembling atmospheric accumulative hinting at a cruel, an inexorably serene time-lessness. . . . Wrey Gardiner scores by aiming at simple bull's-eyes with precision. Only they are not so simple, and through this contented sadness runs more than the surface bitter-sweet of resignation." (*Poetry Quarterly*).

opposed to persecution, are almost always made with intent to deceive. Other words used in variable meanings, in most cases more or less dishonestly, are: *class, totalitarian, science, progressive, reactionary, bourgeois, equality.*

Now that I have made this catalogue of swindles and perversions, let me give another example of the kind of writing that they lead to. This time it must of its nature be an imaginary one. I am going to translate a passage of good English into modern English of the worst sort. Here is a well-known verse from *Ecclesiastes*:

> *I returned and saw under the sun, that the race is not to the swift, nor the battle to the strong, neither yet bread to the wise, nor yet riches to men of understanding, nor yet favour to men of skill; but time and chance happeneth to them all.*

Here it is in modern English:

> *Objective consideration of contemporary phenomena compels the conclusion that success or failure in competitive activities exhibits no tendency to be commensurate with innate capacity, but that a considerable element of the unpredictable must invariably be taken into account.*

This is a parody, but not a very gross one. Exhibit (3), above, for instance, contains several patches of the same kind of English. It will be seen that I have not made a full translation. The beginning and ending of the sentence follow the original meaning fairly closely, but in the middle the concrete illustrations—race, battle, bread—dissolve into the vague phrase "success or failure in competitive activities." This had to be so, because no modern writer of the kind I am discussing—no one capable of using phrases like "objective consideration of contemporary phenomena"—would ever tabulate his thoughts in that precise and detailed way. The whole tendency of modern prose is away from concreteness. Now analyze these two sentences a little more closely. The first contains forty-nine words but only sixty syllables, and all its words are those of everyday life. The second contains thirty-eight words of ninety syllables: eighteen of its words are from Latin roots, and one from Greek. The first sentence contains six vivid images, and only one phrase ("time and chance") that could be called vague. The second contains not a single fresh, arresting phrase, and in spite of its ninety syllables it gives only a shortened version of the meaning contained in the first. Yet without a doubt it is the second

10

kind of sentence that is gaining ground in modern English. I do not want to exaggerate. This kind of writing is not yet universal, and outcrops of simplicity will occur here and there in the worst-written page. Still, if you or I were told to write a few lines on the uncertainty of human fortunes, we should probably come much nearer to my imaginary sentence than to the one from *Ecclesiastes*.

As I have tried to show, modern writing at its worst does not consist in picking out words for the sake of their meaning and inventing images in order to make the meaning clearer. It consists in gumming together long strips of words which have already been set in order by someone else, and making the results presentable by sheer humbug. The attraction of this way of writing is that it is easy. It is easier—even quicker, once you have the habit—to say *In my opinion it is not an unjustifiable assumption that* than to say *I think*. If you use ready-made phrases, you not only don't have to hunt about for words; you also don't have to bother with the rhythms of your sentences, since these phrases are generally so arranged as to be more or less euphonious. When you are composing in a hurry—when you are dictating to a stenographer, for instance, or making a public speech—it is natural to fall into a pretentious, Latinized style. Tags like *a consideration which we should do well to bear in mind* or *a conclusion to which all of us would readily assent* will save many a sentence from coming down with a bump. By using stale metaphors, similes and idioms, you save much mental effort, at the cost of leaving your meaning vague, not only for your reader but for yourself. This is the significance of mixed metaphors. The sole aim of a metaphor is to call up a visual image. When these images clash—as in *The Fascist octopus has sung its swan song, the jackboot is thrown into the melting pot*—it can be taken as certain that the writer is not seeing a mental image of the objects he is naming; in other words he is not really thinking. Look again at the examples I gave at the beginning of this essay. Professor Laski (1) uses five negatives in fifty-three words. One of these is superfluous, making nonsense of the whole passage, and in addition there is the slip *alien* for *akin*, making further nonsense, and several avoidable pieces of clumsiness which increase the general vagueness. Professor Hogben (2) plays ducks and drakes with a battery which is able to write prescriptions, and while, disapproving of the everyday phrase *put up with*, is unwilling to look *egregious* up in the dictionary and see what it means; (3), if one takes an uncharitable attitude towards it, is simply meaningless: probably one could work out its intended meaning by reading the whole of the article in which it occurs. In (4), the writer knows more or less what he wants to say, but an accumulation of stale phrases chokes him like tea leaves blocking a sink. In (5), words and meaning have almost parted company. People who write in this manner usually have a general emotional meaning—they dislike one thing and want to express solidarity with another—but they are not interested in the detail of what they are saying. A scrupulous writer, in every sentence that he writes, will ask himself at least four questions, thus: What am I trying to say? What words will express it? What image or idiom will make it clearer? Is this image fresh enough to have an effect? And he will probably ask himself two more: Could I put it more shortly? Have I said anything that is avoidably ugly? But you are not obliged to go to all this trouble. You can shirk it by simply throwing your mind open and letting the ready-made phrases come crowding in. They will construct your sentences for you—even think your thoughts for you, to a certain extent—and at need they will perform the important service of partially concealing your meaning even from yourself. It is at this point that the special connection between politics and the debasement of language becomes clear.

In our time it is broadly true that political writing is bad writing. Where it is not true, it will generally be found that the writer is some kind of rebel, expressing his private opinions and not a "party line." Orthodoxy, of whatever color, seems to demand a lifeless, imitative style. The political dialects to be found in pamphlets, leading articles, manifestos, White Papers and the speeches of undersecretaries do, of course, vary from party to party, but they are all alike in that one almost never finds in them a fresh, vivid, home-made turn of speech. When one watches some tired hack on the platform mechanically repeating the familiar phrases—*bestial atrocities, iron heel, bloodstained tyranny, free peoples of the world, stand shoulder to shoulder*—one often has a curious feeling that one is not watching a live human being but some kind of dummy: a feeling which suddenly becomes stronger at moments when the light catches the speaker's spectacles and turns them into blank discs which seem to have no eyes behind them. And this is not altogether fanciful. A speaker who uses that kind of phraseology has gone some distance towards turning himself into a machine. The appropriate noises are coming out of his larynx, but his brain is not involved as it would be if he were choosing his words for himself. If the speech he is making is one that he is accustomed to make over and over again, he may be almost unconscious of what he is saying, as one is when one utters the responses in church. And this reduced state of consciousness, if not indispensable, is at any rate favorable to political conformity.

In our time, political speech and writing are largely the defense of the indefensible. Things like the continuance of British rule in India, the Russian purges and deportations, the dropping of the atom bombs on Japan, can indeed be defended, but only by arguments which are too brutal for most people to face, and which do not square with the professed aims of political parties. Thus political language has to consist largely of euphemism, question-begging and sheer cloudy vagueness. Defenseless villages are bombarded from the air, the inhabitants driven out into the countryside, the cattle machine-gunned, the huts set on fire with incendiary bullets: this is called *pacification*. Millions of peasants are robbed of their farms and sent trudging along the roads with no more than they can carry: this is called *transfer of population* or *rectification of frontiers*. People are imprisoned for years without trial, or shot in the back of the neck or sent to die of scurvy in Arctic lumber camps: this is called *elimination of unreliable elements*. Such phraseology is needed if one wants to name things without calling up mental pictures of them. Consider for instance some comfortable English professor defending Russian totalitarianism. He cannot say outright, "I believe in killing off your opponents when you can get good results by doing so." Probably, therefore, he will say something like this:

> While freely conceding that the Soviet regime exhibits certain features which the humanitarian may be inclined to deplore, we must, I think, agree that a certain curtailment of the right to political opposition is an unavoidable concomitant of transitional periods, and that the rigors which the Russian people have been called upon to undergo have been amply justified in the sphere of concrete achievement.

The inflated style is itself a kind of euphemism. A mass of Latin words falls upon the facts like soft snow, blurring the outlines and covering up all the details. The great enemy of clear language is insincerity. When there is a gap between one's real and one's declared aims, one turns as it were instinctively to long words and exhausted idioms, like a cuttlefish squirting out ink. In our age there is no such thing as "keeping out of politics." All issues are political issues, and politics itself is a mass of lies, evasions, folly, hatred and schizophrenia. When the general atmosphere is bad, language must suffer. I should expect to find—this is a guess which I have not sufficient knowledge to verify—that the German, Russian and Italian languages have all deteriorated in the last ten to fifteen years, as a result of dictatorship.

15   But if thought corrupts language, language can also corrupt thought. A bad usage can spread by tradition and imitation, even among people who should and do know better. The debased language that I have been discussing is in some ways very convenient. Phrases like a *not unjustifiable assumption, leaves much to be desired, would serve no good purpose, a consideration which we should do well to bear in mind,* are a continuous temptation, a packet of aspirins always at one's elbow. Look back through this essay, and for certain you will find that I have again and again committed the very faults I am protesting against. By this morning's post I have received a pamphlet dealing with conditions in Germany. The author tells me that he "felt impelled" to write it. I open it at random, and here is almost the first sentence that I see: "[The Allies] have an opportunity not only of achieving a radical transformation of Germany's social and political structure in such a way as to avoid a nationalistic reaction in Germany itself, but at the same time of laying the foundations of a cooperative and unified Europe." You see, he "feels impelled" to write—feels, presumably, that he has something new to say—and yet his words, like cavalry horses answering the bugle, group themselves automatically into the familiar dreary pattern. This invasion of one's mind by ready-made phrases (*lay the foundations, achieve a radical transformation*) can only be prevented if one is constantly on guard against them, and every such phrase anaesthetizes a portion of one's brain.

I said earlier that the decadence of our language is probably curable. Those who deny this would argue, if they produced an argument at all, that language merely reflects existing social conditions, and that we cannot influence its development by any direct tinkering with words and constructions. As far as the general tone or spirit of a language goes, this may be true, but it is not true in detail. Silly words and expressions have often disappeared, not through any evolutionary process but owing to the conscious action of a minority. Two recent examples were *explore every avenue* and *leave no stone unturned*, which were killed by the jeers of a few journalists. There is a long list of flyblown metaphors which could similarly be got rid of if enough people would interest themselves in the job; and it should also be possible to laugh the *not un-* formation out of existence,[3] to reduce the amount of Latin and Greek in the average sentence, to drive out foreign phrases

---

[3] One can cure oneself of the *not un-* formation by memorizing this sentence: *A not unblack dog was chasing a not unsmall rabbit across a not ungreen field.*

and strayed scientific words, and, in general, to make pretentiousness unfashionable. But all these are minor points. The defense of the English language implies more than this, and perhaps it is best to start by saying what it does *not* imply.

To begin with it has nothing to do with archaism, with the salvaging of obsolete words and turns of speech, or with the setting up of a "standard English" which must never be departed from. On the contrary, it is especially concerned with the scrapping of every word or idiom which has outworn its usefulness. It has nothing to do with correct grammar and syntax, which are of no importance so long as one makes one's meaning clear, or with the avoidance of Americanisms, or with having what is called a "good prose style." On the other hand it is not concerned with fake simplicity and the attempt to make written English colloquial. Nor does it even imply in every case preferring the Saxon word to the Latin one, though it does imply using the fewest and shortest words that will cover one's meaning. What is above all needed is to let the meaning choose the word, and not the other way about. In prose, the worst thing one can do with words is to surrender to them. When you think of a concrete object, you think wordlessly, and then, if you want to describe the thing you have been visualizing you probably hunt about till you find the exact words that seem to fit it. When you think of something abstract you are more inclined to use words from the start, and unless you make a conscious effort to prevent it, the existing dialect will come rushing in and do the job for you, at the expense of blurring or even changing your meaning. Probably it is better to put off using words as long as possible and get one's meaning as clear as one can through pictures or sensations. Afterwards one can choose—not simply *accept*—the phrases that will best cover the meaning, and then switch round and decide what impression one's words are likely to make on another person. This last effort of the mind cuts out all stale or mixed images, all prefabricated phrases, needless repetitions, and humbug and vagueness generally. But one can often be in doubt about the effect of a word or a phase, and one needs rules that one can rely on when instinct fails. I think the following rules will cover most cases:

1. Never use a metaphor, simile or other figure of speech which you are used to seeing in print.
2. Never use a long word where a short one will do.
3. If it is possible to cut a word out, always cut it out.
4. Never use the passive where you can use the active.

5. Never use a foreign phrase, a scientific word or a jargon word if you can think of an everyday English equivalent.
6. Break any of these rules sooner than say anything outright barbarous.

These rules sound elementary, and so they are, but they demand a deep change of attitude in anyone who has grown used to writing in the style now fashionable. One could keep all of them and still write bad English, but one could not write the kind of stuff that I quoted in those five specimens at the beginning of this article.

I have not here been considering the literary use of language, but merely language as an instrument for expressing and not for concealing or preventing thought. Stuart Chase and others have come near to claiming that all abstract words are meaningless, and have used this as a pretext for advocating a kind of political quietism. Since you don't know what Fascism is, how can you struggle against Fascism? One need not swallow such absurdities as this, but one ought to recognize that the present political chaos is connected with the decay of language, and that one can probably bring about some improvement by starting at the verbal end. If you simplify your English, you are freed from the worst follies of orthodoxy. You cannot speak any of the necessary dialects, and when you make a stupid remark its stupidity will be obvious, even to yourself. Political language—and with variations this is true of all political parties, from Conservatives to Anarchists—is designed to make lies sound truthful and murder respectable, and to give an appearance of solidity to pure wind. One cannot change this all in a moment, but one can at least change one's own habits, and from time to time one can even, if one jeers loudly enough, send some worn-out and useless phrase—some *jackboot, Achilles' heel, hotbed, melting pot, acid test, veritable inferno* or other lump of verbal refuse—into the dustbin where it belongs.

SUGGESTIONS FOR WRITING

1. According to Orwell, why do politicians speak and write as they do? Find an example of political writing in a recent newspaper or magazine. Using Orwell's rules and suggestions, write an essay that analyzes your choice on his principles.
2. Pick an essay that you have written recently. Now write another essay that analyzes your example from Orwell's point of view.

3. Pick a writer from this chapter. Write an essay that analyzes his or her political writing on the principles Orwell expresses.

Letter from Birmingham Jail   1963

MARTIN LUTHER KING, JR.

Martin Luther King, Jr. was born in Atlanta, Georgia in 1929. He followed his father, Martin Luther King, Sr., into the ministry after a college education that began at the age of fifteen, having skipped part of high school—he was accepted at Morehouse College on the basis of his high college entrance examination scores. After college, he graduated from a seminary and went on to take his doctorate at Boston University.

As head of the Southern Christian Leadership Conference, he was a pivotal figure in the civil rights movement. The essay that follows was to make him a world famous figure, and in 1964 he won the Nobel Peace Prize for his work. He was assassinated in 1968.

My Dear Fellow Clergymen:

While confined here in the Birmingham city jail, I came across your recent statement calling my present activities "unwise and untimely." Seldom do I pause to answer criticism of my work and ideas. If I sought to answer all the criticism that cross my desk, my secretaries would have little time for anything other than such correspondence in the course of the day, and I would have no time for constructive work. But since I feel that you are men of genuine good will and that your criticisms are sincerely set forth, I want to try to answer your statement in what I hope will be patient and reasonable terms.

I think I should indicate why I am here in Birmingham, since you have been influenced by the view which argues against "outsiders coming in." I have the honor of serving as president of the Southern Christian Leadership Conference, an organization operating in every southern state, with headquarters in Atlanta, Georgia. We have some eighty-five affiliated organizations across the South, and one of them is the Alabama Christian Movement for Human Rights. Frequently we share staff, educational and financial resources with our affiliates. Several months ago the affiliate here in Birmingham asked us to be on call to engage in a nonviolent direct-action program if such were deemed necessary. We readily consented, and when the hour came we lived up to our promise. So I, along with several members of my staff, am here because I was invited here. I am here because I have organizational ties here.

But more basically, I am in Birmingham because injustice is here. Just as the prophets of the eighth century B.C. left their villages and carried their "thus saith the Lord" far beyond the boundaries of their home towns, and just as the Apostle Paul left his village of Tarsus and carried the gospel of Jesus Christ to the far corners of the Greco-Roman world, so am I compelled to carry the gospel of freedom beyond my own home town. Like Paul, I must constantly respond to the Macedonian call for aid.

Moreover, I am cognizant of the interrelatedness of all communities and states. I cannot sit idly by in Atlanta and not be concerned about what happens in Birmingham. Injustice anywhere is a threat to justice everywhere. We are caught in an inescapable network of mutuality, tied in a single garment of destiny. Whatever affects one directly, affects all indirectly. Never again can we afford to live with the narrow, provincial "outside agitator" idea. Anyone who lives inside the United States can never be considered an outsider anywhere within its bounds.

5   You deplore the demonstrations taking place in Birmingham. But your statement, I am sorry to say, fails to express a similar concern for the conditions that brought about the demonstrations. I am sure that none of you would want to rest content with the superficial kind of social analysis that deals merely with effects and does not grapple with underlying causes. It is unfortunate that demonstrations are taking place in Birmingham, but it is even more unfortunate that the city's white power structure left the Negro community with no alternative.

In any nonviolent campaign there are four basic steps: collection of the facts to determine whether injustices exist; negotiation; self-purification; and direct action. We have gone through all these steps in Birmingham. There can be no gainsaying the fact that racial injustice engulfs this community. Birmingham is probably the most thoroughly segregated city in the United States. Its ugly record of brutality is widely known. Negroes have experienced grossly unjust treatment in the courts. There have been more unsolved bombings of Negro homes and churches in Birmingham than in any other city in the nation. These are the hard, brutal facts of the case. On the basis of these conditions, Negro leaders sought to negotiate with the city fathers. But the latter consistently refused to engage in good-faith negotiation.

Then, last September, came the opportunity to talk with leaders of Birmingham's economic community. In the course of the negotiations, certain promises were made by the merchants—for example, to remove the stores' humiliating racial signs. On the basis of these promises, the

Reverend Fred Shuttlesworth and the leaders of the Alabama Christian Movement for Human Rights agreed to a moratorium on all demonstrations. As the weeks and months went by, we realized that we were the victims of a broken promise. A few signs, briefly removed, returned; the others remained.

As in so many past experiences, our hopes had been blasted, and the shadow of deep disappointment settled upon us. We had no alternative except to prepare for direct action, whereby we would present our very bodies as a means of laying our case before the conscience of the local and the national community. Mindful of the difficulties involved, we decided to undertake a process of self-purification. We began a series of workshops on nonviolence, and we repeatedly asked ourselves: "Are you able to accept blows without retaliating?" "Are you able to endure the ordeal of jail?" We decided to schedule our direct-action program for the Easter season, realizing that except for Christmas, this is the main shopping period of the year. Knowing that a strong economic-withdrawal program would be the by-product of direct action, we felt that this would be the best time to bring pressure to bear on the merchants for the needed change.

Then it occurred to us that Birmingham's mayoralty election was coming up in March, and we speedily decided to postpone action until after election day. When we discovered that the Commissioner of Public Safety, Eugene "Bull" Connor, had piled up enough votes to be in the run-off, we decided again to postpone action until the day after the run-off so that the demonstrations could not be used to could the issues. Like many others, we waited to see Mr. Connor defeated, and to this end we endured postponement after postponement. Having aided in this community need, we felt that our direct-action program could be delayed no longer.

10   You may well ask: "Why direct action? Why sit-ins, marches and so forth? Isn't negotiation a better path?" You are quite right in calling for negotiation. Indeed, this is the very purpose of direct action. Nonviolent direct action seeks to create such a crisis and foster such a tension that a community which has constantly refused to negotiate is forced to confront the issue. It seeks so to dramatize the issue that it can no longer be ignored. My citing the creation of tension as part of the work of the nonviolent resister may sound rather shocking. But I must confess that I am not afraid of the word "tension." I have earnestly opposed violent tension, but there is a type of constructive, nonviolent tension which is

necessary for growth. Just as Socrates felt that it was necessary to create a tension in the mind so that individuals could rise from the bondage of myths and half-truths to the unfettered realm of creative analysis and objective appraisal, so must we see the need for nonviolent gadflies to create the kind of tension in society that will help men rise from the dark depths of prejudice and racism to the majestic heights of understanding and brotherhood.

The purpose of our direct-action program is to create a situation so crisis-packed that it will inevitably open the door to negotiation. I therefore concur with you in your call for negotiation. Too long has our beloved Southland been bogged down in a tragic effort to live in monologue rather than dialogue.

One of the basic points in your statement is that the action that I and my associates have taken in Birmingham is untimely. Some have asked: "Why didn't you give the new city administration time to act?" The only answer that I can give to this query is that the new Birmingham administration must be prodded about as much as the outgoing one, before it will act. We are sadly mistaken if we feel that the election of Albert Boutwell as mayor will bring the millennium to Birmingham. While Mr. Boutwell is a much more gentle person than Mr. Connor, they are both segregationists, dedicated to maintenance of the status quo. I have hope that Mr. Boutwell will be reasonable enough to see the futility of massive resistance to desegregation. But he will not see this without pressure from devotees of civil rights. My friends, I must say to you that we have not made a single gain in civil rights without determined legal and nonviolent pressure. Lamentably, it is an historical fact that privileged groups seldom give up their privileges voluntarily. Individuals may see the moral light and voluntarily give up their unjust posture; but, as Reinhold Niebuhr has reminded us, groups tend to be more immoral than individuals.

We know through painful experience that freedom is never voluntarily given by the oppressor; it must be demanded by the oppressed. Frankly, I have yet to engage in a direct-action campaign that was "well timed" in the view of those who have not suffered unduly from the disease of segregation. For years now I have heard the word "Wait!" It rings in the ear of every Negro with piercing familiarity. This "Wait" has almost always meant "Never." We must come to see, with one of our distinguished jurists, that "justice too long delayed is justice denied."

We have waited for more than 340 years for our constitutional and God-given rights. The nations of Asia and Africa are moving with jet-like speed toward gaining political independence, but we still creep at horse-and-buggy pace toward gaining a cup of coffee at a lunch counter. Perhaps it is easy for those who have never felt the stinging darts of segregation to say, "Wait." But when you have seen vicious mobs lynch your mothers and fathers at will and drown your sisters and brothers at whim; when you have seen hate-filled policemen curse, kick and even kill your black brothers and sisters; when you see the vast majority of your twenty million Negro brothers smothering in an airtight cage of poverty in the midst of an affluent society; when you suddenly find your tongue twisted and your speech stammering as you seek to explain to your six-year-old daughter why she can't go to the public amusement park that has just been advertised on television, and see tears welling up in her eyes when she is told that Funtown is closed to colored children, and see ominous clouds of inferiority beginning to form in her little mental sky, and see her beginning to distort her personality by developing an unconscious bitterness toward white people; when you have to concoct an answer for a five-year-old son who is asking: "Daddy, why do white people treat colored people so mean?"; when you take a cross-country drive and find it necessary to sleep night after night in the uncomfortable corners of your automobile because no motel will accept you; when you are humiliated day in and day out by nagging signs reading "white" and "colored"; when your first name becomes "nigger," your middle name becomes "boy" (however old you are) and your last name becomes "John," and your wife and mother are never given the respected title "Mrs."; when you are harried by day and haunted by night by the fact that you are a Negro, living constantly at tiptoe stance, never quite knowing what to expect next, and are plagued with inner fears and outer resentments; when you are forever fighting a degenerating sense of "nobodiness"— then you will understand why we find it difficult to wait. There comes a time when the cup of endurance runs over, and men are no longer willing to be plunged into the abyss of despair. I hope, sirs, you can understand our legitimate and unavoidable impatience.

15   You express a great deal of anxiety over our willingness to break laws. This is certainly a legitimate concern. Since we so diligently urge people to obey the Supreme Court's decision of 1954 outlawing segregation in the public schools, at first glance it may seem rather paradoxical for us

consciously to break laws. One may well ask: "How can you advocate breaking some laws and obeying others?" The answer lies in the fact that there are two types of laws: just and unjust. I would be the first to advocate obeying just laws. One has not only a legal but a moral responsibility to obey just laws. Conversely, one has a moral responsibility to disobey unjust laws. I would agree with St. Augustine that "an unjust law is no law at all."

Now, what is the difference between the two? How does one determine whether a law is just or unjust? A just law is a man-made code that squares with the moral law or the law of God. An unjust law is a code that is out of harmony with the moral law. To put it in the terms of St. Thomas Aquinas: An unjust law is a human law that is not rooted in eternal law and natural law. Any law that uplifts human personality is just. Any law that degrades human personality is unjust. All segregation statutes are unjust because segregation distorts the soul and damages the personality. It gives the segregator a false sense of superiority and the segregated a false sense of inferiority. Segregation, to use the terminology of the Jewish philosopher Martin Buber, substitutes an "I-it" relationship for an "I-thou" relationship and ends up relegating persons to the status of things. Hence segregation is not only politically, economically and sociologically unsound, it is morally wrong and sinful. Paul Tillich has said that sin is separation. Is not segregation an existential expression of man's tragic separation, his awful estrangement, his terrible sinfulness? Thus it is that I can urge men to obey the 1954 decision of the Supreme Court, for it is morally right; and I can urge them to disobey segregation ordinances, for they are morally wrong.

Let us consider a more concrete example of just and unjust laws. An unjust law is a code that a numerical or power majority group compels a minority group to obey but does not make binding on itself. This is *difference* made legal. By the same token, a just law is a code that a majority compels a minority to follow and that it is willing to follow itself. This is *sameness* made legal.

Let me give another explanation. A law is unjust if it is inflicted on a minority that, as a result of being denied the right to vote, had no part in enacting or devising the law. Who can say that the legislature of Alabama which set up that state's segregation laws was democratically elected? Throughout Alabama all sorts of devious methods are used to prevent Negroes from becoming registered voters, and there are some counties in which, even though Negroes constitute a majority of the population, not a single Negro is registered. Can any law enacted under such circumstances be considered democratically structured?

Sometimes a law is just on its face and unjust in its application. For instance, I have been arrested on a charge of parading without a permit. Now, there is nothing wrong in having an ordinance which requires a permit for a parade. But such an ordinance becomes unjust when it is used to maintain segregation and to deny citizens the First-Amendment privilege of peaceful assembly and protest.

20   I hope you are able to see the distinction I am trying to point out. In no sense do I advocate evading or defying the law, as would the rabid segregationist. That would lead to anarchy. One who breaks an unjust law must do so openly, lovingly, and with a willingness to accept the penalty. I submit that an individual who breaks a law that conscience tells him is unjust, and who willingly accepts the penalty of imprisonment in order to arouse the conscience of the community over its injustice, is in reality expressing the highest respect for law.

Of course, there is nothing new about this kind of civil disobedience. It was evidenced sublimely in the refusal of Shadrach, Meshach and Abednego to obey the laws of Nebuchadnezzar, on the ground that a higher moral law was at stake. It was practiced superbly by the early Christians, who were willing to face hungry lions and the excruciating pain of chopping blocks rather than submit to certain unjust laws of the Roman Empire. To a degree, academic freedom is a reality today because Socrates practiced civil disobedience. In our own nation, the Boston Tea Party represented a massive act of civil disobedience.

We should never forget that everything Adolf Hitler did in Germany was "legal" and everything the Hungarian freedom fighters did in Hungary was "illegal." It was "illegal" to aid and comfort a Jew in Hitler's Germany. Even so, I am sure that, had I lived in Germany at the time, I would have aided and comforted my Jewish brothers. If today I lived in a Communist country where certain principles dear to the Christian faith are suppressed, I would openly advocate disobeying that country's antireligious laws.

I must make two honest confessions to you, my Christian and Jewish brothers. First, I must confess that over the past few years I have been gravely disappointed with the white moderate. I have almost reached the regrettable conclusion that the Negro's great stumbling block in his stride toward freedom is not the White Citizen's Counciler or the Ku Klux Klanner, but the white moderate, who is more devoted to "order" than to justice; who prefers a negative peace which is the absence of tension to a positive peace which is the presence of justice; who constantly says: "I agree with you in the goal you seek, but I cannot agree with your methods of direct action"; who paternalistically believes he can set the timetable for another man's freedom; who lives by a mythical concept of time and who constantly advises the Negro to wait for a "more convenient season." Shallow understanding from people of good will is more frustrating than absolute misunderstanding from people of ill will. Lukewarm acceptance is much more bewildering than outright rejection.

I had hoped that the white moderate would understand that law and order exist for the purpose of establishing justice and that when they fail in this purpose they become the dangerously structured dams that block the flow of social progress. I had hoped that the white moderate would understand that the present tension in the South is a necessary phase of the transition from an obnoxious negative peace, in which the Negro passively accepted his unjust plight, to a substantive and positive peace, in which all men will respect the dignity and worth of human personality. Actually, we who engage in nonviolent direct action are not the creators of tension. We merely bring to the surface the hidden tension that is already alive. We bring it out in the open, where it can be seen and dealt with. Like a boil that can never be cured so long as it is covered up but must be opened with all its ugliness to the natural medicines of air and light, injustice must be exposed, with all the tension its exposure creates, to the light of human conscience and the air of national opinion before it can be cured.

25   In your statement you assert that our actions, even though peaceful, must be condemned because they precipitate violence. But is this a logical assertion? Isn't this like condemning a robbed man because his possession of money precipitated the evil act of robbery? Isn't this like condemning Socrates because his unswerving commitment to truth and his philosophical inquiries precipitated the act by the misguided populace in which they made him drink hemlock? Isn't this like condemning Jesus because his unique God-consciousness and never-ceasing devotion to God's will precipitated the evil act of crucifixion? We must come to see that, as the federal courts have consistently affirmed, it is wrong to urge an individual to cease his efforts to gain his basic constitutional rights because the quest may precipitate violence. Society must protect the robbed and punish the robber.

I had also hoped that the white moderate would reject the myth concerning time in relation to the struggle for freedom. I have just received a letter from a white brother in Texas. He writes: "All Christians know that the colored people will receive equal rights eventually, but it is possible that you are in too great a religious hurry. It has taken Christianity almost two thousand years to accomplish what it has. The teachings of Christ take time to come to earth." Such an attitude stems from a tragic misconception of time, from the strangely irrational notion that there is something in the very flow of time that will inevitably cure all ills. Actually, time itself is neutral; it can be used either destructively or constructively. More and more I feel that the people of ill will have used time much more effectively than have the people of good will. We will have to repent in this generation not merely for the hateful words and actions of the bad people but for the appalling silence of the good people. Human progress never rolls in on wheels of inevitability; it comes through the tireless efforts of men willing to be coworkers with God, and without this hard work, time itself becomes an ally of the forces of social stagnation. We must use time creatively, in the knowledge that the time is always ripe to do right. Now is the time to make real the promise of democracy and transform our pending national elegy into a creative psalm of brotherhood. Now is the time to lift our national policy from the quicksand of racial injustice to the solid rock of human dignity.

You speak of our activity in Birmingham as extreme. At first I was rather disappointed that fellow clergymen would see my nonviolent efforts as those of an extremist. I began thinking about the fact that I stand in the middle of two opposing forces in the Negro community. One is a force of complacency, made up in part of Negroes who, as a result of long years of oppression, are so drained of self-respect and a sense of "somebodiness" that they have adjusted to segregation; and in part of a few middle-class Negroes who, because of a degree of academic and economic security and because in some ways they profit by segregation, have become insensitive to the problems of masses. The other force is one of bitterness and hatred, and it comes perilously close to advocating violence. It is expressed in the various black nationalist groups that are springing up across the nation, the largest and best-known being Elijah Muhammad's Muslim movement. Nourished by the Negro's frustration over the continued existence of racial discrimination, this movement is made up of people who have lost faith in

America, who have absolutely repudiated Christianity, and who have concluded that the white man is an incorrigible "devil."

I have tried to stand between these two forces, saying that we need emulate neither the "do-nothingism" of the complacent nor the hatred and despair of the black nationalist. For there is the more excellent way of love and nonviolent protest. I am grateful to God that, through the influence of the Negro church, the way of nonviolence became an integral part of our struggle.

If this philosophy had not emerged, by now many streets of the South would, I am convinced, be flowing with blood. And I am further convinced that if our white brothers dismiss as "rabble-rousers" and "outside agitators" those of us who employ nonviolent direct action, and if they refuse to support our nonviolent efforts, millions of Negroes will, out of frustration and despair, seek solace and security in black-nationalist ideologies—a development that would inevitably lead to a frightening racial nightmare.

30   Oppressed people cannot remain oppressed forever. The yearning for freedom eventually manifests itself, and that is what has happened to the American Negro. Something within has reminded him of his birthright of freedom, and something without has reminded him that it can be gained. Consciously or unconsciously, he has been caught up by the *Zeitgeist*, and with his black brothers of Africa and his brown and yellow brothers of Asia, South America and the Caribbean, the United States Negro is moving with a sense of great urgency toward the promised land of racial justice. If one recognizes this vital urge that has engulfed the Negro community, one should readily understand why public demonstrations are taking place. The Negro has many pent-up resentments and latent frustrations, and he must release them. So let him march; let him make prayer pilgrimages to the city hall; let him go on freedom rides—and try to understand why he must do so. If his repressed emotions are not released in nonviolent ways, they will seek expression through violence; this is not a threat but a fact of history. So I have not said to my people: "Get rid of your discontent." Rather, I have tried to say that this normal and healthy discontent can be chan-neled into the creative outlet of nonviolent direct action. And now this approach is being termed extremist.

But though I was initially disappointed at being categorized as an extremist, as I continued to think about the matter I gradually gained a measure of satisfaction from the label. Was not Jesus an extremist for love: "Love your enemies, bless them that curse you, do good to them that hate you, and pray for them which despitefully use you, and persecute you." Was not Amos an extremist for justice: "Let justice roll down like waters and righteousness like an ever-flowing stream." Was not Paul an extremist for the Christian gospel: "I bear in my body the marks of the Lord Jesus." Was not Martin Luther an extremist: "Here I stand; I cannot do otherwise, so help me God." And John Bunyan: "I will stay in jail to the end of my days before I make a butchery of my conscience." And Abraham Lincoln: "This nation cannot survive half slave and half free." And Thomas Jefferson: "We hold these truths to be self-evident, that all men are created equal..." So the question is not whether we will be extremists, but what kind of extremists we will be. Will we be extremists for hate or for love? Will we be extremists for the preservation of injustice or for the extension of justice? In that dramatic scene on Calvary's hill three men were crucified. We must never forget that all three were crucified for the same crime—the crime of extremism. Two were extremists for immorality, and thus fell below their environment. The other, Jesus Christ, was an extremist for love, truth and goodness, and thereby rose above his environment. Perhaps the South, the nation and the world are in dire need of creative extremists.

I had hoped that the white moderate would see this need. Perhaps I was too optimistic; perhaps I expected too much. I suppose I should have realized that few members of the oppressor race can understand the deep groans and passionate yearnings of the oppressed race, and still fewer have the vision to see that injustice must be rooted out by strong, persistent and determined action. I am thankful, however, that some of our white brothers in the South have grasped the meaning of this social revolution and committed themselves to it. They are still all too few in quantity, but they are big in quality. Some—such as Ralph McGill, Lillian Smith, Harry Golden, James McBride Dabbs, Ann Braden and Sarah Patton Boyle—have written about our struggle in eloquent and prophetic terms. Others have marched with us down nameless streets of the South. They have languished in filthy, roach-infested jails, suffering the abuse and brutality of policemen who view them as "dirty niggerlovers," Unlike so many of their moderate brothers and sisters, they have recognized the urgency of the moment and sensed the need for powerful "action" antidotes to combat the disease of segregation.

Let me take note of my other major disappointment. I have been so greatly disappointed with the white church and its leadership.

Of course, there are some notable exceptions. I am not unmindful of the fact that each of you has taken some significant stands on this issue. I commend you, Reverend Stallings, for your Christian stand on this past Sunday, in welcoming Negroes to your worship service on a non-segregated basis. I commend the Catholic leaders of this state for integrating Spring Hill College several years ago.

But despite these notable exceptions, I must honestly reiterate that I have been disappointed with the Church. I do not say this as one of those negative critics who can always find something wrong with the church. I say this as a minister of the gospel, who loves the church; who was nurtured in its bosom; who has been sustained by its spiritual blessings and who will remain true to it as long as the cord of life shall lengthen.

35   When I was suddenly catapulted into the leadership of the bus protest in Montgomery, Alabama, a few years ago, I felt we would be supported by the white church. I felt that the white ministers, priests and rabbis of the South would be among our strongest allies. Instead, some have been outright opponents, refusing to understand the freedom movement and misrepresenting its leaders; all too many others have been more cautious than courageous and have remained silent behind the anesthetizing security of stained-glass windows.

In spite of my shattered dreams, I came to Birmingham with the hope that the white religious leadership of this community would see the justice of our cause and, with deep moral concern, would serve as the channel through which our just grievances could reach the power structure. I had hoped that each of you would understand. But again I have been disappointed.

I have heard numerous southern religious leaders admonish their worshipers to comply with a desegregation decision because it is the law, but I have longed to hear white ministers declare: "Follow this decree because integration is morally right and because the Negro is your brother." In the midst of blatant injustices inflicted upon the Negro, I have watched white churchmen stand on the sideline and mouth pious irrelevancies and sanctimonious trivialities. In the midst of a mighty struggle to rid our nation of racial and economic injustice, I have heard many ministers say: "Those are social issues, with which the gospel has no real concern." And I have watched many churches commit themselves to a completely other-worldly religion which makes a strange, un-Biblical distinction between body and soul, between the sacred and the secular.

I have traveled the length and breadth of Alabama, Mississippi and all the other southern states. On sweltering summer days and crisp autumn mornings I have looked at the South's beautiful churches with their lofty spires pointing heavenward. I have beheld the impressive outlines of her massive religious-education buildings. Over and over I have found myself saying: "What kind of people worship here? Who is their God? Where were their voices when the lips of Governor Barnett dripped with words of interposition and nullification? Where were they when Governor Wallace gave a clarion call for defiance and hatred? Where were their voices of support when bruised and weary Negro men and women decided to rise from the dark dungeons of complacency to the bright hills of creative protest?"

Yes, these questions are still in my mind. In deep disappointment I have wept over the laxity of the church. But be assured that my tears have been tears of love. There can be no deep disappointment where there is not deep love. Yes, I love the church. How could I do otherwise? I am in the rather unique position of being the son, the grandson and the great-grandson of preachers. Yes, I see the church as the body of Christ. But, oh! How we have blemished and scarred that body through social neglect and through fear of being nonconformists.

40 There was a time when the church was very powerful—in the time when the early Christians rejoiced at being deemed worthy to suffer for what they believed. In those days the church was not merely a thermometer that recorded the ideas and principles of popular opinion; it was a thermostat that transformed the mores of society. Whenever the early Christians entered a town, the people in power became disturbed and immediately sought to convict the Christians for being "disturbers of the peace" and "outside agitators." But the Christians pressed on, in the conviction that they were "a colony of heaven," called to obey God rather than man. Small in number, they were big in commitment. They were too God-intoxicated to be "astronomically intimidated." By their effort and example they brought an end to such ancient evils as infanticide and gladiatorial contests.

Things are different now. So often the contemporary church is a weak, ineffectual voice with an uncertain sound. So often it is an archdefender of the status quo. Far from being disturbed by the presence of the church, the power structure of the average community is consoled by the church's silent—and often even vocal—sanction of things as they are.

But the judgment of God is upon the church as never before. If today's church does not recapture the sacrificial spirit of the early church, it will lose its authenticity, forfeit the loyalty of millions, and be dismissed as an irrelevant social club with no meaning for the twentieth century. Every day I meet young people whose disappointment with the church has turned into outright disgust.

Perhaps I have once again been too optimistic. Is organized religion too inextricably bound to the status quo to save our nation and the world? Perhaps I must turn my faith to the inner spiritual church, the church within the church, as the true *ekklesia* and the hope of the world. But again I am thankful to God that some noble souls from the ranks of organized religion have broken loose from the paralyzing chains of conformity and joined us as active partners in the struggle for freedom. They have left their secure congregations and walked the streets of Albany, Georgia, with us. They have gone down the highways of the South on tortuous rides for freedom. Yes, they have gone to jail with us. Some have been dismissed from their churches, have lost the support of their bishops and fellow ministers. But they have acted in the faith that right defeated is stronger than evil triumphant. Their witness has been the spiritual salt that has preserved the true meaning of the gospel in these troubled times. They have carved a tunnel of hope through the dark mountain of disappointment.

I hope the church as a whole will meet the challenge of this decisive hour. But even if the church does not come to the aid of justice, I have no despair about the future. I have no fear about the outcome of our struggle in Birmingham, even if our motives are at present misunderstood. We will reach the goal of freedom in Birmingham and all over the nation, because the goal of America is freedom. Abused and scorned though we may be, our destiny is tied up with America's destiny. Before the pilgrims landed at Plymouth, we were here. Before the pen of Jefferson etched the majestic words of the Declaration of Independence across the pages of history, we were here. For more than two centuries our forebears labored in this country without wages; they made cotton king; they built the homes of their masters while suffering gross injustice and shameful humiliation—and yet out of a bottomless vitality they continued to thrive and develop. If the inexpressible cruelties of slavery could not stop us, the opposition we now face will surely fail. We will win our freedom because the sacred heritage of our nation and the eternal will of God are embodied in our echoing demands.

45   Before closing I feel impelled to mention one other point in your statement that has troubled me profoundly. You warmly commended the Birmingham police force for keeping "order" and "preventing violence." I doubt that you would have so warmly commended the police force if you had seen its dogs sinking their teeth into unarmed, nonviolent Negroes. I doubt that you would so quickly commend the policemen if you were to observe their ugly and inhumane treatment of Negroes here in the city jail; if you were to watch them push and curse old Negro women and young Negro girls; if you were to see them slap and kick old Negro men and young boys; if you were to observe them, as they did on two occasions, refuse to give us food because we wanted to sing our grace together. I cannot join you in your praise of the Birmingham police department.

It is true that the police have exercised a degree of discipline in handling the demonstrators. In this sense they have conducted themselves rather "nonviolently" in public. But for what purpose? To preserve the evil system of segregation. Over the past few years I have consistently preached that nonviolence demands that the means we use must be as pure as the ends we seek. I have tried to make clear that it is wrong to use immoral means to attain moral ends. But now I must affirm that it is just as wrong, or perhaps even more so, to use moral means to preserve immoral ends. Perhaps Mr. Connor and his policemen have been rather nonviolent in public, as was Chief Pritchett in Albany, Georgia, but they have used the moral means of nonviolence to maintain the immoral end of racial injustice. As T. S. Eliot has said: "The last temptation is the greatest treason: To do the right deed for the wrong reason."

I wish you had commended the Negro sit-inners and demonstrators of Birmingham for their sublime courage, their willingness to suffer and their amazing discipline in the midst of great provocation. One day the South will recognize its real heroes. They will be the James Merediths, with the noble sense of purpose that enables them to face jeering and hostile mobs, and with the agonizing loneliness that characterizes the life of the pioneer. They will be old, oppressed, battered Negro women, symbolized in a seventy-two-year-old woman in Montgomery, Alabama, who rose up with a sense of dignity and with her people decided not to ride segregated buses, and who responded with ungrammatical profundity to one who inquired about her weariness: "My feets is tired, but my soul is at rest." They will be the young high school and college students, the young ministers of the gospel and a host of their elders, courageously and nonviolently sitting in at lunch counters and willingly going to jail for conscience sake. One day the South will know that when these disinherited children of God sat down at lunch counters, they were in reality standing up for what is best in the American dream and for the most sacred values in our Judaeo-Christian heritage, thereby bringing our nation back to those great wells of democracy which were dug deep by the founding fathers in their formulation of the Constitution and the Declaration of Independence.

Never before have I written so long a letter. I'm afraid it is much too long to take your precious time. I can assure you that it would have been much shorter if I had been writing from a comfortable desk, but what else can one do when he is alone in a narrow jail cell, other than write long letters, think long thoughts and pray long prayers?

If I have said anything in this letter that overstates the truth and indicates an unreasonable impatience, I beg you to forgive me. If I have said anything that understates the truth and indicates my having a patience that allows me to settle for anything less than brotherhood, I beg God to forgive me.

I hope this letter finds you strong in the faith. I also hope that circumstances will soon make it possible for me to meet each of you, not as an integrationist or a civil-rights leader but as a fellow clergyman and a Christian brother. Let us all hope that the dark clouds of racial prejudice will soon pass away and the deep fog of misunderstanding will be lifted from our fear-drenched communities, and in some not too distant tomorrow the radiant stars of love and brotherhood will shine over our great nation with all their scintillating beauty.

Yours for the cause of Peace and Brotherhood,
Martin Luther King, Jr.

SUGGESTIONS FOR WRITING

1. Write an essay that analyzes the position King takes in his letter on the relationship of government and human rights.
2. In the course of his letter, King refers to Thomas Jefferson and the Declaration of Independence. Write an essay that analyzes the common principles of human rights shared by the two men.
3. King's letter was originally addressed to his fellow clergymen, and he raises many religious issues along with political ones. Write an essay that analyzes the relationship between church and state implied by King's writing.

The Ballot or the Bullet
1964

MALCOLM X

While in prison for burglary, Malcolm X (born Malcolm Little) taught himself to read and write and entered into an investigation of the causes and results of racism in America. He became a convert to Islam and rose high in the ranks of the Black Muslim movement headed by Elijah Mohammed. He delivered the following speech in 1964, in part to present his movement's attitude toward the nonviolent policies of Martin Luther King, Jr. Not quite a year later, Malcolm X was assassinated at a rally in New York City.

If we don't do something real soon, I think you'll have to agree that we're going to be forced either to use the ballot or the bullet. It's one or the other in 1964. It isn't that time is running out—time has run out! 1964 threatens to be the most explosive year America has ever witnessed. The most explosive year. Why? It's also a political year. It's the year when all of the white politicians will be back in the so-called Negro community jiving you and me for some votes. The year when all of the white political crooks will be right back in your and my community with their false promises, building up our hopes for a letdown, with their trickery and their treachery, with their false promises which they don't intend to keep. As they nourish these dissatisfactions, it can only lead to one thing, an explosion; and now we have the type of black man on the scene in America today—I'm sorry, Brother Lomax—who just doesn't intend to turn the other cheek any longer.

Don't let anybody tell you anything about the odds are against you. If they draft you, they send you to Korea and make you face 800 million Chinese. If you can be brave over there, you can be brave right here. These odds aren't as great as those odds. And if you fight here, you will at least know what you're fighting for.

I'm not a politician, not even a student of politics; in fact, I'm not a student of much of anything. I'm not a Democrat, I'm not a Republican, and I don't even consider myself an American. If you and I were Americans, there'd be no problem. Those Hunkies that just got off the boat, they're already Americans; Polacks are already Americans; the Italian refugees are already Americans. Everything that came out of Europe, every blue-eyed thing, is already an American. And as long as you and I have been over here, we aren't Americans yet.

Well, I am one who doesn't believe in deluding myself. I'm not going to sit at your table and watch you eat, with nothing on my plate, and call myself a diner. Sitting at the table doesn't make you a diner, unless you eat some of what's on that plate. Being here in America doesn't make you an American. Being born here in America doesn't make you an American. Why, if birth made you American, you wouldn't need any legislation, you wouldn't need any amendments to the Constitution, you wouldn't be faced with civil-rights filibustering in Washington, D.C., right now. They don't have to pass civil-rights legislation to make a Polack an American.

No, I'm not an American. I'm one of the 22 million black people who are the victims of Americanism. One of the 22 million black people who are the victims of democracy, nothing but disguised hypocrisy. So, I'm not standing here speaking to you as an American, or a patriot, or a flag-saluter, or a flag-waver—no, not I. I'm speaking as a victim of this American system. And I see America through the eyes of the victim. I don't see any American dream; I see an American nightmare. . . .

Last but not least, I must say this concerning the great controversy over rifles and shotguns. The only thing that I've ever said is that in areas where the government has proven itself either unwilling or unable to defend the lives and the property of Negroes, it's time for Negroes to defend themselves. Article number two of the constitutional amendments provides you and me the right to own a rifle or a shotgun. It is constitutionally legal to own a shotgun or a rifle. This doesn't mean you're going to get a rifle and form battalions and go out looking for white folks, although you'd be within your rights—I mean, you'd be justified; but that would be illegal and we don't do anything illegal. If the white man doesn't want the black man buying rifles and shotguns, then let the government do its job. That's all. And don't let the white man come to you and ask you what you think about what Malcolm says— why, you old Uncle Tom. He would never ask you if you thought you were going to say, "Amen!" No, he is making a Tom out of you.

So, this doesn't mean forming rifle clubs and going out looking, for people, but it is time, in 1964, if you are a man, to let that man know. If he's not going to do his job in running the government and providing you and me with the protection that our taxes are supposed to be for, since he spend all those billions for his defense budget, he certainly can't begrudge you and me spending $12 or $15 for a single-shot, or double-action. I hope you understand. Don't go out shooting people, but any time, brothers and sisters, and especially the men in this audience—some of you wearing Congressional Medals of Honor, with shoulders this wide, chests this big, muscles that big— any time you and I sit around and read where they bomb a church and murder in cold blood, not some grownups, but four little girls while they were praying to the same god the white man taught them to pray to, and you and I see the government go down and can't find who did it.

Why, this man—he can find Eichmann hiding down in Argentina somewhere. Let two or three American soldiers, who are minding somebody else's business way over in South Vietnam, get killed, and he'll send battleships, sticking his nose in their business. He wanted to send troops down to Cuba and make them have what he calls free elections—this old cracker who doesn't have free elections in his own country. No, if you never see me another time in your life, if I die in the morning, I'll die saying one thing: the ballot or the bullet, the ballot or the bullet.

If a Negro in 1964 has to sit around and wait for some cracker senator to filibuster when it comes to the rights of black people, why, you and I should hang our heads in shame. You talk about a march on Washington in 1963; you haven't seen anything. There's some more going down in '64. And this time they're not going like they went last year. They're not going singing "We Shall Overcome." They're not going with white friends. They're not going with placards already painted for them. They're not going with round-trip tickets. They're going with one-way tickets.

And if they don't want that non-nonviolent army going down there, tell them to bring the filibuster to a halt. The black nationalists aren't going to wait. Lyndon B. Johnson is the head of the Democratic Party. If he's for civil rights, let him go into the Senate next week and declare himself. Let him go in there right now and declare himself. Let him go in there and denounce the Southern branch of his party. Let him go in there right now and take a moral stand—right now, not later. Tell him, don't wait until election time. If he waits too long, brothers and sisters, he will be responsible for letting a condition develop in this country which will create a climate that will bring seeds up out of the ground with vegetation on the end of them looking like something these people never dreamed of. In 1964, it's the ballot or the bullet. Thank you.

SUGGESTIONS FOR WRITING

1. Malcolm X says: "If you and I were Americans, there'd be no problem." Write an essay that shows how Malcolm X appeals to the political principles of the United States to criticize the country.
2. In your view, what does Malcolm X understand as the proper relationship of government and human rights? Write an essay that explains and defends your answer.
3. In your view, what would Malcolm X say in response to Martin Luther King, Jr.'s letter? Write an essay that explains and defends your view.

INTERDISCIPLINARY CONNECTIONS

1. Thomas Hobbes and Mahatma Gandhi seem most explicitly concerned with the relations of human violence and human government, though of course in very different ways. In your view, which of the other authors has most successfully addressed this issue in his or her thinking? Write an essay that explains and defends your answer.
2. Most if not all of the authors in this chapter seem to operate on strong assumptions about the existence of natural rights and the nature of those rights. Which two of the writers seem in closest agreement? Which two seem to disagree most on this topic? Write an essay explaining and defending your answer.
3. Many authors seem to rely on the idea of a social contract to explain the relations of human rights to government. Write an essay that explores and explains the differences and similarities of thought on this topic represented in this chapter.
4. Which of the writers seems to you most utopian in his or her ideas about government? Write an essay that explains and defends your answer.
5. Only Wollstonecraft and Sanger speak directly to the issue of gender on the topic of government and human rights. Which of the other authors do you think would most agree with them about the special need to address women's rights? Write an essay that explains and defends your answer.

CHAPTER 4

Literature
Life's Mirror and Life's Lamp

Plato	Virginia Woolf
Aristotle	Herman Melville
Samuel Johnson	Louise Barnett
Reuben Brower	Andrew Delbanco
Irving Babbitt	

Introduction

Language is the greatest invention of the human mind. Without language, none of the topics of human life addressed in this book could be discussed, nor would they even exist. And if literature expresses in its style the glory of language, its content expresses the glory and the tragedy of human life. Literature both reflects and illuminates life by means of language. Just as any individual is able to physically observe anyone in the world but also is unable to see him- or herself without the aid of a mirror, so literature has been traditionally figured as a metaphysical mirror for the whole human race, unable to see itself as it really is without the aid of art. Literature has also been described as a lamp, illuminating aspects of life that would remain obscure without its aid. The writers in this chapter take these general defenses of the literary imagination for granted and address more particular aspects of literary art.

The chapter begins with a selection from Plato's *Ion* in which some basic principles of the literary process are addressed in a Socratic dialogue. Where does literature originate and what parts in it are respectively played by inspiration, artistry, and audience? Socrates examines these questions dialectically and the issues he raises have remained relevant to literary criticism ever since.

Plato's most famous pupil, Aristotle, gets at literature from a perspective different from that taken by his master. In a selection from Aristotle's classic critical study *The Poetics*, the philosopher analyzes not only the nature of the literary product but also the means of its literary production, the better to lay down principles for the proper judgment of excellence in the manifestations of the imagination as verbal artifacts.

Samuel Johnson, the leading critic of literature in English during the second half of the eighteenth century, takes up one critical principle of Aristotle that has been in Johnson's view abused by writers and critics who claim Aristotle's support. Johnson claims that an irrational extension of the idea of "unity" has become patently ridiculous by a blind adherence to rules that make no sense. Johnson brings the example of Shakespeare's drama to make his case for a more realistic understanding of the aesthetic experience.

In the next selection Reuben Brower, the famous inventor of an introduction to literature course at Harvard, moves from the theoretical concerns of the earlier essays into those of practical criticism, the interaction of a given reader with a given work of the imagination. Brower's title "Reading in Slow Motion" represents his advice to anyone wishing to foster lifelong habits in the creative reading of creative writing.

Classic and *Romantic* are two indispensable terms of critical categorization for literary students. Where do the terms come from? What do they mean? Irving Babbitt takes you through the history and implications of both words in an excerpt from his classic book, *Rousseau and Romanticism*. Babbitt, who founded the study of comparative literature in the United States, was a professor of French at Harvard early in the twentieth century.

A contemporary of Irving Babbitt, the British novelist and critic Virginia Woolf founded the study of feminist literature with the lectures that led to her book, *A Room of One's Own*. Woolf's lectures in 1928 took place at Girton College of Cambridge University. The college had admitted women from 1869, but was not granted full university status until 1948, a fact that makes a representative example of Woolf's subject— the historical lack of literary opportunity for women—in an excerpt from her book, "Shakespeare's Sister."

Herman Melville is an author who provides a representative example of the history of critical taste that shows how the literary canon—the generally acknowledged group of highly respected literary works—can change over time. A mildly popular novelist when he began his career as a writer, Melville was almost entirely forgotten by the time he died in 1891, and *Moby-Dick*, if it was remembered at all, was remembered as an adventure story for boys. It was not until the 1920s that Melville's writing began to enjoy the status it is granted today, and works like his story included here, "Bartleby the Scrivener," began to receive the attention they deserve.

The chapter closes with two different though not necessarily opposed critical approaches to "Bartleby the Scrivener." The critic and university professor of English and American studies Louise Barnett analyzes Bartleby from the point of view of Karl Marx (Chapter 2), seeing Bartleby as the embodiment of Marx's alienated worker. Andrew Delbanco, a biographer of Melville, takes a psychological approach and sees the dead letter office, which appears at the end of the story, as a symbol of the failure in communication that characterized Bartleby's life.

Ion

About 390 B.C.

PLATO

Plato (428–347 B. C.), a well-educated Athenian from an aristocratic family, became the most famous student of Socrates, and Plato immortalized his master (whose own instructions were strictly oral) by making him the principal figure in his written philosophical dialogues. It is impossible and perhaps unnecessary to separate the views of the two philosophers, who thus remain inseparable for all time. After Socrates was tried, convicted, and executed (by forced suicide) for "corrupting" the youth of Athens, Plato founded a school called the Academy, which endured for almost a thousand years in testimony to the greatness of its founder and that founder's teacher and model. Another excerpt from Plato appears in Chapter 6.

In the part of a dialogue presented here, Socrates uses the metaphor of a magnet that connects iron rings by its force to argue that poetry is not a matter of art but of divine inspiration. People composing poetry, those who recite the compositions, and those who hear them are all in different degrees not in their own minds, which are inspired (or "breathed into") with thoughts and feelings derived from the muses and the supernatural order.

I CANNOT deny what you say, Socrates. Nevertheless I am conscious in my own self, and the world agrees with me, that I do speak better and have more to say about Homer than any other man; but I do not speak equally well about others. After all, there must be some reason for this; what is it?

I see the reason, Ion; and I will proceed to explain to you what I imagine it to be. The gift which you possess of speaking excellently about Homer is not an art, but, as I was just saying, an inspiration; there is a divinity moving you, like that contained in the stone which Euripides calls a magnet, but which is commonly known as the stone of Heraclea. This stone not only attracts iron rings, but also imparts to them a similar power of attracting other rings; and sometimes you may see a number of pieces of iron and rings suspended from one another so as to form quite a long chain: and all of them derive their power of suspension from the original stone. In like manner the Muse first of all inspires men herself; and from these inspired persons a chain of other persons is suspended, who take the inspiration. For all good poets, epic as well as lyric, compose their beautiful poems not by art, but because they are inspired and possessed. And as the Corybantian revellers when they dance are not in their right mind, so the lyric poets are not in their right mind when they are composing their beautiful strains: but when falling under the power of music and metre they are inspired and possessed; like Bacchic maidens who draw milk and honey from the rivers when they are under the influence of Dionysus but not when they are in their right mind. And the soul of the lyric poet does the same, as they themselves say; for they tell us that they bring songs from honeyed fountains, culling them out of the gardens and dells of the Muses; they, like the bees, winging their way from flower to flower. And this is true. For the poet is a light and winged and holy thing, and there is no invention in him until he has been inspired and is out of his senses, and reason is no longer in him: no man, while he retains that faculty, has the oracular gift of poetry.

Many are the noble words in which poets speak concerning the actions of men; but like yourself when speaking about Homer, they do not speak of them by any rules of art: they are simply inspired to utter that to which the Muse impels them, and that only; and when inspired, one of them will make dithyrambs, another hymns of praise, another choral strains, another epic or iambic verses, but not one of them is of any account in the other kinds. For not by art does the poet sing, but by power divine; had he learned by rules of art, he would have known how to speak not of one theme only, but of all; and therefore God takes away reason from poets, and uses them as his ministers, as he also uses the pronouncers of oracles and holy prophets, in order that we who hear them may know them to be speaking not of themselves, who utter these priceless words while bereft of reason, but that God himself is the speaker, and that through them he is addressing us. And Tynnichus the Chalcidian affords a striking instance of what I am saying: he wrote no poem that anyone would care to remember but the famous paean which is in everyone's mouth, one of the finest lyric poems ever written, simply an invention of the Muses, as he himself says. For in this way God would seem to demonstrate to us and not to allow us to doubt that these beautiful poems are not human, not the work of man, but divine and the work of God; and that the poets are only the interpreters of the gods by whom they are severally possessed. Was not this the lesson which God intended to teach when by the mouth of the worst of poets he sang the best of songs? Am I not right, Ion?

Yes, indeed, Socrates, I feel that you are; for your words touch my soul, and I am persuaded that in these works the good poets, under divine inspiration, interpret to us the voice of the Gods.

5   And you rhapsodists are the interpreters of the poets?

There again you are right.

Then you are the interpreters of interpreters?

Precisely.

I wish you would frankly tell me, Ion, what I am going to ask of you: When you produce the greatest effect upon the audience in the recitation of some striking passage, such as the apparition of Odysseus leaping forth on the floor, recognized by the suitors and shaking out his arrows at his feet, or the description of Achilles springing upon Hector, or the sorrows of Andromache, Hecuba, or Priam,—are you in your right mind? Are you not carried out of yourself, and does not your soul in an ecstasy seem to be among the persons or places of which you are speaking, whether they are in Ithaca or in Troy or whatever may be the scene of the poem?

10   That proof strikes home to me, Socrates. For I must frankly confess that at the tale of pity my eyes are filled with tears, and when I speak of horrors, my hair stands on end and my heart throbs.

Well, Ion, and what are we to say of a man who at a sacrifice or festival, when he is dressed in an embroidered robe, and has golden crowns upon his head, of which nobody has robbed him, appears weeping or panic-stricken in the presence of more than twenty thousand friendly faces, when there is no one despoiling or wronging him;—is he in his right mind or is he not?

No indeed, Socrates, I must say that, strictly speaking, he is not in his right mind.

And are you aware that you produce similar effects on most of the spectators?

Only too well; for I look down upon them from the stage, and behold the various emotions of pity, wonder, sternness, stamped upon their countenances when I am speaking: and I am obliged to give my very best attention to them; for if I make them cry I myself shall laugh, and if I make them laugh I myself shall cry, when the time of payment arrives.

15   Do you know that the spectator is the last of the rings which, as I am saying, receive the power of the original magnet from one another? The rhapsode like yourself and the actor are intermediate links, and the poet himself is the first of them. Through all these God sways the souls of men in any direction which He pleases, causing each link to communicate the power to the next. Thus there is a vast chain of dancers and masters and under-masters of choruses, who are suspended, as if from the stone, at the side of the rings which hang down from the Muse. And every poet has some Muse from whom he is suspended, and by whom he is said to be possessed, which is nearly the same thing; for he is taken hold of. And from these first rings, which are the poets, depend others, some deriving their inspiration from Orpheus, others from Musaeus; but the greater number are possessed and held by Homer. Of whom, Ion, you are one, and are possessed by Homer; and when anyone repeats the words of another poet you go to sleep, and know not what to say; but when anyone recites a strain of Homer you wake up in a moment, and your soul leaps within you, and you have plenty to say; for not by art or knowledge about Homer do you say what you say, but by divine inspiration and by possession; just

as the Corybantian revellers too have a quick perception of that strain only which is appropriated to the god by whom they are possessed, and have plenty of dances and words for that, but take no heed of any other. And you, Ion, when the name of Homer is mentioned have plenty to say, and have nothing to say of others. You ask, 'Why is this?' The answer is that your skill in the praise of Homer comes not from art but from divine inspiration.

SUGGESTIONS FOR WRITING

1. There must be few people who have not been moved to feel strong emotions when reading some imaginative work. Yet how is it possible to feel real emotions about unreal people and events? Write an essay that explains how Plato addresses this question in his dialogue between Socrates and Ion.
2. Literary taste is notoriously a matter of individual taste. Write an essay that explains how Plato accounts for this aspect of literature in his dialogue.
3. According to Plato, literature begins in divine inspiration, not in human skill. His view implies that creative writing courses would be of little use. Do you agree? Write an essay that explains and defends your answer.

The Poetics About 335–322 B.C.

ARISTOTLE

For twenty years Artistotle (384–322 B.C.) attended the Academy of Plato mentioned in the preceding head note and became Plato's most famous pupil as Plato was of Socrates. In turn, Aristotle's own most famous pupil was Alexander the Great, who in conquering most of the known world spread Greek philosophy as expressed by Socrates, Plato, and Aristotle himself to an enormous audience that has come to include the educated world in the twenty-first century.

In his philosophic views, Aristotle is as much noted for his differences from his master Plato as for his agreements. In terms of literary theory, Plato tends to examine poetry in relation to other things, while Aristotle examines poetry in itself, trying to distinguish what is best in it and how that excellence is achieved. In the following selections from The Poetics *he begins not with the gods, as Plato does, but with children as examples of what is most natural to human nature.*

IV

Poetry in general seems to have sprung from two causes, each of them lying deep in our nature. First, the instinct of imitation is implanted in man from childhood, one difference between him and other animals being that he is the most imitative of living creatures, and through imitation learns his earliest lessons; and no less universal is the pleasure felt in things imitated. We have evidence of this in the facts of experience. Objects which in themselves we view with pain, we delight to contemplate when reproduced with minute fidelity: such as the forms of the most ignoble animals and of dead bodies. The cause of this again is, that to learn gives the liveliest pleasure, not only to philosophers but to men in general; whose capacity, however, of learning is more limited. Thus the reason why men enjoy seeing a likeness is, that in contemplating it they find themselves learning or inferring, and saying perhaps, 'Ah, that is he.' For if you happen not to have seen the original, the pleasure will be due not to the imitation as such, but to the execution, the colouring, or some such other cause.

Imitation, then, is one instinct of our nature. Next, there is the instinct for 'harmony' and rhythm, metres being manifestly sections of rhythm. Persons, therefore, starting with this natural gift developed by degrees their special aptitudes, till their rude improvisations gave birth to Poetry.

Poetry now diverged in two directions, according to the individual character of the writers. The graver spirits imitated noble actions, and the actions of good men. The more trivial sort imitated the actions of meaner persons, at first composing satires, as the former did hymns to the gods and the praises of famous men. A poem of the satirical kind cannot indeed be put down to any author earlier than Homer; though many such writers probably there were. But from Homer onward, instances can be cited,—his own Margites, for example, and other similar compositions. The appropriate metre was also here introduced; hence the measure is still called the iambic or lampooning measure, being that in which people lampooned one another. Thus the older poets were distinguished as writers of heroic or of lampooning verse.

As, in the serious style, Homer is pre-eminent among poets, for he alone combined dramatic form with excellence of imitation, so he too first laid down the main lines of Comedy, by dramatising the ludicrous instead of writing personal satire. His Margites bears the same relation to Comedy that the Iliad and Odyssey do to Tragedy. But when Tragedy and Comedy came to light, the two classes of poets still followed their natural bent: the lampooners became writers of Comedy, and the Epic poets were succeeded by Tragedians, since the drama was a larger and higher form of art.

5   Whether Tragedy has as yet perfected its proper types or not; and whether it is to be judged in itself, or in relation also to the audience,— this raises another question. Be that as it may, Tragedy—as also Comedy—was at first mere improvisation. The one originated with the authors of the Dithyramb, the other with those of the phallic songs, which are still in use in many of our cities. Tragedy advanced by slow degrees; each new element that showed itself was in turn developed. Having passed through many changes, it found its natural form, and there it stopped.

Aeschylus first introduced a second actor; he diminished the importance of the Chorus, and assigned the leading part to the dialogue. Sophocles raised the number of actors to three, and added scene-painting. Moreover, it was not till late that the short plot was discarded for one of greater compass, and the grotesque diction of the earlier satyric form for the stately manner of Tragedy. The iambic measure then replaced the trochaic tetrameter, which was originally employed when the poetry was of the satyric order, and had greater affinities with dancing. Once dialogue had come in, Nature herself discovered the appropriate measure. For the iambic is, of all measures, the most collo-quial: we see it in the fact that conversational speech runs into iambic lines more frequently than into any other kind of verse; rarely into hexameters, and only when we drop the colloquial intonation. The additions to the number of 'episodes' or acts, and the other accessories of which tradition tells, must be taken as already described; for to discuss them in detail would, doubtless, be a large undertaking.

V

Comedy is, as we have said, an imitation of characters of a lower type,— not, however, in the full sense of the word bad, the Ludicrous being merely a subdivision of the ugly. It consists in some defect or ugliness which is not painful or destructive. To take an obvious example, the comic mask is ugly and distorted, but does not imply pain.

The successive changes through which Tragedy passed, and the authors of these changes, are well known, whereas Comedy has had no history, because it was not at first treated seriously. It was late before the Archon granted a comic chorus to a poet; the performers were till then voluntary. Comedy had already taken definite shape when comic poets, distinctively so called, are heard of. Who furnished it with masks, or prologues, or increased the number of actors,—these and other similar details remain unknown. As for the plot, it came originally from Sicily; but of Athenian writers Crates was the first who, abandoning the 'iambic' or lampooning form, generalised his themes and plots.

Epic poetry agrees with Tragedy in so far as it is an imitation in verse of characters of a higher type. They differ, in that Epic poetry admits but one kind of metre, and is narrative in form. They differ, again, in their length: for Tragedy endeavours, as far as possible, to confine itself to a single revolution of the sun, or but slightly to exceed this limit; whereas the Epic action has no limits of time. This, then, is a second point of difference; though at first the same freedom was admitted in Tragedy as in Epic poetry.

10   Of their constituent parts some are common to both, some peculiar to Tragedy: whoever, therefore, knows what is good or bad Tragedy, knows also about Epic poetry. All the elements of an Epic poem are found in Tragedy, but the elements of a Tragedy are not all found in the Epic poem.

VI

Of the poetry which imitates in hexameter verse, and of Comedy, we will speak hereafter. Let us now discuss Tragedy, resuming its formal definition, as resulting from what has been already said.

Tragedy, then, is an imitation of an action that is serious, complete, and of a certain magnitude; in language embellished with each kind of artistic ornament, the several kinds being found in separate parts of the play; in the form of action, not of narrative; through pity and fear effecting the proper purgation of these emotions. By 'language embellished,' I mean language into which rhythm, 'harmony,' and song enter. By 'the several kinds of separate parts,' I mean, that some parts are rendered through the medium of verse alone, others again with the aid of song.

Now as tragic imitation implies persons acting, it necessarily follows, in the first place, that Spectacular equipment will be a part of

Tragedy. Next, Song and Diction, for these are the medium of imitation. By 'Diction' I mean the mere metrical arrangement of the words: as for 'Song,' it is a term whose sense every one understands.

Again, Tragedy is the imitation of an action; and an action implies personal agents, who necessarily possess certain distinctive qualities both of character and thought; for it is by these that we qualify actions themselves, and these—thought and character—are the two natural causes from which actions spring, and on actions again all success or failure depends. Hence, the Plot is the imitation of the action:—for by plot I here mean the arrangement of the incidents. By Character I mean that in virtue of which we ascribe certain qualities to the agents. Thought is required wherever a statement is proved, or, it may be, a general truth enunciated. Every Tragedy, therefore, must have six parts, which parts determine its quality—namely, Plot, Character, Diction, Thought, Spectacle, Song. Two of the parts constitute the medium of imitation, one the manner, and three the objects of imitation. And these complete the list. These elements have been employed, we may say, by the poets to a man; in fact, every play contains Spectacular elements as well as Character, Plot, Diction, Song, and Thought.

15 But most important of all is the structure of the incidents. For Tragedy is an imitation, not of men, but of an action and of life, and life consists in action, and its end is a mode of action, not a quality. Now character determines men's qualities, but it is by their actions that they are happy or the reverse. Dramatic action, therefore, is not with a view to the representation of character: character comes in as subsidiary to the actions. Hence the incidents and the plot are the end of a tragedy; and the end is the chief thing of all. Again, without action there cannot be a tragedy; there may be without character. The tragedies of most of our modern poets fail in the rendering of character; and of poets in general this is often true. It is the same in painting; and here lies the difference between Zeuxis and Polygnotus. Polygnotus delineates character well: the style of Zeuxis is devoid of ethical quality. Again, if you string together a set of speeches expressive of character, and well finished in point of diction and thought, you will not produce the essential tragic effect nearly so well as with a play which, however deficient in these respects, yet has a plot and artistically constructed incidents. Besides which, the most powerful elements of emotional interest in Tragedy—Peripeteia or Reversal of the Situation, and Recognition scenes—are parts of the plot. A further proof is,

that novices in the art attain to finish of diction and precision of portraiture before they can construct the plot. It is the same with almost all the early poets.

The Plot, then, is the first principle, and, as it were, the soul of a tragedy: Character holds the second place. A similar fact is seen in painting. The most beautiful colours, laid on confusedly, will not give as much pleasure as the chalk outline of a portrait. Thus Tragedy is the imitation of an action, and of the agents mainly with a view to the action.

Third in order is Thought,—that is, the faculty of saying what is possible and pertinent in given circumstances. In the case of oratory, this is the function of the political art and of the art of rhetoric: and so indeed the older poets make their characters speak the language of civic life; the poets of our time, the language of the rhetoricians. Character is that which reveals moral purpose, showing what kind of things a man chooses or avoids. Speeches, therefore, which do not make this manifest, or in which the speaker does not choose or avoid anything whatever, are not expressive of character. Thought, on the other hand, is found where something is proved to be or not to be, or a general maxim is enunciated.

Fourth among the elements enumerated comes Diction; by which I mean, as has been already said, the expression of the meaning in words; and its essence is the same both in verse and prose.

Of the remaining elements Song holds the chief place among the embellishments.

20   The Spectacle has, indeed, an emotional attraction of its own, but, of all the parts, it is the least artistic, and connected least with the art of poetry. For the power of Tragedy, we may be sure, is felt even apart from representation and actors. Besides, the production of spectacular effects depends more on the art of the stage machinist than on that of the poet.

SUGGESTIONS FOR WRITING

1. Aristotle bases his literary theories on the idea that the imaginative imitation of life is natural and instinctive and therefore evident in childhood and children's play. Write an essay that examines some activities of childhood that do or do not support Aristotle's claim.

2. Using examples from Greek literary culture, Aristotle distinguishes higher and lower forms of poetry and drama and describes styles

appropriate to each. Using his writing as a model, classify some works of fiction and their appropriate styles from your own literary experience.

3. Aristotle says in section VI that plot is "the soul of tragedy." Write an essay that explores the reasoning that he brings in support of this claim.

On The Unities 1765

From Preface to *Shakespeare*

SAMUEL JOHNSON

Samuel Johnson (1709–1784) was the leading figure of English literature in the second half of the eighteenth century. His first fame was due to his Dictionary of the English Language, *the first great work of its kind in English. But Johnson also wrote as a poet, essayist, novelist, dramatist, and critic. His conversation was such that great men and women of the period including Adam Smith (Chapter 2) vied to hear him hold forth on any subject whatsoever. The novelist Smollet called him the Grand Cham of Literature.*

The following critical discussion of what were called the unities comes from Johnson's edition of Shakespeare published when Johnson was at the full height of his powers. The critical idea had a history that went back to Aristotle seen earlier in this chapter. Though Aristotle speaks only of the unity of action, French neoclassical figures of the seventeenth century had extrapolated the unities of time and place. Their prestige was such that Johnson was undertaking no light task in his refutation, and the reader will see that Johnson himself is aware of the weight of opinion against him.

It will be thought strange, that, in enumerating the defects of this writer, I have not yet mentioned his neglect of the unities; his violation of those laws which have been instituted and established by the joint authority of poets and of criticks.

For his other deviations from the art of writing, I resign him to critical justice, without making any other demand in his favour, than that which must be indulged to all human excellence: that his virtues be rated with his failings: But, from the censure which this irregularity may bring upon him, I shall, with due reverence to that learning which I must oppose, adventure to try how I can defend him.

His histories, being neither tragedies nor comedies are not subject to any of their laws; nothing more is necessary to all the praise which they expect, than that the changes of action be so prepared as to be understood, that the incidents be various and affecting, and the characters consistent, natural, and distinct. No other unity is intended, and therefore none is to be sought.

In his other works he has well enough preserved the unity of action. He has not, indeed, an intrigue regularly perplexed and regularly unravelled: he does not endeavour to hide his design only to discover it, for this is seldom the order of real events, and Shakespeare is the poet of nature: But his plan has commonly what Aristotle requires, a beginning, a middle, and an end; one event is concatenated with another, and the conclusion follows by easy consequence. There are perhaps some incidents that might be spared, as in other poets there is much talk that only fills up time upon the stage; but the general system makes gradual advances, and the end of the play is the end of expectation.

5   To the unities of time and place he has shewn no regard; and perhaps a nearer view of the principles on which they stand will diminish their value, and withdraw from them the veneration which, from the time of Corneille, they have very generally received, by discovering that they have given more trouble to the poet, than pleasure to the auditor.

The necessity of observing the unities of time and place arises from the supposed necessity of making the drama credible. The criticks hold it impossible, that an action of months or years can be possibly believed to pass in three hours; or that the spectator can suppose himself to sit in the theatre, while ambassadors go and return between distant kings, while armies are levied and towns besieged, while an exile wanders and returns, or till he whom they saw courting his mistress, shall lament the untimely fall of his son. The mind revolts from evident falsehood, and fiction loses its force when it departs from the resemblance of reality.

From the narrow limitation of time necessarily arises the contraction of place. The spectator, who knows that he saw the first act at Alexandria, cannot suppose that he sees the next at Rome, at a distance to which not the dragons of Medea could, in so short a time, have transported him; he knows with certainty that he has not changed his place, and he knows that place cannot change itself; that what was a house cannot become a plain; that what was Thebes can never be Persepolis.

Such is the triumphant language with which a critick exults over the misery of an irregular poet, and exults commonly without resistance or reply. It is time therefore to tell him by the authority of Shakespeare, that he assumes, as an unquestionable principle, a position, which, while his breath is forming it into words, his understanding pronounces to be false. It is false, that any representation is mistaken for reality; that any dramatick fable in its materiality was ever credible, or, for a single moment, was ever credited.

The objection arising from the impossibility of passing the first hour at Alexandria, and the next at Rome, supposes, that when the play opens, the spectator really imagines himself at Alexandria, and believes that his walk to the theatre has been a voyage to Egypt, and that he lives in the days of Antony and Cleopatra. Sure he that imagines this may imagine more. He that can take the stage at one time for the palace of the Ptolemies, may take it in half an hour for the promontory of Actium. Delusion, if delusion be admitted, has no certain limitation; if the spectator can be once persuaded, that his old acquaintance are Alexander and Cæsar, that a room illuminated with candles is the plain of Pharsalia, or the bank of Granicus, he is in a state of elevation above the reach of reason, or of truth, and from the heights of empyrean poetry, may despise the circumscriptions of terrestrial nature. There is no reason why a mind thus wandering in extasy should count the clock, or why an hour should not be a century in that calenture of the brains that can make the stage a field.

10   The truth is, that the spectators are always in their senses, and know, from the first act to the last, that the stage is only a stage, and that the players are only players. They came to hear a certain number of lines recited with just gesture and elegant modulation. The lines relate to some action, and an action must be in some place; but the different actions that compleat a story may be in places very remote from each other; and where is the absurdity of allowing that space to represent first Athens, and then Sicily, which was always known to be neither Sicily nor Athens, but a modern theatre?

By supposition, as place is introduced, time may be extended; the time required by the fable elapses for the most part between the acts; for, of so much of the action as is represented, the real and poetical duration is the same. If, in the first act, preparations for war against Mithridates are represented to be made in Rome, the event of the war may, without absurdity, be represented in the catastrophe, as happening in Pontus; we know that there is neither war, nor preparation for war; we know that we are neither in Rome nor Pontus; that neither Mithridates nor Lucullus are before us. The drama exhibits successive imitations of successive actions; and why may not the second imitation

represent an action that happened years after the first, if it be so connected with it, that nothing but time can be supposed to intervene?
Time is, of all modes of existence, most obsequious to the imagination;
a lapse of years is as easily conceived as a passage of hours. In contemplation we easily contract the time of real actions, and therefore willingly permit it to be contracted when we only see their imitation.

It will be asked, how the drama moves, if it is not credited. It is
credited with all the credit due to a drama. It is credited, whenever it
moves, as a just picture of a real original; as representing to the auditor
what he would himself feel, if he were to do or suffer what is there
feigned to be suffered or to be done. The reflection that strikes the
heart is not, that the evils before us are real evils, but that they are evils
to which we ourselves may be exposed. If there be any fallacy, it is not
that we fancy the players, but that we fancy ourselves unhappy for a
moment; but we rather lament the possibility than suppose the presence of misery, as a mother weeps over her babe, when she remembers
that death may take it from her. The delight of tragedy proceeds from
our consciousness of fiction; if we thought murders and treasons real,
they would please no more.

Imitations produce pain or pleasure, not because they are mistaken
for realities, but because they bring realities to mind. When the imagination is recreated by a painted landscape, the trees are not supposed
capable to give us shade, or the fountains coolness; but we consider,
how we should be pleased with such fountains playing beside us, and
such woods waving over us. We are agitated in reading the history of
Henry the Fifth, yet no man takes his book for the field of Agencourt.
A dramatick exhibition is a book recited with concomitants that
encrease or diminish its effect. Familiar comedy is often more powerful on the theatre, than in the page; imperial tragedy is always less. The
humour of Petruchio may be heightened by grimace; but what voice or
what gesture can hope to add dignity or force to the soliloquy of Cato.

A play read, affects the mind like a play acted. It is therefore
evident, that the action is not supposed to be real; and it follows, that
between the acts a longer or shorter time may be allowed to pass, and
that no more account of space or duration is to be taken by the auditor
of a drama, than by the reader of a narrative, before whom may pass in
an hour the life of a hero, or the revolution of an empire.

15   Whether Shakespeare knew the unities, and rejected them by design,
or deviated from them by happy ignorance, it is, I think, impossible

to decide, and useless to enquire. We may reasonably suppose, that, when he rose to notice, he did not want the counsels and admonitions of scholars and cricks, and that he at last deliberately persisted in a practice, which he might have begun by chance. As nothing is essential to the fable, but unity of action, and as the unities of time and place arise evidently from false assumptions, and, by circumscribing the extent of the drama, lessen its variety, I cannot think it much to be lamented, that they were not known by him, or not observed: Nor, if such another poet could arise, should I very vehemently reproach him, that his first act assed at Venice, and his next in Cyprus. Such violations of rules merely positive, become the comprehensive genius of Shakespeare, and such censures are suitable to the minute and slender criticism of Voltaire:

> *Non usque adea permiscuit imis*
> *Longus summa dies, ut non, si voce Metelli*
> *Serventur leges, malint a Cæsare tolli.*[1]

Yet when I speak thus slightly of dramatick rules, I cannot but recollect how much wit and learning may be produced against me; before such authorities I am afraid to stand, not that I think the present question one of those that are to be decided by mere authority, but because it is to be suspected, that these precepts have not been so easily received but for better reasons than I have yet been able to find. The result of my enquiries, in which it would be ludicrous to boast of impartiality, is, that the unities of time and place are not essential to a just drama, that though they may sometimes conduce to pleasure, they are always to be sacrificed to the nobler beauties of variety and instruction; and that a play, written with nice observation of critical rules, is to be contemplated as an elaborate curiosity, as the product of superfluous and ostentatious art, by which is shewn, rather what is possible, than what is necessary.

He, that, without diminution of any other excellence, shall preserve all the unities unbroken, deserves the like applause with the architect, who shall display all the orders of architecture in a citadel, without any deduction from its strength; but the principal beauty of a citadel is to exclude the enemy; and the greatest graces of a play, are to copy nature and instruct life.

---

[1] A long period of time does not bring such confusion that the laws made by Metellus should need to be abolished by Caesar.

Perhaps, what I have here not dogmatically but deliberately written, may recall the principles of the drama to a new examination. I am almost frighted at my own temerity; and when I estimate the fame and the strength of those that maintain the contrary opinion, am ready to sink down in reverential silence; as Æneas withdrew from the defence of Troy, when he saw Neptune shaking the wall, and Juno heading the besiegers.

SUGGESTIONS FOR WRITING

1. At the end of paragraph 12 Johnson says: "The delight of tragedy pro-ceeds from our consciousness of fiction; if we thought murders and treasons real, they would please no more." Do you agree with Johnson on this point? Write an essay that explains and defends your views on the issue, being sure to take into account Johnson's own reasoning, whether you agree with him or not.

2. In paragraph 13 Johnson makes a related but somewhat different point: "Imitations produce pain or pleasure, not because they are mistaken for realities, but because they bring realities to mind." Do you agree with Johnson here? Write an essay that explains your views on this issue, being sure again to take account of Johnson's own reasoning.

3. Based on your admittedly limited reading of both authors, do you think Aristotle would agree with Samuel Johnson's understanding of tragedy? Write an essay that explains and defends your views.

Reading in Slow Motion   1959

REUBEN BROWER

A much revered teacher of literature, Reuben Brower (1908–1975) was a master of the skill named in the title of his essay. Trained in classical and modern litera-tures at Amherst College and Cambridge University, he took his Ph.D. at Harvard. After many years of teaching at one of his alma maters (Amherst), Brower returned to Harvard to become a teacher of teachers and the inventor of a famous course introducing students to literary study, "Hum. 6." In the essay reprinted here, Brower gets down to basics and discusses the best ways of making the skills and pleasures of literary texts available to everyone.

The Question put to me at a conference on undergraduate education, "How shall we encourage and influence the lifetime reading habit?"

brought to mind the words of Solon that Croesus recalled on the funeral pyre: "I shall not call you fortunate until I learn that the end of your life was happy too." Call no student a lifetime reader until . . . No teacher can be quite sure that he has a lifetime habit of reading, and if asked whether his students have acquired it or formed good reading habits, he will probably feel most uneasy about making an answer. But assuming that we could see each student's life as a whole, *sub specie æternitatis,* we should have to ask the further question: What reading habit are we evaluating? In the age of the New Stupid (a term Aldous Huxley once used for the age of mass literacy), nearly everyone has a reading habit of some sort. Everyone runs through the morning newspaper or *Time* and *Life* strictly as a matter of daily or weekly routine. Each social group has its "great readers," a term of admiration used to cover a wide range of activities that have little more than the printed page in common. There is, for example, reading as anodyne, and reading as extended daydream. There is reading as pursuit of fact or of useful technical knowhow, and reading that may or may not be useful, when we are interested solely in understanding a theory or a point of view. Still more remote from immediate usefulness comes reading as active amusement, a game demanding the highest alertness and the finest degree of sensibility, "judgment ever awake and steady self-possession with enthusiasm and feeling profound or vehement." Reading at this level—to borrow Coleridgean terms a second time—"brings the whole soul of man into activity." Coleridge was speaking of the poet and the power of imagination, but his words describe very well the way we read when we enter into, or rather engage in, experiences of imaginative literature. I say "amusement," not "pleasure," to stress the play of mind, the play of the whole being, that reading of this sort calls for. I am hardly suggesting that literary experience is not a "good," that it is not in some indirect and profound way morally valuable. But if it is to do us any good, it must be fun. The first line of a poem by D. H. Lawrence offers an appropriate motto for teachers and students of literature:

If it's never any fun, don't do it!

Active "amusement" is the reading habit I am concerned with here and more especially with the role played by the teacher of literature in encouraging students to acquire it. I prefer to speak of the "teacher of literature," not the "humanities," because that noble term has become so debased in current usage, and because teachers of texts in humanities courses are or should be teachers of literature. The teacher of Plato or Hobbes or Hume is not only interpreting a system but an expression, an expression that uses many resources of language and uses them in ways that profoundly influence how we take the writer's radical meaning. We cannot subtract from our interpretations the effect of Platonic comedy or of Hobbesian metaphor or of Hume's dispassionate irony. But it remains true that the teacher of literature in the conventional sense has a special interest in encouraging students to respond actively to all the uses of language, from the barely referential to the rhythmic. He is always more or less consciously urging his students to make themselves readers of imagination.

How will the teacher go about reaching this noble aim? By a method that might be described as "slow motion," by slowing down the process of reading to observe what is happening, in order to attend very closely to the words, their uses, and their meanings. Since poetry is literature in its essential and purest form—the mode of writing in which we find at the same time the most varied uses of language and the highest degree of order—the first aim of the teacher of literature will be to make his students better readers of poetry. He will try by every means in his power to bring out the complete and agile response to words that is demanded by a good poem.

5   But in order not to create a wrong impression, a word needs to be said here about method, a term liable to please some and displease others for equally bad reasons. There is certainly no single sacred technique for teaching reading at the level I have in mind. In teaching literature—unlike science, one may suppose—no holds are barred, providing they work and providing that the injury to the work and to the student does not exceed the limits of humanity. The most distinctive feature of the kind of literature course I am about to describe is that the teacher does have some "holds," some ways of reading that he is willing to demonstrate and that his students can imitate. In this respect "Literature X," as I shall call it, differs from the old-time appreciation course in which the teacher mounted the platform and sang a rhapsody which he alone was capable of understanding and which the student memorized, with the usual inaccuracies, for the coming examination.

But why a course in slow reading? The parent who has a son or daughter in college may well feel confused, since almost certainly he has at least one child with a reading difficulty, the most common complaint being that the child cannot read fast enough. As the parent himself watches the mounting lists of important books, and as he scans the rivers of print in the daily paper, he may well feel that like Alice and the Red Queen, he and his children are going faster and faster but getting no where.

The difficulties of parent and child point to conditions that have led to the introduction of how-to-read courses in our colleges and universities. We might note first the sheer mass of printed material to which we are exposed—not to mention the flood of words and images pouring through radio and television. If by temperament or principle we resist the distracting appeals of the press and other media, we must nevertheless read a great deal as we run if we are to perform our tasks as citizens and wage earners. Add to such facts the changes in family life that have altered reading habits of both parents and children. Memorization of Bible texts and poetry is hardly common in school or home, and the family reading circle where books were read aloud and slowly, has all but disappeared even from the idyllic backwaters of academic communities. Yet many if not all of the writers of the past, from Homer to novelists like Jane Austen and Dickens, have assumed reading aloud and a relatively slow rate of intellectual digestion. Literature of the first order calls for lively reading; we must almost act it out as if we were taking parts in a play. As the average high school student reads more and more with less and less wholeness of attention, he may become positively incapacitated for reading the classics of his own or any literature. Incidentally, the parent of the slow reader should take heart: his child may not be stupid, but more than ordinarily sensitive to words. He may in fact have the makings of a poet.

Another change in precollege education is almost certainly connected with the decline in the ability to read literature of the first quality, a change that points also to profound changes in the literary public of the past century and a half. Until thirty or forty years ago a high proportion of students of literature in our liberal arts colleges had received a considerable training in Latin or Greek. If we move back to the much smaller reading publics of the seventeenth and eighteenth centuries, the audiences for whom much of our greatest literature was written, the relative number of readers trained in the classics becomes much higher. The principal method of teaching the ancient languages, translation into English or from English into Latin or Greek, may have had disadvantages compared with the direct method of today, but as a basic preparation for the study of literature it can hardly be surpassed. It may be doubted whether learning of a foreign language can take place without some translation, at least into what experts in linguistics call the "meta-language" of the learner. To translate from Latin and Greek demanded close attention to the printed word, and since the ideas being communicated and the linguistic and literary forms through which they were expressed were often quite unlike those in English, translation compelled the closest scrutiny of meanings and forms of expression in both the ancient and the modern language. Although the old-time classicist may not always have been successful as a teacher of literature, he cannot often be accused of lacking rigor. His students had to spend a good many hours in school and college reading some pieces of literature very attentively. One purpose of a course in slow reading is to offer a larger number of present-day undergraduates an equivalent for the older classical training in interpretation of texts.

It might be noted that Coleridge, who harshly criticized the practice of Latin versemaking in English schools, paid the highest tribute to that "severe master, the Reverend James Bowyer":

> At the same time that we were studying the Greek tragic poets, he made us read Shakespeare and Milton as lessons: and they were the lessons too, which required the most time and trouble to bring up, so as to escape his censure. I learned from him, that poetry, even that of the loftiest and, seemingly, that of the wildest odes, had a logic of its own, as severe as that of science; and more difficult, because more subtle, more complex, and dependent on more and more fugitive causes. In the truly great poets, he would say, there is a reason assignable not only for every word, but for the position of every word; and I well remember that, availing himself of the synonymes to the Homer of Didymus, he made us attempt to show, with regard to each, why it would not have answered the same purpose; and wherein consisted the peculiar fitness of the word in the original text.
>
> In our own English compositions (at least for the last three years of our school education) he showed no mercy to phrase, metaphor, or image, unsupported by a sound sense, or where the same sense might have been conveyed with equal force and dignity in plainer words. Lute, harp, and lyre, Muse, Muses, and inspirations, Pegasus, Parnassus, and Hippocrene were all an abomination to him. In fancy I can almost hear him now, exclaiming: "Harp? Harp? Lyre? Pen and ink, boy, you mean! Muse, boy, Muse? Your nurse's daughter, you mean! Pierian spring? Oh aye! the cloister-pump, I suppose!"

The Reverend James Bowyer and not Coleridge, it appears, was the original New Critic, which is to say that much New Criticism is old criticism writ large. Bowyer's example suggests another important point to which I shall return: that teaching of reading is necessarily teaching of writing. The student cannot show his teacher or himself that he has had an important and relevant literary experience except in writing or in speaking that is as disciplined as good writing.

10   To teach reading or any other subject in the style of the Reverend Bowyer demands an attitude toward the job that is obvious but easily overlooked in our larger universities, where increasing numbers of students often impose mass production methods. The most important requirement for teaching an undergraduate course—beyond belief in what one is doing—is to keep this question in mind: What is happening to the student? Other questions soon follow: What do I want him to do and how can I get him to do it? Planning and teaching from this point of view makes the difference between a course that engages the student and one that merely displays the teacher. The perfect model for the teacher of literature as for the teacher of science is Agassiz, who would come into the laboratory, pour out a basket of bones before the student, and leave him alone to sort them out. We learn that after this introduction to the "material" of the course, Agassiz limited his teaching to infrequent visits, when he checked on the learner's progress by an occasional nod or shake of the head to say "That's right!" or "No, not that!" The great thing in teaching is to get the basket of bones before the student and get him to sorting them for himself as soon as possible. What we must avoid at all costs is sorting out all the bones in advance. Agassiz' principle is of great importance in the teaching of literature, where far too often we present the undergraduate with the end products of literary scholarship without being sure he has read or has the capacity of reading the works we are interpreting.

    If we are interested in fostering a habit of reading well, we must set up our introductory courses on a principle very different from that underlying the older survey or the now more fashionable history-of-ideas course. We are not handing the student a body of knowledge, so much "material"—the history of the Romantic Movement or an anatomy of the concepts labeled "Romanticism"—however useful such knowledge may be at a later stage in literary education. Our aim rather is to get the student in a position where he can learn for himself. If we succeed, we have reason to believe that he may acquire a lifetime habit of learning independently. The teacher who is working toward this noble end will always be working *with* the student, not *for* him or *over* him. Whitehead used to say that the student should feel he is present while the teacher is thinking, present at an occasion when thought is in process. Those who knew Whitehead in the classroom will know what he meant and why he never seemed to be lecturing, even before a class of a hundred or two hundred students. His listeners never knew exactly where he was coming out. Not knowing where one is coming out is an essential part of the experience of thinking.

To get the student to a point where he can learn for himself requires therefore a redefinition of a "lecture." It asks the teacher to share his ignorance with his students as well as his knowledge. Or if professors shrink from admitting less than omniscience, it calls for at least a Socratic simulation of ignorance. What is wanted is the "nonlecture," to borrow E. E. Cummings's happy term, an action performed by the teacher but clearly directed to the next performance of the student. The ideal nonlecturer is setting a job for the student and showing him how he would go about doing it. If he is not in fact setting a job, he will clearly indicate a relevant kind of job to be done. A proper job means setting a question and offering a way, not a formula, for answering it. Student and teacher must clearly understand that a course in interpretation is a course in "right answering." not a course in "right answers."

Let me now attempt to describe Literature X, a course in slow reading that aims to meet the general requirements I have been outlining and that is designed also to meet the needs of young readers in our colleges and universities. I have said that we want students to increase their power of engaging in imaginative experience, and we assume—this was implied by our earlier reference to Coleridge—that a work of literature offers us an experience through words that is different from average, everyday experience. It is different in its mysterious wholeness, in the number of elements embraced and in the variety and closeness of their relationship. When Othello, just before Desdemona's death, says, "Put out the light, and then put out the light," we feel not only the horror of his intention but also a remarkable concentration of much that has gone on before: the moving history of the relations between the lovers and between them and Iago, the echoed presence of earlier moments of "lightness" and "darkness."

We all agree that such experiences in literature are wonderful, but what can a teacher do to guide a student to discover them? He will of course start from his own excitement, and he will do everything he can to infect his students with it: he will try to express in other words what Othello and the audience are experiencing; he will read the passage aloud or get a student to do it; he will exhort and entreat. But finally he cannot hand over his feelings to his students; he cannot force them to be more sensitive than they are. What can he do that the students may also do and that they can imitate when they read another scene or another play? He can do a great deal if he remembers that while he and his students do not have a common nervous system, they do have the same printed page and they share some knowledge of the English language. He will therefore direct their attention to the words, to what they mean and to their connection with other words and meanings. In considering the "put out the light" speech from *Othello*, the teacher may begin by asking what the words mean in terms of stage business. He may then call for a paraphrase: for "put out the light" someone may offer "bring darkness," or "put an end to." The class can next be asked to connect this expression with others used elsewhere in the play. Someone may recall Othello's earlier line associating Desdemona with darkness and death: ". . . when I love thee not,/ Chaos is come again." The reader can now begin to appreciate the poignancy and the irony of Othello's picturing his action as "putting out the light." So by directing attention to words, their meanings, and relationships, the teacher may put his students in a position where they too will feel the pity and terror of this moment in the play.

15 We might describe Literature X as a "mutual demonstration society," the work of the course being carried on mainly through student-teacher explorations of the kind I have been attempting to illustrate. For the students the most important and most strenuous demonstrations will be the exercises that they write on their own after being suitably prepared by the teacher. *Othello* may serve as an example once more. After several classes of reading aloud and exploring connections in the earlier acts of the play, an exercise will be set on a speech or scene from the last act. The students now have an opportunity to show whether they can practice independently the sort of interpretation they have been attempting in class. To guide them, they will be given an exercise sheet with a very carefully planned

series of questions. Beginning with queries on words and phrases, the exercise goes on to ask about relationships of various kinds, and it concludes with a question demanding a generalization about the work as a whole or about a type of literature or experience. An exercise on *Othello* might finally call for a statement about the nature of Othello's tragedy and for a tentative definition of "tragic" as used in Shakespearean drama. But the words "tragic" or "tragedy" will not necessarily appear in the directions; rather, the students will be impelled to talk about these concepts because they are relevant. In the class on the exercise papers the student and his teacher will be admirably prepared to consider what is meant by tragic literature and experience. These discussions of the exercises should be among the most valuable classes in the course. Here the student can learn by comparing where he succeeded or failed as an interpreter, and frequently he may have the pleasure of finding that he has taught his teacher something, an event that can give satisfaction to both parties and that can take place more often in a course where the student is an active participant, not a passive member of an audience.

Literature X as a whole will consist of a series of these exercise waves, with some more terrifying than others, the seventh and last coming when the students are given two or more weeks without classes in which to read new material—poems, plays, or novels—with no teacher to guide them.

The course will not begin with Shakespeare, although Shakespeare is the necessary measure of imaginative experience and of the capacity to engage in it. We shall begin rather with the smaller model of the short poem, because as I have said it offers literary experience in its purest form. By beginning with poems we can be reasonably sure that the student learns early to distinguish between life and literature and not to be unduly distracted by questions of biography and history or by social and psychological problems of the type raised so often by the novel. Most important, the student will learn at the outset to deal with *wholes*, since within the limits of a class hour or a brief paper he can arrive at an interpretation of a whole literary expression. Poems may come to stand in his mind as Platonic forms of true and complete literary experience.

Beginning with poems has another advantage if students are to learn the value of attending closely to language and if they are to see the satisfactions that come from alert and accurate reading. In the small world of a sonnet, a reader can see how a single word may cause a shift in the equilibrium of feeling in the whole poem. So when Shakespeare says:

> For thy sweet love remember'd such wealth brings
> That then I scorn to change my state with kings.

"state" carries connotations of Elizabethan *state*, and as a result the speaker's voice takes on a tone of grandeur, a somewhat stagey grandeur that reminds us of gestures in a play. But the word "state" would hardly impart that quality without the reference to "kings." This fairly simple example brings home the importance in interpretation of considering the context. A course in interpretation is a course in definition by context, in seeing how words are given rich and precise meaning through their interrelations with other words. The student who acquires this habit of definition will be a better reader of philosophy or law or any other type of specialized discourse, and he may learn something about the art of writing, of how to control context in order to express oneself.

Reading poems also offers one of the best ways of lifting the student from adolescent to adult appreciation of literature. The adult reader realizes that reading a work of literature is at once a solitary and a social act. In reading we are alone, but we are also among the company of readers assumed by the poem or play or novel. The poem is more than a personal message, it invites us to move out of ourselves, to get into an "act," to be another self in a fictive drama. The sonnet of Shakespeare we have just quoted seems to call for a very simple identification of the actual reader with the imagined speaker,

> When in disgrace with fortune and men's eyes
> I all alone beweep my outcast stat . . .

(Many will recall their own youthful readings of the poem.) Yet even this simple if not sentimental sonnet asks something more of us in the end; it asks us to take on the demonstrative air of the theatrical lover, to protest in language we would never actually use in our most romantic moments.

20   In Literature X we shall start by reading poems, and start with no apparent method or at least with method well concealed. We begin, as Frost says, with delight, to end in wisdom. "What is it *like*," we say

rather crudely, "to read this poem?" "With what feeling are we left at its close?" "What sort of person is speaking?" "What is he *like*, and where does he reveal himself most clearly?" "In what line or phrase?" We may then ask if there is a key phrase or word in the poem, and we can begin to introduce the notion of the poem as a structure, as an ordered experience built up through various kinds of meaning controlled in turn by various uses of language.

Remembering our questions about the speaker, we first direct attention to dramatic uses of language, to the ways in which the words create a character speaking in a certain role. We may ask, for example, who is speaking in Keats's sonnet on Chapman's *Homer*. An alert student may point out that he is a traveler (many do not see this), and that he uses idioms with a medieval coloring: "realms," "goodly," "bards in fealty," "demesne." But the speaker does not continue to talk in this vein:

Till I heard Chapman speak out loud and bold.

He has changed, and the drama moves into a second act. We hear a voice that is powerful and young, the voice of the New World discoverer and the Renaissance astronomer. We now point out to our young reader (if he is still listening) that the poem is indeed an "act." The poet is speaking *as if* he were a traveler-explorer, and the whole poem is built on a metaphor. So, while reading many poems, we may introduce a few basic notions of literary design and some useful critical terms. But our emphasis will always be on the term as a tool, as a device for calling attention to the poem and how it is made. In time we can turn to study of the poem as an experience of ordered sounds, but not, we hasten to add, of sounds divorced from sense. Our aim in talking about rhythmic pattern, as in considering dramatic and metaphorical design, is to show how the poem "works" and what it expresses. We see, for example, that as Keats's sonnet moves from the medieval to the modern speaker, and as the metaphor also shifts, the rhythm changes from the "broken" couplets and inversions of the octave to the long and steady sweep of the sestet. The whole sonnet in its beautiful interaction of parts gives us the sense of discovery and release into a new world of literary and aesthetic experience.

Following a period of reading poems, the course will move ahead to a play by Shakespeare so that students can see at once that the way in which they have read poems works also for a poetic drama and that there are some basic similarities between the structure of these different types of literature. They may see, for example, that the man speaking in a poem corresponds to the character in a play, that Shakespeare has his large metaphors just as Keats has his smaller ones.

From drama we go to the reading of a novel, often via short stories. The short story like the poem gives us literary experience in microcosm and makes it easier to see analogies between fiction and poetry, to see that a tale by Hawthorne is the unfolding of a single metaphorical vision, or that the narrator in a story by Joyce controls our sense of being within the child's world, exiled from adult society. The novel, especially as we have it in its classic nineteenth century form in Dickens or George Eliot, demands a very different reading from a Shakespearean drama, but by putting the same questions to both genres their likeness and their unlikeness can be defined, and the exact quality of a particular work can be discovered. The student will find, for example, that the "marshes" and "mists" of *Great Expectations* are nearer to the fixed symbols of allegory than to the fluid metaphors of Shakespeare. But he can also see that in a novel as in a poem the narrative voice is of immense importance. Comparison of the opening scene in the film of *Great Expectations* with Dickens's telling shows that when the sanely humorous, entertaining voice of Dickens is removed, we are left with images of pure nightmare. The major themes of *Great Expectations*, guilt and innocence, justice and injustice, are not un-Shakespearean, but we can hardly read the novel without an awareness that unlike *King Lear* and *Macbeth* and like most novels, the imaginative world of *Great Expectations* has a date. Jaggers is an awesome symbol of the link between criminality and legal justice, but he also embodies a sharp criticism of the actual court and prison world of mid-nineteenth century England.

Reading a novel forcibly reminds us that literature is embedded in history, that the meaning of the work in itself changes when we view it in relation to other works and to the social situation in which it first appeared. Literature X will move on in its later phases to some experiments in historical interpretation, "historical" being used here to include the relation of a work to its time, especially to more or less contemporary works, and to literary tradition. If we return to *Othello* or *Coriolanus* after reading the *Iliad* and after gaining some familiarity with the heroic tradition in Renaissance epic and drama, we find that both plays are clearer and richer in their meaning. We see in *Coriolanus* what happens when an Achilles enters the Roman forum: the simple absolutes of the hero, the code that makes

Coriolanus prefer a "noble life before a long" one, bring confusion in a civil society. The teacher of our ideal course will not merely lay a comparison of this sort before his students, he will try to get them into a position where they can make the comparison for themselves. He will use all the ingenuity he can muster to devise assignments in which the student can practice thinking historically about works of literature.

25   In a year in which the class has made some study of the hero in Homer and in the Renaissance, a project might be focused on Fielding's *Tom Jones*. While the students are reading the novel outside class (it takes time!), they would study with their teacher readings useful for interpreting the novel in relation to the heroic tradition and to the climate of moral opinion in the eighteenth century. They could observe in Dryden's *Mac Flecknoe* the shift from the Renaissance "heroick" to the mock-heroic, and in *The Rape of the Lock*, they could see how allusions to the ancient heroic world are used to satirize eighteenth century high society while giving the world of the poem splendor and moral seriousness. After comparing the mock-heroic in Pope and Fielding, they might attempt a definition of the hero in *Tom Jones*. By skillful prodding (in an exercise) they could be led to see that Fielding has created a new type of hero, a youth who is at once ridiculous and charmingly "good-natured," that although he finally gains a modicum of "prudence," he wins his way largely through "benevolence" and "goodness of heart."

As a final step in this experiment, there might be a series of readings in Chesterfield, Hume, and Dr. Johnson, all concerned with social "goodness," and more especially with "prudence" and "benevolence." The students would then be asked to define and place the moral attitudes expressed in *Tom Jones*, through comparing them with similar attitudes expressed in these eighteenth century moralists. By projects of this type undergraduates could be given some practice—at an elementary level— in writing intellectual history. At the same time their earlier practice in interpretation would protect them from reducing the experience of the novel to the abstracted idea. But they would also begin to see that a purely literary judgment is finally impossible, that we are impelled to move back from literature to life. Dr. Johnson's famous comparison of Fielding and Richardson might be used to show that "liking" or "disliking" a novel is an act of moral evaluation. At the end of Literature X, by returning to poetry we could make the point that a choice between poems is a choice between lives.

You may be asking by now what the connection is between our ideal course and the lifetime reading habits of undergraduates. I should reply that Literature X attempts to influence future reading habits by keeping to the principle of student activity. No test or exercise or final examination asks the student to "give back" the "material" of the course. On the contrary, each stage of the work is planned with a view to how the student reads the *next* work, whether poem or play or novel. At the end of the first half of the course the student is sent off to read and interpret on his own another play of Shakespeare and another novel. He is given leading questions that impel him to do likewise "differently." An appropriate midyear examination in the course might consist of a sight poem to interpret and an essay-exercise on a longer work read outside class. The test for the second half-year (whether an examination or a long essay) would ordinarily be based on a set of texts to be used in interpreting a work in the manner of the project on *Tom Jones*.

But the teacher of a course in slow reading will always be haunted by the question once asked by a colleague of mine: "Our students learn *how* to read, but *do* they read?" Do they, for example, ever read an author, read every one of his books they can lay their hands on, with an urge to know the writer's work as a whole? Can we do anything in our ideal course to stimulate this most valuable habit? Some modest experiments can be made, I believe, and with some assurance of success. A model can be set by reading generously in a single poet, preferably a contemporary, such as Frost, Yeats, or Eliot. Or the teacher can give the class a start by reading a few poems in each of a number of writers, and then send the students off to read one of the poets independently. After some weeks they might write an essay "On Reading So-and-So." The essay must have a point (surprisingly few students know what a point is) supported by deft and apt interpretation of particular poems. The novel, the most important form for habitual readers in this generation, presents a problem, since we can hardly read all or even several novels of the same writer within the limits of an introductory course. But two novels and some stories by a single writer may rouse some readers to go ahead on their own, and sometimes the discovery that a difficult writer—James or Joyce—is understandable and rewarding or that an old-fashioned writer—Fielding or Jane Austen—is amusing, will start a student along the right path. The best way to influence later habits is the natural way: recommending without system books we have read with pleasure and without ulterior motives. Students recognize the difference between love and duty, and they will respond to genuine enthusiasm and avoid books that they "ought to" read or—and this is the lowest of all academic appeals—that "fill a gap" in preparing for general examinations or graduate school placement tests.

If we turn our attention from lifetime reading habits to the larger educational influence of courses in slow reading, we can note some possible correlations between classroom and later performances. In this connection we should recall the value for close reading of practice in equally close writing. The student who looks at poems as carefully as we have suggested will understand that poetry begins in grammar and that to express a just appreciation of a poem demands fine control of grammar on the part of the appreciator. But to help the student make such discoveries calls for guidance in small classes or at least careful criticism of written exercises. Good writing is an art not amenable to mass production methods.

30   Attentive criticism of written work is almost certainly of much more value for teaching good reading and writing than the usual discussions or section meetings. The value of a discussion meeting does not depend primarily on size, as many assume, but on the planning that precedes the meeting and the direction of the conversation to a defined goal. In our course in slow reading the discussion is not an addendum, but the culminating act toward which the teacher's demonstration and the student's exercise have been directed. Under these conditions student and teacher are fully prepared to say something meaningful to each other, since they have before them well-defined questions to pursue and alternative expressed answers to compare and judge.

But discussion of this type need not be vocal. The student can carry it on internally during a lecture, if the lecture is an exercise in how to ask and answer a question of interpretation. The indispensable requirement for an active course in literature is not "sections," but some form of independent performance for an attentive critical audience of one. Here is where large-scale production methods break down, and limitations in size are necessary. Very few readers can handle more than twenty to twenty-five papers of the type I have been describing and maintain the necessary vigilance and the power of viewing them as individual performances. A reader can handle them in the usual fashion—grade them and add a complimentary or devastating comment—but he cannot give them critical attention at a high level. The student who is to rise to the kind of reading and writing called for in our ideal course must feel that he has a responsible reader, one who addresses himself to this essay and to this mind. The most valuable discussion a teacher can give is a comment surely directed to an individual written performance. Here we have the ideal section: two actors engaged in a Socratic dialogue. A teacher who is not bewildered and dulled by reading too many papers on the same topic will be able to judge the student's present achievement in relation to what he has done in the past. He can also help him keep track of his development and show him where he is going, and when he has failed, show him how to build on an earlier successful performance. Again Coleridge's Reverend Bowyer may serve as a guide:

> . . . there was one custom of our master's, which I cannot pass over in silence, because I think it imitable and worthy of imitation. He would often permit our exercises, under some pretext of want of time, to accumulate, till each had four or five to be looked over. Then placing the whole number abreast on his desk, he would ask the writer, why this or that sentence might not have found as appropriate a place under this or that other thesis: and if no satisfying answer could be returned, and two faults of the same kind were found in one exercise, the irrevocable verdict followed, the exercise was torn up, and another on the same subject to be produced, in addition to the tasks of the day. The reader will, I trust, excuse this tribute of recollection to a man, whose severities, even now, not seldom furnish the dreams, by which the blind fancy would fain interpret to the mind the painful sensations of distempered sleep; but neither lessen nor dim the sense of my moral and intellectual obligations.

The marker of an English paper, as Coleridge realized though with "painful sensations," is a very important person indeed; he becomes the higher literary conscience, the intellectual guardian angel of his students.

It is evident that education in literature of this kind must be personal, and expensive, though scarcely more expensive than education in the sciences. Let us have at least as generous a supply of readers and conference rooms as we have of laboratory assistants and laboratories. The Humanities cannot flourish without *humanitas*. A protest is in order against the inhumanity of the Humanities when in some of our larger institutions the study of Great Books is reduced to display lectures before audiences of five and six hundred, and when the individual performance is measured by machine-graded examinations.

The teaching of great literary texts in Humanities courses has also had other if less depressing results which the teacher of literature should note if he is to fulfill his proper educational role. Because many works are taught in translation and taught often by staffs including many nonspecialists in language and literature, and because the texts are often presented in some broad historical framework, a work of imaginative literature tends to be treated either as a document for studying the history of ideas or as a text for illustrating and enforcing desirable moral and social attitudes. Though neither of these approaches is in itself harmful or inappropriate to a university, it may involve serious losses, especially in courses in which many students are reading for the first time—or for the first time at an adult level—masterpieces of European literature. There is a danger, which is increased by the large amounts of reading assigned in Great Books courses, that rich and special experiences will be too readily reduced to crude examples of a historic idea or a moral principle. Though the reductions may be necessary and useful for certain purposes, we must not let students make them too soon or too easily, not if we are seriously concerned with lifetime habits of reading. The undergraduate who masters the trick too early and too well may in the process suffer real damage. He may have acquired the dubious art of reading carelessly, of making the reduction *before reading,* and he may have lowered rather than increased his capacity for responding precisely to a particular work and for making fine discriminations between works.

Hence the special function of the teacher of literature, which is not to be confused with that of the historian or the moral philosopher. The teacher of literature in a Humanities course must feel he has betrayed a trust if he has not given the lay reader what he is best qualified to give: training in the literary disciplines of reading and writing. It is pertinent to recall the historic definition of the Humanities as it stands in the *Oxford English Dictionary:* "Learning or literature concerned with human culture, as grammar, rhetoric, poetry, and especially the ancient Latin and Greek classics." I suspect that some of the more enthusiastic general educators may be surprised by the words that follow "human culture": "as grammar, rhetoric, poetry . . ." (The order of items in the list is instructive, too.) The disciplines named are the ones that the teacher of literature has a special responsibility to impart. He is, like Horace's poet, a guardian of the language who shows (as Pope translates it) "no mercy to an empty line." His prime object is to maintain fineness of response to words, and his students rightly assume that he will be adept in discovering and illustrating refinements in writing whether in a great book or a student essay. This guardianship, once performed by teachers of the ancient Latin and Greek classics, now falls to the teachers of English and other modern literatures. Why is this so? Because they are committed to the principle that the study of letters is inseparable from the study of language.

35   Study of literature based on this principle can hardly be carried on in a course based mainly on texts in translation. Translations have their place in a course in interpretation, but only as ancillary to the main business of close reading in the original. The finer distinctions, the finer relationships which we are training our students to discover and make are almost invariably dulled or lost in the process of translation. We want the student to acquire the habit of recognizing and making such distinctions in his *own* language, and we can hardly teach him to do it if the examples before him are relatively crude. Whitehead once remarked when discussing Plato's cosmology, "After all, the translators of Plato have had B+ philosophic minds." With rare exceptions the translators of literature have had literary minds of similar quality. There are of course the handful of translations that are masterpieces, such as Pope's *Illiad*, North's *Plutarch*, and Dryden's *Aeneis*, texts that can bear the close study necessary for literary education. Ironically enough, these are the very translations avoided in most Great Books courses.

In speaking of the necessity for close attention to language, I am not forgetting that teachers of literature are also teachers of human culture and that they are therefore guardians of important values. But they do not set out to teach these values, although they inevitably impart them by the way they talk and act in the presence of works of literature. But they are especially concerned with another task, with teaching ways of discovering and experiencing values expressed through literary objects. The most precious thing they can give their students is some increase of power, some help however humble in getting into Shakespeare or Dr. Johnson or Joyce.

We may hope that a student who has learned how to get into these writers will go back for further experiences after he has left the classroom and the university. That he surely will we cannot say. Even if he does not return to Shakespeare or Johnson, the experiences in the classroom almost certainly have their value and their effect in determining the quality of his later reading. One play well read with a good teacher and well digested in a reflective essay may serve as a touchstone of what literary experience can be. But finally, our belief that students' habits of reading are permanently affected is Platonic. The model for most cultural education is to be found in the third book of the *Republic*:

> ... *our young men, dwelling as it were in a healthy region, may receive benefit from all things about them; the influence that emanates from works of beauty may waft itself to eye or ear like a breeze that brings health from wholesome places, and so from earliest childhood insensibly guide them to likeness, to friendship, to harmony with beautiful reason.*

In the effort to realize this Platonic vision in a modern university the undergraduate library plays its part by surrounding our youth with fair works of literature through which they may come into "harmony with beautiful reason." No one knows how born readers are produced, but we can put books in their way and in the way of the less happily born in the hope that proximity will have its effect as it does in the formation of more mundane habits. Of one thing I am convinced: that a born reader on a library staff can have a tremendous effect on young readers who come his way. I remember with gratitude two librarians of that description, one in school and one in college, who led us to read books we might never have looked into by sharing their love for what they had read. If I were to found a library dedicated to influencing the reading habit, I should place a half-dozen of these enthusiasts at strategic points to ensnare wandering students. They would not necessarily be trained librarians, and they would surely waste students' time and occasionally disturb their colleagues, but like great authors they would create an ever-widening circle of readers. Mere teachers of literature could hardly hope to compete with them, and might in time quietly disappear from the academic scene.

SUGGESTIONS FOR WRITING

1. Brower advocates a particular relation between student and teacher. Make a list of the specific actions each person must perform. Do you find such actions performed and such relations created in your own

experience of literary study? Write an essay that explains your answer.

2. According to Brower, what are the benefits of a good literary education? What are the dangers that stand in the way of its realization? Write an essay that explains your views on the value of studying literature.

3. As an illustration of what might go on in "Literature X," Brower uses the example of Keats's sonnet, "On First Looking Into Chapman's Homer." After looking at the complete poem yourself, write an essay in which you show how Brower does or does not demonstrate the general ideals of Literature X through his particular analysis of a particular poem.

The Terms Classic and Romantic 1919
From *Rousseau and Romanticism*

IRVING BABBITT

Irving Babbitt (1865–1933) was a critic of culture and literature who spent much of his career writing books in opposition to the ideas of romanticism as represented by the works and influence of Jean-Jacques Rousseau (Chapter 3). Babbitt began as a classical scholar but became a teacher of romance languages, first at Williams College and later at Harvard, where he introduced the subject of comparative literature. In 1960 Harvard honored his memory by creating the position of Irving Babbitt Professor of Comparative Literature.

As the selection here shows, "comparative" names a method that Babbitt rigorously employs as a critic and definer. He attempts to get key terms sorted out with increasing degrees of clarity, ultimately basing his definitions on how a given group of writers understands a key word and produces creative writing and criticism in keeping with that understanding. For example, Babbitt faults neoclassical writers for focusing solely on the aspect of classical tradition and doing so with a strictness that subsequently caused a reaction leading to the romantic movement in literature and the romantic sentiment in life as a whole.

Chapter 1
The Terms Classic and Romantic

The words classic and romantic, we are often told, cannot be defined at all, and even if they could be defined, some would add, we should not be much profited. But this inability or unwillingness to define may itself turn out to be only one aspect of a movement that from Rousseau to Bergson has sought to discredit the analytical intellect—what

Wordsworth calls "the false secondary power by which we multiply distinctions." However, those who are with Socrates rather than with Rousseau or Wordsworth in this matter, will insist on the importance of definition, especially in a chaotic era like the present; for nothing is more characteristic of such an era than its irresponsible use of general terms. Now to measure up to the Socratic standard, a definition must not be abstract and metaphysical, but experimental; it must not, that is, reflect our opinion of what a word should mean, but what it actually has meant. Mathematicians may be free at times to frame their own definitions, but in the case of words like classic and romantic, that have been used innumerable times, and used not in one but in many countries, such a method is inadmissible. One must keep one's eye on actual usage. One should indeed allow for a certain amount of freakishness in this usage. Beaumarchais, for example, makes classic synonymous with barbaric.[1] One may disregard an occasional aberration of this kind, but if one can find only confusion and inconsistency in all the main uses of words like classic and romantic, the only procedure for those who speak or write in order to be understood is to banish the words from their vocabulary.

Now to define in a Socratic way two things are necessary: one must learn to see a common element in things that are apparently different and also to discriminate between things that are apparently similar. A Newton, to take the familiar instance of the former process, saw a common element in the fall of an apple and the motion of a planet; and one may perhaps without being a literary Newton discover a common element in all the main uses of the word romantic as well as in all the main uses of the word classic; though some of the things to which the word romantic in particular has been applied seem, it must be admitted, at least as far apart as the fall of an apple and the motion of a planet. The first step is to perceive the something that connects two or more of these things apparently so diverse, and then it may be found necessary to refer this unifying trait itself back to something still more general, and so on until we arrive, not indeed at anything absolute—the absolute will always elude us—but at what Goethe calls the original or underlying phenomenon (*Urphänomen*). A fruitful source of false definition is to take as primary in a more or less closely allied group of facts what is actually secondary—for example, to fix upon the return to the Middle Ages as the central fact in romanticism, whereas this return is only symptomatic; it is very far from being the original phenomenon. Confused and incomplete definitions of romanticism have indeed just that origin—they seek to put at the centre something that though romantic is not central but peripheral, and so the whole subject is thrown out of perspective.

My plan then is to determine to the best of my ability, in connection with a brief historical survey, the common element in the various uses of the words classic and romantic; and then, having thus disposed of the similarities, to turn to the second part of the art of defining and deal, also historically, with the differences. For my subject is not romanticism in general, but only a particular type of romanticism, and this type of romanticism needs to be seen as a recoil, not from classicism in general, but from a particular type of classicism.

I

The word romantic when traced historically is found to go back to the old French *roman* of which still older forms are *romans* and *romant*. These and similar formations derive ultimately from the mediæval Latin adverb *romanice*. *Roman* and like words meant originally the various vernaculars derived from Latin, just as the French still speak of these vernaculars as *les langues romanes*; and then the word *roman* came to be applied to tales written in the various vernaculars, especially in old French. Now with what features of these tales were people most struck? The reply to this question is found in a passage of a fifteenth-century Latin manuscript: "From the reading of certain romantics, that is, books of poetry composed in French on military deeds which are for the most part fictitious." Here the term romantic is applied to books that we should still call romantic and for the very same reason, namely, because of the predominance in these books of the element of fiction over reality.

5   In general a thing is romantic when, as Aristotle would say, it is wonderful rather than probable; in other words, when it violates the normal sequence of cause and effect in favor of adventure. Here is the fundamental contrast between the words classic and romantic which meets us at the outset and in some form or other persists in all the uses of the word down to the present day. A thing is romantic when it is strange, unexpected, intense, superlative, extreme, unique, etc. A thing is classical, on the other hand, when it is not unique, but representative of a class. In this sense medical men may speak correctly of a classic

case of typhoid fever, or a classic case of hysteria. One is even justified in speaking of a classic example of romanticism. By an easy extension of meaning a thing is classical when it belongs to a high class or to the best class. . . .

In the second half of the eighteenth century the increasingly favorable use of words like Gothic and enthusiastic as well as the emergence of words like sentimental and picturesque are among the symptoms of a new movement, and the fortunes of the word romantic were more or less bound up with this movement. Still, apart from its application to natural scenery, the word is as yet far from having acquired a favorable connotation if we are to believe an essay by John Foster on the "Application of the Epithet Romantic" (1805). Foster's point of view is not unlike that of Heidigger. Romantic, he says, had come to be used as a term of vague abuse, whereas it can be used rightly only of the ascendency of imagination over judgment, and is therefore synonymous with such words as wild, visionary, extravagant. "A man possessing so strong a judgment and so subordinate a fancy as Dean Swift would hardly have been made romantic . . . if he had studied all the books in Don Quixote's library." It is not, Foster admits, a sign of high endowment for a youth to be too coldly judicial, too deaf to the blandishments of imaginative illusion. Yet in general a man should strive to bring his imagination under the control of sound reason. But how is it possible thus to prevail against the deceits of fancy? Right knowing, he asserts very un-Socratically, is not enough to ensure right doing. At this point Foster changes from the tone of a literary essay to that of a sermon, and, maintaining a thesis somewhat similar to that of Pascal in the seventeenth century and Heidigger in the eighteenth, he concludes that a man's imagination will run away with his judgment or reason unless he have the aid of divine grace.

II

When Foster wrote his essay there was no question as yet in England of a romantic school. Before considering how the word came to be applied to a particular movement we need first to bring out more fully certain broad conflicts of tendency during the seventeenth and eighteenth centuries, conflicts that are not sufficiently revealed by the occasional uses during this period of the word romantic. In the contrast Foster established between judgment and imagination he is merely following a long series of neo-classical critics and this contrast not only seemed to him and these critics, but still seems to many, the essential contrast between classicism and romanticism. . . .

The following lines of Mulgrave are typical of the neo-classical notion of the relation between fancy and judgment:

> As all is dullness when the Fancy's bad,
> > So without Judgment, Fancy is but mad.
> Reason is that substantial, useful part
> > Which gains the Head, while t' other wins the Heart.

The opposition established by the neo-classicist in passages of this kind is too mechanical. Fancy and judgment do not seem to coöperate but to war with one another. In case of doubt the neo-classicist is always ready to sacrifice fancy to the "substantial, useful part," and so he seems too negative and cool and prosaic in his reason, and this is because his reason is so largely a protest against a previous romantic excess. What had been considered genius in the time of the "metaphysicals" had too often turned out to be only oddity. With this warning before them men kept their eyes fixed very closely on the model of normal human nature that had been set up, and imitated it very literally and timorously. A man was haunted by the fear that he might be "monstrous," and so, as Rymer put it, "satisfy nobody's maggot but his own." Correctness thus became a sort of tyranny. We suffer to the present day from this neo-classical failure to work out a sound conception of the imagination in its relation to good sense. Because the neo-classicist held the imagination lightly as compared with good sense the romantic rebels were led to hold good sense lightly as compared with imagination. The romantic view in short is too much the neo-classical view turned upside down; and, as Sainte-Beuve says, nothing resembles a hollow so much as a swelling.

III

Because the classicism against which romanticism rebelled was inadequate it does not follow that every type of classicism suffers from a similar inadequacy. . . .

We still need, therefore, to return to Greece, not merely for the best practice, but for the best theory of classicism; for this is still found in spite of all its obscurities and incompleteness in the Poetics of Aristotle. If we have recourse to this treatise, however, it must be on condition that we do not, like the critics of the Renaissance, deal with it in an abstract and dogmatic way (the form of the treatise it must be confessed gave them no slight encouragement), but in a spirit akin to Aristotle's own as revealed in the total body of his writings—a spirit that is at its best positive and experimental.

10   Aristotle not only deals positively and experimentally with the natural order and with man so far as he is a part of this order, but he deals in a similar fashion with a side of man that the modern positivist often overlooks. Like all the great Greeks Aristotle recognizes that man is the creature of two laws: he has an ordinary or natural self of impulse and desire and a human self that is known practically as a power of control over impulse and desire. If man is to become human he must not let impulse and desire run wild, but must oppose to everything excessive in his ordinary self, whether in thought or deed or emotion, the law of measure. This insistence on restraint and proportion is rightly taken to be of the essence not merely of the Greek spirit but of the classical spirit in general. The norm or standard that is to set bounds to the ordinary self is got at by different types of classicists in different ways and described variously: for example, as the human law, or the better self, or reason (a word to be discussed more fully later), or nature. Thus when Boileau says, "Let nature be your only study," he does not mean outer nature, nor again the nature of this or that individual, but representative human nature. Having decided what is normal either for man or some particular class of men the classicist takes this normal "nature" for his model and proceeds to imitate it. Whatever accords with the model he has thus set up he pronounces natural or probable, whatever on the other hand departs too far from what he conceives to be the normal type or the normal sequence of cause and effect he holds to be "improbable" and unnatural or even, if it attains an extreme of abnormality, "monstrous." Whatever in conduct or character is duly restrained and proportionate with reference to the model is said to observe decorum. Probability and decorum are identical in some of their aspects and closely related in all. To recapitulate, a general nature, a core of normal experience, is affirmed by all classicists. From this central affirmation derives the doctrine of imitation, and from imitation in turn the doctrines of probability and decorum.

But though all classicists are alike in insisting on nature, imitation, probability and decorum, they differ widely, as I have already intimated, in what they understand by these terms. Let us consider first what Aristotle and the Greeks understand by them. The first point to observe is that according to Aristotle one is to get his general nature not on authority or second hand, but is to disengage it directly for himself from the jumble of particulars that he has before his eyes. He is not, says Aristotle, to imitate things as they are, but as they ought to be. Thus conceived imitation is a creative act. Through all the welter of the actual one penetrates to the real and so succeeds without ceasing to be individual in suggesting the universal. Poetry that is imitative in this sense is, according to Aristotle, more "serious" and "philosophical" than history. History deals merely with what has happened, whereas poetry deals with what may happen according to probability or necessity. Poetry, that is, does not portray life literally but extricates the deeper or ideal truth from the flux of circumstance. One may add with Sydney that if poetry is thus superior to history in being more serious and philosophical it resembles history and is superior to philosophy in being concrete.

The One that the great poet or artist perceives in the Many and that gives to his work its high seriousness is not a fixed absolute. In general the model that the highly serious man (ὁ σπουδαῖος) imitates and that keeps his ordinary self within the bounds of decorum is not to be taken as anything finite, as anything that can be formulated once for all. This point is important for on it hinges every right distinction not merely between the classic and the romantic, but between the classic and the pseudoclassic. Romanticism has claimed for itself a monopoly of imagination and infinitude, but on closer examination, as I hope to show later, this claim, at least so far as genuine classicism is concerned, will be found to be quite unjustified. For the present it is enough to say that true classicism does not rest on the observance of rules or the imitation of models but on an immediate insight into the universal. Aristotle is especially admirable in the account he gives of this insight and of the way it may manifest itself in art and literature. One may be rightly imitative, he says, and so have access to a superior truth and give others access to it only by being a master of illusion. Though the great poet "breathes immortal air," though he sees behind the shows of sense a world of more abiding relationships, he can convey his vision not directly but only imaginatively. Aristotle, one should observe, does not establish any hard and fast opposition between judgment and imagination, an opposition that pervades not only the neo-classical movement but also the romantic revolt from it. He simply affirms a supersensuous order which one can perceive only with the help of fiction. The best art, says Goethe in the true spirit of Aristotle, gives us the "illusion of a higher reality." This has the advantage of being experimental. It is merely a statement of what one feels in the presence of a great painting, let us say, or in reading a great poem. . . .

One must grant, indeed, that must noble work was achieved under the neo-classical dispensation, work that shows a genuine insight into the universal, but it is none the less evident that the view of the imagination held during this period has a formalistic taint.

This taint in neo-classicism is due not merely to its dogmatic and mechanical way of dealing with the doctrine of imitation but also to the fact that it had to reconcile classical with Christian dogma; and the two antiquities, classical and Christian, if interpreted vitally and in the spirit, were in many respects divergent and in some respects contradictory. The general outcome of the attempts at reconciliation made by the literary casuists of Italy and France was that Christianity should have a monopoly of truth and classicism a monopoly of fiction. For the true classicist, it will be remembered, the two things are inseparable—he gets at his truth through a veil of fiction. Many of the neo-classicists came to conceive of art as many romanticists were to conceive of it later as a sort of irresponsible game or play, but they were, it must be confessed, very inferior to the romanticists in the spontaneity of their fiction. They went for this fiction as for everything else to the models, and this meant in practice that they employed the pagan myths, not as imaginative symbols of a higher reality—it is still possible to employ them in that way—but merely in Boileau's phrase as "traditional ornaments" (*ornements reçus*). The neo-classicist to be sure might so employ his "fiction" as to inculcate a moral; in that case he is only too likely to give us instead of the living symbol, dead allegory; instead of high seriousness, its caricature, didacticism. The traditional stock of fiction became at last so intolerably trite as to be rejected even by some of the late neo-classicists. "The rejection and contempt of fiction," said Dr. Johnson (who indulged in it himself on occasion) "is rational and manly." But to reject fiction in the larger sense is to miss the true driving power in human nature—the imagination. Before concluding, however, that Dr. Johnson had no notion of the rôle of the imagination one should read his attack on the theory of the three unities which was later to be turned to account by the romanticists. . . .

One should not however, like Rousseau and the romanticists, judge of decorum by what it degenerated into. Every doctrine of genuine worth is disciplinary and men in the mass do not desire discipline. "Most men," says Aristotle, "would rather live in a disorderly than in a sober manner." But most men do not admit any such preference—that would be crude and inartistic. They incline rather to substitute for the reality of discipline some art of going through the motions. Every great doctrine is thus in constant peril of passing over into some hollow semblance or even, it may be, into some mere caricature of itself. When one wishes therefore to determine the nature of decorum one should think of a Milton, let us say, and not of a Talleyrand or even of a Chesterfield.

15 Milton imitated the models, like any other neo-classicist, but his imitation was not, in Joubert's phrase, that of one book by another book, but of one soul by another soul. His decorum is therefore imaginative; and it is the privilege of the imagination to give the sense of spaciousness and infinitude. On the other hand, the unimaginative way in which many of the neo-classicists held their main tenets—nature, imitation, probability, decorum—narrowed unduly the scope of the human spirit and appeared to close the gates of the future. "Art and diligence have now done their best," says Dr. Johnson of the versification of Pope, "and what shall be added will be the effort of tedious toil and needless curiosity." Nothing is more perilous than thus to seem to confine man in some pinfold; there is something in him that refuses to acquiesce in any position as final; he is in Nietzsche's phrase the being who must always surpass himself. The attempt to oppose external and mechanical barriers to the freedom of the spirit will create in the long run an atmosphere of stuffiness and smugness, and nothing is more intolerable than smugness. Men were guillotined in the French Revolution, as Bagehot suggests, simply because either they or their ancestors had been smug. . . .

I have been trying to build up a background that will make clear why the reason of the eighteenth century (whether we understand by reason logic or good sense) had come to be superficial and therefore oppressive to the imagination. It is only with reference to this "reason" that one can understand the romantic revolt. But neo-classical reason itself can be understood only with reference to its background—as a recoil namely from a previous romantic excess. This excess was manifested not only in the intellectual romanticism of which I have already spoken, but in the cult of the romantic deed that had flourished in the Middle Ages. This cult and the literature that reflected it continued to appeal, even to the cultivated, well on into the neo-classical period. It was therefore felt necessary to frame a definition of reason that should be a rebuke to the extravagance and improbability of the mediæval romances. When men became conscious in the eighteenth century of the neo-classical meagerness on the imaginative side they began to look back with a certain envy to the free efflorescence of fiction in the Middle Ages. They began to ask themselves with Hurd whether the reason and correctness they had won were worth the sacrifice of a "world of fine fabling." We must not, however, like Heine and many others, look on the romantic movement as merely a return to the Middle Ages. We have seen that the men of the Middle Ages themselves understood by romance not simply their own kind of speech and writing in contrast with what was written in Latin, but a kind of writing in which the pursuit of strangeness and adventure predominated. This pursuit of strangeness and adventure will be found to predominate in all types of romanticism. The type of romanticism, however, which came in towards the end of the eighteenth century did not, even when professedly mediæval, simply revert to the older types. It was primarily not a romanticism of thought or of action, the types we have encountered thus far, but a romanticism of feeling. The beginnings of this emotional romanticism antedate considerably the application of the word romantic to a particular literary school. . . .

SUGGESTIONS FOR WRITING

1. In your view, does Irving Babbitt live up to his own high regard for the importance of definition? Write an essay that explores his performance as a definer of terms.
2. Babbitt says that the nineteenth-century romanticism (that of Wordsworth, Coleridge, Keats, Shelley, and Byron, for example) resulted from a recoil against the pseudoclassical spirit in neoclassicism, which in its turn came out of a response to the excesses of an earlier romanticism. Does he thereby seem to view literary history as an evolutionary process, in your view? Write an essay that explains and defends your answer.
3. Almost everyone has seen one or more films in the *Star Wars* series. In your opinion, how would Irving Babbitt categorize the artistic spirit of any one of these films that you have seen. Would he see your film as

classic? Neoclassic? Romantic? Using Babbitt's procedure as a model, write an essay that explores the problem of defining the artistic spirit of a *Star Wars* film.

Shakespeare's Sister
From *A Room of One's Own*

VIRGINIA WOOLF

Virginia Woolf (1882–1941) was born in London and educated in her highly literate and well-connected family. Her father, Sir Leslie Stephen, was a famous editor, critic, and biographer—the widower of Thackeray's daughter and the friend of Henry James. In 1928 Woolf was invited to lecture at Girton and Newham Colleges of Cambridge University. Although Girton was founded in 1869 and was the first college to admit women, it did not receive full university status until 1948. The values, assumptions, and prejudices underlying this fact make the subject of her lectures later turned into a famous book, A Room of One's Own. *In the excerpt reprinted here, Woolf speculates on the literary prospects for "Judith," a sister she invents for William Shakespeare. The result marks the first practical and theoretical critical exploration of feminist literary history.*

WOOLF: SHAKESPEARE'S SISTER

Here am I asking why women did not write poetry in the Elizabethan age, and I am not sure how they were educated; whether they were taught to write; whether they had sitting-rooms to themselves; how many women had children before they were twenty-one; what, in short, they did from eight in the morning till eight at night. They had no money evidently; according to Professor Trevelyan they were married whether they liked it or not before they were out of the nursery, at fifteen or sixteen very likely. It would have been extremely odd, even upon this showing, had one of them suddenly written the plays of Shakespeare, I concluded, and I thought of that old gentleman, who is dead now, but was a bishop, I think, who declared that it was impossible for any woman, past, present, or to come, to have the genius of Shakespeare. He wrote to the papers about it. He also told a lady who applied to him for information that cats do not as a matter of fact go to heaven, though they have, he added, souls of a sort. How much thinking those old gentlemen used to save one! How the borders of ignorance shrank back at their approach! Cats do not go to heaven. Women cannot write the plays of Shakespeare.

Be that as it may, I could not help thinking, as I looked at the works of Shakespeare on the shelf, that the bishop was right at least in this; it would have been impossible, completely and entirely, for any woman to have written the plays of Shakespeare in the age of Shakespeare. Let me imagine, since facts are so hard to come by, what would have happened had Shakespeare had a wonderfully gifted sister, called Judith, let us say. Shakespeare himself went, very probably—his mother was an heiress—to the grammar school, where he may have learnt Latin— Ovid, Virgil and Horace—and the elements of grammar and logic. He was, it is well known, a wild boy who poached rabbits, perhaps shot a deer, and had, rather sooner than he should have done, to marry a woman in the neighbourhood, who bore him a child rather quicker than was right. That escapade sent him to seek his fortune in London. He had, it seemed, a taste for the theatre; he began by holding horses at the stage door. Very soon he got work in the theatre, became a successful actor, and lived at the hub of the universe, meeting everybody, knowing everybody, practising his art on the boards, exercising his wits in the streets, and even getting access to the palace of the queen. Meanwhile his extraordinarily gifted sister, let us suppose, remained at home. She was as adventurous, as imaginative, as agog to see the world as he was. But she was not sent to school. She had no chance of learning grammar and logic, let alone of reading Horace and Virgil. She picked up a book now and then, one of her brother's perhaps, and read a few pages. But then her parents came in and told her to mend the stockings or mind the stew and not moon about with books and papers. They would have spoken sharply but kindly, for they were substantial people who knew the conditions of life for a woman and loved their daughter—indeed, more likely than not she was the apple of her father's eye. Perhaps she scribbled some pages up in an apple loft on the sly, but was careful to hide them or set fire to them. Soon, however, before she was out of her teens, she was to be betrothed to the son of a neighbouring wool-stapler. She cried out that marriage was hateful to her, and for that she was severely beaten by her father. Then he ceased to scold her. He begged her instead not to hurt him, not to shame him in this matter of her marriage. He would give her a chain of beads or a fine petticoat, he said; and there were tears in his eyes. How could she disobey him? How could she break his heart? The force of her own gift alone drove her to it. She made up a small parcel of her belongings, let herself down by a rope one summer's night and took the road to London. She was not seventeen. The birds that sang in the hedge were not more musical than she was. She had the quickest fancy, a gift like her brother's, for the tune of words. Like him, she had a taste for the theatre. She stood at the stage door; she wanted to act, she said. Men laughed in her face. The manager—a fat, loose-lipped man—guffawed. He bellowed something about poodles dancing and women acting— no woman, he said, could possibly be an actress. He hinted—you can imagine what. She could get no training in her craft. Could she even seek her dinner in a tavern or roam the streets at midnight? Yet her genius was for fiction and lusted to feed abundantly upon the lives of men and women and the study of their ways. At last—for she was very young, oddly like Shakespeare the poet in her face, with the same grey eyes and rounded brows—at last Nick Greene the actor-manager took pity on her; she found herself with child by that gentleman and so— who shall measure the heat and violence of the poet's heart when caught and tangled in a woman's body?—killed herself one winter's night and lies buried at some cross-roads where the omnibuses now stop outside the Elephant and Castle.

That, more or less, is how the story would run, I think, if a woman in Shakespeare's day had had Shakespeare's genius. But for my part, I agree with the deceased bishop, if such he was—it is unthinkable that any woman in Shakespeare's day should have had Shakespeare's genius. For genius like Shakespeare's is not born among labouring, uneducated, servile people. It was not born in England among the Saxons and the Britons. It is not born today among the working classes. How, then, could it have been born among women whose work began, according to Professor Trevelyan, almost before they were out of the nursery, who were forced to it by their parents and held to it by all the power of law and custom? Yet genius of a sort must have existed among women as it must have existed among the working classes. Now and again an Emily Brontë or a Robert Burns blazes out and proves its presence. But certainly it never got itself on to paper. When, however, one reads of a witch being ducked, of a woman possessed by devils, of a wise woman selling herbs, or even of a very remarkable man who had a mother, then I think we are on the track of a lost novelist, a suppressed poet, of some mute and inglorious Jane Austen, some Emily Brontë who dashed her brains out on the moor or mopped and mowed about the highways crazed with the torture that her gift had put her to. Indeed, I would venture to guess that Anon, who wrote so many poems without signing them, was often a woman. It was a woman Edward Fitzgerald, I think, suggested who made the ballads and the folk-songs, crooning them to her children, beguiling her spinning with them, or the length of the winter's night.

This may be true or it may be false—who can say?—but what is true in it, so it seemed to me, reviewing the story of Shakespeare's sister as I had made it, is that any woman born with a great gift in the sixteenth century would certainly have gone crazed, shot herself, or ended her days in some lonely cottage outside the village, half witch, half wizard, feared and mocked at. For it needs little skill in psychology to be sure that a highly gifted girl who had tried to use her gift for poetry would have been so thwarted and hindered by other people, so tortured and pulled asunder by her own contrary instincts, that she must have lost her health and sanity to a certainty. No girl could have walked to London and stood at a stage door and forced her way into the presence of actor-managers without doing herself a violence and suffering an anguish which may have been irrational—for chastity may be a fetish invented by certain societies for unknown reasons—but were none the less inevitable. Chastity had then, it has even now, a religious importance in a woman's life, and has so wrapped itself round with nerves and instincts that to cut it free and bring it to the light of day demands courage of the rarest. To have lived a free life in London in the sixteenth century would have meant for a woman who was a poet and a playwright a nervous stress and dilemma which might well have killed her. Had she survived, whatever she had written would have been twisted and deformed, issuing from a strained and morbid imagination. And undoubtedly, I thought, looking at the shelf where there are no plays by women, her work would have gone unsigned. That refuge she would have sought certainly. It was the relic of the sense of chastity that dictated anonymity to women even so late as the nineteenth century. Currer Bell, George Eliot, George Sand, all the victims of inner strife as their writings prove, sought ineffectively to veil themselves by using the name of a man. Thus they did homage to the convention, which if not implanted by the other sex was liberally encouraged by them (the chief glory of a woman is not to be talked of, said Pericles, himself a much-talked-of man), that publicity in women is detestable. Anonymity runs in their blood. The desire to be veiled still possesses them. They are not even now as concerned about the health of their fame as men are, and, speaking generally, will pass a tombstone or a signpost without feeling an irresistible desire to cut their names on it, as Alf, Bert or Chas. must do in obedience to their instinct, which murmurs if it sees a fine woman go by, or even a god, Ce chien est à moi. And, of course, it may not be a dog, I thought, remembering Parliament Square, the Sieges Allee and other avenues; it may be a piece of land or a man with curly black hair. It is one of the great advantages of being a woman that one can pass even a very fine negress without wishing to make an Englishwoman of her.

5   That woman, then, who was born with a gift of poetry in the sixteenth century, was an unhappy woman, a woman at strife against herself. All the conditions of her life, all her own instincts, were hostile to the state of mind which is needed to set free whatever is in the brain. But what is the state of mind that is most propitious to the act of creation, I asked? Can one come by any notion of the state that furthers and makes possible that strange activity? Here I opened the volume containing the Tragedies of Shakespeare. What was Shakespeare's state of mind, for instance, when he wrote *Lear* and *Antony and Cleopatra?* It was certainly the state of mind most favourable to poetry that there has ever existed. But Shakespeare himself said nothing about it. We only know casually and by chance that he "never blotted a line." Nothing indeed was ever said by the artist himself about his state of mind until the eighteenth century perhaps. Rousseau perhaps began it. At any rate, by the nineteenth century self-consciousness had developed so far that it was the habit for men of letters to describe their minds in confessions and autobiographies. Their lives also were written, and their letters were printed after their deaths. Thus, though we do not know what Shakespeare went through when he wrote *Lear*, we do know what Carlyle went through when he wrote *The French Revolution;* what Flaubert went through when he wrote *Madame Bovary;* what Keats was going through when he tried to write poetry against the coming of death and the indifference of the world.

And one gathers from this enormous modern literature of confession and self-analysis that to write a work of genius is almost always a feat of prodigious difficulty. Everything is against the likelihood that it will come from the writer's mind whole and entire. Generally material circumstances are against it. Dogs will bark; people will interrupt; money must be made; health will break down. Further, accentuating all these difficulties and making them harder to bear is the world's notorious indifference. It does not ask people to write poems and novels and histories; it does not need them. It does not care whether Flaubert finds the right word or whether Carlyle scrupulously verifies this or that fact. Naturally, it will not pay for what it does not want. And so the writer, Keats, Flaubert, Carlyle, suffers, especially in the creative years of youth, every form of distraction and discouragement. A curse, a cry of agony, rises from those books of analysis and confession. "Mighty poets in their misery dead"—that is the burden of their song. If anything comes through in spite of all this, it is a miracle, and probably no book is born entire and uncrippled as it was conceived.

But for women, I thought, looking at the empty shelves, these difficulties were infinitely more formidable. In the first place, to have a room of her own, let alone a quiet room or a sound-proof room, was out of the question, unless her parents were exceptionally rich or very noble, even up to the beginning of the nineteenth century. Since her pin money, which depended on the good will of her father, was only enough to keep her clothed, she was debarred from such alleviations as came even to Keats or Tennyson or Carlyle, all poor men, from a walking tour, a little journey to France, from the separate lodging which, even if it were miserable enough, sheltered them from the claims and tyrannies of their families. Such material difficulties were formidable; but much worse were the immaterial. The indifference of the world which Keats and Flaubert and other men of genius have found so hard to bear was in her case not indifference but hostility. The world did not say to her as it said to them, Write if you choose; it makes no difference to me. The world said with a guffaw, Write? What's the good of your writing? Here the psychologists of Newnham and Girton might come to our help. I thought, looking again at the blank spaces on the shelves. For surely it is time that the effect of discouragement upon the mind of the artist should be measured, as I have seen a dairy company measure the effect of ordinary milk and Grade A milk upon the body of the rat. They set two rats in cages side by side, and of the two one was furtive, timid and small, and the other was glossy, bold and big. Now what food do we feed women as artists upon? I asked, remembering, I suppose, that dinner of prunes and custard. To answer that question I had only to open the evening paper and to read that Lord Birkenhead is of opinion— but really I am not going to trouble to copy out Lord Birkenhead's opinion upon the writing of women. What Dean Inge says I will leave in peace. The Harley Street specialist may be allowed to rouse the echoes of Harley Street with his vociferations without raising a hair on my head. I will quote, however, Mr. Oscar Browning, because Mr. Oscar Browning was a great figure in Cambridge at one time, and used to examine the students at Girton and Newnham. Mr. Oscar Browning was wont to declare "that the impression left on his mind, after looking over any set of examination papers, was that, irrespective of the marks he might give, the best woman was intellectually the inferior of the worst man." After saying that Mr. Browning went back to his rooms—and it is this sequel that endears him and makes him a human figure of some bulk and majesty—he went back to his rooms and found a stable-boy lying on the sofa—"a mere skeleton, his cheeks were cavernous and sallow, his teeth were black, and he did not appear to have the full use of his limbs. . . . 'That's Arthur' [said Mr. Browning]. 'He's a dear boy really and most high-minded.'" The two pictures always seem to me to complete each other. And happily in this age of biography the two pictures often do complete each other, so that we are able to interpret the opinions of great men not only by what they say, but by what they do.

But though this is possible now, such opinions coming from the lips of important people must have been formidable enough even fifty years ago. Let us suppose that a father from the highest motives did not wish his daughter to leave home and become writer, painter or scholar. "See what Mr. Oscar Browning says," he would say; and there was not only Mr. Oscar Browning; there was the *Saturday Review*; there was Mr. Greg—the "essentials of a woman's being," said Mr. Greg emphatically, "are that *they are supported by, and they minister to, men*"— there was an enormous body of masculine opinion to the effect that nothing could be expected of women intellectually. Even if her father did not read out loud these opinions, any girl could read them for herself; and the reading, even in the nineteenth century, must have lowered her vitality, and told profoundly upon her work. There would always have been that assertion—you cannot do this, you are incapable of doing that—to protest against, to overcome. Probably for a novelist this germ is no longer of much effect; for there have been women novelists of merit. But for painters it must still have some sting in it; and for musicians, I imagine, is even now active and poisonous in the extreme. The woman composer stands where the actress stood in the time of Shakespeare. Nick Greene, I thought, remembering the story I had made about Shakespeare's sister, said that a woman acting put him in mind of a dog dancing. Johnson repeated the phrase two hundred years later of women preaching. And here, I said, opening a book about music, we have the very words used again in this year of grace, 1928, of women who try to write music. "Of Mlle. Germaine Tailleferre one can only repeat Dr. Johnson's dictum concerning a woman preacher, transposed into terms of music. 'Sir, a woman's composing is like a dog's walking on his hind legs. It is not done well, but you are surprised to find it done at all.'" So accurately does history repeat itself.

Thus, I concluded, shutting Mr. Oscar Browning's life and pushing away the rest, it is fairly evident that even in the nineteenth century a woman was not encouraged to be an artist. On the contrary, she was snubbed, slapped, lectured and exhorted. Her mind must have been strained and her vitality lowered by the need of opposing this, of disproving that. For here again we come within range of that very interesting and obscure masculine complex which has had so much influence upon the woman's movement; that deep-seated desire, not so much that *she* shall be inferior as that *he* shall be superior, which plants him wherever one looks, not only in front of the arts, but barring the way to politics too, even when the risk to himself seems infinitesimal and the suppliants humble and devoted. . . .

SUGGESTIONS FOR WRITING

1. Plato maintains that divine inspiration is the source and cause of literary production. To what extent do you think Virginia Woolf would agree or disagree? Based on your reading of "Shakespeare's Sister," write an essay that imagines a response by Woolf to Plato.

2. In your opinion, does Virginia Woolf's story of Judith Shakespeare's life and death have a plot according to Aristotle's definition? Write an essay that explains and defends your views.

3. Virgina Woolf does not mention Mary Wollstonecraft, but she seems to agree with Wollstonecraft about some of the same "unnatural distinctions established in society." Write an essay that explores Virginia Woolf's views of the "pernicious effects which arise" within literary culture because of those distinctions.

Bartleby, The Scrivener   1853

HERMAN MELVILLE

Herman Melville (1819–1891) was a popular novelist at the beginning of his career with tales of tropical paradises and seagoing life, but he was a writer all but forgotten by the public and critics alike when he died. He was "rediscovered" only in the late teens and early twenties of the following century—his late novella Billy Budd *lay in a tin can for years until its publication in 1924 and* Moby-Dick *was considered an adventure book for boys. With his critical rehabilitation,* Moby-Dick *was seen as one of the great novels of American literature and Melville as one of its greatest writers. His enigmatic story of "Bartleby the Scrivener" was also reevaluated and has delighted and puzzled readers ever since.*

A Story of Wall-street

I am a rather elderly man. The nature of my avocations for the last thirty years has brought me into more than ordinary contact with what would seem an interesting and somewhat singular set of men of whom as yet nothing that I know of has ever been written:—I mean the law-copyists or scriveners. I have known very many of them, professionally and privately, and if I pleased, could relate divers histories, at which good-natured gentlemen might smile, and sentimental souls might weep. But I waive the biographies of all other scriveners for a few passages in the life of Bartleby, who was a scrivener the strangest I ever saw or heard of. While of other law-copyists I might write the complete life, of Bartleby nothing of that sort can be done. I believe that no materials exist for a full and satisfactory biography of this man. It is an irreparable loss to literature. Bartleby was one of those beings of whom nothing is ascertainable, except from the original sources, and in his case those are very small. What my own astonished eyes saw of Bartleby, *that* is all I know of him, except, indeed, one vague report which will appear in the sequel.

Ere introducing the scrivener, as he first appeared to me, it is fit I make some mention of myself, my *employées*, my business, my chambers, and general surroundings; because some such description is indispensable to an adequate understanding of the chief character about to be presented.

Imprimis: I am a man who, from his youth upwards, has been filled with a profound conviction that the easiest way of life is the best. Hence, though I belong to a profession proverbially energetic and nervous, even to turbulence, at times, yet nothing of that sort have I ever suffered to invade my peace. I am one of those unambitious lawyers who never addresses a jury, or in any way draws down public applause; but in the cool tranquillity of a snug retreat, do a snug business among rich men's bonds and mortgages and title-deeds. All who know me, consider me an eminently *safe* man. The late John Jacob

Astor, a personage little given to poetic enthusiasm, had no hesitation in pronouncing my first grand point to be prudence; my next, method. I do not speak it in vanity, but simply record the fact, that I was not un-employed in my profession by the late John Jacob Astor; a name which, I admit, I love to repeat, for it hath a rounded and orbicular sound to it, and rings like unto bullion. I will freely add, that I was not insensible to the late John Jacob Astor's good opinion.

Some time prior to the period at which this little history begins, my avocations had been largely increased. The good old office, now extinct in the State of New York, of a Master in Chancery, had been conferred upon me. It was not a very arduous office, but very pleasantly remuner-ative. I seldom lose my temper; much more seldom indulge in danger-ous indignation at wrongs and outrages; but I must be permitted to be rash here and declare, that I consider the sudden and violent abroga-tion of the office of Master in Chancery, by the new Constitution, as a——premature act; inasmuch as I had counted upon a life-lease of the profits, whereas I only received those of a few short years. But this is by the way.

5   My chambers were up stairs at No.—Wall-street. At one end they looked upon the white wall of the interior of a spacious skylight shaft, penetrating the building from top to bottom. This view might have been considered rather tame than otherwise, deficient in what land-scape painters call "life." But if so, the view from the other end of my chambers offered, at least, a contrast, if nothing more. In that direction my windows commanded an unobstructed view of a lofty brick wall, black by age and everlasting shade; which wall required no spy-glass to bring out its lurking beauties, but for the benefit of all near-sighted spectators, was pushed up to within ten feet of my window panes. Owing to the great height of the surrounding buildings, and my chambers being on the second floor, the interval between this wall and mine not a little resembled a huge square cistern.

At the period just preceding the advent of Bartleby, I had two per-sons as copyists in my employment, and a promising lad as an office-boy. First, Turkey; second, Nippers; third, Ginger Nut. These may seem names, the like of which are not usually found in the Directory. In truth they were nicknames, mutually conferred upon each other by my three clerks, and were deemed expressive of their respective persons or char-acters. Turkey was a short, pursy Englishman of about my own age, that is, somewhere not far from sixty. In the morning, one might say, his face was of a fine florid hue, but after twelve o'clock, meridian—his dinner hour—it blazed like a grate full of Christmas coals; and continued blazing—but, as it were, with a gradual wane—till 6 o'clock, P.M. or thereabouts, after which I saw no more of the proprietor of the face, which gaining its meridian with the sun, seemed to set with it, to rise, culminate, and decline the following day, with the like regularity and undiminished glory. There are many singular coincidences I have known in the course of my life, not the least among which was the fact that exactly when Turkey displayed his fullest beams from his red and radiant countenance, just then, too, at the critical moment, began the daily period when I considered his business capacities as seriously disturbed for the remainder of the twenty-four hours. Not that he was absolutely idle, or averse to business then; far from it. The difficulty was, he was apt to be altogether too energetic. There was a strange, inflamed, flurried, flighty recklessness of activity about him. He would be incautious in dipping his pen into his inkstand. All his blots upon my documents, were dropped there after twelve o'clock, meridian. Indeed, not only would he be reckless and sadly given to making blots in the afternoon, but some days he went further, and was rather noisy. At such times, too, his face flamed with augmented blazonry, as if cannel coal had been heaped on anthracite. He made an unpleasant racket with his chair; spilled his sand-box; in mending his pens, impatiently split them all to pieces, and threw them on the floor in a sudden passion; stood up and leaned over his table, boxing his papers about in a most indecorous manner, very sad to behold in an elderly man like him. Nevertheless, as he was in many ways a most valuable person to me, and all the time before twelve o'clock, meridian, was the quickest, steadiest creature too, accomplishing a great deal of work in a style not easy to be matched—for these reasons, I was willing to overlook his eccentricities, though indeed, occasionally, I remonstrated with him. I did this very gently, however, because, though the civilest, nay, the blandest and most reverential of men in the morning, yet in the afternoon he was disposed, upon provocation, to be slightly rash with his tongue, in fact, insolent. Now, valuing his morning services as I did, and resolved not to lose them; yet, at the same time made uncomfortable by his inflamed ways after twelve o'clock; and being a man of peace, unwilling by my admonitions to call forth unseemingly retorts from him; I took upon me, one Saturday noon (he was always worse on Saturdays), to hint to him, very kindly, that perhaps now that he was growing old, it might be well to abridge his labors; in short, he need not come to my chambers after twelve o'clock, but dinner over, had best go home to his lodgings and rest himself till tea-time. But no; he insisted upon his afternoon devotions. His countenance became intolerably fervid, as he oratorically assured me—gesticulating with a long ruler at the other end of the room—that if his services in the morning were useful, how indispensable, then, in the afternoon?

"With submission, sir," said Turkey on this occasion, "I consider myself your right-hand man. In the morning I but marshal and deploy my columns; but in the afternoon I put myself at their head, and gallantly charge the foe, thus!"—and he made a violent thrust with the ruler.

"But the blots, Turkey," intimated I.

"True,—but, with submission, sir, behold these hairs! I am getting old. Surely, sir, a blot or two of a warm afternoon is not to be severely urged against gray hairs. Old age—even if it blot the page—is honorable. With submission, sir, we *both* are getting old."

10 This appeal to my fellow-feeling was hardly to be resisted. At all events, I saw that go he would not. So I made up my mind to let him stay, resolving, nevertheless, to see to it, that during the afternoon he had to do with my less important papers.

Nippers, the second on my list, was a whiskered, sallow, and, upon the whole, rather piratical-looking young man of about five and twenty. I always deemed him the victim of two evil powers—ambition and indigestion. The ambition was evinced by a certain impatience of the duties of a mere copyist, an unwarrantable usurpation of strictly professional affairs, such as the original drawing up of legal documents. The indigestion seemed betokened in an occasional nervous testiness and grinning irritability, causing the teeth to audibly grind together over mistakes committed in copying; unnecessary maledictions, hissed, rather than spoken, in the heat of business; and especially by a continual discontent with the height of the table where he worked. Though of a very ingenious mechanical turn, Nippers could never get this table to suit him. He put chips under it, blocks of various sorts, bits of pasteboard, and at last went so far as to attempt an exquisite adjustment by final pieces of folded blotting-paper. But no invention would answer. If, for the sake of easing his back, he brought the table lid at a sharp angle well up towards his chin, and wrote there like a man using the steep roof of a Dutch house for his desk:—then he declared that it stopped the circulation in his arms. If now he lowered the table to his waistbands, and stooped over it in writing, then there was a sore aching in his back. In short, the truth of the matter was, Nippers knew not what he wanted. Or, if he wanted anything, it was to be rid of a scrivener's table altogether. Among the manifestations of his diseased ambition was a fondness he had for receiving visits from certain ambiguous-looking fellows in seedy coats, whom he called his clients. Indeed I was aware that not only was he, at times, considerable of a ward-politician, but he occasionally did a little business at the Justices' courts, and was not unknown on the steps of the Tombs. I have good reason to believe, however, that one individual who called upon him at my chambers, and who, with a grand air, he insisted was his client, was no other than a dun, and the alleged title-deed, a bill. But with all his failings, and the annoyances he caused me, Nippers, like his compatriot Turkey, was a very useful man to me; wrote a neat, swift hand; and, when he chose, was not deficient in a gentlemanly sort of deportment. Added to this, he always dressed in a gentlemanly sort of way; and so, incidentally, reflected credit upon my chambers. Whereas with respect to Turkey, I had much ado to keep him from being a reproach to me. His clothes were apt to look oily and smell of eating-houses. He wore his pantaloons very loose and baggy in summer. His coats were execrable; his hat not to be handled. But while the hat was a thing of indifference to me, inasmuch as his natural civility and deference, as a dependent Englishman, always led him to doff it the moment he entered the room, yet his coat was another matter. Concerning his coats, I reasoned with him; but with no effect. The truth was, I suppose, that a man with so small an income, could not afford to sport such a lustrous face and a lustrous coat at one and the same time. As Nippers once observed, Turkey's money went chiefly for red ink. One winter day I presented Turkey with a highly respectable looking coat of my own, a padded gray coat, of a most comfortable warmth, and which buttoned straight up from the knee to the neck. I thought Turkey would appreciate the favor, and abate his rashness and obstreperousness of afternoons. But no. I verily believe that buttoning himself up in so downy and blanket-like a coat had a pernicious effect upon him; upon the same principle that too much oats are bad for horses. In fact, precisely as a rash, restive horse is said to feel his oats, so Turkey felt his coat. It made him insolent. He was a man whom prosperity harmed.

Though concerning the self-indulgent habits of Turkey I had my own private surmises, yet touching Nippers I was well persuaded that whatever might be his faults in other respects, he was, at least, a temperate young man. But indeed, nature herself seemed to have been his vintner, and at his birth charged him so thoroughly with an irritable, brandy-like disposition, that all subsequent potations were needless. When I consider how, amid the stillness of my chambers, Nippers would sometimes impatiently rise from his seat, and stooping over his table, spread his arms wide apart, seize the whole desk, and move it, and jerk it, with a grim, grinding motion on the floor, as if the table were a perverse voluntary agent, intent on thwarting and vexing him; I plainly perceive that for Nippers, brandy and water were altogether superfluous.

It was fortunate for me that, owing to its peculiar cause—indigestion—the irritability and consequent nervousness of Nippers, were mainly observable in the morning, while in the afternoon he was comparatively mild. So that Turkey's paroxysms only coming on about twelve o'clock, I never had to do with their eccentricities at one time. Their fits relieved each other like guards. When Nippers' was on, Turkey's was off; and *vice versa*. This was a good natural arrangement under the circumstances.

Ginger Nut, the third on my list, was a lad some twelve years old. His father was a carman, ambitious of seeing his son on the bench instead of a cart, before he died. So he sent him to my office as student at law, errand boy, and cleaner and sweeper, at the rate of one dollar a week. He had a little desk to himself, but he did not use it much. Upon inspection, the drawer exhibited a great array of the shells of various sorts of nuts. Indeed, to this quick-witted youth the whole noble science of the law was contained in a nut-shell. Not the least among the employments of Ginger Nut, as well as one which he discharged with the most alacrity, was his duty as cake and apple purveyor for Turkey and Nippers. Copying law papers being proverbially a dry, husky sort of business, my two scriveners were fain to moisten their mouths very often with Spitzenbergs to be had at the numerous stalls nigh the Custom House and Post Office. Also, they sent Ginger Nut very frequently for that peculiar cake—small, flat, round, and very spicy—after which he had been named by them. Of a cold morning when business was but dull, Turkey would gobble up scores of these cakes, as if they were mere wafers—indeed they sell them at the rate of six or eight for a penny—the scrape of his pen blending with the crunching of the crisp particles in his mouth. Of all the fiery afternoon blunders and flurried rashnesses of Turkey, was his once moistening a ginger-cake between his lips, and clapping it on to a mortgage for a seal. I came within an ace of dismissing him then. But he mollified me by making an oriental bow, and saying—"With submission, sir, it was generous of me to find you in stationery on my own account."

15   Now my original business—that of a conveyancer and title hunter, and drawer-up of recondite documents of all sorts—was considerably increased by receiving the master's office. There was now great work for scriveners. Not only must I push the clerks already with me, but I must have additional help. In answer to my advertisement, a motionless young man one morning, stood upon my office threshold, the door being open, for it was summer. I can see that figure now—pallidly neat, pitiably respectable, incurably forlorn! It was Bartleby.

After a few words touching his qualifications, I engaged him, glad to have among my corps of copyists a man of so singularly sedate an aspect, which I thought might operate beneficially upon the flighty temper of Turkey, and the fiery one of Nippers.

I should have stated before that ground glass folding-doors divided my premises into two parts, one of which was occupied by my scriveners, the other by myself. According to my humor I threw open these doors, or closed them. I resolved to assign Bartleby a corner by the folding-doors, but on my side of them, so as to have this quiet man within easy call, in case any trifling thing was to be done. I placed his desk close up to a small sidewindow in that part of the room, a window which originally had afforded a lateral view of certain grimy back-yards and bricks, but which, owing to subsequent erections, commanded at present no view at all, though it gave some light. Within three feet of the panes was a wall, and the light came down from far above, between two lofty buildings, as from a very small opening in a dome. Still further to a satisfactory arrangement, I procured a high green folding screen, which might entirely isolate Bartleby from my sight, though not remove him from my voice. And thus, in a manner, privacy and society were conjoined.

At first Bartleby did an extraordinary quantity of writing. As if long famishing for something to copy, he seemed to gorge himself on my documents. There was no pause for digestion. He ran a day and night line, copying by sun-light and by candle-light. I should have been quite delighted with his application, had he been cheerfully industrious. But he wrote on silently, palely, mechanically.

It is, of course, an indispensable part of a scrivener's business to verify the accuracy of his copy, word by word. Where there are two or more scriveners in an office, they assist each other in this examination, one reading from the copy, the other holding the original. It is a very dull, wearisome, and lethargic affair. I can readily imagine that to some sanguine temperaments it would be altogether intolerable. For example, I cannot credit that the mettlesome poet Byron would have contentedly sat down with Bartleby to examine a law document of, say five hundred pages, closely written in a crimpy hand.

20   Now and then, in the haste of business, it had been my habit to assist in comparing some brief document myself, calling Turkey or Nippers for this purpose. One object I had in placing Bartleby so handy to me behind the screen, was to avail myself of his services on such trivial occasions. It was on the third day, I think, of his being with me, and before any necessity had arisen for having his own writing examined, that, being much hurried to complete a small affair I had in hand, I abruptly called to Bartleby. In my haste and natural expectancy of instant compliance, I sat with my head bent over the original on my desk, and my right hand sideways, and somewhat nervously extended with the copy, so that immediately upon emerging from his retreat, Bartleby might snatch it and proceed to business without the least delay.

In this very attitude did I sit when I called to him, rapidly stating what it was I wanted him to do—namely, to examine a small paper with me. Imagine my surprise, nay, my consternation, when without moving from his privacy, Bartleby in a singularly mild, firm voice, replied, "I would prefer not to."

I sat awhile in perfect silence, rallying my stunned faculties. Immediately it occurred to me that my ears had deceived me, or Bartleby had entirely misunderstood my meaning. I repeated my request in the clearest tone I could assume. But in quite as clear a one came the previous reply, "I would prefer not to."

"Prefer not to," echoed I, rising in high excitement, and crossing the room with a stride, "What do you mean? Are you moon-struck? I want you to help me compare this sheet here—take it," and I thrust it towards him.

"I would prefer not to," said he.

I looked at him steadfastly. His face was leanly composed; his gray eye dimly calm. Not a wrinkle of agitation rippled him. Had there been the least uneasiness, anger, impatience or impertinence in his manner; in other words, had there been any thing ordinarily human about him, doubtless I should have violently dismissed him from the premises. But as it was, I should have as soon thought of turning my pale plaster-of-paris bust of Cicero out of doors. I stood gazing at him awhile, as he went on with his own writing, and then reseated myself at my desk. This is very strange, thought I. What had one best do? But my business hurried me. I concluded to forget the matter for the present, reserving it for my future leisure. So calling Nippers from the other room, the paper was speedily examined.

A few days after this, Bartleby concluded four lengthy documents, being quadruplicates of a week's testimony taken before me in my High Court of Chancery. It became necessary to examine them. It was an important suit, and great accuracy was imperative. Having all things arranged I called Turkey, Nippers and Ginger Nut from the next room, meaning to place the four copies in the hands of my four clerks, while I should read from the original. Accordingly Turkey, Nippers and Ginger Nut had taken their seats in a row, each with his document in hand, when I called to Bartleby to join this interesting group.

"Bartleby! quick, I am waiting."

I heard a slow scrape of his chair legs on the unscraped floor, and soon he appeared standing at the entrance of his hermitage.

"What is wanted?" said he mildly.

30 "The copies, the copies," said I hurriedly. "We are going to examine them. There"—and I held towards him the fourth quadruplicate.

"I would prefer not to," he said, and gently disappeared behind the screen.

For a few moments I was turned into a pillar of salt, standing at the head of my seated column of clerks. Recovering myself, I advanced towards the screen, and demanded the reason for such extraordinary conduct.

"*Why* do you refuse?"

"I would prefer not to."

35 With any other man I should have flown outright into a dreadful passion, scorned all further words, and thrust him ignominiously from my presence. But there was something about Bartleby that not only

strangely disarmed me, but in a wonderful manner touched and dis-concerted me. I began to reason with him.

"These are your own copies we are about to examine. It is labor sav-ing to you, because one examination will answer for your four papers. It is common usage. Every copyist is bound to help examine his copy. Is it not so? Will you not speak? Answer!"

"I prefer not to," he replied in a flute-like tone. It seemed to me that while I had been addressing him, he carefully revolved every statement that I made; fully comprehended the meaning; could not gainsay the irresistible conclusion; but, at the same time, some paramount consid-eration prevailed with him to reply as he did.

"You are decided, then, not to comply with my request—a request made according to common usage and common sense?"

He briefly gave me to understand that on that point my judgment was sound. Yes: his decision was irreversible.

40   It is not seldom the case that when a man is browbeaten in some unprecedented and violently unreasonable way, he begins to stagger in his own plainest faith. He begins, as it were, vaguely to surmise that, wonderful as it may be, all the justice and all the reason is on the other side. Accordingly, if any disinterested persons are present, he turns to them for some reinforcement for his own faltering mind.

"Turkey," said I, "what do you think of this? Am I not right?"

"With submission, sir," said Turkey, with his blandest tone, "I think that you are."

"Nippers," said I, "what do you think of it?"

"I think I should kick him out of the office."

(The reader of nice perceptions will here perceive that, it being morning, Turkey's answer is couched in polite and tranquil terms, but Nippers replies in ill-tempered ones. Or, to repeat a previous sentence, Nippers's ugly mood was on duty, and Turkey's off.)

"Ginger Nut," said I, willing to enlist the smallest suffrage in my behalf, "what do you think of it?"

"I think, sir, he's a little *luny*," replied Ginger Nut, with a grin.

"You hear what they say," said I, turning towards the screen, "come forth and do your duty."

But he vouchsafed no reply. I pondered a moment in sore perplexity. But once more business hurried me. I determined again to postpone the consideration of this dilemma to my future leisure. With a little trouble we made out to examine the papers without Bartleby, though at every page or two, Turkey deferentially dropped his opinion that this proceeding was quite out of the common; while Nippers, twitching in his chair with a dyspeptic nervousness, ground out between his set teeth occasional hissing maledictions against the stubborn oaf behind the screen. And for his (Nippers's) part, this was the first and the last time he would do another man's business without pay.

50   Meanwhile Bartleby sat in his hermitage, oblivious to every thing but his own peculiar business there.

Some days passed, the scrivener being employed upon another lengthy work. His late remarkable conduct led me to regard his way narrowly. I observed that he never went to dinner; indeed that he never went any where. As yet I had never of my personal knowledge known him to be outside of my office. He was a perpetual sentry in the corner. At about eleven o'clock though, in the morning, I noticed that Ginger Nut would advance toward the opening in Bartleby's screen, as if silently beckoned thither by a gesture invisible to me where I sat. That boy would then leave the office jingling a few pence, and reappear with a handful of ginger-nuts which he delivered in the hermitage, receiving two of the cakes for his trouble.

He lives, then, on ginger-nuts, thought I; never eats a dinner, properly speaking; he must be a vegetarian then, but no; he never eats even vegetables, he eats nothing but ginger-nuts. My mind then ran on in reveries concerning the probable effects upon the human constitution of living entirely on ginger-nuts. Ginger-nuts are so called because they contain ginger as one of their peculiar constituents, and the final flavoring one. Now what was ginger? A hot, spicy thing. Was Bartleby hot and spicy? Not at all. Ginger, then, had no effect upon Bartleby. Probably he preferred it should have none.

Nothing so aggravates an earnest person as a passive resistance. If the individual so resisted be of a not inhumane temper, and the resisting one perfectly harmless in his passivity; then, in the better moods of the former, he will endeavor charitably to construe to his imagination what proves impossible to be solved by his judgment. Even so, for the most part, I regarded Bartleby and his ways. Poor fellow! thought I, he means no mischief; it is plain he intends no insolence; his aspect sufficiently evinces that his eccentricities are involuntary. He is useful to me. I can get along with him. If I turn him away, the chances are he will fall in with some less indulgent employer, and then he will be rudely treated, and perhaps driven forth miserably to starve. Yes. Here I can cheaply purchase a delicious self-approval. To befriend Bartleby; to humor him in his strange wilfulness, will cost me little or nothing, while I lay up in my soul what will eventually prove a sweet morsel for my conscience. But this mood was not invariable with me. The passiveness of Bartleby sometimes irritated me. I felt strangely goaded on to encounter him in new opposition, to elicit some angry spark from him answerable to my own. But indeed I might as well have essayed to strike fire with my knuckles against a bit of Windsor soap. But one afternoon the evil impulse in me mastered me, and the following little scene ensued:

"Bartleby," said I, "when those papers are all copied, I will compare them with you."

55 "I would prefer not to."

"How? Surely you do not mean to persist in that mulish vagary?"

No answer.

I threw open the folding-doors near by, and turning upon Turkey and Nippers, exclaimed in an excited manner—

"He says, a second time, he won't examine his papers. What do you think of it, Turkey?"

60 It was afternoon, be it remembered. Turkey sat glowing like a brass boiler, his bald head steaming, his hands reeling among his blotted papers.

"Think of it?" roared Turkey; "I think I'll just step behind his screen, and black his eyes for him!"

So saying, Turkey rose to his feet and threw his arms into a pugilistic position. He was hurrying away to make good his promise, when I detained him, alarmed at the effect of incautiously rousing Turkey's combativeness after dinner.

"Sit down, Turkey," said I, "and hear what Nippers has to say. What to do you think of it, Nippers? Would I not be justified in immediately dimissing Bartleby?"

"Excuse me, that is for you to decide, sir. I think his conduct quite unusual, and indeed unjust, as regards Turkey and myself. But it may only be a passing whim."

65 "Ah," exclaimed I, "you have strangely changed your mind then—you speak very gently of him now."

"All beer," cried Turkey; "gentleness is effects of beer—Nippers and I dined together to-day. You see how gentle *I* am, sir. Shall I go and black his eyes?"

"You refer to Bartleby, I suppose. No, not to-day, Turkey," I replied; "pray, put up your fists."

I closed the doors, and again advanced towards Bartleby. I felt additional incentives tempting me to my fate. I burned to be rebelled against again. I remembered that Bartleby never left the office.

"Bartleby," said I, "Ginger Nut is away; just step round to the Post Office, won't you? (it was but a three minutes walk,) and see if there is any thing for me."

70 "I would prefer not to."

"You *will* not?"

"I *prefer* not."

I staggered to my desk, and sat there in a deep study. My blind inveteracy returned. Was there any other thing in which I could procure myself to be ignominiously repulsed by this lean, penniless wight?— my hired clerk? What added thing is there, perfectly reasonable, that he will be sure to refuse to do?

"Bartleby!"

75 No answer.

"Bartleby," in a louder tone.

No answer.

"Bartleby," I roared.

Like a very ghost, agreeably to the laws of magical invocation, at the third summons, he appeared at the entrance of his hermitage.

80 "Go to the next room, and tell Nippers to come to me."

"I prefer not to," he respectfully and slowly said, and mildly disappeared.

"Very good, Bartleby," said I, in a quiet sort of serenely severe self-possessed tone, intimating the unalterable purpose of some terrible retribution very close at hand. At the moment I half intended something of the kind. But upon the whole, as it was drawing towards my dinner-hour, I thought it best to put on my hat and walk home for the day, suffering much from perplexity and distress of mind.

Shall I acknowledge it? The conclusion of this whole business was, that it soon became a fixed fact of my chambers, that a pale young scrivener, by the name of Bartleby, had a desk there; that he copied for me at the usual rate of four cents a folio (one hundred words); but he was permanently exempt from examining the work done by him, that duty being transferred to Turkey and Nippers, one of compliment doubtless to their superior acuteness; moreover, said Bartleby was never on any account to be dispatched on the most trivial errand of any sort; and that even if entreated to take upon him such a matter, it was generally understood that he would prefer not to—in other words, that he would refuse point-blank.

As days passed on, I became considerably reconciled to Bartleby. His steadiness, his freedom from all dissipation, his incessant industry (except when he chose to throw himself into a standing revery behind his screen), his great stillness, his unalterableness of demeanor under all circumstances, made him a valuable acquisition. One prime thing was this,—*he was always there*;—first in the morning, continually through the day, and the last at night. I had a singular confidence in his honesty. I felt my most precious papers perfectly safe in his hands. Sometimes to be sure I could not, for the very soul of me, avoid falling into sudden spasmodic passions with him. For it was exceeding difficult to bear in mind all the time those strange peculiarities, privileges, and unheard of exemptions, forming the tacit stipulations on Bartleby's part under which he remained in my office. Now and then, in the eagerness of dispatching pressing business, I would inadvertently summon Bartleby, in a short, rapid tone, to put his finger, say, on the incipient tie of a bit of red tape with which I was about compressing some papers. Of course, from behind the screen the usual answer, "I prefer not to," was sure to come; and then, how could a human creature with the common infirmities of our nature, refrain from bitterly exclaiming upon such perverseness—such unreasonableness. However, every added repulse of this sort which I received only tended to lessen the probability of my repeating the inadvertence.

85   Here it must be said, that according to the custom of most legal gentlemen occupying chambers in densely-populated law buildings, there were several keys to my door. One was kept by a woman residing in the attic, which person weekly scrubbed and daily swept and dusted my apartments. Another was kept by Turkey for convenience sake. The third I sometimes carried in my own pocket. The fourth I knew not who had.

Now one Sunday morning I happened to go to Trinity Church; to hear a celebrated preacher, and finding myself rather early on the ground, I thought I would walk round to my chambers for a while. Luckily I had my key with me; but upon applying it to the lock, I found it resisted by something inserted from the inside. Quite surprised, I called out; when to my consternation a key was turned from within;

and thrusting his lean visage at me, and holding the door ajar, the apparition of Bartleby appeared, in his shirt sleeves, and otherwise in a strangely tattered dishabille, saying quietly that he was sorry, but he was deeply engaged just then, and—preferred not admitting me at present. In a brief word or two, he moreover added, that perhaps I had better walk round the block two or three times, and by that time he would probably have concluded his affairs.

Now, the utterly unsurmised appearance of Bartleby, tenanting my law-chambers of a Sunday morning, with his cadaverously gentlemanly *nonchalance*, yet withal firm and self-possessed, had such a strange effect upon me, that incontinently I slunk away from my own door, and did as desired. But not without sundry twinges of impotent rebellion against the mild effrontery of this unaccountable scrivener. Indeed, it was his wonderful mildness chiefly, which not only disarmed me, but unmanned me, as it were. For I consider that one, for the time, is a sort of unmanned when he tranquilly permits his hired clerk to dictate to him, and order him away from his own premises. Furthermore, I was full of uneasiness as to what Bartleby could possibly be doing in my office in his shirt sleeves, and in an otherwise dismantled condition of a Sunday morning. Was any thing amiss going on? Nay, that was out of the question. It was not to be thought of for a moment that Bartleby was an immoral person. But what could he be doing there?—copying? Nay again, whatever might be his eccentricities, Bartleby was an eminently decorous person. He would be the last man to sit down to his desk in any state approaching to nudity. Besides, it was Sunday; and there was something about Bartleby that forbade the supposition that he would by any secular occupation violate the proprieties of the day.

Nevertheless, my mind was not pacified; and full of a restless curiosity, at last I returned to the door. Without hindrance I inserted my key, opened it, and entered. Bartleby was not to be seen. I looked round anxiously, peeped behind his screen; but it was very plain that he was gone. Upon more closely examining the place, I surmised that for an indefinite period Bartleby must have ate, dressed, and slept in my office, and that too without plate, mirror, or bed. The cushioned seat of a rickety old sofa in one corner bore the faint impress of a lean, reclining form. Rolled away under his desk, I found a blanket; under the empty grate, a blacking box and brush; on a chair, a tin basin, with soap and a ragged towel; in a newspaper a few crumbs of ginger-nuts and a morsel of cheese. Yes, thought I, it is evident enough that Bartleby has been making his home here, keeping bachelor's hall all by himself. Immediately then the thought came sweeping across me, What miserable friendlessness and loneliness are here revealed! His poverty is great; but his solitude, how horrible! Think of it. Of a Sunday, Wall-street is deserted as Petra; and every night of every day it is an emptiness. This building too, which of week-days hums with industry and life, at night-fall echoes with sheer vacancy, and all through Sunday is forlorn. And here Bartleby makes his home; sole spectator of a solitude which he has seen all populous—a sort of innocent and transformed Marius brooding among the ruins of Carthage!

For the first time in my life a feeling of overpowering stinging melancholy seized me. Before, I had never experienced aught but a not-unpleasing sadness. The bond of a common humanity now drew me irresistibly to gloom. A fraternal melancholy! For both I and Bartleby were sons of Adam. I remembered the bright silks and sparkling faces I had seen that day in gala trim, swan-like sailing down the Mississippi of Broadway; and I contrasted them with the pallid copyist, and thought to myself, Ah, happiness courts the light, so we deem the world is gay; but misery hides aloof, so we deem that misery there is none. These sad fancyings—chimeras, doubtless, of a sick and silly brain—led on to other and more special thoughts, concerning the eccentricities of Bartleby. Presentiments of strange discoveries hovered round me. The scrivener's pale form appeared to me laid out, among uncaring strangers, in its shivering winding sheet.

90 Suddenly I was attracted by Bartleby's closed desk, the key in open sight left in the lock.

I mean no mischief, seek the gratification of no heartless curiosity, thought I; besides, the desk is mine, and its contents too, so I will make bold to look within. Every thing was methodically arranged, the papers smoothly placed. The pigeon holes were deep, and removing the files of documents, I groped into their recesses. Presently I felt something there, and dragged it out. It was an old bandanna handkerchief, heavy and knotted. I opened it, and saw it was a savings' bank.

I now recalled all the quiet mysteries which I had noted in the man. I remembered that he never spoke but to answer; that though at intervals he had considerable time to himself, yet I had never seen him reading—no, not even a newspaper; that for long periods he would stand looking out, at his pale window behind the screen, upon the dead brick wall; I was quite sure he never visited any refectory or eating house; while his pale face clearly indicated that he never drank beer like Turkey, or tea and coffee even, like other men; that he never went any where in particular that I could learn; never went out for a walk, unless indeed that was the case at present; that he had declined telling who he was, or whence he came, or whether he had any relatives in the world; that though so thin and pale, he never complained of ill health. And more than all, I remembered a certain unconscious air of pallid— how shall I call it?—of pallid haughtiness, say, or rather an austere reserve about him, which had positively awed me into my tame compliance with his eccentricities, when I had feared to ask him to do the slightest incidental thing for me, even though I might know, from his long-continued motionlessness, that behind his screen he must be standing in one of those dead-wall reveries of his.

Revolving all these things, and coupling them with the recently discovered fact that he made my office his constant abiding place and home, and not forgetful of his morbid moodiness; revolving all these things, a prudential feeling began to steal over me. My first emotions had been those of pure melancholy and sincerest pity; but just in proportion as the forlornness of Bartleby grew and grew to my imagination, did that same melancholy merge into fear, that pity into repulsion. So true it is, and so terrible too, that up to a certain point the thought or sight of misery enlists our best affections; but, in certain special cases, beyond that point it does not. They err who would assert that invariably this is owing to the inherent selfishness of the human heart. It rather proceeds from a certain hopelessness of remedying excessive and organic ill. To a sensitive being, pity is not seldom pain. And when at last it is perceived that such pity cannot lead to effectual succor, common sense bids the soul be rid of it. What I saw that morning persuaded me that the scrivener was the victim of innate and incurable disorder. I might give alms to his body; but his body did not pain him; it was his soul that suffered, and his soul I could not reach.

I did not accomplish the purpose of going to Trinity Church that morning. Somehow, the things I had seen disqualified me for the time from church-going. I walked homeward, thinking what I would do with Bartleby. Finally, I resolved upon this; I would put certain calm questions to him the next morning, touching his history, &c., and if he declined to answer them openly and unreservedly (and I supposed he would prefer not), then to give him a twenty dollar bill over and above whatever I might owe him, and tell him his services were no longer required; but that if in any other way I could assist him, I would be happy to do so, especially if he desired to return to his native place, wherever that might be, I would willingly help to defray the expenses. Moreover, if after reaching home, he found himself at any time in want of aid, a letter from him would be sure of a reply.

95   The next morning came.

"Bartleby," said I, gently calling to him behind his screen. No reply.

"Bartleby," said I, in a still gentler tone, "come here; I am not going to ask you to do any thing you would prefer not to do I simply wish to speak to you."

Upon this he noiselessly slid into view.

"Will you tell me, Bartleby, where you were born?"

100   "I would prefer not to."

"Will you tell me *any thing* about yourself?"

"I would prefer not to."

"But what reasonable objection can you have to speak to me? I feel friendly towards you."

He did not look at me while I spoke, but kept his glance fixed upon my bust of Cicero, which as I then sat, was directly behind me, some six inches above my head.

105   "What is your answer, Bartleby?" said I, after waiting a considerable time for a reply, during which his countenance remained immovable, only there was the faintest conceivable tremor of the white attenuated mouth.

"At present I prefer to give no answer," he said, and retired into his hermitage.

It was rather weak in me I confess, but his manner on this occasion nettled me. Not only did there seem to lurk in it a certain disdain, but his perverseness seemed ungrateful, considering the undeniable good usage and indulgence he had received from me.

Again I sat ruminating what I should do. Mortified as I was at his behavior, and resolved as I had been to dismiss him when I entered my office, nevertheless I strangely felt something superstitious knocking at my heart, and forbidding me to carry out my purpose, and denouncing me for a villain if I dared to breathe one bitter word against this forlornest of mankind. At last, familiarly drawing my chair behind his screen, I sat down and said: "Bartleby, never mind then about revealing your history; but let me entreat you, as a friend, to comply as far as may be with the usages of this office. Say now you will help to examine papers tomorrow or next day: in short, say now that in a day or two you will begin to be a little reasonable:—say so, Bartleby."

"At present I would prefer not to be a little reasonable," was his mildly cadaverous reply.

110 Just then the folding-doors opened, and Nippers approached. He seemed suffering from an unusually bad night's rest, induced by severer indigestion than common. He overheard those final words of Bartleby.

"*Prefer not*, eh?" gritted Nippers—"I'd *prefer* him, if I were you, sir," addressing me—"I'd *prefer* him; I'd give him preferences, the stubborn mule! What is it, sir, pray, that he *prefers* not to do now?"

Bartleby moved not a limb.

"Mr. Nippers," said I, "I'd prefer that you would withdraw for the present."

Somehow, of late I had got into the way of involuntary using this word "prefer" upon all sorts of not exactly suitable occasions. And I trembled to think that my contact with the scrivener had already and seriously affected me in a mental way. And what further and deeper aberration might it not yet produce? This apprehension had not been without efficacy in determining me to summary means.

115 As Nippers, looking very sour and sulky, was departing, Turkey blandly and deferentially approached.

"With submission, sir," said he, "yesterday I was thinking about Bartleby here, and I think that if he would but prefer to take a quart of good ale every day, it would do much towards mending him, and enabling him to assist in examining his papers."

"So you have got the word too," said I, slightly excited. "With submission, what word, sir," asked Turkey, respectfully crowding himself into the contracted space behind the screen, and by so doing, making me jostle the scrivener. "What word, sir?"

"I would prefer to be left alone here," said Bartleby, as if offended at being mobbed in his privacy.

"*That's* the word, Turkey," said I—"*that's* it."

120 "Oh, *prefer*? oh yes—queer word. I never use it myself. But, sir, as I was saying, if he would but prefer—"

"Turkey," interrupted I, "you will please withdraw." "Oh certainly, sir, if you prefer that I should."

As he opened the folding-door to retire, Nippers at his desk caught a glimpse of me, and asked whether I would prefer to have a certain paper copied on blue paper or white. He did not in the least roguishly accent the word prefer. It was plain that it involuntarily rolled from his tongue. I thought to myself, surely I must get rid of a demented man, who already has in some degree turned the tongues, if not the heads of myself and clerks. But I thought it prudent not to break the dismission at once.

The next day I noticed that Bartleby did nothing but stand at his window in his dead-wall revery. Upon asking him why he did not write, he said that he had decided upon doing no more writing.

"Why, how now? what next?" exclaimed I, "do no more writing?"

125   "No more."

"And what is the reason?"

"Do you not see the reason for yourself," he indifferently replied.

I looked steadfastly at him, and perceived that his eyes looked dull and glazed. Instantly it occurred to me, that his unexampled diligence in copying by his dim window for the first few weeks of his stay with me might have temporarily impaired his vision.

I was touched. I said something in condolence with him. I hinted that of course he did wisely in abstaining from writing for a while; and urged him to embrace that opportunity of taking wholesome exercise in the open air. This, however, he did not do. A few days after this, my other clerks being absent, and being in a great hurry to dispatch certain letters by the mail, I thought that, having nothing else earthly to do, Bartleby would surely be less inflexible than usual, and carry these letters to the post-office. But he blankly declined. So, much to my inconvenience, I went myself.

130   Still added days went by. Whether Bartleby's eyes improved or not, I could not say. To all appearance, I thought they did. But when I asked him if they did, he vouchsafed no answer. At all events, he would do no copying. At last, in reply to my urgings, he informed me that he had permanently given up copying.

"What!" exclaimed I; "suppose your eyes should get entirely well— better than ever before—would you not copy then?"

"I have given up copying," he answered, and slid aside.

He remained as ever, a fixture in my chamber. Nay—if that were possible—he became still more of a fixture than before. What was to be done? He would do nothing in the office: why should he stay there? In plain fact, he had now become a millstone to me, not only useless as a necklace, but afflictive to bear. Yet I was sorry for him.

I speak less than truth when I say that, on his own account, he occasioned me uneasiness. If he would but have named a single relative or friend, I would instantly have written, and urged their taking the poor fellow away to some convenient retreat. But he seemed alone, absolutely alone in the universe. A bit of wreck in the mid Atlantic. At length, necessities connected with my business tyrannized over all other considerations. Decently as I could, I told Bartleby that in six days' time he must unconditionally leave the office. I warned him to take measures, in the interval, for procuring some other abode. I offered to assist him in this endeavor, if he himself would but take the first step towards a removal. "And when you finally quit me, Bartleby," added I, "I shall see that you go not away entirely unprovided. Six days from this hour, remember."

At the expiration of that period, I peeped behind the screen, and lo! Bartleby was there.

135   I buttoned up my coat, balanced myself; advanced slowly towards him, touched his shoulder, and said, "The time has come; you must quit this place; I am sorry for you; here is money; but you must go."

"I would prefer not," he replied, with his back still towards me.

"You *must*."

He remained silent.

Now I had an unbounded confidence in this man's common honesty. He had frequently restored to me six pences and shillings carelessly dropped upon the floor, for I am apt to be very reckless in such shirt-button affairs. The proceeding then which followed will not be deemed extraordinary.

140   "Bartleby," said I, "I owe you twelve dollars on account; here are thirty-two; the odd twenty are yours.—Will you take it?" and I handed the bills towards him.

But he made no motion.

"I will leave them here then," putting them under a weight on the table. Then taking my hat and cane and going to the door I tranquilly turned and added—"After you have removed your things from these offices, Bartleby, you will of course lock the door—since every one is now gone for the day but you—and if you please, slip your key underneath the mat, so that I may have it in the morning. I shall not see you again; so good-bye to you. If hereafter in your new place of abode I can be of any service to you, do not fail to advise me by letter. Good-bye, Bartleby, and fare you well."

But he answered not a word; like the last column of some ruined temple, he remained standing mute and solitary in the middle of the otherwise deserted room.

As I walked home in a pensive mood, my vanity got the better of my pity. I could not but highly plume myself on my masterly management in getting rid of Bartleby. Masterly I call it, and such it must appear to any dispassionate thinker. The beauty of my procedure seemed to consist in its perfect quietness. There was no vulgar bullying, no bravado of any sort, no choleric hectoring, and striding to and fro across the apartment, jerking out vehement commands for Bartleby to bundle himself off with his beggarly traps. Nothing of the kind. Without loudly bidding Bartleby depart—as an inferior genius might have done—I *assumed* the ground that depart he must; and upon the assumption built all I had to say. The more I thought over my procedure, the more I was charmed with it. Nevertheless, next morning, upon awakening, I had my doubts,—I had somehow slept off the fumes of vanity. One of the coolest and wisest hours a man has, is just after he awakes in the morning. My procedure seemed as sagacious as ever,—but only in theory. How it would prove in practice—there was the rub. It was truly a beautiful thought to have assumed Bartleby's departure; but, after all, that assumption was simply my own, and none of Bartleby's. The great point was, not whether I had assumed that he would quit me, but whether he would prefer so to do. He was more a man of preferences than assumptions.

145   After breakfast, I walked down town, arguing the probabilities *pro* and *con.* One moment I thought it would prove a miserable failure, and Bartleby would be found all alive at my office as usual; the next moment it seemed certain that I should see his chair empty. And so I kept veering about. At the corner of Broadway and Canal-street, I saw quite an excited group of people standing in earnest conversation.

"I'll take odds he doesn't," said a voice as I passed.

"Doesn't go?—done!" said I, "put up your money."

I was instinctively putting my hand in my pocket to produce my own, when I remembered that this was an election day. The words I had overheard bore no reference to Bartleby, but to the success or non-success of some candidate for the mayoralty. In my intent frame of mind, I had, as it were, imagined that all Broadway shared in my excitement, and were debating the same question with me. I passed on, very thankful that the uproar of the street screened my momentary absent-mindedness.

As I had intended, I was earlier than usual at my office door. I stood listening for a moment. All was still. He must be gone. I tried the knob. The door was locked. Yes, my procedure had worked to a charm; he indeed must be vanished. Yet a certain melancholy mixed with this: I was almost sorry for my brilliant success. I was fumbling under the door mat for the key, which Bartleby was to have left there for me, when accidentally my knee knocked against a panel, producing a summoning sound, and in response a voice came to me from within— "Not yet; I am occupied."

150   It was Bartleby.

I was thunderstruck. For an instant I stood like the man who, pipe in mouth, was killed one cloudless afternoon long ago in Virginia, by summer lightning; at his own warm open window he was killed, and remained leaning out there upon the dreamy afternoon, till some one touched him, when he fell.

"Not gone!" I murmured at last. But again obeying that wondrous ascendancy which the inscrutable scrivener had over me, and from which ascendency, for all my chafing, I could not completely escape, I slowly went down stairs and out into the street, and while walking round the block, considered what I should next do in this unheard-of perplexity. Turn the man out by an actual thrusting I could not; to drive him away by calling him hard names would not do; calling in the police was an unpleasant idea; and yet, permit him to enjoy his cadaverous triumph over me,—this too I could not think of. What was to be done? or, if nothing could be done, was there any thing further that I could assume in the matter? Yes, as before I had prospectively assumed that Bartleby would depart, so now I might retrospectively assume that departed he was. In the legitimate carrying out of this assumption, I might enter my office in a great hurry, and pretending not to see Bartleby at all, walk straight against him as if he were air. Such a proceeding would in a singular degree have the appearance of a home-thrust. It was hardly possible that Bartleby could withstand such an application of the doctrine of assumptions. But upon second thoughts the success of the plan seemed rather dubious. I resolved to argue the matter over with him again.

"Bartleby," said I, entering the office, with a quietly severe expression, "I am seriously displeased. I am pained, Bartleby. I had thought better of you. I had imagined you of such a gentlemanly organization, that in any delicate dilemma a slight hint would suffice—in short, an assumption. But it appears I am deceived. Why," I added, unaffectedly starting, "you have not even touched that money yet," pointing to it, just where I had left it the evening previous.

He answered nothing.

155 "Will you, or will you not, quit me?" I now demanded in a sudden passion, advancing close to him.

"I would prefer *not* to quit you," he replied, gently emphasizing the *not*.

"What earthly right have you to stay here? Do you pay any rent? Do you pay my taxes? Or is this property yours?"

He answered nothing.

"Are you ready to go on and write now? Are your eyes recovered? Could you copy a small paper for me this morning? or help examine a few lines? or step round to the post-office? In a word, will you do any thing at all, to give a coloring to your refusal to depart the premises?"

160 He silently retired into his hermitage.

I was now in such a state of nervous resentment that I thought it but prudent to check myself at present from further demonstrations. Bartleby and I were alone. I remembered the tragedy of the unfortunate Adams and the still more unfortunate Colt in the solitary office of the latter; and how poor Colt, being dreadfully incensed by Adams, and imprudently permitting himself to get wildly excited, was at unawares hurried into his fatal act—an act which certainly no man could possibly deplore more than the actor himself. Often it had occurred to me in my ponderings upon the subject, that had that altercation taken place in the public street, or at a private residence, it would not have terminated as it did. It was the circumstance of being alone in a solitary office, up stairs, of a building entirely unhallowed by humanizing domestic associations—an uncarpeted office, doubtless, of a dusty, haggard sort of appearance;—this it must have been, which greatly helped to enhance the irritable desperation of the hapless Colt.

But when this old Adam of resentment rose in me and tempted me concerning Bartleby, I grappled him and threw him. How? Why, simply by recalling the divine injunction: "A new commandment give I unto you, that ye love one another." Yes, this it was that saved me. Aside from higher considerations, charity often operates as a vastly wise and prudent principle—a great safeguard to its possessor. Men have committed murder for jealousy's sake, and anger's sake, and hatred's sake, and selfishness' sake, and spiritual pride's sake; but no man that ever I heard of, ever committed a diabolical murder for sweet charity's sake. Mere self-interest, then, if no better motive can be enlisted, should, especially with high-tempered men, prompt all beings to charity and philanthropy. At any rate, upon the occasion in question, I strove to drown my exasperated feelings towards the scrivener by benevolently construing his conduct. Poor fellow, poor fellow! thought I, he don't mean any thing; and besides, he has seen hard times, and ought to be indulged.

I endeavored also immediately to occupy myself, and at the same time to comfort my despondency. I tried to fancy that in the course of the morning, at such time as might prove agreeable to him, Bartleby, of his own free accord, would emerge from his hermitage, and take up some decided line of march in the direction of the door. But no. Half-past twelve o'clock came; Turkey began to glow in the face, overturn his inkstand, and become generally obstreperous; Nippers abated down into quietude and courtesy; Ginger Nut munched his noon apple; and Bartleby remained standing at his window in one of his profoundest deadwall reveries. Will it be credited? Ought I to acknowledge it? That afternoon I left the office without saying one further word to him.

Some days now passed, during which, at leisure intervals I looked a little into "Edwards in the Will," and "Priestley on Necessity." Under the circumstances, those books induced a salutary feeling. Gradually I slid into the persuasion that these troubles of mine touching the scrivener, had been all predestinated from eternity, and Bartleby was billeted upon me for some mysterious purpose of an all-wise Providence, which it was not for a mere mortal like me to fathom. Yes, Bartleby, stay there behind your screen, thought I; I shall persecute you no more; you are harmless and noiseless as any of these old chairs; in short, I never feel so private as when I know you are here. At least I see it, I feel it; I penetrate to the predestinated purpose of my life. I am content. Others may have loftier parts to enact; but my mission in this world, Bartleby, is to furnish you with office-room for such period as you may see fit to remain.

165   I believe that this wise and blessed frame of mind would have continued with me, had it not been for the unsolicited and uncharitable remarks obtruded upon me by my professional friends who visited the rooms. But thus it often is, that the constant friction of illiberal minds wears out at last the best resolves of the more generous. Though to be

sure, when I reflected upon it, it was not strange that people entering my office should be struck by the peculiar aspect of the unaccountable Bartleby, and so be tempted to throw out some sinister observations concerning him. Sometimes an attorney having business with me, and calling at my office, and finding no one but the scrivener there, would undertake to obtain some sort of precise information from him touching my whereabouts; but without heeding his idle talk, Bartleby would remain standing immovable in the middle of the room. So after contemplating him in that position for a time, the attorney would depart, no wiser than he came.

Also, when a Reference was going on, and the room full of lawyers and witnesses and business was driving fast; some deeply occupied legal gentleman present, seeing Bartleby wholly unemployed, would request him to run round to his (the legal gentleman's) office and fetch some papers for him. Thereupon, Bartleby would tranquilly decline, and remain idle as before. Then the lawyer would give a great stare, and turn to me. And what could I say? At last I was made aware that all through the circle of my professional acquaintance, a whisper of wonder was running round, having reference to the strange creature I kept at my office. This worried me very much. And as the idea came upon me of his possibly turning out a long-lived man, and keep occupying my chambers, and denying my authority; and perplexing my visitors; and scandalizing my professional reputation; and casting a general gloom over the premises; keeping soul and body together to the last upon his savings (for doubtless he spent but half a dime a day), and in the end perhaps outlive me, and claim possession of my office by right of his perpetual occupancy: as all these dark anticipations crowded upon me more and more, and my friends continually intruded their relentless remarks upon the apparition in my room; a great change was wrought in me. I resolved to gather all my faculties together, and for ever rid me of this intolerable incubus.

Ere revolving any complicated project, however, adapted to this end, I first simply suggested to Bartleby the propriety of his permanent departure. In a calm and serious tone, I commended the idea to his careful and mature consideration. But having taken three days to meditate upon it, he apprised me that his original determination remained the same; in short, that he still preferred to abide with me.

What shall I do? I now said to myself, buttoning up my coat to the last button. What shall I do? what ought I to do? what does conscience say I *should* do with this man, or rather ghost. Rid myself of him, I must; go, he shall. But how? You will not thrust him, the poor, pale, passive mortal,—you will not thrust such a helpless creature out of your door? you will not dishonor yourself by such cruelty? No, I will not, I cannot do that. Rather would I let him live and die here, and then mason up his remains in the wall. What then will you do? For all your coaxing, he will not budge. Bribes he leaves under your own paper-weight on your table; in short, it is quite plain that he prefers to cling to you.

Then something severe, something unusual must be done. What! surely you will not have him collared by a constable, and commit his innocent pallor to the common jail? And upon what ground could you procure such a thing to be done?—a vagrant, is he? What! he a vagrant, a wanderer, who refuses to budge? It is because he will *not* be a vagrant, then, that you seek to count him *as* a vagrant. That is too absurd. No visible means of support: there I have him. Wrong again: for indubitably he *does* support himself, and that is the only unanswerable proof that any man can show of his possessing the means so to do. No more then. Since he will not quit me, I must quit him. I will change my offices; I will move elsewhere; and give him fair notice, that if I find him on my new premises I will then proceed against him as a common trespasser.

170   Acting accordingly, next day I thus addressed him: "I find these chambers too far from the City Hall; the air is unwholesome. In a word, I propose to remove my offices next week, and shall no longer require your services. I tell you this now, in order that you may seek another place."

He made no reply, and nothing more was said.

On the appointed day I engaged carts and men, proceeded to my chambers, and having but little furniture, every thing was removed in a few hours. Throughout, the scrivener remained standing behind the screen, which I directed to be removed the last thing. It was withdrawn; and being folded up like a huge folio, left him the motionless occupant of a naked room. I stood in the entry watching him a moment, while something from within me upbraided me.

I re-entered, with my hand in my pocket—and—and my heart in my mouth.

"Good-bye, Bartleby; I am going—good-bye, and God some way bless you; and take that," slipping something in his hand. But it dropped upon the floor, and then,—strange to say—I tore myself from him whom I had so longed to be rid of.

175   Established in my new quarters, for a day or two I kept the door locked, and started at every footfall in the passages. When I returned to my rooms after any little absence, I would pause at the threshold for an instant, and attentively listen, ere applying my key. But these fears were needless. Bartleby never came nigh me.

    I thought all was going well, when a perturbed looking stranger visited me, inquiring whether I was the person who had recently occupied rooms at No.—Wall-street.

    Full of forebodings, I replied that I was.

    "Then sir," said the stranger, who proved a lawyer, "you are responsible for the man you left there. He refuses to do any copying; he refuses to do any thing; he says he prefers not to; and he refuses to quit the premises."

    "I am very sorry, sir," said I, with assumed tranquillity, but an inward tremor, "but, really, the man you allude to is nothing to me—he is no relation or apprentice of mine, that you should hold me responsible for him."

180   "In mercy's name, who is he?"

    "I certainly cannot inform you. I know nothing about him. Formerly I employed him as a copyist; but he has done nothing for me now for some time past."

    "I shall settle him then,—good morning, sir."

    Several days passed, and I heard nothing more; and though I often felt a charitable prompting to call at the place and see poor Bartleby, yet a certain squeamishness of I know not what withheld me.

    All is over with him, by this time, thought I at last, when through another week no further intelligence reached me.

185   But coming to my room the day after, I found several persons waiting at my door in a high state of nervous excitement.

    "That's the man—here he comes," cried the foremost one, whom I recognized as the lawyer who had previously called upon me alone.

    "You must take him away, sir, at once," cried a portly person among them, advancing upon me, and whom I knew to be the landlord of No.—Wall-street. "These gentlemen, my tenants, cannot stand it any longer; Mr. B—" pointing to the lawyer, "has turned him out of his room, and he now persists in haunting the building generally, sitting upon the banisters of the stairs by day, and sleeping in the entry by night. Every body is concerned; clients are leaving the offices; some fears are entertained of a mob; something you must do, and that without delay."

Aghast at this torrent, I fell back before it, and would fain have locked myself in my new quarters. In vain I persisted that Bartleby was nothing to me—no more than to any one else. In vain:—I was the last person known to have any thing to do with him, and they held me to the terrible account. Fearful then of being exposed in the papers (as one person present obscurely threatened) I considered the matter, and at length said, that if the lawyer would give me a confidential interview with the scrivener, in his (the lawyer's) own room, I would that afternoon strive my best to rid them of the nuisance they complained of.

Going up stairs to my old haunt, there was Bartleby silently sitting upon the banister at the landing.

190   "What are you doing here, Bartleby?" said I.

"Sitting upon the banister," he mildly replied.

I motioned him into the lawyer's room, who then left us.

"Bartleby," said I, "are you aware that you are the cause of great tribulation to me, by persisting in occupying the entry after being dismissed from the office?"

No answer.

195   "Now one of two things must take place. Either you must do something or something must be done to you. Now what sort of business would you like to engage in? Would you like to re-engage in copying for some one?"

"No; I would prefer not to make any change."

"Would you like a clerkship in a dry-goods store?"

"There is too much confinement about that. No, I would not like a clerkship; but I am not particular."

"Too much confinement," I cried, "why you keep yourself confined all the time!"

200   "I would prefer not to take a clerkship," he rejoined, as if to settle that little item at once.

"How would a bar-tender's business suit you? There is no trying of the eyesight in that."

"I would not like it at all; though, as I said before, I am not particular."

His unwonted wordiness inspirited me. I returned to the charge.

"Well then, would you like to travel through the country collecting bills for the merchants? That would improve your health."

"No, I would prefer to be doing something else."

"How then would going as a companion to Europe, to entertain some young gentleman with your conversation,—how would that suit you?"

"Not at all. It does not strike me that there is any thing definite about that. I like to be stationary. But I am not particular."

"Stationary you shall be then," I cried, now losing all patience, and for the first time in all my exasperating connection with him fairly flying into a passion. "If you do not go away from these premises before night, I shall feel bound—indeed I *am* bound—to—to—to quit the premises myself!" I rather absurdly concluded, knowing not with what possible threat to try to frighten his immobility into compliance. Despairing of all further efforts, I was precipitately leaving him, when a final thought occurred to me—one which had not been wholly unindulged before.

"Bartleby," said I, in the kindest tone I could assume under such exciting circumstances, "will you go home with me now—not to my office, but my dwelling—and remain there till we can conclude upon some convenient arrangement for you at our leisure? Come, let us start now, right away."

"No: at present I would prefer not to make any change at all."

I answered nothing; but effectually dodging every one by the suddenness and rapidity of my flight, rushed from the building, ran up Wall-street towards Broadway, and jumping into the first omnibus was soon removed from pursuit. As soon as tranquillity returned I distinctly perceived that I had now done all that I possibly could, both in respect to the demands of the landlord and his tenants, and with regard to my own desire and sense of duty, to benefit Bartleby, and shield him from rude persecution. I now strove to be entirely care-free and quiescent; and my conscience justified me in the attempt; though indeed it was not so successful as I could have wished. So fearful was I of being again hunted out by the incensed landlord and his exasperated tenants, that, surrendering my business to Nippers, for a few days I drove about the upper part of the town and through the suburbs, in my rockaway; crossed over to Jersey City and Hoboken, and paid fugitive visits to Manhattanville and Astoria. In fact I almost lived in my rockaway for the time.

When again I entered my office, lo, a note from the landlord lay upon the desk. I opened it with trembling hands. It informed me that the writer had sent to the police, and had Bartleby removed to the Tombs as a vagrant. Moreover, since I knew more about him than any one else, he wished me to appear at that place, and make a suitable statement of the facts. These tidings had a conflicting effect upon me. At first I was indignant; but at last almost approved. The landlord's energetic, summary disposition, had led him to adopt a procedure which I do not think I would have decided upon myself; and yet as a last resort, under such peculiar circumstances, it seemed the only plan.

As I afterwards learned, the poor scrivener, when told that he must be conducted to the Tombs, offered not the slightest obstacle, but in his pale unmoving way, silently acquiesced.

Some of the compassionate and curious bystanders joined the party; and headed by one of the constables arm in arm with Bartleby, the silent procession filed its way through all the noise, and heat, and joy of the roaring thoroughfares at noon.

215   The same day I received the note I went to the Tombs, or to speak more properly, the Halls of Justice. Seeking the right officer, I stated the purpose of my call, and was informed that the individual I described was indeed within. I then assured the functionary that Bartleby was a perfectly honest man, and greatly to be compassionated, however unaccountably eccentric. I narrated all I knew, and closed by suggesting the idea of letting him remain in as indulgent confinement as possible till something less harsh might be done—though indeed I hardly knew what. At all events, if nothing else could be decided upon, the alms-house must receive him. I then begged to have an interview.

Being under no disgraceful charge, and quite serene and harmless in all his ways, they had permitted him freely to wander about the prison, and especially in the inclosed grass-platted yards thereof. And so I found him there, standing all alone in the quietest of the yards, his face towards a high wall, while all around, from the narrow slits of the jail windows, I thought I saw peering out upon him the eyes of murderers and thieves.

"Bartleby!"

"I know you," he said, without looking round,—"and I want nothing to say to you."

"It was not I that brought you here, Bartleby," said I, keenly pained at his implied suspicion. "And to you, this should not be so vile a place. Nothing reproachful attaches to you by being here. And see, it is not so sad a place as one might think. Look, there is the sky, and here is the grass."

220 "I know where I am," he replied, but would say nothing more, and so I left him.

As I entered the corridor again, a broad meat-like man, in an apron, accosted me, and jerking his thumb over his shoulder said—"Is that your friend?"

"Yes."

"Does he want to starve? If he does, let him live on the prison fare, that's all."

"Who are you?" asked I, not knowing what to make of such an unofficially speaking person in such a place.

225 "I am the grub-man. Such gentlemen as have friends here, hire me to provide them with something good to eat."

"Is this so?" said I, turning to the turnkey.

He said it was.

"Well then," said I, slipping some silver into the grubman's hands (for so they called him). "I want you to give particular attention to my friend there; let him have the best dinner you can get. And you must be as polite to him as possible."

"Introduce me, will you?" said the grub-man, looking at me with an expression which seemed to say he was all impatience for an opportunity to give a specimen of his breeding.

230 Thinking it would prove of benefit to the scrivener, I acquiesced; and asking the grub-man his name, went up with him to Bartleby.

"Bartleby, this is a friend; you will find him very useful to you."

"Your sarvant, sir, your sarvant," said the grub-man, making a low salutation behind his apron. "Hope you find it pleasant here, sir;—spacious grounds—cool apartments, sir—hope you'll stay with us some time—try to make it agreeable. What will you have for dinner today?"

"I prefer not to dine to-day," said Bartleby, turning away. "It would disagree with me; I am unused to dinners." So saying he slowly moved to the other side of the inclosure, and took up a position fronting the dead-wall.

"How's this?" said the grub-man, addressing me with a stare of astonishment. "He's odd, aint he?"

235 "I think he is a little deranged," said I, sadly.

"Deranged? deranged is it? Well now, upon my word, I thought that friend of yourn was a gentleman forger; they are always pale and genteel-like, them forgers. I can't help pity 'em—can't help it, sir. Did you know Monroe Edwards?" he added touchingly, and paused. Then, laying his hand pityingly on my shoulder, sighed, "he died of consumption at Sing-Sing. So you weren't acquainted with Monroe?"

"No, I was never socially acquainted with any forgers. But I cannot stop longer. Look to my friend yonder. You will not lose by it. I will see you again."

Some few days after this, I again obtained admission to the Tombs, and went through the corridors in quest of Bartleby; but without finding him.

"I saw him coming from his cell not long ago," said a turnkey, "may be he's gone to loiter in the yards."

240 So I went in that direction.

"Are you looking for the silent man?" said another turnkey passing me. "Yonder he lies—sleeping in the yard there. Tis not twenty minutes since I saw him lie down."

The yard was entirely quiet. It was not accessible to the common prisoners. The surrounding walls, of amazing thickness, kept off all sound behind them. The Egyptian character of the masonry weighed upon me with its gloom. But a soft imprisoned turf grew under foot. The heart of the eternal pyramids, it seemed, wherein, by some strange magic, through the clefts, grass-seed, dropped by birds, had sprung.

Strangely huddled at the base of the wall, his knees drawn up, and lying on his side, his head touching the cold stones, I saw the wasted Bartleby. But nothing stirred. I paused; then went close up to him; stooped over, and saw that his dim eyes were open; otherwise he seemed profoundly sleeping. Something prompted me to touch him. I felt his hand, when a tingling shiver ran up my arm and down my spine to my feet.

The round face of the grub-man peered upon me now. "His dinner is ready. Won't he dine to-day, either? Or does he live without dining?"

245 "Lives without dining," said I, and closed the eyes.

"Eh!—He's asleep, aint he?"

"With kings and counsellors," murmured I.

* * * * * * * *

There would seem little need for proceeding further in this history. Imagination will readily supply the meagre recital of poor

Bartleby's interment. But ere parting with the reader, let me say, that if this little narrative has sufficiently interested him, to awaken curiosity as to who Bartleby was, and what manner of life he led prior to the present narrator's making his acquaintance, I can only reply, that in such curiosity I fully share, but am wholly unable to gratify it. Yet here I hardly know whether I should divulge one little item of rumor, which came to my ear a few months after the scrivener's decease. Upon what basis it rested, I could never ascertain; and hence how true it is I cannot now tell. But inasmuch as this vague report has not been without a certain strange suggestive interest to me, however sad, it may prove the same with some others; and so I will briefly mention it. The report was this: that Bartleby had been a subordinate clerk in the Dead Letter Office at Washington, from which he had been suddenly removed by a change in the administration. When I think over this rumor, I cannot adequately express the emotions which seize me. Dead letters! does it not sound like dead men? Conceive a man by nature and misfortune prone to a pallid hopelessness, can any business seem more fitted to heighten it than that of continually handling these dead letters and assorting them for the flames? For by the cartload they are annually burned. Sometimes from out the folded paper the pale clerk takes a ring:—the finger it was meant for, perhaps, moulders in the grave; a bank-note sent in swiftest charity:—he whom it would relieve, nor eats nor hungers any more; pardon for those who died despairing; hope for those who died unhoping; good tidings for those who died stifled by unrelieved calamities. On errands of life, these letters speed to death.

Ah Bartleby! Ah humanity!

SUGGESTIONS FOR WRITING

1. In your opinion does Melville's story satisfy Aristotle's requirements of plot? Write an essay that explains and defends your answer.
2. In your opinion, how would Irving Babbitt classify "Bartleby the Scrivener"? Write an essay that explains and defends your answer.
3. When Bartleby dies, the narrator says Bartleby is "with kings and counselors." Kings presume to derive their powers from natural right and counselors derive theirs from wisdom. Is Bartleby only powerful in death? If you think so, write an essay analyzing the sources of and

reasons for his powerlessness in life. If you think he displays power while alive, write an essay analyzing its sources and rationale.

Bartleby as Alienated Worker 1974

LOUISE BARNETT

Louise Barnett is a professor of English and American studies at Rutgers University where she specializes in nineteenth-century American culture with seven books in that field to her credit. She did her undergraduate work at the University of North Carolina and earned her Ph. D. at Bryn Mawr.

The following essay was first published in the professional journal of criticism Essays in Short Fiction. *In it Barnett applies ideas about class warfare formed by Karl Marx (Chapter 2). The figure of Bartleby is thereby seen not only as a suffering and misunderstood individual but as a representative of a whole class of alienated workers in a newly industrialized America that was in turn representative of the new social and economic dynamics of western civilization.*

A decade after Karl Marx first described the worker's alienation in a capitalistic society, his contemporary, Herman Melville, independently created the perfect exemplum of this condition in his tale of "Bartleby the Scrivener."[1] Although critics have seen Bartleby in a number of interesting and even heroic guises,[2] I believe that he is a figure of another sort: the alienated worker who, realizing that his work is meaningless and without a future, can only protest his humanity by a negative assertion. Defined only by his job, and becoming increasingly dissociated from it, Bartleby sums up the worker's plight. Given a system committed to profits, the only alternative to working under such demeaning conditions is death.

---

[1]Marx's *Economic and Philosophical Manuscripts of 1844* were not published until 1932; the tale of "Bartleby the Scrivener" first appeared in *Putnam's Monthly Magazine* (December, 1853).

[2]Literally dozens of critics have identified Bartleby with Melville or with artists in general. For a thorough review of "Bartleby" criticism through 1965 see Donald M. Fiene, "A Bibliography of Criticism of 'Bartleby the Scrivener,'" *The Melville Annual, 1965, A Symposium: Bartleby the Scrivener,* ed. Howard P. Vincent (Kent, Ohio; Kent University Press, 1966), pp. 140–190. Bartleby as Thoreau is discussed by Egbert S. Oliver, "A Second Look at 'Bartleby,'" *College English,* 6 (1944–1945), 434–439.

According to Marx, the worker experiences alienation for the following reasons: "First, that the work is *external* to the worker, that it is not a part of his nature, that consequently he does not fulfil himself in his work but denies himself, has a feeling of misery, not of well-being, does not develop freely a physical and mental energy, but is physically exhausted and mentally debased. . . . Finally, the alienated character of work for the worker appears in the fact that it is not his work but work for someone else, that in work he does not belong to himself but to another person."[3] All three of the scriveners employed in the lawyer-narrator's office illustrate the aspects of alienation that Marx delineates, but only Bartleby comes to understand the situation and reject it.

That the conditions of labor in the law office are undesirable, likely to produce a feeling of misery rather than well being, is amply confirmed by the narrator. Describing the general surroundings—which, as he rightly notes, have some bearing on the story of Bartleby—he reveals satisfaction in the dehumanized but functional environment. The windows, for example, let in light but present no distracting vistas, only varieties of wall. Placing Bartleby's desk close to one of these viewless openings is part of the narrator's "satisfactory arrangement" for the new employee. Another detail is the use of a folding screen to remove Bartleby from sight while keeping him within easy call, in case any trifling thing was to be done."[4] The narrator is pleased with this way of achieving privacy and society at the same time, but what for him is the best of both these worlds is clearly the worst for Bartleby. Conveniently placed to answer his employer's summons with alacrity, he must inhabit a circumscribed and isolated cell whose lack of outlook mirrors the lack of prospects of his menial occupation.

In his solitary confinement[5] Bartleby works *mechanically*, an adjective well suited to the tedious copying which comprises the chief part of his job. The other duty of a scrivener, verification, is "very dull, wearisome, and lethargic" (p. 24). According to the lawyer such labor

---

[3]*Economic and Philosophical Manuscripts of 1844* in *Karl Marx Selected Writings in Sociology and Social Philosophy,* ed. T. B. Bottomore and Maximilien Rubel, trans. T. B. Bottomore (New York: McGraw-Hill, 1964), pp. 169–70.
[4]Herman Melville, *Piazza Tales,* ed. Egbert S. Oliver (New York, 1948), p. 23. Further references to "Bartleby" in the text are to this edition.
[5]We should keep in mind that by the arrangement which he describes, the narrator isolates Bartleby before the copyist "chooses" isolation.

would be intolerable to anyone of sanguine temperament or mettle—to almost any human being, we might assume.

5   Although the narrator has described himself as an easy-going man in a traditionally hard-driving profession, his description of himself and of office business undercuts this self-characterization. John Jacob Astor is referred to with approval three times in as many sentences; indeed, the narrator confesses that he loves to repeat the name because "it rings like unto bullion" (p. 17).[6] The making of money is the only discernible motive in the lawyer's account of his practice, from his usual traffic in rich men's documents to the remunerative office of Master in Chancery. If a certain indolence is suggested by the lawyer's report of his efforts, it is not characteristic of what he demands from his employees, who are often expected to work at top speed. The account of Bartleby's first refusal to read copy reveals this climate of pressure: "Being much hurried to complete a small affair I had in hand, I abruptly called to Bartleby. In my haste and natural expectancy of instant compliance, I sat with my head bent over the original on my desk, and my right hand sideways, and somewhat nervously extended with the copy, so that, immediately upon emerging from his retreat, Bartleby might snatch it and proceed to business without the least delay" (p. 24). The course of office events is punctuated by words like *speedily, quick, hurriedly, fast.*

In his attitude toward his employees, the narrator is a typically enlightened master[7] who realizes that self-interest will be served by a charitable indulgence. When his scriveners assert their individuality and unconsciously rebel against their dehumanized labors, he tolerates the resulting eccentric behavior because it is still profitable to his business to do so. For all their idiosyncrasies, the other scriveners are an easily managed lot who neither challenge the employer's authority as Bartleby does nor support Bartleby in his disobedience.[8] When Turkey offends the lawyer by sealing a mortgage with a ginger nut, he avoids dismissal by the exaggerated obeisance of "an oriental bow" and a speech beginning with his usual placatory formula: "With submission, sir."

[6]As William Bysshe Stein comments: "John Jacob Astor, the high priest of financial duplicity, incarnates the ruling ethic of callous self-interest." ("Bartleby: the Christian Conscience," *The Melville Annual, 1965,* p. 104).
[7]The lawyer's becoming "Master in Chancery" has led to the advertisement for additional help that Bartleby answers.
[8]As Leo Marx has noted, in acquiring the habit of using the word *prefer,* the other employees assume the form but not the substance of Bartleby's rebellion. ["Melville's Parable of the Walls," *Sewanee Review,* 61 (1953), 620–621.]

As seen through the lawyer's eyes from an amused, paternalistic height, Turkey and Nippers are only caricatures—ludicrously nicknamed bundles of eccentricities. A keener observer might perceive that the monotonous work itself engenders their antics, but the narrator makes only a superficial connection between the conditions of employment and the various foibles of his scriveners. All have hopes of more prestigious and less menial work: Turkey describes himself as the lawyer's right hand man; Nippers is guilty of "an unwarrantable usurpation of strictly professional affairs" (p. 20); and the office boy, Ginger Nut, has been placed in the law office because of his working class father's desire that he rise in life. In the narrator's view these aspirations are only delusions of grandeur. He notices Nippers' endless adjusting of his table, but interprets this as simply a manifestation of indigestion—an affliction vaguely coupled in the narrator's mind with "diseased ambition." The response of Turkey to the gift of his employer's hand-me-down coat is similarly regarded as an example of that scrivener's failure to know his inferior place in the scheme of things: "I thought Turkey would appreciate the favour, and abate his rashness and obstreperousness of afternoons. But no; I verily believe that buttoning himself up in so downy and blanket-like a coat had a pernicious effect upon him—upon the same principle that too much oats are bad for horses. In fact, precisely as a rash, restive horse is said to feel his oats, so Turkey felt his coat. It made him insolent. He was a man whom prosperity harmed" (p. 21).[9] Even Ginger Nut, whose youthful apprenticeship might auger possibility, seems little likely to escape his humble origin and present job. As the lawyer comments: "He had a little desk to himself, but he did not use it much. Upon inspection, the drawer exhibited a great array of the shells of various sorts of nuts" (p. 22).

Physically as well as mentally, the scriveners illustrate Marx's diagnosis of malaise. Turkey's inflamed face witnesses his over-indulgence; Nippers is given to teeth grinding and nervous attacks; Bartleby is pale and thin. Nursing their vain expectations, Turkey and Nippers take what solace they can in cakes and ale and fits of temper. Bartleby chooses not to continue working.

The lawyer's possessive attitude towards the entire world of his law office exemplifies still another Marxian contention: that a factor contributing to the alienated character of work is its belonging not to

[9]Cf. Karl Marx, p. 168: "The proletarian, just like a horse, need only receive so much as enables him to work."

the worker, but to another person. Giving Turkey a coat, the lawyer thinks to control his behavior completely; disobeyed by Bartleby, he feels the shameful anomaly of being stymied by a man who should be his creature: "Was there any other thing in which I could procure myself to be ignominiously repulsed by this lean, penniless wight?—my hired clerk?" (p. 30)[10] Later, he justifies his unlocking of Bartleby's desk, and consequent infringement of his privacy, by his own proprietary right: "The desk is mine, and its contents, too, so I will make bold to look within" (p. 34). Bartleby's family and past, however, are locked within a place that the narrator cannot violate. The scrivener absolutely refuses to respond to any of the narrator's overtures, and thus provokes his employer's exasperation. In the latter's opinion the lowly copyist's life ought to be accessible for his employer's convenience.

10   The narrator's belief in the sanctity of his property is further demonstrated when Bartleby maintains his intransigence. Finding the scrivener still on the premises after receiving an ultimatum to leave, the narrator, in an appropriate simile, compares himself to a man killed by lightning "at his own warm open window"—where presumably he should enjoy security. A similar sense of injured property rights informs the series of questions that he puts to Bartleby: "What earthly right have you to stay here? Do you pay any rent? Do you pay my taxes? Or is this property yours?" (p. 42). Unable to free himself from the exigencies of ownership, the narrator temporarily reconciles himself to Bartleby's continued presence by transforming the scrivener into a piece of his property: "I shall persecute you no more; you are harmless and noiseless as any of these old chairs" (p. 44). Finally, the thought that Bartleby might outlive him and establish the right of occupancy to the office is one of the "dark anticipations" that decide the lawyer to take action against the scrivener.

2

When Bartleby comes to the narrator's office, he appears to be a model employee—quiet, neat, and devoted to copying. Significantly, his first resistance to the lawyer's will is a refusal to perform the most tedious of the scrivener's duties, examination of copy. The astounded employer,

---

[10]The lawyer's chagrin is based on class distinctions as well as on the boss-worker relationship. Bartleby is a "lean, penniless wight," i.e., a nobody, while the lawyer is a man of substance and position.

too hurried to go into the matter fully, eventually decides that the business ethic of buying cheap and selling dear will apply to this peculiar case: "Here I can cheaply purchase a delicious self-approval. To befriend Bartleby; to humour him in his strange wilfulness, will cost me little or nothing, while I lay up in my soul what will eventually prove a sweet morsel for my conscience" (p. 28). Moreover, Bartleby is still useful: while the other malleable scriveners examine copy, he can continue to write and thus earn the narrator's indulgence.

Later, when Bartleby refuses to do any work at all, he exhibits the mental and physical exhaustion characteristic of Marx's alienated worker. "His eyes looked dull and glazed" (p. 38), which the narrator interprets as temporary eyestrain rather than an enduring physical and spiritual anguish. Now the employer's charity is truly tested, for there is no longer any material profit to be made from the recalcitrant scrivener.

Bartleby as neither profit nor loss can be tolerated, but when business begins to suffer, the narrator acts—radically, if not decisively. Rather than confront his inhumanity by taking violent measures, he moves his office, denies responsibility for Bartleby to the new tenant—even when implored "in mercy's name"—and only reassumes the problem under threat of adverse publicity. Then, in their most extensive conversation of the story, Bartleby cryptically explains himself to the narrator. In preferring not to follow any of the unskilled occupations which the lawyer suggests, but at the same time affirming that he is not particular, Bartleby articulates the worker's dilemma. He is willing to do any meaningful work, but none of the jobs enumerated would be any improvement over the body-and-mind-destroying labor he has just given up. Uncomprehending, and desperate to rid himself of a nuisance, the narrator now offers to install Bartleby temporarily in his own home, so that the process of money-making can continue without interruption.[11] Whether or not genuine humanity could now rehabilitate the alienated worker is a useless conjecture: the profit system cannot accommodate it, and Bartleby must necessarily reject an offer so redolent of self-interest.

After this failure to move Bartleby, the lawyer, true to his commercial values, experiences relief *first* at the thought of having done all he

---

[11]The same tone of peremptory command that informed the narrator's office speech to Bartleby is evident in this supposedly benevolent offer: "'Come, let us start now, right away'" (p. 49).

could vis-à-vis the other parties of his class: the landlord and lawyer tenants who had been insisting on his responsibility for Bartleby. Concern for the scrivener takes second place. The narrator's next action is similarly prompted not by the proddings of conscience over Bartleby's now certain eviction but by fear of further bother: "So fearful was I of being again hunted out by the incensed landlord and his exasperated tenants, that, surrendering my business to Nippers, for a few days, I drove about the upper part of the town and through the suburbs. . . ." (p. 50). When Bartleby is safely behind bars, continuing the dead-wall revery he pursued in the law office, the narrator can patronize him once more and encourage him to make the best of it: "'And see, it is not so sad a place as one might think. Look, there is the sky, and here is the grass'" (p. 51). Bartleby will not be deluded into seeing his situation falsely, however. He knows that the natural world is equally constrained in the Tombs and on Wall Street; the man-made wall is omnipresent. Knowing as he does their respective positions, and the lawyer's real unwillingness to blur the distinction between their roles, Bartleby repudiates the narrator firmly: "'I know you, he said, without looking round—'and I want nothing to say to you'" (ibid.).[12] When, on his last visit, the narrator reaches out to touch Bartleby—his first attempt at physical contact—the effort is once more too little and too late. His benediction over the dead scrivener, that he sleeps "with kings and counsellors," is an ironic acknowledgment of the common humanity of all men, an idea subordinated to considerations of class and position in his treatment of the enigmatic Bartleby.[13]

15   The narrator's epilogue is of a piece with his imperceptive evaluation of Bartleby throughout—a failure to see which is unconsciously motivated by self-protection. Wishing to view Bartleby as a man doomed "by nature and misfortune"[14] rather than by the commercial values that have given himself a comfortable existence, the narrator finds Bartleby's past occupation symbolically fitting. The final exclamation, linking Bartleby

[12]Liane Norman, "Bartleby and the Reader," *New England Quarterly*, 44 (1971), 38, similarly interprets this to mean: "I know your freedom and prosperity and I want nothing to do with them. They did not permit me to choose."

[13]The narrator has felt the attraction of Bartleby as *doppelgänger* early on but has never wanted to place "the bond of a common humanity" (p. 33) above business considerations.

[14]Similar statements about Bartleby earlier in the story have the same function of relieving the narrator of responsibility: whatever he does, Bartleby is fated to hopelessness and the narrator thus escapes blame.

and humanity, is a way of merging the individual into the vast human tide for which he need take no responsibility.

To see Bartleby as victim of and protest against the numbing world of capitalistic profit and alienated labor suggested by the story's sub-title, "A Story of Wall Street," is not to insist upon a reductive economic meaning or to deny that other symbolic dimensions are necessarily untenable. The alienated worker can also be the alienated writer; alienation from work—the necessary labor by which most of us live—is the key in Marx's thinking to alienation from self and society as well.

SUGGESTIONS FOR WRITING

1. Barnett's essay is organized around the exploration of a definition by Karl Marx. In your view, how well does she perform as a definer? Write an essay that explains and defends your view of her skill in this regard.
2. In her footnote 8 Barnett cites another critic, Leo Marx, who claims that when Bartleby's fellow workers use the word *prefer* they assume the form but not the substance of Bartleby's rebellion. Write an essay that explains the extent of your agreement or disagreement with this critical formulation.
3. In her next-to-last paragraph Barnett writes: "the narrator's epilogue is of a piece with his imperceptive evaluation of Bartleby throughout." Write an essay that responds to this critical formulation with your own views of the epilogue.

Bartleby   2005

From *Herman Melville*

ANDREW DELBANCO

Andrew Delbanco (b. 1952) is currently the Julian Clarence Levi Professor in The Humanities at Columbia University. In 2001 he was named "America's best social critic" by Time magazine. He is the author of several books and many articles on American literature and the excerpt on Bartleby below is taken from his 2005 biography of Herman Melville. Delbanco sees Bartleby as a deep study in the psychology of an urban casualty who arouses disgust as well as pity. He also focuses on the narrator, as troubled in his own way as Bartleby. Delbanco also records the real world background of the dead letter theme in the story as an image of failed communications.

"Bartleby" touches a nerve with every reader who has ever tried to manage an unmanageable relationship with a parent, child, lover, spouse—anyone who compels our better self to try and try again but pushes us toward cruelty and a final "Enough!" It is the story of one of those Melvillean characters like Pip (and, in works yet to be written, Hunilla in *The Encantadas* and Colonel Moredock in *The Confidence-Man*), who has been shocked by some incommunicable experience that has left him scarred and less than whole. It is a city story about one of those innumerable urban casualties who makes us feel both sympathy and disgust, as well as fear, given that he might be a preview of what could happen to us upon some comparable reversal of fortune. But Melville's aim is far from a pitch for pity or charity. As we follow Bartleby's descent into the New York City jail (known even then as "the Tombs") where he is sent to die alone, the story becomes ineffably sad but also bitterly funny, blending, as Richard Henry Dana, Sr., recognized, "the pathetic and the ludicrous,"[1] as the half-crazy Turkey and Nippers, like a couple of tramps in a Beckett play, climb up to ride tandem on their high horse in order to show Bartleby who's boss.

Perhaps some precipitating event in Melville's life might explain the half-despondent, half-delirious mood of this remarkable story. Perhaps it was a story about Melville's own fall into obscurity or an allegory of Hawthorne's emotional recalcitrance (Melville describes Vine, in *Clarel*, as "opulent in withheld replies"). Searching for some explanation for the despair he had seen in Bartleby's eyes, the lawyer reports in a brief Epilogue a rumor that the young man had once worked in the Dead Letter Office, where the clerks take piles of undeliverable mail and file them away into storage, where they will gather dust for eternity. It may be that the seed of "Bartleby" had been planted in Melville's mind by an article, "The Lawyer's Story," about an odd clerk that was published in February 1853 in the *New York Times*, or by one that had run in September 1852 in the *Albany Register* about the Dead Letter Office, where "great sacks, locked and sealed . . . [are] piled in the halls, containing undelivered love notes, locks of hair . . . Daguerreotype portraits . . . lottery tickets and tickets for rail or ship passage, household keys, diamond ornaments," all tokens of thwarted human dreams. Perhaps Bartleby had had such an encounter with the dead-endedness

---

[1]This mix of pathos and farce is captured well in Jonathan Parker's expressionistic 2002 film adaptation of "Bartleby."

of life and had thereby, as we would say today, "gone postal"—no longer capable of sorting through his fingers the paper traces of a million ruined lives.

Melville's treatment of the lawyer's confusion over how to respond to this mutilated soul is a finely wrought portrait of a morally vexed man. But it is also a meditation on a large moral issue under dispute in antebellum America: how to define collective responsibility at a time when the old ad hoc welfare system of churches and charities could no longer cope with the growing number of workers and families left destitute by the boom-and-bust cycle of the industrial economy. As casualties mounted, the scope of corporate responsibility was being narrowed in the courts by business-friendly judges who routinely ruled against plaintiffs in cases of workplace injury and property loss. (One suit, brought against the Boston & Worcester Railroad in 1842 by an employee who had been injured in a derailment caused by another employee's negligence, had been dismissed in a precedent-setting case by none other than Judge Lemuel Shaw.) In the 1850s, the United States was fast becoming a laissez-faire society with no articulated system for protecting individuals against impersonal power. In this respect, Bartleby—homeless, friendless, the urban equivalent of "a bit of wreck in the mid Atlantic"—was a figure more representative than eccentric.

Yet there was an opposite thrust in midcentury America that Melville also registered in "Bartleby." This was the fundamentally religious impulse, expressed chiefly in the abolitionist movement but also in the whole array of reform movements from temperance to public education, to *expand* the scope of responsibility—to insist, that is, that the sufferings of some people must be the business of all people. This groping toward a widened sense of accountability was driven by multiple forces, among them the force of technology (railroads, canals, steamboats, and, especially, the telegraph) that enabled news to be circulated more broadly and rapidly than ever before, as well as by the evangelical movements that were springing up everywhere from the seaboard cities to the frontier. When the lawyer in "Bartleby" finds himself indisposed to taking his usual seat in his pew at Trinity Church ("the things I had seen disqualified me for a time from church-going"), he looks back, with a penitent sense of his own insufficiency, into the writings of the great evangelical theologian

Jonathan Edwards, for whom religion is "not only . . . the business of Sabbath days, or . . . the business of a month, or a year, or of seven years . . . but the business of life." The lawyer knows that he cannot rise to this impossible standard, which amounts to a call to put away "the old Adam of resentment" and to embrace the new Adam of selfless love in a lifelong act of *imitatio Christi*. But Melville does not write about the lawyer in a prosecutorial spirit. He writes about him as a witness to a good man trying to become a better man in the face of another man's suffering.

What Melville achieved in "Bartleby, the Scrivener" was the integration of the radical insight that the standing social order is morally outrageous and must be rejected with the conservative insight that custom and precedent are precious and fragile and must be defended. "Bartleby" registers the truth of both views. It integrates the moral truth that we owe our fellow human beings our faith and love with the psychological and social truth that sympathy and benevolence have their limits—that, as the historian Thomas Haskell has put it, "the limits of moral responsibility have to be drawn somewhere and . . . the 'somewhere' will always fall far short of much pain and suffering that we could do something to alleviate." The radical voice in Melville says, "Save him, succor him, embrace him as a child of God," while the conservative voice says, "What more can I do for him? And if I turn my whole life over to him, what will become of the others who depend on me?" In "Bartleby," these two voices speak as they do in life: they speak, that is, simultaneously.

SUGGESTIONS FOR WRITING

1. In his first paragraph, Delbanco claims that Bartleby represents modern figures that make us feel both sympathy and disgust. Write an essay that responds to this critical formulation with your own understanding of and response to Bartleby's character.

2. Unlike Barnett, Delbanco in paragraph 3 sees the narrator as "a morally vexed man." Do you agree? Write an essay that explores your own understanding of the narrator's character.

3. In your opinion, are the critical performances of Barnett and Delbanco opposed or complementary? Write an essay that expresses your critical view of their critical views.

INTERDISCIPLINARY CONNECTIONS

1. Louise Barnett's criticism takes an economic view and Virginia Woolf focuses on the issue of gender, to take only two examples of interdisciplinarity in this chapter. In your view does literary criticism seem to lend itself particularly to an interdisciplinary approach? Write an essay that explains and defends your answer.

2. Based on the readings in this chapter, does literary history seem to be an evolutionary process or a history better explained by some other model of change in time? Write an essay that explores the reasoning behind your response.

3. From which of the literary critics in this chapter have you gained the most insight into literature? Write an essay in praise of the author of your choice.

4. Throughout the history of literature, many people have read nothing at all or next to nothing in works of the literary imagination. Yet all the writers in this chapter assume great powers for literary art. In your view, which of these critics seems most utopian in his or her assumptions about the importance for human life of the literary imagination? Write an essay that argues for the justice of your choice.

5. In paragraph 4 Virginia Woolf speculates on the sad fates of women born "with a great gift in the Elizabethan age." Among other destinies, she images someone who "ended her days in some lonely cottage outside the village, half witch, half wizard, feared and mocked at." In Chapter 6 Rose Weitz analyzes some similar figures. Write an essay in which you compare and contrast the views of Virginia Woolf and Rose Weitz on this subject.

Utopias and Dystopias

Secular Heavens and Secular Hells

Thomas More	H. G. Wells
Francis Bacon	Charlotte Perkins Gilman
Jonathan Swift	Ray Bradbury
Mary Shelley	Chairman Mao
Henry David Thoreau	Margaret Atwood

Introduction

Dreams of an ideal world and nightmares about its opposite have long stirred the human imagination, and fictional stories on both themes have provided ways of dramatizing human values and aspirations whether in triumph or defeat. Sir Thomas More gave us the word *utopia* (Latin for *no place*) to stand for imaginative renderings of the ideal, and by analogy *dystopia* has come to name the nightmares. As versions of societies wildly different from our own, utopias and dystopias can serve to express both social critiques and social ambitions by giving us models and mirrors for discussion of the values and assumptions that underlie our own current lives. The imaginary locations naturally lend themselves to interdisciplinary discussion because they are open to the same kinds of analyses that our own world is open to, as the variety of selections in this chapter attests.

We begin with an excerpt from the book by Sir Thomas More that gave its name to a genre. In a plot that was to become familiar, travelers discover a hitherto unknown island republic. Its economic and social organization seems astoundingly rational, producing every necessity and many comforts though the populace labors a mere six hours a day. The strong appeal of improving life by a new social order based on logic has been felt ever since this book's publication.

The social order of Sir Francis Bacon's *The New Atlantis* is organized in large part around the production of scientific knowledge in Solomon's House, a research institute named after the wisest king in the Old Testament. Bacon is revered as the man who initiated the modern scientific method to reveal nature's secrets through experiments to collect facts, which are in turn used to infer the laws of nature. In the excerpt given here, a high official of the New Atlantis tell the explorers who have discovered his country about the experiments in Solomon's House.

Swift's Academy at Logado turns Bacon's Solomon's House upside down. Like his friend, the poet Alexander Pope, Swift thought that "the proper study of mankind is man," and Swift had little patience with the contemporary success of Bacon's methods insofar as they led to the material study of dirt and insects and away from the study of proper human action. Anyone reading a list of nationally funded scientific proposals today will perhaps understand the spirit of Swift's exasperation in this chapter from *Gulliver's Travels*.

Mary Shelley's vision of a utopian experiment that turns into a dystopian tragedy was embodied not in a nation or an institution but in an individual. Dr. Frankenstein creates an entirely new being with no historical ties and hence no inherited responsibilities either to humanity or to a divine creator. The being turns out in his creator's view not to be the creature he hopes could demonstrate new possibilities for mankind but a monster who murders. Still, the creature has his own point of view on the causes of his actions and the possibilities for his future, and justifies himself in an excerpt from the famous novel, *Frankenstein*.

Like Mary Shelley, Henry David Thoreau imagines the creation of new possibilities for the human race, and, like her too, he centers his vision in an individual—in this case, himself. In this excerpt from *Walden*, Thoreau tells us how material comfort may be easily and cheaply obtained through self-reliance with a resulting leisure for higher pursuits greater even in its extent than that enjoyed by the citizens of More's Utopia with their six-hour work days.

Will the future fulfill the promise of a better world through an improved humanity, as Thoreau thought? H. G. Wells was one of the early masters of science fiction. In *The Time Machine*, a scientist invents a vehicle that can travel through time as other vehicles travel through space. Using this machine, a man known only as the Time Traveler brings himself to a very distant future where another idea—evolution—has been at work for thousands of millennia. At first the results of a Darwinian natural selection seem utopian, but they are soon seen to have been combined with a Marxian class struggle and a darker side is revealed.

Charlotte Perkins Gilman's writing is also featured earlier in this book, in Chapter 2, with a selection from her book *Women and Economics*. She appears here in an excerpt from her novel about a feminist utopia, *Herland*. Male travelers come upon a long-isolated country and find it populated entirely by women. In the traditional manner of utopian narratives, the natives explain their origins and ways of life including a new means of human reproduction—parthenogenesis.

Utopias and dystopias are literary forms and they have long appeared as books. In Ray Bradbury's famous novel *Fahrenheit 451*, books are forbidden and firemen exist only to burn them whenever they are discovered. Bradbury's title is an allusion to the temperature at which paper ignites. In the excerpt given here, a fire chief explains why books must be destroyed to a young fireman who is secretly guilty of reading.

Utopians have sometimes left the pages of books for the real world, though the results of such realizations are often far from ideal. Communist China under Chairman Mao set out to create a workers' paradise and ended up resembling a death camp. When dissent went underground, Chairman Mao brought it out of hiding by announcing in a speech that a utopian climate of free speech would henceforth replace repression as the national policy. The idea of the speech, "Let a Hundred Flowers Blossom," was to treat ideas on an evolutionary rather than a revolutionary basis, a process which was supposed to lead to a kind of intellectual survival of the fittest. Of course, those who believed in the truth of the benevolent message did not survive at all.

The chapter ends with a selection from Margaret Atwood's dystopian novel, *The Handmaid's Tale*. The world Atwood imagines seems like Charlotte Perkins Gilman's *Herland* as seen in a dark and tragic mirror image. The two visions, though written at different ends of the twentieth century, make a very interesting topic for comparison and contrast. In Atwood's world, women are assigned to biological functions and strictly controlled. Dissent is punished through a weird ritual described in the excerpt given here.

Utopia

1516

Concerning the Best State of a Republic Book II by Thomas More, Citizen and Undersheriff of London

Translated from the Latin original by Niti Bagchi

SIR THOMAS MORE

Sir Thomas More (1478–1535) gave the word utopia—Latin for no place—to the world in the book of that name about an ideal island published first in 1516. More's career included high office in the legal areas of the English government and he is remembered for his principled stand against Henry VIII's claim to be supreme head of the Church of England. That king drove More from office and had him executed as a traitor. Four hundred years later, More was canonized by Pope Pius XI and was later declared the patron saint of statesmen and lawyers.

If utopia means "no place", the word also implies that the ideal can exist but only somewhere outside our world and its constraints and can be expressed better through fiction than through fact. In the pages excerpted here, an ideal social order is surveyed in a fictional form, after a "realistic" survey of Utopia's physical setting.

The island of the Utopians extends for two hundred miles at the middle part (for it is widest here), and most of the island is not much narrower, except toward both ends, where it tapers gradually. These ends, curved as if in a circle with a circumference of five hundred miles, shape the whole aspect/appearance of the island as a new moon. The sea, flowing between the horns of the crescent, separates them by eleven miles more or less, and spreads through a vast empty space. The sea being surrounded by land on all sides, winds are kept away. It is calm, like a vast lake, rather than being rough. Nearly the whole interior coast of the land makes a harbor, and to the great benefit of the people, ships cross it in all directions. With shoals on this side and rocks on that, the mouth of the harbor is extremely dangerous. A crag projects roughly in the middle of the intervening space, and in itself is harmless. They have built a tower upon it and keep a garrison there. The remaining crags are underwater, and hence are perilous. The channels are known only to the Utopian people, and therefore it occurs that no outsider shall enter this bay easily, unless with a Utopian guide. The entry would be scarcely safe even for Utopians themselves, except that their path is kept on course by certain landmarks on the shore. If these were moved to different places, the Utopians could easily drag an enemy fleet to destruction, no matter how large it was.

Harbors are not infrequent on the other side of the island. But everywhere, the land is so fortified either by nature or by design that large troops could be hindered by only a few defenders. However that may be, it is said—and the appearance of the place confirms it—that at one time, this land was not surrounded by the sea. But Utopus, who conquered the island and whose name it now bears (for before this time it was called Abraxa), and who brought the rude and savage inhabitants to culture and humanity such that they now surpass other mortals, having acquired victory immediately upon landing, saw to it that fifteen miles of land that was joined to the continent was cut away, and he led the sea to circle the country. He put to labor not only the vanquished residents, but also his own soldiers; lest the natives think this work to be disgraceful. With the task distributed among such a multitude of men, the deed was completed with amazing speed so that the bordering people (who at first had laughed at the vanity of the undertaking) were full of admiration and terror at its success.

The island has fifty-four cities, all of which are large and magnificent, and absolutely identical in language, traditions, institutions and laws. As far as the location allows, they are all identically situated, and the same everywhere, and have the same appearance. No city is so far away that one could not travel on foot to another city within one day.

Every year, out of each city come three old and experienced men and they travel to Amaurot to transact the common matters of the island. For this city (that is located just like a navel of the land and is most convenient for ambassadors from all parts of the island) is held as the capital. Fields are so appropriately assigned to the cities that there are no less than twelve miles of farmland from any part of the city. There may even be more, where the cities are a farther distance apart. No city desires to enlarge its boundaries, because the citizens consider themselves to be farmers rather than masters of the lands. They have in the country, throughout all the fields, farmhouses that are situated conveniently and furnished with farming tools. These are inhabited by citizens who move to the country by turns. No country household has fewer than forty men and women, in addition to two bound slaves, above whom are appointed a grave and mature master and mistress of the household. There is one phylarch placed over every thirty households. Twenty people from each family move back to the city every year, and these having completed a two-year stay in the country. In their place are substituted the same number of people newly arrived from the city, so that they may be trained by those who have been in the country for a year and are therefore more experienced in rustic things. The following year, the recent arrivals shall teach others. If all were equally new and unskilled at agriculture, they would make blunders among the crops out of ignorance and inexperience. This custom of introducing new farm workers is the usual mode lest someone unwilling be forced to continue for a long time in such a harsh way of life. Nevertheless, many who enjoy farm work by nature receive permission to live there for more years.

5   The farmers till the land, feed the animals, provide firewood and take it to the city by land or water, whichever way is convenient. They raise a large number of chickens by a marvelous method. The hens do not incubate the eggs, but the farmers keep a great number of them warm at a steady temperature, and they are hatched. These chickens, as soon as they emerge from the shell, recognize and follow men in the place of their mothers.

They raise very few horses, and none but very fierce ones, which are not used for anything except exercising youths in equestrian arts, for oxen undertake all the labor of plowing and drawing. They are agreed to be inferior to horses in the short-term, but they outlast hard times and the farmers think that they are not as vulnerable to diseases as horses are. In addition, they require less expense and less work, and are fit to be eaten when they are too old for labors.

They use grain only for bread, for they drink wine made from grapes, apples or pears, or they drink nothing but pure water. Often, they boil water with honey or licorice, of which they have a copious amount. Although they know for sure (for they know it most certainly) how much grain each city and the districts surrounding it will consume, they produce even more grain and raise more cattle than will suffice for their needs, the excess to be shared with their neighbors. Whatever need there may be for things that are not to be had in the country, the rural people seek all such things from the city, and without anything given in exchange, and with no trouble. They obtain them from the city magistrates. Many of them go once a month to the city on the feast day. When the day for harvesting draws near, the phylarchs of the farmers tell the city magistrates how many urban citizens need to be sent to them. The multitude of harvesters arrives on an opportune day, and in almost one day of fair weather, they harvest the whole crop.

Concerning their Cities, and Namely Amaurot

He who knows one of their cities knows them all, there being such similarities among them (to the degree that the nature of the place allows.) Therefore I shall describe one of them, and it is of no matter which. But which rather than Amaurot? Not only is it worthier than any other city, for the remaining cities acknowledge its as the senate, but also it is better known to me than any other city, as I lived there for five full years.

So, Amaurot is situated on the side of a low hill, and is almost square in shape. Its breadth begins a little below the crown of the hill, and continues for two miles to the river Anyder. Its length, along the bank of the river, is somewhat greater. Anyder rises eighty miles above Amaurot, from a small spring, but is augmented by other smaller streams flowing into it, and two bigger ones. Thus, before the city it has grown to a width of about five hundred yards. It grows still larger, and sixty miles ahead is received by the ocean. In the whole space that lies between the city and the sea, and also for certain miles above the city, flowing continuously for six hours with a swift current, the water alternates between ebb and flow. When the sea flows in, it fills the whole Anyder with salt water for thirty miles, and the freshwater is driven back. Then, somewhat further, it mars the freshness of the water with saltiness. A small distance beyond this, the untainted sweetness of the river flows alongside the city, and with the ebb of the tide, the river is pure and untainted almost all the way to the sea.

10   The city is joined together by a bridge made not upon wooden piles or stakes, but upon arches with remarkable stonework. It is at that part of the city that is most distant from the sea, so that ships may sail unhindered along the entire length of the city. They have also another stream which is not very large but gentle and pleasant. It gushes forth from the same hill upon which the city is situated, and flowing along the slope, goes through the city and into the Anyder. The inhabitants of Amaurot have enclosed the head of the spring with fortifications, since it rises somewhat outside the city, lest the water be poisoned, or cut off and diverted if the strength of some enemies should fall upon them. Water from the stream is diverted to various lower parts of the city by means of brick canals. Where the terrain makes this impossible, rainwater is collected in large cisterns, which are of good use.

A high and thick wall encircles the town, with many towers and ramparts. A dry ditch that is deep and wide, and overgrown with brambles, surrounds the town walls on three sides; on the fourth side, the river itself acts as a ditch. The streets are laid out very conveniently for vehicles and for protection against the wind. The houses are not at all shabby, and stand facing each other down a long, unbroken row on the street. These house-fronts are separated by a street twenty feet wide. Behind the houses lies a garden, as long as the street, and enclosed by the backs of the streets.

Every house has two doors, one leading to the street and a backdoor leading into the garden. The double-doors are easily opened with a push of the hand and on their own allow in anyone entering, because nothing anywhere is private. They exchange the houses themselves every decade, by lot. They make much of their gardens: in these they have vines, fruits, herbs and flowers that are so resplendent and well-grown that I have never seen anywhere more elegant or flourishing gardens. Their zeal for this thing comes not only from pleasure but also from a competition rising among the streets about the raising of the gardens. And certainly you shall not easily find in the whole city anything more useful or pleasant for the citizens. Therefore it may seem that he who founded the city must have had the gardens in mind primarily.

It is held that from the beginning, King Utopus himself planned the whole city. However, he left to posterity matters of adornment and culture, for which he saw that the lifetime of one man would not endure. They have records which begin 1,760 years ago, from the conquest of the island. The history of the years is compiled and written diligently; at the beginning, the houses were low and like cottages or huts, made roughly with wood of any sort, and with mud-covered walls. The roofs, tapering to a point, were thatched with straw. But now every house is worth seeing, formed with three storeys; the exteriors of the walls are constructed with flint stone, concrete or bricks, and the gap between is filled up with rubble. The roofs are flat and covered with a sort of plaster that is of no cost and does not wear away. It is not vulnerable to fire and can withstand the ravages of weather better than lead. Winds are kept out of the windows with glass, which is very frequently used there. They also use a thin linen cloth coated with clear oil or amber, having a double advantage, as by this method, more light is let in and more wind kept out.

Concerning their Officials

Every thirty families selects for themselves a magistrate annually, whom they call the syphogrant in their ancient tongue, and the phylarch in the newer language. An official once called the tranibor and now called the chief phylarch is set over every ten syphogrants and their thirty families. In the election of the chief, all the syphogrants, who are two hundred in number, swear to choose the man they consider best-qualified. By a secret election, they choose as prince one of those four men whom the populace had nominated. Four men are selected from the four quarters of the city to be recommended for senate. The office of the chief lasts for life, unless he is suspected of tyranny. The people elect tranibors annually, but they are not changed lightly. All other officials have office only for one year.

15   Every third day, and more often if need be, the tranibors meet in counsel with the chief. They discuss matters of the republic, and resolve private disputes (if there are any, and there are very few) quickly. The tranibors always admit two syphogrants to senate, but different ones daily. It is decreed that no decision may be made on a matter of state unless it has been discussed in senate for three days. It is considered a capital crime to make plans on public matters outside the senate or public assembly. It is held that this statute was instituted lest there be conspiracy among the prince and tranibors, through which tyranny to oppress the people and change the state of the government. Therefore, matters of great importance are adjudged having been brought before

the assembly of the syphogrants, who having discussed the matter with their households, present their counsel to the senate. Sometimes a matter is brought before an assembly of the whole island.

The senate also has a tradition that a matter is never discussed on the day it is first brought up, but deferred till the next meeting. This is so that no one blurts out rashly the first thought that comes to his mouth, and afterward contrive to defend his own idea, neglecting the common good in favor of his own opinion. There are some men with so perverse and preposterous a sense of shame that they would rather see the negligence of common good than admit to having been short-sighted in the beginning. They should have been fore-sighted in the beginning so that they could have spoken in a considered manner rather than in haste.

Concerning Occupations

The one trade carried out by men and women alike is agriculture, from which no one is exempt. All are instructed in this from childhood, partly being taught theory in school, and partly in the fields near the city where they are taught through play-like instruction, not merely watching, but also learning through the opportunity to exercise their bodies in practice.

Besides agriculture (which is done by the whole public, as I have said), everyone is taught a particular trade of his own. This is generally wool-making, linen-making, masonry, or the art of metalwork or that of carpentry. There is no other work worth mentioning that occupies any number of people in that place. As for clothing—of which, except for the habit that the sexes are distinguished from each other, as well as married and unmarried people—there is one style for the whole island, the same style continuing through all one's life. It is not unattractive and is convenient for free movement of the body. It is suited to both winter and summer. These clothes, I say, each family makes for itself.

Out of those trades, everyone learns a certain one, not only the men, but also the women. As the weaker ones, the women carry out the lighter tasks: they usually work the wool and linen. The remaining, more laborious trades are delegated to the men. For the most part, sons are trained in the arts of their fathers, for many are drawn to these by natural disposition. But if one's spirit draws one to another trade, he is led by adoption to a family practicing that craft. Care is taken not only by his father, but also but the magistrates that he be transferred to a grave and honest householder. Furthermore, if anyone having learned one craft desires to learn another, he is permitted in the same way. Having experienced both, he undertakes the one he prefers, unless the city has need of one more than the other.

20   The foremost and almost only business of the syphogrants is to take care and watch closely lest anyone should sit idle, and to ensure that everyone applies himself diligently to his own trade: Nevertheless, no one need be exhausted from early morning to late night in perpetual labor, like a beast of burden. Such distressing labor, which is worse than slavery, is nearly everywhere the life of workmen, except in Utopia. They divide day and night into twenty-four equal hours, and they devote no more than six hours to work. They work for three hours before noon, at which time they go to lunch. They rest for two hours after lunch, and then another three hours are devoted to working before they go to dinner. Counting the first hour after noon as 'one,' they go to bed at eight o' clock. Sleep claims eight hours.

Whatever hours there are that are not given to labor, sleep and eating are left to the discretion of each person for himself, not so they may be abused in extravagance or inactivity, but so that in the time free from work, one might occupy the mind properly in some study. Many devote these breaks to learning. For it is a usual thing to have daily public lectures in the hours before dawn, at which only they need be present who are expressly selected for learning. A great multitude of the remaining people, both men and women, gather to hear the lectures. Some attend one, some another, each according to his interest. However, if someone prefers to spend this time on his trade, as many do whose minds don't aspire to the contemplation of knowledge, this is not prohibited. In fact, these people are praised as being useful to the republic.

After dinner, they spend an hour in play, in the gardens during summer, and during the winter, in the common halls where they eat. There they play music or refresh themselves in conversation. They do not know about dice and other, similar foolish and destructive games, but they have two games that are not unlike the game of chess. One is a battle of numbers in which one number preys on another, the other is a game in which vices having been brought together fight against virtues in battle. In this game are showed very expertly both the discord of the vices among themselves and their harmony in opposition to the virtues. Then it is shown which vices oppose what virtues, with what forces they fight openly, and with which they attack obliquely with machinations, with what defense the virtues weaken the powers of the vices, with what arts they elude the endeavors of the vices, and finally, the means by which one party or another may have victory.

But at this point, lest you should be mistaken, one point must be considered more closely. Since there are no more than six hours for work, you may perhaps think that a lack of necessary things may follow. But this is not so—for it happens that the time does not merely suffice but is even excessive for the necessities and commodities of life. You shall understand this if you consider with yourselves how large a part of the population among other races spends its life idly. First, hardly any women, who are half the population, work: or wheresoever women are in fact working, there, most of the men snore away in exchange. In addition, there is a large, idle group of priests and those who call themselves religious! Add to them all the rich, especially the land-owners who are commonly called gentlemen and noblemen. Take into this number their attendants, namely that rabble of good-for-nothing swashbucklers. Then include the robust and healthy beggars, feigning some disease as a pretext for their idleness. You shall certainly find that all things used by mortals are produced by the labor of many less people than you had thought.

Consider now with yourself how few out of these are versed in necessary trades; in fact, where all is measured in terms of money, it is necessary that many trades be practiced that are absolutely inane and superfluous, carried out for the sake of luxury and caprice. For if the same multitude that is now occupied at work were divided into so few trades as nature suitably requires, then there would now be such an abundance of things that prices would be too low for workers to make a living. But if such workers who are presently engaged in idle trades, and the whole crowd of them relaxing in idleness and apathy (any one of whom consumes as much of what is furnished by the labors of others as two of the laborers themselves), if these men were set to useful work for common benefit, you would realize easily how little time would be enough, and even abundant, for the furnishing of all things required by necessity and convenience (and yes, even for pleasure, which would be true and natural pleasure.)

25   And this thing in Utopia makes itself evident. For there, in the whole city and the adjacent countryside, scarcely five hundred people out of all men and women whose age and strength make them eligible for work are made exempt from it. Among these are the syphogrants,

whom the laws free from having to work. Nevertheless, they do not exempt themselves, encouraging others to work by their own example. They also enjoy the same exemption from labor, who by the recommendation of the priests and a secret vote of the syphogrants are given a permanent exemption for the pursuit of learning. If any one of these men fails to live up to the hope conceived of him, he is pushed back among the workers. And conversely, it happens not infrequently that a certain handicraftsman devotes his spare hours so zealously to study, and through his diligence makes such progress, that he is exempted from work and promoted to the class of the learned. From this order of the learned are chosen ambassadors, priests, tranibors and finally, the chief himself, whom they called Barzanes in their ancient tongue, but in the modern language is called Ademus. Nearly the whole remaining population is neither idle or occupied with useless crafts, so it is easy to judge in how few hours of work they accomplish so much.

To these things of which I have spoken, they have moreover the ease of the additional fact that in most of the necessary trades they have less work than people in other countries. For first of all, the construction or repairing of houses everywhere requires the assiduous labor of many men, because that which the father built, the insufficiently thrifty heir allows to fall into decay. Thus what could have been kept in good order at minimal cost, his successor is forced to reconstruct to his great expense. In fact, frequently, a man has built a large house at great cost, another with a more refined sensibility condemns it. The house, thus neglected, quickly falls into ruin, and he builds another one in another place, not with small expense. But among the Utopians, where all things are properly composed and the republic is properly established, it happens extremely rarely that a new plot of land is selected upon which to build a new house. Not only are fast remedies administered upon present damages, but imminent ones are also prevented. Thus it is that houses last for a very long time with minimal labor and workmen of this sort so scarcely have anything to do that they are ordered to chop wood at home and to square and make ready stone, by which if any work come about unexpectedly, it may more quickly be done.

Now see how little work is needed for their clothing. Work clothes are plain and covered in leather or pelts, which last for seven years. When they go out in public, they put on a cloak which covers up the rougher work clothes. Throughout the whole island, there is one color and that is the natural color of wool. Thus not only does much less woolen cloth suffice than in other countries, but also the same in much lower in cost. The use of linens is widespread because it is made with less labor than wool. They admire whiteness alone in linen and cleanliness alone in wool, and there is no regard for the fineness of the thread. Thus it is that in other places, on no occasion are four or five woolen cloaks of different colors and as many silk tunics sufficient for one man. For one of the more refined sort, even ten are too few. But there, everyone is content with one cloak, which generally lasts two years. Naturally there is no cause to strive after any more clothes, for even if he had them, he would not be better protected from the cold nor would he appear even a whit more fashionable.

Since all men are exercised in useful trades and less work sufficing in the trades, there is certainly an abundance of all things, they sometimes draw together a great multitude to rebuild public roads, if any are in disrepair. Often, also, when there is no such work, they proclaim publicly that fewer hours shall be devoted to working. For the magistrates do not exercise citizens against their will in unnecessary labor. The custom of the republic considers one goal primarily: that as much as public needs allow, all citizens should be freely able to spend much time away from the service of the body and toward the cultivation of the mind. For they think that in this rests the happiness of life.

SUGGESTIONS FOR WRITING

1. More's narrator obviously approves the virtues of Utopia while looking over his shoulder at the vices of our own world. His story's organization might therefore be described as something like the Utopian "chess" game where virtues fight with vices. Write an essay in which you show how the virtues of Utopia appear as possible cures for the vices of our world.

2. Do you think More's narrative treats women evenhandedly—both the women of Utopia and the women of our world? Write an essay that explains and defends your answer.

3. We are given to understand that the leisure achieved by the economy of Utopia is based on the production of necessities and the elimination of needless luxuries, though we are given very few concrete examples. If you were able to control the economy of our world, what would be the necessary occupations allowed and what occupations would be eliminated? Write an essay that describes and explains some aspects of your ideal economy.

The New Atlantis

1626

FRANCIS BACON

Francis Bacon (1561–1626), a contemporary of Shakespeare, was trained as a lawyer and was created Lord Verulum for his public service in many high offices under Queen Elizabeth I (Chapter 3) and James I, patron of the King James Bible. Bacon fell from power into disgrace in later life and is remembered not as a statesman but as the father of the modern scientific method. Briefly put, Bacon championed a new logic of induction which reached a general conclusion from the observations of many discrete but related facts. This method contrasts to that of Aristotle (Chapter 4), a logic of deduction that derives implications from agreed upon premises and which had dominated methods of inquiry in most areas of intellect for nearly 2000 years.

Bacon wrote his utopian fantasy The New Atlantis *in order to dramatize what a properly organized inquiry into the secrets of nature and its laws might be like. In fact, in spite of some old-fashioned and therefore perhaps quaint-appearing details, his description of "Salomon's House" (Bacon's spelling) in the land of the New Atlantis seems an accurate sketch of a research university in the land of twenty-first century America. Bacon's institution is named for the King of Israel who was reputed to be the wisest man in the world.*

'God bless thee, my son; I will give thee the greatest jewel I have. For I will impart unto thee, for the love of God and men, a relation of the true state of Salomon's House. Son, to make you know the true state of Salomon's House, I will keep this order. First, I will set forth unto you the end of our foundation. Secondly, the preparations and instruments we have for our works. Thirdly, the several employments and functions whereto our fellows are assigned. And fourthly, the ordinances and rites which we observe.

'The end of our foundation is the knowledge of causes, and secret motions of things; and the enlarging of the bounds of human empire, to the effecting of all things possible.

'The preparations and instruments are these. We have large and deep caves of several depths: the deepest are sunk six hundred fathoms; and some of them are digged and made under great hills and mountains; so that if you reckon together the depth of the hill, and the depth of the cave, they are, some of them, above three miles deep. For we find that the depth of a hill, and the depth of a cave from the flat, is the same thing; both remote alike from the sun and heaven's beams, and from the open air. These caves we call the lower region, and we use them for all coagulations, indurations, refrigerations, and conservations of bodies. We use them likewise for the imitation of natural mines, and the producing also of new artificial metals, by compositions and materials which we use, and lay there for many years. We use them also sometimes (which may seem strange) for curing of some diseases, and for prolongation of life, in some hermits that choose to live there, well accommodated of all things necessary, and indeed live very long; by whom also we learn many things.

'We have burials in several earths, where we put divers cements, as the Chinese do their porcelain. But we have them in greater variety, and some of them more fine. We also have great variety of composts and soils, for the making of the earth fruitful.

5   'We have high towers, the highest about half a mile in height, and some of them likewise set upon high mountains, so that the vantage of the hill, with the tower, is in the highest of them three miles at least. And these places we call the upper region, accounting the air between the high places and the low as a middle region. We use these towers, according to their several heights and situations, for insolation, refrigeration, conservation, and for the view of divers meteors—as winds, rain, snow, hail; and some of the fiery meteors also. And upon them, in some places, are dwellings of hermits, whom we visit sometimes, and instruct what to observe.

'We have great lakes, both salt and fresh, whereof we have use for the fish and fowl. We use them also for burials of some natural bodies, for we find a difference in things buried in earth, or in air below the earth, and things buried in water. We have also pools, of which some do strain fresh water out of salt, and others by art do turn fresh water into salt. We have also some rocks in the midst of the sea, and some bays upon the shore for some works, wherein is required the air and vapour of the sea. We have likewise violent streams and cataracts, which serve us for many motions; and likewise engines for multiplying and enforcing of winds to set also on divers motions.

'We have also a number of artificial wells and fountains, made in imitation of the natural sources and baths, as tincted upon vitriol, sulphur, steel, brass, lead, nitre, and other minerals; and again, we have little wells for infusions of many things, where the waters take the virtue quicker and better than in vessels or basins. And amongst them we have a water, which we call Water of Paradise, being by that we do to it made very sovereign for health and prolongation of life.

'We have also great and spacious houses, where we imitate and demonstrate meteors—as snow, hail, rain, some artificial rains of bodies, and not of water, thunders, lightnings; also generations of bodies in air—as frogs, flies, and divers others.

'We have also certain chambers, which we call chambers of health, where we qualify the air as we think good and proper for the cure of divers diseases, and preservation of health.

10   'We have also fair and large baths, of several mixtures, for the cure of diseases, and the restoring of man's body from arefaction; and others for the confirming of it in strength of sinews, vital parts, and the very juice and substance of the body.

'We have also large and various orchards and gardens, wherein we do not so much respect beauty as variety of ground and soil, proper for divers trees and herbs, and some very spacious, where trees and berries are set, whereof we make divers kinds of drinks, besides the vineyards. In these we practise likewise all conclusions of grafting and inoculating, as well of wild-trees as fruit-trees which produceth many effects. And we make by art, in the same orchards and gardens, trees and flowers, to come earlier or later than their seasons, and to come up and bear more speedily than by their natural course they do. We make them also by art greater much than their nature; and their fruit greater and sweeter, and of differing taste, smell, colour, and figure, from their nature. And many of them we so order as they become of medicinal use.

'We have also means to make divers plants rise by mixtures of earths without seeds, and likewise to make divers new plants, differing from the vulgar, and to make one tree or plant turn into another.

'We have also parks, and enclosures of all sorts, of beasts and birds; which we use not only for view or rareness, but likewise for dissections and trials, that thereby we may take light what may be wrought upon the body of man. Where in we we find many strange effects: as continuing life in them, though divers parts, which you account vital, be perished and taken forth; resuscitating of some that seem dead in appearance, and the like. We try also all poisons, and other medicines upon them, as well of chirurgery as physic. By art likewise we make them greater or taller than their kind is, and contrariwise dwarf them and stay their growth; we make them more fruitful and bearing than their kind is, and contrariwise barren and not generative. Also we make them differ in colour, shape, activity, many ways. We find means to make commixtures and copulations of divers kinds, which have produced many new kinds, and them not barren, as the general opinion is. We make a number of kinds, of serpents, worms, flies, fishes, of putrefaction, whereof some are advanced (in effect) to be perfect creatures, like beasts or birds, and have sexes, and do propagate. Neither do we this by chance, but we know beforehand of what matter and commixture, what kind of those creatures will arise.

15 'We have also particular pools where we make trials upon fishes, as we have said before of beasts and birds.

'We have also places for breed and generation of those kinds of worms and flies which are of special use; such as are with you your silkworms and bees.

'I will not hold you long with recounting of our brew-houses, bake-houses and kitchens, where are made divers drinks, breads, and meats, rare and of special effects. Wines we have of grapes, and drinks of other juice, of fruits, of grains, and of roots, and of mixtures with honey, sugar, manna, and fruits dried and decocted; also of the tears or woundings of trees, and of the pulp of canes. And these drinks are of several ages, some to the age or last of forty years. We have drinks also brewed with several herbs, and roots and spices; yea, with several fleshes and white-meats; whereof some of the drinks are such as they are in effect meat and drink both, so that divers, especially in age, do desire to live with them with little or no meat or bread. And above all we strive to have drinks of extreme thin parts, to insinuate into the body, and yet without all biting, sharpness, or fretting; insomuch as some of them, put upon the back of your hand, will with a little stay pass through to the palm, and taste yet mild to the mouth. We have also waters, which we ripen in that fashion, as they become nourishing, so that they are indeed excellent drinks, and many will use no other. Bread we have of several grains, roots, and kernels; yea, and some of flesh, and fish, dried; with divers kinds of leavenings and seasonings; so that some do extremely move appetites, some do nourish so, as divers do live of them, without any other meat, who live very long. So for meats, we have some of them so beaten, and made tender, and mortified, yet without all corrupting, as a weak heat of the stomach will turn them into good chilus, as well as a strong heat would meat other-wise prepared. We have some meats also, and breads, and drinks, which taken by men, enable them to fast long after; and some other, that used make the very flesh of men's bodies sensibly more hard and tough, and their strength far greater than otherwise it would be.

'We have dispensatories or shops of medicines; wherein you may easily think, if we have such variety of plants, and living creatures, more than you have in Europe (for we know what you have), the simples, drugs and ingredients of medicines, must likewise be in so much the greater variety. We have them likewise of divers ages, and long fermentations. And for their preparations, we have not only all manner of exquisite distillations and separations, and especially by gentle heats, and percolations through divers strainers, yea, and substances; but also exact forms of composition, whereby they incorporate almost as they were natural simples.

'We have also divers mechanical arts, which you have not; and stuffs made by them, as papers, linen, silks, tissues, dainty works of feathers of wonderful lustre, excellent dyes, and many others: and shops likewise, as well for such as are not brought into vulgar use amongst us, as for those that are. For you must know, that of the things before recited, many of them are grown into use throughout the kingdom, but yet, if they did flow from our invention, we have of them also for patterns and principles.

'We have also furnaces of great diversities, and that keep great diversity of heats: fierce and quick, strong and constant, soft and mild; blown, quiet, dry, moist, and the like. But above all we have heats, in imitation of the sun's and heavenly bodies' heats, that pass divers inequalities, and (as it were) orbs, progresses, and returns, whereby we produce admirable effects. Besides, we have heats of dungs, and of bellies and maws of living creatures and of their bloods and bodies, and of hays and herbs laid up moist, of lime unquenched, and such like. Instruments also which generate heat only by motion. And farther, places for strong insolations; and again, places under the earth, which by nature or art yield heat. These divers heats we use as the nature of the operation which we intend requireth.

20   'We have also perspective houses, where we make demonstrations of all lights and radiations, and of all colours; and out of things uncoloured and transparent, we can represent unto you all several colours, not in rainbows (as it is in gems and prisms), but of themselves single. We represent also all multiplications of light, which we carry to great distance, and make so sharp, as to discern small points and lines. Also all colourations of light; all delusions and deceits of the sight, in figures, magnitudes, motions, colours; all demonstrations of shadows. We find also divers means yet unknown to you, of producing of light, originally

from divers bodies. We procure means of seeing objects afar off, as in the heaven and remote places; and represent things near as afar off, and things afar off as near; making feigned distances. We have also helps for the sight, far above spectacles and glasses in use. We have also glasses and means to see small and minute bodies, perfectly and distinctly; as the shapes and colours of small flies and worms, grains, and flaws in gems which cannot otherwise be seen, observations in urine and blood not otherwise to be seen. We make artificial rainbows, halos, and circles about light. We represent also all manner of reflections, refractions, and multiplications of visual beams of objects.

'We have also precious stones of all kinds, many of them of great beauty and to you unknown; crystals likewise, and glasses of divers kinds; and amongst them some of metals vitrificated, and other materials, besides those of which you make glass. Also a number of fossils and imperfect minerals, which you have not. Likewise loadstones of prodigious virtue: and other rare stones, both natural and artificial.

'We have also sound-houses, where we practise and demonstrate all sounds and their generation. We have harmonies which you have not, of quarter-sounds and lesser slides of sounds. Divers instruments of music likewise to you unknown, some sweeter than any you have; together with bells and rings that are dainty and sweet. We represent small sounds as great and deep; likewise great sounds, extenuate and sharp; we make divers tremblings and warblings of sounds, which in their original are entire. We represent and imitate all articulate sounds and letters, and the voices and notes of beasts and birds. We have certain helps, which set to the ear do further the hearing greatly. We have also divers strange and artificial echoes, reflecting the voice many times, and as it were tossing it; and some that give back the voice louder than it came, some shriller and some deeper; yea, some rendering the voice, differing in the letters or articulate sound from that they receive. We have also means to convey sounds in trunks and pipes, in strange lines and distances.

'We have also perfume-houses wherewith we join also practices of taste. We multiply smells, which may seem strange: we imitate smells, making all smells to breathe out of other mixtures than those that give them. We make divers imitations of taste likewise, so that they will deceive any man's taste. And in this house we contain also a confiture-house, where we make all sweetmeats, dry and moist, and divers pleasant wines, milks, broths, and salads, far in greater variety than you have.

'We have also engine-houses, where are prepared engines and instruments for all sorts of motions. There we imitate and practise to make swifter motions than any you have, either out of your muskets or any engine that you have; and to make them and multiply them more easily and with small force, by wheels and other means, and to make them stronger and more violent than yours are, exceeding your greatest cannons and basilisks. We represent also ordnance and instruments of war and engines of all kinds; and likewise new mixtures and compositions of gunpowder, wildfires burning in water and unquenchable, also fire-works of all variety, both for pleasure and use. We imitate also fights of birds; we have some degrees of flying in the air. We have ships and boats for going under water and brooking of seas, also swimming-girdles and supporters. We have divers curious clocks, and other like motions of return, and some perpetual motions. We imitate also motions of living creatures by images of men, beasts, birds, fishes, and serpents; we have also a great number of other various motions, strange for equality, fineness, and subtilty.

25   'We have also a mathematical-house, where are represented all instruments, as well of geometry as astronomy, exquisitely made.

'We have also houses of deceits of the senses, where we represent all manner of feats of juggling, false apparitions, impostures and illusions, and their fallacies. And surely you will easily believe that we, that have so many things truly natural which induce admiration, could in a world of particulars deceive the senses if we would disguise those things, and labour to make them seem more miraculous. But we do hate all impostures and lies, insomuch as we have severely forbidden it to all our fellows, under pain of ignominy and fines, that they do not show any natural work or thing adorned or swelling, but only pure as it is, and without all affectation of strangeness.

'These are, my son, the riches of Salomon's House.

'For the several employments and offices of our fellows, we have twelve that sail into foreign countries under the names of other nations (for our own we conceal), who bring us the books and abstracts, and patterns of experiments of all other parts. These we call Merchants of Light.

'We have three that collect the experiments which are in all books. These we call Depredators.

30   'We have three that collect the experiments of mechanical arts, and also of liberal sciences, and also of practices which are not brought into arts. These we call Mystery-men.

'We have three that try new experiments, such as themselves think good. These we call Pioneers or Miners.

'We have three that draw the experiments of the former four into titles and tables, to give the better light for the drawing of observations and axioms out of them. These we call Compilers.

'We have three that bend themselves, looking into the experiments of their fellows, and cast about how to draw out of them things of use and practice for man's life and knowledge, as well for works as for plain demonstration of causes, means of natural divinations, and the easy and clear discovery of the virtues and parts of bodies. These we call dowry-men or Benefactors.

'Then after divers meetings and consults of our whole number, to consider of the former labours and collections, we have three that take care out of them to direct new experiments, of a higher light, more penetrating into Nature than the former. These we call Lamps.

35 'We have three others that do execute the experiments so directed, and report them. These we call Inoculators.

'Lastly, we have three that raise the former discoveries by experiments into greater observations, axioms, and aphorisms. These we call Interpreters of Nature.

'We have also, as you must think, novices and apprentices, that the succession of the former employed men do not fail; besides a great number of servants and attendants, men and women. And this we do also: we have consultations, which of the inventions and experiences which we have discovered shall be published, and which not: and take all an oath of secrecy for the concealing of those which we think fit to keep secret: though some of those we do reveal sometimes to the State, and some not.

'For our ordinances and rites, we have two very long and fair galleries: in one of these we place patterns and samples of all manner of the more rare and excellent inventions: in the other we place the statues of all principal inventors. There we have the statue of your Columbus, that discovered the West Indies: also the inventor of ships: your Monk that was the inventor of ordnance and of gunpowder: the inventor of music: the inventor of letters: the inventor of printing: the inventor of observations of astronomy: the inventor of works in metal: the inventor of glass: the inventor of silk of the worm: the inventor of wine: the inventor of corn and bread: the inventor of sugars: and all these by more certain tradition than you have. Then we have divers inventors of our own, of excellent works, which since you have not seen, it were too long to make descriptions of them; and besides, in the right understanding of those descriptions you might easily err. For upon every invention of value we erect a statue to the inventor, and give him a liberal and honourable reward. These statues are some of brass, some of marble and touchstone, some of cedar and other special woods gilt and adorned; some of iron, some of silver, some of gold.

'We have certain hymns and services, which we say daily, of laud and thanks to God for His marvellous works. And forms of prayer, imploring His aid and blessing for the illumination of our labours, and the turning of them into good and holy uses.

40   'Lastly, we have circuits or visits, of divers principal cities of the kingdom; where, as it cometh to pass, we do publish such new profitable inventions as we think good. And we do also declare natural divinations of diseases, plagues, swarms of hurtful creatures, scarcity, tempests, earthquakes, great inundations, comets, temperature of the year, and divers other things; and we give counsel thereupon, what the people shall do for the prevention and remedy of them.'

And when he had said this he stood up; and I, as I had been taught, knelt down; and he laid his right hand upon my head, and said, 'God bless thee, my son, and God bless this relation which I have made. I give thee leave to publish it, for the good of other nations; for we here are in God's bosom, a land unknown.' And so he left me; having assigned a value of about two thousand ducats for a bounty to me and my fellows. For they give great largesses, where they come, upon all occasions.

SUGGESTIONS FOR WRITING

1. In the second paragraph, the father of Salomon's House gives a stirring account of the goals for a human empire of research in the New Atlantis, before going on to describe some of the results of that research. Write an essay that describes some of the fictional projects that have in fact been realized by scientific research in modern times.

2. Some of the research projects are obviously absurd, being based on false knowledge current in Bacon's time, such as the generation of flies. Write an essay that describes some of the projects in Salomon's House that have not been realized by scientific research in modern times, giving reasons for their status, if possible.

3. The repetitive style of Bacon's transitions ("We have also. . . .") is a striking feature of his writing. Do you find it a virtue or a drawback, given the nature of the selection as a whole? Write an essay that explains and defends your answer.

Gulliver's Travels   1726

JONATHAN SWIFT

Jonathan Swift (1667–1745) still retains his reputation as the greatest satirist in the English language and Gulliver's Travels *remains his most famous book. He was born in Ireland of parents who came there from England. He attended Dublin University but fled to England during the political and religious turmoil stemming from the Glorious Revolution of 1688 when the Roman Catholic James II was forced from the throne and into exile after a civil war. In England, Swift obtained the post of secretary to Sir William Temple, an English diplomat and writer who introduced Swift into the inner circles of British political power, a world that both attracted and repelled him for the rest of his life. Swift was ordained in the protestant Church of Ireland and eventually rose to become Dean of St. Patrick's Cathedral in Dublin, but his career included literature and politics as well as the church.*

In the passages below from Book III of Gulliver's Travels, *Swift makes fun of the kind of "pure" scientific method advocated by Bacon in Solomon's House. In Swift's academy, reason leads to irrationality and objectivity comes to mean ignoring the human in human relations to the world of nature. The Author is Swift's naïve and gullible fictional traveler, Lemuel Gulliver.*

Chapter 5

The Author permitted to see the grand Academy of Lagado. The Academy largely described. The Arts wherein the Professors employ themselves.

This Academy is not an entire single Building, but a Continuation of several Houses on both Sides of a Street; which growing waste, was purchased and applyed to that Use.

I was received very kindly by the Warden, and went for many Days to the Academy. Every Room hath in it one or more Projectors; and I believe I could not be in fewer than five Hundred Rooms.

The first Man I saw was of a meagre Aspect, with sooty Hands and Face, his Hair and Beard long, ragged and singed in several Places. His

Clothes, Shirt, and Skin were all of the same Colour. He had been Eight Years upon a Project for extracting Sun-Beams out of Cucumbers, which were to be put into Vials hermetically sealed, and let out to warm the Air in raw inclement Summers.[1] He told me, he did not doubt in Eight Years more, that he should be able to supply Governors Gardens with Sun-shine at a reasonable Rate; but he complained that his Stock was low, and intreated me to give him something as an Encouragement to Ingenuity, especially since this had been a very dear Season for Cucumbers. I made him a small Present, for my Lord had furnished me with Money on purpose, because he knew their Practice of begging from all who go to see them.

I went into another Chamber, but was ready to hasten back, being almost overcome with a horrible Stink. My Conductor pressed me forward, conjuring me in a Whisper to give no Offence, which would be highly resented; and therefore I durst not so much as stop my Nose. The Projector of this Cell was the most ancient Student of the Academy. His Face and Beard were of a pale Yellow; his Hands and Clothes dawbed over with Filth. When I was presented to him, he gave me a very close Embrace, (a Compliment I could well have excused). His Employment from his first coming into the Academy, was an Operation to reduce human Excrement to its original Food, by separating the several Parts, removing the Tincture which it receives from the Gall, making the Odour exhale, and scumming off the Saliva. He had a weekly Allowance from the Society, of a Vessel filled with human Ordure, about the Bigness of a *Bristol* Barrel.

5   I saw another at work to calcine Ice into Gunpowder; who likewise shewed me a Treatise he had written concerning the Malleability of Fire, which he intended to publish.

There was a most ingenious Architect who had contrived a new Method for building Houses, by beginning at the Roof, and working downwards to the Foundation; which he justified to me by the like Practice of those two prudent Insects the Bee and the Spider.

There was a Man born blind, who had several Apprentices in his own Condition: Their Employment was to mix Colours for Painters, which their Master taught them to distinguish by feeling and smelling. It was indeed my Misfortune to find them at that Time not very perfect in their

---

[1] The experiments described in this chapter are based on actual experiments undertaken or proposed by Swift's contemporaries.

Lessons; and the Professor himself happened to be generally mistaken: This Artist is much encouraged and esteemed by the whole Fraternity.

In another Apartment I was highly pleased with a Projector, who had found a Device of plowing the Ground with Hogs, to save the Charges of Plows, Cattle, and Labour. The Method is this: In an Acre of Ground you bury at six Inches Distance, and eight deep, a Quantity of Acorns, Dates, Chestnuts, and other Maste or Vegetables whereof these Animals are fondest; then you drive six Hundred or more of them into the Field, where in a few Days they will root up the whole Ground in search of their Food, and make it fit for sowing, at the same time manuring it with their Dung. It is true, upon Experiment they found the Charge and Trouble very great, and they had little or no Crop. However, it is not doubted that this Invention may be capable of great Improvement.

I went into another Room, where the Walls and Ceiling were all hung round with Cobwebs, except a narrow Passage for the Artist to go in and out. At my Entrance he called aloud to me not to disturb his Webs. He lamented the fatal Mistake the World had been so long in of using Silk-Worms, while we had such plenty of domestick Insects, who infinitely excelled the former, because they understood how to weave as well as spin. And he proposed farther, that by employing Spiders, the Charge of dying Silks would be wholly saved; whereof I was fully convinced when he shewed me a vast Number of Flies most beautifully coloured, wherewith he fed his Spiders; assuring us, that the Webs would take a Tincture from them; and as he had them of all Hues, he hoped to fit every Body's Fancy, as soon as he could find proper Food for the Flies, of certain Gums, Oyls, and other glutinous Matter, to give a Strength and Consistence to the Threads.

10 There was an Astronomer who had undertaken to place a SunDial upon the great Weather-Cock on the Town-House, by adjusting the annual and diurnal Motions of the Earth and Sun, so as to answer and coincide with all accidental Turnings of the Wind.

I was complaining of a small Fit of the Cholick; upon which my Conductor led me into a Room, where a great Physician resided, who was famous for curing that Disease by contrary Operations from the same Instrument. He had a large Pair of Bellows, with a long slender Muzzle of Ivory. This he conveyed eight Inches up the Anus, and drawing in the Wind, he affirmed he could make the Guts as lank as a dried Bladder. But when the Disease was more stubborn and violent, he let in the Muzzle while the Bellows was full of Wind, which he discharged into the Body of the Patient; then withdrew the Instrument to replenish it, clapping his Thumb strongly against the Orifice of the Fundament; and this being repeated three or four Times, the adventitious Wind would rush out, bringing the noxious along with it (like Water put into a Pump) and the Patient recovers. I saw him try both Experiments upon a Dog, but could not discern any Effect from the former. After the latter, the Animal was ready to burst, and made so violent a Discharge, as was very offensive to me and my Companions. The Dog died on the Spot, and we left the Doctor endeavouring to recover him by the same Operation.

I visited many other Apartments, but shall not trouble my Reader with all the Curiosities I observed, being studious of Brevity.

I had hitherto seen only one Side of the Academy, the other being appropriated to the Advancers of speculative Learning; of whom I shall say something when I have mentioned one illustrious Person more, who is called among them *the universal Artist.* He told us, he had been Thirty Years employing his Thoughts for the Improvement of human Life. He had two large Rooms full of wonderful Curiosities, and Fifty Men at work. Some were condensing Air into a dry tangible Substance, by extracting the Nitre, and letting the aqueous or fluid Particles percolate: Others softening Marble for Pillows and Pin-cushions; others petrifying the Hoofs of a living Horse to preserve them from foundring. The Artist himself was at that Time busy upon two great Designs: The first, to sow Land with Chaff, wherein he affirmed the true seminal Virtue to be contained, as he demonstrated by several Experiments which I was not skilful enough to comprehend. The other was, by a certain Composition of Gums, Minerals, and Vegetables outwardly applied, to prevent the Growth of Wool upon two young Lambs; and he hoped in a reasonable Time to propagate the Breed of naked Sheep all over the Kingdom.

We crossed a Walk to the other Part of the Academy, where, as I have already said, the Projectors in speculative Learning resided.

15   The first Professor I saw was in a very large Room, with Forty Pupils about him. After Salutation, observing me to look earnestly upon a Frame, which took up the greatest Part of both the Length and Breadth of the Room; he said, perhaps I might wonder to see him employed in a Project for improving speculative Knowledge by practical and mechanical Operations. But the World would soon be sensible

of its Usefulness; and he flattered himself, that a more noble exalted Thought never sprang in any other Man's Head. Every one knew how laborious the usual Method is of attaining to Arts and Sciences; whereas by his Contrivance, the most ignorant Person at a reasonable Charge, and with a little bodily Labour, may write Books in Philosophy, Poetry, Politicks, Law, Mathematicks and Theology, without the least Assistance from Genius or Study. He then led me to the Frame, about the Sides whereof all his Pupils stood in Ranks. It was Twenty Foot square, placed in the Middle of the Room. The Superficies was composed of several Bits of Wood, about the Bigness of a Dye, but some larger than others. They were all linked together by slender Wires. These Bits of Wood were covered on every Square with Papers pasted on them; and on these Papers were written all the Words of their Language in their several Moods, Tenses, and Declensions, but without any Order. The Professor then desired me to observe, for he was going to set his Engine at work. The Pupils at his Commond took each of them hold of an Iron Handle, whereof there were Forty fixed round the Edges of the Frame; and giving them a sudden Turn, the whole Disposition of the Words was entirely changed. He then commanded Six and Thirty of the Lads to read the several Lines softly as they appeared upon the Frame; and where they found three or four Words together that might make Part of a Sentence, they dictated to the four remaining Boys who were Scribes. This Work was repeated three or four Times, and at every Turn the Engine was so contrived, that the Words shifted into new Places, as the square Bits of Wood moved upside down.

Six Hours a-Day the young Students were employed in this Labour; and the Professor shewed me several Volumes in large Folio already collected, of broken Sentences, which he intended to piece together; and out of those rich Materials to give the World a compleat Body of all Arts and Sciences; which however might be still improved, and much expedited, if the Publick would raise a Fund for making and employing five Hundred such Frames in *Lagado*, and oblige the Managers to contribute in common their several Collections.

He assured me, that this Invention had employed all his Thoughts from his Youth; that he had emptied the whole Vocabulary into his Frame, and made the strictest Computation of the general Proportion there is in Books between the Numbers of Particles, Nouns, and Verbs, and other Parts of Speech.

I made my humblest Acknowledgments to this illustrious Person for his great Communicativeness; and promised if ever I had the good Fortune to return to my native Country, that I would do him Justice, as the sole Inventor of this wonderful Machine; the Form and Contrivance of which I desired Leave to delineate upon Paper as in the Figure here annexed. I told him, although it were the Custom of our Learned in *Europe* to steal Inventions from each other, who had thereby at least this Advantage, that it became a Controversy which was the right Owner; yet I would take such. Caution, that he should have the Honour entire without a Rival.

We next went to the School of Languages, where three Professors sat in Consultation upon improving that of their own Country.

The first Project was to shorten Discourse by cutting Polysyllables into one, and leaving out Verbs and Participles; because in Reality all things imaginable are but Nouns.

The other, was a Scheme for entirely abolishing all Words whatsoever: And this was urged as a great Advantage in Point of Health as well as Brevity. For, it is plain, that every Word we speak is in some Degree a Diminution of our Lungs by Corrosion; and consequently contributes to the shortening of our Lives. An Expedient was therefore offered, that since Words are only Names for *Things*, it would be more convenient for all Men to carry about them, such *Things* as were necessary to express the particular Business they are to discourse on. And this Invention would certainly have taken Place, to the great Ease as well as Health of the Subject, if the Women in Conjunction with the Vulgar and Illiterate had not threatned to raise a Rebellion, unless they might be allowed the Liberty to speak with their Tongues, after the Manner of their Forefathers: Such constant irreconcileable Enemies to Science are the common People. However, many of the most Learned and Wise adhere to the new Scheme of expressing themselves by *Things*; which hath only this Inconvenience attending it; that if a Man's Business be very great, and of various Kinds, he must be obliged in Proportion to carry a greater Bundle of *Things* upon his Back, unless he can afford one or two strong Servants to attend him. I have often beheld two of those Sages almost sinking under the Weight of their Packs, like Pedlars among us, who when they met in the Streets, would lay down their Loads, open their Sacks, and hold Conversation for an Hour together; then put up their Implements, help each other to resume their Burthens, and take their Leave.

But, for short Conversations a Man may carry Implements in his Pockets and under his Arms, enough to supply him, and in his House he cannot be at a Loss; therefore the Room where Company meet who practice this Art, is full of all *Things* ready at Hand, requisite to furnish Matter for this Kind of artificial Converse.

Another great Advantage proposed by this Invention, was, that it would serve as an universal Language to be understood in all civilized Nations, whose Goods and Utensils are generally of the same Kind, or nearly resembling, so that their Uses might easily be comprehended. And thus, Embassadors would be qualified to treat with foreign Princes or Ministers of State, to whose Tongues they were utter Strangers.

I was at the Mathematical School, where the Master taught his Pupils after a Method scarce imaginable to us in *Europe*. The Proposition and Demonstration were fairly written on a thin Wafer, with Ink composed of a Cephalick Tincture. This the Student was to swallow upon a fasting Stomach, and for three Days following eat nothing but Bread and Water. As the Wafer digested, the Tincture mounted to his Brain, bearing the Proposition along with it. But the Success hath not hitherto been answerable, partly by some Error in the *Quantum* or Composition, and partly by the Perverseness of Lads; to whom this Bolus is so nauseous, that they generally steal aside, and discharge it upwards before it can operate: neither have they been yet persuaded to use so long an Abstinence as the Prescription requires.

SUGGESTIONS FOR WRITING

1. Swift's satire seems informed in part by Solomon's House in Bacon's *New Atlantis*. Write an essay that analyzes some of the ways in which Swift employ's Bacon's style to satirize some of his assumptions about scientific research.

2. If we do live in a world made of things as science assumes, surely the project of reducing all language to nouns makes good sense. Write an essay in which you explain Swift's satire by showing how the project makes no sense at all.

3. Write an essay in which you analyze the project of plowing a field by the use of hogs to show how it is representative of other projects in the Academy at Lagado.

Frankenstein

1818

MARY SHELLEY

*Mary Shelley (1797–1851) was the second daughter of the feminist writer Mary
Wollstonecraft (Chapter 3). Her mother died only ten days after giving birth and
she was raised and privately educated by her father, the radical writer and
thinker William Godwin. At sixteen years of age Mary met the poet Percy Bysshe
Shelley, a freethinker like her father, when Shelley was in the process of becoming
estranged from his first wife. The poet and the teenager fell in love and eloped to
France. The couple formed a literary circle in Geneva with the poet Lord Byron
and a ghost-story writing contest produced her masterpiece* Frankenstein, *a
story that begins with utopian scientific hopes and ends in dystopian scientific
tragedy. In the following passage, the creature and his creator argue over ideal
rights and duties in the context of murderous facts.*

It was nearly noon when I arrived at the top of the ascent. For some
time I sat upon the rock that overlooks the sea of ice. A mist covered
both that and the surrounding mountains. Presently a breeze dissipated the cloud, and I descended upon the glacier. The surface is very
uneven, rising like the waves of a troubled sea, descending low, and
interspersed by rifts that sink deep. The field of ice is almost a league
in width, but I spent nearly two hours in crossing it. The opposite
mountain is a bare perpendicular rock. From the side where I now
stood Montanvert was exactly opposite, at the distance of a league;
and above it rose Mont Blanc, in awful majesty. I remained in a recess
of the rock, gazing on this wonderful and stupendous scene. The sea,
or rather the vast river of ice, wound among its dependent mountains,
whose aerial summits hung over its recesses. Their icy and glittering
peaks shone in the sunlight over the clouds. My heart, which was
before sorrowful, now swelled with something like joy; I exclaimed,
"Wandering spirits, if indeed ye wander, and do not rest in your narrow beds, allow me this faint happiness, or take me, as your companion, away from the joys of life."

As I said this I suddenly beheld the figure of a man, at some distance,
advancing towards me with superhuman speed. He bounded over the
crevices in the ice, among which I had walked with caution; his stature,
also, as he approached, seemed to exceed that of man. I was troubled; a
mist came over my eyes, and I felt a faintness seize me; but I was quickly

restored by the cold gale of the mountains. I perceived, as the shape came nearer (sight tremendous and abhorred!) that it was the wretch whom I had created. I trembled with rage and horror, resolving to wait his approach and then close with him in mortal combat. He approached; his countenance bespoke bitter anguish, combined with disdain and malignity, while its unearthly ugliness rendered it almost too horrible for human eyes. But I scarcely observed this; rage and hatred had at first deprived me of utterance, and I recovered only to overwhelm him with words expressive of furious detestation and contempt.

"Devil," I exclaimed, "do you dare approach me? And do not you fear the fierce vengeance of my arm wreaked on your miserable head? Begone, vile insect! Or rather, stay, that I may trample you to dust! And, oh! That I could, with the extinction of your miserable existence, restore those victims whom you have so diabolically murdered!"

"I expected this reception," said the demon. "All men hate the wretched; how, then, must I be hated, who am miserable beyond all living things! Yet you, my creator, detest and spurn me, thy creature, to whom thou art bound by ties only dissoluble by the annihilation of one of us. You purpose to kill me. How dare you sport thus with life? Do you duty towards me, and I will do mine towards you and the rest of mankind. If you will comply with my conditions, I will leave them and you at peace; but if you refuse, I will glut the maw of death, until it be satiated with the blood of your remaining friends."

5   "Abhorred monster! Fiend that thou art! The tortures of hell are too mild a vengeance for thy crimes. Wretched devil! You reproach me with your creation; come on, then, that I may extinguish the spark which I so negligently bestowed."

My rage was without bounds; I sprang on him, impelled by all the feelings which can arm one being against the existence of another.

He easily eluded me and said, "Be calm! I entreat you to hear me before you give vent to your hatred on my devoted head. Have I not suffered enough, that you seek to increase my misery? Life, although it may only be an accumulation of anguish, is dear to me, and I will defend it. Remember, thou hast made me more powerful than thyself; my height is superior to thine, my joints more supple. But I will not be tempted to set myself in opposition to thee. I am thy creature, and I will be even mild and docile to my natural lord and king if thou wilt also perform thy part, the which thou owest me. Oh, Frankenstein, be not equitable to every other and trample upon me alone, to whom thy justice, and even thy clemency and affection, is most due. Remember that I am thy creature; I ought to be thy Adam, but I am rather the fallen angel, whom thou drivest from joy for no misdeed. Everywhere I see bliss, from which I alone am irrevocably excluded. I was benevolent and good; misery made me a fiend. Make me happy, and I shall again be virtuous."

"Begone! I will not hear you. There can be no community between you and me; we are enemies. Begone, or let us try our strength in a fight, in which one must fall."

"How can I move thee? Will no entreaties cause thee to turn a favourable eye upon thy creature, who implores thy goodness and compassion? Believe me, Frankenstein, I was benevolent; my soul glowed with love and humanity; but am I not alone, miserably alone? You, my creator, abhor me; what hope can I gather from your fellow creatures, who owe me nothing? They spurn and hate me. The desert mountains and dreary glaciers are my refuge. I have wandered here many days; the caves of ice, which I only do not fear, are a dwelling to me, and the only one which man does not grudge. These bleak skies I hail, for they are kinder to me than your fellow beings. If the multitude of mankind knew of my existence, they would do as you do, and arm themselves for my destruction. Shall I not then hate them who abhor me? I will keep no terms with my enemies. I am miserable, and they shall share my wretchedness. Yet it is in your power to recompense me, and deliver them from an evil which it only remains for you to make so great, that not only you and your family, but thousands of others, shall be swallowed up in the whirlwinds of its rage. Let your compassion be moved, and do not disdain me. Listen to my tale; when you have heard that, abandon or commiserate me, as you shall judge that I deserve. But hear me. The guilty are allowed, by human laws, bloody as they are, to speak in their own defence before they are condemned. Listen to me, Frankenstein. You accuse me of murder, and yet you would, with a satisfied conscience, destroy your own creature. Oh, praise the eternal justice of man! Yet I ask you not to spare me; listen to me, and then, if you can, and if you will, destroy the work of your hands."

10 "Why do you call to my remembrance," I rejoined, "circumstances of which I shudder to reflect, that I have been the miserable origin and author? Cursed be the day, abhorred devil, in which you first saw light! Cursed (although I curse myself) be the hands that formed you! You have made me wretched beyond expression. You have left me no power to consider whether I am just to you or not. Begone! Relieve me from the sight of your detested form."

"Thus I relieve thee, my creator," he said, and placed his hated hands before my eyes, which I flung from me with violence; "thus I take from thee a sight which you abhor. Still thou canst listen to me and grant me thy compassion. By the virtues that I once possessed, I demand this from you. Hear my tale; it is long and strange, and the temperature of this place is not fitting to your fine sensations; come to the hut upon the mountain. The sun is yet high in the heavens; before it descends to hide itself behind your snowy precipices and illuminate another world, you will have heard my story and can decide. On you it rests, whether I quit forever the neighbourhood of man and lead a harmless life, or become the scourge of your fellow creatures and the author of your own speedy ruin."

As he said this he led the way across the ice; I followed. My heart was full, and I did not answer him, but as I proceeded, I weighed the various arguments that he had used and determined at least to listen to his tale. I was partly urged by curiosity, and compassion confirmed my resolution. I had hitherto supposed him to be the murderer of my brother, and I eagerly sought a confirmation or denial of this opinion. For the first time, also, I felt what the duties of a creator towards his creature were, and that I ought to render him happy before I complained of his wickedness. These motives urged me to comply with his demand. We crossed the ice, therefore, and ascended the opposite rock.

SUGGESTIONS FOR WRITING

1. Viktor Frankenstein created his creature out of intentions based on scientific utopianism, but found that there were unintended consequences to his acts. He now wants to kill his creature, but the creature argues for the existence of a kind of social contract between them. Write an essay that analyzes the reasoning brought by the creature to support the existence of the natural rights he claims.

2. You have seen in this chapter how scientific activity was held to be admirable by More and Bacon and how it was satirized by Swift. What is Mary Shelley's implied attitude toward science in the passage you have read? Write an essay that explores your sense of those implied attitudes.

3. The creature speaks in a tone that seems a strange mixture of deference and aggressiveness. In what ways does this mixed style express the strange position of one *created* out of dead materials rather than engendered as part of the long history of human generation? Write an essay that explains and defends your answer.

Putting My House in Order   1854

From *Walden or Life in the Woods*

HENRY DAVID THOREAU

Henry David Thoreau (1817–1862) graduated from Harvard in 1837 and went to live in his native Concord, Massachusetts where his friend and fellow native, the philosopher and poet Ralph Waldo Emerson gave Henry permission to build a house on a piece of his land near Walden Pond. The result was Walden, *a book about practical ways to live an ideal life in the transcendental tradition. For Thoreau the ideal always had its echo in the practical; he was a Yankee craftsman as well as a philosopher, and a man who worked with his hands as well as with his head. As both his actions and words show, Thoreau believed that people could better become rich in every sense by limiting their material demands to allow an increase in their spiritual supplies. The way he makes his house his home in the following passage makes a case history in down-to-earth idealism.*

Near the end of March, 1845, I borrowed an axe and went down to the woods by Walden Pond, nearest to where I intended to build my house, and began to cut down some tall, arrowy white pines, still in their youth, for timber. It is difficult to begin without borrowing, but perhaps it is the most generous course thus to permit your fellow-men to have an interest in your enterprise. The owner of the axe, as he released his hold on it, said that it was the apple of his eye; but I returned it sharper than I received it. It was a pleasant hillside where I worked, covered with pine woods, through which I looked out on the pond, and a small open field in the woods where pines and hickories were springing up. The ice in the pond was not yet dissolved, though there were some open spaces, and it was all dark-colored and saturated with water. There were some slight flurries of snow during the days that I worked there; but for the most part when I came out on to the railroad, on my way home, its yellow sand-heap stretched away gleaming in the hazy atmosphere, and the rails shone in the spring sun, and I heard the lark and pewee and other birds already come to commence another year with us. They were pleasant spring days, in which the winter of man's discontent was thawing as well as the earth, and the life that had lain torpid began to stretch itself. One day, when my axe had come off and I had cut a green hickory for a wedge, driving it with a stone, and had placed the whole to soak in a pond-hole in order to swell the wood, I saw a striped snake run into the water, and he lay on the bottom, apparently without inconvenience, as long as I stayed there, or more than a quarter of an hour; perhaps because he had not yet fairly come out of the torpid state. It appeared to me that for a like reason men remain in their present low and primitive condition; but if they should feel the influence of the spring of springs arousing them, they would of necessity rise to a higher and more ethereal life. I had previously seen the snakes in frosty mornings in my path with portions of their bodies still numb and inflexible, waiting for the sun to thaw them. On the 1st of April it rained and melted the ice, and in the early part of the day, which was very foggy, I heard a stray goose groping about over the pond and cackling as if lost, or like the spirit of the fog.

So I went on for some days cutting and hewing timber, and also studs and rafters, all with my narrow axe, not having many communicable or scholar-like thoughts, singing to myself,—

> Men say they know many things;
> But lo! they have taken wings,—
> The arts and sciences,
> And a thousand appliances:
> The wind that blows
> Is all that anybody knows.

I hewed the main timbers six inches square, most of the studs on two sides only, and the rafters and floor timbers on one side, leaving the rest of the bark on, so that they were just as straight and much stronger than sawed ones. Each stick was carefully mortised or tenoned by its stump, for I had borrowed other tools by this time. My days in the woods were not very long ones; yet I usually carried my dinner of bread and butter, and read the newspaper in which it was wrapped, at noon, sitting amid the green pine boughs which I had cut off, and to my bread was imparted some of their fragrance, for my hands were covered with a thick coat of pitch. Before I had done I was more the friend than the foe of the pine tree, though I had cut down some of them, having become better acquainted with it. Sometimes a rambler in the wood was attracted by the sound of my axe, and we chatted pleasantly over the chips which I had made.

By the middle of April, for I made no haste in my work, but rather made the most of it, my house was framed and ready for the raising. I had already bought the shanty of James Collins, an Irishman who worked on the Fitchburg Railroad, for boards. James Collins' shanty was considered an uncommonly fine one. When I called to see it he was not at home. I walked about the outside, at first unobserved from within, the window was so deep and high. It was of small dimensions, with a peaked cottage roof, and not much else to be seen, the dirt being raised five feet all around as if it were a compost heap. The roof was the soundest part, though a good deal warped and made brittle by the sun. Doorsill there was none, but a perennial passage for the hens under the door-board. Mrs. C. came to the door and asked me to view it from the inside. The hens were driven in by my approach. It was dark, and had a dirt floor for the most part, dank, clammy, and aguish, only here a board and there a board which would not bear removal. She lighted a lamp to show me the inside of the roof and the walls, and also that the board floor extended under the bed, warning me not to step into the cellar, a sort of dust hole two feet deep. In her own words, they were "good boards overhead, good boards all around, and a good window,"—of two whole squares originally, only the cat had passed out that way lately. There was a stove, a bed; and a place to sit, an infant in the house where it was born, a silk parasol, gilt-framed looking-glass, and a patent new coffee-mill nailed to an oak sapling, all told. The bargain was soon concluded, for James had in the meanwhile returned. I to pay four dollars and twenty-five cents to-night, he to vacate at five to-morrow morning, selling to nobody else meanwhile: I to take possession at six. It were well, he said, to be there early, and anticipate certain indistinct but wholly unjust claims on the score of ground rent and fuel. This he assured me was the only encumbrance. At six I passed him and his family on the road. One large bundle held their all,—bed, coffee-mill, looking-glass, hens,—all but the cat; she took to the woods and became a wild cat, and, as I learned afterward, trod in a trap set for woodchucks, and so became a dead cat at last.

5   I took down this dwelling the same morning, drawing the nails, and removed it to the pond-side by small cartloads, spreading the boards on the grass there to bleach and warp back again in the sun. One early thrush gave me a note or two as I drove along the woodland path. I was informed treacherously by a young Patrick that neighbor Seeley, an Irishman, in the intervals of the carting, transferred the still tolerable, straight, and drivable nails, staples, and spikes to his pocket, and then stood when I came back to pass the time of day, and look freshly up, unconcerned, with spring thoughts, at the devastation; there being a dearth of work, as he said. He was there to represent spectatordom, and help make this seemingly insignificant event one with the removal of the gods of Troy.

I dug my cellar in the side of a hill sloping to the south, where a woodchuck had formerly dug his burrow, down through sumach and blackberry roots, and the lowest stain of vegetation, six feet square by seven deep, to a fine sand where potatoes would not freeze in any winter. The sides were left shelving, and not stoned; but the sun having never shone on them, the sand still keeps its place. It was but two hours' work. I took particular pleasure in this breaking of ground, for in almost all latitudes men dig into the earth for an equable temperature. Under the most splendid house in the city is still to be found the cellar where they store their roots as of old, and long after the superstructure has disappeared posterity remark its dent in the earth. The house is still but a sort of porch at the entrance of a burrow.

At length, in the beginning of May, with the help of some of my acquaintances, rather to improve so good an occasion for neighborliness than from any necessity, I set up the frame of my house. No man was ever more honored in the character of his raisers than I. They are destined, I trust, to assist at the raising of loftier structures one day. I began to occupy my house on the 4th of July, as soon as it was boarded and roofed, for the boards were carefully feather-edged and lapped, so that it was perfectly impervious to rain, but before boarding I laid the foundation of a chimney at one end, bringing two cartloads of stones up the hill from the pond in my arms. I built the chimney after my hoeing in the fall, before a fire became necessary for warmth, doing my cooking in the meanwhile out of doors on the ground, early in the morning: which mode I still think is in some respects more convenient and agreeable than the usual one. When it stormed before my bread was baked, I fixed a few boards over the fire, and sat under them to watch my loaf, and passed some pleasant hours in that way. In those days, when my hands were much employed, I read but little, but the least scraps of paper which lay on the ground, my holder, or tablecloth, afforded me as much entertainment, in fact answered the same purpose as the Iliad.

It would be worth the while to build still more deliberately than I did, considering, for instance, what foundation a door, a window, a cellar, a garret, have in the nature of man, and perchance never raising any superstructure until we found a better reason for it than our temporal necessities even. There is some of the same fitness in a man's building his own house that there is in a bird's building its own nest. Who knows but if men constructed their dwellings with their own hands, and provided food for themselves and families simply and honestly enough, the poetic faculty would be universally developed, as birds universally sing when they are so engaged? But alas! we do like cowbirds and cuckoos, which lay their eggs in nests which other birds have built, and cheer no traveller with their chattering and unmusical notes. Shall we forever resign the pleasure of construction to the carpenter? What does architecture amount to in the experience of the mass of men? I never in all my walks came across a man engaged in so simple and natural an occupation as building his house. We belong to the community. It is not the tailor alone who is the ninth part of a man; it is as much the preacher, and the merchant, and the farmer. Where is this division of labor to end? and what object does it finally serve? No doubt another *may* also think for me; but it is not therefore desirable that he should do so to the exclusion of my thinking for myself.

True, there are architects so called in this country, and I have heard of one at least possessed with the idea of making architectural ornaments have a core of truth, a necessity, and hence a beauty, as if it were a revelation to him. All very well perhaps from his point of view, but only a little better than the common dilettantism. A sentimental reformer in architecture, he began at the cornice, not at the foundation. It was only how to put a core of truth within the ornaments, that every sugarplum, in fact, might have an almond or caraway seed in it,—though I hold that almonds are most wholesome without the sugar,—and not how the inhabitant, the indweller, might build truly within and without, and let the ornaments take care of themselves. What reasonable man ever supposed that ornaments were something outward and in the skin merely,—that the tortoise got his spotted shell, or the shell-fish its mother-o'-pearl tints, by such a contract as the inhabitants of Broadway their Trinity Church? But a man has no more to do with the style of architecture of his house than a tortoise with that of its shell: nor need the soldier be so idle as to try to paint the precise *color* of his virtue on his standard. The enemy will find it out. He may turn pale when the trial comes. This man seemed to me to lean over the cornice, and timidly whisper his half truth to the rude occupants who really knew it better than he. What of architectural beauty I now see, I know has gradually grown from within outward, out of the necessities and character of the indweller, who is the only builder,—out of some unconscious truthfulness, and nobleness, without ever a thought for the appearance and whatever additional beauty of this kind is destined to be produced will be preceded by a like unconscious beauty of life. The most interesting dwellings in this country, as the painter knows, are the most unpretending, humble log huts and cottages of the poor commonly; it is the life of the inhabitants whose shells they are, and not any peculiarity in their surfaces merely, which makes them *picturesque*: and equally interesting will be the citizen's suburban box, when his life shall be as simple and as agreeable to the imagination and there is as little straining after effect in the style of his dwelling. A great proportion of architectural ornaments are literally hollow, and a September gale would strip them off, like borrowed plumes, without injury to the substantials. They can do without *architecture* who have no olives nor wines in the cellar. What if an equal ado were made about the ornaments of style in literature, and the architects of our Bibles spent as much time about their cornices as the architects of our churches do? So are made the *belles-lettres* and the *beaux-arts* and their professors. Much it concerns a man, forsooth, how a few sticks are slanted over him or under him, and what colors are daubed upon his box. It would signify somewhat, if, in any earnest sense, *he* slanted them and daubed it; but the spirit having departed out of the tenant, it is of a piece with constructing his own coffin,—the architecture of the grave,—and "carpenter" is but another name for "coffin-maker." One man says, in his despair or indifference to life, take up a handful of the earth at your feet, and paint your house that color. Is he thinking of his last and narrow house? Toss up a copper for it as well. What an abundance of leisure he must have! Why do you take up a handful of dirt? Better paint your house your own complexion; let it turn pale or blush for you. An enterprise to improve the style of cottage architecture! When you have got my ornaments ready, I will wear them.

10   Before winter I built a chimney, and shingled the sides of my house, which were already impervious to rain, with imperfect and sappy shingles made of the first slice of the log, whose edges I was obliged to straighten with a plane.

I have thus a tight shingled and plastered house, ten feet wide by fifteen long, and eight-feet posts, with a garret and a closet, a large window on each side, two trap-doors, one door at the end, and a brick fireplace opposite. The exact cost of my house, paying the usual price for such materials as I used, but not counting the work, all of which was done by myself, was as follows; and I give the details because very few are able to tell exactly what their houses cost, and fewer still, if any, the separate cost of the various materials which compose them:—

Boards	$8 03½,	mostly shanty boards.
Refuse shingles for roof and sides	4 00	
Laths	1 25	
Two second-hand windows with glass	2 43	
One thousand old brick .	4 00	
Two casks of lime	2 40	That was high.
Hair	0 31	More than I needed.
Mantle-tree iron	0 15	
Nails	3 90	
Hinges and screws	0 14	
Latch	0 10	
Chalk	0 01	
Transportation	1 40	{ I carried a good part on my back.
In all	$28 12½	

These are all the materials, excepting the timber, stones, and sand, which I claimed by squatter's right. I have also a small woodshed adjoining, made chiefly of the stuff which was left after building the house.

I intend to build me a house which will surpass any on the main street in Concord in grandeur and luxury, as soon as it pleases me as much and will cost me no more than my present one.

I thus found that the student who wishes for a shelter can obtain one for a lifetime at an expense not greater than the rent which he now pays annually. If I seem to boast more than is becoming, my excuse is that I brag for humanity rather than for myself; and my shortcomings and inconsistencies do not affect the truth of my statement. Notwithstanding much cant and hypocrisy,—chaff which I find it difficult to separate from my wheat, but for which I am as sorry as any man,—I will breathe freely and stretch myself in this respect, it is such a relief to both the moral and physical system; and I am resolved that I will not through humility become the devil's attorney. I will endeavor to speak a good word for the truth. At Cambridge College the mere rent of a student's room, which is only a little larger than my own, is thirty dollars each year, though the corporation had the advantage of building thirty-two side by side and under one roof, and the occupant suffers the inconvenience of many and noisy neighbors, and perhaps a residence in the fourth story. I cannot but think that if we had more true wisdom in these respects, not only less education would be needed, because, forsooth, more would already have been acquired, but the pecuniary expense of getting an education would in a great measure vanish. Those conveniences which the student requires at Cambridge or elsewhere cost him or somebody else ten times as great a sacrifice of life as they would with proper management on both sides. Those things for which the most money is demanded are never the things which the student most wants. Tuition, for instance, is an important item in the term bill, while for the far more valuable education which he gets by associating with the most cultivated of his contemporaries no charge is made. The mode of founding a college is, commonly, to get up a subscription of dollars and cents, and then, following blindly the principles of a division of labor to its extreme,—a principle which should never be followed but with circumspection,—to call in a contractor who makes this a subject of speculation, and he employs Irishmen or other operatives actually to lay the foundations, while the students that are to be are said to be fitting themselves for it; and for these oversights successive generations have to pay. I think that it would be *better than this,* for the students, or those who desire to be benefited by it, even to lay the foundation themselves. The student who secures his coveted leisure and retirement by systematically shirking any labor necessary to man obtains but an ignoble and unprofitable leisure, defrauding himself of the experience which alone can make leisure fruitful. "But," says one, "you do not mean that the students should go to work with their hands instead of their heads?" I do not mean that exactly, but I mean something which he might think a good deal like that; I mean that they should not *play* life, or *study* it merely, while the community supports them at this expensive game, but earnestly *live* it from beginning to end. How could youths better learn to live than by at once trying the experiment of living?

SUGGESTIONS FOR WRITING

1. Do you think that Thomas More would find a kindred spirit in Thoreau? Write an essay that explores similarities among the attitudes and ideas of More and Thoreau.
2. Thoreau tells us with a straight face that he first occupied his house on July 4th, that is, on Independence Day. Write an essay that shows by the analysis of other examples how this detail is representative of Thoreau's humor and the uses he makes of humor generally.

3. Thoreau sometimes seems to speak of the two Irish immigrants in the passage as though they were members of a different race from a different world. Write an essay that explains how Thoreau uses the economic values and assumptions of the two figures as a means to better express his own by an implied extremity of contrast.

The Time Machine   1895

H. G. WELLS

H. G. Wells (1866–1946) was born in England to a father who combined shopkeeping with professional cricket and a mother who sometimes worked as a housekeeper. After his father's business failed, Wells was apprenticed to a clothing shop owner. He started his rise from trade to the world of letters as a teacher-pupil at a grammar school and as a brilliant student was able to obtain a university scholarship in London to study science under the great Victorian scientist T. H. Huxley. From 1893 Wells became a fulltime writer, going on to write an enormously popular group of works in philosophically speculative science fiction of which The Time Machine *(1895) is the first. It was admired not only by the reading public for popular fiction, but by the most distinguished novelist of the time, Henry James, who became a friend.*

*The Time Machine *speculates on possible future implications of Darwin's theory of natural selection (Chapter 1) and foresees humanity evolving into two species that mirror Marx's division of bourgeois and working class (Chapter 2). The two classes have become the beautiful but frail and helpless Eloi who have degenerated into "little people," and the ape-like Morlocks, who live underground and provide for the material needs of the Eloi, but only for the purpose of harvesting them as a food supply. We join the Time Traveler in 802,701 A.D. as he attempts to regain his machine accompanied by the Eloi, Weena, whom he has rescued and befriended.*

X

When the Night Came

"Now, indeed, I seemed in a worse case than before. Hitherto, except during my night's anguish at the loss of the Time Machine, I had felt a sustaining hope of ultimate escape, but that hope was staggered by these new discoveries. Hitherto I had merely thought myself impeded by the childish simplicity of the little people, and by some unknown forces which I had only to understand to overcome; but there was an altogether new element in the sickening quality of the Morlocks—a something inhuman and malign. Instinctively I loathed them. Before, I had felt as a man might feel who had fallen into a pit: my concern was with the pit and how to get out of it. Now I felt like a beast in a trap, whose enemy would come upon him soon.

"The enemy I dreaded may surprise you. It was the darkness of the new moon. Weena had put this into my head by some at first incomprehensible remarks about the Dark Nights. It was not now such a very difficult problem to guess what the coming Dark Nights might mean. The moon was on the wane: each night there was a longer interval of darkness. And I now understood to some slight degree at least the reason of the fear of the little upper-world people for the dark. I wondered vaguely what foul villainy it might be that the Morlocks did under the new moon. I felt pretty sure now that my second hypothesis was all wrong. The upper-world people might once have been the favoured aristocracy, and the Morlocks their mechanical servants; but that had long since passed away. The two species that had resulted from the evolution of man were sliding down towards, or had already arrived at, an altogether new relationship. The Eloi, like the Carlovignan kings, had decayed to a mere beautiful futility. They still possessed the earth on sufferance: since the Morlocks, subterranean for innumerable genera-tions, had come at last to find the daylit surface intolerable. And the Morlocks made their garments, I inferred, and maintained them in their habitual needs, perhaps through the survival of an old habit of service. They did it as a standing horse paws with his foot, or as a man enjoys killing animals in sport: because ancient and departed necessities had impressed it on the organism. But, clearly, the old order was already in part reversed. The Nemesis of the delicate ones was creeping on apace. Ages ago, thousands of generations ago, man had thrust his brother man out of the ease and the sunshine. And now that brother was coming back—changed! Already the Eloi had begun to learn one old lesson anew. They were becoming re-acquainted with Fear. And suddenly there came into my head the memory of the meat I had seen in the under-world. It seemed odd how it floated into my mind: not stirred up as it were by the current of my meditations, but coming in almost like a question from outside. I tried to recall the form of it. I had a vague sense of something familiar, but I could not tell what it was at the time:

"Still, however helpless the little people in the presence of their mysterious Fear, I was differently constituted. I came out of this age of ours, this ripe prime of the human race, when Fear does not paralyze and mystery has lost its terrors. I at least would defend myself. Without further delay I determined to make myself arms and a fastness where I might sleep. With that refuge as a base, I could face this strange world with some of that confidence I had lost in realizing to what creatures night by night I lay exposed. I felt I could never sleep again until my bed was secure from them. I shuddered with horror to think how they must already have examined me.

"I wandered during the afternoon along the valley of the Thames, but found nothing that commended itself to my mind as inaccessible. All the buildings and trees seemed easily practicable to such dexterous climbers as the Morlocks, to judge by their wells, must be. Then the tall pinnacles of the Palace of Green Porcelain and the polished gleam of its walls came back to my memory; and in the evening, taking Weena like a child upon my shoulder, I went up the hills towards the south-west. The distance, I had reckoned, was seven or eight miles, but it must have been nearer eighteen. I had first seen the place on a moist afternoon when distances are deceptively diminished. In addition, the heel of one of my shoes was loose, and a nail was working through the sole—they were comfortable old shoes I wore about indoors—so that I was lame. And it was already long past sunset when I came in sight of the palace, silhouetted black against the pale yellow of the sky.

5 "Weena had been hugely delighted when I began to carry her, but after a time she desired me to let her down, and ran along by the side of me, occasionally darting off on either hand to pick flowers to stick in my pockets. My pockets had always puzzled Weena, but at the last she had concluded that they were an eccentric kind of vases for floral decoration. At least she utilized them for that purpose. And that reminds me! In changing my jacket I found . . ."

The Time Traveller paused, put his hand into his pocket, and silently placed two withered flowers, not unlike very large white mallows, upon the little table. Then he resumed his narrative.

"As the hush of evening crept over the world and we proceeded over the hill crest towards Wimbledon, Weena grew tired and wanted to return to the house of grey stone. But I pointed out the distant pinnacles of the Palace of Green Porcelain to her, and contrived to make her understand that we were seeking a refuge there from her Fear. . . .

. . ."I awakened Weena, and we went down into the wood, now green and pleasant instead of black and forbidding. We found some fruit wherewith to break our fast. We soon met others of the dainty ones, laughing and dancing in the sunlight as though there was no such thing in nature as the night. And then I thought once more of the meat that I had been. I felt assured now of what it was, and from the bottom of my heart I pitied this last feeble rill from the great flood of humanity. Clearly, at some time in the Long-Ago of human decay the Morlocks' food had run short. Possibly they had lived on rats and such like vermin. Even now man is far less discriminating and exclusive in his food than he was—far less than any monkey. His prejudice against human flesh is no deep-seated instinct. And so these inhuman sons of men—! I tried to look at the thing in a scientific spirit. After all, they were less human and more remote than our cannibal ancestors of three or four thousand years ago. And the intelligence that would have made this state of things a torment had gone. Why should I trouble myself? These Eloi were mere fatted cattle, which the ant-like Morlocks preserved and preyed upon—probably saw to the breeding of. And there was Weena dancing at my side!

"Then I tried to preserve myself from the horror that was coming upon me, by regarding it as a rigorous punishment of human selfishness. Man had been content to live in ease and delight upon the labours of his fellow-man, had taken Necessity as his watchword and excuse, and in the fulness of time Necessity had come home to him. I even tried a Carlyle-like scorn of this wretched aristocracy-in-decay. But this attitude of mind was impossible. However great their intellectual degradation, the Eloi had kept too much of the human form not to claim my sympathy, and to make me perforce a sharer in their degradation and their Fear.

10 "I had at that time very vague ideas as to the course I should pursue. My first was to secure some safe place of refuge, and to make myself such arms of metal or stone as I could contrive. That necessity was immediate. In the next place, I hoped to procure some means of fire, so that I should have the weapon of a torch at hand, for nothing, I knew, would be more efficient against these Morlocks. Then I wanted to arrange some contrivance to break open the doors of bronze under the White Sphinx. I had in mind a battering-ram. I had a persuasion that if I could enter these doors and carry a blaze of light before me I should discover the Time Machine and escape. I could not imagine the Morlocks were strong enough to move it far away. Weena I had resolved to bring with me to our own time. And turning such schemes over in my mind I pursued our way towards the building which my fancy had chosen as our dwelling.

"I grieved to think how brief the dream of the human intellect had been. It had committed suicide. It had set itself steadfastly towards comfort and ease, a balanced society with security and permanency as its watchword, it had attained its hopes—to come to this at last. Once, life and property must have reached almost absolute safety. The rich had been assured of his wealth and comfort, the toiler assured of his life and work. No doubt in that perfect world there had been no unemployed problem, no social question left unsolved. And a great quiet had followed.

"It is a law of nature we overlook, that intellectual versatility is the compensation for change, danger, and trouble. An animal perfectly in harmony with its environment is a perfect mechanism. Nature never appeals to intelligence until habit and instinct are useless. There is no intelligence where there is no change and no need of change. Only those animals partake of intelligence that have to meet a huge variety of needs and dangers.

"So, as I see it, the upper-world man had drifted towards his feeble prettiness, and the under-world to mere mechanical industry. But that perfect state had lacked one thing even for mechanical perfection—absolute permanency. Apparently as time went on, the feeling of the under-world, however it was effected, had become disjointed. Mother Necessity, who had been staved off for a few thousand years, came back again, and she began below. The under-world being in contact with machinery, which, however perfect, still needs some little thought outside habit, had probably retained perforce rather more initiative, if less of every other human character, than the upper. And when other meat failed them, they turned to what old habit had hitherto forbidden. So I say I saw it in my last view of the world of Eight Hundred and Two Thousand Seven Hundred and One. It may be as wrong an explanation as mortal wit could invent. It is how the thing shaped itself to me, and as that I give it to you.

SUGGESTIONS FOR WRITING

1. It seems clear that the future changes imagined in *The Time Machine* come from economic causes linked to biological ones. Write an essay that recounts in your own words how it is H. G. Wells imagines that human evolution might continue.

2. Though economic class struggle seems important in Wells's notions of a possible future history, that struggle does not seem entirely Marxist in its

nature. Write an essay in which you compare and contrast the relations between economic classes as imagined by Karl Marx and H. G. Wells.

3. Jorge Luis Borges has noted the striking strangeness of one detail—the flowers from the future that the Time Traveler shows to his listeners. Do they seem strange to you? Write an essay that explores the implications for time involved in the existence of these flowers in the narrative.

Herland   1915

CHARLOTTE PERKINS GILMAN

Charlotte Perkins Gilman (1860–1935), perhaps most famous for her short story "The Yellow Wallpaper," is widely considered the most important author in the women's movement of the early twentieth century. She energetically maintained a rigorous program of self-education and social criticism throughout a long and troubled life that began with the desertion of her father and included marriage troubles. She is represented in this book by two selections, the one below from her utopian fantasy Herland *(1915) and the essay from* Women and Economics *(1898) in Chapter 2.*

A group of men happen on the isolated country of Herland where long ago all the males have been killed. Miraculously, the remaining women have evolved in such a way as to reproduce themselves without any need of men, and in the excerpt below the resulting feminist utopia is explained to the sometimes dubious male explorers.

IT IS NO USE for me to try to piece out this account with adventures. If the people who read it are not interested in these amazing women and their history, they will not be interested at all.

As for us—three young men to a whole landful of women—what could we do? We did get away, as described, and were peacefully brought back again without, as Terry complained, even the satisfaction of hitting anybody.

There were no adventures because there was nothing to fight. There were no wild beasts in the country and very few tame ones. Of these I might as well stop to describe the one common pet of the country. Cats, of course. But such cats!

What do you suppose these lady Burbanks had done with their cats? By the most prolonged and careful selection and exclusion they had developed a race of cats that did not sing! That's a fact.

5   The most those poor dumb brutes could do was to make a kind of squeak when they were hungry or wanted the door open; and, of course, to purr, and make the various mother-noises to their kittens.

Moreover they had ceased to kill birds. They were rigorously bred to destroy mice and moles and all such enemies of the food supply; but the birds were numerous and safe.

While we were discussing birds, Terry asked them if they used feathers for their hats, and they seemed amused at the idea. He made a few sketches of our women's hats, with plumes and quills and those various tickling things that stick out so far; and they were eagerly interested, as at everything about our women.

As for them, they said they only wore hats for shade when working in the sun; and those were big light straw hats, something like those used in China and Japan. In cold weather they wore caps or hoods.

"But for decorative purposes—don't you think they would be becoming?" pursued Terry, making a picture as [best] he could of a lady with a plumed straw hat.

10   They by no means agreed to that, asking quite simply if the men wore the same kind. We hastened to assure her that they did not—and drew for them our kind of headgear.

"And do no men wear feathers in their hats?"

"Only Indians," Jeff explained, "savages, you know." And he sketched a warbonnet to show them.

"And soldiers," I added, drawing a military hat with plumes.

They never expressed horror or disapproval, nor indeed much surprise—just a keen interest. And the notes they made!—miles of them!

15   But to return to our pussy-cats. We were a good deal impressed by this achievement in breeding, and when they questioned us—I can tell you we were well pumped for information—we told of what had been done for dogs and horses and cattle, but that there was no effort applied to cats, except for show purposes.

I wish I could represent the kind, quiet, steady, ingenious way they questioned us. It was not just curiosity—they weren't a bit more curious about us than we were about them, if as much. But they were bent on understanding our kind of civilization and their lines of interrogation would gradually surround us and drive us in till we found ourselves up against some admissions we did not want to make.

"Are all these breeds of dogs you have made useful?" they asked.

"Oh—useful! Why, the hunting dogs and watch-dogs and sheep-dogs are useful—and sled-dogs of course!—and ratters, I suppose, but we don't keep dogs for their *usefulness*. The dog is 'the friend of men,' we say—we love them."

That they understood. "We love our cats that way. They surely are our friends, and helpers too. You can see how intelligent and affection-ate they are."

20   It was a fact. I'd never seen such cats, except in a few rare instances. Big, handsome silky things, friendly with everyone and devotedly attached to their special owners.

"You must have a heartbreaking time drowning kittens," we suggested.

But they said: "Oh, no! You see we care for them as you do for your valuable cattle. The fathers are few compared to the mothers, just a few very fine ones in each town; they live quite happily in walled gardens and the houses of their friends. But they only have a mating season once a year."

"Rather hard on Thomas, isn't it?" suggested Terry.

"Oh, no—truly! You see it is many centuries that we have been breeding the kind of cats we wanted. They are healthy and happy and friendly, as you see. How do you manage with your dogs? Do you keep them in pairs, or segregate the fathers, or what?"

25   Then we explained that—well, that it wasn't a question of fathers exactly; that nobody wanted a—a mother dog; that, well, that practi-cally all our dogs were males—there was only a very small percentage of females allowed to live.

Then Zava, observing Terry with her grave sweet smile, quoted back at him: "Rather hard on Thomas, isn't it? Do they enjoy it—living with-out mates? Are your dogs as uniformly healthy and sweet-tempered as our cats?"

Jeff laughed, eyeing Terry mischievously. As a matter of fact we began to feel Jeff something of a traitor—he so often flopped over and took their side of things; also his medical knowledge gave him a different point of view somehow.

"I'm sorry to admit," he told them, "that the dog, with us, is the most diseased of any animal—next to man. And as to temper—there are always some dogs who bite people[,] especially children."

That was pure malice. You see children were the—the *raison d'être* in this country. All our interlocutors sat up straight at once. They were still gentle, still restrained, but there was a note of deep amazement in their voices.

30 "Do we understand that you keep an animal—an unmated male animal—that bites children? About how many are there of them, please?"

"Thousands—in a large city," said Jeff, "and nearly every family has one in the country."

Terry broke in at this. "You must not imagine they are all dangerous—it's not one in a hundred that ever bites anybody. Why, they are the best friends of the children—a boy doesn't have half a chance that hasn't a dog to play with!"

"And the girls?" asked Somel.

"Oh—girls—why they like them too," he said, but his voice flattened a little. They always noticed little things like that, we found later.

Little by little they wrung from us the fact that the friend of man, in the city, was a prisoner; was taken out for his meager exercise on a leash; was liable not only to many diseases, but to the one destroying horror of rabies, and, in many cases, for the safety of the citizens, he had to go muzzled. Jeff maliciously added vivid instances he had known or read of injury and death from mad dogs.

35 They did not scold or fuss about it. Calm as judges, those women were. But they made notes; Moadine read them to us.

"Please tell me if I have the facts correct," she said. "In your country—and in others too?"

"Yes," we admitted, "in most civilized countries."

"In most civilized countries a kind of animal is kept which is no longer useful—"

"They are a protection," Terry insisted. "They bark if burglars try to get in."

40 Then she made notes of "burglars" and went on: "because of the love which people bear to this animal."

Zava interrupted here. "Is it the men or the women who love this animal so much?"

"Both!" insisted Terry.

"Equally?" she inquired.

And Jeff said: "Nonsense, Terry—you know men like dogs better than women do—as a whole."

45 "Because they love it so much—especially men. This animal is kept shut up, or chained."

"Why?" suddenly asked Somel. "We keep our father cats shut up because we do not want too much fathering; but they are not chained—they have large grounds to run in."

"A valuable dog would be stolen if he was let loose," I said. "We put collars on them, with the owner's name, in case they do stray. Besides, they get into fights—a valuable dog might easily be killed by a bigger one."

"I see," she said. "They fight when they meet—is that common?" We admitted that it was.

"They are kept shut up, or chained." She paused again, and asked, "Is not a dog fond/of running? Are they not built for speed?" That we admitted too, and Jeff, still malicious, enlightened them farther.

50 "I've always thought it was a pathetic sight, both ways—to see a man or a woman taking a dog to walk—at the end of a string."

"Have you bred them to be as neat in their habits as cats are?" was the next question. And when Jeff told them of the effect of dogs on sidewalk merchandise and the streets generally, they found it hard to believe.

You see their country was as neat as a Dutch kitchen, and as to sanitation—but I might as well start in now with as much as I can remember of the history of this amazing country before further description.

And I'll summarize here a bit as to our opportunities for learning it. I will not try to repeat the careful, detailed account I lost; I'll just say that we were kept in that fortress a good six months all told; and after that, three in a pleasant enough city where—to Terry's infinite disgust—there were only "Colonels" and little children—no young women whatever. Then we were under surveillance for three more—always with a tutor or a guard or both. But those months were pleasant because we were really getting acquainted with the girls. That was a chapter!—or will be—I will try to do justice to it.

We learned their language pretty thoroughly—had to; and they learned ours much more quickly and used it to hasten our own studies.

55 Jeff, who was never without reading matter of some sort, had two little books with him, a novel, and a little anthology of verse; and I had one of those pocket encyclopedias—a fat little thing, bursting with facts. These were used in our education—and theirs. Then as soon as we were up to it, they furnished us with plenty of their own books, and I went in for the history part—I wanted to understand the genesis of this miracle of theirs.

And this is what happened, according to their records:

As to geography—at about the time of the Christian era this land had a free passage to the sea. I'm not saying where, for good reasons. But there was a fairly easy pass through that wall of mountains behind us, and there is no doubt in my mind that these people were of Aryan stock, and were once in contact with the best civilization of the old world. They were "white," but somewhat darker than our northern races because of their constant exposure to sun and air.

The country was far larger then, including much land beyond the pass, and a strip of coast. They had ships, commerce, an army, a king—for at that time they were what they so calmly called us—a bi-sexual race.

What happened to them first was merely a succession of historic misfortunes such as have befallen other nations often enough. They were decimated by war, driven up from their coast line till finally the reduced population with many of the men killed in battle, occupied this hinterland, and defended it for years, in the mountain passes. Where it was open to any possible attack from below they strengthened the natural defences so that it became unscalably secure, as we found it.

60   They were a polygamous people, and a slave-holding people, like all of their time; and during the generation or two of this struggle to defend their mountain home they built the fortresses, such as the one we were held in, and other of their oldest buildings, some still in use. Nothing but earthquakes could destroy such architecture—huge solid blocks, holding by their own weight. They must have had efficient workmen and enough of them in those days.

They made a brave fight for their existence, but no nation can stand up against what the steamship companies call "an act of God." While the whole fighting force was doing its best to defend their mountain pathway, there occurred a volcanic outburst, with some local tremors, and the result was the complete filling up of the pass—their only outlet. Instead of a passage, a new ridge, sheer and high, stood between them and the sea; they were walled in, and beneath that wall lay their whole little army. Very few men were left alive, save the slaves; and these now seized their opportunity, rose in revolt, killed their remaining masters even to the youngest boy, killed the old women too, and the mothers, intending to take possession of the country with the remaining young women and girls.

But this succession of misfortunes was too much for those infuriated virgins. There were many of them, and but few of these would be masters, so the young women, instead of submitting, rose in sheer desperation, and slew their brutal conquerors.

This sounds like Titus Andronicus, I know, but that is their account. I suppose they were about crazy—can you blame them?

There was literally no one left on this beautiful high garden land but a bunch of hysterical girls and some older slave women.

65   That was about two thousand years ago.

At first there was a period of sheer despair. The mountains towered between them and their old enemies, but also between them and escape. There was no way up or down or out—they simply had to stay there. Some were for suicide, but not the majority. They must have been a plucky lot, as a whole, and they decided to live—as long as they did live. Of course they had hope, as youth must, that something would happen to change their fate.

So they set to work, to bury the dead, to plow and sow, to care for one another.

Speaking of burying the dead, I will set down while I think of it, that they had adopted cremation about the thirteenth century, for the same reason that they had left off raising cattle—they could not spare the room. They were much surprised to learn that we were still burying—asked our reasons for it, and were much dissatisfied with what we gave. We told them of the belief in the resurrection of the body, and they asked if our God was not as well able to resurrect from ashes as from long corruption. We told them of how people thought it repugnant to have their loved ones burn, and they asked if it was less repugnant to have them decay. They were inconveniently reasonable, those women.

Well—that original bunch of girls set to work to clean up the place and make their livings as best they could. Some of the remaining slave women rendered invaluable service, teaching such trades as they knew. They had such records as were then kept, all the tools and implements of the time, and a most fertile land to work in.

70   There were a handful of the younger matrons who had escaped slaughter, and a few babies were born after the cataclysm—but only two boys and they both died.

For five or ten years they worked together, growing stronger and wiser and more and more mutually attached, and then the miracle happened—one of these young women bore a child. Of course they all thought there must be a man somewhere, but none was found. Then they decided it must be a direct gift from the gods, and placed the proud mother in the Temple of Maaia—their Goddess of Motherhood—under strict watch. And there, as years passed, this wonder-woman bore child after child, five of them—all girls.

I did my best, keenly interested as I have always been in sociology and social psychology, to reconstruct in my mind the real position of these ancient women. There were some five or six hundred of them, and they were harembred; yet for the few preceding generations they had been reared in the atmosphere of such heroic struggle that the stock must have been toughened somewhat. Left alone in that terrific orphanhood, they had clung together, supporting one another and their little sisters, and developing unknown powers in the stress of new necessity. To this pain-hardened and work-strengthened group, who had lost not only the love and care of parents, but the hope of ever having children of their own, there now dawned the new hope.

Here at last was Motherhood, and though it was not for all of them personally, it might—if the Power was inherited—found here a new race.

It may be imagined how those five Daughters of Maaia, Children of the Temple, Mothers of the Future—they had all the titles that love and hope and reverence could give—were reared. The whole little nation of women surrounded them with loving service, and waited, between a boundless hope and an as boundless despair, to see if they too would be Mothers.

75   And they were! As fast as they reached the age of twenty-five they began bearing. Each of them, like her mother, bore five daughters. Presently there were twenty-five New Women, Mothers in their own right, and the whole spirit of the country changed from mourning and mere courageous resignation, to proud joy. The older women, those who remembered men, died off; the youngest of all the first lot of course died too, after a while, and by that time there were left one hundred and fifty-five parthenogenetic women, founding a new race.

They inherited all that the devoted care of that declining band of original ones could leave them. Their little country was quite safe. Their farms and gardens were all in full production. Such industries as they had were in careful order. The records of their past were all preserved, and for years the older women had spent their time in the best teaching they were capable of, that they might leave to the little group of sisters and mothers all they possessed of skill and knowledge.

There you have the start of Herland! One family, all descended from one mother! She lived to be a hundred years old; lived to see her hundred and twenty-five great-granddaughters born; lived as Queen-Priestess-Mother of them all; and died with a noble pride and a fuller joy than perhaps any human soul has ever known—she alone had founded a new race!

The first five daughters had grown up in an atmosphere of holy calm, of awed watchful waiting, of breathless prayer. To them the longed-for Motherhood was not only a personal joy, but a nation's hope. Their twenty-five daughters in turn, with a stronger hope, a richer, wider outlook, with the devoted love and care of all the surviving population, grew up as a holy sisterhood, their whole ardent youth looking forward to their great office. And at last they were left alone; the white-haired First Mother was gone, and this one family, five sisters, twenty-five first cousins, and a hundred and twenty-five second cousins, began a new race.

Here you have human beings, unquestionably, but what we were slow in understanding was how these ultra-women, inheriting only from women, had eliminated not only certain masculine characteristics, which of course we did not look for; but so much of what we had always thought essentially feminine.

80   The tradition of men as guardians and protectors had quite died out. These stalwart virgins had no men to fear and therefore no need of protection. As to wild beasts—there were none in their sheltered land.

The power of mother-love, that maternal instinct we so highly laud, was theirs of course, raised to its highest power; and a sister-love which, even while recognizing the actual relationship, we found it hard to credit.

Terry, incredulous, even contemptuous, when we were alone, refused to believe the story. "A lot of traditions as old as Herodotus—and about as trustworthy!" he said. "It's likely women—just a pack of women—would have hung together like that! We all know women can't organize—that they scrap like anything—are frightfully jealous."

"But these New Ladies didn't have anyone to be jealous of, remember," drawled Jeff.

"That's a likely story," Terry sneered.

85   "Why don't you invent a likelier one?" I asked him. "Here *are* the women—nothing but women, and you admit yourself there's no trace of a man in the country." This was after we had been about a good deal.

"I'll admit that," he growled. "And it's a big miss, too. There's not only no fun without 'em—no real sport—no competition: but these women aren't *womanly*. You know they aren't."

That kind of talk always set Jeff going; and I gradually grew to side with him.

"Then you don't call a breed of women whose one concern is Motherhood—womanly?" he asked.

"Indeed I don't," snapped Terry. "What does a man care for motherhood—when he hasn't a ghost of a chance at fatherhood? And besides—what's the good of talking sentiment when we are just men together? What a man wants of women is a good deal more than this 'motherhood'!"

We were as patient as possible with Terry. He had lived about nine months among the Colonels when he made that outburst; and with no chance at any more strenuous excitement than our gymnastics gave us—save for our escape fiasco. I don't suppose Terry had ever lived so long with neither Love, Combat, nor Danger to employ his superabundant energies, and he was irritable. Neither Jeff nor I found it so wearing. I was so much interested intellectually that our confinement did not wear on me; and as for Jeff, bless his heart!—he enjoyed the society of that tutor of his almost as much as if she had been a girl—I don't know but more.

90   As to Terry's criticism, it was true. These women, whose essential distinction of Motherhood was the dominant note of their whole culture, were strikingly deficient in what we call "femininity." This led me very promptly to the conviction that these "feminine charms" we are so fond of are not feminine at all, but mere reflected masculinity—developed to please us because they had to please us—and in no way essential to the real fulfillment of their great process. But Terry came to no such conclusion.

"Just you wait till I get out!" he muttered.

Then we both cautioned him. "Look here, Terry, my boy! You be careful! They've been mighty good to us—but do you remember the anaesthesia? If you do any mischief in this virgin land, beware of the vengeance of the Maiden Aunts! Come, be a man! It won't be forever."

To return to the history:

They began at once to plan and build for their children, all the Strength and intelligence of the whole of them devoted to that one thing. Each girl, of course, was reared in full knowledge of her Crowning

Office, and they had, even then, very high ideas of the moulding powers of the mother as well as those of education.

95   Such high ideals as they had! Beauty, Health, Strength, Intellect, Goodness—for these they prayed and worked.

They had no enemies; they themselves were all sisters and friends; the land was fair before them, and a great Future began to form itself in their minds.

The religion they had to begin with was much like that of old Greece—a number of gods and goddesses; but they lost all interest in deities of war and plunder, and gradually centered on their Mother Goddess altogether. Then, as they grew more intelligent, this had turned into a sort of Maternal Pantheism.

Here was Mother Earth, bearing fruit. All that they are was fruit of motherhood, from seed or egg or their product. By motherhood they were born and by motherhood they lived—life was, to them, just the long cycle of motherhood.

But very early they recognized the need of improvement as well as of mere repetition, and devoted their combined intelligence to that problem—how to make the best kind of people. First this was merely the hope of bearing better ones, and then they recognized that however the children differed at birth, the real growth lay later—through education.

100   Then things began to hum.

As I learned more and more to appreciate what these women had accomplished, the less proud I was of what we, with all our manhood, had done.

You see, they had had no wars. They had had no kings, and no priests, and no aristocracies. They were sisters, and as they grew, they grew together; not by competition, but by united action.

We tried to put in a good word for competition, and they were keenly interested. Indeed we soon found, from their earnest questions of us, that they were prepared to believe our world must be better than theirs. They were not sure; they wanted to know; but there was no such arrogance about them as might have been expected.

We rather spread ourselves, telling of the advantages of competition; how it developed fine qualities; that without it there would be "no stimulus to industry." Terry was very strong on that point.

105   "No stimulus to industry," they repeated, with that puzzled look we had learned to know so well. "*Stimulus? To Industry?* But don't you *like* to work?"

"No man would work unless he had to," Terry declared.

"Oh, no *man!* You mean that is one of your sex distinctions?"

"No, indeed!" he said hastily. "No one, I mean, man or woman, would work without incentive. Competition is the—the motor power, you see."

"It is not with us," they explained gently, "so it is hard for us to understand. Do you mean, for instance, that with you no mother would work for her children without the stimulus of competition?"

110   No, he admitted that he did not mean that. Mothers, he supposed, would of course work for their children in the home; but the world's work was different—that had to be done by men, and required the competitive element.

All our teachers were eagerly interested.

"We want so much to know—you have the whole world to tell us of, and we have only our little land! And there are two of you—the two sexes—to love and help one another. It must be a rich and wonderful world. Tell us—what is the work of the world,—that men do—which we have not here?"

"Oh, everything," Terry said, grandly. "The men do everything, with us." He squared his broad shoulders and lifted his chest. "We do not allow our women to work. Women are loved—idolized—honored— kept in the home to care for the children."

"What is 'the home'?" asked Somel a little wistfully.

115   But Zava begged: "Tell me first, do no women work, really?"

"Why, yes," Terry admitted. "Some have to, of the poorer sort."

"About how many—in your country?"

"About seven or eight million," said Jeff, as mischievous as ever.

SUGGESTIONS FOR WRITING

1. Write an essay that explores some of the ways in which the treatment of cats becomes representative of other ideas about evolution expressed in *Herland.*

2. In paragraph 73 the narrator says: "Here at last was Motherhood." Why "at last?" Write an essay in which you explore the significances of the phrase "at last" given by the context of the story as a whole.

3. Write an essay that describes some of the ways that "masculine" and "feminine" traits imagined in Herland are seen by the characters in the story as different from those traits referred to by the same names in our world.

Fahrenheit 451 1953

RAY BRADBURY

Ray Bradbury was born in 1922 and has been considered America's foremost writer of science fiction in the twentieth century. He was raised in Waukegan, Illinois and spent a large part of his early youth absorbed in a wide program of self-directed reading at the local college library. His family eventually settled in Los Angeles where Bradbury graduated from high school in 1938. Choosing life as a writer over higher education, he immediately began to publish science fiction stories in pulp magazines. After wide success as an author in the 1950s, he began to work also in the new medium of television and later went on to help Walt Disney to design the futuristic theme park Epcot. For his work in movies, Bradbury has been given a star on the Hollywood Walk of Fame.

His still popular novel Fahrenheit 451 *(1953) depicts a futuristic dystopian world of censorship where "firemen" are charged with burning books. In this excerpt the policy is defended by the fire captain Beatty who visits the hero, Montag, at home.*

Captain Beatty sat down in the most comfortable chair with a peaceful look on his ruddy face. He took time to prepare and light his brass pipe and puff out a great smoke cloud. "Just thought I'd come by and see how the sick man is."

"How'd you guess?"

Beatty smiled his smile which showed the candy pinkness of his gums and the tiny candy whiteness of his teeth. "I've seen it all. You were going to call for a night off."

Montag sat in bed.

5   "Well," said Beatty, "*take* the night off!" He examined his eternal matchbox, the lid of which said GUARANTEED: ONE MILLION LIGHTS IN THIS IGNITER, and began to strike the chemical match abstractedly, blow out, strike, blow out strike, speak a few words, blow out. He looked at the flame. He blew, he looked at the smoke. "When will you be well?"

"Tomorrow. The next day maybe. First of the week."

Beatty puffed his pipe. "Every fireman, sooner or later, hits this. They only need understanding, to know how the wheels run. Need to know the history of our profession. They don't feed it to rookies like they used to. Damn shame." Puff. "Only fire chiefs remember it now." Puff. "I'll let you in on it."

Mildred fidgeted.

Beatty took a full minute to settle himself in and think back for what he wanted to say.

10 "When did it all start, you ask, this job of ours, how did it come about, where, when? Well, I'd say it really got started around about a thing called the Civil War. Even though our rule book claims it was founded earlier. The fact is we didn't get along well until photography came into its own. Then—motion pictures in the early twentieth century. Radio. Television. Things began to have *mass*."

Montag sat in bed, not moving.

"And because they had mass, they became simpler," said Beatty. "Once, books appealed to a few people, here, there, everywhere. They could afford to be different. The world was roomy. But then the world got full of eyes and elbows and mouths. Double, triple, quadruple population. Films and radios, magazines, books leveled down to a sort of paste pudding norm, do you follow me?"

"I think so."

Beatty peered at the smoke pattern he had put out on the air. "Picture it. Nineteenth-century man with his horses, dogs, carts, slow motion. Then, in the twentieth century, speed up your camera. Books cut shorter. Condensations. Digests, Taboids. Everything boils down to the gag, the snap ending."

"Snap ending." Mildred nodded.

15 "Classics cut to fit fifteen-minute radio shows, then cut again to fill a two-minute book column, winding up at last as a ten- or twelve-line dictionary resume. I exaggerate, of course. The dictionaries were for reference. But many were those whose sole knowledge of *Hamlet* (you know the title certainly, Montag; it is probably only a faint rumor of a title to you, Mrs. Montag), whose sole knowledge, as I say, of *Hamlet* was a one-page digest in a book that claimed: *now at last you can read all the classics; keep up with your neighbors.* Do you see? Out of the nursery into the college and back to the nursery; there's your intellectual pattern for the past five centuries or more."

Mildred arose and began to move around the room, picking things up and putting them down. Beatty ignored her and continued:

"Speed up the film, Montag, quick. *Click, Pic, Look, Eye, Now, Flick, Here, There, Swift, Pace, Up, Down, In, Out, Why, How, Who, What,*

Where, Eh? Uh! Bang! Smack! Wallop, Bing, Bong, Boom! Digest-digests, digest-digest-digests. Politics? One column, two sentences, a headline! Then, in mid-air, all vanishes! Whirl man's mind around about so fast under the pumping hands of publishers, exploiters, broadcasters that the centrifuge flings off all unnecessary, time-wasting thought!"

Mildred smoothed the bedclothes. Montag felt his heart jump and jump again as she patted his pillow. Right now she was pulling at his shoulder to try to get him to move so she could take the pillow out and fix it nicely and put it back. And perhaps cry out and stare or simply reach down her hand and say, "What's this?" and hold up the hidden book with touching innocence.

20   "School is shortened, discipline relaxed, philosophies, histories, languages dropped, English and spelling gradually gradually neglected, finally almost completely ignored. Life is immediate, the job counts, pleasure lies all about after work. Why learn anything save pressing buttons, pulling switches, fitting nuts and bolts?"

"Let me fix your pillow," said Mildred.

"No!" whispered Montag.

"The zipper displaces the button and a man lacks just that much time to think while dressing at dawn, a philosophical hour, and thus a melancholy hour."

Mildred said, "Here."

25   "Get away," said Montag.

"Life becomes one big pratfall, Montag; everything bang, boff, and wow!"

"Wow," said Mildred, yanking at the pillow.

"For God's sake, let me be!" cried Montag passionately.

Beatty opened his eyes wide.

30   Mildred's hand had frozen behind the pillow. Her fingers were tracing the book's outline and as the shape became familiar her face looked surprised and then stunned. Her mouth opened to ask a question. . . .

"Empty the theaters save for clowns and furnish the rooms with glass walls and pretty colors running up and down the walls like confetti or blood or sherry or sauterne. You like baseball, don't you, Montag?"

"Baseball's a fine game."

Now Beatty was almost invisible, a voice somewhere behind a screen of smoke.

"What's this?" asked Mildred, almost with delight. Montag heaved back against her arms. "What's this here?"

35 "Sit down!" Montag shouted. She jumped away, her hands empty. "We're talking!"

Beatty went on as if nothing had happened. "You like bowling, don't you, Montag?"

"Bowling, yes."

"And golf?"

"Golf is a fine game."

40 "Basketball?"

"A fine game."

"Billiards, pool? Football?"

"Fine games, all of them."

"More sports for everyone, group spirit, fun, and you don't have to think, eh? Organize and organize and super organize super-super sports. More cartoons in books. More pictures. The mind drinks less and less. Impatience. Highways full of crowds going somewhere, somewhere, somewhere, nowhere. The gasoline refugee. Towns turn into motels, people in nomadic surges from place to place, following the moon tides, living tonight in the room where you slept this noon and I the night before."

45 Mildred went out of the room and slammed the door. The parlor "aunts" began to laugh at the parlor "uncles."

"Now let's take up the minorities in our civilization, shall we? Bigger the population, the more minorities. Don't step on the toes of the dog-lovers, the cat-lovers, doctors, lawyers, merchants, chiefs, Mormons, Baptists, Unitarians, second-generation Chinese, Swedes, Italians, Germans, Texans, Brooklynites, Irishmen, people from Oregon or Mexico. The people in this book, this play, this TV serial are not meant to represent any actual painters, cartographers, mechanics anywhere. The bigger your market, Montag, the less you handle controversy, remember that! All the minor minorities with their navels to be kept clean. Authors, full of evil thoughts, lock up your typewriters. They *did*. Magazines became a nice blend of vanilla tapioca. Books, so the damned snobbish critics said, were dishwater. No *wonder* books stopped selling, the critics said. But the public, knowing what it wanted, spinning happily, let the comic books survive. And the three-dimensional sex magazines, of course. There you have it, Montag. It didn't come from the Government down. There was no dictum, no declaration, no censorship, to start with, no! Technology, mass exploitation, and minority pressure carried the trick, thank God. Today, thanks to them, you can stay happy all the time, you are allowed to read comics, the good old confessions, or trade journals."

"Yes, but what about the firemen, then?" asked Montag.

"Ah." Beatty leaned forward in the faint mist of smoke from his pipe. "What more easily explained and natural? With school turning out more runners, jumpers, racers, tinkerers, grabbers, snatchers, fliers, and swimmers instead of examiners, critics, knowers, and imaginative creators, the word 'intellectual,' of course, became the swear word it deserved to be. You always dread the unfamiliar. Surely you remember the boy in your own school class who was exceptionally 'bright,' did most of the reciting and answering while the others sat like so many leaden idols, hating him. And wasn't it this bright boy you selected for beatings and tortures after hours? Of course it was. We must all be alike. Not everyone born free and equal, as the Constitution says, but everyone *made* equal. Each man the image of every other; then all are happy, for there are no mountains to make them cower, to judge themselves against. So! A book is a loaded gun in the house next door. Burn it. Take the shot from the weapon. Breach man's mind. Who knows who might be the target of the well-read man? Me? I won't stomach them for a minute. And so when houses were finally fireproofed completely, all over the world (you were correct in your assumption the other night) there was no longer need of firemen for the old purposes. They were given the new job, as custodians of our peace of mind, the focus of our understandable and rightful dread of being inferior; official censors, judges, and executors. That's you, Montag, and that's me."

The door to the parlor opened and Mildred stood there looking in at them, looking at Beatty and then at Montag. Behind her the walls of the room were flooded with green and yellow and orange fireworks sizzling and bursting to some music composed almost completely of trap drums, tom-toms, and cymbals. Her mouth moved and she was saying something but the sound covered it.

50   Beatty knocked his pipe into the palm of his pink hand, studied the ashes as if they were a symbol to be diagnosed and searched for meaning.

"You must understand that our civilization is so vast that we can't have our minorities upset and stirred. Ask yourself, What do we want in this country, above all? People want to be happy, isn't that right?

Haven't you heard it all your life? I want to be happy, people say. Well, aren't they? Don't we keep them moving, don't we give them fun? That's all we live for, isn't it? For pleasure, for titillation? And you must admit our culture provides plenty of these."

"Yes."

Montag could lip-read what Mildred was saying in the doorway. He tried not to look at her mouth, because then Beatty might turn and read what was there, too.

"Colored people don't like *Little Black Sambo*. Burn it. White people don't feel good about *Uncle Tom's Cabin*. Burn it. Someone's written a book on tobacco and cancer of the lungs? The cigarette people are weeping? Burn the book. Serenity, Montag. Peace, Montag. Take your fight outside. Better yet, into the incinerator. Funerals are unhappy and pagan? Eliminate them, too. Five minutes after a person is dead he's on his way to the Big Flue, the Incinerators serviced by helicopters all over the country. Ten minutes after death a man's a speck of black dust. Let's not quibble over individuals with memoriams. Forget them. Burn all, burn everything. Fire is bright and fire is clean."

55   The fireworks died in the parlor behind Mildred. She had stopped talking at the same time; a miraculous coincidence. Montag held his breath.

"There was a girl next door," he said, slowly. "She's gone now, I think, dead. I can't even remember her face. But she was different. How—how did she *happen?*"

Beatty smiled. "Here or there, that's bound to occur. Clarisse McClellan? We've a record on her family. We've watched them carefully. Heredity and environment are funny things. You can't rid yourselves of all the odd ducks in just a few years. The home environment can undo a lot you try to do at school. That's why we've lowered the kindergarten age year after year until now we're almost snatching them from the cradle. We had some false alarms on the McClellans, when they lived in Chicago. Never found a book. Uncle had a mixed record; antisocial. The girl? She was a time bomb. The family had been feeding her subconscious, I'm sure, from what I saw of her school record. She didn't want to know *how* a thing was done, but *why*. That can be embarrassing. You ask Why to a lot of things and you wind up very unhappy indeed, if you keep at it. The poor girl's better off dead."

"Yes, dead."

"Luckily, queer ones like her don't happen often. We know how to nip most of them in the bud, early. You can't build a house without nails and wood. If you don't want a house built, hide the nails and wood. If you don't want man unhappy politically, don't give him two sides to a question to worry him; give him one. Better yet, give him none. Let him forget there is such a thing as war. If the government is inefficient, top-heavy, and tax-mad, better it be all those than that people worry over it. Peace, Montag. Give the people contests they win by remembering the words to more popular songs or the names of state capitals or how much corn Iowa grew last year. Cram them full of noncombustible data, chock them so damned full of 'facts' they feel stuffed, but absolutely 'brilliant' with information. Then they'll feel they're thinking, they'll get a *sense* of motion without moving. And they'll be happy, because facts of that sort don't change. Don't give them any slippery stuff like philosophy or sociology to tie things up with. That way lies melancholy. Any man who can take a TV wall apart and put it back together again, and most men can, nowadays, is happier than any man who tries to slide rule, measure, and equate the universe, which just won't be measured or equated without making man feel bestial and lonely. I know, I've tried it; to hell with it. So bring on your clubs and parties, your acrobats and magicians, your daredevils, jet cars, motorcycle helicopters, your sex and heroin, more of everything to do with automatic reflex. If the drama is bad, if the film says nothing, if the play is hollow, sting me with the Theremin, loudly. I'll think I'm responding to the play, when it's only a tactile reaction to vibration. But I don't care. I just like solid entertainment."

60 Beatty got up. "I must be going. Lecture's over. I hope I've clarified things. The important thing for you to remember, Montag, is we're the Happiness Boys, the Dixie Duo, you and I and the others. We stand against the small tide of those who want to make everyone unhappy with conflicting theory and thought. We have our fingers in the dike. Hold steady. Don't let the torrent of melancholy and drear philosophy drown our world. We depend on you. I don't think you realize how important *you* are, *we* are, to our happy world as it stands now."

Beatty shook Montag's limp hand. Montag still sat, as if the house were collapsing about him and he could not move, in the bed. Mildred had vanished from the door.

"One last thing," said Beatty. "At least once in his career, every fireman gets an itch. What do the books *say,* he wonders. Oh, to *scratch* that itch, eh? Well, Montag, take my word for it, I've had to read a few in my time, to know what I was about, and the books say *nothing!* Nothing you can teach or believe. They're about nonexistent people, figments of imagination, if they're fiction. And if they're nonfiction, it's worse, one professor calling another an idiot, one philosopher screaming down another's gullet. All of them running about, putting out the stars and extinguishing the sun. You come away lost."

"Well, then, what if a fireman accidentally, really not intending anything, takes a book home with him?"

Montag twitched. The open door looked at him with its great vacant eye.

65 "A natural error. Curiosity alone," said Beatty. "We don't get overanxious or mad. We let the fireman keep the book twenty-four hours. If he hasn't burned it by then, we simply come burn it for him."

"Of course." Montag's mouth was dry.

"Well, Montag. Will you take another, later shift, today? Will we see you tonight perhaps?"

"I don't know," said Montag.

"What?" Beatty looked faintly surprised.

Montag shut his eyes. "I'll be in later. Maybe."

70 "We'd certainly miss you if you didn't show," said Beatty, putting his pipe in his pocket thoughtfully.

I'll never come in again, thought Montag.

"Get well and keep well," said Beatty.

He turned and went out through the open door.

SUGGESTIONS FOR WRITING

1. The "aunts" and "uncles" who make up the "parlor relatives" are the people who appear on Montag's television. Write an essay that explores some of the ways people who appear on our contemporary television might be characterized as "relatives" in the attitudes they both project toward and encourage in their viewers.

2. Write an essay that summarizes in your own words Captain Beatty's theory of literary evolution.

3. Write an essay that summarizes in your own words the reasoning behind Beatty's contention that the purpose of a fireman's burning books is to create happiness.

Let a Hundred Flowers Blossom

1957

Translated from the Chinese by Lily Wei

CHAIRMAN MAO

Mao Zedong (1893–1976) was the Chinese Marxist political and military leader who ruled China from 1949, following victory in a long civil war, until his death. He has the infamous distinction of having killed more of his fellow citizens than any other ruler in the history of the earth—at least 60 million of them. After coming to power, he combated internal resistances to the large-scale sweeping changes he imposed on China with direct repression. Naturally, people soon ceased to object openly. Mao then adopted the policy announced in the famous speech printed below. Here utopian ideals and dystopian facts may be seen at odds. By showering praise on the virtues of unrestrained free speech, Mao convinced dissenters that their ideas would be respected on the bases of Darwinian and Marxist ideas of evolution outlined in earlier chapters of this book. Many were convinced and spoke out; they were all either killed or sent to "re-education" camps, the central institution of his dystopia.

How have the slogans "Letting a Hundred Flowers Blossom," "Letting a Hundred Schools of Thought Contend," "Achieving a Long-Term Coexistence among a Variety of Forms and Styles in Art and Different Theories in Science" and "Supervising Each Other to Strive" developed? They developed based on China's particular situation, and the recognition that various conflicts would continue to exist in the socialist society, as well as the urgent demand on our nation's economic and cultural developments. "Letting a Hundred Flowers Blossom and Letting a Hundred Schools of Thought Contend" is the policy, which will promote the development of art and advancement on science. It is the policy, which will flourish our socialist nation's culture. Different forms and styles in art should be allowed to develop liberally. Different theories in science should be allowed to contend freely. To use a political power, to force a single style or one theory into practice or to ban the style or theory which differs from the advocated will harm, we believe, sound developments of art and science. The conflicts between the notion of right vs. wrong should be resolved through the free discussions among intellectuals and scientists and through practice. We should not use a simple method to resolve the conflict. Identifying the right thing from the wrong thing requires time to do so. From the historical viewpoint, new and correct things often are unacceptable by people at first, and can only develop through a long-term struggle. New and correct things, so often at its beginning, are not recognized as fragrant flowers, but as poisonous weeds. Copernicus's theory of the solar system and Darwin's theory of evolution were once deemed as erroneous ideas and, therefore, they encountered many harsh contentions. Our history also has numerous similar examples. Compared with the old society, the socialist society has provided us with a much better condition for new things to develop, which is radically different from the ways of old society. However, to oppress newly-developed ideas or reasonable opinions are still a common phenomenon in our society. Sometimes, the people do not intentionally try to disrupt the development of new things, but are just unable to distinguish good things from bad things. As a result, the development of new things is interrupted. Therefore, as to the issue of right vs. wrong in art and science, we should take a prudent approach, and use the free-speech method to avoid a hasty conclusion. We deem that adopting the aforementioned approach can provide our nation with a sound development in the areas of art and science.

The development of Marxism has also been through struggle. The theory of Marxism, at first, was criticized harshly, and was deemed as poisonous weeds. Even now, the theory of Marxism is still criticized in many countries and is defined as poisonous weeds. Certainly, the position of Marxism in a socialist society is different. However, the non-Marxist and anti-Marxist in our nation will continue to exist. In our nation, even though socialist transformation in reference to the change in the system of ownership has been basically completed, and the large-scaled, violent mass struggle in the revolutionary period has mainly finished, the residue of the overthrown landlord and comprador classes still exist, the bourgeoisie still exists, and the task of reshaping the petty bourgeoisie's ideology has just begun. Therefore, class struggle is not yet over. The class struggle between the proletariat and bourgeoisie, each a political faction, the ideologies of the proletariat and bourgeoisie will continue to exist for a long period of time. These struggles will appear to be torturous and, sometimes, will appear to be brutal. The proletariat wants to change the world according to its own ideology. In a similar manner, the bourgeoisie wants to change the world according to its own ideology. In this respect, the outcome of whether socialism or capitalism will win the battle in the ideological field is not certain. Marxists are still a minority either in the entire population or among the intellectuals. Thus, Marxism will still develop through struggle. In fact, Marxism must strive through struggle. This fact was not only evidenced in the past as well as now, but also will be evidenced in the future. The development of correct things is always based on the process of fighting evil things, because truthful, virtuous and beautiful things can only exist in comparison with false, wicked and evil things, and, therefore, good things can only develop through struggle with bad things. Further, when some erroneous things are universally abandoned, and some truths are unanimously accepted by mankind, some newer ideas of truth, again, will begin to struggle with some new-found erroneous ideas. This kind of struggle will never end. It is the law of the development of truth. Certainly, this law also applies to the development of Marxism.

The outcome of whether, in China, socialism or capitalism will win as ideologies will remain unknown for a long period of time. This is because the influence of the bourgeoisie and the intellectuals whose minds were educated by the old society will continue to exist in society for a long period of time. Thus, the struggle between two different ideologies will stay alive. If we are not adequately aware of this situation, or pay no attention to this situation, we will commit a grave mistake, the ignorance of ideological struggle. Ideological struggle is different from the other struggle. To confront with ideological struggle, people can not adopt a rude attitude, but a persuasive approach. Nowadays, the socialist country in ideological struggle has its advantage because political power is held in the working class people under the leadership of the proletariat. Our communist party possesses a strong political power and enjoys high prestige. Although our job performances are not perfect and we, sometimes, make mistakes, every Chinese citizen observes that we are loyal to the people, and are determined, as well as are capable of establishing, together with our people, a new country. In fact, we have already achieved enormous successes, and will continue to achieve greater successes. Basically, the majority of bourgeoisies and the intellectuals who come from the old society love the country, and are willing to serve our flourishing socialist nation. They also understand that if they separate themselves from the socialist society, and the working class people under the leadership of the communist party, they will have no place to survive, and will not have any bright future.

People might ask: In our country, since the majority of the people have accepted the theory of Marxism as a guiding ideology, can it be criticized? The answer is that Marxism certainly can be criticized. Marxism represents a scientific truth, therefore it fears no criticism. If Marxism fears criticism and if its theory can be defeated due to criticism, the truth of Marxism will become questionable. As a matter of fact, some "idealists" have been criticizing Marxism every day by a variety of means. Don't those people who cherish the ideologies of the bourgeoisie and the petty bourgeoisie and who refuse to reshape their thinking—don't they do the same thing and criticize Marxism by many methods in our country? Marxists should not be afraid of being criticized by any people. On the contrary, Marxists should prepare and develop themselves through criticisms and intense confrontations with the opposing people in order to expand their battlefield. Fighting with erroneous ideologies is the same as getting the smallpox vaccination. After the smallpox vaccination is given, the body's immune system will be greatly enhanced. The things which are cultivated in a comfortable indoor environment will not have strong capacity to live. Thus, implementing the policy of "Letting a Hundred Flowers Blossom and Letting a Hundred Schools of Thought Contend" will not weaken the leading position of Marxism in the field of ideology, but will strengthen it.

SUGGESTIONS FOR WRITING

1. The principal metaphor of flowers blossoming makes a striking and memorable title for the speech, especially given the violent context of political revolution surrounding it. One implication of the figure of speech is the diverse natural beauty in different flowers; another, the short life of beautiful flowers. What are some other implications? By examining this and other metaphors in the speech, write an essay about some ways metaphorical implications create Mao's meaning.

2. Mao mentions both Darwin and Marx as examples. Write an essay that explores some of the ways in which Chairman Mao's speech views political and social change as an evolutionary processes.

3. As the head note to this selection explains, those who reacted to the speech by proclaiming views independent of the Chinese Communist Party line were quickly repressed, punished, and in many cases killed. Do these results necessarily turn the content of the speech into a lie? Or can that content be read in ways compatible with the ensuing repression? Write an essay in which you explore the sincerity or insincerity attributable to Chairman Mao from the meaning of his words in this famous speech.

The Handmaid's Tale   1986

MARGARET ATWOOD

The Canadian writer Margaret Atwood was born in Ottawa, Ontario in 1939. In 1957 she began her studies at Victoria University in the University of Toronto, but she had begun to write even earlier. After a book of poems won a prestigious prize, she pursued graduate studies at Harvard, earning an M. A. Her subsequent writing led to teaching posts at many Canadian and American universities.

The futuristic dystopia in her award-winning The Handmaid's Tale *has found many ways to repress its women. One involves the way subordinate females are used to produce offspring for the infertile members of the ruling elite and are called "handmaids" after the similar function performed in the Bible for Jacob's wives Rachel and Leah by their servants. In the excerpt below, the values and assumptions of the society are reaffirmed in one of its horrible rituals.*

The bell is tolling; we can hear it from a long way off. It's morning, and today we've had no breakfast. When we reach the main gate we file through it, two by two. There's a heavy contingent of guards, special-detail Angels, with riot gear—the helmets with the bulging dark Plexiglas visors that make them look like beetles, the long clubs, the gas-canister guns—in cordon around the outside of the Wall. That's in case of hysteria. The hooks on the Wall are empty.

This is a district Salvaging, for women only. Salvagings are always segregated. It was announced yesterday. They tell you only the day before. It's not enough time, to get used to it.

To the tolling of the bell we walk along the paths once used by students, past buildings that were once lecture halls and dormitories. It's very strange to be in here again. From the outside you can't tell that anything's changed, except that the blinds on most of the windows are drawn down. These buildings belong to the Eyes now.

We file onto the wide lawn in front of what used to be the library. The white steps going up are still the same, the main entrance is unaltered. There's a wooden stage erected on the lawn, something like the one they used every spring, for commencement, in the time before. I think of hats, pastel hats worn by some of the mothers, and of the black gowns the students would put on, and the red ones. But this stage is not the same after all, because of the three wooden posts that stand on it, with the loops of rope.

5   At the front of the stage there is a microphone; the television camera is discreetly off to the side.

I've only been to one of these before, two years ago. Women's Salvagings are not frequent. There is less need for them. These days we are so well behaved.

I don't want to be telling this story.

We take our places in the standard order: Wives and daughters on the folding wooden chairs placed towards the back, Econowives and Marthas around the edges and on the library steps, and Handmaids at the front, where everyone can keep an eye on us. We don't sit on chairs, but kneel, and this time we have cushions, small red velvet ones with nothing written on them, not even *Faith*.

Luckily the weather is all right: not too hot, cloudy bright. It would be miserable kneeling here in the rain. Maybe that's why they leave it so late to tell us: so they'll know what the weather will be like. That's as good a reason as any.

10   I kneel on my red velvet cushion. I try to think about tonight, about making love, in the dark, in the light reflected off the white walls. I remember being held.

There's a long piece of rope that winds like a snake in front of the first row of cushions, along the second, and back through the lines of chairs, bending like a very old, very slow river viewed from the air, down to the back. The rope is thick and brown and smells of tar. The front end of the rope runs up onto the stage. It's like a fuse, or the string of a balloon.

On the stage, to the left, are those who are to be salvaged: two Handmaids, one Wife. Wives are unusual, and despite myself I look at this one with interest. I want to know what she has done.

They have been placed here before the gates were opened. All of them sit on folding wooden chairs, like graduating students who are about to be given prizes. Their hands rest in their laps, looking as if they are folded sedately. They sway a little, they've probably been given injections or pills, so they won't make a fuss. It's better if things go smoothly. Are they attached to their chairs? Impossible to say, under all that drapery.

Now the official procession is approaching the stage, mounting the steps at the right: three women, one Aunt in front, two Salvagers in their black hoods and cloaks a pace behind her. Behind them are the other Aunts. The whisperings among us hush. The three arrange themselves, turn towards us, the Aunt flanked by the two black-robed Salvagers.

15   It's Aunt Lydia. How many years since I've seen her? I'd begun to think she existed only in my head, but here she is, a little older. I have a good view, I can see the deepening furrows to either side of her nose, the engraved frown. Her eyes blink, she smiles nervously, peering to left and right, checking out the audience, and lifts a hand to fidget with her headdress. An odd strangling sound comes over the PA system: she is clearing her throat.

I've begun to shiver. Hatred fills my mouth like spit.

The sun comes out, and the stage and its occupants light up like a Christmas crèche. I can see the wrinkles under Aunt Lydia's eyes, the pallor of the seated women, the hairs on the rope in front of me on the grass, the blades of grass. There is a dandelion, right in front of me, the color of egg yolk. I feel hungry. The bell stops tolling.

Aunt Lydia stands up, smooths down her skirt with both hands, and steps forward to the mike. "*Good afternoon, ladies,*" she says, and there is an instant and earsplitting feedback whine from the PA system. From among us, incredibly, there is laughter. It's hard not to laugh, it's the tension, and the look of irritation on Aunt Lydia's face as she adjusts the sound. This is supposed to be dignified.

"Good afternoon, ladies," she says again, her voice now tinny and flattened. It's *ladies* instead of *girls* because of the Wives. "I'm sure we are all aware of the unfortunate circumstances that bring us all here together on this beautiful morning, when I am certain we would all rather be doing something else, at least I speak for myself, but duty is a hard taskmaster, or may I say on this occasion taskmistress, and it is in the name of duty that we are here today."

20   She goes on like this for some minutes, but I don't listen. I've heard this speech, or one like it, often enough before: the same platitudes, the same slogans, the same phrases: the torch of the future, the cradle of the race, the task before us. It's hard to believe there will not be polite clapping after this speech, and tea and cookies served on the lawn.

That was the prologue, I think. Now she'll get down to it.

Aunt Lydia rummages in her pocket, produces a crumpled piece of paper. This she takes an undue length of time to unfold and scan. She's rubbing our noses in it, letting us know exactly who she is, making us watch her as she silently reads, flaunting her prerogative. Obscene, I think. Let's get this over with.

"In the past," says Aunt Lydia, "it has been the custom to precede the actual Salvagings with a detailed account of the crimes of which the prisoners stand convicted. However, we have found that such a public account, especially when televised, is invariably followed by a rash, if I may call it that, an outbreak I should say, of exactly similar crimes. So we have decided in the best interests of all to discontinue this practice. The Salvagings will proceed without further ado."

A collective murmur goes up from us. The crimes of others are a secret language among us. Through them we show ourselves what we might be capable of, after all. This is not a popular announcement. But you would never know it from Aunt Lydia, who smiles and blinks as if washed in applause. Now we are left to our own devices, our own speculations. The first one, the one they're now raising from her chair, black-gloved hands on her upper arms: Reading? No, that's only a hand cut off, on the third conviction. Unchastity, or an attempt on the life of her Commander? Or the Commander's Wife, more likely. That's what we're thinking. As for the Wife, there's mostly just one thing they get salvaged for. They can do almost anything to us, but they aren't allowed to kill us, not legally. Not with knitting needles or garden shears, or knives purloined from the kitchen, and especially not when we are pregnant. It could be adultery, of course. It could always be that.

25 Or attempted escape.

"Ofcharles," Aunt Lydia announces. No one I know. The woman is brought forward; she walks as if she's really concentrating on it, one foot, the other foot, she's definitely drugged. There's a groggy off-center smile on her mouth. One side of her face contracts, an uncoordinated wink, aimed at the camera. They'll never show it of course, this isn't live. The two Salvagers tie her hands, behind her back.

From behind me there's a sound of retching.

That's why we don't get breakfast.

"Janine, most likely," Ofglen whispers.

30 I've seen it before, the white bag placed over the head, the woman helped up onto the high stool as if she's being helped up the steps of a bus, steadied there, the noose adjusted delicately around the neck, like a vestment, the stool kicked away. I've heard the long sigh go up, from around me, the sigh like air coming out of an air mattress, I've seen Aunt Lydia place her hand over the mike, to stifle the other sounds

coming from behind her, I've leaned forward to touch the rope in front of me, in time with the others, both hands on it, the rope hairy, sticky with tar in the hot sun, then placed my hand on my heart to show my unity with the Salvagers and my consent, and my complicity in the death of this woman. I have seen the kicking feet and the two in black who now seize hold of them and drag downward with all their weight. I don't want to see it anymore. I look at the grass instead. I describe the rope.

SUGGESTIONS FOR WRITING

1. Make a list of those aspects of a "Salvaging" that resemble an academic ceremony. Now write an essay on the implied meanings of the academic analogy for the dystopian world of *The Handmaid's Tale*.
2. Why do the authorities omit the announcement of the women's "crimes" from the Salvaging? Write an essay on the psychological motivations in both "criminals" and "authorities" implied by the omission.
3. The passage ends with a focus on the long rope. Write an essay on the implied function of that long rope in the intentions of the authorities to salvage what is salvaged in a Salvaging.

INTERDISCIPLINARY CONNECTIONS

1. All the selections imply some kind of evolution in the fictional worlds they imagine. Pick one of these worlds and write an essay that explores the stages and causes of the evolutionary processes involved.
2. Pick two selections that focus on economic issues. Write an essay that explores some ways in which the selections dramatize economic issues by literary means.
3. Pick two selections that focus on issues of human rights. Write an essay that explores some ways in which the selections dramatize their issues by literary means.
4. Which of the selections seems to you most "utopian" in the common current sense of that word? Most "dystopian"? Write an essay that explains and defends your answers.
5. Pick two selections that focus on issues of gender. Write an essay that explores some ways in which the selections dramatize their issues by literary means.

CHAPTER 6

Gender
Human Conditioning and the Human Condition

Plato

Elizabeth Cady
Stanton

Carol Gilligan

bell hooks

Edmund White

Rose Weitz

James Reed

Pratima Cranse

Camille Paglia

Susan Faludi

Introduction

Gender is an old word that has taken on new meanings and new importance within relatively recent times. The root meaning of the word is *kind* or *class* or *type* and the primary meaning came to be *sex* as in *male* and *female*. The word also appeared in the vocabulary of grammar, but there its meaning was often arbitrary and not always related to "natural" gender. The flexibility of its grammatical sense came to serve the word when questions of sexual identity were pursued beyond traditional simple limits provided by male and female. The social identity of sexual identity is another area in which gender has played a principal part. The selections here address both categories of interest and show in a representative way how gender serves as an interdisciplinary theme throughout the humanities and social sciences.

We begin with a selection from Plato's *Republic* on "The Role of Women in the Ideal Society" that serves as segue from the utopias of the last chapter to the social questions addressed in this one. Plato's Guardians of the Republic are his ideal leaders, and the questions arise: Are women to figure among them? And If so, how shall they be trained and educated to be worthy of such high functions?

Some 2000 years, later women not only were denied high office in the American Republic, but were not even allowed to vote on who should hold such a position. Elizabeth Cady Stanton was a pioneering American feminist and leader in the woman's suffrage movement. In the speech given here, she addresses a convention that had come together to find ways of furthering voting rights for women. Stanton bases her argument not on a woman's identity as a woman, but on her identity as an individual.

Elizabeth Cady Stanton was an abolitionist as well as a suffragette, but the two causes were not always allied in harmony as shown by the next essay, "Racism and Feminism." Author bell hooks traces a historical conflict between white and black women that has hindered each group in both political advancement and social harmony. Gender, it seems, may be defined and constrained by aspects of race and class as well as by sex.

Early in the twentieth century, the equality of political rights that Stanton fought for was achieved. But did those rights lead to equality of treatment outside the political sphere? Educational researcher Carol Gilligan explores her own field and finds an ironic answer. Her essay "Woman's Place in Man's Life Cycle" shows, among other things, how most of the classical evidence used to support theories of developmental education in the twentieth century has in fact been derived by studies of boys rather than girls.

What is sexual identity and how far does it create a social or cultural identity for anyone? In "Sexual Culture," novelist and critic Edmund White explores the social identities of gay men, identities that even the best disposed of their fellow citizens seem almost completely in the dark about. White sketches out both the problem for the larger society and the cultural conditions that define male homosexuals as beings in whose lives are far from fully defined by a sexual orientation.

Next Rose Weitz looks at some women outside the mainstream of traditionally gendered social roles in "What Price Independence: Social Reactions to Lesbians, Spinsters, Widows, and Nuns." In taking a historical and a sociological approach, Weitz tallies up the costs incurred by individuals who have maintained independence from society as a whole and from more usual gendered roles within it. Her essay has the form of an article in a professional publication complete with footnotes and other scholarly apparatus.

One of the first, if not the first, to use the term gender in its more modern senses was the pioneering psychologist and sex researcher John Money. Money opened up the meanings of the term to indicate the range of socially constructed sexual identities that were not constrained by anatomical facts. A professor of history, James Reed takes us through the story of Money's rise and fall as a hero to those who used his liberation of the term in fields far beyond Money's own.

As the essays in this chapter have indicated, sex and gender are far from equivalent terms, with gender covering the public functions of sexual identity. But how do people of different sexes view the very private and intimate matters that make up the subject matter in sex education and what are the implications for the concept of gender? Pratima Cranse shows in her essay "Fear and Loathing in Sex Education" that there is a generally gendered response to the topic and gives us real-life examples of the forms it takes.

The chapter and the book close with two opposing views on a controversial topic: date rape. The problem is one that may be studied from many of the points of view embodied in other chapters. Here two women disagree on the issue. In "It's a Jungle Out There, So Get Used To It," Camille Paglia argues that some feminist ideas about gender equality have ignored cultural facts deeply based in biology and history, facts that traditional social customs have endeavored to deal with. We disregard those customs, she says, at the peril of our young women. Susan Faludi takes a different view of the causes involved in the issue and in its debate. She claims in "Whose Hype?" that debunkers of date rape are in fact part of a backlash against real gains made by feminists in the area of women's rights.

The Role of Women in the Ideal Society

From *The Republic*

PLATO

Plato (428–347 B. C.), a well-educated Athenian from an aristocratic family, became the most famous student of Socrates and Plato immortalized his master (whose own instructions were strictly oral) by making him the principal figure in his written philosophical dialogues. It is impossible and perhaps unnecessary to separate the views of the two philosophers, who thus remain inseparable for all time. After Socrates was tried, convicted, and executed (by forced suicide) for "corrupting" the youth of Athens, Plato founded a school called the Academy, which endured for almost a thousand years in testimony to the greatness of its founder and that founder's teacher and model. Another excerpt from Plato appears in Chapter 4.

In the dialogue that follows, Socrates and Glaucon discuss how women might take their places within the society of Plato's ideal Republic. As you will see, many of the questions they raised thousands of years ago are still matters of debate today. For example, women obviously differ from men physically in some important ways; but to what degree, if any, should those differences affect their functions and positions in the world?

Well, I replied, I suppose that I must retrace my steps and say what I perhaps ought to have said before in the proper place. The part of the men has been played out, and now properly enough comes the turn of the women. Of them I will proceed to speak, and the more readily since I am invited by you.

For men born and educated like our citizens, the only way, in my opinion, of arriving at a right conclusion about the possession and use of women and children is to follow the path on which we originally started, when we said that the men were to be the guardians and watchdogs of the herd.

True.

Let us further suppose the birth and education of our women to be subject to similar or nearly similar regulations; then we shall see whether the result accords with our design.

5   What do you mean?

What I mean may be put into the form of a question, I said: Are dogs divided into has and shes, or do they both share equally in hunting and in keeping watch and in the other duties of dogs? or do we entrust to the males the entire and exclusive care of the flocks, while we leave the females at home, under the idea that the bearing and suckling their puppies is labour enough for them?

No, he said, they share alike; the only difference between them is that the males are stronger and the females weaker.

But can you use different animals for the same purpose, unless they are bred and fed in the same way?

You cannot.

10 Then, if women are to have the same duties as men, they must have the same nurture and education?

Yes.

The education which was assigned to the men was music and gymnastic.

Yes.

Then women must be taught music and gymnastic and also the art of war, which they must practise like the men?

15 That is the inference, I suppose.

I should rather expect, I said, that several of our proposals, if they are carried out, being unusual, may appear ridiculous.

No doubt of it.

Yes, and the most ridiculous thing of all will be the sight of women naked in the palaestra, exercising with the men, especially when they are no longer young; they certainly will not be a vision of beauty, any more than the enthusiastic old men who in spite of wrinkles and ugliness continue to frequent the gymnasia.

Yes, indeed, he said: according to present notions the proposal would be thought ridiculous.

20 But then, I said, as we have determined to speak our minds, we must not fear the jests of the wits which will be directed against this sort of innovation; how they will talk of women's attainments both in music and gymnastic, and above all about their wearing armour and riding upon horseback!

Very true, he replied.

Yet having begun we must go forward to the rough places of the law; at the same time begging of these gentlemen for once in their life to be serious. Not long ago, as we shall remind them, the Hellenes were of the opinion, which is still generally received among the barbarians, that the sight of a naked man was ridiculous and improper; and when first the Cretans and then the Lacedaemonians introduced the custom, the wits of that day might equally have ridiculed the innovation.

No doubt.

But when experience showed that to let all things be uncovered was far better than to cover them up, and the ludicrous effect to the outward eye vanished before the better principle which reason asserted, then the man was perceived to be a fool who directs the shafts of his ridicule at any other sight but that of folly and vice, or seriously inclines to weigh the beautiful by any other standard but that of the good.

25   Very true, he replied.

First, then, whether the question is to be put in jest or in earnest, let us come to an understanding about the nature of woman: Is she capable of sharing either wholly or partially in the actions of men, or not at all? And is the art of war one of those arts in which she can or can not share? That will be the best way of commencing the enquiry, and will probably lead to the fairest conclusion.

That will be much the best way.

Shall we take the other side first and begin by arguing against ourselves; in this manner the adversary's position will not be undefended.

Why not? he said.

30   Then let us put a speech into the mouths of our opponents. They will say: 'Socrates and Glaucon, no adversary need convict you, for you yourselves, at the first foundation of the State, admitted the principle that everybody was to do the one work suited to his own nature.' And certainly, if I am not mistaken, such an admission was made by us. 'And do not the natures of men and women differ very much indeed?' And we shall reply: Of course they do. Then we shall be asked, 'Whether the tasks assigned to men and to women should not be different, and such as are agreeable to their different natures? Certainly they should. But if so, have you not fallen into a serious inconsistency in saying that men and women, whose natures are so entirely different, ought to perform the same actions?—What defence will you make for us, my good Sir, against any one who offers these objections?

That is not an easy question to answer when asked suddenly; and I shall and I do beg of you to draw out the case on our side.

These are the objections, Glaucon, and there are many others of a like kind, which I foresaw long ago; they made me afraid and reluctant to take in hand any law about the possession and nurture of women and children.

By Zeus, he said, the problem to be solved is anything but easy.

Why yes, I said, but the fact is that when a man is out of his depth, whether he has fallen into a little swimming bath or into mid-ocean, he has to swim all the same.

35 Very true.

And must not we swim and try to reach the shore: we will hope that Arion's dolphin or some other miraculous help may save us?

I suppose so, he said.

Well then, let us see if any way of escape can be found. We acknowledged—did we not? that different natures ought to have different pursuits, and that men's and women's natures are different. And now what are we saying?—that different natures ought to have the same pursuits,—this is the inconsistency which is charged upon us.

Precisely.

40 Verily, Glaucon, I said, glorious is the power of the art of contradiction!

Why do you say so?

Because I think that many a man falls into the practice against his will. When he thinks that he is reasoning he is really disputing, just because he cannot define and divide, and so know that of which he is speaking; and he will pursue a merely verbal opposition in the spirit of contention and not of fair discussion.

Yes, he replied, such is very often the case; but what has that to do with us and our argument?

A great deal; for there is certainly a danger of our getting unintentionally into a verbal opposition.

45 In what way?

Why we valiantly and pugnaciously insist upon the verbal truth, that different natures ought to have different pursuits, but we never considered at all what was the meaning of sameness or difference of nature, or why we distinguished them when we assigned different pursuits to different natures and the same to the same natures.

Why, no, he said, that was never considered by us.

I said: Suppose that by way of illustration we were to ask the question whether there is not an opposition in nature between bald men and hairy men; and if this is admitted by us, then, if bald men are cobblers, we should forbid the hairy men to be cobblers, and conversely?

That would be a jest, he said.

50 Yes, I said, a jest; and why? because we never meant when we constructed the State, that the opposition of natures should extend to

every difference, but only to those differences which affected the pursuit in which the individual is engaged; we should have argued, for example, that a physician and one who is in mind a physician may be said to have the same nature.

True.

Whereas the physician and the carpenter have different natures?

Certainly.

And if, I said, the male and female sex appear to differ in their fitness for any art or pursuit, we should say that such pursuit or art ought to be assigned to one or the other of them; but if the difference consists only in women bearing and men begetting children, this does not amount to a proof that a woman differs from a man in respect of the sort of education she should receive; and we shall therefore continue to maintain that our guardians and their wives ought to have the same pursuits.

55 Very true, he said.

Next, we shall ask our opponent how, in reference to any of the pursuits or arts of civic life, the nature of a woman differs from that of a man?

That will be quite fair.

And perhaps he, like yourself, will reply that to give a sufficient answer on the instant is not easy; but after a little reflection there is no difficulty.

Yes, perhaps.

60 Suppose then that we invite him to accompany us in the argument, and then we may hope to show him that there is nothing peculiar in the constitution of women which would affect them in the administration of the State.

By all means.

Let us say to him: Come now, and we will ask you a question:—when you spoke of a nature gifted or not gifted in any respect, did you mean to say that one man will acquire a thing easily, another with difficulty; a little learning will lead the one to discover a great deal; whereas the other, after much study and application, no sooner learns than he forgets; or again, did you mean, that the one has a body which is a good servant to his mind, while the body of the other is a hindrance to him?—would not these be the sort of differences which distinguish the man gifted by nature from the one who is ungifted?

No one will deny that.

And can you mention any pursuit of mankind in which the male sex has not all these gifts and qualities in a higher degree than the female? Need I waste time in speaking of the art of weaving, and the management of pancakes and preserves, in which womankind does really appear to be great, and in which for her to be beaten by a man is of all things the most absurd?

65 You are quite right, he replied, in maintaining the general inferiority of the female sex: although many women are in many things superior to many men, yet on the whole what you say is true.

And if so, my friend, I said, there is no special faculty of administration in a state which a woman has because she is a woman, or which a man has by virtue of his sex; but the gifts of nature are alike diffused in both; all the pursuits of men are the pursuits of women also, but in all of them a woman is inferior to a man.

Very true.

Then are we to impose all our enactments on men and none of them on women?

That will never do.

70 One woman has a gift of healing, another not; one is a musician, and another has no music in her nature?

Very true.

And one woman has a turn for gymnastic and military exercises, and another is unwarlike and hates gymnastics?

Certainly.

And one woman is a philosopher, and another is an enemy of philosophy; one has spirit, and another is without spirit?

75 That is also true.

Then one woman will have the temper of a guardian, and another not. Was not the selection of the male guardians determined by differences of this sort?

Yes.

Men and women alike possess the qualities which make a guardian; they differ only in their comparative strength or weakness.

Obviously.

80 And those women who have such qualities are to be selected as the companions and colleagues of men who have similar qualities and whom they resemble in capacity and in character?

Very true.

And ought not the same natures to have the same pursuits?

They ought.

Then, as we were saying before, there is nothing unnatural in assigning music and gymnastic to the wives of the guardians—to that point we come round again.

85 Certainly not.

The law which we then enacted was agreeable to nature, and therefore not an impossibility or mere aspiration; and the contrary practice, which prevails at present, is in reality a violation of nature.

That appears to be true.

We had to consider, first, whether our proposals were possible, and secondly whether they were the most beneficial?

90 Yes.

And the possibility has been acknowledged?

Yes.

The very great benefit has next to be established?

Quite so.

You will admit that the same education which makes a man a good guardian will make a woman a good guardian; for their original nature is the same?

95 Yes.

I should like to ask you a question.

What is it?

Would you say that all men are equal in excellence or is one man better than another?

The latter.

100 And in the commonwealth which we were founding do you conceive the guardians who have been brought up on our model system to be more perfect men, or the cobblers whose education has been cobbling?

What a ridiculous question!

You have answered me, I replied: Well, and may we not further say that our guardians are the best of our citizens?

By far the best.

And will not their wives be the best women?

105 Yes, by far the best.

And can there be anything better for the interests of the State than that the men and women of a State should be as good as possible?

There can be nothing better.

And this is what the arts of music and gymnastic, when present in such manner as we have described, will accomplish?

Certainly.

110 Then we have made an enactment not only possible but in the highest degree beneficial to the State?

True.

Then let the wives of our guardians strip, for their virtue will be their robe, and let them share in the toils of war and the defence of their country; only in the distribution of labours the lighter are to be assigned to the women, who are the weaker natures, but in other respects their duties are to be the same. And as for the man who laughs at naked women exercising their bodies from the best of motives, in his laughter he is plucking 'A fruit of unripe wisdom,' and he himself is ignorant of what he is laughing at, or what he is about;—for that is, and ever will be, the best of sayings, *That the useful is the noble and the hurtful is the base.*

Very true.

Here, then, is one difficulty in our law about women, which we may say that we have now escaped; the wave has not swallowed us up alive for enacting that the guardians of either sex should have all their pursuits in common; to the utility and also to the possibility of this arrangement the consistency of the argument with itself bears witness.

SUGGESTIONS FOR WRITING

1. In their dialogue, Socrates and Glaucon try to discriminate between nature and nurture. Write an essay that explains their conclusions and the reasoning behind them.
2. Socrates makes a point about confusions created merely by verbal causes. Write an essay about how verbal confusions may create misunderstandings in a discussion on the differences and similarities of men and women.
3. Socrates uses the analogy of guard dogs or watchdogs. Write an essay on the ways in which that analogy helps to clarify the question of male and female nature in the dialogue.

Address to the National Woman Suffrage Convention   1848

ELIZABETH CADY STANTON

Elizabeth Cady Stanton (1815–1902) was a social activist and leader of the women's rights movement during the nineteenth century. She began her career in public life by becoming a force in the temperance movement before the Civil War, shocking some by claiming that drunkenness by itself made fully sufficient grounds for divorce. She was also an ardent abolitionist. Taking up the cause of woman suffrage, she helped to organize the historical Seneca Falls Convention in 1848. After the Civil War, she worked even more extensively to gain voting rights for women. However, her address below shows that her views on women began from basic principles, being pre-political and existential and seeing women first and foremost as individuals.

A great idea of progress is near its consummation, when statesmen in the councils of the nation propose to frame it into statutes and constitutions: when Reverend Fathers recognize it by a new interpretation of their creeds and canons; when the Bar and Bench at its command set aside the legislation of centuries, and girls of twenty put their heels on the Cokes and Blackstones of the past.

Those who represent what is called "the Woman's Rights Movement," have argued their right to political equality from every standpoint of justice, religion, and logic, for the last twenty years. They have quoted the Constitution, the Declaration of Independence, the Bible, the opinions of great men and women in all ages: they have plead the theory of our government; suffrage a natural, inalienable rights: shown from the lessons of history, that one class can not legislate for another; the disfranchised classes must ever be neglected and degraded; and that all privileges are but mockery to the citizen, until he has a voice in the making and administering of law. Such arguments have been made over and over in conventions and before the legislatures of the several States. Judges, lawyers, priests, and politicians have said again and again, that our logic was unanswerable, and although much nonsense has emanated from the male tongue and pen on this subject no man has yet made a fair argument on the other side. Knowing that we hold the Gibraltar rock of reason on this question they resort to ridicule and petty objections. Compelled to follow our assailants, wherever they go, and fight them with their own weapons; when cornered with wit and sarcasm, some cry out, you have no logic on your platform, forgetting that we have no use for logic until they give us logicians at whom to hurl it, and if, for the pure love of it, we now and then rehearse the logic that is like a, b, c, to all of us, others cry out—the same old speeches we have heard these twenty years. It would be safe to say a hundred years, for they are the same our fathers used when battling old King George and the British Parliament for their right to representation, and a voice in the laws by which they were governed. There are no new arguments to be made on human rights, our work to-day is to apply to ourselves those so familiar to all; to teach man that woman is not an anomalous being, outside all laws and constitutions, but one whose rights are to be established by the same process of reason as that by which he demands his own.

When our Fathers made out their famous bill of impeachment against England, they specified eighteen grievances. When the women of this country surveyed the situation in their first convention, they found they had precisely that number, and quite similar in character; and reading over the old revolutionary arguments of Jefferson, Patrick Henry, Otis, and Adams, they found they applied remarkably well to their case. The same arguments made in this country for extending suffrage from time to time, to white men, native born citizens, without property and education, and to foreigners; the same used by John Bright in England, to extend it to a million new voters, and the same used by the great Republican party to enfranchise a million black men in the South, all these arguments we have to-day to offer for woman, and one, in addition, stronger than all besides, the difference in man and woman. Because man and woman are the complement of one another, we need woman's thought in national affairs to make a safe and stable government.

The Republican party to-day congratulates itself on having carried the Fifteenth Amendment of the Constitution, thus securing "manhood suffrage" and establishing an aristocracy of sex on this continent. As several bills to secure Woman's Suffrage in the District and the Territories have been already presented in both houses of Congress, and as by Mr. Julian's bill, the question of so amending the Constitution as to extend suffrage to all the women of the country has been presented to the nation for consideration, it is not only the right but the duty of every thoughtful woman to express her opinion on a Sixteenth Amendment. While I hail the late discussions in Congress and the various bills presented as so many signs of progress, I am especially gratified with those of Messrs. Julian and Pomeroy, which forbid any State to deny the right of suffrage to any of its citizens on account of sex or color.

5   This fundamental principle of our government—the equality of all the citizens of the republic—should be incorporated in the Federal Constitution, there to remain forever. To leave this question to the States and partial acts of Congress, is to defer indefinitely its settlement,

for what is done by this Congress may be repealed by the next; and politics in the several States differ so widely, that no harmonious action on any question can ever be secured, except as a strict party measure. Hence, we appeal to the party now in power, everywhere, to end this protracted debate on suffrage, and declare it the inalienable right of every citizen who is amenable to the laws of the land, who pays taxes and the penalty of crime. We have a splendid theory of a genuine republic, why not realize it and make our government homogeneous, from Maine to California. The Republican party has the power to do this, and now is its only opportunity. Woman's Suffrage, in 1872, may be as good a card for the Republicans as Gen. Grant was in the last election. It is said that the Republican party made him President, not because they thought him the most desirable man in the nation for that office, but they were afraid the Democrats would take him if they did not. We would suggest, there may be the same danger of Democrats taking up Woman Suffrage if they do not. God, in his providence, may have purified that party in the furnace of affliction. They have had the opportunity, safe from the turmoil of political life and the temptations of office, to study and apply the divine principles of justice and equality to life: for minorities are always in a position to carry principles to their logical results, while majorities are governed only by votes. You see my faith in Democrats is based on sound philosophy. In the next Congress, the Democratic party will gain thirty-four new member, hence the Republicans have had their last chance to do justice to woman. It will be no enviable record for the Fortieth Congress that in the darkest days of the republic it placed our free institutions in the care and keeping of every type of manhood, ignoring womanhood, all the elevating and purifying influences of the most virtuous and humane half of the American people. . . .

I urge a speedy adoption of a Sixteenth Amendment for the following reasons:

1. A government, based on the principle of caste and class, can not stand. The aristocratic idea, in any form, is opposed to the genius of our free institutions to our own declaration of rights and to the civilization of the age. All artificial distinctions whether of family, blood, wealth, color or sex are equally oppressive to the subject classes and equally destructive to national life and prosperity. Governments based on every form of aristocracy on every degree and variety of inequality have been tried in despotisms, monarchies and

republics and all alike have perished. In the panorama of the past behold the mighty nations that have risen, one by one but to fall. Behold their temples thrones and pyramids their gorgeous palaces and stately monuments now crumbled all to dust. Behold every monarch in Europe at this very hour trembling on his throne. Behold the republics on this Western continent convulsed distracted divided the hosts scattered the leaders fallen the scouts lost in the wilderness, the once inspired prophets blind and dumb while on all sides the cry is echoed, "Republicanism is a failure." though that great principle of a government "by the people, of the people for the people" has never been tried. Thus far all nations have been built on caste and failed. Why, in this hour of reconstruction with the experience of generations before us, make another experiment in the same direction? If serfdom, peasantry, and slavery have shattered kingdoms, deluged continents with blood, scattered republics like dust before the wind, and rent our own Union asunder, what kind of a government, think you, American statesmen, you can build, with the mothers of the race crouching at your feet, while iron-heeled peasants, serfs, and slaves, exalted by your hands, tread our inalienable rights into the dust? While all men, everywhere, are rejoicing in new-found liberties, shall woman alone be denied the rights, privileges, and immunities of citizenship? While in England men are coming up from the coal mines of Cornwall, from the factories of Birmingham and Manchester, demanding the suffrage; while in frigid Russia the 22,000,000 newly-emancipated serfs are already claiming a voice in the government; while here, in our own land, slaves, but just rejoicing in the proclamation of emancipation, ignorant alike of its power and significance, have the ballot unasked, unsought, already laid at their feet—think you the daughters of Adams, Jefferson, and Patrick Henry, in whose veins flows the blood of two Revolutions, will forever linger round the campfires of an old barbarism, with no longings to join this grand army of freedom in its onward march to roll back the golden gates of a higher and better civilization? Of all kinds of aristocracy, that of sex is the most odious and unnatural; invading, as it does, our homes, desecrating our family altars, dividing those whom God has joined together, exalting the son above the mother who bore him, and subjugating, everywhere, moral power to brute force. Such a government would not be worth the blood and treasure so freely poured out in its long struggles for freedom. . . .

2. I urge a Sixteenth Amendment, because "manhood suffrage" or a man's government, is civil, religious, and social disorganization. The male element is a destructive force, stern, selfish, aggrandizing, loving war, violence, conquest, acquisition, breeding in the material and moral world alike discord, disorder, disease, and death. See what a record of blood and cruelty the pages of history reveal! Through what slavery, slaughter, and sacrifice, through what inquisitions and imprisonments, pains and persecutions, black codes and gloomy creeds, the soul of humanity has struggled for the centuries, while mercy has veiled her face and all hearts have been dead alike to love and hope! The male element has held high carnival thus far, it has fairly run riot from the beginning, overpowering the feminine element everywhere, crushing out all the diviner qualities in human nature, until we know but little of true manhood and womanhood, of the latter comparatively nothing, for it has scarce been recognized as a power until within the last century. Society is but the reflection of man himself, untempered by woman's thought, the hard iron rule we feel alike in the church, the state, and the home. No one need wonder at the disorganization, at the fragmentary condition of everything, when we remember that man, who represents but half a complete being, with but half an idea on every subject, has undertaken the absolute control of all sublunary matters.

People object to the demands of those whom they choose to call the strong-minded, because they say, "the right of suffrage will make the women masculine." That is just the difficulty in which we are involved today. Though disfranchised we have few women in the best sense, we have simply so many reflections, varieties, and dilutions of the masculine gender. The strong, natural characteristics of womanhood are repressed and ignored in dependence, for so long as man feeds woman she will try to please the giver and adapt herself to his condition. To keep a foothold in society woman must be as near like man as possible, reflect his ideas, opinions, virtues, motives, prejudices, and vices. She must respect his statutes, though they strip her of every inalienable right, and conflict with that higher law written by the finger of God on her own soul. She must believe his theology, though it pave the highways of hell with the skulls of newborn infants, and make God a monster of vengeance and hypocrisy. She must look at everything from its dollar and cent point of view, or she is a mere romancer. She must accept things as they are and make the best of them. To mourn over the miseries of others, the poverty of the poor, their hardships in jails, prisons asylums, the horrors of war, cruelty, and brutality in every form, all this would be mere sentimentalizing. To protest against the intrigue, bribery, and corruption of public life, to desire that her sons might follow some business that did not involve lying, cheating, and a hard grinding selfishness would be arrant nonsense. In this way man has been molding woman to his ideas by direct and positive influences while she, if not a negation, has used indirect means to control him and in most cases developed the very characteristics both in him and herself that needed repression. And now man himself stands appalled at the results of his own excesses, and mourns in bitterness that falsehood, selfishness and violence are the law of life. The need of this hour is not territory, gold mines, railroads, or specie payments, but a new evangel of womanhood, to exalt purity, virtue, morality, true religion, to lift man up into the higher realms of thought and action.

10   We ask woman's enfranchisement as the first step toward the recognition of that essential element in government that can only secure the health strength and prosperity of the nation. Whatever is done to lift woman to her true position will help to usher in a new day of peace and perfection for the race. In speaking of the masculine element, I do not wish to be understood to say that all men are hard, selfish, and brutal, for many of the most beautiful spirits the world has known have been clothed with manhood: but I refer to those characteristics, though often marked in woman, that distinguish what is called the stronger sex. For example the love of acquisition and conquest the very pioneers of civilization when expended on the earth, the sea, the elements, the riches and forces of Nature are powers of destruction when used to subjugate one man to another or to sacrifice nations to ambition. Here that great conservator of woman's love, if permitted to assert itself as it naturally would in freedom against oppression, violence, and war, would hold all these destructive forces in check, for woman knows the cost of life better than man does, and not with her consent would one drop of blood ever be shed, one life sacrificed in vain. With violence and disturbance in the natural world, we see a constant effort to maintain an equilibrium of forces. Nature, like a loving mother, is ever trying to keep land and sea, mountain and valley, each in its place, to hush the angry winds and waves, balance the extremes of heat and cold, of rain and drought, that peace, harmony, and beauty may reign supreme. There is a striking analogy between matter and mind, and

the present disorganization of society warns us, that in the dethrone-ment of woman we have let loose the elements of violence and ruin that she only has the power to curb. If the civilization of the age calls for an extension of the suffrage, surely a government of the most virtu-ous, educated men and women would better represent the whole, and protect the interests of all than could the representation of either sex alone. But government gains no new element of strength in admitting all men to the ballot-box, for we have too much of the man-power there already. We see this in every department of legislation, and it is a common remark, that unless some new virtue is infused into our pub-lic life the nation is doomed to destruction. Will the foreign element, the dregs of China, Germany, England, Ireland, and Africa, supply this needed force, or the nobler types of American womanhood who have taught our presidents, senators, and congressmen the rudiments of all they know?

3. I urge a Sixteenth Amendment because, when "manhood suffrage" is established from Maine to California, woman has reached the lowest depths of political degradation. So long as there is a disfran-chised class in this country, and that class is women, a man's govern-ment is worse than a white man's government with suffrage limited by property and educational qualifications, because in proportion as you multiply the rulers, the condition of the politically ostracised is more hopeless and degraded. John Stuart Mill, in his work on "Liberty," shows that the condition of one disfranchised man in a nation is worse than when the whole nation is under one man, because in the latter case, if the one man is despotic, the nation can easily throw him off, but what can one man do with a nation of tyrants over him? If American women find it hard to bear the oppressions of their own Saxon fathers, the best orders of manhood, what may they not be called to endure when all the lower orders of foreigners now crowding our shores legislate for them and their daughters. Think of Patrick and Sambo and Hans and Yung Tung, who do not know the difference between a monarchy and a republic, who can not read the Declaration of Independence or Web-ster's spelling-book, making laws for Lucretia Mott, Ernestine L. Rose, and Anna E. Dickinson. Think of jurors and jailors drawn from these ranks to watch and try young girls for the crime of infanticide, to decide the moral code by which the mothers of this Republic shall be gov-erned? This manhood suffrage is an appalling question, and it would be well for thinking women, who seem to consider it so magnanimous to

hold their own claims in abeyance until all men are crowned with citizenship, to remember that the most ignorant men are ever the most hostile to the equality of women, as they have know them only in slavery and degradation.

Go to our courts of justice, our jails and prisons; go into the world of work; into the trades and professions; into the temples of science and learning, and see what is meted out everywhere to women—to those who have no advocates in our courts, no representatives in the councils of the nation. Shall we prolong and perpetuate such injustice, and by increasing this power risk worse oppressions for ourselves and daughters? It is an open, deliberate insult to American womanhood to be cast down under the iron-heeled peasantry of the Old World and the slaves of the New, as we shall be in the practical working of the Fifteenth Amendment, and the only atonement the Republican party can make is now to complete its work, by enfranchising the women of the nation. I have not forgotten their action four years ago, when Article XIV., Sec. 2, was amended* by invidiously introducing the word "male" into the Federal Constitution, where it had never been before, thus counting out of the basis of representation all men not permitted to vote, thereby making it the interest of every State to enfranchise its male citizens, and virtually declaring it no crime to disfranchise its women. As political sagacity moved our rulers thus to guard the interests of the negro for party purposes, common justice might have compelled them to show like respect for their own mothers, by counting woman too out of the basis of representation, that she might no longer swell the numbers to legislate adversely to her interests. And this desecration of the last will and testament of the fathers, this retrogressive legislation for woman, was in the face of the earnest protests of thousands of the best educated, most refined and cultivated women of the North.

Now, when the attention of the whole world is turned to this question of suffrage, and women themselves are throwing off the lethargy of ages, and in England, France, Germany, Switzerland, and Russia are holding their conventions, and their rulers are everywhere

*The amendment as proposed by the Hon. Thaddeus Stevens, of Pennsylvania, extended the right of suffrage to "all citizens," which included both white and black women. At the bare thought of such an impending calamity, the more timid Republicans were filled with alarm, and the word "male" promptly inserted.

giving them a respectful hearing, shall American statesmen, claiming to be liberal, so amend their constitutions as to make their wives and mothers the political inferiors of unlettered and unwashed ditch-diggers, boot-blacks, butchers, and barbers, fresh from the slave plantations of the South, and the effete civilizations of the Old World? While poets and philosophers, statesmen and men of science are all alike pointing to woman as the new hope for the redemption of the race, shall the freest Government on the earth be the first to establish an aristocracy based on sex alone? to exalt ignorance above education, vice above virtue, brutality and barbarism above refinement and religion? Not since God first called light out of darkness and order out of chaos, was there ever made so base a proposition as "manhood suffrage" in this American Republic, after all the discussions we have had on human rights in the last century. On all the blackest pages of history there is no record of an act like this, in any nation, where native born citizens, having the same religion, speaking the same language, equal to their rulers in wealth, family, and education, have been politically ostracised by their own countrymen, outlawed with savages, and subjected to the government of outside barbarians. Remember the Fifteenth Amendment takes in a larger population than the 2,000,000 black men on the Southern plantation. It takes in all the foreigners daily landing in our eastern cities, the Chinese crowding our western shores, the inhabitants of Alaska, and all those western isles that will soon be ours. American statesmen may flatter themselves that by superior intelligence and political sagacity the higher orders of men will always govern, but when the ignorant foreign vote already holds the balance of power in all the large cities by sheer force of numbers, it is simply a question of impulse or passion, bribery or fraud, how our elections will be carried. When the highest offices in the gift of the people are bought and sold in Wall Street, it is a mere chance who will be our rulers. Whither is a nation tending when brains count for less than bullion, and clowns make laws for queens? It is a startling assertion, but nevertheless true, that in none of the nations of modern Europe are the higher classes of women politically so degraded as are the women of this Republic to-day. In the Old World, where the government is the aristocracy, where it is considered a mark of nobility to share its offices and powers, women of rank have certain hereditary rights which raise them above a majority of the men, certain honors and privileges not granted to serfs and peasants. There women are queens, hold subordinate offices, and vote on many questions. In our Southern States even, before the war, women were not degraded below the working population. They were not humiliated in seeing their coachmen, gardeners, and waiters go to the polls to legislate for them; but here, in this boasted Northern civilization, women of wealth and education, who pay taxes and obey the laws, who in morals and intellect are the peers of their proudest rulers, are thrust outside the pale of political consideration with minors, paupers, lunatics, traitors, idiots, with those guilty of bribery, larceny, and infamous crimes.

Would those gentlemen who are on all sides telling the women of the nation not to press their claims until the negro is safe beyond peradventure, be willing themselves to stand aside and trust all their interests to hands like these? The educated women of this nation feel as much interest in republican institutions, the preservation of the country, the good of the race, their own elevation and success, as any man possibly can, and we have the same distrust in man's power to legislate for us, that he has in woman's power to legislate wisely for herself.

SUGGESTIONS FOR WRITING

1. Elizabeth Cady Stanton discusses feminism primarily as an existential, pre-political matter. Write an essay on the difference her approach makes for the political views she advocates.
2. What in your view is the greatest strength of Elizabeth Cady Stanton as a writer? Write an essay that analyzes the literary skill of her address.
3. Where would Elizabeth Cady Stanton's views place her within the current spectrum of feminism as you understand it? Write an essay that explains and defends your views.

Woman's Place in Man's Life Cycle   1982

CAROL GILLIGAN

A professor of education at Harvard, Carol Gilligan (b. 1936) has explored many areas in the field of psychological development. One aspect of this field makes a theme in her essay below: the tendency of experts in development to base their conclusions almost entirely on studies dealing almost entirely with boys rather than girls. The ironic spirit of her essay's title playfully refers to the resulting slant of such studies, which Gilligan naturally finds of severely limited value.

In the second act of *The Cherry Orchard*, Lopahin, a young merchant, describes his life of hard work and success. Failing to convince Madame Ranevskaya to cut down the cherry orchard to save her estate, he will go on in the next act to buy it himself. He is the self-made man who, in purchasing the estate where his father and grandfather were slaves, seeks to eradicate the "awkward, unhappy life" of the past, replacing the cherry orchard with summer cottages where coming generations "will see a new life." In elaborating this developmental vision, he reveals the image of man that underlies and supports his activity: "At times when I can't go to sleep, I think: Lord, thou gavest us immense forests, unbounded fields and the widest horizons, and living in the midst of them we should indeed be giants"—at which point, Madame Ranevskaya interrupts him, saying, "You feel the need for giants—They are good only in fairy tales, anywhere else they only frighten us."

Conceptions of the human life cycle represent attempts to order and make coherent the unfolding experiences and perceptions, the changing wishes and realities of everyday life. But the nature of such conceptions depends in part on the position of the observer. The brief excerpt from Chekhov's play suggest that when the observer is a woman, the perspective may be of a different sort. Different judgments of the image of man as giant imply different ideas about human development, different ways of imagining the human condition, different notions of what is of value in life.

At a time when efforts are being made to eradicate discrimination between the sexes in the search for social equality and justice, the differences between the sexes are being rediscovered in the social sciences. This discovery occurs when theories formerly considered to be sexually neutral in their scientific objectivity are found instead to reflect a consistent observational and evaluative bias. Then the presumed neutrality of science, like that of language itself, gives way to the recognition that the categories of knowledge are human constructions. The fascination with point of view that has informed the fiction of the twentieth century and the corresponding recognition of the relativity of judgment infuse our scientific understanding as well when we begin to notice how accustomed we have become to seeing life through men's eyes.

A recent discovery of this sort pertains to the apparently innocent classic *The Elements of Style* by William Strunk and E. B. White. A Supreme Court ruling on the subject of sex discrimination led one teacher of English to notice that the elementary rules of English usage were being taught through examples which counterposed the birth of Napoleon, the writings of Coleridge, and statements such as "He was an interesting talker. A man who had traveled all over the world and lived in half a dozen countries," with "Well, Susan, this is a fine mess you are in" or, less drastically, "He saw a woman, accompanied by two children, walking slowly down the road."

5   Psychological theorists have fallen as innocently as Strunk and White into the same observational bias. Implicitly adopting the male life as the norm, they have tried to fashion women out of a masculine cloth. It all goes back, of course, to Adam and Eve—a story which shows, among other things, that if you make a woman out of a man, you are bound to get into trouble. In the life cycle, as in the Garden of Eden, the woman has been the deviant.

The penchant of developmental theorists to project a masculine image, and one that appears frightening to women, goes back at least to Freud (1905), who built his theory of psychosexual development around the experiences of the male child that culminate in the Oedipus complex. In the 1920s, Freud struggled to resolve the contradictions posed for his theory by the differences in female anatomy and the different configuration of the young girl's early family relationships. After trying to fit women into his masculine conception, seeing them as envying that which they missed, he came instead to acknowledge, in the strength and persistence of women's pre-Oedipal attachments to their mothers, a developmental difference. He considered this difference in women's development to be responsible for what he saw as women's developmental failure.

Having tied the formation of the superego or conscience to castration anxiety, Freud considered women to be deprived by nature of the impetus for a clear-cut Oedipal resolution. Consequently, women's superego—the heir to the Oedipus complex—was compromised: it was never "so inexorable, so impersonal, so independent of its emotional origins as we require it to be in men." From this observation of difference, that "for women the level of what is ethically normal is different from what it is in men," Freud concluded that women "show less sense of justice than men, that they are less ready to submit to the great exigencies of life, that they are more often influenced in their judgements by feelings of affection or hostility" (1925, pp. 257–258).

Thus a problem in theory became cast as a problem in women's development, and the problem in women's development was located in their experience of relationships. Nancy Chodorow (1974), attempting to account for "the reproduction within each generation of certain general and nearly universal differences that characterize masculine and feminine personality and roles," attributes these differences between the sexes not to anatomy but rather to "the fact that women, universally, are largely responsible for early child care." Because this early social environment differs for and is experienced differently by male and female children, basic sex differences recurin personality development. As a result, "in any given society, feminine personality comes to define itself in relation and connection to other people more than masculine personality does" (pp. 43–44).

In her analysis, Chodorow relies primarily on Robert Stoller's studies which indicate that gender identity, the unchanging core of personality formation, is "with rare exception firmly and irreversibly established for both sexes by the time a child is around three." Given that for both sexes the primary caretaker in the first three years of life is typically female, the interpersonal dynamics of gender identity formation are different for boys and girls. Female identity formation takes place in a context of ongoing relationship since "mothers tend to experience their daughters as more like, and continuous with, themselves." Correspondingly, girls, in identifying themselves as female, experience themselves as like their mothers, thus fusing the experience of attachment with the process of identity formation. In contrast, "mothers experience their sons as a male opposite," and boys, in defining themselves as masculine, separate their mothers from themselves, thus curtailing "their primary love and sense of empathic tie." Consequently, male development entails a "more emphatic individuation and a more defensive firming of experienced ego boundaries." For boys, but not girls, "issues of differentiation have become intertwined with sexual issues" (1978, pp. 150, 166–167).

10   Writing against the masculine bias of psychoanalytic theory, Chodorow argues that the existence of sex differences in the early

experiences of individuation and relationship "does not mean that women have 'weaker' ego boundaries than men or are more prone to psychosis." It means instead that "girls emerge from this period with a basis for 'empathy' built into their primary definition of self in a way that boys do not." Chodorow thus replaces Freud's negative and derivative description of female psychology with a positive and direct account of her own: "Girls emerge with a stronger basis for experiencing another's needs or feelings as one's own (or of thinking that one is so experiencing another's needs and feelings). Furthermore, girls do not define themselves in terms of the denial of pre-Oedipal relational modes to the same extent as do boys. Therefore, regression to these modes tends not to feel as much a basic threat to their ego. From very early, then, because they are parented by a person of the same gender . . . girls come to experience themselves as less differentiated than boys, as more continuous with and related to the external object-world, and as differently oriented to their inner object-world as well" (p. 167).

Consequently, relationships, and particularly issues of dependency, are experienced differently by women and men. For boys and men, separation and individuation are critically tied to gender identity since separation from the mother is essential for the development of masculinity. For girls and women, issues of femininity or feminine identity do not depend on the achievement of separation from the mother or on the progress of individuation. Since masculinity is defined through separation while femininity is defined through attachment, male gender identity is threatened by intimacy while female gender identity is threatened by separation. Thus males tend to have difficulty with relationships, while females tend to have problems with individuation. The quality of embeddedness in social interaction and personal relationships that characterizes women's lives in contrast to men's, however, becomes not only a descriptive difference but also a developmental liability when the milestones of childhood and adolescent development in the psychological literature are markers of increasing separation. Women's failure to separate then becomes by definition a failure to develop.

The sex differences in personality formation that Chodorow describes in early childhood appear during the middle childhood years in studies of children's games. Children's games are considered by George Herbert Mead (1934) and Jean Piaget (1932) as the crucible of social development during the school years. In games, children learn to take the role of the other and come to see themselves through another's eyes. In games, they learn respect for rules and come to understand the ways rules can be made and changed.

Janet Lever (1976), considering the peer group to be the agent of socialization during the elementary school years and play to be a major activity of socialization at that time, set out to discover whether there are sex differences in the games that children play. Studying 181 fifth-grade, white, middle-class children, ages ten and eleven, she observed the organization and structure of their playtime activities. She watched the children as they played at school during recess and in physical education class, and in addition kept diaries of their accounts as to how they spent their out-of-school time. From this study, Lever reports sex differences: boys play out of doors more often than girls do; boys play more often in large and age-heterogeneous groups; they play competitive games more often, and their games last longer than girls' games. The last is in some ways the most interesting finding. Boys' games appeared to last longer not only because they required a higher level of skill and were thus less likely to become boring, but also because, when disputes arose in the course of a game, boys were able to resolve the disputes more effectively than girls: "During the course of this study, boys were seen quarrelling all the time, but not once was a game terminated because of a quarrel and no game was interrupted for more than seven minutes. In the gravest debates, the final word was always, to 'repeat the play,' generally followed by a chorus of 'cheater's proof'" (p. 482). In fact, it seemed that the boys enjoyed the legal debates as much as they did the game itself, and even marginal players of lesser size or skill participated equally in these recurrent squabbles. In contrast, the eruption of disputes among girls tended to end the game.

Thus Lever extends and corroborates the observations of Piaget in his study of the rules of the game, where he finds boys becoming through childhood increasingly fascinated with the legal elaboration of rules and the development of fair procedures for adjudicating conflicts, a fascination that, he notes, does not hold for girls. Girls, Piaget observes, have a more "pragmatic" attitude toward rules, "regarding a rule as good as long as the game repaid it" (p. 83). Girls are more tolerant in their attitudes toward rules, more willing to make exceptions, and more easily reconciled to innovations. As a result, the legal sense, which Piaget considers essential to moral development, "is far less developed in little girls than in boys" (p. 77).

15   The bias that leads Piaget to equate male development with child development also colors Lever's work. The assumption that shapes her discussion of results is that the male model is the better one since it fits the requirements for modern corporate success. In contrast, the sensitivity and care for the feelings of others that girls develop through their play have little market value and can even impede professional success. Lever implies that, given the realities of adult life, if a girl does not want to be left dependent on men, she will have to learn to play like a boy.

To Piaget's argument that children learn the respect for rules necessary for moral development by playing rule-bound games, Lawrence Kohlberg (1969) adds that these lessons are most effectively learned through the opportunities for role-taking that arise in the course of resolving disputes. Consequently, the moral lessons inherent in girls' play appear to be fewer than in boys'. Traditional girls' games like jump rope and hopscotch are turn-taking games, where competition is indirect since one person's success does not necessarily signify another's failure. Consequently, disputes requiring adjudication are less likely to occur. In fact, most of the girls whom Lever interviewed claimed that when a quarrel broke out, they ended the game. Rather than elaborating a system of rules for resolving disputes, girls subordinated the continuation of the game to the continuation of relationships.

Lever concludes that from the games they play, boys learn both the independence and the organizational skills necessary for coordinating the activities of large and diverse groups of people. By participating in controlled and socially approved competitive situations, they learn to deal with competition in a relatively forthright manner—to play with their enemies and to compete with their friends—all in accordance with the rules of the game. In contrast, girls' play tends to occur in smaller, more intimate groups, often the best-friend dyad, and in private places. This play replicates the social pattern of primary human relationships in that its organization is more cooperative. Thus, it points less, in Mead's terms, toward learning to take the role of "the generalized other," less toward the abstraction of human relationships. But it fosters the development of the empathy and sensitivity necessary for taking the role of "the particular other" and points more toward knowing the other as different from the self.

The sex differences in personality formation in early childhood that Chodorow derives from her analysis of the mother-child relationship are thus extended by Lever's observations of sex differences in the play activities of middle childhood. Together these accounts suggest that boys and girls arrive at puberty with a different interpersonal orientation and a different range of social experiences. Yet, since adolescence is considered a crucial time for separation, the period of "the second individuation process" (Blos, 1967), female development has appeared most divergent and thus most problematic at this time.

"Puberty," Freud says, "which brings about so great an accession of libido in boys, is marked in girls by a fresh wave of *repression*," necessary for the transformation of the young girl's "masculine sexuality" into the specifically feminine sexuality of her adulthood (1905, pp. 220–221). Freud posits this transformation on the girl's acknowledgment and acceptance of "the fact of her castration" (1931, p. 229). To the girl, Freud explains, puberty brings a new awareness of "the wound to her narcissism" and leads her to develop, "like a scar, a sense of inferiority" (1925, p. 253). Since in Erik Erikson's expansion of Freud's psychoanalytic account, adolescence is the time when development hinges on identity, the girl arrives at this juncture either psychologically at risk or with a different agenda.

20   The problem that female adolescence presents for theorists of human development is apparent in Erikson's scheme. Erikson (1950) charts eight stages of psychosocial development, of which adolescence is the fifth. The task at this stage is to forge a coherent sense of self, to verify an identity that can span the discontinuity of puberty and make possible the adult capacity to love and work. The preparation for the successful resolution of the adolescent identity crisis is delineated in Erikson's description of the crises that characterize the preceding four stages. Although the initial crisis in infancy of "trust versus mistrust" anchors development in the experience of relationship, the task then clearly becomes one of individuation. Erikson's second stage centers on the crisis of "autonomy versus shame and doubt," which marks the walking child's emerging sense of separateness and agency. From there, development goes on through the crisis of "initiative versus guilt," successful resolution of which represents a further move in the direction of autonomy. Next, following the inevitable disappointment of the magical wishes of the Oedipal period, children realize that to compete with their parents, they must first join them and learn to do what they do so well. Thus in the middle childhood years, development turns on the crisis of "industry versus inferiority," as the demonstration of competence becomes critical to the child's developing self-esteem. This is the time when children strive to learn and master the technology of

their culture, in order to recognize themselves and to be recognized by others as capable of becoming adults. Next comes adolescence, the celebration of the autonomous, initiating, industrious self through the forging of an identity based on an ideology that can support and justify adult commitments. But about whom is Erikson talking?

Once again it turns out to be the male child. For the female, Erikson (1968) says, the sequence is a bit different. She holds her identity in abeyance as she prepares to attract the man by whose name she will be known, by whose status she will be defined, the man who will rescue her from emptiness and loneliness by filling "the inner space." While for men, identity precedes intimacy and generativity in the optimal cycle of human separation and attachment, for women these tasks seem instead to be fused. Intimacy goes along with identity, as the female comes to know herself as she is known, through her relationships with others.

Yet despite Erikson's observation of sex differences, his chart of life-cycle stages remains unchanged: identity continues to precede intimacy as male experience continues to define his life-cycle conception. But in this male life cycle there is little preparation for the intimacy of the first adult stage. Only the initial stage of trust versus mistrust suggests the type of mutuality that Erikson means by intimacy and generativity and Freud means by genitality. The rest is separateness, with the result that development itself comes to be identified with separation, and attachments appear to be developmental impediments, as is repeatedly the case in the assessment of women.

Erikson's description of male identity as forged in relation to the world and of female identity as awakened in a relationship of intimacy with another person is hardly new. In the fairy tales that Bruno Bettelheim (1976) describes an identical portrayal appears. The dynamics of male adolescence are illustrated archetypically by the conflict between father and son in "The Three Languages." Here a son, considered hopelessly stupid by his father, is given one last chance at education and sent for a year to study with a master. But when he returns, all he has learned is "what the dogs bark." After two further attempts of this sort, the father gives up in disgust and orders his servants to take the child into the forest and kill him. But the servants, those perpetual rescuers of disowned and abandoned children, take pity on the child and decide simply to leave him in the forest. From there, his wanderings take him to a land beset by furious dogs whose barking permits nobody to rest and who periodically devour one of the inhabitants.

Now it turns out that our hero has learned just the right thing: he can talk with the dogs and is able to quiet them, thus restoring peace to the land. Since the other knowledge he acquires serves him equally well, he emerges triumphant from his adolescent confrontation with his father, a giant of the life-cycle conception.

In contrast, the dynamics of female adolescence are depicted through the telling of a very different story. In the world of the fairy tale, the girl's first bleeding is followed by a period of intense passivity in which nothing seems to be happening. Yet in the deep sleeps of Snow White and Sleeping Beauty, Bettelheim sees that inner concentration which he considers to be the necessary counterpart to the activity of adventure. Since the adolescent heroines awake from their sleep, not to conquer the world, but to marry the prince, their identity is inwardly and interpersonally defined. For women, in Bettelheim's as in Erikson's account, identity and intimacy are intricately conjoined. The sex differences depicted in the world of fairy tales, like the fantasy of the woman warrior in Maxine Hong Kingston's (1977) recent autobiographical novel which echoes the old stories of Troilus and Cressida and Tancred and Chlorinda, indicate repeatedly that active adventure is a male activity, and that if a woman is to embark on such endeavors, she must at least dress like a man.

25   These observations about sex difference support the conclusion reached by David McClelland (1975) that "sex role turns out to be one of the most important determinants of human behavior; psychologists have found sex differences in their studies from the moment they started doing empirical research." But since it is difficult to say "different" without saying "better" or "worse," since there is a tendency to construct a single scale of measurement, and since that scale has generally been derived from and standardized on the basis of men's interpretations of research data drawn predominantly or exclusively from studies of males, psychologists "have tended to regard male behavior as the 'norm' and female behavior as some kind of deviation from that norm" (p. 81). Thus, when women do not conform to the standards of psychological expectation, the conclusion has generally been that something is wrong with the women.

What Matina Horner (1972) found to be wrong with women was the anxiety they showed about competitive achievement. From the beginning, research on human motivation using the Thematic Apperception Test (TAT) was plagued by evidence of sex differences which appeared to confuse and complicate data analysis. The TAT presents for interpretation an ambiguous cue—a picture about which a story is to be written or a segment of a story that is to be completed. Such stories, in reflecting projective imagination, are considered by psychologists to reveal the ways in which people construe what they perceive, that is, the concepts and interpretations they bring to their experience and thus presumably the kind of sense that they make of their lives. Prior to Horner's work it was clear that women made a different kind of sense than men of situations of competitive achievement, that in some way they saw the situations differently or the situations aroused in them some different response.

On the basis of his studies of men, McClelland divided the concept of achievement motivation into what appeared to be its two logical components, a motive to approach success ("hope success") and a motive to avoid failure ("fear failure"). From her studies of women, Horner identified as a third category the unlikely motivation to avoid success ("fear success"). Women appeared to have a problem with competitive achievement, and that problem seemed to emanate from a perceived conflict between femininity and success, the dilemma of the female adolescent who struggles to integrate her feminine aspirations and the identifications of her early childhood with the more masculine competence she has acquired at school. From her analysis of women's completions of a story that began, "after first term finals, Anne finds herself at the top of her medical school class," and from her observation of women's performance in competitive achievement situations, Horner reports that, "when success is likely or possible, threatened by the negative consequences they expect to follow success, young women become anxious and their positive achievement strivings become thwarted" (p. 171). She concludes that this fear "exists because for most women, the anticipation of success in competitive achievement activity, especially against men, produces anticipation of certain negative consequences, for example, threat of social rejection and loss of femininity" (1968, p. 125).

Such conflicts about success, however, may be viewed in a different light. Georgia Sassen (1980) suggests that the conflicts expressed by the women might instead indicate "a heightened perception of the 'other side' of competitive success, that is, the great emotional costs at which success achieved through competition is often gained—an understanding which, though confused, indicates some underlying sense that something is rotten in the state in which success is defined as having better grades than everyone else" (p. 15). Sassen points out that Horner found success anxiety to be present in women only when achievement was directly competitive, that is, when one person's success was at the expense of another's failure.

In his elaboration of the identity crisis, Erikson (1968) cites the life of George Bernard Shaw to illustrate the young person's sense of being co-opted prematurely by success in a career he cannot wholeheartedly endorse. Shaw at seventy, reflecting upon his life, described his crisis at the age of twenty as having been caused not by the lack of success or the absence of recognition, but by too much of both: "I made good in spite of myself, and found, to my dismay, that Business, instead of expelling me as the worthless imposter I was, was fastening upon me with no intention of letting me go. Behold me, therefore, in my twentieth year, with a business training, in an occupation which I detested as cordially as any sane person lets himself detest anything he cannot escape from. In March 1876 I broke loose" (p. 143). At this point Shaw settled down to study and write as he pleased. Hardly interpreted as evidence of neurotic anxiety about achievement and competition. Shaw's refusal suggests to Erikson "the extraordinary workings of an extraordinary personality [coming] to the fore" (p. 144).

30   We might on these grounds begin to ask, not why women have conflicts about competitive success, but why men show such readiness to adopt and celebrate a rather narrow vision of success. Remembering Piaget's observation, corroborated by Lever, that boys in their games are more concerned with rules while girls are more concerned with relationships, often at the expense of the game itself—and given Chodorow's conclusion that men's social orientation is positional while women's is personal—we begin to understand why, when "Anne" becomes "John" in Horner's tale of competitive success and the story is completed by men, fear of success tends to disappear. John is considered to have played by the rules and won. He has the *right* to feel good about his success. Confirmed in the sense of his own identity as separate from those who, compared to him, are less competent, his positional sense of self is affirmed. For Anne, it is possible that the position she could obtain by being at the top of her medical school class may not, in fact, be what she wants.

"It is obvious," Virginia Woolf says, "that the values of women differ very often from the values which have been made by the other sex" (1929, p. 76). Yet, she adds, "it is the masculine values that prevail." As a result, women come to question the normality of their feelings and to alter their judgments in deference to the opinion of others. In the nineteenth century novels written by women, Woolf sees at work "a mind which was slightly pulled from the straight and made to alter its clear vision in deference to external authority." The same deference to the values and opinions of others can be seen in the judgments of twentieth century women. The difficulty women experience in finding or speaking publicly in their own voices emerges repeatedly in the form of qualification and self-doubt, but also in intimations of a divided judgment, a public assessment and private assessment which are fundamentally at odds.

Yet the deference and confusion that Woolf criticizes in women derive from the values she sees as their strength. Women's deference is rooted not only in their social subordination but also in the substance of their moral concern. Sensitivity to the needs of others and the assumption of responsibility for taking care lead women to attend to voices other than their own and to include in their judgment other points of view. Women's moral weakness, manifest in an apparent diffusion and confusion of judgment, is thus inseparable from women's moral strength, an overriding concern with relationships and responsibilities. The reluctance to judge may itself be indicative of the care and concern for others that infuse the psychology of women's development and are responsible for what is generally seen as problematic in its nature.

Thus women not only define themselves in a context of human relationship but also judge themselves in terms of their ability to care. Women's place in man's life cycle has been that of nurturer, caretaker, and helpmate, the weaver of those networks of relationships on which she in turn relies. But while women have thus taken care of men, men have, in their theories of psychological development, as in their economic arrangements, tended to assume or devalue that care. When the focus on individuation and individual achievement extends into adulthood and maturity is equated with personal autonomy, concern with relationships appears as a weakness of women rather than as a human strength (Miller, 1976).

The discrepancy between womanhood and adulthood is nowhere more evident than in the studies on sex-role stereotypes reported by Broverman, Vogel, Broverman, Clarkson, and Rosenkrantz (1972). The repeated finding of these studies is that the qualities deemed necessary for adulthood—the capacity for autonomous thinking, clear decision-making, and responsible action—are those associated with masculinity and considered undesirable as attributes of the feminine self. The stereotypes suggest a splitting of love and work that relegates expressive capacities to women while placing instrumental abilities in the masculine domain. Yet looked at from a different perspective, these stereotypes reflect a conception of adulthood that is itself out of balance, favoring the separateness of the individual self over connection to others, and leaning more toward an autonomous life of work than toward the interdependence of love and care.

35   The discovery now being celebrated by men in mid-life of the importance of intimacy, relationships, and care is something that women have known from the beginning. However, because that knowledge in women has been considered "intuitive" or "instinctive," a function of anatomy coupled with destiny, psychologists have neglected to describe its development. In my research, I have found that women's moral development centers on the elaboration of that knowledge and thus delineates a critical line of psychological development in the lives of both of the sexes. The subject of moral development not only provides the final illustration of the reiterative pattern in the observation and assessment of sex differences in the literature on human development, but also indicates more particularly why the nature and significance of women's development has been for so long obscured and shrouded in mystery.

The criticism that Freud makes of women's sense of justice, seeing it as compromised in its refusal of blind impartiality, reappears not only in the work of Piaget but also in that of Kohlberg. While in Piaget's account (1932) of the moral judgment of the child, girls are an aside, a curiosity to whom he devotes four brief entries in an index that omits "boys" altogether because "the child" is assumed to be male, in the research from which Kohlberg derives his theory, females simply do not exist. Kohlberg's (1958, 1981) six stages that describe the development of moral judgment from childhood to adulthood are based empirically on a study of eighty-four boys whose development Kohlberg has followed for a period of over twenty years. Although Kohlberg claims universality for his stage sequence, those groups not included in his original sample rarely reach his higher stages (Edwards, 1975; Holstein, 1976; Simpson, 1974). Prominent among those who thus appear to be deficient in moral development when measured by Kohlberg's scale are women, whose judgments seem to exemplify the third stage of his six-stage sequence. At this stage morality is conceived in interpersonal terms and goodness is equated with helping and pleasing others. This conception of goodness is considered by Kohlberg and Kramer (1969) to be functional in the lives of mature women insofar as their lives take place in the home. Kohlberg and Kramer imply that only if women enter the traditional arena of male activity will they recognize the inadequacy of this moral perspective and progress like men toward higher stages where relationships are subordinated to rules (stage four) and rules to universal principles of justice (stages five and six).

Yet herein lies a paradox, for the very traits that traditionally have defined the "goodness" of women, their care for and sensitivity to the needs of others, are those that mark them as deficient in moral development. In this version of moral development, however, the conception of maturity is derived from the study of men's lives and reflects the importance of individuation in their development. Piaget (1970), challenging the common impression that a developmental theory is built like a pyramid from its base in infancy, points out that a conception of development instead hangs from its vertex of maturity, the point toward which progress is traced. Thus, a change in the definition of maturity does not simply alter the description of the highest stage but recasts the understanding of development, changing the entire account.

When one begins with the study of women and derives developmental constructs from their lives, the outline of a moral conception different from that described by Freud, Piaget, or Kohlberg begins to emerge and informs a different description of development. In this conception, the moral problem arises from conflicting responsibilities rather than from competing rights and requires for its resolution a mode of thinking that is contextual and narrative rather than formal and abstract. This conception of morality as concerned with the activity of care centers moral development around the understanding of responsibility and relationships, just as the conception of morality as fairness ties moral development to the understanding of rights and rules.

This different construction of the moral problem by women may be seen as the critical reason for their failure to develop within the constraints of Kohlberg's system. Regarding all constructions of responsibility as evidence of a conventional moral understanding, Kohlberg defines the highest stages of moral development as deriving from a reflective understanding of human rights. That the morality of rights differs from the morality of responsibility in its emphasis on separation rather than connection, in its consideration of the individual rather than the relationship as primary, is illustrated by two responses to interview questions about the nature of morality. The first comes from a twenty-five-year-old man, one of the participants in Kohlberg's study:

> [What does the word morality mean to you?] Nobody in the world knows the answer. I think it is recognizing the right of the individual, the rights of other individuals, not interfering with those rights. Act as fairly as you would have them treat you. I think it is basically to preserve the human being's right to existence I think that is the most important. Secondly, the human being's right to do as he pleases, again without interfering with somebody's else's rights.
>
> [How have your views on morality changed since the last interview?] I think I am more aware of an individual's rights now. I used to be looking at it strictly from my point of view, just for me. Now I think I am more aware of what the individual has a right to.

Kohlberg (1973) cites this man's response as illustrative of the principled conception of human rights that exemplifies his fifth and sixth stages. Commenting on the response, Kohlberg says: "Moving to a perspective outside of that of his society, he identifies morality with justice (fairness, rights, the Golden Rule), with recognition of the rights of others as these are defined naturally or intrinsically. The human's being right to do as he pleases without interfering with somebody else's rights is a formula defining rights prior to social legislation" (pp.29–30).

40   The second response comes from a woman who participated in the rights and responsibilities study. She also was twenty-five and, at the time, a third-year law student:

> [Is there really some correct solution to moral problems, or is everybody's opinion equally right?] No, I don't think everybody's opinion is equally right. I think that in some situations there may be opinions that are equally valid, and one could conscientiously adopt one of several courses of action. But there are other situations in which I think there are right and wrong answers, that sort of inhere in the nature of existence, of all individuals here who need to live with each other to live. We need to depend on each other, and hopefully it is not only a physical need but a

need of fulfillment in ourselves, that a person's life is enriched by cooper-
ating with other people and striving to live in harmony with everybody
else, and to that end, there are right and wrong, there are things which
promote that end and that move away from it, and in that way it is
possible to choose in certain cases among different courses of action
that obviously promote or harm that goal.

[Is there a time in the past when you would have thought about
these things differently?] Oh, yeah, I think that I went through a time
when I thought that things were pretty relative, that I can't tell you
what to do and you can't tell me what to do, because you've got your
conscience and I've got mine.

[When was that?] When I was in high school. I guess that it just
sort of dawned on me that my own ideas changed, and because my
own judgment changed, I felt I couldn't judge another person's judg-
ment. But now I think even when it is only the person himself who is
going to be affected, I say it is wrong to the extent it doesn't cohere
with what I know about human nature and what I know about you,
and just from what I think is true about the operation of the universe,
I could say I think you are making a mistake.

[What led you to change, do you think?] Just seeing more of life,
just recognizing that there are an awful lot of things that are common
among people. There are certain things that you come to learn promote
a better life and better relationships and more personal fulfillment
than other things that in general tend to do the opposite, and the
things that promote these things, you would call morally right.

This response also represents a personal reconstruction of morality
following a period of questioning and doubt, but the reconstruction of
moral understanding is based not on the primacy and universality of
individual rights, but rather on what she describes as a "very strong sense
of being responsible to the world." Within this construction, the moral
dilemma changes from how to exercise one's rights without interfering
with the rights of others to how "to lead a moral life which includes obligations to myself and my family and people in general." The problem
then becomes one of limiting responsibilities without abandoning
moral concern. When asked to describe herself, this woman says that she
values "having other people that I am tied to, and also having people that
I am responsible to. I have a very strong sense of being responsible to
the world, that I can't just live for my enjoyment, but just the fact of being

in the world gives me an obligation to do what I can to make the world a better place to live in, no matter how small a scale that may be on." Thus while Kohlberg's subject worries about people interfering with each other's rights, this woman worries about "the possibility of omission, of your not helping others when you could help them."

The issue that this woman raises is addressed by Jane Loevinger's fifth "autonomous" stage of ego development, where autonomy, placed in a context of relationships, is defined as modulating an excessive sense of responsibility through the recognition that other people have responsibility for their own destiny. The autonomous stage in Loevinger's account (1970) witnesses a relinquishing of moral dichotomies and their replacement with "a feeling for the complexity and multifaceted character of real people and real situations" (p. 6). Whereas the rights conception of morality that informs Kohlberg's principled level (stages five and six) is geared to arriving at an objectively fair or just resolution to moral dilemmas upon which all rational persons could agree, the responsibility conception focuses instead on the limitations of any particular resolution and describes the conflicts that remain.

Thus it becomes clear why a morality of rights and noninterference may appear frightening to women in its potential justification of indifference and unconcern. At the same time, it becomes clear why, from a male perspective, a morality of responsibility appears inconclusive and diffuse, given its insistent contextual relativism. Women's moral judgments thus elucidate the pattern observed in the description of the developmental differences between the sexes, but they also provide an alternative conception of maturity by which these differences can be assessed and their implications traced. The psychology of women that has consistently been described as distinctive in its greater orientation toward relationships and interdependence implies a more contextual mode of judgment and a different moral understanding. Given the differences in women's conceptions of self and morality, women bring to the life cycle a different point of view and order human experience in terms of different priorities.

The myth of Demeter and Persephone, which McClelland (1975) cites as exemplifying the feminine attitude toward power, was associated with the Eleusinian Mysteries celebrated in ancient Greece for over two thousand years. As told in the Homeric *Hymn to Demeter*, the story of Persephone indicates the strengths of interdependence, building up resources and giving, that McClelland found in his research on power motivation to characterize the mature feminine style. Although,

McClelland says, "it is fashionable to conclude that no one knows what went on in the Mysteries, it is known that they were probably the most important religious ceremonies, even partly on the historical record, which were organized by and for women, especially at the onset before men by means of the cult of Dionysos began to take them over." Thus McClelland regards the myth as "a special presentation of feminine psychology" (p. 96). It is, as well, a life-cycle story par excellence.

45   Persephone, the daughter of Demeter, while playing in a meadow with her girlfriends, sees a beautiful narcissus which she runs to pick. As she does so, the earth opens and she is snatched away by Hades, who takes her to his underworld kingdom. Demeter, goddess of the earth, so mourns the loss of her daughter that she refuses to allow anything to grow. The crops that sustain life on earth shrivel up, killing men and animals alike, until Zeus takes pity on man's suffering and persuades his brother to return Persephone to her mother. But before she leaves, Persephone eats some pomegranate seeds, which ensures that she will spend part of every year with Hades in the underworld.

The elusive mystery of women's development lies in its recognition of the continuing importance of attachment in the human life cycle. Woman's place in man's life cycle is to protect this recognition while the developmental litany intones the celebration of separation, autonomy, individuation, and natural rights. The myth of Persephone speaks directly to the distortion in this view by reminding us that narcissism leads to death, that the fertility of the earth is in some mysterious way tied to the continuation of the mother-daughter relationship, and that the life cycle itself arises from an alternation between the world of women and that of men. Only when life-cycle theorists divide their attention and begin to live with women as they have lived with men will their vision encompass the experience of both sexes and their theories become correspondingly more fertile.

SUGGESTIONS FOR WRITING

1. Do you agree with Gilligan that men and women tend to observe things differently? Write an essay that uses examples to explain and defend your answer.
2. Gilligan points to a famous short guide to writing, *The Elements of Style*. Write an essay that analyzes the ways in which Gilligan uses this particular example to support her general argument in her essay as a whole.

3. In your opinion, to what extent does Gilligan reflect the views of Virginia Woolf in "Shakespeare's Sister?" Write an essay that explains what you see as the common grounds (or the lack of them) shared by the two women in their positions.

Racism and Feminism 1981

BELL HOOKS

bell hooks (the lower case letters are her choice) was born Gloria Jean Watkins in 1952. Writing largely from a black perspective, she has addressed a variety of issues as a social critic and literary scholar. Her early education took place in segregated schools, but she went on to graduate from Stanford, to earn an M.A. from Wisconsin, and a Ph. D. from the University of California at Santa Cruz. In the following essay, she discusses the historical interactions of racism and the feminist movement, finding that all too often that intersection saw "white and black women compete to be the chosen female group," instead of uniting against a common enemy or combining to pursue common goals.

I am a black woman. I attended all-black public schools. I grew up in the south where all around me was the fact of racial discrimination, hatred, and forced segregation. Yet my education as to the politics of race in American society was not that different from that of white female students I met in integrated high schools, in college, or in various women's groups. The majority of us understood racism as a social evil perpetuated by prejudiced white people that could be overcome through bonding between blacks and liberal whites, through militant protest, changing of laws or racial integration. Higher educational institutions did nothing to increase our limited understanding of racism as a political ideology. Instead professors systematically denied us truth, teaching us to accept racial polarity in the form of white supremacy and sexual polarity in the form of male dominance.

American women have been socialized, even brainwashed, to accept a version of American history that was created to uphold and maintain racial imperialism in the form of white supremacy and sexual imperialism in the form of patriarchy. One measure of the success of such indoctrination is that we perpetuate both consciously and unconsciously the very evils that oppress us. I am certain that the black female sixth grade teacher who taught us history, who taught us to identify with the American government, who loved those students who could best recite the pledge of allegiance to the American flag was not aware of the contradiction; that we should love this government that segregated us, that failed to send schools with all black students supplies that went to schools with only white pupils. Unknowingly she implanted in our psyches a seed of the racial imperialism that would keep us forever in bondage. For how does one overthrow, change, or even challenge a system that you have been taught to admire, to love, to believe in? Her innocence does not change the reality that she was teaching black children to embrace the very system that oppressed us, that she encouraged us to support it, to stand in awe of it, die for it.

That American women, irrespective of their education, economic status, or racial identification, have undergone years of sexist and racist socialization that has taught us to blindly trust our knowledge of history and its effect on present reality, even though that knowledge has been formed and shaped by an oppressive system, is nowhere more evident than in the recent feminist movement. The group of college-educated white middle and upper class women who came together to organize a women's movement brought a new energy to the concept of women's rights in America. They were not merely advocating social equality with men. They demanded a transformation of society, a revolution, a change in the American social structure. Yet as they attempted to take feminism beyond the realm of radical rhetoric and into the realm of American life, they revealed that they had not changed, had not undone the sexist and racist brainwashing that had taught them to regard women like themselves as Others. Consequently, the Sisterhood they talked about has not become a reality, and the women's movement they envisioned would have a transformative effect on American culture has not emerged. Instead, the hierarchical pattern of race and sex relationships already established in American society merely took a different form under "feminism": the form of women being classed as an oppressed group under affirmative action programs further perpetuating the myth that the social status of all women in America is the same; the form of women's studies programs being established with all-white faculty teaching literature almost exclusively by white women about white women and frequently from racist perspectives; the form of white women writing books that purport to be about the experience of American women when in fact they concentrate solely on the experience of white women; and finally the form of endless argument and debate as to whether or not racism was a feminist issue.

Every women's movement in America from its earliest origin to the present day has been built on a racist foundation–a fact which in no way invalidates feminism as a political ideology. The racial apartheid social structure that characterized 19th and early 20th century American life was mirrored in the women's rights movement. The first white women's rights advocates were never seeking social equality for all women; they were seeking social equality for white women. Because many 19th century white women's rights advocates were also active in the abolitionist movement, it is often assumed they were anti-racist. Historiographers and especially recent feminist writing have created a version of American history in which white women's rights advocates are presented as champions of oppressed black people. This fierce romanticism has informed most studies of the abolitionist movement. In contemporary times there is a general tendency to equate abolitionism with a repudiation of racism. In actuality, most white abolitionists, male and female, though vehement in their antislavery protest, were totally opposed to granting social equality to black people. Joel Kovel, in his study *White Racism: A Psychohistory*, emphasizes that the "actual aim of the reform movement, so nobly and bravely begun, was not the liberation of the black, but the fortification of the white, conscience and all."

5   It is a commonly accepted belief that white female reformist empathy with the oppressed black slave, coupled with her recognition that she was powerless to end slavery, led to the development of a feminist consciousness and feminist revolt. Contemporary historiographers and in particular white female scholars accept the theory that the white women's rights advocates' feelings of solidarity with black slaves were an indication that they were anti-racist and were supportive of social equality of blacks. It is this glorification of the role white women played that leads Adrienne Rich to assert:

> . . . It is important for white feminists to remember that–despite lack of constitutional citizenship, educational deprivation, economic bondage to men, laws and customs forbidding women to speak in public or to disobey fathers, husbands, and brothers–our white foresisters have, in Lillian Smith's words, repeatedly been "disloyal to civilization" and have "smelled death in the word 'segregation,'" often defying patriarchy for the first time,

not on their own behalf but for the sake of black men, women, and
children. We have a strong anti-racist female tradition despite all efforts by
the white patriarchy to polarize its creature-objects, creating dichotomies of
privilege and caste, skin color, and age and condition of servitude.

There is little historical evidence to document Rich's assertion that white women as a collective group or white women's rights advocates are part of an anti-racist tradition. When white women reformers in the 1830s chose to work to free the slave, they were motivated by religious sentiment. They attacked slavery, not racism. The basis of their attack was moral reform. That they were not demanding social equality for black people is an indication that they remained committed to white racist supremacy despite their anti-slavery work. While they strongly advocated an end to slavery, they never advocated a change in the racial hierarchy that allowed their caste status to be higher than that of black women or men. In fact, they wanted that hierarchy to be maintained. Consequently, the white women's rights movement which had a luke-warm beginning in earlier reform activities emerged in full force in the wake of efforts to gain rights for black people precisely because white women wanted to see no change in the social status of blacks until they were assured that their demands for more rights were met.

White women's rights advocate and abolitionist Abby Kelly's comment, "We have good cause to be grateful to the slave for the benefit we have received to ourselves, in working for him. In striving to strike his irons off, we found most surely, that we were manacled ourselves," is often quoted by scholars as evidence that white women became conscious of their own limited rights as they worked to end slavery. Despite popular 19th century rhetoric, the notion that white women had to learn from their efforts to free the slave of their own limited rights is simply erroneous. No 19th century white woman could grow to maturity without an awareness of institutionalized sexism. White women did learn via their efforts to free the slave that white men were willing to advocate rights for blacks while denouncing rights for women. As a result of negative reaction to their reform activity and public effort to curtail and prevent their anti-slavery work, they were forced to acknowledge that without out-spoken demands for equal rights with white men they might ultimately be lumped in the same social category with blacks—or even worse, black men might gain a higher social status than theirs.

It did not enhance the cause of oppressed black slaves for white women to make synonymous their plight and the plight of the slave. Despite Abby Klein's dramatic statement, there was very little if any similarity between the day-to-day life experiences of white women and the day-to-day experiences of the black slave. Theoretically, the white woman's legal status under patriarchy may have been that of "property," but she was in no way subjected to the de-humanization and brutal oppression that was the lot of the slave. When white reformers made synonymous the impact of sexism on their lives, they were not revealing an awareness of or sensitivity to the slave's lot; they were simply appropriating the horror of the slave experience to enhance their own cause.

The fact that the majority of white women reformers did not feel political solidarity with black people was made evident in the conflict over the vote. When it appeared that white men might grant black men the right to vote while leaving white women disenfranchised, white suffragists did not respond as a group by demanding that all women and men deserved the right to vote. They simply expressed anger and outrage that white men were more committed to maintaining sexual hierarchies than racial hierarchies in the political arena. Ardent white women's rights advocates like Elizabeth Cady Stanton who had never before argued for women's rights on a racially imperialistic platform expressed outrage that inferior "niggers" should be granted the vote while "superior" white women remained disenfranchised. Stanton argued:

> *If Saxon men have legislated thus for their own mothers, wives and daughters, what can we hope for at the hands of Chinese, Indians, and Africans? . . . I protest against the enfranchisement of another man of any race or clime until the daughters of Jefferson, Hancock, and Adams are crowned with their rights.*

10 White suffragists felt that white men were insulting white womanhood by refusing to grant them privileges that were to be granted black men. They admonished white men not for their sexism but for their willingness to allow sexism to overshadow racial alliances. Stanton, along with other white women's rights supporters, did not want to see blacks enslaved, but neither did she wish to see the status of black people improved while the status of white women remained the same.

Animosity between black and white women's liberationists was not due solely to disagreement over racism within the women's movement;

it was the end result of years of jealousy, envy, competition, and anger between the two groups. Conflict between black and white women did not begin with the 20th century women's movement. It began during slavery. The social status of white women in America has to a large extent been determined by white people's relationship to black people. It was the enslavement of African people in colonized America that marked the beginning of a change in the social status of white women. Prior to slavery, patriarchal law decreed white women were lowly inferior beings, the subordinate group in society. The subjugation of black people allowed them to vacate their despised position and assume the role of a superior.

Consequently, it can be easily argued that even though white men institutionalized slavery, white women were its most immediate beneficiaries. Slavery in no way altered the hierarchical social status of the white male but it created a new status for the white female. The only way that her new status could be maintained was through the constant assertion of her superiority over the black woman and man. All too often colonial white women, particularly those who were slave mistresses, chose to differentiate their status from the slave's by treating the slave in a brutal and cruel manner. It was in her relationship to the black female slave that the white woman could best assert her power. Individual black slave women were quick to learn that sex-role differentiation did not mean that the white mistress was not to be regarded as an authority figure. Because they had been socialized via patriarchy to respect male authority and resent female authority, black women were reluctant to acknowledge the "power" of the white mistress. When the enslaved black woman expressed contempt and disregard for white female authority, the white mistress often resorted to brutal punishment to assert her authority. But even brutal punishment could not change the fact that black women were not inclined to regard the white female with the awe and respect they showed to the white male.

By flaunting their sexual lust for the bodies of black women and their preference for them as sexual partners, white men successfully pitted white women and enslaved black women against one another. In most instances, the white mistress did not envy the black female slave her role as sexual object; she feared only that her newly acquired social status might be threatened by white male sexual interaction with black women. His sexual involvement with black women (even if that involvement was rape) in effect reminded the white female of her subordinate position in relationship to him. For he could exercise his power as racial imperialist and sexual imperialist to rape or seduce black women, while white women were not free to rape or seduce black men without fear of punishment. Though the white female might condemn the actions of a white male who chose to interact sexually with black female slaves, she was unable to dictate to him proper behavior. Nor could she retaliate by engaging in sexual relationships with enslaved or free black men. Not surprisingly, she directed her anger and rage at the enslaved black women. In those cases where emotional ties developed between white men and black female slaves, white mistresses would go to great lengths to punish the female. Severe beatings were the method most white women used to punish black female slaves. Often in a jealous rage a mistress might use disfigurement to punish a lusted-after black female slave. The mistress might cut off her breast, blind an eye, or cut off another body part. Such treatment naturally caused hostility between white women and enslaved black women. To the enslaved black woman, the white mistress living in relative comfort was the representative symbol of white womanhood. She was both envied and despised—envied for her material comfort, despised because she felt little concern or compassion for the slave woman's lot. Since the white woman's privileged social status could not exist if a group of women were present to assume the lowly position she had abdicated, it follows that black and white women would be at odds with one another. If the white woman struggled to change the lot of the black slave woman, her own social position on the race-sex hierarchy would be altered.

Manumission did not bring an end to conflicts between black and white women; it heightened them. To maintain the apartheid structure slavery had institutionalized, white colonizers, male and female, created a variety of myths and stereotypes to differentiate the status of black women from that of white women. White racists and even some black people who had absorbed the colonizer's mentality depicted the white woman as a symbol of perfect womanhood and encouraged black women to strive to attain such perfection by using the white female as her model. The jealousy and envy of white women that had erupted in the black woman's consciousness during slavery was deliberately encouraged by the dominant white culture. Advertisements, newspaper articles, books, etc., were constant reminders to black women of the difference between their social status and that of white women, and they bitterly resented it. Nowhere was this dichotomy as clearly demonstrated as in the materially privileged white household where the black female domestic worked as an employee of the white family. In these relationships, black women workers were exploited to enhance the social standing of white families. In the white community, employing domestic help was a sign of material privilege and the person who directly benefited from a servant's work was the white woman, since without the servant she would have performed domestic chores. Not surprisingly, the black female domestic tended to see the white female as her "boss," her oppressor, not the white male whose earnings usually paid her wage.

15   Throughout American history white men have deliberately promoted hostility and divisiveness between white and black women. The white patriarchal power structure pits the two groups against each other, preventing the growth of solidarity between women and ensuring that women's status as a subordinate group under patriarchy remains intact. To this end, white men have supported changes in the white woman's social standing only if there exists another female group to assume that role. Consequently, the white patriarch undergoes no radical change in his sexist assumption that woman is inherently inferior. He neither relinquishes his dominant position nor alters the patriarchal structure of society. He is, however, able to convince many white women that fundamental changes in "woman's status" have occurred because he has successfully socialized her, via racism, to assume that no connection exists between her and black women.

Because women's liberation has been equated with gaining privileges within the white male power structure, white men–and not women, either white or black–have dictated the terms by which women are allowed entrance into the system. One of the terms male patriarchs have set is that one group of women is granted privileges that they obtain by actively supporting the oppression and exploitation of other groups of women. White and black women have been socialized to accept and honor these terms, hence the fierce competition between the two groups; a competition that has always been centered in the arena of sexual politics, with white and black women competing against one another for male favor. This competition is part of an overall battle between various groups of women to be the chosen female group.

The contemporary move toward feminist revolution was continually undermined by competition between various factions. In regards to race, the women's movement has become simply another arena in which white and black women compete to be the chosen female group. This power struggle has not been resolved by the formation of opposing interest groups. Such groups are symptomatic of the problem and are no solution. Black and white women have for so long allowed their idea of liberation to be formed by the existing status quo that they have not yet devised a strategy by which we can come together. They have had only a slave's idea of freedom. And to the slave, the master's way of life represents the ideal free lifestyle.

Women's liberationists, white and black, will always be at odds with one another as long as our idea of liberation is based on having the power white men have. For that power denies unity, denies common connections, and is inherently divisive. It is woman's acceptance of divisiveness as a natural order that has caused black and white women to cling religiously to the belief that bonding across racial boundaries is impossible, to passively accept the notion that the distances that separate women are immutable.

SUGGESTIONS FOR WRITING

1. In her title, bell hooks joins feminism and racism grammatically. Write an essay that analyzes some of the ways in which she relates them in ideological terms.

2. According to bell hooks, even abolitionists and suffragettes of the nineteenth century were racists. Does she support these contentions satisfactorily in your opinion? Write an essay that analyzes her arguments and use of evidence on this topic.

3. Do you agree with the conclusions of hook's last paragraph? Write an essay that responds to its claims.

Sexual Culture   1983

EDMUND WHITE

Edmund White was born in 1941. A novelist, short story writer, and literary critic whose work has been widely praised by fellow writers including the likes of Valdimir Nabokov, he served as the Director of Creative Writing at Princeton University. In his work as an influential social critic, he has for decades openly discussed his own HIV positive status. In his essay here, White addresses assumptions about the social lives of homosexuals widely held by the larger society of which they make a part. He argues that sexual orientation alone can no more define homosexual identities than it can define heterosexual ones.

"Do gay men have friends–I mean," she said, "are they friends with each other?" Since the woman asking was a New Yorker, the owner of one of the city's simplest and priciest restaurants, someone who's known gays all her life, I found the question honest, shocking, and revealing of a narrow but bottomless abyss between us.

Of course New York is a city of total, even absolute strangers rubbing shoulders: the Hasidim in their yellow school bus being conveyed back to Brooklyn from the jewelry district, beards and black hats glimpsed through mud-splattered windows in a sun-dimmed daguerreotype; the junkie pushing the baby carriage and telling his wife, the prostitute, as he points to his tattooed biceps, "I haven't partied in this vein for years"; Moonies doing calisthenics at midnight in their Eighth Avenue center high above empty Thirty-fourth Street. . . . But this alienation wasn't religious or ethnic. The woman and I spoke the same language, knew the same people; we both considered Marcella Hazan fun but no substitute for Simone Beck. How odd that she, as lower-upper-middle-class as I, shouldn't know whether gay men befriended one another.

It was then that I saw how mysterious gay culture is–not homosexuality, which is merely an erotic tropism; but modern American gay culture, which is a special way of laughing, spending money, ordering priorities, encoding everything from song lyrics to mirror-shiny military shoes. None of the usual modes for a subculture will do, for gay men are brought up by heterosexuals to be straight, they seek other men through what feels very much like a compulsion though they enter the ghetto by choice, yet once they make that choice it reshapes their lives, even their bodies, certainly their wardrobes. Many gay men live among straights as Marranos, those Spanish Jews who pretended during the Inquisition to convert to Christianity but continued to observe the old rites in cellars, when alone, in the greatest secrecy. Gays aren't *like* blacks or Jews since they often *are* black or Jewish, and their affectional preference isn't a color or a religion though it has spawned a culture not unlike an ethnic minority's. Few Jews have Christian siblings, but most gays have straight brothers and sisters or at least straight parents. Many American Jews have been raised to feel they belong to the Chosen People, at once superior and inferior to gentiles, but every gay discovers his sexual nature with a combination of pain and relief, regret at being excluded from the tribe but elation at discovering the solution to the puzzle.

Gays aren't a nationality. They aren't Chicanos or Italo-Americans or Irish-Americans, but they do constitute one of the most potent political forces in big cities such as New York, Philadelphia, Washington (where gays and blacks elected Marion Barry mayor), Houston, Los Angeles, and San Francisco (where gays are so numerous they've splintered into countless factions, including the lesbian S/M group Samois and the Sisters of Perpetual Indulgence, a group of drag nuns, one of whose members ran in a cowl and wimple as a candidate in the last citywide election). Not ethnic but a minority, not a polis but political, not a nationality but possessed of a costume, customs, and a patois, not a class but an economic force (not only as a market for records, films, vacations, and clothes but also as an army of worker ants who, for better or worse, have gentrified the center cities, thereby creating a better tomorrow for single young white heterosexual professionals).

Imagine a religion one enters against one's parents' will—and against one's own. Imagine a race one joins at sixteen or sixty without
5 changing one's hue or hair texture (unless at the tanning or beauty salon). Imagine a sterile nation without descendants but with a long, misty regress of ancestors, without an articulated self-definition but with a venerable history. Imagine an exclusive club that includes a P.R. (Puerto Rican) boy of sixteen wearing ankle-high black-and-white Converse basketball shoes and a petrol green shirt sawed off to reveal a Praxitelean stomach—and also includes a P.R. (Public Relations) WASP executive of forty in his Prince of Wales plaids and Cole-Haan tasseled loafers.

If one is gay, one is always in a crucial relationship to gayness as such, a defining category that is so full it is nearly empty (Renaud Camus writes: "Homosexuality is always elsewhere because it is everywhere"). No straight man stands in rapt contemplation of his straightness unless he's an ass. To be sure, heterosexuals may wonder over the significance of their homosexual fantasies, though even that morbid exercise is less popular now than formerly; as Barbara Ehrenreich acutely observes in her new study of the heterosexual male revolt, *The Hearts of Men*, the emergence of gay liberation ended the period in which everyone suspected everyone else of being "latently" homosexual. Now there are open homosexuals, and heterosexual men are exempt from the automatic suspicion of deviance.

No homosexual can take his homosexuality for granted. He must sound it, palpate it, auscultate it as though it were the dead limb of a tree or the living but tricky limb of a body; for that reason all homosexuals are "gay philosophers" in that they must invent themselves. At a certain point one undergoes a violent conversion into a new state, the unknown, which one then sets about knowing as one will. Surely everyone experiences his or her life as an artifact, as molten glass being twirled and pinched into a shape to cool, or as a novel at once capacious and suspenseful, but no one is more a *Homo faber* (in the sense of both "fabricator" and "fabulist") than a homo. It would be vain, of course, to suggest that this creativity is praiseworthy, an ambition rather than a response.

Sometimes I try to imagine how straights–not fundamentalist know-nothings, not rural innocents, not Freudian bigots, but educated urban heterosexuals—look at gay men (do they even see lesbians?). When they see gay men, what do they see? A mustache, a pumped-up body in black jeans and a tank top, an eye-catching tattoo (braided rope around the biceps)? And what do they think ("they," in this case, *hypocrite lecteur*, being *you*)? Do you see something at once ludicrous and mildly enviable in the still youthful but overexercised body of this forty-year-old clone with the aggressive stare and soft voice? If you're a woman, do you find so much preening over appearance in a grown man . . . well, if not offensive, at least unappetizing; energy better spent on a career, on a family–on you? If you're a man, does it incense you that this jerk is out of harness, too loose, too free, has so lightly made a mockery of manhood? Once, on a radio call-in show a cop called in to tell me he had to admire the old-style queens back when it was rough being queer but that now, jeez, these guys swapping spit wit' a goil one week, wit' a guy the next, they're too lazy, they just don't know the fine art of being a man, it's all just too easy.

Your sentiments, perhaps?

Do you see gays as menacing satyrs, sex fiends around whom it's dangerous to drop your soap, *and* as feeble sissies, frail wood nymphs locked within massive trunks and limbs? Or, more positively if just as narrowly, are you a sybaritic het who greets the sight of gays with cries of glee, convinced you've stumbled on liberty hall, where sexual license of every sort–including your sort–is bound to reign? In fact, such sybarites often do regard gay men as comrades in arms, fellow libertines, and fellow victims in a country phobic to pleasure.

Or do gays just irk you? Do you regard them as a tinselly distraction in your peripheral vision? As errant, obstinate atoms that can't be drawn into any of the usual social molecules, men who if they insist on their gayness won't really do at any of the solemnities, from dinner parties to debutante balls, all of which depend on strict gender dimorphism for a rational seating plan? Since any proper gathering requires the threat of adultery for excitement and the prospect of marriage as a justification, of what earthly use are gays? Even the few fearless straight guys who've invaded my gay gym drift toward one another, not out of soap-dropping panic but because otherwise their dirty jokes fall on deaf or prettily blushing ears and their taunting, butt-slapping mix of rivalry and camaraderie provokes a weird hostility or a still weirder thrill.

And how do gays look at straights? In Andrew Holleran's superb new novel, *Nights in Aruba*, the narrator wonders "what it would be like to be the head of a family, as if with that all my problems would drop away, when in fact they would have merely been replaced by another set. I would not have worried about the size of my penis, the restrictions of age, the difficulty of finding love; I would have worried about mortgages, tuition, my youngest daughter's asthma, my competition at Shearson Loeb Rhoades." What makes this speculation so characteristically gay is that it is so focused on the family man, for if the nineteenth-century tart required, even invented the convent-bred virgin to contemplate, in the same way the homosexual man today must insult and revere, mock and envy this purely imaginary bourgeois paterfamilias, a creature extinct except in gay fantasies. Meanwhile, of course, the family man devotes his time to scream therapy and tai chi, ticking off Personals in the *Village Voice* and wriggling out of visits from his kids, two punked-out teens who live in a feminist compound with his divorced wife, now a lesbian potter of great sensitivity and verve if low energy.

So much for how the two sexes (straight and gay) regard each other. If the camera were to pull back and frame both worlds in the lens, how would the two systems compare?

The most obvious difference is that whereas heterosexuality does include two sexes, since homosexuality does not it must improvise a new polarity moment by moment. Such a polarity seems necessary to sexual desire, at least as it is constructed in our culture. No wonder that some gay men search out the most extreme opposites (someone of a distant race, a remote language, another class or age); no wonder that even that convinced heterosexual Flaubert was finally able to unbend with a boy prostitute in Egypt, an exotic who provided him with all the difference desire might demand. Other gay men seek out their twins— so that the beloved, I suppose, can stand in for oneself as one bows down to this false god and plays in turn his father, teacher, son, godfather, or god. Still others institutionalize the polarity in that next-best thing to heterosexuality: sadomasochism, the only vice that anthologizes all family and romantic relationships.

15   Because every gay man loves men, he comes to learn at first hand how to soothe the savage breast of the male ego. No matter how passive or girlish or shy the new beau might be in the boudoir, he will become the autocrat of the dinner table. Women's magazines are always planning articles on gay men and straight women; I'd say what they have most in common, aside from a few shared sexual techniques, is a body of folk wisdom about that hardhead, that bully, that maddeningly self-involved creature, the human male. As studies have surprisingly shown, men talk more than women, interrupt them more often, and determine the topics of conversation and object to women's assertions with more authority and frequency. When two gay men get together, especially after the first romantic urge to oblige the other wanes, a struggle for conversational dominance ensues, a conflict only symptomatic of larger arguments over every issue from where to live to how and whom to entertain.

To be sure, in this way the gay couple resembles the straight duo that includes an assertive, liberated woman. But while most of the young straight liberated women I know, at least, may protect their real long-range interests (career, mode of life, emotional needs) with vigilance, they're still willing to accommodate *him* in little social ways essential to harmony.

One benign side of straight life is that women conceive of men as "characters," as full-bodied, multifaceted beings who are first social, second familial, third amorous or amicable, and only finally physical. I'm trying politely to say that women are lousy judges of male beauty; they're easily taken in by such superficial traits as loyalty, dependability, charm, a sense of humor. Women don't, or at least didn't, judge men as so much beefcake. But men, both straight and gay, start with looks, the most obvious currency of value, worth, price. Let's say that women see men as characters in a long family novel in which the men are introduced complete with phrenology, genealogy, and one annoying and two endearing traits, whereas men see their partners (whether male or female) as cars, makes to be instantly spotted, appraised, envied, made. A woman wants to be envied for her husband's goodness, his character, whereas a man wants to be envied for his wife's beauty, rarity, status— her drivability. Straight life combines the warmth and *Gemütlichkeit* of the nineteenth-century bourgeois (the woman) with the steely corporate ethos of the twentieth-century functionary (the man). If gay male life, freed of this dialectic, has become supremely efficient (the trapdoor beside the bed) and only momentarily intimate (a whole life cycle compressed into the one-night stand), then the gain is dubious, albeit an extreme expression of one trend in our cultural economy.

But of course most morality, that is, popular morality—not real morals, which are unaffected by consensus, but mores, which are a form of fashion—is nothing but a species of nostalgia, a cover-up for pleasurable and profitable but not yet admissible innovations. If so many people condemn promiscuity, they do so at least partly because there is no available rhetoric that could condone, much less glamorize, impermanence in love. Nevertheless, it strikes me that homosexuals, masters of improvisation fully at home with the arbitrary and equipped with an internal compass that orients them instantly to any social novelty, are perhaps the most sensitive indicators of the future.

The birthrate declines, the divorce rate climbs, and popular culture (movies, television, song lyrics, advertising, fashions, journalism) is so completely and irrevocably secularized that the so-called religious revival is of no more lasting importance than the fad for Kabuki in a transistorized Japan—a temporary throwback, a slight brake on the wheel. In such a world the rate of change is so rapid that children, once they are in school, can learn little from their parents but must assimilate new forms of behavior from their peers and new information from specialized instructors. As a result, parental authority declines, and the demarcations between the generations become ever more formidable.

Nor do the parents regret their loss of control, since they're devoting all their energy to cultivating the inner self in the wholesale transition of our society from an ethic of self-sacrifice to one of self-indulgence, the so-called aristocraticization of middle-class life that has dominated the peaceful parts of this century in the industrialized West.

20   In the contemporary world the nineteenth-century experiment of compassionate marriage, never very workable, has collapsed utterly. The exact nature of the collapse isn't very clear yet because of our distracting, probably irrelevant habit of psychologizing every crisis (thus the endless speculations in the lowbrow press on the Irresponsible Male and the Defeminized Female or the paradoxical and cruelly impracticable advice to women readers to "go for it all—family, career, marriage, romance, *and* the reveries of solitude"). We treat the failure of marriage as though it were the failure of individuals to achieve it— a decline in grit or maturity or commitment or stamina rather than the unraveling of a poorly tied knot. Bourgeois marriage was meant to concentrate friendship, romance, and sex into an institution at once familial and economic. Only the most intense surveillance could keep such a bulky, ill-assorted load from bursting at the seams. Once the hedonism of the 60s' relaxed that tension, people began to admit that friendship tranquilizes sexual desires (when mates become siblings, the incest taboo sets in) and that romance is by its very nature evanescent though indefinitely renewable given an endless supply of fresh partners. Neither sexual nor romantic attraction, so capricious, so passionate, so unstable, could ever serve as the basis for an enduring relationship, which can be balanced only on the plinth of esteem, that easy, undramatic, intimate kind of love one would say resembled family love if families were more loving.

It is this love that so many gay couples know about, aim for, and sometimes even express. If all goes well, two gay men will meet through sex, become lovers, weather the storms of jealousy and the diminution of lust, develop shared interests (a hobby, a business, a house, a circle), and end up with a long-term, probably sexless camaraderie that is not as disinterested as friendship or as seismic as passion or as charged with contradiction as fraternity. Younger gay couples feel that this sort of relationship, when it happens to them, is incomplete, a compromise, and they break up in order to find total fulfillment (i.e., tireless passion) elsewhere. But older gay couples stay together, cultivate their mild, reasonable love, and defend it against the ever-present danger of the sexual allure exercised by a newcomer. For the weak point of such marriages is the eternally recurring fantasy, first in one partner and then the other, of "total fulfillment." Needless to say, such couples can wreak havoc on the newcomer who fails to grasp that Bob and Fred are not just roommates. They may have separate bedrooms and regular extracurricular sex partners or even beaux, but Bob monitors Fred's infatuations with an eye attuned to nuance, and at a certain point will intervene to banish a potential rival.

I think most straight people would find these arrangements more scandalous than the infamous sexual high jinks of gays. Because these arrangements have no name, no mythology, no public or private acknowledgment, they're almost invisible even to the participants. Thus if you asked Bob in a survey what he wanted, he might say he wanted a "real" lover. He might also say Fred was "just a roommate, my best friend, we used to be lovers." So much for explicit analysis, but over the years Bob has cannily steered his affair with Fred between the Scylla of excessive fidelity (which is finally so dull no two imaginative gay men could endure it) and the Charybdis of excessive tolerance (which could leave both men feeling so neglected they'd seek love elsewhere for sure).

There are, of course, countless variants to this pattern. The men live together or they don't. If they don't, they can maintain the civilized fiction of romance for years. They plan dates, honeymoons, take turns sleeping over at each other's house, and avoid conflicts about domestic details. They keep their extracurricular sex lives separate, they agree not to snoop—or they have threeways. Or one of the pair has an active sex life and the other has abandoned the erotic arena.

Are gay men friends with each other? the woman asked me.

25   The question may assume that gays are only sexual, and that a man eternally on the prowl can never pause for mere affection that a gay Don Juan is lonely. Or perhaps the question reveals a confusion about a society of one gender. Since a straight woman has other women for friends and men for lovers, my questioner might have wondered how the same sex could serve in both capacities.

The first supposition—that gay men are only sexual—is an ancient prejudice, and like all prejudices mostly untrue but in one sense occasionally accurate. If politically conscious homosexuals prefer the word *gay* to *homosexual*, they do so because they want to make the world regard attraction to members of the same gender as an affectional preference as well as a sexual orientation.

For instance, there are some gay men who prefer the feel of women's bodies to men's, who are even more comfortable sexually with women, but whose emotions crave contact with other men. Gay men have unfinished emotional business with other men—scary, promising, troubling, absorbing business—whereas their sentiments toward women (at least women not in their family) are much simpler, more stable, less fraught. Affection, passionate affection, is never simple; it is built out of equal parts of yearning, fear, and appetite. For that reason the friendship of one gay man fiercely drawn to another is as tense as any heterosexual passion, whereas a sexless, more disinterested gay friendship is as relaxed, as good-tempered as a friendship, say, between two straight men.

Gay men, then, do divide other gays into two camps—those who are potential partners (lovers) and those who are not (friends). But where gay life is more ambiguous than the world at large (and possibly for that reason more baffling to outsiders) is that the members of the two camps, lovers and friends, are always switching places or hovering somewhere in the margin between. It is these unconfessed feelings that have always intrigued me the most as a novelist—the unspoken love between two gay men, say, who pretend they are just friends, cruising buddies, merely filling in until Mr. Right comes along (mercifully, he never does).

In one sense, the public's prejudice about a gay obsession with sex is valid. The right to have sex, even to look for it, has been so stringently denied to gays for so many centuries that the drive toward sexual freedom remains a bright, throbbing banner in the fierce winds whipping over the ghetto. Laws against sex have always created the biggest problems for homosexuals; they helped to define the very category of homosexuality. For that reason, the gay community, despite its invention of a culture no more eroticized than any other, still cannot give up its origin in sexual desire and its suppression.

30   But what about the "excessive" promiscuity of gay men, the infamous quickies, a phenomenon only temporarily held in check by the AIDS crisis? Don't the quickies prove that gay men are essentially bizarre, fundamentally lacking in judgment—*oversexed?* Of course, gay men behave as all men would were they free of the strictures of female tastes, needs, prohibitions, and expectations. There is nothing in gay male life that cannot be attributed either to its minority status or to its all-male population. All men want quick uncomplicated sexual adventure (as well as sustained romantic passion); in a world of all men, that desire is granted.

The very universality of sexual opportunity within the modern gay ghetto has, paradoxically, increased the importance of friendship. In a society not based on the measured denial or canalization of sexual desire, there is more energy left over for friendship. Relationships are less loaded in gay life (hence the celebrated gay irony, a levity equivalent to seeing through conventions). In so many ways gays are still prisoners of the dominant society, but in this one regard gays are freer than their jailers: because gay relationships are not disciplined by religious, legal, economic, and political ceremonies but only by the dictates of conscience and the impulses of the heart, they don's stand for anything larger. They aren't symbols but realities, not laws but entities sufficient unto themselves, not consequential but ecstatic.

SUGGESTIONS FOR WRITING

1. In paragraph 3, White distinguishes between gay culture and homosexuality. Write an essay that analyzes the reasoning and evidence that White brings to support his claim.
2. In paragraph 7 White says: "No homosexual can take his homosexuality for granted." Write an essay that analyzes the reasoning and evidence that White brings to support this claim.
3. White writes about the different nature of gay culture, but shows through examples how difficult it is to find analogies from other areas of life, the better to understand the nature of those differences. Write an essay that analyzes the importance of this problem as White understands it.

What Price Independence? 1984

Social Reactions to Lesbians, Spinsters, Widows, and Nuns

ROSE WEITZ

Rose Weitz is a sociologist and professor in the Women's Studies Department at the University of Arizona. She is the author or co-author of many books on various aspects of women's health and sexuality, her latest publication being Rapunzel's Daughters: What Women's Hair Tells Us About Women's Lives. In the essay that follows, Weitz explores multifarious facts of history to note the ways in which independent women—that is, women independent of conventional relations with men, such as lesbians, spinsters, widows, and nuns—have often been forced to pay a high social price for their exceptional social status.

For seven days in 1981, nineteen-year-old Stephanie Riethmiller was held captive by two men and a woman in a secluded Alabama cabin. During that time, according to Riethmiller, her captors constantly harangued her on the sinfulness of homosexuality, and one captor raped her nightly. Riethmiller's parents, who feared that their daughter was involved in a lesbian relationship with her roommate, had paid $8,000 for this "deprogramming"; her mother remained in the next room throughout her captivity. When the kidnappers were brought to trial, the jury, in the opinion of the judge, "permit[ted] their moral evaluations to enter into their legal conculsions" and failed to bring in a guilty verdict (Raskin 1982, 19).

As the Riethmiller case shows, the individual who identifies herself as a lesbian—or who is so labeled by others—may face severe social, economic, and legal sanctions. Along with communists, the diseased, and the insane, persons who openly acknowledge their homosexuality may be denied admission to the United States. In most U.S. jurisdictions, discrimination against homosexuals in housing, employment, child custody and other areas of life is legal, while homosexual behavior is illegal. Gay persons are not covered under any of the national civil rights acts, and most court decisions have held that they are not covered under the equal protection clause of the United States Constitution. (For an excellent review of the legal status of homosexuality, see Rivera 1979.)

These legal restrictions reflect generally held social attitudes. Surveys conducted during the 1970s using large national probability samples found that between 70 percent and 75 percent of the Americans interviewed believed that sexual relations between two members of the same sex were always wrong (Glenn and Weaver 1979).

Cross-Cultural and Historical Views of Lesbianism

To most Americans, stigmatization and punishment of lesbianism seem perfectly natural. Yet such has not always been the case. In fact, a study of attitudes toward homosexuality in seventy-six cultures around the world found that in 64 percent of those cultures "homosexual activities of one sort or another" are considered normal and socially acceptable for certain members of the community" (Ford and Beach 1951, 130).

5   In the Western world, male homosexuality, which had been an accepted part of Greek and Roman culture, was increasingly rejected by society as the power of the Christian church grew (Barrett 1979). Yet lesbianism generally remained unrecognized legally and socially until the beginning of the modern age. Instead, beginning with the Renaissance, intimate "romantic friendship" between women were a common part of life, at least among the middle and upper classes (Faderman 1981)[1]

> *Women who were romantic friends were everything to each other. They lived to be together. They thought of each other constantly. They made each other deliriously happy or horribly miserable by the increase or abatement of their proffered love. They were jealous of other female friends (and certainly of male friends) who impinged on their beloved's time or threatened to carry away a portion of her affections. They vowed that if it were at all possible they would someday live together, or at least die together, and they declared that both eventualities would be their greatest happiness. They embraced and kissed and walked hand in hand, and some even held each other all night in sleep. But unless they were transvestites or considered "unwomanly" in some male's conception, there was little chance that their relationships would be considered lesbian [Faderman 1981, 84].*

We cannot know whether most romantic friends expressed their love for women genitally, and we do know that most were married to men (at least in part for economic survival). A reading of letters and journals from this period leaves no doubt, however, of the erotic and emotional intensity of these relationships between women and little doubt that in another era the relationships would have been expressed sexually (Smith-Rosenberg 1975; Faderman 1981). Yet belief in the purity of these relationships lingered even into the twentieth century. For example, when the British Parliament attempted in 1885 to add mention of lesbianism to its criminal code, Queen Victoria refused to sign the bill, on the ground that such behavior did not exist (Ettorre 1980).

Given that lesbianism has not always elicited negative social reactions, the current intolerance of it cannot derive from some universal

---

[1]We have little first-hand data about the intimate lives of lower-class women. Few poorer women could write, and, even if they could and did record their lives, their letters and journals were rarely preserved.

biological or ethical law. What, then, causes these negative social reactions? I suggest in this article that at least part of the answer lies in the threat that lesbianism presents to the power of males in society. Furthermore, I suggest that whenever men fear women's sexual or economic independence, all unmarried women face an increased risk of stigmatization and punishment. The experience of such diverse groups as lesbians, medieval nuns, and Hindu widows shows the interrelated social fates of all women not under the direct control of men.

Lesbians and the Threat to Male Power

Western culture teaches that women are the weaker sex, that they cannot flourish—or perhaps even survive—without the protection of men. Women are taught that they cannot live happy and fulfilled lives without a Prince Charming, who is superior to them in all ways. In the struggle to find and keep their men, women learn to view each other as untrustworthy competitors. They subordinate the development of their own psychological, physical, and professional strengths to the task of finding male protectors who will make up for their shortcomings. In this way, Western culture keeps women from developing bonds with each other, while it maintains their dependence on men.

Lesbians[2] throw a large wrench into the works of this cultural system. In a society that denigrates women, lesbians value women enough to spend their lives with women rather than with men. Lesbians therefore do not and cannot rely on the protection of men. Knowing that they will not have that protection, lesbians are forced to develop their own resources. The very survival of lesbians therefore suggests the potential strength of all women and their ability to transcend their traditional roles. At the same time since lesbians do not have even the illusion of male protection that marriage provides, and since they are likely to see their fate as tied to other women rather than to individual men, lesbians may be more likely than heterosexual women to believe in the necessity of fighting for women's rights; the

[2] I am using the terms *lesbian* and *heterosexual* as nouns simply to ease the flow of the writing. This article focuses on stigmatization, not on some intrinsic quality of individuals. Hence, in this article, *lesbian* and *heterosexual* refer to persons who adopt a particular lifestyle or who are labeled as doing so by significant others. These terms reflect shared social fates, not some essential, inflexible aspect of the individual.

heavy involvement of lesbians in the feminist movement seems to support this thesis (Abbott and Love 1972).

10 Lesbians also threaten the dominant cultural system by presenting, or at least appearing to present, an alternative to the typical inequality of heterosexual relationships. Partners attempting to equalize power in a heterosexual relationships must first neutralize deeply ingrained traditional sex roles. Since lesbian relationships generally contain no built-in assumption of the superiority of one partner,[3] developing an egalitarian relationship may be easier. Lesbian relationships suggest both that a love between equals is possible and that an alternative way of obtaining such a love may exist. Regardless of the actual likelihood of achieving equality in a lesbian relationship, the threat to the system remains, as long as lesbian relationship are believed to be more egalitarian. This threat increases significantly when, as in the past few years, lesbians express pride in and satisfaction with their life-style.

If lesbianism incurs social wrath because of the threat it presents to existing sexist social arrangements, then we should find that lesbianism is most negatively viewed by persons who hold sexist beliefs. Evidence from various studies (summarized in Weinberger and Millham 1979) supports this hypothesis. Homophobia (i.e., fear and hatred of homosexuals) appears strongly correlated with support for traditional sex roles. Survey data suggest that support for traditional sex roles explains homophobia better than do negative or conservative attitudes toward sex in general (MacDonald et al. 1973; MacDonald and Games 1974).

Historical data on when and under what circumstances lesbianism became stigmatized also support the contention of a link between that stigma and the threat lesbianism poses to male power. As described above, romantic friendships between women were common in both Europe and America from the Renaissance through the late nineteenth century. The women involved were generally accepted or at least tolerated by society even in the few cases where their relationships were openly sexual. That acceptance ceased, however, if either of the women attempted to usurp male privilege in some way—by wearing men's

[3]While there is no way to ascertain exactly what proportion of lesbian couples adopted butch-femme relationships in the past, recent studies suggest that such relationships have all but disappeared, especially among younger and more feminist lesbians (Wolf 1979; Tanner 1978).

clothing, using a dildo, or passing as a man. Only in these circumstances were premodern-era lesbians likely to suffer social sanctions. In looking at both historical records and fiction from the thirteenth through the nineteenth centuries, Faderman (1981) found that women were, at most, lightly punished for lesbianism unless they wore male clothing.[4] She therefore concludes that "at the base it was not the sexual aspects of lesbianism as much as the attempted usurpation of male prerogative by women who behaved like men that many societies appeared to find most disturbing" (Faderman 1981, 17).

As long as the women involved did not attempt to obtain male privileges, romantic friends ran little risk of censure before the late nineteenth century. The factors behind the shift in attitude that occurred at that time again suggest the importance of the threat that lesbianism seemed to pose to male power.

Before the twentieth century, only a small number of independently wealthy women (such as the Ladies of Llangollen [Mayor 1973]) were able to establish their own households and live out their lives with their female companions (Faderman 1981). By the second half of the nineteenth century, however, the combined effects of the Civil War in this country and of male migration away from rural areas in both the United States and Europe had created a surplus of unmarried women in many communities. At the same time, the growth of the feminist movement had led to increased educational opportunities for women. These factors, coupled with the growth of industrialization, opened the possibility of employment and an independent existence to significant numbers of women.

15   Once female independence became a real economic possibility, it became a serious concern to those intent on maintaining the sexual status quo. Relationships between women, which previously had seemed harmless, now took on a new and threatening appearance. Only at this point do new theories emerge that reject the Victorian image of the passionless woman (Cott 1978), acknowledge females as sexual beings, and define lesbianism as pathological.

Stereotypes of lesbianism, first developed in the early twentieth century, reduce the threat to existing social arrangements by defusing the power of lesbianism as a viable alternative life-style. According to

[4]The crime for which Joan of Arc was eventually condemned was not witchcraft but the heretical act of wearing male clothing.

these stereotypes, all lesbians are either butches or femmes,[5] and their relationships merely mimic heterosexual relationships. Lesbianism, therefore, seems to offer no advantages over heterosexuality.

Cultural stereotypes defuse lesbian sexuality by alternately denying and exaggerating it. These stereotypes hold that women become lesbians because of either their inability to find a man or their hatred of men. Such stereotypes deny that lesbianism may be a positive choice, while suggesting that lesbianism can be cured by the right man. The supposed futility of lesbian sexuality was summed up by best-selling author Dr. David Reuben in the phrase, "one vagina plus another vagina still equals zero" (1969, 217). (Reuben further invalidated lesbianism by locating his entire discussion of the subject within his chapter on prostitution; male homosexuality was "honored" with its own chapter.) In other cultural arenas, lesbians and lesbianism are defined in purely sexual terms, stripped of all romantic, social, or political content. In this incarnation, lesbianism can be subverted into a vehicle for male sexual pleasure; in the world of pornographic films, men frequently construct lesbian scenes to play out their own sexual fantasies.

In sum, strong evidence suggests that the negative social reactions to lesbianism reflect male fears of female independence, and the social sanctions and cultural stereotypes serve to lessen the threat that these independent women pose to male power.

If this hypothesis is true, then it should also hold for other groups of women not under direct male control. Next, I briefly discuss how, historically, negative social reactions to such women seem most likely to develop whenever men fear women's sexual or economic independence.

Spinsters, Widows, and Women Religious

20 The inquisition against witches that occurred from the fifteenth through the seventeenth centuries represents the most extreme response in the Western world to the threat posed by independent women. The vast majority of the persons executed for witchcraft were women; estimates of the number killed range from under one hundred thousand to several million (Daly 1978). Accusations of witchcraft typically involved charges

[5]*butches . . . femmes*: women who adopt particularly masculine or feminine appearance and behavior.

that the women healed sickness, engaged in prohibited sexual practices, or controlled reproduction (Ehrenreich and English 1973). Such activities threatened the power of the church by giving individuals (especially women) greater control over their own lives, reducing their dependence on the church for divine intervention while inhibiting the natural increase of the Catholic population.

The witchcraft trials occurred in a society undergoing the first throes of industrialization and urbanization (Nelson 1979). The weakening of the rural extended family forced many women to look for employment outside the home. These unattached women proved especially vulnerable to accusations of witchcraft (Nelson 1979; Daly 1978). As Mary Daly points out, "The targets of attack in the witchcraze were not women defined by assimilation into the patriarchal family. Rather, the witchcraze focused predominantly upon women who had rejected marriage (Spinsters) [sic] and some who had survived it (widows)" (1978, 184).

Contemporary theological beliefs regarding female sexuality magnified the perceived economic and social threat posed by unmarried women. The medieval church viewed all aspects of female sexuality with distrust; unless a woman was virginal or proven chaste, she was believed to be ruled by her sexual desires (Ehrenreich and English 1973). Catholic doctrine blamed Eve's licentiousness for the fall from grace in the Garden of Eden. According to the most popular medieval "manual" for witchhunters, the *Malleus Maleficarum*, most witches were women because "all witchcraft comes from carnal lust, which is in women insatiable" (Kramer and Sprenger 1971, 120). Given this theology, any woman not under the direct sexual control of a man would appear suspect, if not outright dangerous.

For most women living before the nineteenth century who wished to or were forced to remain unmarried, entering the religious life was the only socially acceptable option.[6] During the Middle Ages, a woman could either become a nun or join one of the "secular convents" known as *Beguines* (Nelson 1979; Boulding 1976). Beguines arose to serve the population of surplus unmarried women that had developed in the

---

[6]However, it should be realized that convent life was not always a chosen refuge. Just as a father could marry his daughter to whatever man he chose, so too could he "marry" his daughter to the church.

early European cities. Residents of Beguines took a vow of chasity and obedience while living there, but they could marry thereafter. They spent their days in work and prayer.

Beguines threatened the monopolies of both the guilds and the church. The guilds feared the economic competition of these organized skilled women workers, while the church feared their social and religious independence (Nelson 1979); the Beguines' uncloistered life seemed likely to lead women into sin, while the lack of perpetual vows freed them from direct church supervision. For these reasons, the church in the fourteenth century ordered the Beguine houses dissolved, although some have continued nonetheless to the present day. Residents were urged either to marry or to become nuns (Boulding 1976).

25   The history of convents similarly illustrates the church's distrust of independent women (Eckenstein 1963). In the early medieval period, many nuns lived with their families. Some nuns showed their religious vocation through the wearing of a veil, while others wore no distinctive dress. Convents served as centers of learning for women, providing educational opportunities not available elsewhere. During this period, many "double monasteries" flourished, in which male and female residents lived and shared decision-making authority.

Given medieval ideas regarding the spiritual weakness and inherent carnality of women, the independence of early medieval nuns could not be allowed to last long. The developing laws of feudalism increasingly restricted the right of women to own land, so that, by the Renaissance, women faced increasing difficulties in attempting to found or to endow convents, while friars began to take over the management of existing convents (Eckenstein 1963). The church gradually closed all double monasteries, pressuring nuns to enter cloisters and to wear religious habits. Education for nuns to increasingly seemed unnecessary or even dangerous. For this reason, by the sixteenth century church authorities had significantly decreased the educational opportunities available in most convents, although some convents did manage to preserve their intellectual traditions. Once Latin ceased to be taught, nuns were effectively excluded from all major church decisions.

As Protestant ideas began to infiltrate Europe, the status of unmarried women declined. One of the few areas in which Catholics and early Protestants agreed was the danger presented by independent women. Responding to flagrant sexual offenses in medieval monasteries, Protestants concluded that few men—let alone women, given their basically carnal nature–could maintain a celibate life. They therefore viewed "the religious profession [as] a thing of evil and temptation in which it was not possible to keep holy" (Charitas Perckheimer, quoted in Eckenstein 1963, 467). To Protestants, "marriage was the most acceptable state before God and . . . a woman has no claim to consideration except in her capacity as wife and mother" (Eckenstein 1963, 433). These beliefs, coupled with the political aims of Protestant rulers, culminated in the forced dissolution of convents and monasteries in many parts of Europe. In Protestant Europe, women were left without a socially acceptable alternative to marriage, while, in Catholic Europe, nuns had been stripped of their autonomy.

The belief in female carnality continued until the nineteenth century. At that point, while lower-class women were still considered sexually wanton by their social betters, prescriptive literature began to paint an image of upper-class women as passionless (Cott 1978). In this situation, unmarried lower-class women continued to suffer severe social sanctions as real or suspected prostitutes. Unmarried upper-class women continued to be stigmatized as unnatural, since they were not fulfilling their allotted role as wives and mothers. These upper-class women did not seem particularly threatening, however, since they were assumed, at least in public discourse, to be asexual beings. As a result, social sanctions against them diminished sharply, not to emerge again until women's newfound economic independence significantly changed the social context of romantic friendships among women.

In this historical overview I have so far discussed only events in the Western world. In the West, widows probably evoke less of a sense of threat than do other unmarried women, since widows do not generally seem to have chosen their fate. It is instructive to compare the fate of Hindu widows, who are believed to have caused their husbands' deaths by sins they committed in this or a previous life (Daly 1978; Stein 1978).

30   Since a Hindu woman's status is determined by her relationship to a man, and since Hindu custom forbids remarriage, widows literally have no place in that society. A widow is a superfluous economic burden on her family. She is also viewed as a potential source of dishonor, since Hindus believe that "women are by nature sexually unreliable and incapable of leading chaste lives without a husband to control them" (Stein 1978, 255). For the benefit of her family and for her own happiness in future lives, a widow was in the past expected to commit suttee–to

throw herself alive onto her husband's burning funeral pyre.[7] The horror of suttee was multiplied by the practice of polygamy and by the practice of marrying young girls to grown men, which resulted in the widowing of many young girls before they even reached puberty (Stein 1978; Daly 1978). Suttee, child marriage, and polygamy are illegal under the current government, but they do still occur.

As her only alternative to suttee, a widow was allowed to adopt a life of such poverty and austerity that she rarely survived for long. Her life was made even more miserable by the fact that only faithful wives were permitted to commit suttee. The refusal to commit suttee might therefore be regarded as an admission of infidelity. If a woman declined to immolate herself, her relatives might force her to do so, to protect both her honor and the honor of her family.

Stigmatization of Male Homosexuals

... this article has discussed male homosexuality only in passing. Nevertheless, it cannot be ignored that the sanctions against male homosexuality appear even stronger than those against lesbianism. Why might this be so? First, I would argue that anything women do is considered relatively trivial—be it housework, mothering, or lesbianism. Second, whereas lesbians threaten the status quo by refusing to accept their inferior position as women, gay males may threaten it even more by appearing to reject their privileged status as men. Prevailing cultural mythology holds that lesbians want to be males. In a paradoxical way, therefore, lesbians may be perceived as upholding "male" values. Male homosexuality, on the other hand, is regarded as a rejection of masculine values; gay males are regarded as feminized "sissies" and "queens." Thus male homosexuality, with its implied rejection of male privilege, may seem even more incomprehensible and threatening than lesbianism. Finally, research indicates that people in general are more fearful and intolerant of homosexuals of their own sex than of homosexuals belonging to the opposite sex (Weinberger and Millham 1979). The greater stigmatization of male than female homosexuality may therefore simply reflect the greater ability of males to enforce their prejudices.

[7]Suttee was most common among the upper castes (where a widow meant an extra mouth, but not an extra pair of hands), but it occurred throughout Hindu society (Stein 1978).

Conclusions

The stigmatization of independent women–whether spinster, widow, nun, or lesbian–is neither automatic nor natural. Rather, it seems to derive from a particular social constellation in which men fear women's sexual and economic independence. Sociological theory explains how stigmatizing individuals as deviant may serve certain purposes for the dominant community, regardless of the accuracy of the accusations leveled (Erikson 1962). First, particularly when social norms are changing rapidly, labeling and punishing certain behaviors as deviant emphasizes the new or continued unacceptability of those behaviors. The stigmatization of "romantic friendships" in the early twentieth century, for example, forced all members of society to recognize that social norms had changed and that such relationships would no longer be tolerated. Second, stigmatizing certain groups as deviant may increase solidarity within the dominant group, as the dominant group unites against its common enemy. Third, stigmatizing as deviant the individuals who challenge traditional ideas may reduce the threat of social change, if those individuals either lose credibility or are removed from the community altogether.

These principles apply to the stigmatization of independent women, from the labeling of nontraditional women as witches in medieval society to the condemnation of lesbians in contemporary society. Medieval inquisitors used the label *witch* to reinforce the normative boundaries of their community, to unite that community against the perceived source of its problems, and to eliminate completely women who seemed to threaten the social order. Currently, the word *lesbian* is used not only to describe women who love other women but also to censure women who overstep the bounds of the traditional female role and to teach all women that such behavior will not be tolerated. Feminists, women athletes, professional women, and others risk being labeled lesbian for their actions and beliefs. Awareness of the potential social consequences of that label exerts significant pressure on all women to remain in their traditional roles.

35   Antifeminist forces have used the lesbian label to denigrate all feminists, incite community wrath against them, and dismiss their political claims. In 1969 and 1970, some feminists responded to this social pressure by purging lesbians from their midst and proclaiming their moral purity (Abbott and Love 1972). This tactic proved extremely

self-destructive, as movement organizations collapsed in bitterness and dissension. In addition, eliminating lesbian members had little effect, since lesbian-baiting by antifeminists was equally damaging to the movement whether or not it was accurate.

By late 1970, many feminists had realized that trying to remove lesbians from their organizations was both self-destructive and ineffective. In response to this knowledge, various feminist organizations went on record acknowledging sexual preference as a feminist and a civil rights issue and supporting the rights of lesbians (Abbott and Love 1972). In a press conference held in December 1970, various women's liberation activists stated:

> Women's Liberation and Homosexual Liberation are both struggling toward a common goal: a society free from defining and categorizing people by virtue of gender and/or sexual preference. "Lesbian" is a label used as a psychic weapon to keep women locked into their male-defined "feminine role." The essence of that role is that a woman is defined in terms of her relationship to men. A woman is called a Lesbian when she functions autonomously. Women's autonomy is what Women's Liberation is all about [quoted in Abbott and Love 1972, 124).

A leaflet distributed the same month by the New York branch of the National Organization for Women acknowledged that, when charges of lesbianism are made, "it is not one woman's sexual preference that is under attack—it is the freedom of all women to openly state values that fundamentally challenge the basic structure of patriarchy" (quoted in Abbott and Love 1972, 122).

It seems, then, that the fates of feminists and lesbians are inextricably intertwined. Unless and until women's independence is accepted, lesbians will be stigmatized, and unless and until the stigma attached to lesbianism diminishes, the lesbian label will be used as a weapon against those who work for women's independence.

Works Cited

Abbott, Sidney and Barbara Love. *Sappho Was a Right-on Woman: A Liberated View of Lesbianism.* New York: Stein and Day Publishers, 1972.

Barrett, Ellen M. "Legal Homophobia and the Christian Church." *Hastings Law Journal* 30(4): 1019–27, 1979.

Boulding, Elise. *The Underside of History*. Boulder, Colo.: Westview Press, 1976.

Cott, Nancy. "Passionlessness: An Interpretation of Victorian Sexual Ideology, 1790–1850." *Signs: Journal of Women in Culture and Society* 4(2): 219–36, 1978.

Daly, Mary. *Gyn/ecology: The Metaethics of Radical Feminism*. Boston: Beacon Press, 1978.

Eckenstein, Lina. *Women under Monasticism*. New York: Russell and Russell, 1963.

Ehrenreich, Barbara, and Deirdre English. *Witches, Midwives and Nurses: A History of Women Healers*. Old Westbury, N.Y.: Feminist Press, 1973.

Erikson, Kai T. "Notes on the Sociology of Deviance." *Social Problems* 9(Spring): 307–14, 1962.

Ettorre, E. M. *Lesbians, Women and Society*. London: Routledge and Kegan Paul, 1980.

Faderman, Lillian. *Surpassing the Love of Men: Romantic Friendship and Love between Women from the Renaissance to the Present*. New York: William Morrow and Co., 1981.

Ford, Clellan S., and Frank A. Beach. *Patterns of Sexual Behavior*. New York: Harper and Row, 1951.

Glenn, Norval D., and Charles N. Weaver. "Attitudes towards Premarital, Extramarital and Homosexual Relationships in the United States in the 1970s." *Journal of Sex Research* 15(2): 108–17, 1979.

Kramer, H., and J. Sprenger. *Malleus Maleficarum*. Translated by Montague Summers. New York: Dover Publications, 1971.

MacDonald, A. P., and R. G. Games. "Some Characteristics of Those Who Have Positive and Negative Attitudes towards Homosexuals." *Journal of Homosexuality* 1(1): 9–28, 1974.

MacDonald, A. P., J. Huggins, S. Young, and R. A. Swanson. "Attitudes toward Homosexuality: Preservation of Sex Morality or the Double Standard." *Journal of Consulting and Clinical Psychology* 40(1): 161, 1973.

Mayor, Elizabeth. *The Ladies of Llangollen: A Study of Romantic Friendship*. New York Penguin Books, 1973.

Nelson, Mary. "Why Witches Were Women." In Jo Freeman (ed.), *Women: A Feminist Perspective*, 2d ed. Palo Alto, Calif.: Mayfield Publishing Co., 1979.

Raskin, Richard. "The 'Deprogramming' of Stephanie Riethmiller," *Ms.*, Sept. 1982, 19.

Reuben, David. *Everything You Always Wanted to Know about Sex But Were Afraid Ask*. New York: David McKay Co., 1969.

Rivera, Rhonda R. "Our Straight-laced Judges: The Legal Position of Homosexual Persons in the United States." *Hastings Law Journal* 30(4): 799–956, 1979

Smith-Rosenberg, Carroll. "The Female World of Love and Ritual: Relations Between Women in Nineteenth Century America." *Signs: Journal of Women Culture and Society* 1(1): 1–29, 1975.

Stein, Dorothy K. "Women to Burn: Suttee as a Normative Institution." *Signs: Journal of Women in Culture and Society* 4(2): 253–68, 1978.

Tanner, Donna M. *The Lesbian Couple.* Lexington, Mass.: D. C. Heath and Co., 1978.

Weinberger, Linda E., and Jim Millham. "Attitudinal Homophobia and Support Traditional Sex Roles." *Journal of Homosexuality* 4(3): 237–45, 1979.

Wolf, Deborah Goleman. *The Lesbian Community.* Berkeley: University of California Press, 1979.

SUGGESTIONS FOR WRITING

1. Weitz's title connects different categories that are usually not considered to be related. Write an essay that analyzes the arguments Weitz brings in support of her contention that they are so related.

2. According to Weitz, many factors beyond genital sexuality make lesbianism threatening to some societies. Write an essay that analyzes the arguments she makes in support of these claims.

3. Based on the information Weitz supplies and any additional knowledge you may command, write an essay that compares and contrasts the situation of widowhood in Western and Hindu societies.

Gender Role: The Early History of a Concept   2007

JAMES REED

James Reed (b. 1944) is a professor of history at Rutgers University where he served as dean of Rutgers College for many years. He was born and educated in New Orleans and took his Ph. D. at Harvard. Reed is currently at work on a biomedical history of sex research in the United States and the following essay makes a part of that larger project. In his brief history of John Money's work, Reed reveals that the term gender in its current and widely used sense of socially constructed identity was first so used by Money as a way of breaking down rigid formulations of sexualized types. The refashioning of a grammatical term was, Money saw, an act of necessity, because the kinds of people he studied and tried to help could not always be described conventionally, even in anatomical terms.

". . . the social history of our era cannot be written without naming gender, gender role, and gender identity as organizing principles."
John Money (1994)[i]

We invent new words and concepts in an effort to comprehend and to manage our environment. New meaning is found in old words and new language is coined as we struggle to make sense of social change. Twenty-first century American undergraduates use many newly coined acronyms that reflect advances in science and technology, *pc* and *DNA* for example, but their vocabulary also includes such terms as *racist* and *sexist* that were not part of the English language in 1900. The cosmopolitan academics who constructed the discipline of cultural anthropology in the early twentieth century developed a new vocabulary that reflected their desire to redeem non-Western peoples from the cultural condescension of physical anthropologists who claimed to have discovered differences in the bodies of human groups that explained the perceived cultural inferiority of non-Caucasians. The Columbia University anthropologists Franz Boas and Ruth Benedict professed a new science of cultural relativism based upon careful study and comparison of other cultures, and they coined the term *racist* as a pejorative label for those who insisted upon the natural superiority of white men. Armed with the ethos of anti-racism constructed by the Boas school in the first half of the twentieth century, radical women undergraduates of the 1960s enlisted in the struggle to dismantle Jim Crow, the racial caste system in the United States. As they labored for racial justice in such organizations as the Student Non-Violent Coordinating Committee, some women became disillusioned with the attitudes of male social activists toward them. They added *sexist* to our vocabulary as a label for those who still assumed male superiority over women, and these "second-wave feminists" found a mass audience among working women who had encountered *the glass ceiling*. A society in which a majority of women worked outside the home for wages needed new words and concepts to explain social tensions and conflicts of interest that could not be ignored.

[i]"The Concept of Gender Identity Disorder in Childhood and Adolescence After 39 Years," *Journal of Sex & Marital Therapy* 20:3 (Fall 1994):176.

As liberationist movements for racial equality and women's liberation gained traction, other *minorities* developed group-consciousness and made claims for justice, including *gays*, lesbians, *transsexuals*, and the *intersexed*. By the turn of the twenty-first century there were academic programs in *gender studies*, and college student life deans invited faculty members to workshops on how to be an "ally" for the LGBT (lesbian-gay-bisexual-transgender) community. Those who were comfortable in conventional *gender identities* were sometimes challenged by *gender benders*. The mass media featured stories about *gender dysphoria*, and debate raged among psychiatrists and clinical psychologists over the criteria for the sex change operations sought by thousands of *transgendered* persons, including some prison inmates, one of whom sued the government for surgical relief. The felon lost his suit for a sex-change operation, but the court ruled that he did have a right for treatment of his gender dysphoria. In media coverage of this legal case, we find a new language of gender that spoke to tensions and possibilities of *post-modernity*. According to the *Oxford English Dictionary Online*, distinguished by its word genealogies, in modern usage, *gender* is "a euphemism for the sex of a human being, often intended to emphasize the social and cultural, as opposed to the biological, distinctions between the sexes." The first usage cited by *OEDO* is Alex Comfort's *Sex in Society* (1963), where one learns that "The gender role learned by the age of two years is for most individual almost irreversible, even if it runs counter to the physical sex of the subject." Comfort's assertion that a person's genetic and hormonal sex might be overridden by other factors such as the sexual identity assigned at birth, reflected the growing influence of John Money, a Johns Hopkins University clinical psychologist who, beginning in the 1950s, would make major contributions to new language for discussing human sexuality. Money sought to build a scientific discipline of sexology that would encompass every aspect of human sexual behavior. One of Money's first contributions was the concept of gender role which he developed in the 1950s in a pioneering study of the emotional lives of hermaphrodites, whose bodies and behavior, he argued, demanded a reassessment of what it meant to be a man or a woman.

Money (b. 1921) began his study of hermaphrodites in the late 1940s as a graduate student in clinical psychology at Harvard. He had emigrated to the United States from New Zealand in 1947 with masters degrees in both education and psychology, eager to take advantage of the rapidly expanding job market for mental health personnel in a country where, in the wake of World War II, there were more available job openings for clinical psychologists in Veterans Administration Hospitals than there were certified psychological counselors. Money also sought perspective on personal issues related to his revolt against the repressive sexual values of his Christian evangelical family, in which male lust was demonized. He had embraced psychology as a scientific discipline that might explain his strong erotic attraction to men and inhibitions in relationships with women, and perhaps place his own sexual suffering in an affirming context. Money thought that he might write his doctoral dissertation on psychoanalytic theories of sexuality until a seminar taught by a physician from a child guidance center suggested a more promising subject, the psychology of persons with ambiguous genitals. The seminar case study was a seventeen-year-old boy with a condition that is now called androgen insensitivity syndrome (AIS). In AIS, the cells throughout the body of a genetic male (XY) child fail to respond to androgens. As a result the child developed a female body shape and genitals, but at seventeen he had a strong male identity and no interest in treatment to complete the process of feminization. Money was fascinated by the apparent paradox that the sex of the mind could be at odds with the visible sex of the body. His dissertation, *Hermaphroditism: An Inquiry into the Nature of a Human Paradox* (1952), provided a comprehensive review of the several hundred cases reported in the medical literature and ten extensive case studies of the emotional life of different types of intersex persons recruited for the study, thanks to an appointment in the department of psychiatry at the Massachusetts General Hospital.

Money's medical mentors were eager to have his help in understanding and treating conditions that took on new interest because rapid developments in genetics and endocrinology, as well as the availability of synthetic steroids, created new expectations about the possibilities for treating sex errors of the body and related syndromes. In his dissertation Money argued that his subjects adjusted remarkably well to the physical and emotional challenges they faced, and they exhibited no more psychopathology than the population at large. Money found his most important mentor when he asked the Johns Hopkins University pediatrician Lawson Wilkins for access to patient records. Wilkins had begun to use the newly synthesized hormone cortisol (1950) to treat congenital adrenal hyperplasia (CAH), a condition in which female children are masculinized by excessive production of androgens by their own adrenal glands. Wilkins not only invited Money for a research visit but wrote him into grant applications that provided Money with a new institutional home as a protégé of "the father of pediatric endocrinology." Money's legitimacy as an authority on human sexuality rested heavily on the rich clinical experience that he tapped as a staff member of the Pediatric Endocrinology Clinic at Johns Hopkins, but his ambition to build a science of sexology led him to draw the largest possible theoretical conclusions from the case histories of the patients that he counseled.

5   By the late 1950s Money's prolific publications had won a wide and admiring audience among physicians and psychologists. His impressive monographs were distinguished by empathy for individual patients, whose struggles to find their way in the world despite great physical and emotional challenges were described in vivid detail, and by theoretical verve. For example, in "An Examination of Some Basic Sexual Concepts: the Evidence of Human Hermaphroditism" (1955),[ii] Money made a startling assertion, based on seventy-six cases, that the unitary definition of sex as male or female based upon chromosomes, gonads, and hormone levels should be abandoned. Instead, he identified seven variables of sex that might interact in contradictory ways. They were:

1. Assigned sex and sex of rearing
2. External genital morphology
3. Internal accessory reproductive structures
4. Hormonal sex and secondary sexual characteristics
5. Gonadal sex
6. Chromosomal sex
7. Gender role and orientation as male or female, established while growing up

He defined the new concept of gender role as "all those things that a person says or does to disclose himself or herself as having the status of boy or man, girl or woman respectively. It includes but is not restricted to sexuality in the sense of eroticism. Gender role is appraised in relation to the following: general mannerisms, deportment and demeanor; play

[ii]Money was the lead author but this author had two coauthors, Hopkins Department of Psychiatry colleagues Joan G. Hampson and John L. Hampson. *Bulletin of the Johns Hopkins University Hospital* 97:301–19.

preferences and recreational interests; spontaneous topics of talk in unprompted conversation and casual comment; content of dreams, day-dreams and fantasies; replies to oblique inquiries and projective tests; evidence of erotic practices and, finally, the person's own replies to direct inquiry." Of most importance, he argued, "In place of a theory of masculinity or femininity which is innate, the evidence of hermaphroditism lends support to a conception that, psychologically sexuality is undifferentiated at birth and that it becomes differentiated as masculine or feminine in the course of the various experiences of growing up." The most potent determinant of sexual identity in Money's cases seemed to be the sex assigned after birth by adults. One's gender might contradict the evidence of chromosomes, hormones, or other somatic signs of sex! The concept of gender role was needed to reconcile the multiple sequential factors that determined the sexual identity of a human being.

Money's startling claim for conceptualizing sexual development in a radical new way that recognized the power of post-natal nurture and experience might seem to contradict accepted wisdom about American culture in the 1950s, where many historians have found a Cold War atmosphere of conformity and repression that included celebration of traditional family values and denigration as domestic subversives of those who challenged them in world or deed. Physicians are often included among the social conservatives of the era, but Money softened resistance to his request for a new understanding of sex with evocative testimony from his clients whose photographed bodies and candid descriptions of struggles to manage their lives made strong claims on the sympathies of readers. Money concluded "An Examination of Some Basic Sexual Concepts" with the "case illustration" of a twenty-four-year-old subject who was a genetic female but had lived his whole life as a male. Despite a tiny hypospadic phallus and absence of testicles, the subject had been declared a boy at birth and reared as such in an academic family. When his breasts began to enlarge at the age of eleven, he was treated with androgens and internal female organs were removed. The desire to marry brought the subject to the pediatrics unit at Johns Hopkins, where Money noted that "At first sight and throughout the first meeting with this man, I kept thinking that nothing in his general appearance, manner or conversation betrayed a single hint of the information filed away in his medical record. He would pass anywhere as the advanced graduate student that he was."

After discussing the high IQ, work ethic, open disposition, and academic achievements of his subject, Money quoted his client at length on his mechanisms for coping with his genital anomalies. His mother had attempted to dissuade him from thinking of marriage from an early age, but this had simply heightened his desire to find a female mate and to have a happy family like the one in which he had been reared. After falling in love with a Roman Catholic woman, and their mutual conclusion after much soul searching and consultation with priests and a family physician that they could get married, the young man had plastic surgery that improved the salience of his micropenis. He explained that he and his bride ". . . make out very well now, of course we're still just married, but it's a rough day when we don't get to bed at least once." "Of course we have to experiment quite a bit, to find the best ways for Rae always to have an orgasm. If she doesn't that makes me very unhappy."

Money's narrative took on a more subjective tone as he brought this story to a conclusion after more than five papers of close description. "A spontaneous gaiety in their marriage was clearly reflected in a passage of free association. 'And we had good fun in bed the other day; gee it must have been two hours. We've felt good ever since.' At this point he paused, checked himself, awakened from somnolence, laughed and said he had been thinking about . . . the day when she may get ambitious enough for fellatio in love making." After reviewing the obstacles to construction of an effective identity that his subject had overcome, Money concluded his "psychological appraisal" with frank praise. His subject "passed simply as an ordinary male college graduate—one of the more stable and well-adjusted." "He was meeting life most successfully without any suspicion of psychopathology. There was every reason to believe that he would continue to do so. His life is an eloquent and incisive testimony to the stamina of human personality." The good news from the new academic discipline of pediatric psychoendocrinology was that nurture might trump nature in the pursuit of human possibilities.

Money's work with the intersexed prepared him for a sympathetic response to somatically normal adults who were unhappy with their genitals. Although the surgical reconstruction of the anomalous genitals of intersex children was becoming standard practice by the mid-1960s, genitally normal adults who sought sex reassignment found no relief from American surgeons who feared that they would be vulnerable under common law "mayhem" statutes that forbade the amputation of healthy body parts and who often doubted the sanity of those who were unhappy with their sex. In the cultural ferment of the 1960s, a lobby for sex change operations began to coalesce, however, thanks to the funding provided by Reed Erickson, a wealthy female-to-male transsexual, and the scientific rationale provided by Money, whose tireless lobbying led to the opening of the Johns Hopkins Gender Identity Clinic in 1966, where sex-reassignment surgery was available in a university-based hospital for the first time.

Money claimed a high level of success in the surgical treatment of gender disphoria and became a national celebrity associated with many aspects of sexual liberation and reform that flourished at the time. His command of the literatures of the life sciences and of anthropology was exhibited in widely-read books such as *Man & Woman, Boy & Girl* (1972) and *Sexual Signatures: On Being A Man or A Woman* (1975). His message was that the scientific study of sexuality was demolishing old stereotypes of masculinity and femininity and opening the way for "pioneers" of new lifestyles, including bi-sexual swinging, who were pushing forward the frontiers of human possibility. "The traditional assumption has been that just two sexual possibilities exist, one deriving from XY chromosomes at conception, resulting in manhood, the other from XX chromosomes, resulting in womanhood. But the exceptions—hermaphrodites, transvestites, transsexuals, homosexuals, and bi-sexuals—have always raised puzzling questions. In attempting to help these people fit comfortably into society's sexual schemas, scientists have arrived at startling discoveries: the fact is, a person becomes male or female by stages, and there is a great deal more flexibility than is ordinarily supposed."

By the 1970s one of Money's favorite case histories, which lent tremendous "clinical authority" to his ideas, detailed the successful sex reassignment of a normal male child whose penis was destroyed at the age of eight months in a botched circumcision. David Reimer's working-class Canadian parents had sought help at the Menninger Clinic in Minnesota but had been told that there was little that could be done for their child. By chance, they saw Money discussing the successful work with transsexuals at Johns Hopkins on a British television news magazine, sought his counsel, and were encouraged by his opinion that it might be possible to rear their child as a woman. The Reimer case provided a rare opportunity for Money because David had a twin brother, and it would be possible to compare the development of two normal genetic males, one of whom would be reassigned as female. In 1967 David Reimer was castrated at Johns Hopkins. Money provided "after care" for the whole family, which included detailed instructions to the parents on how to rear a female child and yearly family visits to Baltimore, where much time was devoted to interviewing the twins and teaching them their respective gender roles. In numerous publications and talks, Money used the Reimer case to bolster his hypothesis that the sex of assignment and rearing trumped all other variables in the formation of gender identity, not only in the intersexed but possibly in normal children as well. In Money's reports, despite her XY genotype and male genital and endocrine profile at birth, "Brenda" Reimer was a normal little girl who "preferred dresses to pants, enjoyed wearing her hair ribbons, bracelets and frilly blouses, and loved being her Daddy's little sweetheart."

The Reimer's new daughter desperately resisted the sex reassignment. She was taunted as "Cave Woman" by her school mates, refused for several years to accept the further genital surgery that Money hoped would complete the project of constructing a girl from the body of a boy, and finally got her parents to stop cooperating with Money's program by threatening suicide at age fourteen. Money gradually dropped this case from his repertoire and evaded dozens of inquiries from well meaning teachers and counselors who had read his publications and requested updates. Persistent efforts by scientific rivals to discredit Money's hypothesis that human beings are psychosexually neutral at birth eventually led them to David Reimer, who was living as a man after phalloplasty, eager to renounce Money's theories, and willing to recount his dreadful suffering at the hands of his Johns Hopkins therapist. The journalist John Colapinto publicized the Reimer case in a 1997 *Rolling Stone* article, followed by *As Nature Made Him: The Boy Who Was Raised As A Girl* (2000). The deconstruction of Money's reputation continued with a "NOVA" public television documentary, "Sex Unknown" (2001), that explored "the fateful consequences of gender reassignment" and echoed Colapinto's story line of nurture theory run amuck. David Reimer committed suicide in 2004, at the age of thirty-eight, following the 2002 example of his twin brother. His mother told reporters that she had never forgiven Money for the harm he had caused her family.

Long before Money's work on the determinants of sexual identity came under attack, the concept of gender role had taken on a life of its own. Money complained that his multi-variate, sequential theory of psychosexual development was torn from its biological context. He claimed that nature could never be disentangled from nurture and especially disputed feminist accounts that supposed differences between men and women were simply social artifact without basis in biological reality. He regretted the "neutering of gender," "man-bashing" and the "demonization of lust" which he found in much feminist theory, but the nature/nurture debated roared on with or without him, and partisans on all sides adopted useful vocabulary from the vast edifice of Money's sexology.

SUGGESTIONS FOR WRITING

1. Reed analyzes the importance of new language to reliable analysis in general and Money's research in particular. Write an essay that explores the importance of the term *gender* as used by Money in the examination and discussion of the issues he raised in his career.

2. Write an essay that analyzes and exemplifies Money's arguments to the effect that "the unitary definition of sex as male or female . . . should be abandoned." [paragraph 5]

3. Reed records some of the attacks on Money's reputation. What in your view are the principal reasons for Money's later lack of success? Write an essay that explains and defends your answer.

Fear and Loathing in Sex Education

2003

PRATIMA CRANSE

Pratima Cranse (b. 1978) is now a registered nurse who undertook a volunteer assignment to participate as an instructor in a peer-education course in sex education while still an undergraduate at Rutgers University in the late 1990s. As is well known, talking in public about sex among strangers makes people nervous. The idea of the course was that students would be less shy and more forthcoming about the important matters of sexuality, including sexually transmitted diseases and infections, if they were addressed by a fellow student. In her report, we see how that idea played out in practice with both triumphs and setbacks in the effort to create a better informed student population.

The elevator doors slide open and I walk into the third-floor hallway of a freshmen dorm. There is a large corkboard on my left with various posters: "Join the Army, Be All That You Can Be," "Study abroad for a year and become a different person!" "NJ film festival starts on March 4," "Sign up for your FREE credit card today," "Sexual Health Program, 'Lets Talk About Sex' on the third-floor lounge at 9:00." This one is hastily drawn up on typing paper and reproduced by a photocopier. Copies are pinned not only to the corkboard but also taped all over the hallway walls. One poster has been vandalized with "Suck my Cock" boldly scrawled and, as the meaning of that particular phrase might be unclear to the reader, there is an accompanying hand-drawn graphic of would-be sexy, bee-stung lips performing fellatio on a free-floating penis.

I enter the lounge, which is carpeted yellowish-orange and a few students carrying books or cell phones are scattered about. I shrug off my winter jacket and immediately start to set up shop, dragging a table to one end of the room and taping up three sheets of butcher paper on the wall behind me. On the first sheet of paper I write the word "vagina," on the second I write "penis," and on the last I write "sex." On the table I arrange thick packets of informational brochures about sexual health: STDs (Sexually Transmitted Diseases), STIs (Sexually Transmitted Infections)[1], contraceptives, sexual assault, STD and STI testing, abstinence, pregnancy, alcohol and other drug abuse, self-examination for breast cancer and self-examination for testicular cancer. I empty a paper bag filled with flavored and unflavored condoms, an empty pack of birth control pills, tubes of lubricant, sheets of dental dams, spermicide, and diaphragms. To this I add, from a larger bag, a model of a penis and a sort of fallopian tube and cervix model. Students began to buzz and hum around me. I feign a grin of total confidence when I hear mocking laughter from a few passing girls, all of them very pretty and also, no doubt, feigning confidence.

---

[1]Sexually Transmitted Diseases are viral and often incurable. Sexually Transmitted Infections are treatable with antibiotics. Herpes, for example, is a disease. Chlamydia is an infection.

By 9 P.M. a crowd has gathered consisting of 30 or so students, all of them about 18 or 19 years old. A group of five or six athletic, handsome young men huddle up in the back corner of the room. They control the atmosphere in the lounge with their good looks and bravado. Making jokes, laughing, talking over each other and me, I know from experience that these guys are my ticket to conducting a good program. For the rest of the program I will play a game with these young men. The goal of the game, on my part, and perhaps theirs, is to contain their distracting behavior and make them listen.

5   There are about 10 women who sit right in front of me. They seem pensive and mildly interested and their expressions will grow more serious throughout the program, but they will speak little. The rest are a relaxed bunch of both sexes, just taking a break from their homework. I ask everyone to quiet down so we can begin. Most listen but the guys in the back keep talking, then my heroine reveals herself.

"Shut the hell up! Can't you see she's trying to talk?"

The words come loudly and yet surprisingly calmly, from a young black woman, who will, for the rest the program, be my champion. She is the only person in the room who does not feign confidence or, more likely, feigns confidence in ways (and for reasons) that are much more complicated than I am attuned to clearly understand or even perceive. The room more or less quiets down and the girl nods to me to proceed.

I introduce myself and my purpose, "My name is Pratima Cranse, I am a junior at Rutgers College and a sexual health advocate. I work out of the health education department at the health center. Do you all know where that is?"

Silence. Somewhere in the distance a cell phone rings.

10   I explain that I am here to conduct a workshop about sexual health: How to protect yourself, get tested, communicate with your partner or partners, use contraceptives, and/or practice abstinence. I go over a set of ground rules for the program. The ground rules are about respect, listening, tolerance, and refraining from making assumptions.

"I do not assume that all or any members of this group are sexually active. I make no assumptions about the sexual orientation of anyone in this group and I expect you to do me the same courtesy."

"Any fags here?" Asks one of the guys from the back and the whole room, with few exceptions, bursts out laughing.

"If you're too nervous to handle talking about sex then please leave," I say without looking at the group of guys. This dirty trick works and for five minutes I get no more interruptions. Since many people assume my heterosexuality (which may stifle certain questions or sanction certain jokes), I often wear a sweatshirt with a picture of a lovely, half-naked Japaname girl coyly staring at the crowd. The audience response to this shirt is always varied and always interesting. Homophobic comments are made with less frequency or not made at all. But the shirt is in the wash and probably wouldn't have worked on this young crowd anyway.

I conduct a warm-up or exercise intended to get the students loosened up and ready to talk and listen. The exercise consists of thinking of synonyms for the three words written on the butcher paper. The crowd begins to nervously then rapturously shout out a colorful array of slang terms for penis, vagina, and sex. Many of the words for sex, like banging or cutting, are also violent actions. At the end of the exercise I ask the audience why the slang words for sex are so violent sounding. A vague, disjointed conversation about the media and pop culture follows. Some newly minted feminist studies students stumble over theories about sex and violence, but the audience does not seem too excited or interested in the topic.

The slang terms for penis are generally humorous (mini me, shlong) but often implicitly degrading (equipment, meat). The slang terms for vagina are, in my personal estimation, the most ugly sounding (cunt, cut, hole, box). I ask the audience what they think of slang words for male and female genitalia and a spirited discussion follows. The women and some of the men argue that the words for vagina are more negative and inappropriate than the slang words for penis. One can say "dick" with near impunity in everyday conversation but "cunt," on the other hand, is the societal equivalent of a swear word or worse; something not to be said aloud in certain company.

15   I mediate the discussion by asking if anyone thinks that the argument exaggerates, is altogether untrue, or if the reverse is true. Some of the men in the back speak up, more or less arguing that the words "cunt" and "hole" are funny and meant to be taken in a lighthearted manner. The discussion ends with eye rolling and insult trading so I close the topic, remind people that we agreed to respect each other, and hurry along to the next exercise.

With the assistance of my champion, the young woman who effectively hushed the crowd at the beginning of the program, I pass around pencils and paper.

"Please write down a question, fold the paper in half, and pass the paper back up to me. I will answer any questions you have about sex, sexually transmitted infections or diseases, contraceptives, getting testing, and, if I can, anything else you want to know about."

After a few minutes one of the quiet girls in front raises her hand and asks, with a challenge in her eye, if she must write down a question.

"Of course not" and I smile, trying to reassure her. She nods and throws the crumpled piece of paper in the wastebasket. I collect the cards and sort through them, weeding out questions that are blatantly inappropriate (not always an easy task). Some of the cards ask for my phone number, one asks if I am a "dyke," and yet another asks how you can tell when a woman is "asking for it." I pause on this last one, then decide to keep it in the pile from which I will read aloud.

20   As usual, almost all the questions are about statistics. Again as usual, many of the questions are also unfortunately based in myths and misinformation. "What are the chances of a white female aged 18 catching AIDS?" "What are the chances of getting pregnant if you use a condom only sometimes?" "When is the best time to have sex without out a condom?" "What is the percent of people who get Herpes from going down on their partner?" "How many women get cancer from the pill?" "What are my chances of getting warts if I am black, monogamous and male?" "Can women give each other STDs?" "How can I give my girl friend an orgasm?" "Where is the g-spot!!??"

I read each question aloud and answer each one. I ask if anyone in the audience knows the answer before I answer myself. I explode some myths about the pill (it does not cause cancer, but women who smoke should seriously consider quitting if they want to take the birth control pill because it can lead to blood clots and, in rare cases, a stroke). I observe the audience's response to my description of the test one can get for Chlamydia and Gonorrhea. Testing for women is a lot like getting a typical annual checkup. You lie flat on your back with your legs spread and feet placed onto two metal handles that look like stirrups. A plastic tube, which is a little uncomfortable, is used to take a culture from the inside of the vaginal wall. As I describe this procedure the audience remains pretty calm, a few people flinch and say "gross."

The procedure for men to get tested can be considered a little more invasive and it produces some physical discomfort that last a few minutes. A metal swab must be inserted into the head of the penis to get a culture. The guys in the back of the audience, clearly in an absolute panic, begin to laugh crazily and joke privately. Moments later a couple of them ask in bored, disdainful tones when they will be able to get the free condoms and leave. I tell them that they can leave whenever they want and I will set aside some condoms for them to pick up after the program is finished. They shrug, still disdainful, but do not leave.

When I get into the statistical questions, the whole audience listens intently. People ask statistical questions, of course, because they want to know what their own chances are of getting an STI or STD. I can rattle off a whole series of statistics and, as I do so, I observe about half the audience concerted in calculations, factoring in their various sexual encounters along with their race and sex and the extent to which they used protection. I'm empathetic to their need to know their "chances," but I also try to steer them away from such misleading calculations, like a math teacher trying to convey to students that comprehension of the equation, not the answer itself, is the real value in the lesson.

* * * * * * * *

There is a great deal of controversy in the United States today about sexual practices among young people. There is even controversy about the *facts* of sexually transmitted diseases and infections. One of my main functions as a sexual health advocate is to convey facts to college students about STDs and STIs. I have little to no interest in whether or not my conveying the facts inflames the controversy.

25   It is a fact that Chlamydia is the most common sexually transmitted infection among college students. There are an estimated 3 million cases annually with the highest rates among those who are 15 to 30 years old. The infection is spread through unprotected vaginal, anal, and/or oral intercourse with infected partners. About 80% of women and most men who have Chlamydia are asymptomatic, meaning they have no symptoms. But if symptoms do occur, they appear about 1–3 weeks after the first exposure (sexual contact). Men may experience painful urination and discharge from the penis. Infected women may experience vaginal discharge or painful intercourse and urination. They may also bleed between menstrual periods. If Chlamydia goes untreated it can cause sterility in men. In women Chlamydia can lead to Pelvic Inflammatory Disease (PID), which can leave a woman infertile. It can also be transmitted to infants during childbirth. Chlamydia is treatable with antibiotics; however; all partners must be treated at the same time to avoid reinfection. To avoid initial infection you can practice abstinence, use latex or polyurethane condoms

both for intercourse and oral sex performed on men, and use dental dams or nonperforated plastic wrap if performing oral sex on women.

Like Chlamydia, Gonorrhea's highest rates are among those who are 15 to 30 years old and it is spread through unprotected vaginal, anal, and/or oral intercourse with infected partners. Men and women may also experience rectal pain or discharge, sore throat and pink eye. If Gonorrhea goes untreated it can lead to infertility or sterility in both men and women. It can lead to blindness, heart problems, skin disease, and arthritis. It can be transmitted to infants during childbirth. To avoid infection you must use the same precautions as you would for preventing Chlamydia.

In 1998 there were 38,000 cases of Syphilis primarily occurring in the 20–39 year age group. African Americans are disproportionately represented in the rates of Syphilis being 34 times more likely than whites to contract it. Syphilis first appears as a painless lesion on the genital area that heals and goes away, followed by the flu-like symptoms that also go away. Because the symptoms disappear, many people do not seek treatment. If left untreated, Syphilis affects major body organs and ultimately leads to death. If caught in its early stages, Syphilis is treatable with antibiotics. The precautionary measures taken to avoid Chlamydia and Gonorrhea are the same for Syphilis.

In the United States, an estimated one in five people age 12 or older have HSV 2 or genital Herpes. Herpes is another disease in which African Americans are disproportionately represented although in proportions not as extreme as those associated with Syphilis. Herpes can be asymptomatic or can appear as pink or fluid-filled sores that can itch or be painful. Herpes can also cause flu-like symptoms two weeks after the initial transmission. Vaginal, anal, or oral intercourse are not necessary to transmit Herpes; it can be contracted simply by coming into contact with a lesion or infected area, and Herpes *can* be contracted even if the infected person is *not* having an outbreak. However, Herpes is more infectious if it is in an active phase or outbreak.

Herpes is treatable but not curable. In most people, if in good health, Herpes does not leave long-term effects. But it is possible, although rare, for a mother to transmit Herpes to her infant at birth, which can lead to brain damage or death to the infant. Condoms and dental dams offer some protection from Herpes but do not guarantee against contracting the virus. Abstinence, communication, and safer sex are all ways to prevent or cope with Herpes and all STIs and STDs.

30   Genital warts or Human Papilloma Virus (HPV) occurs in astounding rates among college-age women and, presumably, the rates are just as high for college-age men. HPV is notoriously asymptomatic or undetectable, so women will often find out that they have it only if they are getting their annual check-up or OBGYN, a check-up for which there is no regulated male equivalent. HPV can look like small, flesh colored, cauliflower-like growths that appear on or around the genitals or inside the cervix. Again, *many women do not know they have HPV until abnormal cells are detected in their annual pap smears.* HPV warts can be treated with topical creams or they can be frozen off. If left untreated, HPV will grow and become more difficult to get rid of. A mother can pass HPV to her infant at birth and some strains of HPV may lead to cervical cancer.

As with Herpes, HPV is transmissible through any sort of contact with an infected area regardless of whether it is in an active or inactive phase. Safer sex precautions (condoms and dental dams) only provide partial protection.

* * * * * * * *

"What do you mean by 'partial protection?'"

"Partial protection means that condoms and dental dams aren't guaranteed to protect you from contracting or spreading HPV."

"Then what are you supposed to do?"

35   The audience gets nervous and angry when I start to talk about Herpes and HPV. I don't blame them. They are used to thinking of cures and guarantees and neither disease seems to provide either. "Okay," I say, "what *are* you supposed to do?" People shuffle around and look at their watches. No one wants to talk about it.

"You insist that your partner get tested before you mess around," says my champion, tapping her foot impatiently.

"That's a great idea, but there isn't really a test for HPV. Lots of men are completely asymptomatic and don't know that they are spreading it."

"So if you're a guy and asymptomatic, it doesn't really mess with you?" asks one of the guys from the back.

I'm not sure how to answer the question, so I answer with a question, "What do you mean by 'mess with you?'"

40   "What I'm saying is, if a guy has it and it doesn't mess with him then he can do whatever he wants."

"But he'd be spreading it to other people, and it might 'mess with them,' as you say."

"Whatever. If it doesn't affect the guy then he doesn't have to worry about that."

The audience explodes. The women start insulting him by calling him a dick or a cocksucker.

"Everybody calm down. No one can hear each other. Please be quiet." Me, my champion, and few others form a chorus of appeal to the crowd. Eventually people stop yelling and look to me for a final verdict.

45 "I would hope that no one in this audience would ever willingly or disinterestedly spread a disease to another human being. I realize that these diseases are scary and many of you might express that fear with anger or general nastiness. If you're scared, say you're scared, okay? I'll be here for awhile after the program for anyone who wants to speak with me privately." A couple people in the audience nod to me. The guy in the back fiddles with his cell phone and grins at his buddies, all of whom seem, finally, a little unsure.

The program has now gone on for two hours and there is still an enormous amount of information to cover. It's getting late and a few kids are yawning or studying. I'm thinking about my car, or rather the walk to my car and the recent reports of muggings and assaults near this area.

"Okay, everyone, let's just focus while I run through the last couple of questions." The crowd is much too defensive and exhausted to deal with the 'How can you tell if a woman is asking for it' question. I read the question outloud anyway and ask if anyone wants to talk about it. Nobody does.

"Whoever wrote this question can see me after the program. We can just chill out and have a soda and talk, okay? I won't get angry."

To answer the many questions about the female orgasm I draw a diagram on the butcher paper showing where the g-spot and clitoris are and explain that, for vaginal sex, many women find that being on top helps them to have an orgasm but, in the end, different people have different needs.

50 "Communication is the key. Many people, both women and men, may know how to pleasure themselves but do not know how to communicate their needs to their partner or partners. Listen. Talk. Watch. Practice. Learn. The same principles you use for learning about soccer or literature or science apply to learning about sex and all its glories." The audience giggles appreciatively.

"Now let's talk about AIDS."

* * * * * * * *

Many health workers say that when it comes to AIDS, Americans are living in a period of denial. "Cocktail drugs" (which 30% of the population is allergic to) can slow down the progress of HIV from becoming full-blown AIDS and/or slow down the progress of AIDS deteriorating the immune system. AIDS is not a "gay" or "heroin addict" disease. Women are the fastest growing population of people with AIDS, and worldwide women make up the majority of AIDS cases.

HIV, the virus that causes AIDS, spreads through contact with blood, semen, vaginal fluid, and breast milk. It is contracted through unprotected vaginal, anal, or oral sex. It is also contracted through infected shared needles for injecting drugs, tattoos, acupuncture, etc. HIV causes a breakdown in the immune system, which eventually leads to AIDS, opportunistic infections, various forms of cancer, and death. Prevention includes abstinence, using a condom and/or dental dam, spermicide (nonoxynol-9 is a particularly effective spermicide although some people are allergic to it), and not sharing needles.

* * * * * * * *

"In the United States AIDS is the leading cause of death among people ages 25 to 44. Since AIDS has a period of latency, those who are dying from it in their mid-twenties contracted it in their late teens or early twenties."

55 Silence.

"Any questions?"

Silence.

"I'll be here to answer any questions or speak to any of you privately. Feel free to take condoms, dental dams, lubricants, spermicide, and pamphlets. Thank you for listening, you've been a great audience."

The crowd more or less applauds and people get up to stretch and yawn. Almost everyone from the audience comes up to the table to take free samples. A few people, including my champion, ask how I became a sexual health advocate and if they can become one as well. I tell them that I took a year-long course in STDs and STIs that is offered by the health department, and give them application information. The crowd thins out and many people head back to their rooms. A handful of girls (the silent, somber group who sat in front during the program) ask me some more detailed questions about symptoms they've been having.

60 "I think I was, like, raped. Do I have to get tested?" whispers a girl with oversized glasses and long, straight red hair. I give her some

phone numbers to call and encourage her to get tested and report her assault. Like many rape victims I've spoken to, she is a confused mixture of distraught and perfectly calm. She takes the phone numbers and asks if the doctor she sees will report what she says to the police.

"No, your doctor will not report anything unless you want to. If the assault occurred very recently, within the last couple of days, (the girl shakes her head positively) the doctor could collect and save evidence if you chose to press charges later on. Do you have any bruises or anything?"

"No, look do I have to get tested or what?" she starts backing away and continues to do so as our conversation ends.

"I can't tell you what to do," I say softly, "but personally I think it's a good idea to get tested. The phone numbers I gave you will connect you with professional people who can really help. In the meantime, do you have someone, a friend, to talk to about this?"

"Yeah."

65   The room is now completely empty. As I am about to leave, one of the loud guys who sat in the back, perhaps the most handsome of them all, comes into the lounge.

"Hey."

"What's up?"

"I have this shit on my dick."

"Does it hurt or itch?"

70   "It itches."

"What does it look like?"

"Weird."

"Is it like any of the symptoms I described?"

"No."

75   "No?"

"No."

"Alright, well, there's a lot of other diseases that I didn't get to talk about. I just went over some of the most common ones. You should really get it looked at by a doctor as soon as possible."

"Shit."

"It's okay, the tests aren't that bad. It can be harder for guys mentally than physically, you know?" He is losing interest or pretending to. I give him a pamphlet and the number to make an appointment. I tell him to inform his partners if he has an infection. He thanks me and walks back to his room.

I push the elevator button to go down as my champion emerges from the ladies room.

"It's late," she says. "Me and my boyfriend will walk you home."

"Thank you so much. I really just need a walk to my car."

"Even better."

They walk me to my car as I tell them about the other programs I've facilitated. I have some great stories and we all have a good laugh. I thank them again and, as I warm up my ancient car, watch them slowly saunter back to the dorm, their pinkies gently linked.

* * * * * * * *

85 My experience as a sexual health advocate for the health department at my school gave me special insight into the subject of this essay. Being a sexual health advocate made me an educator, but when I came face to face with my peers, what I most often found was nonchalance, fear, or a strange mixture of both. I spoke to my audience as a peer, as someone who was or might be going through the same experiences they were. For my audience, my youth and relative awkwardness as a public speaker added to my credibility as did my unsophisticated vocabulary: "plastic tube thingie, cotton swab-type thing." When writing this essay I chose not to hide my vulnerability and so-so ability to control the crowd. On a bright note, my champion is not a fictitious creation, and versions of her have appeared in almost every program I have ever facilitated.

The people who came up to me after the program and asked me their hurried, deeply personal, questions have made lasting impressions. Many young women had frantic stories about late periods, broken condoms, or a boyfriend's adamant refusal to wear a condom. Occasionally a student would protest my being there at all, saying that the services offered by the health education department were too "prosex." I engaged one such student in a discussion and I think he was grateful to talk about sex with somebody.

Yet it's the conversations I didn't get to have that trouble me the most. There were situations I didn't handle with authority. A shy, chubby, myopic boy who waited for me while I spoke to someone else, then someone else; people who wanted condoms and their own questions answered pushed in front of him. He patiently waited his turn until he got embarrassed or tired and then left without having asked me anything. And it didn't occur to me until just now that the person who asked the question, "How do you know if a woman is asking for it?" was the girl with the big glasses and long red hair.

SUGGESTIONS FOR WRITING

1. Cranse blends an expository essay on sexual diseases and infections with a dramatized account of her lecture on the topics. Do you find the blend well managed as a literary enterprise? Write an essay that explains and defends your answer.

2. In some parts of her essay, Cranse uses common but socially vulgar words that do not usually appear in formal writing. Write an essay in which you defend or attack her strategy as a writer in using these terms.

3. Cranse's anecdotes seem to suggest a gender-based difference in attitudes toward sex education. Do you agree with that suggestion? Write an essay that explains and defends your answer.

It's a Jungle Out There, So Get Used to It! 1992

CAMILLE PAGLIA

Camille Paglia was born in 1947 in New York State. She was a relatively unknown professor of art history at the Philadelphia College of Art when her book Sexual Personae: Art and Decadence from Nefertiti to Emily Dickinson *was published in 1990 and she achieved instant notoriety. Subsequently she was named as one of the world's top 100 living intellectuals by the British magazine* Prospect. *She has also been called the feminist that feminists love to hate.*

Paglia's ideas, which are always controversial and incendiary, center around the natural sexual forces that she believes are an unavoidable part of the human condition. In the essay that follows she considers vital questions: What is rape and what can be done about it? Here she examines the dynamics on rape on campus and claims that young women have been made more and more vulnerable by misinformation and ideology.

Rape is an outrage that cannot be tolerated in civilized society. Yet feminism, which has waged a crusade for rape to be taken more seriously, has put young women in danger by hiding the truth about sex from them.

In dramatizing the pervasiveness of rape, feminists have told young women that before they have sex with a man, they must give consent as explicit as a legal contract's. In this way, young women have been convinced that they have been the victims of rape. On elite campuses in the Northeast and on the West Coast, they have held consciousness-raising sessions, petitioned administrations, demanded inquests. At Brown University, outraged, panicky "victims" have scrawled the names of alleged attackers on the walls of women's rest rooms. What marital rape was to the '70s, "date rape" is to the '90s.

The incidence and seriousness of rape do not require this kind of exaggeration. Real acquaintance rape is nothing new. It has been a horrible problem for women for all of recorded history. Once fathers and brothers protected women from rape. Once the penalty for rape was death. I come from a fierce Italian tradition where, not so long ago in the motherland, a rapist would end up knifed, castrated, and hung out to dry.

But the old clans and small rural communities have broken down. In our cities, on our campuses far from home, young women are vulnerable and defenseless. Feminism has not prepared them for this. Feminism keeps saying the sexes are the same. It keeps telling women they can do anything, go anywhere, say anything, wear anything. No, they can't. Women will always be in sexual danger.

5   One of my male students recently slept overnight with a friend in a passageway of the Great Pyramid in Egypt. He described the moon and sand, the ancient silence and eerie echoes. I will never experience that. I am a woman. I am not stupid enough to believe I could ever be safe there. There is a world of solitary adventure I will never have. Women have always known these somber truths. But feminism, with its pie-in-the-sky fantasies about the perfect world, keeps young women from seeing life as it is.

We must remedy social injustice whenever we can. But there are some things we cannot change. There are sexual differences that are based in biology. Academic feminism is lost in a fog of social constructionism. It believes we are totally the product of our environment. This idea was invented by Rousseau. He was wrong. Emboldened by dumb French language theory, academic feminists repeat the same hollow slogans over and over to each other. Their view of sex is naive and prudish. Leaving sex to the feminists is like letting your dog vacation at the taxidermist's.

The sexes are at war. Men must struggle for identity against the overwhelming power of their mothers. Women have menstruation to tell them they are women. Men must do or risk something to be men. Men become masculine only when other men say they are. Having sex with a woman is one way a boy becomes a man.

College men are at their hormonal peak. They have just left their mothers and are questing for their male identity. In groups, they are dangerous. A woman going to a fraternity party is walking into Testosterone Flats, full of prickly cacti and blazing guns. If she goes, she should be armed with resolute alertness. She should arrive with girlfriends and leave with them. A girl who lets herself get dead drunk at a fraternity party is a fool. A girl who goes upstairs alone with a brother at a fraternity party is an idiot. Feminists call this "blaming the victim." I call it common sense.

For a decade, feminists have drilled their disciples to say, "Rape is a crime of violence but not of sex." This sugar-coated Shirley Temple nonsense has exposed young women to disaster. Misled by feminism, they do not expect rape from the nice boys from good homes who sit next to them in class.

10   Aggression and eroticism are deeply intertwined. Hunt, pursuit, and capture are biologically programmed into male sexuality. Generation after generation, men must be educated, refined, and ethically persuaded away from their tendency toward anarchy and brutishness. Society is not the enemy, as feminism ignorantly claims. Society is woman's protection against rape. Feminism, with its solemn Carry Nation repressiveness, does not see what is for men the eroticism or fun element in rape, especially the wild, infectious delirium of gang rape. Women who do not understand rape cannot defend themselves against it.

The date-rape controversy shows feminism hitting the wall of its own broken promises. The women of my '60s generation were the first respectable girls in history to swear like sailors, get drunk, stay out all night—in short, to act like men. We sought total sexual freedom and equality. But as time passed, we woke up to cold reality. The old double standard protected women. When anything goes, it's women who lose.

Today's young women don't know what they want. They see that feminism has not brought sexual happiness. The theatrics of public rage over date rape are their way of restoring the old sexual rules that were shattered by my generation. Because nothing about the sexes has really changed. The comic film *Where the Boys Are* (1960), the ultimate expression of '50s man-chasing, still speaks directly to our time. It shows smart, lively women skillfully anticipating and fending off the dozens of strategies with which horny men try to get them into bed. The agonizing date-rape subplot and climax are brilliantly done. The victim, Yvette Mimieux, makes mistake after mistake, obvious to the other girls. She allows herself to be lured away from her girlfriends and into isolation with boys whose character and intentions she misreads. *Where the Boys Are* tells the truth. It shows courtship as a dangerous game in which the signals are not verbal but subliminal.

Neither militant feminism, which is obsessed with politically correct language, nor academic feminism, which believes that knowledge and experience are "constituted by" language, can understand pre-verbal or non-verbal communication. Feminism, focusing on sexual politics, cannot see that sex exists in and through the body. Sexual desire and arousal cannot be fully translated into verbal terms. This is why men and women misunderstand each other.

Trying to remake the future, feminism cut itself off from sexual history. It discarded and suppressed the sexual myths of literature, art, and religion. Those myths show us the turbulence, the mysteries and passions of sex. In mythology we see men's sexual anxiety, their fear of women's dominance. Much sexual violence is rooted in men's sense of psychological weakness toward women. It takes many men to deal with one woman. Woman's voracity is a persistent motif. Clara Bow, it was rumored, took on the USC football team on weekends. Marilyn Monroe, singing "Diamonds Are a Girl's Best Friend," rules a conga line of men in tuxes. Halfclad Cher, in the video for "If I Could Turn Back Time," deranges a battleship of screaming sailors and straddles a pink-lit cannon. Feminism, coveting social power, is blind to woman's cosmic sexual power.

15   To understand rape, you must study the past. There never was and never will be sexual harmony. Every woman must take personal responsibility for her sexuality, which is nature's red flame. She must be prudent and cautious about where she goes and with whom. When she makes a mistake, she must accept the consequences and, through self-criticism, resolve never to make that mistake again. Running to Mommy and Daddy on the campus grievance committee is unworthy of strong women. Posting lists of guilty men in the toilet is cowardly, infantile stuff.

The Italian philosophy of life espouses high-energy confrontation. A male student makes a vulgar remark about your breasts? Don't slink off to whimper and simper with the campus shrinking violets. Deal with it. On the spot. Say, "Shut up, you jerk! And crawl back to the barnyard where you belong!" In general, women who project this take-charge attitude toward life get harassed less often. I see too many dopey, immature, self-pitying women walking around like melting sticks of butter. It's the Yvette Mimieux syndrome: Make me happy. And listen to me weep when I'm not.

The date-rape debate is already smothering in propaganda churned out by the expensive Northeastern colleges and universities, with their overconcentration of boring, uptight academic feminists and spoiled, affluent students. Beware of the deep manipulativeness of rich students who were neglected by their parents. They love to turn the campus into hysterical psychodramas of sexual transgression, followed by assertions of parental authority and concern. And don't look for sexual enlightenment from academe, which spews out mountains of books but never looks at life directly.

As a fan of football and rock music, I see in the simple, swaggering masculinity of the jock and in the noisy posturing of the heavy-metal guitarist certain fundamental, unchanging truths about sex. Masculinity is aggressive, unstable, combustible. It is also the most creative cultural force in history. Women must reorient themselves toward the elemental powers of sex, which can strengthen or destroy.

The only solution to date rape is female self-awareness and self-control. A woman's number one line of defense is herself. When a real rape occurs, she should report it to the police. Complaining to college committees because the courts "take too long" is ridiculous. College administrations are not a branch of the judiciary. They are not equipped or trained for legal inquiry. Colleges must alert incoming students to the problems and dangers of adulthood. Then colleges must stand back and get out of the sex game.

SUGGESTIONS FOR WRITING

1. Paglia says: "Women who do not understand rape cannot defend themselves against it." Do you agree? Write an essay that supports, disagrees with, or qualifies her contention.
2. According to Paglia, common sense, prudence, caution, self-awareness, and self-control are what women need and not "dumb French language theory" or "running to Mommy and Daddy on the campus grievance committee." Write an essay that responds to these claims with your own views.
3. Write an essay in which you analyze the differences between men and women in their relations to sexual violence.

Whose Hype?   1993

SUSAN FALUDI

Susan Faludi was born in 1959 in New York City and graduated from Harvard in
1981. She is a Pulitzer Prize-winning journalist and author of a widely famous
book, Backlash: The Undeclared War Against American Women *(1992).*

As Camille Paglia suggests in the preceeding essay, the subject of what con-
stitutes a rape has become more controversial and more politicized in recent
times. According to Susan Faludi, however, a sudden wave of "date rape revision-
ism" is not merely an expression of an effort to address the issue by rethinking it,
but rather an attempt to belittle a serious crime that has shown signs of spread-
ing in epidemic proportions.

Did you get the same irksome feeling of *déja vu* as I did reading about
Katie Roiphe's book, "The Morning After," that much-ballyhooed attack
on so-called victim feminism? You're not imagining things. You may
have read an excerpt from the book "Rape Hype Betrays Feminism" in
the June 13 *New York Times Magazine,* or you may remember Roiphe's
"Date Rape Hysteria" on the *Times's* op-ed page of Nov. 20, 1991. Or
maybe you saw a reprint of her op-ed piece—in *Playboy.* Strange times
we live in when *Playboy* finds its best misogynist fare in the pages of
the *Times.*

Or maybe you didn't enter the Roiphe echo chamber but just
read one of the many recent features that deem acquaintance rape
a nonproblem and paint feminists as "neo-Victorian" prudes terror-
izing gals with rape tall tales. What you probably missed was the coverage that viewed acquaintance rape as legitimate. Not your fault; it
went by in a flash. When the media discover a feminist concern, it
gets less than five minutes of serious consideration; then comes
a five-year attack. Most stories have raised a doubting eyebrow:
"Crying Rape" or "Date Rape, Part 2: The Making of a Crisis" (complete with cartoons).

Roiphe and others "prove" their case by recycling the same anecdotes of false accusations; they all quote the same "expert" who dispar-
ages reports of high rape rates. And they never interview any real rape
victims. They advise us that a feeling of victimization is no longer
a reasonable response to sexual violence; it's a hallucinatory state of
mind induced by witchy feminists who cast a spell on impressionable

coeds. These date-rape revisionists claim to be liberating young women from the victim mind-set. But is women's sexual victimization just a mind trip—or a reality?

Roiphe's book says the feminist assertion that one in four women is a victim of rape or attempted rape can't be right because, "If 25 percent of my women friends were being raped—wouldn't I know it?" Roiphe must've skipped Statistics 101: one's friends don't constitute a scientific sample. She then bases her entire argument on the "findings" of University of California professor Neil Gilbert. Gilbert has actually never done any research on rape, but he's denounced feminist scholarship on rape in such conservative periodicals as *The Public Interest*. And he's not a neutral academic; he successfully campaigned to cancel a California school sex-abuse prevention program and is now crusading against federal funds for rape prevention. He argues that the one-in-four rape/attempted rape figure is based on a "radical feminist" study that labeled anything from "the slightest pressure" to "sweet talk" as rape. The real number, he says, is one in 1,000.

5   Gilbert gets this figure from the National Crime Survey (NCS), a poll that even its own researchers fault for undercounting rape. Until recently, the NCS asked the people polled if they had experienced just about every crime *but* rape; victims had to volunteer it on their own. The survey uses an old definition of rape that doesn't fit current laws; for instance, the NCS doesn't term forced oral or anal sex as rape. And the one-in-1,000 figure is based on rapes and attempted rapes in a six-month period; the one-in-four figure reflects how many occurred since a college-age woman turned 14.

Despite Gilbert's claim, the one-in-four figure does not include women who felt sweet-talked into sex. It's true the survey (funded not by a feminist cabal but by the National Institute of Mental Health) asked women if they ever felt pressured into sex, but that data was not included in the final count. Numerous other studies bear these figures out. The bottom line: the number of sexual assaults in the FBI files has risen four times as fast as the total crime rate in the last decade.

The date-rape revisionists claim a feminist-provoked rape hysteria is causing young women to "wallow in victimhood." According to a Senate report, at least 84 percent of rapes go unreported. So where exactly have these chroniclers of "rape hype" spied hordes of victim-emoting gals anyway? Maybe in Hollywood films or on TV where "women in jep" clot the screen. Maybe in the fashion ads featuring wan, cowering waifs. But not in feminist circles where the most striking recent development has been a massive influx not of hanky-clutching neo-Victorians but of such stand-tall feminist groups as Riot GRRRL, Guerrilla Girls, WHAM, YELL, and, my personal favorite, Random Pissed Off Women. These new feminists use wit, not whining, megaphones, not moping, to deliver their point.

There is indeed a national "hysteria" over this new forceful feminism—but it's *male* hysteria. The real cultural fear is not that women are becoming too Victorian but that they're becoming too damn aggressive—in and out of bed. Let's recall where this victimhood argument first surfaced: in conservative journal articles by men. Nearly two years before the *Times* printed Roiphe's "Rape Hype," Commentary published Norman Podhoretz's seven-page denial of date rape. This "brazen campaign" by feminists, he warned, will deny men their privilege of "normal seduction" and "male initiative." "The number of 'wimps'. . . . will multiply apace," as will—drum roll—"the incidence of male impotence."

Now I ask you, just who's spouting hype?

SUGGESTIONS FOR WRITING

1. Faludi attacks several of the date-rape revisionists for (among other things) their poor scholarship and logical errors. In your view, are her accusations valid? Write an essay that explains and defends your answer.
2. In an essay that addresses the issue of date rape, make sure to come up with your own definition of the term.
3. Write an essay of your own that compares the essays of Camille Paglia and Susan Faludi.

INTERDISCIPLINARY CONNECTIONS

1. In your view, what part does human evolution through natural selection play in issues of human gender? Write an essay that explains and defends your views.
2. Other writers earlier in this book have spoken to some of the economic issues related to the topic of gender. Do any of the writers in the current chapter help you to understand those issues better? Write an essay that explains and defends your answer.

3. Some writers in other chapters of this book have spoken to some of the human rights issues related to the topic of gender. Do any of the writers in the current chapter help you to understand those issues better? Write an essay that explains and defends your answer.

4. Plato, White, and Reid pay particular attention to problems of language in their analyses of gender issues. Using the materials of this chapter and any other knowledge at your command, write an essay that explores the particularly verbal issues involved in the topic of human gender.

5. Plato writes of the place of women in his utopia. Given your understanding of the issues involved, write an essay that sketches your idea of a utopia of gender.

Chapter One—Evolution: Inceptions and Implications

Chapter Two—Economics: The Production and Consumption of Wealth

Jared Diamond, "Geographical Selection and Economic Evolution" from GUNS, GERMS AND STEEL: THE FATES OF HUMAN SOCIETIES by Jared Diamond. Copyright © 1997 by Jared Diamond. Used by permission of W. W. Norton & Company, Inc.

Hannah Arendt, "The Labour of Our Body and the Work of Our Hands" reprinted by permission of University of Chicago Press.

John Maynard Keynes, "The End of Laissez Faire" (1926) Macmillan. Reprinted by permission of Palgrave Macmillan.

Milton Friedman, "Occupational Licensure" from *Capitalism and Freedom* reprinted by permission of University of Chicago Press.

Chapter Three—Human Rights: Liberty and Law

Jean-Jacques Rousseau, "The Origins of Civil Society" from *Social Contract*. Translation reprinted by permission of Ronah Sadan.

Margaret Sanger, "Awakening and Revolt" from *My Fight for Birth Control*, reprinted by permission of Alexander Sanger, executor of the estate of Margaret Sanger.

George Orwell, "Politics and the English Language", from SHOOTING AN ELEPHANT AND OTHER ESSAYS by George Orwell, copyright 1950 by Sonia Orwell and renewed 1978 by Sonia Pitt-Rivers, reprinted by permission of Harcourt, Inc.

Martin Luther King, Jr. "Letter from Birmingham Jail", reprinted by arrangement with The Heirs to the Estate of Martin Luther King Jr., c/o Writers House as agent for the proprietor New York, NY. Copyright 1963 Martin Luther King Jr,. copyright renewed 1991 Coretta Scott King.

Malcolm X, "The Ballot or the Bullet" Copyright © 1965, 1989 by Betty Shabazz and Pathfinder Press. Reprinted by permission.

Chapter Four—Literature: Life's Mirror and Life's Lamp

Virginia Woolf, "Shakespeare's Sister" Excerpt from "Shakesperare's Sister" in A ROOM OF ONE'S OWN by Virginia Woolf, copyright 1929 by Harcourt, Inc. and renewed 1957 by Leonard Woolf, reprinted by permission of the publisher.

Louise Barnett, "Bartleby as Alienated Worker". Reprinted by permission of the author.

Andrew Delbanco, "Bartleby" from MELVILLE: HIS WORLD AND WORK by Andrew Delbanco, copyright © 2005 by Andrew Delbanco. Used by permission of Alfred A. Knopf, a division of Random House, Inc.

Chapter Five—Utopias and Dystopias: Secular Heavens and Secular Hells

Thomas More, from *Utopia*. Translated by Niti Bagchi, reprinted by permission of the translator.

Ray Bradbury, from *Fahrenheit 451* (1951) reprinted by permission of Don Congdon Associates, Inc. Copyright © 1953, renewed 1981 by Ray Bradbury.

Chairman Mao, "Let a Hundred Flowers Blossom" (1957) Translated by Lily Wei. Reprinted by permission of the translator.

Margaret Atwood, from *The Handmaid's Tale* (1986) Excerpt from "Salvaging," from THE HANDMAID'S TALE by Margaret Atwood. Copyright © 1986 by O. W. Toad, Ltd. Reprinted by permission of Houghton Mifflin Company. All rights reserved.

Chapter Six—Gender: Human Conditioning and the Human Condition

Carol Gilligan, "Woman's Place in Man's Life Cycle", reprinted by permission of the publisher from IN A DIFFERENT VOICE: PSYCHOLOGICAL THEORY AND WOMEN'S DEVELOPMENT by Carol Gilligan, pp. 5–23, Cambridge, Mass.: Harvard University Press, Copyright © 1982, 1993 by Carol Gilligan.

bell hooks, "Racism and Feminism" from AIN'T I A WOMAN? South End Press. By permission.

Edmund White, "Sexual Culture" Reprinted by permission of International Creative Management, Inc. Copyright © 1983 by Edmund White.

index

additional titles of interest

Allison, Dorothy, *Bastard Out of Carolina*
Alvarez, Julia, *How the Garcia Girls Lost Their Accent*
Austen, Jane, *Persuasion*
Austen, Jane, *Pride and Prejudice*
Austen, Jane, *Sense and Sensibility*
Bloom, Harold, *Shakespeare: The Invention of the Human*
Brontë, Charlotte, *Jane Eyre*
Brontë, Emily, *Wuthering Heights*
Burke, Edmund, *Reflections on the Revolution in France*
Cather, Willa, *My Antonia*
Cather, Willa, *O Pioneers!*
Cellini, Benvenuto, *The Autobiography of Benvenuto Cellini*
Chapman, Abraham, *Black Voices*
Chesnutt, Charles W., *The Marrow of Tradition*
Chopin, Kate, *The Awakening and Selected Stories*
Conrad, Joseph, *Heart of Darkness*
Conrad, Joseph, *Nostromo: A Tale of the Seaboard*
Coraghessan Boyle, T., *The Tortilla Curtain*
Defoe, Daniel, *The Life and Adventures of Robinson Crusoe*
Descartes, René, *Discourse on Method and Meditations*
Descartes, René, *Meditations and Other Metaphysical Writings*
de Tocqueville, *Democracy in America*
Dickens, Charles, *Hard Times*
Douglass, Frederick, *Narrative of the Life of Frederick Douglass: An American Slave*
DuBois, W. E. B., *Souls of Black Folk*
Equiano, Olaudah, *The Interesting Narrative and Other Writings*
Gore, Al, *Earth in the Balance: Ecology and the Human Spirit*

Grossman, Lawrence K., *Electronic Republic*

Hawthorne, Nathaniel, *The Scarlet Letter: A Romance*

Hutner, Gordon, *Immigrant Voices: Twenty-Four Narratives on Becoming an American*

Jacobs, Harriet, *Incidents in the Life of a Slave Girl*

Jen, Gish, *Typical American*

King, Martin Luther, Jr., *Why We Can't Wait*

Lewis, Sinclair, *Babbit*

Machiavelli, *The Prince*

Marx, Karl, *The Communist Manifesto*

Mill, Stuart John, *On Liberty*

More, Sir Thomas, *Utopia and Other Essential Writings*

Orwell, George, *1984*

Paine, Thomas, *Common Sense*

Plato, *The Republic*

Postman, Neil, *Amusing Ourselves to Death*

Rose, Mike, *Lives on the Boundary*

Rossiter, *The Federalist Papers*

Rousseau, Jean-Jaques, *The Social Contract*

Shelley, Mary, *Frankenstein*

Sinclair, Upton, *The Jungle*

St. Augustine, *The Confessions of St. Augustine*

Steinbeck, John, *Of Mice and Men*

Stevenson, Robert Louis, *The Strange Case of Dr. Jekyll and Mr. Hyde*

Stoker, Bram, *Dracula*

Stowe, Harriet Beecher, *Uncle Tom's Cabin*

Swift, Jonathan, *Gulliver's Travels*

Taulbert, Clifton L., *Once Upon a Time When We Were Colored*

Thoreau, Henry David, *Walden: Or, Life in the Woods* and *On the Duty of Civil Disobedience*

Truth, Sojourner, *The Narrative of Sojourner Truth*

Woolf, Virginia, *Jacob's Room*

Zola, Emile, *Germinal*